THE PAPERS OF MARTIN LUTHER KING, JR.

Sponsored by

The Martin Luther King, Jr.,
Center for Nonviolent Social Change, Inc.,

in association with

Stanford University and Emory University

Martin Luther King, Jr. Photograph submitted to Boston University
with his dissertation, April 1955. Photo courtesy of
Martin Luther King, Jr., Papers, Boston University.

THE PAPERS OF MARTIN LUTHER KING, JR.

VOLUME II:

Rediscovering Precious Values
July 1951–November 1955

Senior Editor

Clayborne Carson

Volume Editors

Ralph E. Luker
Penny A. Russell
Peter Holloran

Advisory Editor

Louis R. Harlan

UNIVERSITY OF CALIFORNIA PRESS

Berkeley   Los Angeles   London

University of California Press
Berkeley and Los Angeles, California

University of California Press, Ltd.
London, England

Library of Congress Cataloging-in-Publication Data

King, Martin Luther, Jr., 1929–1968.
    The papers of Martin Luther King, Jr.
    Includes bibliographical references and index.
    v. 2. Rediscovering precious values, July 1951–Nov. 1955.
    Contents: v. 1. Called to serve, January 1929–June 1951—
    1. Afro-Americans—Civil rights. 2. Civil rights move-
ments—United States—History—20th century. 3. King, Martin
Luther, Jr., 1929–1968—Archives. 4. United States—Race rela-
tions. I. Carson, Clayborne, 1944–   . II. Luker, Ralph.
III. Russell, Penny A. IV. Title.
E185.97.K5A2 1992   323'.092   91-42336
ISBN 0-520-07951-5 (cloth alk. paper)

Printed in the United States of America
9 8 7 6 5 4 3 2 1

The paper used in this publication meets the minimum requirements of American National Standard for Information Sciences—
Permanence of Paper for Printed Library Materials, ANSI Z39.48-
1984.∞

*If we are to go forward, we must
go back and rediscover these
precious values—that all reality
hinges on moral foundations and
that all reality has spiritual
control.*

MARTIN LUTHER KING, JR.
28 February 1954

The editors of the Martin Luther King, Jr., Papers Project wish to acknowledge the financial and material support of the following major contributors, without whose support this volume would not have been possible:

Major Contributors

National Endowment for the Humanities
National Historical Publications and Records Commission
James Irvine Foundation
Lilly Endowment
Stanford University
Emory University
Houghton Mifflin Company, School Division
Nordson Corporation Foundation
The H. W. Wilson Foundation
The David and Lucile Packard Foundation

Patrons

Ruth M. Batson Educational Foundation
Diane F. and James A. Geocaris
William P. Madar
The Mercury News
National City Bank
Emory Tolbert
Elizabeth Traugott

Donors

Ann Appleman
Keith Archuleta
Carolyn Barnes
Stanford University Black Community Services Center
J. Herman Blake
Taylor Branch

W. Don Cornell
Wayne Duckworth
Mary McKinney Edmonds
Ernst and Young, Northern California Division
Richard B. Fields
The First Hebrew Congregation of Oakland, Temple Sinai
Ira D. Hall, Jr.
Ronne and Donald Hess
L. Tyrone Holt
Benson Kanemoto
Martin Luther King, Jr., Association of Santa Clara Valley
KNTV San Jose
Lockheed Missiles and Space Co., Inc.
Leanne MacDougall
Kim M. Metters
The Mid-Peninsula NAACP
Woodrow A. and Debra J. Myers
Henry Organ
James N. and Janice G. Rosse
University National Bank and Trust Co.
University of Newcastle upon Tyne
Viola and Andrew White
Wyse Technology

The publishers acknowledge gratefully the many
individuals and foundations that have contributed to the
publication of the Papers of Martin Luther King, Jr.

Our special thanks to Maya Angelou, Mary Jane Hewitt,
Sukey Garcetti, Maxine Griggs, Franklin Murphy, Joan
Palevsky, and Marilyn Solomon for their leadership
during the campaign.

Challenge Grant
Times Mirror Foundation

Leadership Grants
The Ahmanson Foundation
AT&T Foundation

Partners
ARCO Foundation
William H. Cosby, Jr., and Camille O. Cosby
The George Gund Foundation
The Walter & Elise Haas Fund
LEF Foundation
Sally Lilienthal
J. Michael Mahoney
The Andrew W. Mellon Foundation
National Historical Publications and
Records Commission
Peter Norton Family Foundation
Joan Palevsky
The Ralph M. Parsons Foundation

Benefactors
Anonymous
BankAmerica Foundation
David Geffen Foundation
Fleishhacker Foundation
Koret Foundation
Lilly Endowment Inc.

TABLE OF CONTENTS

Illustrations follow p. 37

I : BOSTON UNIVERSITY

II : MONTGOMERY, ALABAMA

ACKNOWLEDGMENTS

Most of the individuals and institutions that were acknowledged in Volume I of the papers of Martin Luther King, Jr., also contributed to this volume. Until it became obvious that we had located an unexpectedly large number of significant documents on King's early years, the first two volumes were to be published as one. Rather than simply repeat my earlier words of appreciation to contributors to the initial manuscript, I will acknowledge those whose work has been especially important to the completion of the present volume. Furthermore, I wish to thank many individuals and institutions whose contributions to the Project's work were not adequately acknowledged or were erroneously omitted in the first volume. As I indicated in the prior volume, the King Papers Project is similar to the social movements that made possible King's achievements, in that the sacrifices of many dedicated people will never be sufficiently recognized.

Institutional Support

The Martin Luther King, Jr., Center for Nonviolent Social Change, Inc., is the sponsor of the King Papers Project. I continue to benefit from the support of the King Center's founding president and chief executive officer, Mrs. Coretta Scott King. The publication of this edition would not be possible without her long-standing insistence that movement documents be preserved and her recognition of the need for a documentary edition such as this. As executrix of the King estate, she has been deeply involved in the King Papers Project from its inception and has allowed us to use photographs from her personal collection. I have been particularly impressed by her willingness to interrupt her busy schedule for extended discussions, sometimes lasting many hours, of Project-related matters. In addition, I continue to rely on the help of Mrs. King's assistants, particularly Delores Harmon, Beni Ivey, Doris Ford, and Lynn Cothren.

The King Center's senior vice-president and treasurer, Mrs. Christine King Farris, has continued to offer vital support to the Project. She met with me on several occasions during the past few years to discuss Project issues, and she generously made available her priceless collection of King family documents and photographs, enriching the first two volumes of King's papers.

The King Papers Project has benefited from the cooperation of other members of the King family as well. On one occasion during 1992, I was pleased to have an extended meeting not only with Mrs. King, but also with the heirs to the King estate: Yolanda, Bernice, Dexter, and Martin III. During the past few years, Dexter King in particular has become more involved in Project issues, including its future relationship to the estate. He and the agent for the

King estate, Michele Clark Jenkins, have devoted considerable time to the needs of the King Papers Project.

Other officers of the King Center have also made important contributions to the Project. I learned much about King and the civil rights movement from my talks with the late Cleveland Dennard, who served as Mrs. King's executive aide; he met with me often, thereby strengthening the relationship between the Project and the King Center. Since the arrival in 1991 of the King Center's executive director, Ronald L. Quincy, the King Papers Project has worked closely with him and other dedicated professionals at the Center. These individuals include Marsha Turner, director of research; Bruce Keys and Danny Bellinger of the King Library and Archives; and Johnny Mack, James Price, and Isaac Clark of the business office. We also wish to thank collectively the many other King Center staff members who expressed support for the Project and offered assistance in various ways.

Because the King Papers Project is conducted in association with Stanford University and Emory University, it relies on the support of administrators at both institutions. At Stanford, President Donald Kennedy and Provost James Rosse provided essential backing until they left office in 1992. Since 1991, the King Papers Project has been under the auspices of the School of Humanities and Sciences, where I have benefited from the counsel and support of Dean Ewart Thomas. Since 1992, I have reported to Associate Dean Albert Camarillo, an old friend and colleague from the history department. Associate Dean of Graduate Studies Cecilia Burciago offered steady support while overseeing the Project's Irvine Foundation grant along with grant coordinator Daniel Ramirez. Humanities and Sciences' Director of Finance, Nancy Padgett, has helped the project with budget matters. Further assistance was provided by Norman Roth, Bo Parker and Charles Stewart from the Stanford Data Center. Iris Brest and Jasper Williams in the General Counsel's office have provided useful legal advice. Henry Organ, Michael Britt, Steven Suda, John Cash, and Evelyn Kelsey of the Office of Development have been helpful in assisting the Project in pursuing funding sources. We have continued to rely on the support of Director James Clark and Assistant Director Lynne Withey at the University of California Press. Other staff with whom the Project has worked include Denise Cicourel, Susan Markey, Kim Darwin, Erika Büky, Fran Mitchell, and Marta Gasoi.

At Emory, the King Papers Project office expanded its operations under the direction of Volume IV editor Virginia Shadron. The Project has received crucial support from Emory administrators at every level, including President James T. Laney, Provost Billy E. Frye, Vice-President for Arts and Sciences David F. Bright, Dean of the School of Arts and Sciences and Vice-President for Research George Jones, Associate Vice-President of Graduate Studies Eleanor Main, Associate Dean Alice Benston, Graduate School Business Manager Tom Stitt, and Administrative Assistant Carl Reid. Deans Jones and Main and history department chairs Thomas Burns and James Roark have been especially helpful to Virginia Shadron as she expanded the Project's capacities at Emory. The following faculty members at Emory served on the Project's informal faculty advisory committee: Delores Aldridge, Rudolph Byrd, Dan T.

Carter, Leroy Davis, Robert M. Franklin, Robin D. G. Kelley, Theophus Smith, and Margaret Spencer.

The King Papers Project's Advisory Board, members of which are listed at the front of the volume, has remained a valued source of advice and critical suggestions. Mrs. King and Mrs. Christine King Farris are, of course, the Board members with the most extensive contact with the Project, but other members have unselfishly assisted us. John Hope Franklin has remained a source of sage advice and participated in a special session devoted to Volumes I and II, held at the 1992 meeting of the Southern Historical Association. Board member Vincent Harding has become a treasured friend, and his summer 1992 visit to the Project was a memorable event for the student interns. Robert A. Hill, John Maguire, and Harris Wofford similarly offered inspiration as well as advice during visits to the King Papers Project in 1991 and 1992. I also appreciated my occasional discussions with Darlene Clark Hine, Otis Moss, Louis R. Harlan, and Ira Berlin. Preston N. Williams and Vincent Harding offered helpful comments regarding drafts of the introductory essay.

Financial Supporters

The King Papers Project could not have survived without funding from numerous generous and enlightened donors. Major contributors to this volume included the National Endowment for the Humanities (NEH), the National Historical Publications and Records Commission (NHPRC), the James Irvine Foundation, the Lilly Endowment, Stanford University, Emory University, Houghton Mifflin Company–School Division, the Nordson Corporation Foundation, and the H. W. Wilson Foundation. Individuals at these institutions have often indicated that their concern for the King Project extends beyond their professional responsibilities. I wish to mention in particular Program Officer Douglas M. Arnold and Grants Officer Alice Hutchins of the NEH. The NHPRC has funded the Project from its inception, and in recent years Executive Director Gerald George, Deputy Executive Director Roger Bruns, Program Director Nancy Sahli, and Assistant Program Director Richard Sheldon have provided support as well as oversight. NHPRC Archivist Donald L. Singer also helped us on several occasions. I am especially grateful for the wonderful reception in February 1992 at the Capitol hosted by National Archivist Don Wilson to celebrate the publication of Volume I. In addition, I have appreciated the support of Irvine Foundation President Dennis Collins and Lilly Endowment Program Director Jacqui Burton. Constance Haqq and Carolyn Gibson were helpful in securing funding from the Nordson Corporation Foundation for summer interns.

Since the beginning of 1992, many individuals have accepted the invitation to join the Stanford University Associates, the support group for the Project's Stanford office. Ira D. Hall, Jr., of IBM has continued to serve as chairperson of the Associates. Associates in the Patron category are: Ruth M. Batson Educational Foundation, Diane F. and James A. Geocaris, William P. Madar, The Mercury News, National City Bank, Emory Tolbert, and Elizabeth Traugott.

Donors have included: Ann Appleman, Keith Archuleta, Carolyn Barnes, Stanford University Black Community Services Center, J. Herman Blake, Taylor Branch, W. Don Cornell, Wayne Duckworth, Mary McKinney Edmonds, Ernst and Young Northern California Division, Richard B. Fields, The First Hebrew Congregation of Oakland, Temple Sinai, Ira D. Hall, Jr., Ronne and Donald Hess, L. Tyrone Holt, Benson Kanemoto, Martin Luther King, Jr., Association of Santa Clara Valley, KNTV San Jose, Lockheed Missiles and Space Company, Inc., Leanne MacDougall, Kim M. Metters, The Mid-Peninsula NAACP, Woodrow A. and Debra J. Myers, Henry Organ, James N. and Janice G. Rosse, University National Bank and Trust Co., University of Newcastle upon Tyne, Viola and Andrew White, and Wyse Technology.

Sustaining members included: Marian Adams, Michael Britt, Roger and Ora Clay, Harvey L. and Fannie L. Cole, George M. Fredrickson, Marvin Goodman, Kenneth P. Jameson, Clinton O'Keefe Killian, Richard H. King, K. C. Morrison, Gary Nash, Jerry Nightingale, Nell Irvin Painter, Gregory Reed, Joni Reid, Beverly P. Ryder, S. Paul Schilling, Terrence and Susan Shea, J. F. Sandy and Susana Gancedo Smith, Michael Tuohy, Richard Wylie, and Bill Walsh. Other members of the Associates have included: Joel and Miriam Beinin, Paul Berman, Julian Bond, Edwin C. Bridges, Jackie Brown, Ralph Carlson, James I. Chatman, Sharon Chatman, John A. Dittmer, Ellious W. and Betty B. Dunson, Larry Elswit, The Frente Foundation, Michon Fulgham, Eva Goodwin, Gloria Guth, Louis Harlan, Stanley L. and Juanita Schuck Harris, Nancy A. Hewitt, Robert Hill, Michael Honey, Gerald and Myra Jackson, Alice Kawazoe, Michael Kazin, Lydia Kennard, Stanley Kutler, Steven Lawson, The Lawyer's Committee for Civil Rights, Douglas J. McAdam, David Oppenheimer, David Pasta, Lynne H. and David B. Posner, Ruth Rosen, Pauline Sanchez, Robert Smith, The Stanford Black Alumni Club Northern California Division, Sheila Troupe, Cheryl and Lonnie Washington, and Gail and Ray Westergard.

Staff Members

The editors listed on the title page have, of course, each made essential contributions to this volume. Ralph Luker, Penny Russell, and Peter Holloran were part of the Project during its early years and have continued to work together as the King Papers Project has grown and matured. Ralph's exceptional expertise regarding modern American religious history has enriched us all. His varied contributions included initiating and directing the Emory office until 1990 and helping to draft many of the annotations for this volume. Penny supervised the process of preparing volume documents for publication and has returned to work with the Project at the Emory University office as a contributing editor of Volume IV. Peter's work on Volume II became even more important after the departure of Ralph and Penny. His assignments have included preparation of the introductory essay and of the document section. During 1992, researcher Stephanie Brookins worked with Peter in the preparation of a new draft of the introductory essay.

Other staff members who assisted on this volume included Associate Editor Stewart Burns, who took time away from his editing of Volume III, and

NHPRC Editing Fellow James Tracy. After joining the Project in July 1993, editorial assistant Dana L. H. Powell assumed the difficult task of guiding this manuscript toward publication. Since June 1993, Aylin Altan has coordinated the Project's fundraising activities.

The cataloging of the enormous number of documents assembled by the Project and preparation of the document calendar was supervised by Librarian-Archivist Susan Carson. From 1989 to 1991, she was assisted by Megan Maxwell. Since the fall of 1991, Susan has worked with Elizabeth Báez, a former Irvine intern who now serves as assistant archivist at the Project.

Other members of the King Papers Project staff during the period of the preparation of Volume II have included office administrator Karl Knapper and IBM loan executives Norma Pugh and Ellious Dunson. Researchers Judy Wu and Amy Whitcomb, talented Stanford graduates, worked with the staff from 1991 to 1993 and became indispensable to our efforts.

Student Researchers: Stanford Office

The Project has always depended on the skills and resources of the undergraduate and graduate students at Stanford. These students, working as interns, volunteers, or for academic credit, have contributed their dedication and enthusiasm. Undergraduate researchers who worked on Volume II or whose work was not acknowledged in Volume I include Michelle Atkins, Lily Batchelder, Kofi Bruce, Doug Bruha, Alan Burnce, Sheila Cain, Linda Chen, Theo Emery, Claudine Gay, Jamie Green, Christy Halvorson, Heidi Hess, Chip Heuisler, Mark Jeter, Linda Jolivet, Katherine Kershner, Andrea Kohn, Becky Marcus, Tasha McNeil, Daralene Montoya, Mary Anne Morgan, Aresa Pecot, Dev Puri, Cheryl Richardson, Jehni Robinson, Matthew Scelza, Michelle Scott, Hillary Skillings, Sarah Stevenson, Rebecca Tamel, Chris Walcott, Michelle Walsh, Heather Williams, Stephen Williams, and Ivy Wilson. Diahanne Starks worked as a volunteer during 1991. Graduate students Victoria Griffith, Leslie Harris, Russell Post, and Susan Stedem also participated. William Tucker's years of dedicated volunteer service to the Project is especially appreciated.

The Project has also benefited from the participation of a number of graduate and undergraduate students from other universities and colleges who worked at our Stanford offices under an internship program funded by the Irvine Foundation. The Irvine interns for the summer of 1992 were Angela Brown (Harvard University), Amanda Kemp (Northwestern University), and Maria Kolby (University of Puget Sound). Landon Reid of Morehouse College was able to participate because of a special grant from the Nordson Foundation, while Helene Fisher of Howard University was sponsored by her institution. Holly Bass (Sarah Lawrence College) and Theresa Napson (American University) participated in the Irvine Program during the summer of 1991.

Student Researchers: King Center and Emory Offices

The work of the editors in Atlanta also depended on the help of graduate and undergraduate students from Emory and other Atlanta-area universi-   xxiii ties. Andrea Simpson acted as the assistant to the Atlanta editor. Graduate students included Gilbert Bond, Josephine Boyd Bradley, Jonathan Byrd, Luther Ivory, Michael McMillen, James Miller, Ed Munn, and Shirley Toland. Undergraduates included Natasha Marcus, David Nuwirth, Audia Wells, and Brian Woods.

Acquisition and Research Assistance

Volume II, like Volume I, would not have been possible without the King-related documents provided by numerous individuals and institutions. The King collection at the King Center is the core of our selection. In addition, the King collection at Boston University, which is the largest archive of pre-1962 King materials, has been critically important to this volume in particular. We are especially grateful for the generous assistance of Special Collections Director Howard Gotlieb and Assistant Director Margaret Goostray. Boston is also the depository of other valuable collections.

In addition to documents obtained from the King Center and Boston University, we identified more than one hundred fifty other manuscript collections with King-related material. Archives that assisted us in locating documents for this volume include the Alabama Department of Archives and History; Antioch College Archives; the Chicago Historical Society; Colgate-Rochester Divinity School; Emory University Special Collections; the Moorland-Spingarn Research Center at Howard University; the Manuscripts Division of the Library of Congress; New York Public Library, Schomburg Collection; the Southern Baptist Convention Historical Commission; Temple University; and the State Historical Society of Wisconsin.

Among the most important sources of King-related documents have been Dr. King's acquaintances and colleagues during his Boston years. Of those whom we were able to contact, many graciously allowed us to make photocopies of documents in their possession, which until now have not been published or made available to the public. Among those individuals who donated documents or photocopies of documents pertaining to Volume II are Thelma B. Archer, Jeanne Martin Brayboy, Lawrence Edward Carter, Sr., Percy A. Carter, Jr., Julian O. Grayson, Nathaniel Leach, John T. Porter, Mark A. Rouch, S. Paul Schilling, Francis E. Stewart, and Ira Zepp, Jr. The following individuals and institutions also permitted us to publish their documents: Gladys Bean, Mrs. Brailsford R. Brazeal, Theodore Enslin, Hazel Yates Gray, Phoebe Burney Hart, Karen Jefferson of the Moorland-Spingarn Research Center, Isabella M. Tobin, Joan Blanton Tucker, and David F. Wright of the University of Edinburgh. Before her death, Mrs. Woodie Brown, the Reverend M. L. King, Sr.'s sister, graciously talked with us about her family.

The Project has also gained access to several collections of papers from institutions in which Dr. King participated. The papers of Dexter Avenue King Memorial Baptist Church and Ebenezer Baptist Church have been made available to us, providing important documents from King's life as pastor of the two churches. Nathaniel Leach of Second Baptist Church in Detroit, Dean Lawrence Edward Carter, Sr., of the Martin Luther King, Jr., Memorial Chapel at Morehouse College, and the First United Baptist Church of Lowell, Massachusetts, also provided important documents and assistance.

Several people without official ties to the Project also provided assistance. John Holloran examined the Howard Thurman collection at Boston University. Cara L. Shelly examined papers at Detroit and Ann Arbor. Bill O'Brien searched the Montgomery Branch NAACP collection at the New York Public Library. André Namphy examined Volume II documents from the King Collection at Boston University.

The following individuals generously consented to formal interviews in connection with this volume: David Briddell, E. Evans Crawford, Jewelle Taylor Gibbs, W. T. Handy, Coretta Scott King, Joel King, George K. MacKechnie, and Sybil Haydel Morial.

A few individuals have enhanced the work of the King Papers Project simply by visiting us and talking to us about their involvement with King and the civil rights movement. Among the prominent visitors in recent years, not listed above, have been Dorothy Cotton, Mary McKinnley Edmonds, Rosemary and Vincent Harding, Bob Moses, Jesse Jackson, Anne Romaine, Harold Sims, Harris Wofford, and Prathia Hall Wynn.

Finally, I sincerely thank Taylor Branch, James Cone, and Nell Irvin Painter, the distinguished scholars who offered helpful criticisms of Volumes I and II as members of a panel, chaired by John Hope Franklin, at the 1992 meeting of the Southern Historical Association in Atlanta. Certainly there are other individuals and organizations that participated in and contributed to the success of the King Papers Project. Failure to mention them simply reflects the limits of my memory rather than of my gratitude.

CLAYBORNE CARSON
15 OCTOBER 1992

In the spring of 1951, Martin Luther King, Jr., twenty-two years old and in his final year at Crozer Theological Seminary, accepted an admission offer from Boston University's Graduate School. Because King had already completed seven years of higher education, his decision to continue with graduate studies in theology set him apart from the great majority of Baptist ministers. His father and grandfather had furthered their careers by acquiring degrees from Morehouse College, but in 1951 less than ten percent of African-American Baptist ministers had pursued formal seminary training, and only a few dozen had earned doctoral degrees. Though the elder King still wanted a permanent co-pastor of Ebenezer Baptist Church, he was pleased that his son "was moving forward into a modern, advanced sort of ministry" and thus was willing to provide financial support for graduate study in systematic theology. Even as his son's theological studies provided a gloss of erudition, King, Sr., remained convinced that the stamp of the African-American Baptist church on his son's religious beliefs was indelible. He admired his son's ability to combine "the Bible's truths with the wisdom of the modern world" but still saw him as "a son of the Baptist South." The young minister's occasional sermons at Ebenezer displayed, in the opinion of his admiring father, "the probing quality of his mind, the urgency, the fire that makes for brilliance in every theological setting."[1]

The academic papers that King, Jr., wrote during his three years at Crozer Theological Seminary record his movement from teenage religious skepticism toward a theological eclecticism that was consistent with his Baptist religious roots. Never having had an "abrupt conversion experience," King felt that his religious beliefs resulted from the "gradual intaking of the noble ideals" of his family and community. "Even in moments of theological doubt I could never turn away" from those ideals, he insisted.[2] Growing up as the son and grandson of preachers and choir directors, King had acquired his basic convictions through daily immersion in the life of Ebenezer. "Religion has just

---

1. The Rev. Martin Luther King, Sr., with Clayton Riley, *Daddy King: An Autobiography* (New York: William Morrow, 1980), p. 147. For an early study of the black Baptist ministry, see Ira De A. Reid, "The Negro Baptist Ministry: An Analysis of Its Profession, Preparation, and Practices," 1951, BEMP-DHU: Box 77. See also Charles Shelby Rooks, *Revolution in Zion: Reshaping African American Ministry, 1960–1974* (New York: Pilgrim, 1990).

2. Martin Luther King, Jr., "An Autobiography of Religious Development," in *The Papers of Martin Luther King, Jr.*, vol. 1: *Called to Serve: January 1929–June 1951*, ed. Clayborne Carson, Ralph E. Luker, and Penny A. Russell (Berkeley and Los Angeles: University of California Press, 1992), pp. 361, 363. King later acknowledged that at an early stage in his religious development he was embarrassed by "the emotionalism of much of Negro religion, the shouting and stamping. I didn't understand it" (King, quoted in William Peters, "Our Weapon Is Love," *Redbook*, August 1956, p. 72).

been something that I grew up in," he noted. The example of his "saintly" grandmother, Jennie Celeste Williams, an influential figure at Ebenezer, was instrumental in his religious development, while his father "also had a great deal to do with my going in[to] the ministry. He set forth a noble example that I didn't min[d] following."[3]

In addition to influencing his choice of a career, King's family and church shaped his theological perspective. As King's undergraduate mentor, Morehouse president Benjamin Mays, wrote in his survey of religious beliefs in the African-American community, there were two traditions of thought about God, one that enabled blacks "to endure hardship, suffer pain, and withstand maladjustment" and another that motivated them "to strive to eliminate the source of the ills they suffer."[4] King's family connected him to the latter tradition, which rejected the notion that Christians should abide this world while awaiting a better one in heaven. "The church is to touch every phase of the community life," King, Sr., once urged his fellow black Baptist ministers. "We are to do something about the broken-hearted, poor, unemployed, the captive, the blind, and the bruised." The elder King exhorted his colleagues to become politically active: "God hasten the time when every minister will become a registered voter and a part of every movement for the betterment of our people."[5]

Theological study became the means by which King, Jr., reconciled his desire to pursue a social gospel ministry with his deep-seated distrust of the emotionalism that sometimes accompanied Baptist religious practice. He later recalled that at the age of seven he had formally joined Ebenezer in the midst of a revival meeting "not out of any dynamic conviction, but out of a childhood desire to keep up with my sister." He rejected scriptural literalism, explaining that he "couldn't see how many of the facts of science squared with religion."[6] At one point as a teenager, he even denied the bodily resurrection of Jesus. His religious doubts began to subside, however, when Morehouse professor George D. Kelsey reassured him "that behind the legends and myths of the Book were many profound truths which one could not escape."[7] Kelsey and Mays provided King with role models of academically trained ministers, and their example inspired him to continue his theological studies. "Both were ministers, both deeply religious," King said in a later interview, "and yet both were learned men, aware of all the trends of modern thinking. I could see in their lives an ideal of what I wanted a minister to be."[8]

Drawn to Crozer because of its liberal reputation, King deepened his theological understanding while at the seminary. By the end of his studies there,

---

3. King, "Autobiography of Religious Development," in *Papers* 1:361, 359, 363.

4. Benjamin E. Mays, *The Negro's God as Reflected in His Literature* (New York: Russell & Russell, 1938), pp. 23–24.

5. King, Sr., "Moderator's Annual Address, Atlanta Missionary Baptist Association," 17 October 1940, CKFC.

6. King, quoted in Peters, "Our Weapon Is Love," p. 72.

7. King, "Autobiography of Religious Development," in *Papers* 1:362.

8. King, quoted in Peters, p. 72.

his papers had begun to express an awareness of the limitations of social gospel theology, even while King identified himself with theological perspectives that stressed transcendent moral values and the importance of religious experience. His seminary program included many courses on theology with George W. Davis, a Baptist theologian who combined social gospel teachings with a critical understanding of modern theology. King initially believed that Christian liberalism provided answers to "new problems of cultural and social change," unlike its theological adversary, fundamentalism, which sought "to preserve the old faith in a changing milieu."[9] As he continued his studies, though, King found his initial uncritical attraction to liberal theology "going through a state of transition." His personal experience with "a vicious race problem" had made it "very difficult . . . to believe in the essential goodness of man"; nevertheless, his recognition of "the gradual improvements of this same race problem" led him "to see some noble possibilities in human nature." While continuing to reject biblical literalism and doctrinal conservatism, King was becoming, he acknowledged, "a victim of eclecticism," seeking to "synthesize the best in liberal theology with the best in neo-o[r]thodox theology."[10]

Davis also introduced King to personalism, a philosophical school of thought that satisfied King's desire for both intellectual cogency and experiential religious understanding. In an essay for Davis, King reviewed a text by Boston University professor Edgar S. Brightman, a leading personalist theologian. Excited by Brightman's analysis of various conceptions of God, King reported that he was "amazed to find that the conception of God is so complex and one about which opinions differ so widely." Conceding that he was still "quite confused as to which definition [of God] was the most adequate," King decided that Brightman's personalist theology held the greatest appeal.[11] Its emphasis on the reality of personal religious experience validated King's own belief that "every man, from the ordinary simplehearted believer to the philosophical intellectual giant, may find God through religious experience."[12] His reading of Brightman suggested to him that his early skepticism may not have undermined his inherited religiosity:

> How I long now for that religious experience which Dr. Brightman so cogently speaks of throughout his book. It seems to be an experience, the lack of which life becomes dull and meaningless. As I reflect on the matter, however, I do remember moments that I have been awe awakened; there have been times that I have been carried out of myself by something greater than myself and to that something I gave myself. Has this great something been God? Maybe after all I have been religious for a number of years, and am now only becoming aware of it.[13]

---

9. King, "The Sources of Fundamentalism and Liberalism Considered Historically and Psychologically," in *Papers* 1:240.

10. King, "How Modern Christians Should Think of Man," in *Papers* 1:274.

11. King, "A Conception and Impression of Religion Drawn from Dr. Brightman's Book Entitled *A Philosophy of Religion*," in *Papers* 1:410, 411.

12. King, "The Place of Reason and Experience in Finding God," in *Papers* 1:234.

13. King, "A Conception and Impression of Religion," in *Papers* 1:415–416.

Brightman's personalism reassured King that he had experienced God's powerful presence in his own life even without the benefit of an "abrupt" religious conversion. Even as personalist theology became the focus of King's studies, it strengthened his belief that experience as well as intellectual reflection could be the basis of religious belief. "It is through experience that we come to realize that some things are out of harmony with God's will," King wrote in an essay for Davis. "No theology is needed to tell us that love is the law of life and to disobey it means to suffer the consequences."[14]

To continue his theological training, King applied to Edinburgh University, which accepted him, and to Yale University, which did not, but it was to Boston University, a stronghold of personalism, that he was particularly attracted. Boston was the alma mater of Raymond Bean, one of King's favorite professors at Crozer. He indicated in his application that Bean's "great influence over me has turned my eyes toward his former school."[15] He was also aware of several African Americans who had studied at the school, which had a long-established reputation as a hospitable environment for black theology students.[16] Unlike Crozer, where there were less than a dozen African-American seminarians, Boston University had a larger number of black students, and its close proximity to other colleges helped to create a community of African-American students with whom King could interact.

King knew that at Boston he could refine his personalism in classes with Brightman and other noted theologians. King explained that he had a "general knowledge" of systematic theology but sought "intensified study" in graduate school to gain "a thorough grasp of knowledge in my field." He announced that theology, his chosen field, should be "as scientific, as thorough, and as realistic as any other discipline. In a word, scholarship is my goal."[17] Even while expressing a desire to teach theology after he completed his studies, King had already begun to incorporate his theological training into his preaching. King's studies at Crozer had encouraged him to question many aspects of his religious heritage, but the church of his parents and grandparents had imparted an understanding of God and the Christian mission that theological learning enhanced rather than displaced. He later explained that personalism's "insistence that only personality—finite and infinite—is ultimately real strengthened me in two convictions: it gave me a

---

14. King, "Place of Reason and Experience," in *Papers* 1:234.

15. King, Fragment of Application to Boston University, in *Papers* 1:390.

16. In the fall of 1950, when considering various graduate schools, King met Crozer alumnus Samuel D. Proctor at a campus lecture and learned about Proctor's training at Boston University, where he had received his Th.D. that year. Dean Walter Muelder later estimated that Boston University awarded half of the doctorates in religion received by African Americans during the decade after King's arrival. He explained: "When the reason for this was sought, blacks said to me, 'We know where Boston University stands and the word gets around'" (Walter G. Muelder, "Philosophical and Theological Influences in the Thought and Action of Martin Luther King, Jr.," *Debate and Understanding* 1 [1977]: 183). See also Muelder, "Recruitment of Negroes for Theological Studies," *Review of Religious Research* 5 (Spring 1964): 152–156.

4   17. King, Fragment of Application to Boston University, in *Papers* 1:390.

metaphysical and philosophical grounding for the idea of a personal God,
and it gave me a metaphysical basis for the dignity and worth of all human
personality."[18]

⋙⋘

In the fall of 1951, after driving from Atlanta in the green Chevrolet his
father had given him and moving into an apartment on St. Botolph Street in
Boston, King immersed himself in his courses at Boston University's School
of Theology. During his first semester he came into contact with the leading
proponents of personalist theological studies. Edgar Brightman had studied
with Borden Parker Bowne, the first notable American advocate of personalism and a member of Boston's faculty until his death in 1910. Since 1925
Brightman had held an endowed chair at Boston named for his mentor. Sixty-
seven years old when King arrived, Brightman taught the core course on the
philosophy of religion, assigning his own work, *A Philosophy of Religion*, as the
required text.[19] Under Brightman's guidance, King would continue developing
his theological outlook by critically evaluating the ideas of leading theologians
from a personalist perspective. He also took two courses—one on personalism
and the other a directed study in systematic theology—with L. Harold De-
Wolf, a Methodist minister and Brightman's protégé. DeWolf had taught at
Boston University for twenty years and would become King's most important
mentor after Brightman's death in 1953.[20]

---

18. King, *Stride Toward Freedom* (New York: Harper & Brothers, 1958), p. 100.

19. Borden Parker Bowne (1847–1910) taught at Boston University in the Liberal Arts College and the School of Theology and became the first dean of Boston's Graduate School. He
published numerous books and articles, including *The Theory of Thought and Knowledge* (1897)
and *Personalism* (1908). Edgar Sheffield Brightman (1884–1953) received his S.T.B. in 1910 and
Ph.D. in 1912 from Boston University. Brightman taught at Nebraska Wesleyan University from
1912 to 1915 and at Wesleyan University from 1915 to 1919. In 1919 he returned to Boston
University as a professor of philosophy, and remained there until his death. His publications
include *Introduction to Philosophy* (1925), *The Problem of God* (1930), *The Finding of God* (1931),
Moral Laws (1933), *A Philosophy of Religion* (1940), and *Nature and Values* (1945). Brightman is
noted for his theistic finitism, and particularly his view that God's power to combat evil is limited.
See Brightman's intellectual autobiography, "Religion as Truth," in *Contemporary American The-
ology*, ed. Vergilius Ferm (New York: Round Table, 1932), pp. 53–81; Brightman, *Person and
Reality*, ed. Peter A. Bertocci (New York: Ronald Press, 1958); and Walter G. Muelder, "Edgar S.
Brightman: Person and Moral Philosopher," in *The Boston Personalist Tradition in Philosophy, Social
Ethics, and Theology*, ed. Paul Deats and Carol Robb (Macon, Ga.: Mercer University Press, 1986),
pp. 105–20.

20. L. Harold DeWolf (1905–1986) received his A.B. from Nebraska Wesleyan University in
1924, his S.T.B. in 1926, and his Ph.D. in 1935 from Boston University. He served as a Methodist
pastor in Nebraska and Massachusetts between 1926 and 1936. He taught in the department of
philosophy at Boston University from 1934 until 1944, when he became professor of systematic
theology in the School of Theology. He left Boston University in 1965 to become dean and
professor of systematic theology at Wesley Theological Seminary in Washington, D.C. He retired
in 1972. He also taught in central and east Africa during 1955–1956 and 1962–1963. His publications include *The Religious Revolt Against Reason* (1949), *A Theology of the Living Church* (1953),
The Case for Theology in Liberal Perspective (1959), *Present Trends in Christian Thought* (1960), *The
Enduring Message of the Bible* (1960), *Responsible Freedom: Guidelines to Christian Action* (1971), and
Crime and Justice in America: A Paradox of Conscience (1975). King remained in contact with DeWolf

During his first semester at Boston, King clarified his personalist views in papers that explored various forms of personalism and critically assessed the writings of non-personalist theologians. King's essays for his classes with Brightman and DeWolf were not as personally revealing as were some of those he had written at Crozer, but they did provide opportunities for him to express his theological opinions. As was the case during his Crozer years, King's arguments were sufficiently consistent and convincing to persuade his teachers of his competency; yet they were also derivative, often relying on appropriated words and phrases. In his essays King acknowledged drawing from others as he refined his theological beliefs, but, especially in the essays for DeWolf, he often failed to cite his sources precisely and appropriated the words of others without adequate attribution.[21] The significance of King's academic papers lies not in their cogency or originality, therefore, but in their reliability as expressions of his theological preferences. The Boston essays trace the course of King's theological development, revealing how he constructed a theological identity by carefully selecting insights from various perspectives that were consistent with his own. These borrowed insights would contribute to his subsequent religious leadership.

In first-semester papers written for Brightman and DeWolf, for example, King distinguished his views from the personalism of the British Hegelian J. M. E. McTaggart, who found belief in an omnipotent and creative God "metaphysically unsound." King labeled McTaggart an atheist, asserting that he failed to "recognize the necessity of one all-embracing or controlling Person." Although King identified himself with Brightman's theological perspective, he offered mild criticisms of his professor's notion that the existence of evil implied that God's power was limited, arguing, for example, that this theistic finitism left "faith in a supreme God endangered."[22] Nevertheless, his formulation of the problem of theodicy placed him close to Brightman's views. "God's power is finite," King wrote on his final examination for Brightman's class, "but his goodness is infinite. . . . After a somewhat extensive study of the idea I am all but convinced that [this] is the only ad[e]quate explanation for the existence of evil."[23] King's defense of personalism from the chal-

---

after graduating in 1955. DeWolf facilitated the 1964 donation of King's personal papers to Boston University, traveling to Atlanta to help pack the boxes for shipment. For DeWolf's assessment of his former student, see L. Harold DeWolf, "Martin Luther King, Jr., as Theologian," *Journal of the Interdenominational Theological Center* 4 (1977): 1–11. For more on DeWolf, see his intellectual autobiography, "Ethical Implications for Criminal Justice," in *The Boston Personalist Tradition in Philosophy, Social Ethics, and Theology*, ed. Paul Deats and Carol Robb (Macon, Ga.: Mercer University Press, 1986), pp. 221–235.

21. For discussions of plagiarism in King's student writings, see the Martin Luther King, Jr., Papers Project, "The Student Papers of Martin Luther King, Jr.: A Summary Statement on Research," *Journal of American History* 78, no. 1 (June 1991): 23–31; and Clayborne Carson, Peter Holloran, Ralph E. Luker, and Penny A. Russell, "Martin Luther King, Jr., as Scholar: A Reexamination of His Theological Writings," ibid., pp. 93–105.

22. King, "A Comparison and Evaluation of the Views Set Forth in J. M. E. McTaggart's *Some Dogmas of Religion* with Those Set Forth by Edgar S. Brightman in His Course on 'Philosophy of Religion,'" 25 October 1951, MLKP-MBU: Box 112.

23. King, Final examination answers, Philosophy of Religion, p. 109 in this volume.

lenges of alternative theological schools gained the approval of Brightman and DeWolf, although the two professors sometimes debated King's points in the margins of his papers.

King received an A— for the course he took with Brightman and grades of A and A— for the two courses with DeWolf, but the latter professor was more effusive in applauding King's work during the first semester. Less critical than Brightman in his evaluations of King's papers, DeWolf gradually assumed the role of King's primary mentor, as he would for many other black students at Boston. DeWolf called one of King's essays "superior," adding that it exhibited "excellent, incisive criticism." He praised another paper on the Swiss neo-orthodox theologian Karl Barth as an "excellent study," awarding King an A. In assessing the Barth paper, DeWolf did not note that King largely restated the views of his professors, both at Crozer and at Boston. Challenging Barth's view of God as "Wholly Other," King conceded that he had been "greatly influence by the liberal theology" to which he was exposed at Crozer and proceeded to use the words of Crozer professor George W. Davis when acknowledging that neo-orthodoxy served as a "necessary corrective" for "shallow" liberalism: "[Barth's] cry does call attention to the desperateness of the human situation. He does insist that religion begins with God and that man cannot have faith apart from him. He does proclaim that apart from God our human efforts turn to ashes and our sunrises into darkest night."[24] King would continue to use Davis's vivid mode of expression on subsequent occasions to praise an author's affirmation of God's transcendence in the world.[25]

In another essay written for DeWolf entitled "Contemporary Continental Theology," King's tendency to appropriate the insights of others was even more evident: lengthy sections of the essay were taken verbatim from *Contemporary Continental Theology* by Walter Marshall Horton.[26] King obscured his reliance on Horton by referring to him only once, when he acknowledged that a passage was quoted from Horton. King cited several European theologians, including Anders Nygren, but his quotations from them and the corresponding interpretations were in fact appropriated from Horton.[27] Although the ideas expressed in the essay were consistent with King's later writings on *agape*, his explication of Nygren's *Agape and Eros* was identical to Horton's. Thus, although King's understanding of the distinction between romantic

---

24. George W. Davis, "Some Theological Continuities in the Crisis Theology," *Crozer Quarterly* 27, no. 3 (July 1950): 217–218, quoted in King, "Karl Barth's Conception of God," p. 106 in this volume. In addition to this concluding statement on Barth's prophetic message, King appropriated many of his criticisms from Davis and another source, Alvin Sylvester Zerbe's *The Karl Barth Theology, or The New Transcendentalism* (Cleveland: Central Publishing House, 1930).

25. In two other Boston essays ("A Comparison and Evaluation of the Theology of Luther with that of Calvin" and "Contemporary Continental Theology," pp. 191 and 138, respectively, in this volume) and in his dissertation, King appropriated the passage to praise such diverse theologians as John Calvin, Martin Luther, Paul Tillich, and Henry Nelson Wieman.

26. Walter Marshall Horton, *Contemporary Continental Theology: An Interpretation for Anglo-Saxons* (New York: Harper & Brothers, 1938).

27. A more extended discussion of King's plagiarism of Horton is in "Student Papers of Martin Luther King, Jr.," pp. 24–25.

love and the Greek concept of *agape* may have been shaped by Nygren's ideas, the evidence in "Contemporary Continental Theology" suggests that King's ideas were drawn from Horton's analysis rather than from his own reading of Nygren.

DeWolf had little reason to suspect plagiarism given his student's good performance in written examinations and in the classroom. He later remembered King as "a very good student, all business, a scholar's scholar, one digging deeply to work out and think through his philosophy of religion and life."[28] DeWolf's obliviousness regarding King's plagiaries is partially explained by the consistency of the theological perspective that emerged in the papers, but it also suggests that he did not demand of King the analytical precision and originality that might have prepared his student for a career of scholarly writing. DeWolf's failure to note the plagiarized passages in King's essays suggests that he asked little more of King than accurate explication and judicious synthesis. Brightman was more demanding. He insisted, for example, on careful citation practices, as outlined in an essay on writing bibliographies in his *Manual for Students of Philosophy*. He told King to consult the manual after the bibliography to King's first essay failed to meet his exacting standards. In his next paper, King indicated an awareness of his professor's expectations by appending a note to the essay, apologizing for footnotes that were "in somewhat bad condition" and a block quotation that had not been properly arranged, both errors attributed to a poor typist.[29]

During his second semester at Boston, King continued his exploration of personalist theology in courses with DeWolf and broadened his studies with a course at Harvard University in the history of modern philosophy with Raphael Demos.[30] King expanded his criticisms of theological liberalism in an outline written for DeWolf on Reinhold Niebuhr, whose writings led King to acknowledge "the fundamental weaknesses and inevitable sterility of the humanistic emphasis" of liberalism in the twentieth century.[31] King was particularly receptive to Niebuhr's criticism of love and justice as conceived in liberal and orthodox theology. In orthodoxy, "individual perfection is too often made an end in itself," but liberalism "vainly seeks to overcome justice th[r]ough purely moral and rational suasions." Liberalism, King wrote, "confuses the ideal itself with the realistic means which must be employed to coerce society into an approximation of that ideal." King was also drawn to Niebuhr's eco-

---

28. L. Harold DeWolf, interview with John H. Britton, 23 April 1968, Ralph J. Bunche Oral History Collection, Moorland-Spingarn Research Center, Howard University.

29. King, "A Comparison and Evaluation of McTaggart and Brightman"; and King to Brightman, 6 December 1951, appended to "A Comparison and Evaluation of the Philosophical Views Set Forth in J. M. E. McTaggart's *Some Dogmas of Religion*, and William E. Hocking's *The Meaning of God in Human Experience* with Those Set Forth in Edgar S. Brightman's Course on 'Philosophy of Religion,'" p. 76 in this volume.

30. King passed over courses with such titles as Seminar in Gandhi, Social Christianity, Methods of Changing Social Attitudes, and Christianity and Race Relations. See Boston University catalogs, 1951–1953.

31. King, "Reinhold Niebuhr," p. 141 in this volume.

nomic and moral critique of capitalism, which King saw as responsible for "appalling injustices," particularly the "concentration of power and resources in the hands of a relatively small wealthy class."[32]

In his conclusion King applauded Niebuhr's emphasis on making realistic moral choices and found "very little to disagree with" in Niebuhr's social analysis. King did, however, criticize Niebuhr for an inadequate explanation of how *agape* operates in human history: "He fails to see that the availability of the divine *Agape* is an essential affirmati[on] of the Christian religion."[33] King would later emphasize the redemptive power of *agape* in his dissertation and in his public statements as a civil rights leader.[34]

༺ஓ๛

At Boston University King encountered an urban environment quite different from the sheltered seminary atmosphere he had left at Crozer, but he quickly adjusted, establishing contacts with other black students attending Boston's many colleges and seminaries. He actively sought out southern students, particularly those from Atlanta, and served as their link to the South. "Martin was in the center of it all," one friend later commented, "as we discussed topics of interest."[35] Traveling south for the holidays and other occasions, King would bring back news about Morehouse College and other Atlanta-area schools.[36]

King's easy warmth and charm made him an attractive figure on campus. One friend described him as a "very amiable" person who liked parties and was generous with his money: "He was like a prince," one friend recalled. A skilled mimic and comic, King developed a private language with the other students. Biting into a hot dog at his favorite restaurant, King would say, "Doctor, this is a great institution." The expression became his signature, and he would apply it in many situations.[37] His acquaintances were eager to hear King speak at Boston-area churches. "We always found our way to those churches," one friend recalled, "as much to hear his message, but also his style was so entertaining."[38] Gathering together in the school cafeteria or in

32. King, "Reinhold Niebuhr's Ethical Dualism," pp. 146, 142 in this volume.

33. King, "Reinhold Niebuhr's Ethical Dualism," p. 150 in this volume. DeWolf gave the essay an A −, calling it an "excellent interpretation and exposition," but wished that "the critical evaluation had been carried further."

34. See, for instance, King, "A Comparison of the Conceptions of God in the Thinking of Paul Tillich and Henry Nelson Wieman," p. 441 in this volume; and King, *Stride Toward Freedom*, pp. 104–106. King's discussion of *agape* in *Stride* may also derive from Harry Emerson Fosdick, *On Being Fit to Live With: Sermons on Post-War Christianity* (New York: Harper & Brothers, 1946), pp. 6–7; and George Kelsey, "The Christian Way in Race Relations," in *The Christian Way in Race Relations*, ed. William Stuart Nelson (New York: Harper & Brothers, 1948), p. 40.

35. Willard A. Williams, "Remembering Martin Luther King, Jr.," 1986, WAWP-GAMK. See also "Conversation Between Cornish Rogers and David Thelen," *Journal of American History* 78, no. 1 (June 1991): 44–46.

36. "Conversation Between Cornish Rogers and David Thelen," p. 45.

37. Williams, "Remembering Martin Luther King, Jr."

38. Sybil Haydel Morial, interview with Clayborne Carson, 25 June 1992.

dormitory rooms, King and the other students explored issues not covered in the classroom. A friend who left Boston after King's first year nostalgically called the group "the gang in the room solving the problems of the world, politically, socially, and in the theological realm."[39] Although participants sometimes discussed racial discrimination, issues such as the positive role of the church in the black community generally engaged them more than discussions of civil rights and black-white relations. Unlike Benjamin Mays and other black academics who had focused on racial issues in their academic studies, King and most others in his group sought advanced training in areas not directly related to their heritage as African Americans.

Over time these gatherings were formalized as meetings of the Dialectical Society. Perhaps modeled after a Philosophical Society initiated by Brightman thirty years before, the group comprised a dozen theological students who met monthly, usually at King's apartment, to discuss a paper presented by one of the participants. "It was a group," one member recalled, "that was mainly interested in certain philosophical and theological ideas and applied them to the black situation in the country."[40] King generally presided over the sessions, helping choose the topics for discussion or engaging a guest speaker such as his advisor, Professor DeWolf. One participant later reflected that King's leadership "was not aggressive, but always available." King "would speak in the discussions, but I never got the impression that he was insisting that if he said it, it had to be right"; instead, King encouraged the others to see that "we're here to cooperate and not compete."[41] King drew upon his academic study of the theology of Reinhold Niebuhr in one of his own talks to the Dialectical Society. Though King's presentation did not directly refer to racial issues, he questioned Niebuhr's notion of the inherent imperfectibility of human nature. "The result of this view is that there can be no real moral progress in man's social, political, and religious life," King complained. "Within such a view is there no hope for man?"[42]

During his first year at Boston University, King strengthened his reputation as a skilled preacher. In September 1951, while driving to Boston for the first time, King preached at Concord Baptist Church in Brooklyn, one of the largest congregations in the country. Its pastor was the Reverend Gardner Taylor, a gifted preacher in the National Baptist Convention and an associate of King, Sr. In addition to Taylor, King was familiar from an early age with other prominent black ministers, many of whom knew his father well and had preached at Ebenezer. King's admiration for the talented preachers who passed through Ebenezer was evident; during one discussion at Boston University, King proudly listed some of the most powerful orators of the African-American Baptist church—Gardner Taylor, Sandy Ray, Mordecai Johnson,

---

39. W. T. Handy, Jr., to King, 18 November 1952, p. 161 in this volume.
40. "Conversation Between Cornish Rogers and David Thelen," p. 46.
41. Ibid., p. 48.
42. King, "The Theology of Reinhold Niebuhr," p. 275 in this volume.

and Benjamin Mays—and challenged the Methodists to do the same. The Methodist seminarians could produce only one name.[43] King's student acquaintances often accompanied him when he delivered guest sermons and recognized his special oratorical talent. A classmate commented that she and other students thought he was a "phenomenal preacher" who could "mesmerize" the audience.[44] His developing reputation as a rising young star of the Baptist church opened up guest pulpits along the eastern seaboard. Churches in Washington, D.C., Baltimore, Philadelphia, and New York offered welcome havens for King as he traveled back and forth between Atlanta and Boston.

An old friend of King, Sr., the Reverend William H. Hester, was particularly supportive of King and other black graduate students, welcoming them to the pulpit of Twelfth Baptist Church in Roxbury. King preached at the church occasionally and participated regularly in the young adults group on Sunday evenings. King once gave a sermon on black women as a "great institution," a female friend remembered, in which he "talked about how resourceful we were and how persevering we were, and how caring and strong."[45] Later, during the Montgomery bus boycott, a parishioner wrote to King recalling "the great sermon" he had heard at Twelfth. In the sermon, probably entitled "Loving Your Enemies," King had preached from a passage in the book of Matthew: "But I say unto you, Love your enemies, bless them that curse you, do good to them that hate you, and pray for them which despitefully use you, and persecute you."[46] If we can judge from their titles, several of King's sermons from this period would later become standards in his repertoire. There is little documentation of these early homilies, but the fragmentary extant evidence suggests that King apparently did not alter a sermon drastically after he initially composed it.[47] In a later version of "Loving Your Enemies," King stressed the importance of forgiveness, noting that "there is some good in the worst of us and some evil in the best of us." King indicated that this love was not "some sentimental outpouring," but *agape*, or "redemptive good will for all men." Love could transform "an enemy into a friend," because "only by loving them can we know God and experience the beauty of his holiness."[48]

King maintained his close ties to Ebenezer Baptist Church and his family

---

43. Williams, "Remembering Martin Luther King, Jr."

44. Sybil Haydel Morial, interview with Clayborne Carson. See also Williams, "Remembering Martin Luther King, Jr."

45. Sybil Haydel Morial, interview with Clayborne Carson.

46. Milton Britton to King, 5 February 1956, MLKP-MBU: Box 15; Matthew 6:44.

47. See, for example, the transcript of King's "Rediscovering Lost Values," 28 February 1954, and the discussion of it in this introduction, pp. 248–256 and 26–28, respectively, in this volume. During the Montgomery bus boycott King gave this sermon several times, occasionally with the title "Going Forward by Going Backwards." Complete transcripts have not been found, but contemporary reports indicate that the structure and language of these versions were similar to the one King preached in 1954.

48. King, *Strength to Love* (New York: Harper & Row, 1963), pp. 48, 49, 50, 52, 53.

while at school in Boston, speaking with his mother by telephone, "often for hours at a time, three or four times a week."[49] In late November 1951, he drove to Atlanta to celebrate his parents' twenty-fifth wedding anniversary, making the first of four trips home that school year. The next month, he traveled to Atlanta again to participate in the Christmas and New Year's services at Ebenezer. His discussions with his parents often concerned his future plans regarding marriage. They expected him to find a wife quickly, as social mores required that preachers be married, but King made slow progress toward that goal. "When I knew M. L.," W. T. Handy later remembered, "he wasn't running after the girls; the girls were running after him. And he was a good catch."[50] After hearing about King's popularity from Handy, who had visited the King family in Atlanta, Alberta Williams King expressed concern about her son's marriage prospects in a sober letter to Martin, Jr., which he shared with Handy. Handy later quoted King's mother in a teasing letter to him: "Remember M. L., 'we are expecting great things from you'"—adding that only King himself would "restrain our expectations from bearing fruit."[51]

Six months after arriving in Boston, King asked Mary Powell, a friend from Atlanta, if she knew any young women who might suit him. Powell immediately thought of Coretta Scott, a fellow student at the New England Conservatory of Music. More interested in a musical career than in marrying a Baptist minister, Coretta Scott, as Powell described her, was a poised, attractive, intelligent young woman with a mind of her own. As Scott later recalled, King called her to see if they could meet. When she agreed and met with King the next day, she remembered feeling initially unimpressed with King's height—five feet seven inches. But when King began talking, he "grew in stature." As she recalled, "This young man became increasingly better-looking as he talked, so strongly and convincingly. . . . He seemed to know exactly where he was going and how he was going to get there." At the end of their first date she remembered King telling her, "You have everything I have ever wanted in a wife. There are only four things, and you have them all . . . character, intelligence, personality, and beauty."[52] King and Scott began dating, and their courtship progressed rapidly; within several months Scott began to consider seriously King's talk of marriage.[53]

Compared to King's relatively privileged childhood in Atlanta's "Sweet Auburn," Coretta Scott's youth had been less advantaged. She grew up on a farm in rural Alabama twenty miles outside the county seat of Marion. Her father,

49. King, Sr., *Daddy King*, p. 148.

50. W. T. Handy, Jr., interview with Clayborne Carson, 1 July 1992.

51. W. T. Handy, Jr., to King, 18 November 1952, p. 163 in this volume. Alberta Williams King's letter to her son is not extant.

52. Coretta Scott King, *My Life with Martin Luther King, Jr.* (New York: Holt, Rinehart & Winston, 1969), pp. 54–55.

53. King, *My Life*, pp. 20–64. See also L. D. Reddick, *Crusader Without Violence* (New York: Harper & Brothers, 1959), pp. 90–105.

Obadiah Scott, was a hardworking farmer who ran a barbershop in his home at night to earn extra money. His industriousness brought the family material comfort and stability, but it also caused Coretta Scott to worry about her father's safety. In a time when successful blacks often encountered racist violence, she later marveled, "It is a wonder that my own father did not end up in the swamp."[54] Her fears for her father were not unfounded. In November 1942, the Scott home had burned to the ground, and the following spring another fire destroyed their newly purchased sawmill after Scott refused to sell it to a white logger.[55]

Determined to advance her education, Coretta Scott decided to attend Antioch College in Yellow Springs, Ohio, where her older sister, Edythe, had been a student. Scott enrolled in 1945 "with a good deal of doubt" and "with a good deal of fear" about northern culture. Her decision to go north to college stemmed from her conviction that "a good education . . . should be as free as possible—and that means free from Jim Crow as well as free in classroom teaching."[56] Taking voice lessons and pursuing a program of music education, Scott became aware of northern racial discrimination when she attempted to fulfill her student teaching requirement in a local elementary school: the school board prohibited her from joining the all-white faculty even though the student body was integrated. When administrators at Antioch discouraged her from protesting this injustice, Scott complained, "I came here from Alabama to be free of segregation." The incident motivated her to join the Antioch chapter of the National Association for the Advancement of Colored People (NAACP) and other civil rights organizations. In addition to civil rights activism, she was also drawn toward the pacifist movement. As a member of the Young Progressives, Scott supported Henry Wallace's presidential campaign in 1948 and attended the Progressive party convention as a student delegate.[57] A few years later, when she first met King in Boston, Scott saw herself as more of a political activist than he was; nevertheless, the two students shared a strong commitment to social reform.

As the courtship continued during the spring, King and Scott found many areas of agreement in their dissenting political and economic views. According to a later memoir, King had undertaken a serious examination of Karl Marx's writings during the Christmas holidays of 1949. Although he rejected Marxian materialism, ethical relativism, and totalitarianism, King was attracted to Marx's critique of capitalism. "I was deeply concerned from my early teen days about the gulf between superfluous wealth and abject poverty, and my reading of Marx made me ever more conscious of this gulf," he

---

54. King, *My Life*, p. 25.

55. Ibid., pp. 38–39.

56. Coretta Scott, "Why I Came To College," *Opportunity* 26 (1948): 42, 71.

57. Coretta Scott King, interview with Donna Ruth Duvigneaud, in Duvigneaud, "The Spirit and Vision of Coretta Scott King: A Case Study of Her Contributions to Nonviolent Social Change" (M.A. thesis, New York University, 1984); King, *My Life*, p. 43.

explained in *Stride Toward Freedom*.[58] Scott recalled that King told her he "could never be a Communist," nor "a thoroughgoing capitalist" like his father. "A society based on making all the money you can and ignoring people's needs is wrong. I don't want to *own* a lot of things," she remembered him saying.[59] King, Sr., recalled political arguments—"sharp exchanges"—with his son, who "seemed to be drifting away from the basics of capitalism and Western democracy."[60] Such disagreements may have been stimulated by King, Jr.'s August 1952 lecture at Ebenezer on "The Challenge of Communism to Christianity."[61]

That same August, King arranged for Coretta Scott to visit Atlanta in an effort to win his parents' approval of their relationship. Scott recalled being wary during this first encounter with the King family—"all I could think of was the well-known, rather closed social life of the black middle class of Atlanta." She discovered that the Kings "were dedicated people who judged others on their own merits," but concluded that her visit "was not an unqualified success." King, Sr., remained unsure about the couple's seriousness. King was not able to meet Scott's family that summer, and they returned to Boston in September without either family's approval of their plans to marry.[62]

ᴓᴓᴓ

Back at school for his second year, King was troubled by the unresolved tensions with his father over his courtship of Coretta Scott, and he spoke of his frustration in conversations with friends. That fall former Crozer classmate H. Edward Whitaker teased him about his unfulfilled intentions: "By the way you told me two years ago you would be married by the next summer. Apparently you are still meeting these girls who are one-time wreckers." W. T. Handy also expressed an interest in the personal life of "the most eligible and popular bachelor in town": "I know you are now married? Which one was

---

58. King, *Stride Toward Freedom*, p. 94. King wrote: "In so far as Marx posited a metaphysical materialism, an ethical relativism, and a strangulating totalitarianism, I responded with an unambiguous 'no'; but in so far as he pointed to weaknesses of traditional capitalism, contributed to the growth of a definite self-consciousness in the masses, and challenged the social conscience of the Christian churches, I responded with a definite 'yes'" (p. 95).

59. King, *My Life*, p. 56.

60. King, Sr., *Daddy King*, p. 147.

61. Melvin H. Watson, dean of the Morehouse School of Religion, commented that King did not adequately clarify the difference between the materialism of the Greek philosophical atomists and that of Karl Marx. Watson corrected King's understanding of Karl Marx, who argued, as Watson explained, that "the culture, thoughts, in fact the whole life of man is conditioned . . . by his relationship to the instruments necessary to the making of a living." Watson also pointed out that "Stalin would certainly not make the question of *race* a sub-point as you did on Sunday," maintaining that Soviet Communism had taken a much stronger official position against racism. Watson reminded King that his comments "by no means indicate a lack of appreciation for the fine job you did on Sunday." See Melvin Watson to King, 14 August 1952, pp. 156–157 in this volume. Watson had written an article on a similar topic in the *Journal of Religious Thought*. In 1963 King published a sermon with a similar title ("How Should a Christian View Communism") in *Strength to Love*, pp. 97–106.

62. King, *My Life*, pp. 63–67.

it?"[63] In addition to these concerns, King was experiencing difficulties with his course work after registering for a heavy academic load: two lecture courses with DeWolf, a seminar on the history of philosophy with Peter Bertocci, and a yearlong course on the philosophy of Hegel with his advisor, Brightman. He also took a class at Harvard with Raphael Demos on the philosophy of Plato.

The first sign of a troubled term came when King stumbled through an exploratory quiz for the Hegel seminar, missing such basic definitions as "logos" and "naturalism."[64] King had studied Hegel in other courses at Boston University, including Richard Millard's History of Recent Philosophy, but the seminar with Brightman constituted King's first prolonged exposure to Hegel's thought. A less than thorough knowledge of German heightened King's difficulty with the course, and—perhaps an indication of his frustration with the philosopher's abstruse language—his essays for the seminar were appropriated largely from a synopsis of Hegel's philosophy.[65] The loss of his mentor's guidance added to King's difficulties. Two weeks after the beginning of the semester a cerebral hemorrhage disabled Brightman, who was replaced by Peter Bertocci as leader of the seminar. Following Brightman's death several months later, King chose DeWolf as his advisor.

Not long after the beginning of the term King encountered difficulties in his other classes as well. After receiving an A on his first midterm examination for DeWolf's course on the history of Christian doctrine, DeWolf chastened King for his weak performance on the second: "Alas! You were to 'illustrate concretely some influences.' You have mostly paraphrased lecture material on the non-Christian philosophies themselves and in telling of their influences— abstractly, not concretely—have added some highly doubtful views." King's poor grade on the examination (68/100) prompted his concerned professor to ask: "Do you have a heavier program than you can swing this term? Let's face it together quickly. Something seems wrong. Can I be of any help?"[66] Two weeks later King took two midterm examinations on the same day, one at Harvard on the philosophy of Plato and another at Boston for a seminar in the history of philosophy. He received C's on both, though Bertocci tried to

---

63. H. Edward Whitaker to King, 31 October 1952; and W. T. Handy, Jr., to King, 18 November 1952; pp. 159, 163, respectively, in this volume.

64. King, Exploratory quiz, Seminar in Hegel, 24 September 1952, MLKP-MBU: Box 113.

65. King failed a German language examination early in the semester. King's main source was W. T. Stace's *The Philosophy of Hegel: A Systematic Exposition* (London: Macmillan, 1924). King's writings for the seminar included "The Development of Hegel's Thought as Revealed in His Early Theological Writings," 1 October 1952; "The Transition from Sense-Certainty to Sense-Perception in Hegel's Analysis of Consciousness," 15 October 1952; "The Transition from Sense-Perception to Understanding," 29 October 1952; "Objective Spirit," 4 February–22 May 1953; and "An Exposition of the First Triad of Categories of the Hegelian Logic—Being, Non-Being, Becoming," 4 February–22 May 1953; all in MLKP-MBU: Box 115. The last essay cited is published in this volume, pp. 196–201.

66. King, Examination answers, Religious Teachings of the Old Testament, 3 October 1952; and Examination answers, History of Christian Doctrine, 28 October 1952; both in MLKP-MBU: Box 115.

be sympathetic: "Too much of this is good to make me want to discourage you, but it does need <u>more careful</u> attention to <u>detail & connection.</u>"[67]

Shortly after these examinations, King confronted his father during his parents' visit to Boston in late November. Scott stopped by King's apartment every day during the visit, and King took his mother aside to tell her about his marriage plans.[68] Alberta Williams King had worried about her son earlier in the semester. She "was the first to notice that M. L. had stopped calling home as much as he had when he'd first gone up to Boston to study." Upon arriving in Boston and seeing the young couple's devotion to each other— "the young man was so much in love, stars were just glittering in his eyes"— King, Sr., decided to challenge them. "Let me ask you very directly," he later remembered saying to Scott. "Do you take my son seriously, Coretta?" Thinking that King, Sr., was referring to his son's sense of humor, Scott answered, "Why, no, Reverend King, not really." King, Sr., exploded in reply to the cheerful answer, mentioning the other women his son had dated: King "has gone out with the daughters of some fine, solid Atlanta families, folks we've known for many years, people we respect, and whose feelings we'd never trample on. I'm talking, Coretta, about people who have much to share and much to offer." When King, Sr., talked with his son in private after confronting Scott, the younger King insisted that he was going to marry her. "She's the most important person to come into my life, Dad," King, Sr., remembered his son saying; "I know you don't really approve, but this is what I have to do."[69] King, Sr., left Boston without giving his assent, but he eventually relented. Within a few months, King, Jr., and Scott were making plans for their wedding, and in April 1953 King, Sr., announced the engagement from Ebenezer's pulpit.[70]

Shortly after the confrontation with his father, King began to recover from his weak midterm grades. He wrote a strong examination on the religious teachings of the Old Testament, prompting DeWolf to comment, "Back in stride! Good work." In fact, DeWolf was so convinced of King's recovery that, despite low grades on the earlier examinations, he gave King an A and an A− for the two classes.[71] DeWolf's course on the religious teachings of the Old Testament was particularly interesting to King, offering the young minister an opportunity to enrich his preaching through detailed analysis of the Bible. King's notes from the course reveal his evolving thoughts about the nature of divinity. He wrote more than a thousand notecards of informal biblical exegesis on many books in the Old Testament, including one famous passage

---

67. King, Examination answers, Seminar in History of Philosophy, 13 November 1952; and Examination answers, Philosophy of Plato, 13 November 1952; both in MLKP-MBU: Box 113.

68. King, *My Life*, p. 68.

69. King, Sr., *Daddy King*, pp. 149–151.

70. *Atlanta Daily World*, 5 April 1953.

71. See King, Examination answers, Religious Teachings of the Old Testament, 22 September 1952–28 January 1953, MLKP-MBU: Box 115; and King, Final examination answers, History of Christian Doctrine, 20 January 1953, MLKP-MBU: Box 113.

from Amos ("let judgment run down as waters, and righteousness as a mighty stream") that King later included in many of his most famous orations. In his notes King argued that the God of Amos was "a God that demands justice rather than sacrifice; righteousness rather than ritual."[72] In his final examination for the course King declared a strong affinity for the Old Testament prophets, noting that they provided the "most illuminating conceptions of God," namely, an ethical monotheism: "For Amos God is a God of righteousness who demands ethical actions from his children. . . . For Hosea God is a God of love, and even his justice is but an expression of his love."[73]

In his notecards King emphasized that Christians should actively struggle for social justice. He praised Amos's condemnation of religious worshipers who neglected the importance of living ethically. "The external forms of worship mean nothing," King maintained, "unless a man's heart is right." King's belief that modern culture placed too much faith in human nature attracted him to Jeremiah, a prophet who stressed faith in God. Noting the similarity on this issue between Jeremiah and neo-orthodox theologians, King declared that "one of the great services of neo-orthodoxy, notwithstanding its e[xt]remes, is its revolt against all forms of humanistic perfectionism." At the same time, in a reading of another passage in Jeremiah, King insisted that human nature contains the potential for ethical action: "No matter how low an individual sinks in sin, there is still a spark of good within him." King's reading of Jeremiah, Amos, and other books affirmed his long-standing conviction that "whenever Christianity has remained true to its prophetic mission, it has taken a deep interest in social justice." Echoing an explanation he had made in an Ebenezer sermon regarding communism's appeal, King said that "the success of communism in the world today is due to the failure of Christians to live to the highest ethical ten[et]s inherent in its system."[74] King's abiding faith in the power of Christianity to create a just society led him to conclude, in an essay for DeWolf on St. Augustine, that the ultimate solution to the problem of evil was "not intellectual but spiritual." King argued that "the Christian answer to the problem of evil is ultimately contained in what he does with it, itself the result of what Christ did with evil on the cross."[75]

Completing his formal course work, King took fewer classes during the second term, but continued to struggle. Entering his final semester of courses on Christian doctrine and on the philosophy of Hegel, King also enrolled in a directed study in dissertation writing and a Harvard course with Nathaniel Lawrence on the philosophy of Alfred North Whitehead. His essays during the term were undistinguished. However, the Whitehead course did prompt

---

72. King, Notecards on books of the Old Testament, p. 165 in this volume.

73. King, Final examination answers, Religious Teachings of the Old Testament, p. 169 in this volume.

74. King, Notecards on books of the Old Testament, p. 165–167 in this volume.

75. King, "A Critical Evaluation of Augustine's Conception of Evil," 9 January 1953, MLKP-MBU: Box 115. His main source was Marion Burton, *The Problem of Evil* (Chicago: Open Court, 1909).

Courses at Boston University

Year & Course, grouped by semester	Instructor	Grade	Credit Hours
1951–1952			
Directed Study in Systematic Theology	L. Harold DeWolf	A –	4
Personalism	L. Harold DeWolf	A	3
Philosophy of Religion	Edgar S. Brightman	A –	2
Formal Logic (without graduate credit)	David S. Scarrow	C	(3)
Religious Teachings of the New Testament	L. Harold DeWolf	B	3
Seminar in Systematic Theology	L. Harold DeWolf	A	3
Directed Study in Systematic Theology	L. Harold DeWolf	A –	3
History of Modern Philosophy [1]	Raphael Demos		3
1952 Intersession			
History of Recent Philosophy	Richard M. Millard	A –	3
Seminar in Historical Theology	Edward P. Booth	B +	3
1952–1953			
Religious Teachings of the Old Testament	L. Harold DeWolf	A –	3
Seminar in History of Philosophy	Peter A. Bertocci	B +	3
Seminar in Philosophy	Edgar S. Brightman	B +	2
History of Christian Doctrine I	L. Harold DeWolf	A	2
Philosophy of Plato [2]	Raphael Demos	B	3
Directed Study in Thesis and Dissertation Writing	Jannette E. Newhall	A	3
Seminar in Philosophy	Peter A. Bertocci	B	2
History of Christian Doctrine II	L. Harold DeWolf	A	2
Philosophy of Whitehead [3]	Nathaniel Lawrence	A –	3

[1] Course taken at Harvard University.
[2] Course taken at Harvard University.
[3] Course taken at Harvard University.

him to write hundreds of notecards on Whitehead's philosophy in preparation for a lengthy term paper on the philosophical paradox of "the one and the many"—that is, the question of whether reality is composed of a unified whole or of numerous parts. King's essay, an expository exercise that explored few of the theological implications of Whitehead's views, received faint praise from Lawrence: "The worst that can be said of this essay is that it is not scintillating. You really wrestle with nothing."[76]

In King's most revealing paper of this term, he evaluated the theology of Martin Luther and John Calvin in an essay for DeWolf's course on Christian doctrine. According to King, Calvin's emphasis on God's power and justice was notable, but the Protestant reformer neglected the importance of God's love. "God is first and foremost an all loving Father," King affirmed, "and any theology which fails to recognize this, in an attempt to maintain the sovereignty of God, is betraying everything that is best in the Christian tradition." King also found Luther's and Calvin's doctrine of original sin undermined by modern discoveries about evolution. Noting that "it has become increasingly difficult to imagine any such original state of perfection for man," King felt "compelled, therefore, to reject the idea of a catastrophic fall." He espoused a notion of human nature that owed more to the evangelical liberalism of Davis and DeWolf than to the neo-orthodoxy of Barth and Niebuhr. Man's fall from grace, he argued, "is not due to some falling away from an original righteousness, but to a failure to rise to a higher level of his present existence."[77]

Shortly after completing his courses at Harvard and Boston University, King traveled to rural Perry County, Alabama, for his marriage to Coretta Scott on 18 June 1953. King's father performed the ceremony in the yard of the Scott family home. After the reception, the Kings drove to nearby Marion for their wedding night, which they spent in a black funeral home because the white-owned hotels in town would not allow the young couple to register. Forgoing a honeymoon, they attended a large reception in their honor at Ebenezer the next evening and settled into the King family home near the church for the remainder of the summer. On the following Sunday, Coretta Scott King, who had been raised a Methodist, joined Ebenezer and was baptized by her father-in-law. King, Jr.'s parents then departed for a summer vacation, leaving him as pastor in charge of the church. Coretta Scott King was quickly welcomed into the community, serving as Ebenezer's "First Lady of the Summer" and working as a clerk at Citizens' Trust Company, a black-owned bank of which King, Sr., was a director.[78]

As a result of Ebenezer's prominence in the community, WERD, an Atlanta

76. King, "Whitehead and the Problem of the One and the Many," 26 January–2 June 1953, MLKP-MBU: Box 112.

77. King, "A Comparison and Evaluation of the Theology of Luther with That of Calvin," pp. 188, 190 in this volume.

78. For additional details about the wedding and the summer of 1953, see King, *My Life*, pp. 71–75.

radio station—the first owned and operated by African Americans—began broadcasting King's sermons that summer. Although these homilies have not been located, transcripts of similarly titled sermons delivered later suggest that King urged the Ebenezer congregation to continue its struggle against injustice and inequality. In a later version of "Transformed Nonconformists," for example, based on a text from Paul's letter to the Romans, King singled out the organized church for yielding "more to the authority of the world than to the authority of God." King argued that "the hope of a secure and livable world lies with disciplined nonconformists, who are dedicated to justice, peace, and brotherhood."[79] King affirmed a similar trust in the transforming power of Christianity in "The Dimensions of a Complete Life." Belief in a "Supreme, Infinite Person," or God, he asserted, stood at the core of a "complete life," but "the rushing tide of materialism" in the modern world had caused Christians to neglect faith.[80] In these and other sermons, King derided the church's traditional separation of spiritual and political concerns, arguing that Christianity contained both the potential and the obligation to strive for a more just world.

In September, a few days after delivering "The Dimensions of a Complete Life" at Ebenezer, King traveled to Miami to attend the annual meeting of the National Baptist Convention with fifteen thousand other Baptists. The convention represented the nation's largest African-American denomination and had been a focus of the King family's religious activities since its inception. King's grandfather, the Reverend A. D. Williams, had attended its founding in 1895 and became a prominent leader in Georgia's affiliated state convention. In their work in the convention, both Williams and King, Sr., stressed the need for a politically active ministry. In 1942, King, Sr., spearheaded an effort in the convention to press President Franklin D. Roosevelt to eliminate racial discrimination on trains.[81] Although the convention supported some of King, Sr.'s efforts to expand the role of ministers to meet the African-American community's changing needs, by the 1950s it had come to be dominated by more conservative ministers who abjured involvement in political issues.

Activist ministers saw an opportunity in Miami to reform the organization

---

79. King, *Strength to Love*, pp. 17, 21, 23.

80. Martin Luther King, Jr., *The Measure of a Man* (Philadelphia: Christian Education Press, 1959), pp. 56, 37, 50.

81. Introduction to the *Papers*, 1:9, 13–14, 17, 33–34. After the *Brown* decision on 17 May 1954, King, Sr., stepped up his challenges to segregation. In June of that year he gave a rousing address to ten thousand Baptists gathered in Birmingham for the National Sunday School and Baptist Training Union Congress. Directing his ire at the city's mayor and superintendent of schools in the audience, King, Sr., declared that "we have learned the way to the Supreme Court and we will call upon it again and again for those rights guaranteed by the Constitution. It took the highest court eighty-nine years to interpret a law that was already on the statute books; now, how long will it take for the law to be enforced?" ("We Want to Live, Says Ga. Pastor," *Pittsburgh Courier*, 3 July 1954).

when president D. V. Jemison announced that he would retire rather than follow the pattern of previous presidents who often retained office until death. Seventy-one-year-old E. W. Perry, who had served as vice-president for many years, was the immediate favorite in the race to succeed Jemison, but other younger and more dynamic ministers announced their candidacy for the position, including King family friends Sandy Ray of Brooklyn and J. Raymond Henderson of Los Angeles. Some activist ministers supported Perry: Gardner Taylor served as his campaign manager, and Atlanta minister William Holmes Borders was on Perry's slate as vice president at large. But King, Sr., who chose not to attend the gathering, almost certainly supported Jackson.[82]

King, Jr., and his uncle, the Rev. Joel King, were among those gathered in Miami to witness the contentious presidential campaign. Henderson ultimately withdrew in favor of Perry, but the latter's support declined after T. J. Jemison, the president's son and leader of a recent Baton Rouge boycott against segregated buses, surprised the delegates by seconding Jackson's nomination instead of supporting Perry, his father's contemporary. After a dramatic all-night roll call vote, the Jackson forces prevailed over Perry's, leading to celebrations among the exhausted Baptists: "A Rev. Mr. King [probably Joel King] came up with a broom from somewhere and went through the crowd wildly sweeping the air to demonstrate that the progressives had made a clean sweep."[83] Although the extant documents do not indicate King, Jr.'s role in the presidential election, the younger King was probably pleased with the convention, which ended with numerous associates holding major positions in the organization. Although the new president did not follow Benjamin Mays's suggestion to name King, Jr., as one of the delegates to the quadrennial World Council of Churches, he selected King, Sr., to serve on the Convention's Board of Directors. J. Pius Barbour retained his post as editor of the *National Baptist Voice*.[84] Twenty-four years old and still a student, King, Jr.,

---

82. A letter to King, Sr., from J. Timothy Boddie, who supported Jackson, suggests that King supported Jackson. Boddie expressed his disappointment that King, Sr., did not attend the convention, but added that "things worked out as we wanted them anyhow" (J. Timothy Boddie to Martin Luther King, Sr., 3 November 1953, p. 210 in this volume). See also "State Leaders Endorse Rev. Jackson for President of Baptist, Inc.," 26 August 1953, Barnett Papers, part 1, reel 52.

83. *Baltimore Afro-American*, 19 September 1953. See also proceedings of the 10 September session in *Record of the Seventy-third Annual Session of the National Baptist Convention, U.S.A., Incorporated . . . , Miami, Florida, September 9–13, 1953* (n. d.), pp. 60–61.

84. *Record of the Seventy-third Annual Session*, pp. 66, 67. In the months before the Miami meeting, Mays, head of the National Baptist Convention's delegation to the World Council of Churches, recommended to President Jemison that King be named as one of the nine members. Jackson later removed the youthful King and several others from his list and appointed replacements with less academic training than those of Mays's list. See D. V. Jemison to Benjamin E. Mays, 18 July 1953; Mays to Jemison, 25 July; Jemison to Mays, 27 July; Jemison to Mays, 4 August; J. H. Jackson to Mays, 16 September; Mays to Jackson, 19 September; Mays to Robert S. Bilheimer, 25 September; Bilheimer to Mays, 3 December; and Mays to Bilheimer, 11 December 1953; all in BEMP-DHU. See also Gerald F. Gilmore's report "Negro Baptist Politics and the World Council of Churches," ca. 1954, in Barnett Papers, part 3, series J, reel 1.

already enjoyed family and personal ties to the ministers who would be prominent in national Baptist affairs for many years to come.[85]

〰〰〰〰

After the convention the newlyweds returned to Boston and moved into an apartment at 396 Northampton Street for their last year in that city. They led a hectic life, continuing their academic studies in addition to entertaining friends and hosting occasional meetings of the Dialectical Society. Coretta Scott King enrolled in thirteen courses that year, practicing four instruments and teaching in local schools in order to graduate from the conservatory in June. King, who had completed his formal course work, cheerfully offered to do the cleaning and washing. Coretta Scott King recalled being "very appreciative" of his help, "but I would wish to myself that he had let me do the job."[86] In addition to preaching, King was studying for several written qualifying examinations before continuing work on his dissertation.

By the time he finished his course work, King had come to affirm some of the enduring values of his religious heritage. In one qualifying examination he declared that, despite modern society's moral relativism, God's judgment was final and eternal: "God has planted in the fiber of the universe certain eternal laws which forever confront every man. They are absolute and not relative. There is an eternal and absolute distinction between right and wrong." One indispensable answer to the theodicy question, King argued, was contained in the concept of the suffering servant, one of the "most noble" teachings of the Old Testament. "His suffering is not due to something that he has done, but it is <u>vicarious</u> and <u>redemptive</u>. Through his suffering knowledge of God is sp[r]ead to the unbelieving Gentiles and those unbelievers seeing that this suffering servant is innocent will become conscious of their sins and repent and thereby be redeemed. The nation would be healed by his wo[unds]." King saw the death of Jesus Christ on the cross as the fulfillment of the prophecy of the suffering servant, but argued that humanity should not wait on God's saving grace. An individual's "faith and fellowship with God," King wrote, were the "ultimate solution to the problem of suffering."[87]

Late that fall, having completed two of his four examinations, King reflected on his intellectual development at Boston in a revealing letter to George Davis. Agreeing with Davis's positive review of DeWolf's new book, King found a "great deal of similarity" between the professors and indicated that "it was not difficult at all for me to emerge from your classroom to Dr. DeWolf's." King assured Davis that he had not abandoned his mentor's "warm evangelical liberalism," even as he was becoming more sympathetic to neo-

---

85. Although Jackson's election in part resulted from dissatisfaction with aging leadership that did not change with the times, he later disappointed many reformers, including King, Jr., when he refused to accept limits on his tenure. In 1961, King was forced out of the convention for supporting Gardner Taylor's campaign against Jackson, who retained the organization's presidency for nearly thirty years.

86. King, *My Life*, p. 90.

87. King, Qualifying examination answers, Theology of the Bible, pp. 206, 208 in this volume.

orthodox theology.[88] In the letter King indicated that his progress at Boston was proceeding rapidly. Both DeWolf and the late Edgar Brightman were "quite impressed" with his performance. King attributed his success to Davis: "In the most decisive moments, I find your influence creeping forth." Updating Davis on his recent work, he indicated that he had finished taking courses and was working on his dissertation. "So far, my Dissertation title is: 'A comparison of the concept of God in the thought of Paul Tillich and Henry Nelson Wieman'. I am finding the study quite fascinating." He hoped to be finished by the end of the following summer.[89]

King's choice of a dissertation topic reflected an interest in the nature of God that derived from both his academic studies and his preaching. In addition to several term papers on the topic, King wove the theme into a number of sermons while at Boston, including one entitled "What Does It Mean to Believe in God?"[90] In his introduction to the dissertation King explained that the concept of God should be examined because of "the central place which it occupies in any religion" and because of "the ever present need to interpret and clarify the God-concept."[91]

King had not formally studied either Tillich or Wieman, but their rejection of the personality of God provided important contrasts to Boston personalism. King described the two men as "fountainhead personalities" who have "had increasing influence upon the climate of theological and philosophical thought."[92] Wieman was influential as a proponent of theocentrism verified by empirical observation.[93] Tillich shared some of Wieman's concerns about the limitations of liberal theology but was more sympathetic to such neo-

---

88. King to George W. Davis, 1 December 1953, pp. 223–224 in this volume. King noted that on this point he was indebted to a "quite influential" article by Davis—an article from which King appropriated passages for several essays at Boston. See George W. Davis, "Some Theological Continuities in the Crisis Theology," *Crozer Quarterly* 27, no. 3 (July 1950): 208–219.

89. King to George W. Davis, 1 December 1953, p. 224 in this volume. In his response Davis remarked, "You have chosen an excellent dissertation topic. It presents striking contrasts in method and content and I think you can do a good piece of work with it" (Davis to King, 7 December 1953, p. 225 in this volume).

90. King gave this sermon at First United Baptist Church in Lowell, Massachusetts, on 12 April 1953.

91. King, diss. chap. 1, p. 346 in this volume.

92. Ibid.

93. Henry Nelson Wieman (1884–1975) received his B.A. at Park College in 1906 and his B.D. at San Francisco Theological Seminary in 1910. After studies at the universities of Jena and Heidelberg and service as a Presbyterian minister, he studied with William Ernest Hocking at Harvard University, where he received his Ph.D. in 1917. After teaching at Occidental College for ten years, he became a professor at the University of Chicago Divinity School, where he remained until 1947. He also taught at the University of Oregon (1949–1951), the University of Houston (1951–1953), and Southern Illinois University (1956–1975). For a listing of Wieman's publications up to 1955, see King's dissertation bibliography, pp. 541–544 in this volume. See also Wieman's theological autobiography in *Contemporary American Theology*, ed. Vergilius Ferm (New York: Round Table press, 1932), pp. 339–352; and essays in *The Empirical Theology of Henry Nelson Wieman*, ed. Robert W. Bretall (New York: Macmillan, 1963).

orthodox theologians as Karl Barth and Emil Brunner.[94] Wieman's ideas contrasted well with Tillich's: "Nothing brings out [Tillich's] position with greater clarity," one theologian observed, "than a study of his relationship with the empirical theology and religious naturalism of Henry Nelson Wieman."[95]

Both Tillich and Wieman objected to conceiving of God as a personality. Personalism's anthropocentric tendency was, according to Wieman, an obstruction to religious knowledge: "We [should] not allow our wishes and needs to shape our idea of God, but shall shape it solely in the light of objective evidence."[96] God was not a being that created the universe, but the creative process that sustains good in opposition to evil. Wieman described God as "the growth of meaning and value in the world."[97] Tillich identified God as neither a being nor a process but as "being-itself," the "ground" or source of all existence. According to Tillich, the term "a personal God" was a useful religious symbol that implied but did not describe God. "To speak of God as a person," Tillich wrote, "would mean making him an object besides other objects, a being among beings, maybe the highest, but anyhow a being."[98] Tillich believed that reducing God to a mere being was blasphemous.

By early 1953, when King enrolled in a course on dissertation writing at the beginning of his research, he was fairly certain about the conclusions he would reach in his dissertation. He jotted his thoughts about the two theologians' "great weakness" on a note card written that spring as he was outlining the thesis. "Both overstress one side of the divine life," he wrote, "while minimiz[ing] another basic aspect. Wieman stress[es] the goodness of God while mi[ni]mizing His power. Tillich stresses the power of God while min[im]izing His goodness."[99]

Rooted in an African-American religious tradition that perceived God as a personal force interceding in history, King found Tillich's and Wieman's con-

94. Paul Johannes Tillich (1886–1965) studied at the universities of Berlin, Tübingen, Halle, and Breslau, where he received his doctorate in philosophy in 1910. After serving as a chaplain in the German army during World War I, he taught theology at the universities of Berlin, Marburg, Dresden, Leipzig, and Frankfurt. Forced by his association with religious socialists to leave Germany in 1933, he came to the United States, where he was an instructor at New York's Union Theological Seminary until 1954. He then taught at Harvard University until leaving in 1962 for a position at the University of Chicago. For his publications up to 1955, see King's dissertation bibliography, pp. 539–541 in this volume. For more information, see *The Theology of Paul Tillich*, ed. Charles W. Kegley and Robert W. Bretall (New York: Macmillan, 1952); and Wilhelm Pauck and Marion Pauck, *Paul Tillich: His Life and Thought* (New York: Harper & Row, 1989).

95. Walter Marshall Horton, "Tillich's Role in Contemporary Theology," in Kegley and Bretall, eds., *The Theology of Paul Tillich*, p. 36.

96. Wieman, "Theocentric Religion," in Ferm, ed., *Contemporary American Theology*, p. 346.

97. Henry Nelson Wieman and Regina Westcott-Wieman, *Normative Psychology of Religion* (New York: Thomas Y. Crowell, 1935), p. 137.

98. Paul Tillich, "The Idea of a Personal God," *Union Review* 2 (1940): 9.

99. King, Notes on "A Comparison of the Conceptions of God in the Thinking of Paul Tillich and Henry Nelson Wieman," 4 February–22 May 1953, MLKP-MBU: Box 107. For a longer description of King's drafting of the dissertation, see the headnote to the dissertation, pp. 339–341 in this volume.

ceptions of divinity unworthy of worship. In the evaluative chapter of the dissertation, King expressed belief in a "living" God, not Tillich's "being-itself" or Wieman's "source of human good." "In God there is feeling and will, responsive to the deepest yearnings of the human heart; this God both evokes and answers prayer." Conceiving of such a God as a person was preferable to Tillich's and Wieman's use of abstract philosophical terms: "It would be better by far to admit that there are difficulties with an idea we know—such as personality—than to employ a term which is practically unknown to us in our experience." King concluded that Tillich and Wieman both set forth a God who is less than personal, despite their comments to the contrary that God was more than personal, or unable to be defined by the concept of personality. "Both Tillich and Wieman reject the conception of a personal God, and with this goes a rejection of the rationality, goodness and love of God in the full sense of the words."[100]

Despite his disagreement with certain aspects of Tillich's and Wieman's conceptions of divinity, King appreciated their criticism of humanism. King approvingly noted that they both emphasized God's immanence, or "the primacy of God over everything else in the universe." "Such an emphasis," he argued, "sounds a much needed note in the face of a supernaturalism that finds nature so irrational that the order of creation can no longer be discerned in it, and history so meaningless that it all bears the 'minus sign' of alienation from God." Characteristically seeking to synthesize dialectically opposed positions, King asserted that "both Wieman and Tillich are partially correct in what they affirm and partially wrong in what they deny. Wieman is right in emphasizing the goodness of God, but wrong in minimizing his power. Likewise Tillich is right in emphasizing the power of God, but wrong in minimizing his goodness."[101]

As in his other academic essays, King often appropriated the words of others without attribution. He frequently used the language of Tillich and Wieman, though it was clear from the context that he was describing their ideas. In addition to his improper use of Tillich and Wieman, King also borrowed from secondary sources without giving adequate citations. These sources included a review of Tillich's *Systematic Theology*, a prominent collection of essays on Tillich, and a dissertation on Tillich that had been completed under DeWolf's supervision three years earlier.[102]

The readers of King's dissertation, DeWolf and S. Paul Schilling, a professor of systematic theology who had recently arrived at Boston University, failed to notice King's flawed use of citations. After reading a draft copy DeWolf criticized him for failing to make explicit the "presuppositions and norms employed in the critical evaluation," but his comments were largely

---

100. King, diss. chap. 5, pp. 512, 524, 512, 510, 506 in this volume.

101. Ibid., pp. 518, 519, 516, 525 in this volume.

102. See Raphael Demos, Review of *Systematic Theology* by Paul Tillich, *Journal of Philosophy* 49 (1952): 692–708; articles in Kegley and Bretall, eds., *The Theology of Paul Tillich*; and Jack Boozer, "The Place of Reason in Tillich's Conception of God" (Ph.D. diss., Boston University, 1951).

positive. He commended King for his handling of a "difficult" topic "with broad learning, impressive ability and convincing mastery of the works immediately involved." Schilling, for his part, found two problems with King's citation practices but dismissed these as anomalous and praised the dissertation in his Second Reader's report. When informed of the plagiaries many years later, Schilling conceded that in certain respects King was "guilty of shoddy scholarship" but argued that "his appropriation of the language of others does not entail inaccurate interpretation of the thought of writers cited." Schilling concluded that his assessment of the dissertation at the time of his first reading was correct: "I stand by the comment in my Second Reader's report: 'The comparisons and evaluations are fair-minded, balanced, and cogent. The author shows sound comprehension and critical capacity.'"[103]

As was true of King's other academic papers, the plagiaries in his dissertation escaped detection during his lifetime. His professors at Boston, like those at Crozer, saw King as an earnest and even gifted student who presented a consistent, though evolving, theological identity in his essays, exams, and classroom comments. King's reputation for excellent memory and his tendency to synthesize conflicting viewpoints may have obscured his reliance on borrowed ideas and words. Although the extent of King's plagiaries suggests that he knew that he was at least skirting academic norms, the extant documents offer no direct evidence on this matter. King's decision to save his papers and to place them in an archive suggests that his academic performance was a source of pride rather than guilt. Thus he may have simply become convinced, on the basis of his grades at Crozer and Boston, that his papers were sufficiently competent to withstand critical scrutiny. Moreover, King's actions during his early adulthood indicate that he increasingly saw himself as a preacher appropriating theological scholarship rather than as an academic producing such scholarship.

Standing in the pulpit, King expressed his concept of God using more vivid language than in the dissertation, skillfully incorporating into his sermons only those aspects of his theological training that affirmed his ties to the religion of his parents and grandparents. King's ability to blend these elements can be seen in his earliest known recorded sermon, "Rediscovering Lost Values."[104] He delivered this sermon to a large Baptist church in Detroit in late February 1954, just days after finishing his final comprehensive examination and a few weeks before the graduate school approved his dissertation outline.

In "Rediscovering," King referred to the account in the gospel of Luke in which Mary and Joseph, while returning to Nazareth after attending a Passover feast in Jerusalem, discover that they have unintentionally left behind

---

103. Schilling to King Papers Project, 5 November 1990. See also "Conversation Between S. Paul Schilling and David Thelen," *Journal of American History* 78, no. 1 (June 1991): 63–80.

104. A tape recording of the sermon at Second Baptist Church was preserved by the church's historical committee. The recording served as the basis for the transcription of "Rediscovering Lost Values," pp. 248–256 in this volume.

twelve-year-old Jesus. In his sermon King used the story to illustrate the tendency of individuals caught up in the tumult of the modern world to move ahead without appreciating the enduring values of the past. "If we are to go forward," he said, "if we are to make this a better world in which to live, we've got to go back. We've got to rediscover these precious values that we've left behind." Despite the many technological advances and material comforts of American society, King argued, humanity had lost the spiritual compass provided by a deep and abiding faith in God. "The real problem is that through our scientific genius we've made of the world a neighborhood, but through our moral and spiritual genius we've failed to make of it a brotherhood." King insisted that "*all* reality hinges on moral foundations," that "this is a moral universe, and that there are moral laws of the universe, just as abiding as the physical laws." Decrying ethical relativism—"Now, I'm not trying to use a big word here"—King expressed a belief in moral absolutes that evoked enthusiastic responses from the congregation.

> I'm here to say to you this morning that some things are right and some things are wrong. (*Yes*) Eternally so, absolutely so. It's *wrong* to hate. (*Yes, That's right*) It always has been wrong and it always will be wrong! (*Amen*) It's wrong in America, it's wrong in Germany, it's wrong in Russia, it's wrong in China! (*Lord help him*) It was wrong in two thousand B.C., and it's wrong in nineteen fifty-four A.D.! It always has been wrong, (*That's right*) and it always will be wrong! . . . Some things in this universe are absolute. The God of the universe has made it so.[105]

Contemporary society had lost sight of this "mighty precious value," adopting instead "a pragmatic test for right and wrong." In the modern world, he asserted, most people believed that "it's all right to disobey the Ten Commandments, but just don't disobey the Eleventh, Thou shall not get caught." The moral decay that King identified in modern culture could be recovered only by ethical living: "The thing that we need in the world today, is a group of men and women who will stand up for right and be opposed to wrong, wherever it is."[106]

King argued that making ethical decisions was impossible without rediscovering the precious value of faith in God. Employing language from his study of Wieman, King affirmed a belief in "a God behind the process." Many people, however, including those who attended church every Sunday, had lost their faith in God. "We must remember that it's possible to affirm the existence of God with your lips and deny his existence with your life." The materialism of American consumer culture had caused some to lose sight of God; yet King cautioned, "automobiles and subways, televisions and radios, dollars and cents, can *never* be substitutes for God."[107]

---

105. King, "Rediscovering Lost Values," pp. 251–252 in this volume. Here the congregation's responses, indicated in italics and parentheses, have been retained in this lengthy quotation, but they are omitted in other quotations below from "Rediscovering." They are preserved in the complete transcription.

106. Ibid., pp. 249, 252 in this volume.

107. Ibid., pp. 253–254 in this volume.

King's most important sources for his sermon were the traditional ones of the African-American Baptist pulpit: the Bible and well-known hymns. Referring to a verse in Psalm 23 and a familiar hymn, King concluded by affirming faith in the God "who walks with us through the valley of the shadow of death, and causes us to fear no evil," and in the God "who has been our help in ages past, and our hope for years to come, and our shelter in the time of storm, and our eternal home."[108] King concluded with a rousing affirmation of God as an integral part of his life: "As a young man with most of my life ahead of me, I decided early to give my life to something eternal and absolute. Not to these little gods that are here today and gone tomorrow. But to God who is the same yesterday, today, and forever."[109]

After completing the taxing qualifying examinations, King began to search for a job, apparently convinced that he could hold a full-time position while finishing his dissertation. He may also have sensed that he had already overcome the most difficult obstacles in his doctoral studies. As one of King's fellow students later commented, "The rejoicing came when you finished your qualifying exams and the rest, writing the dissertation, was just a hurdle that you want to get finished with."[110] King's professors had nominated him for academic positions, and offers came in from several colleges. In a letter recommending King for a position as dean of a school of religion, Crozer president Sankey L. Blanton indicated that King had "great ability" and "would do more for you while finishing the dissertation than the average man would do without any other duties besides."[111] Attaining such a position at an early age would have prepared King for one of his career ambitions: to serve as president of a historically black college such as Morehouse.[112] At the same time, however, King's colleagues in the ministry informed him of prominent churches that were looking for a pastor. The most tempting offers were those that combined the best elements of academic life and preaching, such as college chaplain or minister of a church that welcomed well-educated ministers.

With these considerations in mind, King responded positively to an invitation to deliver a guest sermon in January 1954 at Dexter Avenue Baptist Church in Montgomery, Alabama. Two months before, his parents had informed him that one of Dexter's deacons, J. T. Brooks, had written the Kings to express Dexter's interest in their son. After hearing "so many fine things about him and his ability and possibility," Brooks was "intensely interested" in

---

108. King alluded to the hymn "O God, Our Help in Ages Past."

109. King, "Rediscovering Lost Values," pp. 254–255 in this volume.

110. "Conversation Between Cornish Rogers and David Thelen," p. 60.

111. King received an offer from Shaw University to become dean of its School of Religion. See William R. Strassner to King, 6 November 1952; and Sankey L. Blanton to William R. Strassner, 3 December 1952; pp. 159–160 and 164 in this volume, respectively.

112. Sybil Haydel Morial, interview with Clayborne Carson; and W. T. Handy, Jr., interview with Clayborne Carson.

having King preach at Dexter. Brooks indicated that the church was "now in process of hearing a series of prospects and would like if possible to make a decision sometime in the not too distant future."[113] One of the men scheduled to speak prior to King was his friend from Crozer Walter R. McCall. On the recommendation of Melvin Watson, the First Baptist Church in Chattanooga, Tennessee, was also considering King for its pastorate, but Dexter offered greater opportunities.[114] Its educated congregation would be receptive to King's blend of theological scholarship and the methods of southern Baptist oratory; its pastors, moreover, had long been among the best educated in the country. The church was much smaller than other Montgomery churches, with only 365 members compared to Bethel's 1,500 and Holt Street's 1,200; nevertheless, its reputation well exceeded its size.

On 24 January King delivered a well-rehearsed sermon entitled "The Three Dimensions of a Complete Life," which was received by "a large and appreciative audience at Dexter."[115] King had delivered many other sermons as a minister, but he recalled feeling "conscious this time that I was on trial." He assured himself that all would be well if he remembered that he was the "channel of the gospel, not the source."[116] Several weeks later McCall returned to the church at its behest to preach a second trial sermon. A ministerial colleague reported to King that McCall "came and fell through" and that the congregation "forgot all about him as a prospect."[117]

Despite the competition between the two classmates, McCall was gracious in his letters to King. "If you are <u>interested in getting</u> that church," he wrote, "I would be glad to put in a plug for you. Take it from me, that is a Great Church, Mike. Much honor will go to the man who gets it." Downplaying the church's history of conflict with its pastors, McCall advised, "Don't let anybody tell you that that church is such a hell raiser!"[118] King was aware that the church was not without problems. His father and others had warned him about its contentious history and its reputation as a "silk stocking church" for professionals.[119] But King's predecessor at Dexter, Vernon Johns, may have allayed King's misgivings when they spoke later about the church. King admired Johns, who had preached at Ebenezer that winter, later describing him

---

113. J. T. Brooks to Martin Luther King, Sr., and Alberta Williams King, 16 November 1953, p. 211 in this volume.

114. King gave a trial sermon at First Baptist the Sunday before his sermon at Dexter.

115. *Montgomery Examiner*, 28 January 1954.

116. King, *Stride Toward Freedom*, p. 17.

117. Joseph C. Parker, Sr., to King, 10 March 1954, p. 258 in this volume. Some accounts suggest that McCall tried to best King with a sermon entitled "Four Dimensions of a Complete Life"; see Taylor Branch, *Parting the Waters: America in the King Years, 1954–1963* (New York: Simon & Schuster, 1988), p. 110; and Ralph David Abernathy, *And the Walls Came Tumbling Down* (New York: Harper & Row, 1989), pp. 127–128.

118. Walter R. McCall to King, 17 January 1954, p. 236 in this volume.

119. For King's discussion of Dexter Avenue Baptist Church and his first visits to it, see King, *Stride Toward Freedom*, pp. 16–18.

as "a real iconoclast, bound neither by folkways or mores . . . who never allowed any conditions of injustice to come to his attention without lashing out against [them] in no uncertain terms."[120]

In considering Dexter, King also weighed his wife's objections to the limited educational and cultural opportunities available to blacks in the segregated South. Coretta Scott King was finishing her requirements for a degree in music education and feared that moving to the South would not only limit her musical career but also restrict teaching opportunities in the poorly funded segregated schools. King brought the dilemma to their friends in the Dialectical Society, outlining at some length the three options available to him: the pulpit in Chattanooga, Dexter's pastorate, or a teaching position at a college such as Morehouse. Dexter's attractiveness to King was enhanced by the opportunity to succeed Vernon Johns, a clergyman who combined theological brilliance with social commitment. Under Johns's leadership Dexter had become less provincial and more prepared for the kind of ministry King wished to provide.

Before extending a call to King, Dexter's pulpit committee expressed concern that King might stay at Dexter for only a few years before moving on to a teaching position. They communicated their apprehension to the Reverend Joseph C. Parker, Sr., a pastor of a Baptist church in Montgomery and a friend of King's from Morehouse. Parker warned King that the committee wanted someone "who would stay with them a long time and not resort to teaching." Parker advised them that "no minister knew how long he would stay with a church. But, I told them that the type of salary they offered a minister would have a great deal to do with how long he stayed with them." With a large number of middle-class black professionals, many of whom were affiliated with Alabama State College for Negroes, Dexter could afford to pay its pastor well. When it unanimously called King to the pastorate, it offered him a salary that would make him the highest-paid black minister in the city.[121]

After considering his various options King accepted the offer, but because he had several more months of dissertation research to complete he arranged to spend the summer commuting between Montgomery and Boston. At the end of May, two weeks after the U.S. Supreme Court declared segregation in public schools unconstitutional in *Brown v. Board of Education*, King preached his first sermon as Dexter's pastor, "Loving Your Enemies." That summer King began working with the congregation to ensure that the transition to his leadership went smoothly. He insisted that the church raise funds to repair the parsonage and make other necessary improvements to the church's facilities. On 1 September, the Kings moved into the rebuilt parsonage, and shortly thereafter King presented the congregation with his "Recommendations to the Dexter Avenue Baptist Church for the Fiscal Year 1954–1955." Starting with a strong assertion of pastoral authority, King argued that his call as a

---

120. King, draft of *Stride Toward Freedom*, June 1957–May 1958, MLKP-MBU: Box 86A. See also King, *Stride Toward Freedom*, p. 38.

121. Joseph C. Parker, Sr., to King, 10 March 1954, p. 257 in this volume.

preacher came primarily from God and only secondarily from the congregation. His call to Dexter's pastorate, he said, implied "the unconditional willingness of the people to accept the pastor's leadership." Yet he also suggested that the congregation should not "blindly and ignorantly genuflect" before him, "as if he were possessed of some infallible or superhuman attributes." Referring obliquely to previous tensions between Dexter's deacons and its pastor, King noted that he would neither "needlessly interfere" with the workings of the church nor assume "unnecessary dictatorial authority." He asked instead that he "be respected and accepted as the central figure around which the policies and programs of the church revolve."[122]

After invoking broad authority on church matters, King proposed wide-ranging changes in the church's organization and finances. Relying in part on his acquaintance with his father's centralization of fiscal authority at Ebenezer, he concentrated church finances in a unified budget and treasury and suggested more than a dozen committees, including one to organize social and political action. When the congregation accepted the extensive reorganization without modification, King shared his "Recommendations" with his ministerial friends, including Melvin Watson, who praised the report as one that "happily . . . departs from the beaten path." Watson singled out the many committees as a potential problem, however. "Hectic activity in the church i[s] not necessarily an indication that the cause of the Kingdom is being promoted."[123]

Six weeks after King presented the recommendations, Dexter officially installed him as its pastor. King's family and Ebenezer Baptist Church played integral roles in his transition to Dexter. Several buses of Ebenezer's parishioners traveled to Montgomery to participate in the service, which featured an installation sermon by King, Sr., and the Ebenezer choir directed by Alberta Williams King.[124] Afterward King expressed his enduring gratitude to the members of Ebenezer. "You can never know what your presence in such large numbers meant to me at the beginning of my pastorate," he wrote, adding that "whatever success I might achieve in my life's work you will have helped make it possible."[125]

In addition to writing his dissertation, King set about becoming acquainted with his congregation and the Montgomery community. He visited the sick, met with the local ministerial associations, began implementing his recommendations, and prepared his weekly sermons. In addition to ones he had written earlier, King delivered several new sermons during his first year at Dexter, different versions of which would later be published, including "The Death of Evil upon the Seashore." Although no texts of King's sermons from this period survive, a text of "Death of Evil" delivered months later reveals

---

122. King, "Recommendations to the Dexter Avenue Baptist Church for the Fiscal Year 1954–1955," 5 September 1954, p. 287 in this volume.

123. Melvin Watson to King, 20 October 1954, p. 303 in this volume.

124. Dexter Avenue Baptist Church, "Program, Installation of Rev. Martin Luther King, Jr., as Pastor," 31 October 1954, figure facing p. 236 in this volume.

125. King to Ebenezer Baptist Church Members, 6 November 1954, p. 314 in this volume.

his enduring interest in questions he had explored in graduate school. The presence of evil in the world was undeniable, he argued, but "in the long struggle between good and evil, good eventually emerges as the victor." Evil must eventually "give way to the magnetic redemptive power of a humble servant on an uplifted cross." Taking his theme from the story in Exodus of the Israelites' escape from the "gripping yoke of Egyptian rule," King saw a similar struggle between good and evil occurring in the twentieth century. "Gradually we have seen the forces of freedom and justice emerge victoriously out of some Red Sea," King noted, "only to look back and see the forces of oppression and colonialism dead upon the seashore." Assured by his faith in God that injustice would not survive "the rushing waters of historical necessity," King exhorted his congregation to join the struggle. King's confidence in humanity made him optimistic about the future: "We must believe that a prejudiced mind can be changed, and that man, by the grace of God, can be lifted from the valley of hate to the high mountain of love."[126]

Calling on his expanding network of Baptist ministers, King asked his colleagues to speak at Dexter's special programs, including such events as Men's Day, Women's Day, and the church's anniversary. King invited Walter McCall to preach at Dexter for the annual Youth Day program and initiated a Spring Lecture Series with Virginia Union University president Samuel D. Proctor as the first guest. In his letter inviting Proctor, King indicated his intention to "bring some of the best minds" to the church "to discuss some of the major doctrines and issues of the Christian Faith," explaining that "most church people are appallingly ignorant at this point."[127] In 1955, Morehouse president Mays accepted an invitation to serve as Men's Day speaker, though King's choice for the following year, Howard Thurman, had to decline the invitation. Thurman, the celebrated black theologian who had become dean of Boston University's Marsh Chapel in 1953, noted, however, that he was "delighted" to learn of King's work at "historic" Dexter Avenue.[128]

King's growing prominence in the Baptist community brought numerous invitations for him to speak at other churches. In addition to his forty-six sermons at Dexter that first year, King gave twenty sermons and lectures at churches and colleges throughout the South, including the Anniversary sermon at Ebenezer and a week-long lecture series at Georgia's Fort Valley State College, where McCall served as dean of men. News of King's achievements spread rapidly among his friends and colleagues in the Baptist community. J. Raymond Henderson complimented his old friend King, Sr., on his son's success: "They told me you have a son that can preach rings around you any day you ascend the pulpit. How about that? If it is so, it is a compliment to you." In a letter to King, Jr., Henderson praised the young minister but also urged him to remember his responsibilities: "You have a great heritage in your grandfather and father. I understand you are developing into a good

126. King, "The Death of Evil upon the Seashore," 17 May 1956, MLKP-MBU: Box 119A. King preached this sermon at Dexter on 24 July 1955.

127. King to Samuel D. Proctor, October 1954, p. 297 in this volume.

128. Howard Thurman to King, 14 November 1955, p. 588 in this volume.

preacher in your own right. Remain careful of your conduct. Steer away from 'trashy' preachers. Be worthy of the best. It may come to you some day."[129] On another occasion, fearing that King's popularity might have negative effects on his personal and spiritual well-being, his father wrote him a cautionary letter: "You see young man you are becoming very popular. As I told you you must be much in prayer. Persons like yourself are the ones the devil turns all of his forces aloose to destroy."[130]

In addition to representing Dexter in the various Montgomery church associations, King strengthened his ties to the National Baptist Convention. During his first year at Dexter he attended ten conclaves of the convention, speaking at several of them, including the annual meeting of the Woman's Auxiliary. Afterward Nannie Helen Burroughs, the auxiliary's president, thanked him for "the challenging message" and informed him that "the delegates were profoundly impressed. What your message did to their thinking and to their faith is 'bread cast upon the water' that will be seen day by day in their good works in their communities."[131] In addition to providing service at the convention's annual meeting, King joined an advisory council to the convention's National Baptist Training Union Board.[132] Shortly after King's arrival in Montgomery, the local affiliate of the convention in the area, the Montgomery-Antioch District Association, elected him as the group's reporter.[133] National Baptist Convention president J. H. Jackson declined King's invitation to preach at Dexter, but he noted cordially that "I am delighted to know of the great work that you are doing at Dexter."[134]

J. Pius Barbour, the iconoclastic editor of the *National Baptist Voice* and King's friend and mentor from his Crozer days, was alone in suggesting that King's intellectual talents would be better served outside Montgomery and the South. Drawing on his own experience as a minister in Montgomery, Barbour derided the city's "superficial intellectuality" and advised that King should not be deceived by his success at Dexter, by the "Triple Attendance and Triple collection." "Son," Barbour wrote, "hard liberty is to be prefe[r]red to servile pomp!"[135] In a later letter, Barbour commented on King's choice of a dissertation topic: "Tillich is all wet. . . . Being-Itself is a meaningless abstraction." He also reiterated his warning about King's southern pastorate, noting that he felt "sorry for you with all that learning." "Don['[t get stuck there," he wrote, "move on to a big metropolitan center in THE NORTH, or some town as ATLANTA. You will dry rot there."[136]

---

129. Letters from J. Raymond Henderson to King, Sr., and King, Jr., 12 May 1955, pp. 555–556 in this volume.

130. Martin Luther King, Sr., to King, Jr., 2 December 1954, p. 320 in this volume.

131. Nannie Helen Burroughs to King, 21 September 1954, p. 296 in this volume.

132. Roland Smith to King, 10 December 1954, p. 320 in this volume.

133. King, "Montgomery-Antioch Ass'n. Endorses Wilson and Washington," *Baptist Leader*, 4 November 1954, p. 312 in this volume.

134. J. H. Jackson to King, 28 September 1955, p. 573 in this volume.

135. J. Pius Barbour to King, 21 December 1954, p. 323 in this volume.

136. J. Pius Barbour to King, 21 July 1955, pp. 565–566 in this volume.

Barbour's warnings notwithstanding, King found an active community committed to challenging the status quo. Several organizations and institutions in Montgomery offered opportunities for King to emulate his father's and grandfather's model of the politically active preacher. He quickly sought out the local racial reform groups, meeting most of the politically active black community leaders during his first year. King attended the monthly meetings of the Alabama Council on Human Relations, an affiliate of the Southern Regional Council, the only significant interracial reform group in Montgomery. He also served briefly as the organization's vice president. Though not involved in protest activity per se, the group served "to keep the desperately needed channels of communication open between the races."[137] Several members of King's own congregation were among the most dedicated community activists in the city. Rufus Lewis, a former Alabama State football coach and owner of a funeral home, formed the Citizens Club in the late 1940s to facilitate voter registration and voting, and Mary Fair Burks and Jo Ann Robinson, both professors at Alabama State, each served a term as president of the Women's Political Council, which promoted voter registration and protested the treatment of African Americans on city buses. After the arrest on 2 March 1955 of a young black woman, Claudette Colvin, for violating the city's segregation laws, Robinson initiated two meetings with the mayor and bus company officials to discuss the case. Robinson, Lewis, and Burks were joined by longtime NAACP activists E. D. Nixon and Rosa Parks at the meetings; King, who had been in the city for just six months, accompanied his parishioners to one of the meetings.[138]

King appreciated the civil rights activities of the members of his congregation and, as part of his reorganization of the church, appointed several activists to the newly formed Social and Political Action Committee. Chaired by Robinson and Burks, the committee encouraged voter registration and urged every church member to join the NAACP.[139] In its reports to the congregation, the committee provided information about local and national politics, including a special briefing on the second *Brown v. Board of Education* case.[140] It also published the name of every registered voter in the congregation, a group that, by late 1955, constituted more than half the congregation and both Kings.[141]

---

137. King, *Stride Toward Freedom*, pp. 32–33.

138. Jo Ann Gibson Robinson, *The Montgomery Bus Boycott and the Women Who Started It*, ed. David J. Garrow (Knoxville: University of Tennessee Press, 1987), pp. 40–41.

139. Guided by Robinson, Burks, and Lewis, Dexter encouraged voter registration prior to King's arrival. At a church service the week before King delivered his trial sermon, Dexter's board of ushers urged everyone to register for the upcoming election. See *Montgomery Examiner*, 21 January 1954.

140. Elmer Heningburg Reynolds and Mary Fair Burks, "The NAACP and the Supreme Court," in Dexter Avenue Baptist Church, Social and Political Action Committee Digest, June 1955, MLKP-MBU: Box 77.

141. Dexter Avenue Baptist Church, Social and Political Action Committee Digest, December 1955, MLKP-MBU: Box 77. According to the committee's report, approximately 200 Dexter members were registered voters, out of a congregation of 367.

In addition to encouraging Dexter members to join the NAACP, King himself became increasingly involved in that group, attending the local branch's monthly meetings and on occasion speaking at NAACP gatherings. The Reverend Ralph David Abernathy, the young pastor of First Baptist Church and chaplain of Alabama State College, stimulated King's increasing involvement and became a strong supporter of the newly arrived minister. Abernathy and King had met several years before when King, still a student at Crozer, delivered a sermon at Ebenezer. Abernathy was at the time enrolled at Atlanta University and had heard about the young preacher's powerful style; he therefore visited Ebenezer, where he listened to the sermon "burning with envy at [King's] learning and confidence."[142] When King arrived at Dexter, Abernathy had already become one of Montgomery's more prominent ministers.[143] Following the *Brown* decision, he chaired the state Sunday School and Baptist Training Union Congress's committee to assess the ruling, issuing a report which insisted that Christians should struggle against injustice: "Segregation is an evil that sep[a]rates men and hampers true brotherhood. Jesus is against it and He wants us to fight it. . . . Our business as Christians is to get rid of a system that creates bad men." He then urged the ministers to "return to their respective communities determined to fight this evil until Black Men of Alabama are privileged to enjoy every God-given opportunity as any other man."[144] Early in January 1955, Abernathy arranged for King to give the installation address for the officers and executive committee of the Montgomery branch of the NAACP and its women's auxiliary. According to notes taken by branch secretary Rosa Parks, King "called for a great deal of work, reserve and thinking." He told the branch members: "We have come a long way, but still have a long way to go. We owe a debt of gratitude to those [who] made possible the Supreme Court decision of May 17."[145]

A few weeks later, King delivered a stronger statement of his views when the Birmingham branch of the NAACP invited him to speak at the installation ceremony for its officers. He criticized the apathy of church leaders on political issues: "'You must do more than pray and read the Bible' to destroy segregation and second-class citizenship," the local newspaper reported him as saying; "'you must do something about it.'" Registering for the vote and supporting the NAACP with "big money" would prove critical in the struggle against segregation: "A voteless people," King reportedly said, "is a powerless people." Likewise, he "recommended using the courts more to obtain unjustly denied rights" and "called for an immediate start toward the implementation

---

142. Abernathy, *And the Walls Came Tumbling Down*, p. 89. Abernathy (1926–1990) received his B.S. from Alabama State College in 1950 and studied for his M.S. at Atlanta University in the early 1950s, receiving the degree in 1958. He became pastor of First Baptist Church in 1952 and served until 1961, when he became pastor of Atlanta's West Hunter Street Baptist Church.

143. Abernathy's activities are noted in *Baptist Leader*, 4 November 1954, 17 March 1955.

144. Abernathy, "The Report of the Committee on the Recent Supreme Court Ruling on Segregation in Public Education," *Baptist Leader*, 2 September 1954. As King was in the process of moving to Montgomery after a summer of commuting, he did not attend the congress.

145. Rosa Parks, Minutes, Montgomery Branch NAACP meeting, 9 January 1955, MNAACP-NN-Sc.

of the May 17 U.S. Supreme Court decision banning the segregated school system."[146] After seeing an announcement for King's speech, one veteran NAACP activist in Georgia congratulated King for his support of the association. "I have followed with interest all of your activities," W. W. Law wrote, "and am very happy over the very rapid strides you have made." Law remembered that King's involvement in the NAACP began at Morehouse, noting that "to see you continue interest in this very worthwhile organization (I like to think of it as a movement) in Freedom's cause, now that you have assumed community leadership, is heartwarming."[147]

On 19 June 1955, King was the featured speaker at a mass meeting of the Montgomery branch. Introducing his pastor to the gathering, R. D. Nesbitt lauded King as a great asset to black Montgomery, distinguishing himself "in everything for the betterment of the community" and launching "an extensive campaign" at Dexter to recruit voters and NAACP members. King's address on the "Peril of Complacency in the Fight for Civil Rights" reiterated many of the points he had made in his Birmingham speech. According to Rosa Parks's notes, he stated:

> Jim Crow is on his deathbed but the battle is not yet won. There is no time to pause and be complacent. We must do everything to keep it down. [King] gave a brief history of progress made by Negroes in the past 50 years. We must pay for our freedom, [develop] courageous leaders and not be afraid to take a stand for our freedom. We must continue to get the ballot and speak through our vote. With the NAACP we must fight through legislation, and teach love through education.[148]

After the speech, King accepted an invitation to join the branch's executive committee. Parks welcomed him to the staff in a cordial letter, explaining that King's "outstanding contribution" merited his appointment.[149]

As he ended his first year as pastor of Dexter, King used the annual report to his congregation as an opportunity to reflect on his accomplishments as a minister and community leader. In addition to reporting increased church membership and financial receipts, King celebrated the congregation's enthusiastic participation on the various boards and committees initiated the previous year. He singled out for special praise the "superb" work of the Social and Political Action Committee: "Through the work of this committee many persons have become registered voters and Dexter has led all other church[es] of Montgomery in contributions to the NAACP." King heaped accolades on all aspects of the church, noting that "the wonders that have come about at Dex-

---

146. "Apathy Among Church Leaders Hit in Talk by Rev. M. L. King," *Birmingham World*, 25 January 1955, p. 331 in this volume. King would later deliver the speech, entitled "A Realistic Approach to Progress in Race Relations," on many occasions.

147. W. W. Law to King, 14 January 1955, p. 329 in this volume.

148. Rosa Parks, Minutes, Montgomery Branch NAACP mass meeting, 19 June 1955, MNAACP-NN-Sc.

149. Rosa Parks to King, 26 August 1955, p. 572 in this volume. See also Parks, Minutes, Montgomery Branch NAACP meeting, 14 August 1955, MNAACP-NN-Sc.

ter this year were not due so much to my leadership, but to the greatness of your followship." King warned the congregation, though, that it should not forget its "tremendous responsibilities" to continue its spiritual growth and remain politically active: "Institutions, like men, can so easily fall into moribund conditions when they project their visions merely to past achievements rather than future challenges. There is nothing more tragic than to see a church drowning in the deep waters of spiritual stagnancy, and at the last moment reaching out for some thin straw of past achievement in an attempt to survive." In a prophetic concluding invocation, King encouraged the congregation to expand its activities in the Montgomery community: "Let each of us go out at this moment with grim and bold determination to extend the horizons of Dexter to new boundaries, and lift the spire of her influence to new heights, so that we will be able to inject new spiritual blood into the veins of this community, transforming its jangling discords into meaningful symphonies of spiritual harmony."[150]

As King reflected on his successful first year as pastor, he also moved to a new stage in his family life. On 17 November 1955, Coretta Scott King gave birth to the Kings' first child, Yolanda Denise. King wrote his friend H. Edward Whitaker, "I am now the proud father of a little daughter. . . . Yolanda Denise. She is now about thirteen days old, and she is keeping her father quite busy walking the floor."[151] Having become a father as well as an increasingly influential pastor and civil rights leader, King was prepared to realize his longstanding ambition to "serve humanity." During his first years at Crozer, King had been estranged from his roots, but by the time he entered Boston University he had rediscovered the liberating potential of his African-American Baptist heritage. Forging an eclectic synthesis from such diverse sources as personalism, theological liberalism, neo-orthodox theology, and the activist, Bible-centered religion of his family, King affirmed his abiding faith in a God who was both a comforting personal presence and a powerful spiritual force acting in history for righteousness. This faith would sustain him as the movement irreversibly transformed his life. Several weeks after his report to the Dexter congregation, he used similar language to praise the united African-American community at the initial mass meeting of the Montgomery bus boycott. "Right here in Montgomery, when the history books are written in the future, somebody will have to say, 'There lived a race of people, a *black* people, fleecy locks and black complexion, but a people who had the moral courage to stand up for their rights. And thereby they injected a new meaning into the veins of history and of civilization.'"[152]

150. King, Dexter Avenue Baptist Church Annual Report, 1 October 1954–31 October 1955, pp. 578–580 in this volume.

151. King to H. Edward Whitaker, 30 November 1955, p. 593 in this volume.

152. Montgomery Improvement Association, "First mass meeting, Holt Street Baptist Church." 5 December 1955, MLKJrP-GAMK; to be published in *Papers* 3.

(*Above*) Martin Luther King, Jr., and other Morehouse College
alumni at the National Freedom Day observance in Philadelphia,
1951. Photo and permission courtesy of *Morehouse College Bulletin.*

(*Opposite, top*) Celebration of the King family at the twenty-fifth an-
niversary of the marriage of Martin Luther King, Sr., and Alberta
Williams King, 22 November 1951. From left to right: Christine
King, Martin Luther King, Jr., Martin Luther King, Sr., Alberta
Williams King, Alveda King, Naomi Barber King, A. D. King.
Photo and permission courtesy of Christine King Farris.

(*Opposite*) Martin Luther King, Sr., and Alberta Williams King
at the celebration of their twenty-fifth wedding anniversary,
22 November 1951. Photo and permission courtesy of
Christine King Farris.

Coretta Scott at Progressive Party convention, Philadelphia,
July 1948. Photo courtesy of Charles L. Blockson
Afro-American Collection, Temple University.

Coretta Scott while a student at Antioch College, ca. 1951.
Photo courtesy of Bahnsen Negative Collection,
Antioch College.

Martin Luther King, Jr., and Coretta Scott on the grounds of
Boston University during the academic year 1952–1953.
Photo and permission courtesy of Coretta Scott King.

Martin Luther King, Jr., and Coretta Scott in front of the
chapel at Boston University during the academic year 1952–
1953. Photos and permission courtesy of Coretta Scott King.

Wedding party of Martin Luther King, Jr., and Coretta Scott King, 18 June 1953. From left to right: Christine King, A. D. King, Betty Ann Hill, Martin Luther King, Jr., Naomi Barber King, Coretta Scott King, Martin Luther King, Sr., Edythe Scott, Bernice Scott, Alberta Williams King, Obadiah Scott, and, in front, Alveda King. Photo and permission courtesy of Christine King Farris.

Martin Luther King, Jr., and Coretta Scott King in
their wedding attire, June 1953. Photo courtesy of the
King Center.

Wayman McLaughlin (partly obscured), Zenobia McLaughlin, Ella Clark, Jack Clark, Coretta Scott King, and Martin Luther King, Jr., participants in the Dialectical Society, Boston, 1953–1954. Photo and permission courtesy of Percy A. Carter, Jr.

(*Opposite, top*) Martin Luther King, Jr., with Sybil Haydel Morial and Reuben Dawkins in Boston, February 1953. Photo and permission courtesy of Jeanne Martin Brayboy.

(*Opposite, bottom*) Martin Luther King, Jr. (seated in front), with (clockwise) Eloise Jones, Lemuel Wells, Ida Wood, Jeanne Martin Brayboy, Sybil Haydel Morial, Reuben Dawkins, Mable Carter, and Phillip Lenud in Boston, February 1953. Photo and permission courtesy of Jeanne Martin Brayboy.

Gathering of Morehouse College graduates at the National
Baptist Convention, U.S.A., Inc., in Miami, Florida,
September 1953. Martin Luther King, Jr., is seated in the
front row on the far right. Benjamin Elijah Mays is standing,
sixth from the left. Photo and permission courtesy of
Lawrence Edward Carter, Sr.

Martin Luther King, Jr., at the home of James A. McFall, after his sermon at
Second Baptist Church, Detroit, Michigan, 28 February 1954. Photo and
permission courtesy of Julian Townsend and Nathaniel Leach.

Martin Luther King, Jr., with Justina Leach and Charles Nicks, Jr., after King's sermon at Second Baptist Church, Detroit, Michigan, 28 February 1954. Photo courtesy of Second Baptist Church.

Dexter Avenue Baptist Church, Montgomery, Alabama,
in the early 1950s. Photo courtesy of the Richard Kaplan
Collection, State Historical Society of Wisconsin.

Martin Luther King, Jr., and John Thomas Porter at Alabama State commencement, 16 May 1955. Photo and permission courtesy of John Thomas Porter.

2 Sept 1951	Martin Luther King, Jr., preaches "What Is Man?" and "What Think Ye of Christ?" at Ebenezer.
13 Sept 1951– 15 Jan 1952	During his first term at Boston University's School of Theology, King enrolls in Personalism, Formal Logic, Philosophy of Religion, Directed Study in Systematic Theology, and Seminar in Systematic Theology.
16 Sept	King is the guest preacher at the Reverend Gardner Taylor's Concord Baptist Church in Brooklyn.
2 Oct	Boston University approves King's outline of study.
22 Nov	King, Jr., attends his parents' twenty-fifth wedding anniversary celebration in Atlanta.
23 Jan–16 May 1952	For his second semester at Boston, King takes three courses: Religious Teachings of the New Testament, Directed Study in Systematic Theology, and Seminar in Systematic Theology.
Feb	King begins to date Coretta Scott, a student at the New England Conservatory of Music.
4 Feb–10 June	As a "special student" at Harvard University, King enrolls in the History of Modern Philosophy.
15 Feb	King passes French examination at Boston University, partially fulfilling the language requirement.
16 Mar	King preaches at Ebenezer's celebration of its sixty-fifth anniversary and of King, Sr.'s twentieth anniversary as its pastor.
18 May	King preaches "The Relevance of the Holy Spirit" at Ebenezer.
25 May	King delivers "The Prevalence of Practical Atheism" at Ebenezer.
26 May–5 July	King takes two courses during the intersession at Boston University: Seminar in Historical Theology and History of Recent Philosophy.
22 June	King is initiated into Boston's Sigma chapter of the Alpha Phi Alpha social fraternity.
12 July–7 Sept	King serves as pastor in charge at Ebenezer.
24 July	King attends the annual session of Georgia's Sunday School and Baptist Training Union Congress in Atlanta.
Aug	Coretta Scott visits Atlanta and meets the King family for the first time.

39

10 Aug	King preaches "The Challenge of Communism to Christianity" at Ebenezer.
24 Aug	King is Youth Day speaker at Pilgrim Baptist Church in Atlanta.
7 Sept	King preaches "Mental and Spiritual Slavery" at Ebenezer.
22 Sept 1952– 28 Jan 1953	During the first term of his second year at Boston, King takes four courses: Religious Teachings of the Old Testament, History of Christian Doctrine I, Seminar in Philosophy (Hegel), and Seminar in the History of Philosophy.
22 Sept 1952– 26 Jan 1953	King enrolls in the Philosophy of Plato at Harvard.
10 Oct	King fails Boston University's German examination.
6 Nov	Shaw University President William R. Strassner asks King to apply to become the university's dean of religion.
Nov	King, Sr., and Alberta Williams King visit Boston.
Fall	King preaches at John Street Baptist Church in Worcester, Massachusetts.
26 Jan–2 June 1953	King's final course at Harvard is on the philosophy of Alfred North Whitehead.
4 Feb–22 May	King enrolls in his last courses at Boston: History of Christian Doctrine II, Seminar in Philosophy (Hegel), and Directed Study in Thesis and Dissertation Writing.
18 Feb	On his second attempt, King passes the German examination, thus completing Boston University's language requirement.
25 Feb	King's academic advisor at Boston University, Edgar S. Brightman, dies. King later chooses L. Harold DeWolf as his new advisor.
Apr	Obadiah and Bernice Scott announce the engagement of Coretta Scott and Martin Luther King, Jr.
12 Apr	King speaks at First United Baptist Church in Lowell, Massachusetts, at the invitation of its pastor, the Reverend Otto R. Loverude. King gives a talk on "What it means to be a Negro in the Deep South" and preaches the sermon "What Does It Mean to Believe in God?"
7 May	In a public debate with John Wesley Dobbs, King, Sr., supports Atlanta Mayor William B. Hartsfield's campaign for reelection.
18 June	King, Sr., performs the marriage ceremony of King, Jr., and Coretta Scott at the Scott home near Marion, Alabama.
21 June	King preaches "By These Things Men Live" at Ebenezer's morning services and "Does It Pay to

Be Faithful?" in the evening. King, Sr., baptizes Coretta Scott King.

Summer — Martin Luther and Coretta Scott King spend the summer in Atlanta. King serves as Ebenezer's pastor in charge, and Coretta Scott King works in a local bank.

King attends an interseminary conference at Virginia Union University in Richmond, Virginia.

28 June — King preaches "Accepting Responsibility for Your Actions" at Ebenezer.

5 July — Atlanta's WERD, the nation's first radio station owned and operated by African-Americans, begins broadcasting from Ebenezer for several months.

12 July — King preaches "Transformed Non-Conformists" at Ebenezer.

19 July — Clark College Dean of Women Phoebe Burney is the Women's Day speaker at Ebenezer. Coretta Scott King is the featured soloist at the morning service.

26 July — King preaches "God's Revelation to the World" at Ebenezer.

2 Aug — King preaches "Dressing Christ in False Robes" at Ebenezer.

9 Aug — King delivers the sermon "The Tragedy of Almost" at Ebenezer.

16 Aug — King preaches "Lord, Is It I?" at Ebenezer.

23 Aug — King delivers the sermon "Self-Examination" at Ebenezer.

30 Aug — King delivers the sermon "Opportunity, Fidelity, and Reward" at Ebenezer's morning services; in the evening, he preaches at Pilgrim Baptist Church.

6 Sept — King preaches "The Dimensions of a Complete Life" at Ebenezer.

8–14 Sept — King attends the annual meeting of the National Baptist Convention in Miami. The Reverend J. H. Jackson, pastor of Olivet Baptist Church in Chicago, is elected president of the convention.

Sept — The Kings rent an apartment at 396 Northampton Street in Boston and resume their studies.

Nov — Alberta Williams King and King, Sr., spend two weeks in New York and Boston.

15 Nov — King preaches at the Reverend J. Timothy Boddie's New Shiloh Baptist Church in Baltimore, Maryland.

22 Nov — King preaches at the Reverend J. L. Henry's Tenth Street Baptist Church in Washington, D.C.

21 Dec — King leaves Boston for vacation in Atlanta.

41

1 Jan 1954	King attends the Emancipation Day celebration sponsored by the Atlanta branch of the National Association for the Advancement of Colored People (NAACP) at the City Auditorium. The Reverend J. H. Jackson gives the annual address.
3 Jan	King preaches in the morning at Ebenezer.
10 Jan	King preaches in the morning at Ebenezer.
17 Jan	King delivers a trial sermon at First Baptist Church in Chattanooga, Tennessee.
24 Jan	King delivers a trial sermon, "The Three Dimensions of a Complete Life," at Dexter Avenue Baptist Church in Montgomery, Alabama.
	Dexter's former pastor Vernon Johns preaches "Segregation After Death" at Ebenezer.
28 Feb	At the invitation of the Reverend A. A. Banks, Jr., King preaches "Rediscovering Lost Values" at Second Baptist Church in Detroit.
7 Mar	King is in Lansing, Michigan, to preach at his uncle Joel Lawrence King's church in the morning and evening. He also addresses the local branch of the NAACP in the afternoon.
	By a unanimous vote, Dexter Avenue Baptist Church calls King to its pastorate.
1 Apr	King's Boston University transcript indicates that he has passed his qualifying examinations.
4 Apr	King meets with the pulpit committee at Dexter.
9 Apr	Boston University approves King's outline of his dissertation.
14 Apr	King accepts the call to Dexter's pastorate.
25 Apr	King preaches at the Reverend Leonard G. Carr's Vine Memorial Baptist Church in Philadelphia.
26 Apr	The Kings host a meeting of a black graduate study group, the Dialectical Society, at their Boston apartment.
10 May	Professor L. Harold DeWolf lectures at a meeting of the Dialectical Society; King offers the opening prayer.
16 May	King preaches at the Thirty-third Annual Memorial Service of the Pullman Porters' Benefit Association of America at Union Baptist Church in Cambridge, Massachusetts.
17 May	In *Brown v. Board of Education of Topeka*, the U.S. Supreme Court declares racial segregation in public schools unconstitutional.
30 May	King preaches "Loving Your Enemies" at Dexter and presides over the ordination of deacons. He spends the summer commuting between Boston and Montgomery.

13 June	At the invitation of the Reverend Thomas Kilgore, Jr., King preaches at Friendship Baptist Church in Harlem, New York City.
15 June	Coretta Scott King receives her bachelor of music degree in music education from the New England Conservatory of Music in Boston.
22 June	King, Sr., addresses the opening session of the National Baptist Sunday School and Baptist Training Union Congress in Birmingham, Alabama.
11 July	King preaches "What Is Man?" for Men's Day at Dexter.
1 Sept	King begins his pastorate at Dexter.
5 Sept	King delivers his first sermon as pastor of Dexter and presents his "Recommendations to the Dexter Avenue Baptist Church for the Fiscal Year 1954–1955," which are accepted by the congregation.
6–11 Sept	King, Jr., Alberta Williams King, and King, Sr., attend the National Baptist Convention in St. Louis.
9 Sept	King, Jr., speaks to the Women's Convention at the request of its president, Nannie Helen Burroughs. King's noonday message is "The Vision of the World Made New."
4–10 Oct	Phoebe Burney is the guest speaker for Women's Emphasis Week at Dexter.
20–21 Oct	King attends the Montgomery-Antioch District Association's annual meeting at Hutchinson Street Baptist Church in Montgomery. King is appointed to serve as reporter.
31 Oct	At King, Jr.'s installation as pastor of Dexter, King, Sr., preaches the sermon, and Alberta Williams King conducts Ebenezer's choir.
Nov	King and Coretta Scott King spend two weeks in Boston working on a draft of his dissertation.
14 Nov	King preaches at the Reverend William H. Hester's Twelfth Baptist Church in Boston.
25 Nov	The annual Thanksgiving program at Montgomery's First Baptist Church features a solo by Coretta Scott King.
28 Nov	King delivers the Men's Day sermon at Atlanta's Friendship Baptist Church, whose pastor is the Reverend Samuel W. Williams, his Morehouse philosophy professor.
12 Dec	The Reverend Melvin H. Watson, the son of Ebenezer clerk P. O. Watson, delivers the Seventy-eighth Anniversary sermon at Dexter.
Jan 1955	King and H. Councill Trenholm, president of Alabama State College, Montgomery, deliver eulo-

	gies at the funeral of Alabama State professor James Milton Reynolds.
1 Jan	Coretta Scott King sings a solo at an Emancipation Proclamation anniversary celebration at Holt Street Baptist Church.
11–13 Jan?	King attends the national board meeting of the National Baptist Convention in Hot Springs, Arkansas. The featured preacher is the Reverend C. L. Franklin, who delivers the sermon "God's Wheels of Progress."
23 Jan	King delivers the speech "A Realistic Look at Race Relations" at a meeting of the Birmingham NAACP.
2 Feb	The adjourned session of the Alabama Baptist State Convention meets at First Baptist Church. On 1 Feb King gives the invocation at a service for the group's newly elected officers.
25 Feb	King delivers the evening inspirational message on the final day of the Montgomery Baptist Bible Institute at the Holt Street Baptist Church.
1 Mar	Following the Reverend M. C. Cleveland's sermon, King speaks at a mass meeting for the National Baptist Convention's Home Mission Board. The event, sponsored by the Baptist Ministers' Conference of Montgomery, is held at Beulah Baptist Church.
2 Mar	Claudette Colvin, 15, is arrested for allegedly violating Montgomery's ordinance requiring segregation on the city's buses. King, Jo Ann Robinson of the Women's Political Council, Rosa Parks of the Montgomery NAACP, and others later meet with city and bus company officials.
6 Mar	Coretta Scott King gives a voice recital at First Baptist Church.
8 Mar	Coretta Scott King directs a "talent night" featuring local youth as part of Dexter's Youth Emphasis Week.
13 Mar	King's Morehouse and Crozer classmate the Reverend Walter R. McCall is the guest speaker for Youth Emphasis Week at Dexter. The church's Baptist Youth Fellowship holds a symposium on "The Meaning of Integration for American Society," featuring among other speakers Dexter member Cleveland Dennard and the Reverend Robert E. Hughes, executive director of the Alabama Council on Human Relations.
20 Mar	King delivers the Sixty-eighth Anniversary sermon at Ebenezer.

23–24 Mar	King attends a meeting in Nashville of the Advisory Council on Literature and Curriculum, National Baptist Training Union Board of the National Baptist Convention.
10 Apr	King preaches for Easter services at Dexter.
15 Apr	King delivers the final draft of his dissertation to Boston University.
17 Apr	At the invitation of the Reverend Marvin Gibson, King preaches at Union Baptist Church in Cambridge, Massachusetts.
21 Apr	King defends his dissertation before a faculty committee at Boston University.
24 Apr	Alberta Williams King directs Ebenezer's choir in a Sunday afternoon concert at Dexter.
27–29 Apr	The Reverend Samuel D. Proctor, president of Virginia Union University in Richmond, gives a series of speeches for Dexter's Spring Lecture Series.
30 Apr	King serves as a resource and discussion leader at the annual state meeting of Hi-Y clubs at Alabama State College in Montgomery.
8 May	King preaches "[The] Crisis Facing Present-Day Family Life in America" at Dexter's Mother's Day service.
15 May	King delivers the baccalaureate sermon at the Alabama State College commencement in Montgomery.
22 May	King preaches the baccalaureate sermon at Talladega County Training School in Renfroe, Alabama.
31 May	The faculty of Boston University votes to confer the doctorate on King. The Supreme Court issues an order to implement the May 1954 *Brown v. Board of Education* school desegregation ruling.
1 June	The Reverend Archibald J. Carey, Jr., speaks at a citizenship rally sponsored by Alabama State College's Alpha Phi Alpha fraternity. King gives the benediction.
5 June	King is awarded his doctorate from Boston University; he does not attend the commencement ceremony.
12 June	The Reverend Major J. Jones preaches at Ebenezer.
19 June	King preaches "Who Is Truly Great?" at Dexter. King delivers the keynote address at an Alabama NAACP regional mass meeting at Holt Street CME Church.

26 June	King delivers a sermon titled "Discerning the Signs of History" at Dexter.
27 June–3 July	King attends the National Baptist Sunday School and Baptist Training Union Congress in Atlantic City, New Jersey.
3 July	King preaches at Friendship Baptist Church in Harlem.
8 July–3 Aug	King, Sr., Alberta Williams King, and Christine King attend the Baptist World Alliance meeting in London, England.
10 July	Morehouse president Benjamin Mays is the guest speaker for Men's Day at Dexter.
17 July	King preaches "Am I My Brother's Keeper?" at Dexter.
22 July	At the invitation of Dillard University president Albert W. Dent, King flies to New Orleans to discuss taking a position as dean of the new university chapel.
24 July	King preaches "The Death of Evil upon the Seashore" at Dexter.
31 July	King delivers "The Three Dimensions of a Complete Life" at the Tuskegee Institute chapel.
July	King speaks on "The Three Levels of Love" at the monthly meeting of Dexter's Young Matrons Club.
2–5 Aug	King attends the Alabama Baptist State Sunday School and Baptist Training Union Congress at Holt Street Baptist Church in Montgomery. He serves on the Committee on Youth Parade with the Reverends Ralph D. Abernathy, U. J. Fields, J. C. Parker, A. W. Wilson, and other local ministers.
14 Aug	King addresses the Montgomery NAACP.
18 Aug	King hosts the monthly meeting of the Montgomery chapter of the Alabama Council of Human Relations at Dexter.
26 Aug	Rosa Parks, secretary of the Montgomery NAACP, informs King that he has been elected to the executive committee.
28 Aug	King preaches in the morning and evening for Men's Day at the Reverend J. E. Moss's Jackson Street Baptist Church in Birmingham. Fourteen-year-old Emmett Till, a black teenager from Chicago, is murdered while vacationing with relatives near Money, Mississippi.
Aug	The Montgomery NAACP submits a petition to the school board to integrate the city's public schools.

6–11 Sept	King, Jr., Alberta Williams King, and King, Sr., attend the annual meeting of the National Baptist Convention in Memphis, Tennessee. King, Sr., serves as a member of the convention's board of directors.	Chronology
9 Oct	Lynette Saine Bickers, associate professor of education at Atlanta University, is the guest speaker for Women's Day at Dexter.	
16 Oct	King delivers "The Three Dimensions of a Complete Life" at Southern University in Baton Rouge, Louisiana.	
17–23 Oct	At the invitation of Dean of Students Walter R. McCall, King is the guest speaker for Religious Emphasis Week at Fort Valley State College in Fort Valley, Georgia. The theme of the week is "Christ in Human Relations." King preaches "The Dimensions of a Complete Life," "What Is Man?" "Going Forward by Turning Back," and "The Death of Evil upon the Seashore." He also participates in panel discussions on "How Christianity Affects Our Fears," "Christ and Race Relations," "What Has Christianity to Say About Sex Standards?" "Christ and Business Relations," and "Christ and Our Physical Surroundings."	
30 Oct	King preaches "The Seeking God" at Dexter.	
7 Nov	King speaks at the fall institute of the local Baptist Training Union in Chattanooga, Tennessee.	
17 Nov	Yolanda Denise King, the Kings' first child, is born.	
20 Nov	King preaches "The One-sided Approach of the Good Samaritan" at Dexter.	

The central goal of the Martin Luther King, Jr., Papers Project is to produce an authoritative, multivolume edition of King's works. The chronologically arranged volumes provide accurate, annotated transcriptions of King's most important sermons, speeches, correspondence, published writings, unpublished manuscripts, and other papers. We have examined thousands of King-related documents and recordings and selected those that were biographically or historically significant to King's life, thought, and leadership. Because only a small proportion of all the available documents could be published, we developed the following principles and priorities to guide our selection process.

Of the documents produced during the period covered by this volume, King's writings and statements were assigned highest priority for inclusion. Correspondence was included when letters contained significant information about King's thought or activities. Incoming letters that illuminated his relationships with and impact on others were also included. Routine correspondence and office-generated replies to unsolicited letters were excluded. King's unpublished manuscripts, such as his student papers, were included when they provided significant information about the sources and development of his ideas. We have also included a transcript of the only extant recorded sermon given by King during the period of this volume.

Documents produced by others were selected when they contained significant biographical information regarding King's attitudes, activities, or accomplishments. This category includes confidential academic evaluations. Correspondence not directly involving King and time-specific printed matter concerning King's activities (such as church programs) were selected only if they had exceptional historical value.

To assist scholars and others seeking further information on King-related primary documents, this volume includes a "Calendar of Documents" that describes items not chosen for publication as well as those in the volume. In addition, the project's descriptions of King-related document collections are available in the electronic database of the Research Libraries Information Network (RLIN). This edition of King's papers is part of a broader, long-term effort to facilitate access, through various print and electronic media, to all the research material that the King Papers Project has located.

EDITORIAL ANNOTATIONS

Annotations to document texts are intended to enhance readers' understanding of documents. We have preceded most documents with headnotes explaining the context of their creation and briefly summarizing their contents. Such headnotes, as well as editorial footnotes, may also identify individuals, organizations, and other references in the document. Significant comments written in the margins of the original documents have been annotated as well.

49

In the first two volumes, these marginal comments consist mainly of the remarks of King's professors, although not every correction of King's grammar or spelling is noted. Editorial footnotes are placed at the bottom of the page. For those papers that King annotated, his footnotes are placed as close to the accompanying callouts as feasible. To enable readers to understand King's citation practices, we have provided footnotes that give full references to, and quotations from, sources containing substantial passages similar or identical to King's. We do not indicate whether his use of sources conforms to academic rules regarding plagiarism. We have generally not annotated theological ideas and persons likely to be discussed in standard reference works, and in only a few instances do we make cross-references to documents slated for future volumes. On occasion editorial footnotes also describe variations contained in different versions of documents.

Each document is introduced in almost all cases by a title, date, and place of origin. Existing titles are used when available and are designated by quotation marks. For untitled items, we have created descriptive titles reflecting the content of documents (e.g., A. A. Banks, Jr., to Martin Luther King, Sr.), with errors or irregularities in punctuation, capitalization, and spelling silently corrected and names standardized. In King's correspondence, the title contains the author or the recipient in the document (From Rosa L. Parks), leaving King's participation implied. The date and place of origin (if known) appear after the title. When the date was not specified in the document but was determined through research, we have presented it in italics enclosed in brackets. We provided a range date when a specific date was not available. (A more detailed explanation of procedures for assigning titles, dates, and other cataloging information appears at the end of the volume in the "Calendar of Documents.")

The source note following each document provides information on the characteristics of the original document and its provenance. Codes are used to describe the document's format, type, version, and form of signature. The code "TLS," for example, identifies the letter as a typed letter with a signature. The location of the original document is described next, using standard abbreviations from *Symbols of American Libraries*. (See "List of Abbreviations" for all codes used.)

TRANSCRIPTION PRACTICES

Our transcriptions are intended to reproduce the source document or recording as accurately as possible, adhering to the exact wording and punctuation of the original. Errors in spelling, punctuation, and grammar have been neither corrected nor indicated by *sic*. Such errors and stylistic irregularities may offer important insights into the author's state of mind and conditions under which a document was composed. Other features that could not be adequately reproduced, such as signatures and handwritten marginal comments, are noted and described in the text or footnotes. All editorial explanations are rendered in italics and enclosed by square brackets. In a few cases, the document has been presented as a facsimile.

Audio Recordings. The King Papers Project's transcription practices for audio recordings are intended to reproduce the recorded address accurately. Such transcriptions, however, do not attempt to reproduce all of the aspects of a speech or sermon because written transcriptions could never fully reflect nor interpret oral presentations, particularly those that include a significant degree of interaction between speaker and audience. The primary objective of an audio transcription is to replicate Kings's public statements as they were delivered, excluding only those interjections (e.g., stutters and pause words, such as "uh") that do not convey meaning or that would distract from readers' understanding of King's statement. Certain sharply stressed phrases are italicized to indicate the speaker's emphasis. When available, King's written text is used to clarify ambiguous phrases and as a guide to delineating sentences, paragraphs, and punctuation. In cases where the written text is not available, editors have supplied punctuation for clarity.

Respect for the oral tradition challenged the Project to represent, to the extent practical, audience responses to King's orations. These responses are enclosed italicized, with the first word capitalized, and placed without punctuation appropriately within King's text. The audience's words are enclosed in parentheses; editors' descriptions of audience participation are enclosed in square brackets. The first instance of audience response to a speech is indicated as follows: [*Audience:*] *(Preach)*. Subsequent audience interjections are enclosed, as is appropriate, in brackets—[*Applause*] or [*Singing*] or [*Laughter*]—or in parentheses: *(Yes)* or *(Lord help him)*. Multiple audience responses are indicated in order of occurrence, separated with commas: *(Tell it, Don't stop)*. The loudness of audience responses is not indicated in the transcription, although the duration may be suggested: [*Applause continues*].

General comments regarding the recording and the context in which it was made are indicated in the headnote; the incomplete or indeterminate nature of the recording or the transcriptions may be indicated by editorial annotations—i.e., [*Gap in tape*] or [*Two words inaudible*]. Editorial deletions to eliminate repetitive or extraneous segments of recordings are indicated by ellipses or by explanatory comment: [. . . .] or [*Prayer by Rev. Alford*].

Other transcription practices include the following:

1. Capitalization, boldface, symbols, subscripts, abbreviations, strikeouts, and deletions are replicated regardless of inconsistency or usage.
2. The line breaks, pagination, and vertical and horizontal spacing of the original are not replicated. A blank line signals a break in the text other than a straightforward paragraph break. The transcription regularizes spacing and indentation of paragraphs, outlines, and lists, as well as the spacing of words, initials, and ellipses.
3. The underlining of book titles, court cases, or other words and phrases in typescripts is reproduced. Since underlining practices were often inconsistent (sometimes breaking between words, sometimes not), we regularized the various types to continuous underscoring.
4. Silent editorial corrections have been made only in cases of malformed letters, single-letter corrections of typescript words, and the superimposition of two characters.

51

"A Comparison and Evaluation of the
Theology of Luther with That of Calvin"

15 May 1953
[*Boston, Mass.*]

In this version, written for DeWolf, King differs with Luther and Calvin's undue emphasis on the sovereignty of God, arguing that "God is first and foremost an all loving Father." DeWolf graded the paper "A. Very good–" but added: "awkwardly worded title."

Calvin's doctrine of the Church is quite similar to that of Luther. According to Calvin the Church is the means by which we are nourished in the Christian Life. "To those whom God is Father, the Church must be a mother."[16]

Following the line already marked out by Wyclif, Huss and Zwingli, Calvin defines the Church as "all the elect of God, including in the number even those who have departed this life."*[17] Like Luther, he sees the Church as both visible and invisible, and its marks are the word and the sacrament. Where the word is truly taught and the sacrament rightly administered there is the

* Insti., IV. I. 2.

THDS. MLKP-MBU: Box 112.

16. This paragraph does not appear in the earlier version of this essay.

17. Walker, *Calvin*, pp.418–419: "[The Church] is the means by which we are nourished in the Christian life. 'To those to whom [God] is a Father, the Church must also be a mother.' Following the line already marked out by Wyclif, Huss and Zwinglie, Calvin defines the Church in the last analysis as 'all the elect of God, including in the number even those who have departed this life.'"

5. The author's use of hyphens is replicated, but end-of-line hyphens have been silently deleted unless the usage is ambiguous. Dashes between numbers are rendered as en-dashes. Em-dashes, which appeared in several styles in the original manuscripts, have been regularized.

6. Insertions in the text by the author (usually handwritten) are indicated by curly braces ({ }) and placed as precisely as possible.

7. Footnotes in King's academic essays, which appear in various styles in the original, are rendered as sidenotes (except in his doctoral dissertation, where they appear as footnotes above the editors' notes). Instead of King's numbering systems, we use a sequence of symbols in the following order: asterisk (*), dagger (†), double dagger (‡), section mark (§), parallels (‖), number sign (#). If more than six such notes appear on a page, the symbols are doubled as needed.

8. Telegrams and forms are simulated using small capital letters. In the latter case, King's handwritten or typed responses are set in boldface.

9. Conjectural renderings of text are set in italic type and placed within brackets: [*rousers?*].

10. In cases of illegible text, the extent of the illegibility is indicated: [2 *words illegible*]; and crossed-out words are indicated with the phrase [*strikeout illegible*]. If the strikeout was by someone other than the author, it has been not replicated but is described in a footnote. If part of a document is lost or unintelligible, the condition is described: [*remainder missing*].

11. In rare instances, long documents have been excerpted to highlight passages that were most significant with respect to King. Editorial omissions within a transcription are designated by bracketed ellipses ([. . .]) and described in the annotation.

12. Signatures are reproduced as follows:

Sincerely,
[*signed*]
Benjamin E. Mays

or

Yours sincerely,
[*signed*] Kelly
Kelly Miller Smith

13. Examination questions, when available from archival sources, are indicated in italics and brackets before the answers.

14. Printed letterheads are not reproduced, but significant information contained in them may be explained in the headnote or in a footnote. The internal address, salutation, and complimentary closing of a letter have been reproduced left-aligned, regardless of the original format.

LIST OF ABBREVIATIONS

COLLECTIONS AND REPOSITORIES

A-Ar	Alabama Department of Archives and History, Montgomery, Ala.
AJC-ICHi	Archibald James Carey Collection, Chicago Historical Society, Chicago, Ill.
BEMP-DHU	Benjamin E. Mays Papers, Moorland-Spingarn Research Center, Howard University, Washington, D.C.
BNC-OYesA	Bahnsen Negative Collection, Antioch College, Yellow Springs, Ohio
BUR-MBU	Office of the Registrar Records, Boston University, Boston, Mass.
CKFC	Christine King Farris Collection (in private hands)
CLBAA-PPT	Charles L. Blockson Afro-American Collection, Temple University, Philadelphia, Pa.
CSKC	Coretta Scott King Collection (in private hands)
CRO-NRCR	Crozer Theological Seminary Records, Colgate-Rochester Divinity School, Rochester, N.Y.
DABCC	Dexter Avenue King Memorial Baptist Church Collection (in private hands)
EBCR	Ebenezer Baptist Church, Miscellaneous Records (in private hands)
ESBC-MBU	Edgar Sheffield Brightman Collection, Boston University, Boston, Mass.
FESP	Francis E. Stewart Papers (in private hands)
FUBCR	First United Baptist Church (Lowell, Mass.) Records (in private hands)
HTC-MBU	Howard Thurman Papers, Boston University, Boston, Mass.
IGZ	Ira G. Zepp, Jr., Papers (in private hands)
JMBC	Jeanne Martin Brayboy Collection (in private hands)
JOG	Julian O. Grayson Papers (in private hands)
JTPP	John Thomas Porter Papers (in private hands)
LECC	Lawrence Edward Carter, Sr., Collection (in private hands)
MLKP-MBU	Martin Luther King, Jr., Papers, 1954–1968, Boston University, Boston, Mass.
MLKJrP-GAMK	Martin Luther King, Jr., Papers, 1950–1968, King Library and Archives, Atlanta, Ga.
MNAACP-NN-Sc	Montgomery Branch, National Association for the Advancement of Colored People Minutes, 1954–1955, New York Public Library, Schomburg Collection

MRP-GAMK	Mark A. Rouch Miscellaneous Papers, King Library and Archives, Atlanta, Ga.
NHBP-DLC	Nannie H. Burroughs Papers, Library of Congress, Washington, D.C.
PACC	Percy A. Carter, Jr., Collection (in private hands)
RKC-WHI	Richard Kaplan Collection, State Historical Society of Wisconsin, Madison, Wis.
SBHL-TNSB	Southern Baptist Historical Library and Archives, Southern Baptist Convention Historical Commission, Nashville, Tenn.
SdBCC	Second Baptist Church (Detroit, Mich.) Historical Committee Collection (in private hands)
SPS	S. Paul Schilling Collection (in private hands)
TAP	Thelma B. Archer Papers (in private hands)
WAWP-GAMK	Willard A. Williams Papers, King Library and Archives, Atlanta, Ga.
WHP-GEU	William B. Hartsfield Papers, Emory University Special Collections, Atlanta, Ga.
WMP-MBU	Walter Muelder Papers, Boston University, Boston, Mass.

ABBREVIATIONS USED IN SOURCE NOTES

The following symbols are used to describe the original documents:

Format
A	Autograph—author's hand
H	Handwritten—other than author's hand
P	Printed
T	Typed

Type
At	Audio tape
D	Document
Fm	Form
L	Letter or memo
Ph	Photo
W	Wire or telegram

Version
c	Copy
d	Draft
f	Fragment

Signature
I	Initialed
S	Signed
Sr	Signed with representation of author

I

Boston University

To Sankey L. Blanton

15 October 1951
Boston, Mass.

*King thanks Sankey L. Blanton, who in 1950 replaced E. E. Aubrey as president
of Crozer Theological Seminary, for sending him the first fellowship check helping
him to study at Boston University. The J. Lewis Crozer Fellowship required him to
remain enrolled in graduate school and "show proficiency" in advanced study.*

Dr. Sankey L. Blanton
Crozer Theological Seminary
Chester, Pennsylvania

Dear Dr. Blanton:

Your letter of October 3 was received along with the check for $300 which
constitutes one half of the fellowship grant for 1951–52. I can hardly express
in words my appreciation to you and Crozer Seminary for this generous
grant. Certainly it will be of tremendous aid to me in facing financial difficulties. And I assure you that it will be used very wisely.

So far I am enjoying my work here at Boston University to the highest.
Although the student is very large, I find an intimacy between faculty and
students which is quite reminicent of Crozer. All of my professors have a very
high respect for Crozer and the quality of men it produces. Naturally this
attitude has made me feel good. I feel that my background from Crozer will
be of a great help to me in my work here.

I am very happy to know that you are having an unusually fine year at
Crozer with such an excellent student body. I plan to be in that vicinity in the
near future and I wll be sure to stop in to see you.

TLc. MLKP-MBU: Box 116.

From Morton Scott Enslin

26 October 1951
Chester, Pa.

*The students in L. Harold DeWolf's Seminar in Systematic Theology reviewed
a number of theological journals, among them the* Crozer Quarterly.[1] *Preparing
to give the presentation on the Crozer journal, King wrote a letter to Enslin, his*

---

1. See L. Harold DeWolf, Syllabus, Seminar in Systematic Theology, 13 September 1951–15
January 1952, MLKP-MBU: Box 114.

former teacher and the editor of the journal, inquiring about the history of the publication. Enslin's minuscule handwriting makes portions of his letter in response nearly illegible.

Dear Mr. King,

Your good letter reached me. It is pleasant to hear from you and to learn of your work at Boston University. Please give my most cordial greetings to Professors Brightman and DeWolf.

I am interested in your historical discussion of <u>Crozer Quarterly</u> in connection with the course in contemporary American theology. I think that you will find about all the real historical data in the complete file of the Quarterly itself. I presume that at Boston University or Harvard there is a complete file. It was started with the January issue in 1924. Dr. Pollard was the first editor. It was the result of a feeling by the faculty at that time, under the direction of Dr. Evans, that such a journal was needed. Andover and Rochester were invited to join in the project but found it impossible to accept. Accordingly Crozer has continued it alone from the start.[2] The several editors who have successively directed it have been: Edward B. Pollard, Spenser B. Meeser, A. Stewart Woodburne, R. E. E. Harkness, and Morton S. Enslin. You will find from a study of the various numbers that generally each editor had some column or department in which he gave expression to his own slant or policy for the journal.

Book reviews have always been a part of the Quarterly. In recent years they have become a very important section. And the publishers are eager to have their books in our paper. We have had many indications from here (or the Library of Congress) and abroad that our pages are widely used as a source of standard review. Reviewers are entirely free from editorial pressure as regards the [*tone*] and slant of their reviews.

We have had a bit wider field of interest than many so-called "theological" journals, and a glance at back issues will show the wide field in which our authors and reviewers have worked.

Until Jan 1950 the price was kept at the [*original*] figure $1.50; then it was raised to $2.50. It has never been financially self-supporting and was not intended to be. Its aim was to provide a journal of liberal authors and general values at a figure ministers on limited salary could afford, and we have regarded it in part a missionary effort. I also feel that it has been of value to the Seminary [*through*] the resultant [*publicity*], as it is widely found in the libraries of universities and colleges here and abroad.

I shall be interested to see the result of your study if you have to present it in written form.

Sincerely,
[*signed*] Morton S. Enslin

---

2. King used the preceding three sentences, with minor adjustments, in his presentation. See King, "*Crozer Quarterly*," 12 December 1951, p. 93 in this volume.

Mrs. Heacock is still away from the office in consequence of the broken ankle she suffered last July; hence my letter is long hand. I hope that you can decipher it.

ALS. MLKP-MBU: Box 117.

"The Personalism of
J. M. E. McTaggart Under Criticism"

4 December 1951
[*Boston, Mass.*]

Writing for DeWolf's course on Personalism, King presents and criticizes the views of J. M. E. McTaggart, whose ideas King had contrasted with Edgar S. Brightman's six weeks earlier.[1] King takes issue with McTaggart's atheism: "We shall also notice that many of McTaggart's arguments against an omnipotent God are far from adequate. Indeed, the reader gets the impression sometimes that McTaggart is simply indulging in logical trifling, that the discredited theistic doctrine is unworthy of serious consideration and may be caricatured to any extent." Throughout this paper King rejects many of McTaggart's views, concluding: "We have also seen that McTaggart is usually negative on the idea of freedom. For these and many other reasons, we have found it necessary to reject most of McTaggart's views. Any system which seeks to establish itself on the unreality of time seems to me rationally unsound and empirically unverified." DeWolf gave King an A for the paper and commented: "Excellent, incisive criticism. A superior paper."

Personalism is usually thought of as being theistic in nature. Indeed, the very word was used in the beginning as a general term descriptive of theism, by way of distinction from pantheism. This, however, must not lead one to assume that all Personalism has been theistic. While it is true that most Personalistic philosophies have remained true to their theistic origin, it is also true that there have been exceptions to

---

1. King took a course on the philosophy of religion from Brightman during the same semester. King's two essays for Brightman included sections on J. M. E. McTaggart. The outline of McTaggart's philosophy in this paper is closely related to King's earlier essay for Brightman. See "A Comparison and Evaluation of the Views Set Forth in J. M. E. McTaggart's Some Dogmas of Religion with Those Set Forth by Edgar S. Brightman in His Course on 'Philosophy of Religion,'" 25 October 1951, MLKP-MBU: Box 112; and "A Comparison and Evaluation of the Philosophical Views Set Forth in J. M. E. McTaggart's Some Dogmas of Religion, and William E. Hocking's The Meaning of God in Human Experience with Those Set Forth in Edgar S. Brightman's Course on 'Philosophy of Religion,'" 6 December 1951, pp. 76–92 in this volume.

the rule. We have both an atheistic personalism and a pantheistic personalism.[2] In the present paper, it is our purpose to present and criticise the atheistic personalism of J. M. E. McTaggart. To speak of McTaggart as a personalist is by no means thrusting upon him a label that he would have denied. Says he, "I am also, in one sense of the term, a Personal Idealist. For I believe that every part of the content of spirit falls within some self, and that in part of it falls within more than one self; and that the only substances are selves, parts of selves, and groups of selves or parts of selves."[*]

John McTaggart Ellis McTaggart was born in 1866, and was educated at Clifton and Trinity College, Cambridge. In 1888, he was placed alone in the first class of the Moral Sciences of Tripos. In 1891, he was elected to a prize-fellowship at Trinity. Soon after this, he paid a long visit to New Zealand. In 1897, he was made College Lecturer in the Moral Sciences, an office which he held until 1923. Two years later, after a short but painful illness, he died in London, at the age of 58.[4] While he lived, he published the following books: Studies in Hegelian Dialectic, Studies in Hegelian Cosmology, Some Dogmas of Religion, A Commentary to Hegel's Logic, and the first volume of The Nature of Existence. At the time of his death, he was in the midst of the third draft of the remaining volume of The Nature of Existence. This volume was published a few years after his death.[5]

[*] Muirhead, J. H. (ed.): CBP, 249[3]

---

2. Albert C. Knudson, *The Philosophy of Personalism* (New York: Abingdon Press, 1927), pp. 21–22: "One would expect, then, that a philosophy, bearing the name of personalism or that might properly be called such, would be theistic; and, on the whole, the history of thought does not disappoint this expectation. The personalistic philosophies have, for the most part, been true to their theistic and Christian origin. But there are exceptions to the rule. We have both an *atheistic* personalism and a *pantheistic* personalism."

3. The citation should be J. M. E. McTaggart, "An Ontological Idealism," in *Contemporary British Philosophy*, ed. J. H. Muirhead (New York: Macmillan, 1924), p. 251.

4. C. D. Broad, "Introduction" to J. M. E. McTaggart, *Some Dogmas of Religion* (London: Edward Arnold, 1930), p. xxv: "John McTaggart Ellis McTaggart was born in 1866, and educated at Clifton and Trinity College, Cambridge. In 1888 he was placed alone in the first class of the Moral Science Tripos. In 1890 he became president of the Union Society. He was elected to a prize-fellowship at Trinity in 1891. Soon after this he paid a long visit to New Zealand. In 1899 he married Miss Margaret Elizabeth Bird of Taranki. In 1897 he was made College Lecturer in the Moral Sciences, an office which he held until 1923. . . . After a short but painful illness, borne with admirable courage and patience, he died on the 18th of January, 1925, in a nursing home in London at the age of 58."

5. Broad, "Introduction," p. xxvi: "While he lived he published the following books: *Studies in Hegelian Dialectic, Studies in Hegelian Cosmology, Some Dogmas of Religion, A Commentary to Hegel's*

As stated above, the purpose of this paper is to present and criticise the views of McTaggart's personalistic system. We may conveniently discuss his system under two main headings—Epistemalogy and Metaphysics.

Epistemology

McTaggart's epistemological position is well summarized in the following statement:

> I should say that epistemologically I was a Realist. I should say that knowledge was a true belief, and I should say that a belief was true when, and only when, it stands in a relation of correspondence to a fact. I do not think that this particular relations of correspondence can be defined further, but it may be remarked that it is not a relation of copying or of similarity. Of facts, I should say that whenever anything is anything, using both "anything" and "is" in the widest possible sense, it is a fact that it is so.*

* Ibid, 249.[6]

This is another way of saying he is an epistemological dualist. The thought series and the thing series are "numerically two" and not "one." One wonders how such an ardent disciple of Hegel can come to such a radically different epistemological position. Hegel is an epistemological monist. For him, the identity of knowing and being is a basic principle. The Absolute is himself Thought or Experience, and beyond Thought or Experience, there is no reality. But not so with McTaggart. For him, there is an otherness to individual consciousness which implies a distinction between knowing and being.

At this point, McTaggart is much more in accord with typical personalism than he is at many other points. The dualism of thought and thing, or idea and object is one of the main articles in the epistemological creed of personalism. Typical Personalists would insist, contrary to "pan-subjectivists" and "pan-objectivists", that if personality is to maintain its integrity, it must be kept "a handbreath off", both from the

Logic, and the first volume of *The Nature of Existence*. At the time of his death he had completed the second draft of the remaining volume of *The Nature of Existence* and was engaged in writing the third draft."

6. "Ibid" in fact refers to McTaggart, "Ontological Idealism."

Absolute and from things; and this means epistemological dualism.

Yet it must be stated that although McTaggart and
typical personalists are in accord as to the validity of
epistemological dualism, they are at variance as to
how this dualism is to be explained. The typical personalist finds the only satisfactory explanation of it in
a theistic monism. He would argue that if an intelligent Being is the ultimate source both of the thing
series and the thought series, it is possible to understand at once their dualism and their parallelism.
McTaggart's anti-theistic bias would cause him to immediately reject this explanation. How he explains
this dualism, I have not been able to discern. It so
happens that McTaggart's predominant concern is
with metaphysics and only occasionally does he refer
to his epistemology.

McTaggart's failure to accept theistic monism can
certainly serve as a valid criticism against his epistemological position. While he is basically sound in his starting point, viz., in accepting epistemological dualism,
he is basically unsound in his explanation of this dualism. Apart from an intelligent Being who is the ultimate source both of the thought series and the thing
series, the parallelism of thought and thing remains
an insoluble riddle. McTaggart's epistemological dualism requires a theistic monism for its completion.[7]

Metaphysics

We turn now to a consideration of McTaggart's
metaphysics. Indeed, this is the most important phase
of his philosphy. Some philosophers are concerned
primarily with epistemology. while others are primarily concerned with metaphysics. McTaggart belongs
to the latter class. He is one of the few English thinkers who is the author of a truly original metaphysical
system.[8]

For the last half century or so, the labours of philosophers have been devoted rather to the investiga-

---

7. DeWolf commented in the margin, "Good criticism. It would apply also to [Roy Wood] Sellars, and, indeed more pointedly."

8. Hastings Rashdall, *Philosophy and Religion* (New York: Scribner, 1914), p. 96: "I cannot here undertake a full exposition or criticism of one of the ablest thinkers of our day—one of the very few English thinkers who is the author of a truly original metaphysical system."

tion of the nature and certainty of alleged scientific knowledge than to the attempt to determine the nature of Reality as a whole by abstract reasoning. This limitation has been mainly the result of bitter experience of the futility of previous attempts at speculative metaphysics. A distrust of elaborate philosophical systems has always characterized England in general. To all of these, McTaggart is an eminent exception. He always held that important facts can be proved of Reality as a whole by processes of deductive reasoning.

We may conveniently discuss McTaggart's metaphysics under four headings: 1. The nature of the Absolute, 2. The nature and destiny of the finite self, 3. The doctrine of freedom, and 4. The infinite value of love. Each of these principles will need to be carefully studied if we are to fully understand McTaggart's metaphysical system. In the following discussion, they will be taken up in the order just given.

The Nature
of the Absolute

It has been stated above that McTaggart would readily qualify as a personalist on the grounds that he held that ultimate reality consists of a society of persons. But his personalism is atheistic since he does not recognize the necessity for one all-embracing or controlling Person. He recognizes in the traditional language of Philosophy, an Absolute, but this Absolute is not a Person. {The} Absolute is spiritual, is a unity, and is a harmonious whole, and yet is still not a person. It is a unity of persons, not a personal unity. It consists of conscious individuals, but is not itself a conscious individual. McTaggart comes to this conclusion by a somewhat peculiar process of argument. The Absolute being concrete, is a unity of differentiations. But differences may exist in the unity, and the unity may be in and for the differences without that unity being personal. For this it is necessary that the difference exist for the unity. Now, in the Absolute, unity and differences are identical only in the sense that these two aspects are also distinct, the one would be the other, and the nature of the Absolute becomes meaningless, because barren and inexpressible. But if the differences exist for the unity as the unity exist for the differences, there is no distinction of content between the two aspects, and, hence, it is impossible to speak of one being for the other at all; In that case not mrerely the Absolute but the individuals which make it up cease to be intelligible, for they can have no relation unless by being in some way distinct. Thus, says McTaggart, while we may in virtue of the validity of the "category of teleology," assert that the unity exist in and for the differences, we cannot maintain that the differences exist for the unity, and therefore, must abandon the claim to regard the Absolute as itself personal.

Although this is McTaggart's main argument, he supplements it by further consideration. He points out that for personality "as we know it", the consciousness of a non-ego is essential. But a non-ego is in some sense outside the ego; on the other hand, nothing in any sense can be outside the Absolute. In McTaggart's own words, "such a consciousness the Absolute cannot possess. For there is nothing outside from which it can distinguish itself."* Hence, for the Absolute, there is no non-ego of which it can be conscious, and thus no personality.

* S.H.C., 68

From this discussion on the nature of the Absolute one can easily see that McTaggart's attitude toward the existence of God is essentially negative. He sees the doctrine of an omnipotent and creative God as metaphysically unsound. He is willing to admit the possibility of a non-omnipotent God, whom he styles "the director of the universe", "a person of appreciable importance when measured against the whole of the universe", but such a belief is not at all necessary. The only reason why we should not believe in the existence of such a God, he says, with a dash of cynicism, is that there is no reason why we should believe in it. The ultimate outcome of McTaggart's God concept is found in this phrase, "the Absolute is not God, and in consequence there is no God."†

† Ibid, 94

In spite of its acuteness, and in spite of its novelty, this view of McTaggart seems to me open to insuperable difficulties. First, it fails to satisfy the mind's demand for unity. No system can explain itself. Beneath the "harmonious system of selves", there must be a unitary being that binds the selves together. This unitary being must be more than a mere concept; such a being must be a person.[9] As knudson laconically

---

9. Knudson, *Philosophy of Personalism*, p. 24: "Beyond the harmonious system of selves there must be some unitary principle that binds the selves together, and this principle must be some-

states, in a criticism of McTaggart at this same point: "His theory of a 'harmonious spiritual system' thus requires for its completion a personal God."*

There is a second point in this view which leads to further difficulties/. As an Idealist, McTaggart has to admit that the material world exists only in and for Mind. It is quite apparent that no human mind knows the whole of this world. What kind of existence then have the parts of the universe which are not known to any mind. To follow his view to its logical conculsion, McTaggart would have to admit that they do not exist at all. This would represent a subjective idealism of the most extreme kind.[10] Again we must conclude that McTaggart needs a supreme mind which both knows and wills the existence and the mutual relation of the spirits to complete his system.†

† For an elaboration of this criticism, see Rashdall's, PR, 123–6

We shall also notice that many of McTaggart's arguments against an omnipotent God are far from adequate. Indeed, the reader gets the impression sometimes that McTaggart is simply indulging in logical trifling, that the discredited theistic doctrine is unworthy of serious consideration and may be caricatured to any extent. What other impression is possible from such paragraphs as the following:

> An omnipotent person is one who can do anything. Now suppose that God had willed to create a universe, and had not willed that the law of Identity should be valid. It seems that we have no alternative but to be inconsistent or to be completely unmeaning. To suppose that the universe would not have been created, although God had willed that it should, would be inconsistent with his omnipotence. But the assertion that the universe could be created without being a universe, and without being created is unmeaning. And yet, how can the universe be the universe, or creation be creation unless the law of Identity be true. Again, is there any meaning in the

---

thing other than the selves and something more than a mere concept. To interpret unity as a 'system of differentiations' does not satisfy the mind's demand for unity. To meet this demand there must be a unitary being deeper than the system, and on McTaggart's own principles such a being must be a person."

10. Rashdall, *Philosophy and Religion*, p. 123: "It is admitted that the material world exists only in and for Mind. There is no reason to think that any human mind . . . knows the whole of this world. What kind of existence then have the parts of the Universe which are not known to any mind? It seems to me that Dr. McTaggart would be compelled to admit that they do not exist at all. The world postulated by Science would thus be admitted to be a delusion. This represents a subjective Idealism of an exteme and staggering kind."

supposition that God could create a man who was not a man, or that he could create a being who was neither man nor not man. But, if he could not, then he is bound by the law of Contradiction and the law of Excluded Middle, and, once more, he is not omnipotent.*

* McTaggart: SDR, 202, 203

Certainly few, if any, modern theologians believing in the omnipotence of God would take omnipotence in such an absolutely abstract sense.[11] When God is said to possess omnipotence, the meaning is that there is nothing which can prevent Him realizing any purpose His wisdom and goodness, e.g., decided Him to attempt. Evidently, McTaggart completely overlooked this.[12]

The Nature and Destiny of the Finite Self

In order to understand McTaggart's views on the nature and destiny of the finite self, we must turn immediately to his doctrine of immortality. At this point, McTaggart is thoroughly positive. He never wearies of pointing out the validity of this doctrine. He is convinced that the presumtion against immortality, produced in many people by supposed results of physical science, should be discarded. Science is concerned solely with uniformities in the routine of our perceptions. Physical science can have nothing to say, for example on the questions of the independent existence of matter, which is only one theory about the causes of our sensations, and a theory which, on examination, is found to be ~~invalid~~ {involved} in inconsistency. The "self", therefore, cannot be treated as an activity of the body. Its conscious existence is, on the contrary, a primary reality.

As McTaggart continues his argument, he attempts to connect the belief in immortality with the belief in pre-existence. He says in an interesting passage:

The present attitude of most Western thinkers to the doctrine of pre-existence is curious. Of the many who

---

11. DeWolf underlined "modern" and asked, "Why say modern only? Even Anselm took account of such rational limitations of God, though he declined to call them limitations."

12. In the margin by the last two sentences of this paragraph DeWolf commented, "Good."

4 Dec
1951

regard our life, after the death of our bodies, as certain or probable, scarcely one regards our life before the birth of those bodies as a possibility which deserves discussion, and yet it was taught by Buddha and by Plato, and it is usually associated with the belief in immortality in the Far East. Why should men who are so anxious today to prove that we shall live after this life is ended, regard the hypothesis that we have already survived the end of a life as one which is beneath consideration?*

* Ibid, 112

McTaggart himself believes that any evidence which will prove immortality will also prove pre-existence.

McTaggart has no use for the ethical argument for immortality. He feels that we must fall back on "purely metaphysical arguments". These turn out to be based on abstract considerations as to the nature of substance. The perdurability of substance naturally refers just as much to the past as to the future. McTaggart believes, accordingly, that our present existence has been preceded by a plurality of lives, and will be followed in like manner by a plurality of lives. The obvious objection to this theory is the fact that we retain no memory of those previous lives, and McTaggart, it is to be noted, does not imply that in the lives to come we shall have any memory of our present existence. "An existence that is cut up into separate lives, in none of which memory extends to a previous life, may be thought to have no practical value."† McTaggart labours hard to prove that this is not so, the most important argument being that though the actual experiences are forgotten, their results in the training of mind and character may be carried forward into the next life, so that the man will be wiser and better in the second life because of what has happened in the first. He will, as it were, have a better start; he will build in the new life upon the foundations in the old.

† Ibid, 127.

This argument sounds far more plausible than it really is, and depends upon the ambiguity of the word "person". "In spite of the loss of memory", says McTaggart, "It is the same person who lives in the successive lives".[13] Now it is exceedingly difficult to

---

13. The quotation is from J. M. E. McTaggart, *Some Dogmas of Religion* (London: Edward Arnold, 1906), p. 130.

determine precisely what we mean by personal identity, and what its limits are/. Obviously, within the present life, countless items of our experience lapse from conscious memory and survive only in aptitudes, dispositions, and tendencies. Yet they play their role in training the mind and tempering the character. Still, although much may persist only in the subconscious fashion, it seems clear that a continuity of conscious memory within certain limits is involved in the ordinary notion of personality, so that a complete break of such continuity would make the assertion of personal identity in the two lives unmeaning. It seems that Locke is much nearer the truth than McTaggart when he (Locke) argues in his well-known chapter that "personal identity consists not in the identity of substance, but in the identity of consciousness".[14] So with Rashdall we must conclude that "the theory of pre-existent souls is opposed to all the probabilities suggested by experience"[*15]

* Rashdall: PR, 134

We may also criticise McTaggart's argument for the validity of the doctrine of immortality. As was stated above, he cast out the ethical argument with the contention that we are forced back "on purely metaphysical arguments". But these, as partially revealed in <u>Some Dogmas of Religion</u> and more fully in <u>Studies in Hegelian Cosmology</u>[†] turn out to be based on abstract considerations as to the nature of substance. They are indeed curiously pre-Kantian in character, and it is strange to find so profound a student of Hegel using substance throughout as the ultimate category in speaking both of the self and of God.

† See McTaggart, SDR II, and SHC III.

McTaggart's casting out of the ethical argument for immortality was somewhat ineluctable because of his anti-theistic bias. At this point, however, he was casting out what seems to me the only vigorous argument for immortality, viz., the goodness of God. As Brightman has succinctly put it, "If there is a supreme Cosmic Person, then there is an infinitely good being committed to the eternal conservation of values."[‡] Certainly, God the conserver of values must be God the conserver of Persons, since Persons are of highest

‡ Brightman: POR, 401.

---

14. The quotation is from John Locke, *Essay Concerning Human Understanding*, book 1, chap. 27, sec. 19.

15. DeWolf wrote in the margin, "Good use of sources." The quotation is actually from p. 124.

value. At bottom, faith in immortality is faith in the goodness of God.[16]

A theoretical as well as a practical basis for the belief is to be found in the nature of God. Every argument for his obligation to conserve Persons as intrinsic values. To him, we may therefore safely trust the future, confident that he will conserve the highest values. As Carlyle puts it, in one of the pathetic outbursts of the <u>Autobiography</u>: "Perhaps we shall all meet yonder, and the tears be wiped from all eyes. One thing is no Perhaps; surely we shall all meet, if it be the will of the Maker of us. If it be not His will, then is it not better so?"

One wonders how McTaggart can hold so firmly to a doctrine of immortality and at the same time deny theism. Certainly, this is an enigma to me. Apparently McTaggart is unique in this position, for no other well-known philosopher has held such a view. We may be safe in saying that every other philosophical believer in immortality has affirmed theism.[17] So we might conclude that theists are much sounder than McTaggart in affirming that arguments for God are at the same time arguments for immortality.[18]

Doctrine of Freedom

On the question of the freedom of the will, McTaggart is almost exclusively negative. Not only does he set himself to demolish the ordinary arguments by which the doctrine is supported, but he holds that an metaphysical grounds it can be shown to be untrue. There is no reason, according to McTaggart, why human volitions should be exceptions to any law of the complete determination of events.

---

16. Edgar S. Brightman, *A Philosophy of Religion* (New York: Prentice-Hall, 1940), pp. 400–401: "There is only one vigorous argument for immortality (which reduces to the argument for a theistic philosophy). If there is a God—a supreme, creative, cosmic person—then there is an infinitely good being committed to the eternal conservation of values. . . . God, the conserver of values, must be God, the conserver of persons."

17. Brightman, *Philosophy of Religion*, p. 402: "That the arguments for God are at the same time arguments for immortality is indicated by the fact that there has been only one well-known philosophical believer in immortality who denied theism, namely, J. M. E. McTaggart, and the correlative fact that substantially every theist has accepted immortality."

18. DeWolf commented, "Good."

McTaggart's views on freedom of the will seem to be far below his usual level of freshness and incisiveness. He attacks a "freedom of indetermination" which I do not think any champion would enter the lists. What upholder of freedom, for example, would accept the statement that "according to the indeterminist theory our choice between motives is not determined by anything at all"?* And when McTaggart says that "on the determinist hypothesis an omnipotent God could have prevented all sin by creating us with better natures and in more favorable surroundings", and that "he cannot see what extraordinary value lies in the incompleteness of the determination of the will, which should counterbalance all the sin, and the consequent unhappiness caused by the misuse of that will",† the answer is that creatures so turned out would not be moral beings at all; they would be things and not persons.

Freedom is the central and essential foundation of ethics. As Brightman has cogently put it: "If choice is not possible, the science of ethics is not possible. If rational, purposive choice is not effective in the central of life, goodness is not possible."‡ It is this necessity of moral freedom that McTaggart constantly overlooked. So at times his arguments remind us of the words of Thomas Huxley: "If some great Power would agree to make me think always what is true and do what is right on condition of being turned into a sort of clock, I should instantly close the bargain. The only freedom I care about is the freedom to do right; the freedom to do wrong, I am ready to part with".§[19] But no "sort of clock" can do what is right or think what is true, or indeed think at all. Nor can any man learn without the possibility of going wrong, any more than a child can learn to walk without the possibility of falling. If we are to be persons rather than mere ~~autonoms~~ {automatons}, freedom must be maintained.

Not only is freedom necessary for moral choices, but it is also necessary for the act of reason. To quote Brightman again, "Without freedom, we are not free

* McTaggart, SDR, 143

† Ibid, 164

‡ Brightman, ML, 74

§ CE, I, 192

---

19. The quotation is inaccurate; it should read: "I protest that if some great power would agree to make me always think what is true and do what is right, on condition of being turned into a sort of clock and wound up every morning before I got out of bed, I should instantly close with the offer. The only freedom I care about is the freedom to do right; the freedom to do wrong I am ready to part with on the cheapest terms to any one who will take it of me" (Thomas Huxley, *Collected Essays*, vol. 1: *Method and Results* [New York: Appleton, 1898], pp. 192–93).

to think, for the power to think means that the individual can impose on himself the ideal of logic or scientific method and hold it through thick and thin." [20] 4 Dec 1951
Certainly without freedom, reason would go shipwreck. It was probably Bowne who, more than any other, stressed the significance of this point. For him, freedom has both epistemological and metaphysical significance. I believe that a more sympathetic study of the great masters in ethics and thinkers like Bowne would have made McTaggart's chapter on "Free Will" more adequate to its theme. In rejecting freedom, McTaggart was rejecting the most important characteristic of personality.

The Metaphysical Significance of Love

It is plain to the reader of McTaggart that one of his fundamental connections was that the love of one man for another is of infinite value and profound metaphysical significance. He sets out on his journey to establish the metaphysical significance of love with the attempt to determine the nature of spirit. Since human consciousness has only three modes, Knowledge, Conation,[21] and Feeling, it must be in one of these ways, or in some kind of combination of the, that the ultimate form of the activity of spirit is to be found. Now, both knowledge and volition postulate a perfection which they can never attain unless by losing themselves in what transcends them.[22] For they are distinct, and as they stand opposed forms of activity; one accepts facts, the other judges them. But no such opposition can exist in absolute perfection. Hence, neither knowledge, nor volition, nor the two together gives us the true nature of spirit. Similarly, feeling must be rejected as the ultimate mode of spirit, for it is "pure self reference of the subject;" it

---

20. A footnote number appears in the text without a corresponding citation at the bottom of the page. The quotation is from Edgar S. Brightman, *Moral Laws* (New York: Abingdon Press, 1930), p. 282.

21. King means "Volition" rather than "Conation."

22. J. M. E. McTaggart, *Studies in Hegelian Cosmology* (Cambridge: Cambridge University Press, 1918), p. 262: "If we look close enough we shall find, I think, that both knowledge and volition postulate a perfection to which they can never attain."

"has nothing to do with objects", and cannot therefore fully express the nature of spirit, which necessarily implies an "appreciation of an object".* The only state left to reveal spirit in its perfection is one which will involve all three elements, Knowledge, Volition, and Feeling. This state is Emotion. This is the "concrete unity" in which spirit is fully realized, and for which those three elements are "abstractions". Now emotion made perfect, i.e., in complete harmony, is Love. This, then, is what gives "interest and value to knowledge and volition"; "this resolves their contradictions;" this is the "concrete material of the life of spirit." It is not "benevolence", nor "Love of Truth and Virtue and Beauty, or anything else whose name can be found in the dictionary. It is passionate, all-absorbing, all-consuming love."† It is again not love of God, for love is of persons, and God is not a person.‡ Nor is it love of mankind, for the human race is an aggregate, not an organism; and we cannot love "an indefinitely extended post-office directory." And the same is true of nations, churches, and families.[23] "The nearest approach to it is the love for which no cause can be given, of which we can only say that two people belong to each other—all the love of the Vita Nuova, and of In Memoriam"§

* McTaggart seems to have forgotten this when discussing personality where the difference between personality and spirit turned on the fact that while the former involved reference to an object, the latter, it was said, need not.

† McTaggart, SHC, 260

‡ Ibid, 289

§ Ibid, 291

Closely connected with this is his view that all good is inclusive perception. So when one preceives a person as he is, he really loves him. The more perception, the more love; the more love, the more good. Because this inclusive perception always is on the increase, the future is always better than the past and the distant future will be better than the near future. Here is a doctrine of inevitable progress that out-Spencers Spencer.

As I read McTaggart's views at this point, I could not help but wonder how an atheist could find so much meaning in the universe. McTaggart contends that the Universe constitutes not merely a physical but also a moral order. He would not deny that the universe means something; that the series of events tends toward and end, an end which is good. And yet, this purpose exists in no controlling mind whatso-

---

23. McTaggart, *Studies in Hegelian Cosmology*, p. 290: "If we cannot, properly speaking, love God, it is still more impossible to love mankind. . . . The human race, viewed as such, is only an aggregate, not even an organism. We might as well try to love an indefinitely extended Post Office Directory. And the same will hold true of all subordinate aggregates—nations, churches, and families."

ever, and is due to no controlling will. I confess I do not understand the idea of a purpose which operates, but is not the purpose of a Mind and a Will.

We come now to the end of a study of McTaggart. I have tried to point out what seems to me to be weaknesses in his theories, althought I may be, to some extent, disqualified as a critic.[24] We have seen that he is totally negative on the idea of a Personal, creative God. To affirm the reality of a creative God would mean to affirm the reality of time, and this McTaggart will not do. Says he, "It seems to me that one empirically known characterisitc which cannot really belong to anything that exists is the characteristic of Time."* We have also seen that McTaggart is usually negative on the idea of freedom. For these and many other reasons, we have found it necessary to reject most of McTaggart's views. Any system which seeks to establish itself on the unreality of time seems to me rationally unsound and empirically unverified.

* Muirhead (ed.): CBP, 258

BIBLIOGRAPHY

Brightman, Edgar Sheffield.—ML
    Moral Laws.
    New York: The Abingdon Press, 1930.
———.—POR
    A Philosophy of Religion.
    New York: Prentice Hall, Inc., 1940.
Knudson, Albert C.—POP
    The Philosophy of Personalism.
    New York: The Abingdon Press, 1927.
McTaggart, J. M. E.—SDR
    Some Dogmas of Religion.
    London: Edward Arnold, 1906.
———.—SHC
    Studies in Hegelian Cosmology.
    Cambridge: University Press, 1918.
Muirhead, J. H. (ed.)—CBP
    Contemporary British Philosophy.
    New York: The Macmillan Co., 1924.
Rashdall, Hastings.—PR
    Philosophy and Religion.
    London: Duckwarth & Co., 1948.

THDS. MLKP-MBU: Box 112.

24. DeWolf asked, "Why?" in the margin.

To Edgar S. Brightman

[*6 December 1951*]
[*Boston, Mass.*]

*Brightman received this note with the following paper on J. M. E. McTaggart,
William E. Hocking, and Brightman. He wrote at the bottom of the note: "I'm
certainly going to take this into account. Thank you for your frankness."*

Dr. Brightman

I am almost ashame to turn this paper in because of the numerous errors
found in it. How the typist made such error, I cannot understand. I have tried
to correct as many of the mistakes as possible, but some of them I couldn't.
For an instance there is a long quotation on page 10 ~~wh~~ from Hocking which
should have been single-spaced without quotation marks, indented, and set
off by an omitted line before and after it. The footnotes are also in somewhat
bad condition. I have corrected them as much as possible.

I hope that this ~~can~~ {will} be taken under consideration in your correcting
the paper. It so happens that I am financially unable to have it retyped.

[*signed*] Martin L. King

AHLS. MLKP-MBU: Box 114.

"A Comparison and Evaluation of the
Philosophical Views Set Forth in
J. M. E. McTaggart's *Some Dogmas of Religion*,
and William E. Hocking's *The Meaning of God
in Human Experience* with Those Set Forth
in Edgar S. Brightman's Course on
'Philosophy of Religion'"

[*6 December 1951*]
[*Boston, Mass.*]

*Following Brightman's instructions, King builds on his earlier comparison of
McTaggart and Brightman, bringing the philosophy of William E. Hocking
into his discussion.[1] King concludes that Brightman "is much more sound*

---

1. William Ernest Hocking (1873–1966) was a noted American philosopher of religion and
proponent of what may be termed "objective idealism." He attended Harvard University, receiving his B.A. in 1901, his M.A. in 1902, and his Ph.D. in 1904. After additional study in German

philosophically" than Hocking, who "fails to take seriously the fact that all truth, including religious, is based on the assumption that the human mind is valid and that the cosmos is rational." Brightman gave this paper an A and commented: "This is an unusually thoughtful paper. It is a bit oversimplified, but it grasps central issues soundly. It would have been stronger had you restated your critique of my view, but you show real insight."

Contents

---

universities, he taught at Andover Theological Seminary, the University of California, and Yale before returning to Harvard in 1914 as a professor of philosophy. He retired in 1943. Among his many published works are *The Meaning of God in Human Experience* (1912), *Human Nature and Its Remaking* (1918), and *The Meaning of Immortality in Human Experience* (1957). For more information, see Leroy S. Rouner, *Within Human Experience: The Philosophy of William Ernest Hocking* (Cambridge, Mass.: Harvard University Press, 1969); and *Philosophy, Religion, and the Coming World Civilization: Essays in Honor of William Ernest Hocking*, ed. Leroy S. Rouner (The Hague: Martinus Nijhoff, 1966).

  2. Brightman underlined "impossibility" and wrote, "as absolute proof."

The purpose of this paper is to compare and evaluate the philosophical views set forth in J. M. E. McTaggart's Some Dogmas of Religion, and William E. Hocking's The Meaning of God in Human Experience with those set forth in Edgar S. Brightman's course on "Philosophy of Religion". Before comparing these views, however, we may devote a few paragraphs to a summary of Hocking's The Meaning of God in Human Experience. A summary of McTaggart's Some Dogmas of Religion has already been given in a previous paper.[4]

In this momentous work by Professor Hocking, a serious endeavor is made to reinterpret idealism in a way which will afford a positive groundwork for religion. The author, at the outset, states his cognizance of a deep distrust of the services of recent thought for the purposes of religion. Pragmatism has exposed the weakness of classical {idealism for} religious needs, but pragmatism itself is not considered constructive in this field. Idealism fails to work, not because it has a wrong point of view, but because it is "unfinished".[5] It does "not give credence to the authoritative Object; shows so far, no adequate comprehension of the attitude of worship".[6] It supplies too much a religion of idea, not adequately rooted in passion, fact and institutional life. Hocking thinks that these limitations may be supplied to Idealism by Mysticism of a certain type. The entire volume may be said, to be an attempt to achieve this task. The first part, in three chapters, deals with a statement of the nature of religion in pragmatic terms, by means of its effects in history and in persons.

Part II discusses "Religious Feeling and Religious Theory", and outlines the motives which have led to

---

3. At the bottom of the table of contents, Brightman wrote, "Well outlined!"

4. King, "A Comparison and Evaluation of the Views Set Forth in J. M. E. McTaggart's *Some Dogmas of Religion* with Those Set Forth by Edgar S. Brightman in His Course on 'Philosophy of Religion,'" 25 October 1951, MLKP-MBU: Box 112.

5. This quotation is from William E. Hocking, *The Meaning of God in Human Experience* (New Haven: Yale University Press, 1912), p. x.

6. The quotation is from Hocking, *Meaning of God*, p. xi.

the retirement of reason in religion. A study of religious movements shows that "religion renews its life in great bursts of impulse which emanate not from new thoughts, but from rarely impressive personalities . . . Their utterances are poetic, oracular, couched in figure and parable, not in t[h]eses . . . As passion cools, theology spreads, and as theology spreads, passion cools still more."[7] After reading this passage and more like it, the reader is almost lead to believe that the author makes religion merely a matter of feeling. (It seems to be a favorite knack of Hocking to argue a view which he does not believe with such a positive bent that the reader is left with the impression that is is his view and then in the next instance to refute that view with a positive stating of his true belief.)[8] But Hocking goes on to make it clear that he is not content to make religion a matter of feeling, apart from ideation. It is his conviction that "feeling" does not work apart from its guiding idea", and that ideas are alive and vital only through such feelings as love and sympathy.[9]

6 Dec
1951

Part III is a discussion of "The Need of God." Different types of monism are reviewed with a view to determining what kind and degree of optimism is compatible with each, "for surely we will ~~will~~ have no world in which it is not possible to be optimistic and without danger to our moral fiber."[10] Some kind of monism is necessary to give character to the world. Without this, optimism is impossible.[11]

There is also need of an Absolute—a changeless framework within which we may have the sense of real and progressive improvement. This is shown in the demand of the epistemologist: What can I surely know?—and also in the demand of the moralist: What ought I to do?[12]

But not only do we need a One and an Absolute;

---

7. This passage is from Hocking, *Meaning of God*, p. 41.

8. Brightman remarked, "True!"

9. Brightman commented, "Also, what is love without ideas and ideals?" King misquoted Hocking; the phrase should read, "feeling does no work apart from its guiding idea" (*Meaning of God*, p. 69).

10. The quotation is from Hocking, *Meaning of God*, p. 166.

11. Brightman asked, "Is optimism an a priori?"

12. Brightman changed "demand" to "question" in both cases. These questions are also in Hocking, *Meaning of God*, pp. 191–193.

we need God.[13] "The crux of this problem is the presence of pain and evil in the world, and this must be dealt with in thorough fashion. Basing the discussion here upon a criticism of McTaggart's Some Dogmas of Religion, the conclusion is reached that pain and evil are assuaged through companionship, especially through the sense of association with the Divine. I need this relation with an "Other whose relati[o]n to me is not subject to evil through its own defects."[14]

Part IV is an attempt to show "How men knew God." This is through Nature and social experience. In defining nature, he says, "Nature is pre-eminently the world of socially verifiable things, the world of scientific research—which is general human collaboration on a common object. We look at Nature through the eyes of a social world."[15] There is thus present to us everywhere Other Mind. All our social experience presupposes a fundamental relation with an Other. This social experience could not exist, it is asserted, if there were only empirical knowers in the world.[16] "Our first and fundamental social experience is an experience of God."[17] From this position it is not far to a restatement and adoption of the ontological argument. The reality of God is found in the necessity of the idea in all our limited and negative experience. The consciousness of defects and limits implies the consciousness of God. All other arguments conclude that because the world is, God is, but the ontological arument reasons that "because the world is not, God is".[18] But God thus found is not an object among objects, natural or physical. "As an object in the world of objects, God is next to nothing".[19] The development of the knowledge of God (Chap. xxii) is traced from the beliefs of primitive man to the conception of personality which includes law. "Religion becomes

---

13. Brightman commented in the margin, "Note the difference."

14. The quotation is from Hocking, *Meaning of God*, pp. 223–224.

15. The quotation is from Hocking, *Meaning of God*, p. 280.

16. Hocking, *Meaning of God*, p. 294: "But if there are none but empirical knowers in the world there is no social experience."

17. Brightman noted this sentence and commented in the margin: "Basic for WEH!" The quotation is from Hocking, *Meaning of God*, p. 295.

18. Hocking, *Meaning of God*, p. 312: "These other arguments reason that *because the world is, God is*. The ontological argument reasons that *because the world is not, God is*."

19. Brightman wrote in the margin, "What, then, is he? Cf. p. 5" (see note 22 below). The quotation is from Hocking, *Meaning of God*, p. 323.

universal at the same time that it becomes most peculiarly personal."[20]

Part V presents a treatment of "Worship and the Mystics". The importance of this section is revealed in this statement: "Worship brings the experience of God to pass in self-consciousness with a searching valency not obligating upon the pure thinker: in some way it enacts the presence of God, sets God into the will to work there."[21] Mysticism is taken not so much in terms of its doctrine as its deed. It is pointed out that religion throughout its history has been a matter of overt activity—of ceremonial, rite, dramatic enactment—more than a system of thought. The identification of worship with thinking is therefore a perversion. The author goes on to present an illuminating analysis and description of the mystical experience. Chaps xxvi, xxvii, and xxviii present a suggestive psychological account of the mystic way, through negation of the world and the self, to the passive attitude through which God enters and energizes the soul. The mystic seeks the whole, rather than any particulars of reality. Through this totality, experienced in worship, the details of one's occupations and interest are set in a luminous perceptive and given meaning and worth. But these two spheres of work and worship must alternate and thus enrich and support each other. "Prayer and Its Answer" are discussed in connection with this mystical experience and partake of its essence. Prayer is mystic insight and "the answer to prayer is whatever of simplicity, of naturalness, of original appreciation, is brought into our view of things by this act of obedience of the mind to its absolute object."[22]

Part VI discusses "The Fruits of Religion". It deals with revelation, inspiration, and the prophetic consciousness. This discussion is controlled by the conception of mysticism just preceded.

The book ends with several important notes. They deal with the Subconscious, the Relations between

20. The chapter on the development of the knowledge of God is actually chapter xxiii. The quotation is from Hocking, *Meaning of God*, p. 337.

21. The quotation is from Hocking, *Meaning of God*, p. 342. Hocking used "obligatory" rather than "obligating."

22. Brightman underlined "its absolute object" and wrote, "Cf. p. 4" (see above, note 19). The quotation is from Hocking, *Meaning of God*, p. 439.

Idea and Value, the Knowledge of Independent Reality, and the Nature of the Mystic's Love of God.

With this somewhat brief summary of Hocking's The Meaning of God in Human Experience, we may now turn to a comparison and evaluation of the views set forth {in this book with those set forth} by McTaggart in his Some Dogmas of Religion, and by Edgar S. Brightman in his course on "Philosophy of Religion".[23] We may conveniently discuss the views of these men under four headings: 1. The Doctrine of God, 2. Religious Experience, 3. Religious certainty, and 4. The doctrine of immortality.

The Doctrine of God

As was stated in my previous paper, McTaggart's attitude toward the existence of God is essentially negative. For him, the doctrine of an omnipotent and creative God is metaphysically unsound.*[24] With such a negative attitude toward the God concept neither Brightman nor Hocking would concur. Both men affirm belief in a personal God.[25] Indeed, Hocking affirms that any other conception of divine unity than the personal is "thinner and weaker".†[26] With McTaggart's view that belief in a personal God is unnecessary and metaphysically unsound, neither Hocking nor Brightman would agree. Their views of God are "evolutionary", while McTaggart's view is "revolutionary".[27]

* See my last paper, P. 4

† MGHE, 334.

---

23. Underlining "brief summary," Brightman commented: "But satisfactory."

24. The preceding two sentences and the next two also appear in King's earlier essay on McTaggart and Brightman. In that essay his comments on McTaggart were more extensive: "[McTaggart] is willing to admit the possibility of a non-omnipotent God, whom he styles 'the director of the universe,' 'a person of appreciable importance when measured against the whole of the universe,' but such a belief is not at all necessary. The only reason why we should not believe in the existence of such a God, he says, is that there is no reason why we should believe in it." Commenting on the earlier essay, Brightman underlined "necessary" and wrote "'theoretical relativism'" above it. He also asked King to "specify reasons" in the margin next to "no reason why we should believe in it" (King, "Comparison and Evaluation of McTaggart and Brightman").

25. Brightman emended this sentence to read: "Both men affirm belief in a personal and creative God who knows all that is knowable."

26. Cf. "There is neither merit nor truth in rarefying the thought of God; nor in presenting him to our conceptions in terms of some thinner and weaker sort of world-unity easier to image and believe in than a personal world-unity" (Hocking, *Meaning of God*, p. 334).

27. Brightman commented, "or rather, negative."

There is one point in the God concept, however, at which McTaggart and Brightman are in essential agreement over against Hocking. Both argue that the existence of evil in the world is incompatible with the belief in an omnipotent being who is also good. But while belief in a non-omnipotent God leads McTaggart to the verge of Atheism, it leads Brightman to a modified theism. As stated in my last paper, it seems to me that Brightman, although rejecting theistic absolutism, faces his task with much more sympathy and understanding for contrary views than does McTaggart. Indeed, the reader gets the impression sometimes that McTaggart is simply indulging in logical trifling, that the discredited theistic doctrine is unworthy of serious consideration and may be caricatured to any extent.*[28] McTagart's insistence on taking omnipotence as implying the power to make contradictions true makes his whole discussion at this point rather profitless.

* See quotation from McTaggart's SDR, p. 4, my last paper.

We discussed Dr. Brightman's conception of the finite God in the last paper, but since certain details were omitted, we may restate those views in a more detailed form. Dr. Brightman's conception of the finite God begins with the contention that evil in the world is apparently outside the purpose of God and to some extent beyond his control;[29] this suggests, therefore, a deity "whose creative will is limited both by eternal necessities of reason and by eternal experiences of brute fact"† These limits in God's nature Brightman calls "The Given". The Given consists of the "eternal, uncreated laws of reason", including logic, mathmetical relations, and Platonic Ideas, and

† POR, 337

---

28. The preceding four sentences also appear in King's earlier essay. The quotation from McTaggart, *Some Dogmas of Religion*, pp. 202–203, reads: "An omnipotent person is one who can do anything. Now suppose that God had willed to create a universe, and had not willed that the law of Identity should be valid. It seems that we have no alternative but to be inconsistent or to be completely unmeaning. To suppose that the universe would not have been created, although God had willed that it should, would be inconsistent with his omnipotence. But the assertion that the universe could be created without being a universe, and without being created is unmeaning. And yet how can the universe be the universe, or creation be creation unless the law of Identity be true. Again is there any meaning in the supposition that God could creat a man who was not a man, or that he could create a being who was neither man nor not man? But, if he could not then he is bound by the law of Contradiction and the Law of Excluded Middle, and, once more, he is not omnipotent" (King, "Comparison and Evaluation of McTaggart and Brightman"). In his remarks on the earlier essay Brightman wrote next to the quotation, "This is only an affirmation of a 'rational Given.'"

29. Brightman underlined "beyond his control" and wrote, "beyond his creation."

also of equally eternal uncreated nonrational aspects, "which exhibit all the ultimate qualities of sense objects, disorderly impulses and desires, such experiences as pain and suffering, the forms of space and time, and whatever in God is the source of surd evil."* The Given, although eternally within the experience of God, is not a product of will or created activity.

* POR, 337

Not only does God eternally find "The Given" in his experience, but he also eternally controls it. God's control of "The Given" does not mean complete determination, for in some instances, "The Given", with its purposeless processes, constitutes so great an obstacle to the divine will that God's endeavors are temporarily defeated. God's control of the Given means that his defeat is never final and that even in the face of the most firm obstacles, he finds "new avenues of advance".† He never allows the Given to run wild, but he always subjects it to law and uses it, as far as possible, as an instrument for the expression of his divine purposes.[30]

† Ibid, 338

According to this view, God is not in perfect possession of life and truth, although He is actually on the way to such possession. The perfect God is future possibility, not present actuality.[31] It must be emphasized in passing that Brightman never places limitations on God's ethical nature. Although God's power is finite, His goodness is infinite.[32] Moreover, Brightman's God is infinite in time and space, "by the sense of his unbegun and unedning duration and by his inclusion of all nature within his experience".‡[33] So that Brightman's God is "A Finite-Infinite God".

‡ Ibid, 337

There is much that can be said to commend Dr. Brightman's view at this point. It has the advantage of accounting for the evil in the world without involving

---

30. Brightman marked the last half of the paragraph, underlined "never final" and "'new avenues of advance,'" and wrote, "Good."

31. Brightman underlined "perfect," "such," and "future possibility" in these two sentences and remarked in the margin, "unclear." These sentences, which are also in King's previous essay, had earlier elicited another comment from Brightman: "I don't like the idea of a completed God who has nothing to do. This contradicts both" (King, "Comparison and Evaluation of McTaggart and Brightman").

32. This sentence and the following one are also in King's earlier essay. Brightman wrote in the margin of that essay that "He is always perfectly ethical."

33. Brightman corrected "by the sense" to "in the sense" and changed King's spelling of "unending."

the character of God. Moreover, it has the advantage of establishing the Christian ideal of sacrificial love on metaphysical grounds. But there are also some difficulties inherent in this view. Some of these I tried to point out in the last paper* and for that reason, I will not present them here.[34]

* See my last paper, P. 6

In contrast to Brightman's view, Hocking is a theistic absolutist. He expresses agreement with McTaggart's contention that the finite God is "of no worth".†
So that Hocking rejects finitism as a means of accounting for the fact of evil. He believes that only a type of monism can lead to a genuinely optimistic outlook.[35] Though "no one can doubt that evil is evil", nevertheless, a radical pluralism or even an ultimate dualism in this respect is impossible; "there must be a unity in overcoming evils", such that overcoming makes a difference to the whole. "No man", he writes, "can be content to accept evil as finality; each must have his theory of evil, as a means of bringing that evil under the conception of the whole, and so . . . of disposing of it." Evil, in other words, is "transmutable", apparent evils are seen to be goods in broader contexts, and experience reveals that pain can be "overcome" in courageous devotion to a certain cause. The "untransmuted" evils of a "closed life" are ultimate only if one assumes that no absolute mind exists, which, in its timeless perspective, creates a moral continuity beyond the present and the apparent. We must believe that the Real is the Good, and that evil is somehow "less real". No optimism can "take evil straight"; it must rather be based upon a clear and

† Hocking, MGHE, 225–6. McTaggart differs from Hacking in holding that arguments for theistic finition are more valid than those for absolutism. Of course, he ultimately sees no value in either.

---

34. This paragraph appears in King's earlier essay with a lengthier critique of Brightman's idea of God: "First, Dr. Brightman does not completely escape dualism. It is true that he escapes cosmic dualism, but only to leave a dualism in the nature of God. Does not such dualism leave faith in a supreme God endangered and triumph over the non-rational Given uncertain? What evidence is there that God is winning a gradual mastery over the limitations in His nature? Then, too, this theory seems to establish too sharp a dichotomy between God's nature and his will. We use these terms to denote different aspects of the divine life, but at bottom they involve each other. God's nature gives content to His will and His will gives meaning to His nature. It is the union of the two which constitutes the divine Personality" (King, "Comparison and Evaluation of McTaggart and Brightman"). King placed a footnote after this sentence: "For an elaboration of this criticism see Knudson, DG, 274" (referring to Albert C. Knudson, *The Doctrine of God* [New York: Abingdon Press, 1930].) Brightman underlined "a dualism in the nature of God" and wrote, "All personality is <u>unitas multiplex</u>." Brightman wrote after King's last question, "If there is none, then certainly there is none for an absolute God!" Brightman wrote after the last sentence, "But explain how will could change logic!"

35. Brightman underlined "monism" and remarked, "Monism might be finitistic."

satisfying view of the Whole, in its infinite past and future, whose reality is ulitimately good.* God, then, is "moral" as "He-Who is". It is only as One beyond good and evil that He can transmute evil into good, as the allpowerful One whose "sun shines upon the just and the unjust". The ultimate triumph over evil is found in an "association which cannot be corrupted", with an "Other-than-all-men", through whom pain and evil are seen, "from the outside". God is the "Tao", the "still, small voice".†[36]

* Hacking, MGHE, 166–206, 220–225.

† Ibid, 330–332.

When it comes to his attempt to establish the existence of God, Hocking again parts company with Brightman and McTaggart. He feels that the ontological argument for the existence of God is the only persuasive and necessary argument, and also truly "empirical". This argument, he says is the "only one which is faithful to the history, the anthropology of religion. It is the only proof of God."[37] It is "empirical" and not a priori because such an idea could not have arisen apart from some appropriate "experience". It is impossible that my idea should be a "mere" idea, for it is only possible for me to take this standpoint, external to nature and myself, an idea insofar as I do at the same time take it in experience also . . . The ontological arguments, in its true form, is a report of experience".[38] And the true form of the argument, he says, is not thus: I have an idea of God; therefore, God exists. But rather thus: I have an idea of God; therefore, I have an experience of God. Reality can only be proved by the ontological argument; and conversely, the ontological argument can only be applied to reality. But insofar as reality dwells in self, or Other Mind, or Nature, an ontological argument may be stated in proof of their existence. Thus, the Cartesian certitude may with greater validity be put into this form: I think myself, therefore I exist . . . I have an idea of physical Nature, Nature exists . . . In whatever sense I can think the independence of beings, in that sense independence obtains between them. That which is most independent of me, namely the Other Mind, has been the first object of our on-

---

36. The term "Other-than-all-men" and the comparison of God with Tao are in Hocking, *Meaning of God*, p. 224.

37. The quotation is from Hocking, *Meaning of God*, p. 307.

38. The quotation begins with "It is impossible" and is from Hocking, *Meaning of God*, p. 312.

tological findings. The object of certain knowledge has this threefold structure, Self, Nature, and Other Mind; and God, the appropriate object of ontological proof, includes these three.*[39]

* Hocking, MGHE, 315; 310–316.

This argument does not seem convincing to either Brightman or McTaggart. McTaggart's atheism immediately eliminates him. Brightman on the other hand finds evidences for God in the the law and order of nature, the adaptation of means to ends and the presence of a directive force in evolution, the fact that value as a personal expe[r]ience must have a personal source, and the trend toward monotheism in the history of religion.[40] In the midst of all of these, however, Brightman never points to the antilogical argument as presenting valid evidence for the existence of God. Hacking seems to be one of the few modern theists holding to antilogical argument.[41]

Religious Experiences

The question of religious experience is one that receives fruitful discussion in both the works of Brightman and Hocking. McTaggart's anti-theistic bias causes him to face this problem from a totally negative perspective.[42] Hocking begins his thought at this point with the view that the specifically religious experiences are those of powerful natural phenomena and of social crisis, experiences characterized by a sense of awe and mystery which leads to a recognition of ignorance and stimulates theoretical and practical activity. And the decisive and unique "experience of The Whole" is to be discovered in religious worship and mystical experience. The worth of worship lies in the ambition to find the ultimate powerful reality to which man must adjust himself and by which he is judged. Worship seeks perspective on all the major issues of life; bringing all established habits of thought

---

39. The quotation begins with "I have an idea of God; therefore, God exists" and is from Hocking, *Meaning of God*, pp. 314–315. King referred to the improper format of this block quotation in his letter to Brightman that accompanied this paper. See p. 76 in this volume.

40. Brightman wrote in the margin, "<u>also values</u> & religious experience."

41. Brightman corrected "antilogical" to "ontological." He commented, "Knudson finds some appreciation of it."

42. Brightman underlined "McTaggart" and wrote "Love."

under judgment, it makes possible fresh perceptions. It is an "essay in detachment", beyond the partial detachments of art and science. In mysticism, this aim at detachment is expressed in the <u>via negativa</u>; concentration and unification of thought prepares the way for the "loss" of the self in deeper insights.*

* Ibid, 356, 386

For Hocking, the valid mystical experience is not a matter of "pure thought" alone; rather, "purity of heart" is a necessary precondition. And, through the "principle of alternation", worship must bear fruit in work, and vice-versa. Only through such an "alternation" can spiritual staleness and fatigue be oversome and the sense of the worth of living be recovered.

Hocking insists that the "experience of the Whole" is different in kind from all other types of experience. Surely all sensory experience, at least is experience of definite particulars, or perhaps of definable complexes, and thus of "parts". Even value-experiences have specific referents. But the experience of the Whole is ultimately undifferentiated.

Brightman agrees with Hacking that "apart from specifically religious experience there is no basis for belief in a specifically religious reality";† nevertheless, he cannot agree with him that any one type of religious experience is self-authenticating or normative. He prefers, rather, to define religious experience broadly as "any experience of any person taken in relation to his God".‡ He is appreciative of various types of phenomena which could fall within this classification, but refuses to take any specific form as determinative. Meditation, prayer, mystical insight, religiously motivated activity in society in the interest of ideals—all of these may be religious experience. He accepts, in the main, Hocking's analysis of worship.§ But he does not go so far as to believe that there is a kind of "pure" experience uncolored by the assumption of the experient. "Pure" religious experience, he says,

† Fern, (ed), CAT, 61[43]

‡ Brightman, POR, 415

§ Brightman, R.V., 190 ff.[44]

> is an abstraction as unreal as "pure" sensation in psychology. Some mystics and empiricists in religion appear to have forgotten this fact. On the other hand,

---

43. The citation should read Edgar S. Brightman, "Religion as Truth," in *Contemporary American Theology*, ed. Vergilius Ferm (New York: Round Table Press, 1932), p. 61.

44. This citation, which is not listed in King's bibliography, is to Edgar S. Brightman, *Religious Values* (New York: Abingdon Press, 1925).

religious beliefs, apart from the experience out of which they grew and on which they are nourished are abstractions equally unreal.*[45]

* Ibid, 9.

This is in line with Brightman's view that coherence is the final criterion of truth. No single experience carries its truth with it; all must be tested in terms of "coherence" and synoptic insight into experience as a whole.†

† Brightman, POR, 436.

It is encouraging to find two of the most eminent philosophers of our time taking such an active interest in religious experience. {Although,} as we have seen, they differ in some detail, both are at one in giving equal recognition {to} the rational and the mystical—{to} logic and religious experience. May it not be that the profound insights of great minds like Hocking and Brightman will serve to defend religion and religious experience in the face of philosophers and psychologists who are contemptuous of religion in general and Christianity in particular.

Religious Certainty

We have not had much opportunity to speak of the philosophical methods of McTaggart, Hocking and Brightman in this study, mainly because McTaggart and Hocking make little if any reference to their methods in the works under discussion. It is clear, however, that Brightman's method is that of rational empiricism. "Experience", he writes, "is the necessary starting point of any philosophy of religion".‡ His conception of empirical method is bound up with the idea of coherence as a criterion of truth. "Coherence is no repudiation of empiricism. It is simply an insistence that empiricism must be complete, well-ordered, clearly defined, and rationally interpreted."§ Now, this empirical emphasis has profound implications in Brightman's views on religious knowledge and religious certainty. It leads him to abandon the rationalistic ideal of "finished" truth. Whereas Hocking, even

‡ Brightman, POR, 9

§ Ibid, 193

---

45. Cf. Brightman, *Religious Values*, p. 9: "'Pure' religious experience . . . is an abstraction as unreal as is 'pure' sensation in psychology. Some mystics and empiricists in religion appear to have forgotten this fact. On the other hand, religious beliefs, apart from the life out of which they grow and by which they are nourished, are abstractions equally unreal."

though admitting the values of empiricism, still insists upon the relevance and possiblity of "eternal truth" and certainty. For him, God as the Whole is an object of certain experiences, and not a metaphysical hypothesis: Hypothetical belief in God is worthless, he feels; only certain knowledge qualifies for committment and devotion. The certainty of the experience of the Whole makes possible the free and experimental character of the scientific method itself. So that he can speak of theoretical certainty in religion as well as in scientific inquiry. Brightman agrees more fully with James and Dewey at this point, than he does with Hocking. All truth is held by him to be hypothetical. All propositions, including propositions about God, are seen to be constantly subject to revision or capable or achieving higher degrees of probability, though never certainty. But, though we must be content with "theoretical relativism", rather than certainty, we can accept a "practical absolutism" since our most coherent hypotheses at least enable us to move towards further truth.

I cannot help but feel that Brightman's is much more sound philosophically at this point than is Hocking. At this point, Hocking's empiricism is not empirical enough. I cannot see how Hocking can insist upon a theoretical rather than a "practical" certainty in the whole field of scientific inquiry. It seems that he fails to take seriously the significance of the particular and the contingent with which the natural sciences have to deal. Moreover, he fails to take seriously the fact that all truth, including religious, is based on the assumption that the human mind is valid and that the cosmos is rational.[46]

The Doctrine of
Immortality

At last we come to a point on which all of our thinkers under discussion are agreed. They are all at one in affirming the validity of the doctrine of immortality. They differ, however, in arguments used to establish the validity of the doctrine. As I pointed out in my last paper, McTaggart, because of his anti-

---

46. Brightman marked this paragraph and wrote "Good" in the margin.

theistic thinking, has no use for the ethical argument for immortality.* He feels that we {must} always fall back "on purely metaphysical arguments." These turn out to be based on abstract considerations as to the nature of substance. The perdurability of substance naturally refers just as much to the past as to the future. McTaggart believes, accordingly, that our present existence has been preceded by a plurality of future lives.[47]

One wonders how McTaggart can hold so firmly to a doctrine of immortality and at the same time deny theism. Certainly this is an enigma to me. Apparently McTaggart is unique in this position, for no other well-known philosopher has held such a view. We may be safe in saying that every other philosophical believer in immortality has affirmed theism.†

Hocking holds that immortality is an achievement. The reality of the self is not a fixed quantity. Justice demands that the matter be determined by the degree of reality which the self attains. This is a philosophical interpreation of the orthodox view that one's destiny in heaven or hell is determined by how he has lived. In Hocking's view, those who accept life as an invitation to become real achieve immortality. Only God knows the fate of the others. It must be noted that Hacking is not as certain about immortality as McTaggart. McTaggart feels that there can be absolute metaphysical proof for the doctrine. Hocking, on the other hand, admits that there can be no complete certainty about immortality. It is an empirical problem with no empirical evidence.

Brightman, unlike McTaggart, finds the only vigorous argument for immortality resting on a theistic basis, namely the goodness of God. If there is a supreme creative cosmic Person, says Brightman, then "there is an infinitely good being committed to the eternal conversation of values". Certainly God the conserver of values must be God the conserver of Persons, since Persons are of highest value. Brightman would agree with Hocking that there can be no complete certainty about immortality. For him, faith in immortality is faith in the goodness of God. Brightman's belief in a finite God never leads him to believe

* See my last paper, p. 7

† Brightman, POR, 402

---

47. This paragraph and the following one also appear in King, "Comparison and Evaluation of McTaggart and Brightman."

that God is so finite that he cannot conserve values. He holds that every argument for God, whether as absolute or as finite, is an argument for God's power to control His universe so as to achieve value, and every argument for His goodness is an argument for his obligation to conserve Persons as intrinsic values.[48]

Bibliography

Brightman, Edgar Sheffield.—PG
    The Problem of God.
    New York: The Abingdon Press, 1930
———ML
    Moral Laws,
    New York: The Abingdon Press, 1933
———POR
    A Philosophy of Religion,
    New York: Prentice Hall, Inc., 1940
Ferm, Vergilius (ed.)—CAT
    Contemporary American Theology,
    New York: Round Table Press, Inc., 1932
McTaggart, J. M. E.—SDR
    Some Dogmas of Religion,
    London: Edward Arnold, 1906
Hocking, William Ernest—MGHE
    The Meaning of God in Human Experience,
    New Haven: Yale University Press, 1912

THDS. MLKP-MBU: Box 112.

---

48. This paragraph also appears in King's earlier essay for Brightman. In that essay he attributed the quotation correctly to Brightman, *Philosophy of Religion*, p. 401. The original passage reads: "There is no sufficient reason for supposing [God's power] to be so finite that he cannot conserve values. In a word, every argument for God, whether as absolute or as finite, is an argument for God's power to control his universe so as to achieve value; and every argument for God's goodness is an argument for his obligation to maintain persons in existence as intrinsic values."

"Crozer Quarterly"

[*12 December 1951*]
[*Boston, Mass.*]

During the first semester of DeWolf's Seminar in Systematic Theology, students were required to give a twenty-to-thirty-minute oral report on a religious journal, chosen from a list of twelve journals compiled by DeWolf, and to submit a one-page

*typed review. In preparation for the review King had contacted his former Crozer
professor Morton S. Enslin, editor of the* Crozer Quarterly. *In his summary
King uses some of the information Enslin provided and comments on an article
by his former professor, George W. Davis.*[1] *King reveals a dissatisfaction with
liberalism's doctrine of man: "Any theology which does not have an adequate
anthropology is not worth the name." King's analysis of Davis was considerably
longer in the draft of this report (see below, note 2); he shortened his critique to
meet length limitations.*

1. The Crozer Quarterly was begun in 1924. It was the result of a feeling
   by the faculty at that time, under the direction of Dr. Milton G. Evans,
   that such a journal was needed. Andover Theological Seminary was invited to join in the project but found it impossible to accept. Accordingly
   Crozer has continued it alone from the start. The journal has had several
   editors, namely, Edward B. Pollard, A. S. Woodburn, R. E. E. Harkness,
   and Morton S. Enslin.
2. Subscription rate for the Crozer Quarterly is $2.50 per year; single cop-
   ies are $.75. Publishers: Crozer Theological Seminary, Chester, Pa.
3. The journal is intended chiefly for professional students of religion and
   also for intelligent laymen.
4. The literary style is of the highest quality with few typographical errors.
   The type is small.
5. Dr. Morton Scott Enslin is the editor of the journal. He is Prof. of N. T.
   Literature at Crozer Seminary. b. March 8, 1897, Somerville, Mass. Educated Harvard College, B.A., 1919, Newton, B.D., 1922; Harvard U.,
   Th.D. Author: "The Ethics of Paul, 1930; Christian Beginnings, 1938.
6. Typical contributors include, Vergilius Ferm (Philosopher), Edwin E.
   Aubrey (Theologian), Albert C. Knudson (Dean emeritus of B.U. School
   of Theology).
7. Fields of interest other than theology: (1) Biblical Lit., (2) Psychology of
   Religion, (3) Pastoral Counseling, (4) Worship, (5) Religious Education,
   (6) Church History.
8. Regular features—Five or six articles. A number of book reviews (usually about 20). Several shorter notices and a list of books received. Identification of current contributors and reviewers.
9. Dominant point of View—Liberalism is definitely the dominant point of
   view. Occasionally very controversial issues are discussed with opposing
   views represented.
10. Values appreciated: Its many articles representing profound scholar-
    ship. Its superb book reviews.
11. Defects: None
12. Fifteen to twenty book reviews and notices of the highest quality.
13. Summary of "Liberalism and a Theology of Depth" by George W. Davis
    in The Crozer Quarterly, Vol XXVIII, No. 3, July, 1951.

---

1. See Morton Scott Enslin to King, 26 October 1951, p. 59 in this volume.

Dr. Davis begins his challeging article with the affirmation that Christianity is a religion of depth. By depth as here employed, he means that Christianity breaks through the surface phenomena of reality, bringing an apprehension of what lies beyond these phenomena. He admits that Christianity has its surface and subsurface phenomena, but interest in these must never obscure the significance of depth phenomena. Liberalism, with its emphasis on higher criticism, important as this emphasis is, has devoted much to the surface and subsurface factors to the complete concealment of the depth phenomena originally responsible for biblical religion. If liberalism is to produce anything more than a secular and surface arrangement of intellectual propositions, it must explore and recognize the depths in Christianity. Some of the depths in Christianity which liberalism must recognize are: (1) The Moral foundations of Reality, (2) Spiritual Control, (3) Specific Action, i.e. the faith that specific divine action for human redemption occurred in Jesus of Nazareth, (4) Continuing Divine Concern and Human Opportunity. Can liberal theology, now on the defensive, experience a rebirth? Dr. Davis feels that it can if it takes full cognizance of the depths of the Christian faith.

Critical Comment: I feel that Dr. Davis is grappling with a profound problem and one that all liberals should take cognizance of. It seems to me, however, that Dr. Davis fails to even mention one aspect of a theology of depth which is all important namely, the doctrine of man. Any theology which does not have an adequate anthropology is not worth the name. It is essentially at this point that liberalism has been criticised for being all too shallow. How Dr. Davis could overlook the significance of an adequate anthropology in a theology of depth is quite incomprehensible to me.[2]

TD. MLKP-MBU: Box 114.

---

2. King's rough draft provides a fuller expression of his thinking about Davis: "In this article Dr. Davis is grappling with a profound problem. Indeed it is one that all liberals should take cognizance of. No true Christian thinker can fail to see the necessity of delving to the depths of the Christian faith. Yet Dr Davis is right in affirming that liberalism has all to[o] often been overly concerned with the surface and subsurface phenomena of the Christian faith to the total exclusion of the depth phenomena. Neo-orthodox theologians have reminded us, on every hand, of [liberalism's] appalling failure at this point. Reinhold [Niebuhr,] probably more than any other thinker in America, has stressed the need of a 'dimension of depth,' transcending nature, transcending history, if ethical action here and now is to be sustained by a faith that touches absolute bottom. But such a criticism was expected to come from neo-orthodox circles. Now that the same plea for a dimension of depth comes from a man who is an avowed liberal, makes this article all the more significant.

"Yet even though Dr. Davis' article is a significant and necessary one, I must confess that he fails to go the limit in calling liberalism back to a theology of depth. He fails to even mention one aspect of a theology of depth which seems to me all important, viz., the doctrine of man. Any theology which does not have an [adequate] anthropology is not worthy of the name. I'm sure that Dr. Davis, after such a brilliant analysis, would not be so naive or optimistic as to believe that liberalism has always been depthful in its doctrine of man. It is essentially at this point that liberalism has been criticised for being all [too] shallow. Who can doubt that the criticism has been warranted? There is a strong tendency in liberal Protestantism toward [sentimentality] about man. Man who has come so far in wisdom and [decency] may be expected to go much further as

"Karl Barth's Conception of God"

2 January 1952
[*Boston, Mass.*]

*In this essay for a directed study in systematic theology with DeWolf, King
examines alternative conceptions of God, a theme that would become the topic of his
dissertation. He disagrees with the dialectical nature of Barth's logic and his view
of the transcendence and unknowableness of God. King's analysis, while sharply
critical, is largely appropriated from an article by George W. Davis and a book by
Alvin Sylvester Zerbe.*[1] *Referring to his own studies with Davis and other Crozer
professors, King acknowledges that "most of my criticisms stem from the fact that I
have been greatly influenced by liberal theology, maintaining a healthy respect for
reason and a strong belief in the immanence as well as the transcendence of God."
Echoing the words of Davis, King concludes that Barth's neo-orthodoxy was
important as "a necessary corrective for a liberalism that at times becomes all to[o]
shallow." DeWolf gave the paper an A, terming it an "excellent study."*

The purpose of this paper is to present and criticize
Karl Barth's doctrine of God. We may conveniently
discuss his doctrine of God under three main headings: 1. The transcendent God 2. The unknown God,
and 3. the revelation of God in Jesus Christ. Our
chief sources for the present study are: <u>The Epistle to
the Romans</u>, <u>The Word of God and the Word of
Man</u>, <u>The Knowledge of God and the Service of God</u>

---

his methods of attaining and applying knowledge are improved. Although such ethical religion
is humane and its vision a lofty one, it has obvious shortcomings. This particular sort of optimism
has been discredited by the brutal logic of events. Instead of assured progress in wisdom and
decency man faces the ever present possibility of swift relapse not merely to animalism but into
such calculated cruelty as no other animal can practice.

"Maybe man is more of a sinner than liberals are willing to admit. I realize that the sinfullness
of man is often over-emphasized by some Neo orthodox theologians, but at least we must admit
that many of the ills in the world are due to plain sin. The tendency on the part of some liberal
theologians to see sin as a mere 'lag of nature' which will be progressively eliminated as man
climbs the evolutionary ladder seems to me perilous. I will readily agree that that many of man's
shortcomings are due to natural necessities, but ignorance and finiteness and hampering circumstances, and the pressure of animal [impulse], are all insufficient to account for many of man's
shortcomings. We have to recognize that man has misused his kingly prerogative as a social animal by making others bear the burden of his selfishness. This seems to be an important aspect of
any depth theology" (Draft, "*Crozer Quarterly*," 12 December 1951, MLKP-MBU: Box 114). The
last four sentences of the second paragraph also appear in King, "The Theology of Reinhold
Niebuhr," April 1953–June 1954, p. 278 in this volume.

1. See George W. Davis, "Some Theological Continuities in the Crisis Theology," *Crozer Quarterly* 27, no. 3 (July 1950): 208–219; and Alvin Sylvester Zerbe, *The Karl Barth Theology, or The
New Transcendentalism* (Cleveland: Central Publishing House, 1930). Several of King's quotations
from Barth do not correspond to the translation he cited or to Davis's or Zerbe's translations,
which suggests that King used another unidentified source.

according to the Teaching of the Reformation, and Dogmatics in Outline. Before undertaking the above stated task we may mention something of the life and career of Karl Barth.

Karl Barth was born in Basel, Switzerland in 1886. He was educated at Bern (where his father held a theological chair), Berlin, Tuebingen, and Marburg. During the first world war he was engaged in Pastoral work in Geneva and Safenwil, Switzerland. In 1921 he was appointed professor of Reformed theology at the University of Goettingen. Afterwards he taught at Muenter, and Bonn. In 1934 he was expelled from Germany. Since 1935 he held a professorship in the University of Basel. While a student at Berlin and Marburg he came under the influence of the two great Ritschlian scholars, Harnack and W. Hermann.[2] For a short while he was associate editor of the Ritschlian journal Die Christliche Welt. But this liberal influence was not long to remain a positive factor in Barth's life. As Sasse put it, "in Karl Barth liberal theology brought forth its own conquerer. He could overcome the liberal theology because he was bone of its bone and flesh of its flesh."*

* Stasse, HWS, 155[3]

The Transcendent God

One of the cardinal points of Barth's doctrine of God is that He is the transcendent God. On every hand Barth is out to set God immensely above the dieties of the world, and the substitutes for God which modern philosophy and scientific research into Nature's forces have put into "modern" man's mind. "The power of God," says Barth, "can be detected neither in the world of nature nor in the souls of men. It must not be confounded with any high, exalted, force, known or knowable."† All modern ideas of immanence are thus set aside by this emphasis on God's transcendence.

† Barth, ETR, 30[4]

From the foregoing we can see that Barth procal-

2. King refers to Albrecht Ritschl (1822–1889), Carl Gustav Adolf von Harnack (1851–1930), and Wilhelm Herrmann (1846–1922).

3. Hermann Sasse, *Here We Stand*, trans. T. G. Tappert (New York: Harper, 1938).

4. The quotation is actually from p. 36 (Karl Barth, *The Epistle to the Romans*, trans. Edwyn C. Hoskyns [London: Oxford University Press, 1933]).

ims the utter separation of the high God and the world. The two are totally unlike and exclusive. At no point does God touch the external world with its corrupted nature and evil matter. No part of the world is, therefore, a manifestation or revelation of the infinite, majestic Deity. Barth's God is "above us, above space and time, and above all concepts and opinions and all potentialities."* In other words God is the "Wholly Other." Here "otherness" implies "exclusive separation." Such thinking ends in the entire divorcement of God and our human experience. Take, for an instance, the following passage from <u>The Epistle to the Romans</u>,

* Barth, KOG, 28

> God, the pure limit and pure beginning of all that we are, have, and do, standing over in infinite qualitative difference to man and all that is human, nowhere and never identical with that which we call God, experience, surmise, and pray to as God, the unconditioned Halt as opposed to all human rest, the yes in our no and the no in our yes, the first and last and as such unknown, but nowhere and never a magnitude amongst others in the medium known to us, God the Lord, the Creator and Redeemer . . . that is the living God.†[5]

† ETR, 315f

Such a passage reveals that we are complete aliens until God wills to give himself to us. If we are not to end up defining ourselves when we think that we are defining God, we can only take the second way and therefore "hold fast to the incomprehensible majesty in which God meets us in His revelation, the majesty of His person as Father, Son and Holy Spirit."‡[6]

‡ KOG, 33

In harmony with his general position Barth asserts that man cannot find God by the study of the soul of man. The qualitative distinction between God and man makes this totally impossible. "It is evident that the relation to God with which the Bible is concerned does not have its source in the purple depths of the subconscious, and cannot be identical with what the deep-sea psychical research of our day describes in

---

5. This passage is translated differently on pp. 330–331 of Hoskyns's translation of *Epistle to the Romans*.

6. Karl Barth, *The Knowledge of God and the Service of God According to the Teachings of the Reformation*, trans. J. L. M. Haire and Ian Henderson (London: Hodder & Stoughton, 1938), p. 33: "If we do not wish to end by really defining ourselves, when we think that we are defining God, we can only take the second way and therefore hold fast to the *incomprehensible* majesty in which God meets us in His revelation, the majesty of His person as Father, Son and Holy Spirit."

the narrower or broader sense as libido fulfilment."*

God is the one who stands above our highest and deepest feelings, strivings and intuitions.†[7]

It is to be noted that Barth is explicit in rejecting each and every acknowledgment of a theologia naturalis. This rejection came about primarily because of Barth's emphasis on God's transcendence and man's impotence. The rejection of Natural Theology put Barth in a peculiar position when he was invited by the Senatus of the University of Aberdeen 1935, to deliver the Gifford foundation {Lectures on Natural Theology.} Barth would have had "to promote, advance, teach, and diffuse," the study of natural Theology "among all classes of society," and among the whole population of Scotland as was the intention of the late Lord Gifford.‡ This Barth could not do and remain loyal to his calling as a Reformed theologian. He could make this task his own only indirectly, namely, "to confer on Natural Theology the loyal and real service of reminding it of its partner in the conversation."§ Barth delivered the lectures in 1937 and 1938. Their title is The Knowledge of God and the Service of God According to the Teaching of the Reformation (published 1939). He is very frank as regards his rejection of any sort of a Natural Theology. However there is an emphasis in this work which is somewhat a modification of his former emphasis on the "infinite difference between time and eternity." Barth now says, "While it is beyond our comprehension that eternity should meet us in time, yet it is true because in Jesus Christ eternity has become time."‖ And again: Eternity is here (in the stable at Bethlehem and on the cross of Calvary) in time."# This view expresses the reality of God in time. A detailed discussion of this view may be reserved for our section on "the revelation of God in Christ."

The Unknown God

Barth makes it explicit from the beginning that God is the unknowable and indescribable God. The hidden God remains hidden. Even when we say we

---

7. Karl Barth, *Dogmatics in Outline*, trans. G. T. Thomson (New York: Philosophical Library, 1949), p. 37: "He is the One who stands *above* us and also above our highest and deepest feelings, strivings, intuitions."

know him our knowledge is of an imcomprehensible Reality. Consider, for instance, the personality of God. Barth writes: "God is personal, but personal in an incomprehensible way, in so far as the conception of his personality surpasses all our views of personality."*[8]

Barth also contends that even through the knowledge which comes by faith, than which "no more objective and strict form of knowledge can lay claim more definitely to universal validity,"†[9] no full knowledge comes to us. Even when God reveals himself to the man of faith, or, more accurately, to the man to whom he gives faith, still that man with faith "will confess God as the God of majesty and therefore as the God unknown to us."‡[10] Man as man can never know God: His wishing, seeking, and striving are all in vain.§[11]

In order to understand Barth at this point it is necessary to understand his objectivism. The absolutely objective, the transcendental (Kant) cannot be reached by man. It can only be reached in <u>actus</u> and such <u>actus</u> Barth finds in Scripture and pre-eminently in Christ and the Holy Spirit. And yet, as stated above, even in his revelation of himself God is ontlogically unknown and unknowable.[12] On Romans 1:19, 20, Barth says:

> We know that God is He whom we do not know, and that our ignorance is precisely the problem and the source of our knowledge. The Epistle to the Romans

* Ibid, 31

† Ibid, 25

‡ Ibid, 28

§ ETR, 91

---

8. Davis, "Some Theological Continuities," pp. 208–209: "Barth is always true to his conviction that the infinite God is always unknowable and indescribable. The hidden God remains hidden. . . . Even when we say we know him our knowledge is of an incomprehensible Reality. Consider, for instance, the personality of God. Barth writes: 'God is personal, but personal in an *incomprehensible* way, in so far as the conception of His personality surpasses all our views of personality.'"

9. The quotation should read, " . . . strict form of knowledge can exist, and no type of knowledge can lay claim . . ." (Barth, *Knowledge of God*, p. 25).

10. Davis, "Some Theological Continuities," p. 209: "Barth also contends that even through the knowledge which comes by faith, than which 'no more objective and strict form of knowledge can exist, and [than which] no type of knowledge can lay claim more definitely to universal validity,' no full knowledge of God comes to us. Even when God reveals himself to the man of faith, or, more accurately, to the man to whom he gives faith, still that man with faith 'will confess God as the God of majesty and therefore as the God unknown to us.'"

11. This quotation does not appear on p. 91 of Hoskyns's translation of *Epistle to the Romans*.

12. Zerbe, *Barth Theology*, p. 77: "Much depends upon one's understanding of Barth's objectivism. The absolutely objective, the transcendental (Kant) cannot be reached by man. It can be reached, or cognized, if cognized at all, only in *actus* and such *actus* Barth finds in Scripture and pre-eminently in Christ and the Holy Spirit. . . . Even in his revelation of Himself God is ontologically unknown and unknowable."

is a revelation of the unknown God; God chooses to come to man, not man to God. Even after the revelation man cannot know God, for he is ever the unknown God. In manifesting himself to man he is farther away than before.*[13]

* ETR, 48

The more we know of God the more he is yet to be known.

> The revelation in Jesus, just because it is the revelation of the righteousness of God is at the same time the strongest conceivable veiling and unknowableness of God. In Jesus, God really becomes a mystery, makes himself known as the unknown, speaks as the eternally Silent One.†[14]

† ETR, 73

We give another passage from <u>Dogmatics in Outline</u>, on God's unknowablility, in which Barth's characteristic ideas and modes of expression are closely joined together.

> When attempts were later made to speak systematically about God and to describe His nature, men became more talkative. They spoke of God's aseity, His being grounded in Himself; they spoke of God's infinity in space and time, and therefore of God's eternity. And men spoke on the other hand of God's holiness and righteousness, mercifulness and patience. We must be clear that whatever we say of God in such human concepts can never be more than an indication of Him; no such concept can really conceive the nature of God. God is inconceivable.‡

‡ DO, 46

Barth's contention is summed up in the dictum: <u>Finitum non Capax</u> infiniti, the finite has no capacity

---

13. Zerbe, *Barth Theology*, p. 78: "On Romans 1:19, 20, Barth says: 'We know that God is he whom we do not know and that this not-knowing is the origin of our knowing . . . What do we know of the acts and works of God? Here is the greatest misconception . . . The Epistle to the Romans is a revelation of the unknown God; God chooses to come to man, not man to God. Even after the revelation man cannot know God, for he is ever the unknown God. In manifesting himself to man he is farther away than before' (*Rbr.* p. 353)." Ellipses in original. The quotation is not found on p. 48 of Hoskyns's translation of *Epistle to the Romans*.

14. Zerbe, *Barth Theology*, p. 78: "The more we know of God, the more is yet to be known. 'The revelation in Jesus, just because it is the revelation of the righteousness of God is at the same time the strongest conceivable veiling and unknowableness of God. In Jesus, God really becomes a mystery, makes Himself known as the unknown, speaks as the eternally Silent One.'" Hoskyns's translation of this passage is substantially different: "The revelation which is in Jesus, because it is the revelation of the righteousness of God, must be the most complete veiling of His incomprehensibility. In Jesus, God becomes veritably a secret: He is made known as the Unknown, speaking in eternal silence" (*Epistle to the Romans*, p. 98).

* WG, 177

for the Infinite.[15] "There is no way from us to God—not even via negativa not even a <u>via dialectica</u> nor <u>paradoxa</u>. The god who stood at the end of some human way—even of this way—would not be God."*

In order to understand Barth at this point it is necessary to know something of his method. Barth constantly reiterates that his method is dialectical, proceeding by affirmation and denial, the yes and no, with no safe, ascertainable midway resting place. Astounding as it may seem, Barth boldy affirms that his affirmations and denials are meant to be, not God's absolute truth, but as most human and fallible concepts thereof.

The language of dialectic is that of paradox. Paradox is the juxtaposition of an opinion alongside of it, implicated with it. Examples given by Barth are: The glory of God in creation and yet his concealment; death and its transitory quality alongside of the majesty of another life; man's creation in the image of God conjoined with his fallen being; sin so awful, yet only known when it is forgiven. In God we see the same contrasts. Creation, and Providence; grace and judgment; promise and fulfilment; forgiveness and penalty—"Thou forgavest them though thou tookest vengeance of their inventions." In man's religious experience the same speech of paradox has to be used. Flesh with spirit; faith and obedience; freedom, yet under law still; "autonomy and heteronomy; "justified, yet still a sinner"—these are examples frequently appearing in Barth's works.

The method of dialectic is to counter the no by its opposite yes: the thesis by the antithesis. Barth uses the procedure of the examination room where questions are put requiring answers. The answer contains the question and the question implies the answer. We pass from one side to the other, and often the no is but a concealed yes. Often in the commentary on the Romans, Barth has recourse to algebraical formulae. The minus sign placed before the series of plus terms enclosed in brackets, changes the values, and conversely, the plus sign transforms the minus sign. Every positive implies a negative and every negative hints at a positive.

---

15. Zerbe, *Barth Theology*, p. 79: "Barth's contention is summed up in the dictum: *Finitum non capax infiniti*, the finite has no capacity for the Infinite."

It is quite difficult at times to recognize which method of dialectics Barth prefers—the Platonic-Socratic, the Aristotelian or the Hegelian. Sometimes Barth writes as if truth lies, as with Aristotle, in the mean between two extremes. At other times he seems to incline to Hegel's neat scheme: thesis, antithesis, synthesis, which combines the preceding two in a higher unity. Usually, however Barth takes another line; he passes back behind the contraries to the previous state from which they emerged into contradiction. "The truth," says Barth, "lies not in the yes and not in the no, but in the knowledge and the beginning from which the yes and the no arise."* And again: "Our yes towards life from the very beginning carries within it the Divine No which breaks forth from the antithesis and points away from what now was the thesis to the original and final synthesis. The No is not the last and highest truth, but the call from home which comes in answer to our asking for God in the world."†

* WGWM, 72 f

† Ibid, 312

What is the ultimate way out of this arena of paradox? It is found in God. The contradictions will be solved not in time, nor on this plane of earth, but "from God who is our Home" prior to, subsequent to, Creation—"not now, but in the Better Land".

The Revelation Of God In
Jesus Christ

On every hand Barth speaks of time and eternity as two distinct realms, an unbridged chasm between God and man, and the unknown God. All of this ends up in the view that there is no way from man to God. There is a way, however, from God to man through Jesus Christ. "He who hath seen me hath seen the Father."[16] This Christ who is the Word of God is no "Jesus of history."‡ That "historical Jesus is but a construct of historians' minds, designed to reconcile contradiction which will not down. The Christ of the flesh is not proclaimed by Barth any more than by

‡ WGWM, 277

---

16. Zerbe, *Barth Theology*, p. 133: "Time and eternity two distinct realms, an unbridged chasm between God and man, God unknown to man. . . . There is no way from man to God. There is a way from God to man through Jesus Christ. 'He who hath seen me hath seen the Father.'"

* ETR, 144; WGWM, 201
† ETR, 276 f.

Paul, but the Christ, crucified and risen.[17] It is in him that the impossibilities are combined, the irreconcilables are here reconciled: God and man, eternity and time, death and resurrection.* Here in him, the conflict is somehow resolved,† and thus we are saved. At this point we might give a rather long quotation from the Romans which well summarizes Barth's view at this point:

> In this name (the name of Jesus) two worlds meet and go apart, two planes intersect, the one known and the other unknown. The known plane is God's creation, fallen out of its union with Him, and therefore the world of the flesh needing redemption, the world of men, and of time, and of things—our world. This known plane is intersected by another plane that is unknown—the world of the Father, of the Primal Creation, and of the final Redemption. The relation between us and God, between this world and His world presses for recognition, but the line of intersection is not self-evident. The point on the line of intersection at which the relation becomes observable and observed is Jesus, Jesus of Nazereth, the historical Jesus,—born of the seed of David according to the flesh. The name Jesus defines an historical occurence and marks the point where the unknown world cuts the known world . . . as Christ Jesus is the plane which lies beyond our comprehension. The plane which is known to us, He intersects vertically, from above. Within history Jesus as the Christ can be understood only as Problem or Myth. As the Christ He brings the world of the Father. But we who stand in this concrete world know nothing, and are incapable of knowning anything, of that other world. The Resurrection from the dead is, however, the transformation: the establishing or declaration of that point from above, and the corresponding discerning of it below. The Resurrection is the revelation: the disclosing of Jesus as the Christ, the appearing of God, and the apprehending of God in Jesus. The Resurrection is the emergence of the necessity of giving glory to God: the reckoning with what is unknown and unobservable in Jesus, the recognition of Him as Paradox, Victor and Primal History. In the Resurrection the new world of the Holy Spirit touches the old world of the flesh, but touches it as a tangent touches a circle, that is, without

---

17. Zerbe, *Barth Theology*, p. 134: "The Christ of the flesh is not proclaimed by Barth any more than by Paul; but the Christ crucified and risen."

touching it. And, precisely because it does not touch it, it touches it as its frontier—as the new world.*   * ETR, 29 f

The above passage exhibits the characteristic features of what may be called a theology. In Jesus Christ we have the solution of the problems raised to the mind by the transcendence of God, the brokeness of humanity, and the unknown God. It is the mark of this kind of theology, in contrast to the usual method of procedure followed for almost a century now, to start from above, from the God-side, and work down to man.

Criticism of Barth's Views

The leading ideas of Barth's doctrine of God have been presented in the preceding paragraphs: it remians for us, in this closing section, to indicate the main lines of criticism which they have called forth in my mind. Most of my criticisms stem from the fact that I have been greatly influenced by liberal theology, maintaining a healthy respect for reason and a strong belief in the immanence as well as the transcendence of God.

First let us take the point of God's transcendecne, for it is here that Barthianism irks the liberal Christian mind probably more than elsewhere. Not that God is not transcendent. The liberal so believes, but he also contends that God is also immanent, expressing his creative genius throughout the universe which he is ever creating and always sustaining as well as through the essentail goodness of th world and human life. It is not that God is above us to which the liberal objects, but he does demur when he is asked to affirm that God is with us only in a tiny segment of "experience." (Barth would not use the term, but rather "revelation" or "divine confrontation"); namely, in that which comes only when God gives his word to us. The liberal also finds God in the beauty of the world, in the unpremeditated goodness of men, and in the moral order of reality.[18]

---

18. Davis, "Some Theological Continuities," p. 218: "The point at which Barthianism irks the liberal Christian mind and leaves it cold is in its twin and exclusive emphases of the divine transcendence and our human impotence. Not that God is not transcendent. The liberal so believes, but he also contends that God is also immanent, expressing his creative genius throughout the

Another point at which Barth irks the liberal is his emphasis on the unknowableness of God. "A God about whom we dare not think is a God a thinking mind cannot worhsip."* Note that Barth says that the Word of God is the norm and standard of truth. Let us turn to it.

* Brightman, FG, 26[19]

Job ask: "Canst thou find out the Almighty unto perfection?"† This verse is typical of the Bible representation generally. We can know God as we know anything else, only imperfectly. In the book of Exodus, in the scene in which God appears to Moses we read; "Thou canst not see my face" but "thou shalt see my back".‡ A signal proof that God reveals himself in nature is seen in Psalms 19: "The heavens declare the glory of God, etc." The New Testament writers are even more explicit at this point. According to Paul, man through reason, may have sufficient knowledge of God to render him inexcusable."§[20] This passage, found in the Epistle to the Romans, is practically ignored by Barth. He says: "We know that God is the one whom we do not know and this not-knowing is the problem and origin of our knowing. . . . What are God's works in their absolute riddeness (absolution Raelhselhaftigkeit) other than questions without an answer."‖[21]

† Job 11:16

‡ Exodus 33:20

§ Romans 1:18–23

‖ ETR, 45

---

universe which he is ever creating and always sustaining, as well as through the essential goodness of the world and human life. It is not that God is above us to which the liberal objects, but he does demur when he is asked to affirm that God is with us only in a tiny segment of 'experience' (Barth would not use this term, but rather 'revelation' or 'divine confrontation'); namely, in that which comes only when God gives his Word to us. The liberal also finds God in the beauty of the world, in the unpremeditated goodness of men, and in the moral order of reality within and without himself."

19. This reference, which is not listed in the bibliography, is to Edgar S. Brightman, *The Finding of God* (New York: Abingdon Press, 1931).

20. DeWolf wrote "Quot.?" after this sentence.

21. Zerbe, *Barth Theology*, pp. 81–82: "Job asks: 'Canst thou find out the Almighty unto perfection?' (11:6.) This verse is typical of the Bible representation generally. We can know God as we know anything else, only imperfectly. In Ex. 33, in the scene in which God appears to Moses we read; 'Thou canst not see my face' (v. 20) but 'thou shalt see my back.' . . . A signal proof that God reveals himself in nature is seen in Ps. 19: 'The heavens declare the glory of God, etc.' . . . The New Testament writers are more explicit. According to Paul, man through reason, may have sufficient knowledge of God to render him 'inexcusable.' The classic passage is Rom. 1:18–23, every word of which is significant. Barth, however, practically ignores it, saying: 'We know that God is the one whom we do not know and this not-knowing is the problem and the origin of our knowing . . . What are God's works in their absolute riddleness (*absolution Räthselhaftigkeit*) other than questions without an answer' (*Rbr.* p. 22)." Ellipses in quotation from Barth in original. Hoskyns's translation of this passage is different: "We know that God is He whom we do not know, and that our ignorance is precisely the problem and the source of our knowledge. . . . What are all those enigmatic creatures of God—a zoological garden, for example—but so many problems to which we have no answer?" (*Epistle to the Romans*, pp. 45–46).

It must also be noted at this point that Barth speaks of the generally accepted metaphysical and ethical attributes of God, sovereignity, majesty, holiness, ect., with a degree of certainty. It was once said of Herbert Spencer that he knew a great deal about the "Unknowable" so of Barth, one wonders how he came to know so much of the "Unknown God."[22]

In criticism of Barth's method we may say that there is the danger that one may take a side, the No, or yes, without carrying the dialogue through. This is precisely what Lenin did, with such disastrous consequences to religion in Russia.[23] Again, if a position implies a negation, and a negation a position, then faith carries disbelief with it, theism, atheism, and if one member of the pair comes to be doubted the result may be disastrous to religion itself.

These seem to me, to be some of the great difficulties implicit in the Barthian position. In spite of our somewhat severe criticisms of Barth, however, we do not in the least want to minimize the importance of his message. His cry does call attention to the desperateness of the human situation. He does insist that religion begins with God and that man cannot have faith apart from him. He does proclaim that apart from God our human efforts turn to ashes and our sunrises into darkest night. He does suggest that man is not sufficient unto himself for life, but is dependent upon the proclamatiom of God's living Word, through which by means of Bible, preacher, and revealed Word, God himself comes to the consciences of men. Much of this is good, and may it not be that it will serve as a necessary corrective for a liberalism that at times becomes all to shallow?[24]

---

22. DeWolf commented in the margin, "Good." Zerbe, *Barth Theology*, p. 84: "Barth speaks of the generally accepted metaphysical and ethical attributes of God, sovereignty, majesty, holiness, etc. It was said of Herbert Spencer that he knew a great deal about the 'Unknowable'; so of Barth, one wonders how he came to know so much of the 'Unknown God.'"

23. DeWolf placed an asterisk beside this sentence and remarked at the bottom of the page: "I am interested in this comparison. As a graduate student I once defended the thesis that Lenin was Hegel's 'antithesis on horseback,' indicating the many stages of Hegel's dialectic of which Lenin took the antithesis as the truth. Have you made such a study too? Have you found such a study by someone else?"

24. Davis, "Some Theological Continuities," pp. 217–218: "[Barth's and Emil Brunner's] cries do call attention to the desperateness of the human situation. They do insist that religion begins with God and that men cannot have faith apart from him. . . . They do proclaim that apart from God our human efforts turn to ashes and our sunrises into darkest night. They do suggest that man is not sufficient unto himself for life, but is dependent upon the proclamation of God's living Word, through which, by means of Bible, preacher, and revealed Word, God himself comes to the consciences of men. Much of this is good."

Barth, Karl.—WGWM
The Word of God and The Word Of Man
(Tr. Douglas Horton)
Boston: Pilgrim Press, 1928
—— ETR
The Epistle to the Romans (Tr. Hoskyns)
London: Oxford Press, 1933
—— KOG
The Knowledge of God and the Service of God
according to the Teaching of the Reformation
(Tr. J. L. M. Haire and Ian Henderson)
New York: Charles Scribner's Sons, 1939
—— DO
Dogmatics in Outline (Tr. G. T. Thomson)
New York: Philosophical Library, 1949

THDS. MLKP-MBU: Box 113.

Final Examination Answers, Philosophy of Religion

[*9 January 1952*]
[*Boston, Mass.*]

*In these examination answers for Brightman's course, King expresses enthusiasm
for his professor's concept of a "finite God." He concludes that "after a somewhat
extensive study of the idea I am all but convinced that it is the only ad[e]quate
explanation for the existence of evil. Moreover, it is significant and ad[e]quate
from a religious point of view because it establishes the Christian idea of sacrificial
love on metaphysical grounds." King's answers to several questions of definition
are omitted.*[1] *Brightman gave King 92 points for the exam and an A − for the
course.*

---

1. The first four questions were: (1) "(Required of all.) Define 'the prophetic movement'
precisely: its dates, its chief representatives and their countries, its central ideas, and its importance for philosophy of religion"; (2) "What is the definition of a good hypothesis, according to Professor Reyes? Test a materialistic hypothesis about personality by this definition";
(3) "Define situations-experienced and situations-believed-in. According to the text, how can
we test the validity of situations-believed-in? State concisely how skepticism, naturalism, and
personalistic theism meet the test"; and (4) "Define and distinguish clearly: value and dis-
value; intrinsic and instrumental values; values and norms; the uniqueness of religious values
and their coalescence." King did not answer the second question; his answers to the remaining
three questions are omitted here. The required text for the course was Brightman's *Philosophy of
Religion*.

[5. *Define and evaluate mystical experience.*]

4.[2] Define and evaluate mystical experience

Mystical experience is immediate experience with what is believed to be the source of value. In his Giffort lectures William Janes said that the mystical experience is characterized by four traits: (1) Ineffibility (2) Noetic quality (3) transciency (4) Passivity.[3] These traits are accepted by most psychologists as characteristic of mystical experience.

Certainly no one can doubt that the mystical experience is an important aspect of religion. But we must admit that it can be misused. Often it has been used as a means of escape from this world, moral initia, and even antinomeniasm.[4] This however must not cause one to lose sight of the value of mysticism. Certainly no one can accuse many Quaker mystics of otherworliness and lack of social concern. One needs only know of their stand against slavery, poverty and war.[5]

The mystical experience when rightly used can be an important and meaningful aspect in the life of any one. When misused it can be an injurious force. To say that the mystical experience is unreal and of no value, as Professor Leuba intimated, because similar experience can come from the use of drugs is tantamount to denying the reality of the external world because some ~~peaplle~~ people have hallucinations.[6]

[6. *What is treated in the text as the chief argument for immortality? Evaluate it, treating also one other argument that you regard as important either for or against the belief.*]

5. The chief argument for immortality treated in the text is that of the goodness of God.[7] The argument goes that if God is a good God and the cosmic axiogenetic and axiosoteric power, then he will conserve persons who are of supreme value. God the conserver ~~It~~ of values must be God the conserver of persons.

I feel that this is the only argument that can be set forth for immortality with any weight. Certainly it is coherent. Any argument for God must at the same time be an argument for immortality.

---

2. Brightman had crossed out the "2" next to King's second answer (to question 3) and written, "Use numbers found on exam sheet." He similarly corrected the subsequent numbering (3–6 to 4–7).

3. Brightman corrected "Giffort" to "Gifford" and "Janes" to "James." He also underlined "transciency" twice and wrote a question mark next to it. This list of traits is from Brightman, *Philosophy of Religion*, p. 69.

4. Brightman corrected "initia" to "inertia."

5. Brightman wrote in the margin: "Not the great mystical saints."

6. This argument by James Henry Leuba (1868–1946) is cited in Brightman, *Philosophy of Religion*, p. 70.

7. Brightman underlined "goodness of God" and wrote, "Value of personality."

The most important argument against immortality is that set forth by the materaistic interpretation of ~~philosop~~ physiological psychology. This argument states that there is an inseperable relationship between brain and consciousness. So that without the nervous system or the brain ~~the~~ human consciousness cannot exist. This argument however, may be refuted by a personalistic on the grounds that the body including the brain and nervous system are phenomenal occasions of the divine energizing.

[7. *Define the "finite God" as treated in this course. Criticize the idea; give your present evaluation, both on philosophical and on religious grounds.*]

6. Define the "finite God" as treated in this course.
   The argument for the "finite God" goes as follows:
   God is a ~~consciousnes~~ conscious Person of ~~unending~~ eternal duration. He eternally finds and controls the Given in every moment of his experience. The Given consist of eternal uncreated laws of reason and equally eternal uncreated processes of nonrational consciousness. His will did not create the Given but it is in his experience at every moment.
   This view may be compared to that of Plato. There were three factors in Plato's universe (1) God (the Demiurge) (2) the Pattern (the eternal Ideal) and (3) the Receptacle (the chaos of space). The world came into existence through the interaction of the Pattern with the Receptacle.
   Plato's Patterns is similar to what Brightman calls the formal aspect of the Given. The Receptacle is similar to what he calls the content aspect of the Given. There is one important difference, however, between Plato and Brightman at this point. For Plato the Pattern and the Receptacle are external to God. For Brightman the Given is within God.[8]
   It is significant to note that Brightman never limits God's ethical nature. God's power is finite, but his goodness is infinite.
   At present I am quite sympathetic with this idea. After a somewhat extensive study of the idea I am all but convinced that it is the only adaquate explanation for the existence of evil. Moreover, it is significant and adaquate from a religious point of view because it establishes the Christian idea of sacrificial love on metaphysical grounds. It is the most empirical explanation that we can set forth in relation to the God idea. It makes a thorough distinction between good and evil, given an explanation for the existence of both. This theistic absolutetism fails to do.[9]

---

8. Brightman underlined this sentence and wrote, "Very important."
9. Brightman wrote at the end of this paragraph, "Good analysis."

January 1952
[Boston, Mass.]

*In his final examination answers for DeWolf's course on personalism, King
suggests that "the most serious criticism of personalism is in the area of the mind-
body problem." He praises DeWolf's "double aspect theory" as an "important and
brilliant attempt to solve this pressing problem." King also asserts that "one
of the most important problems confronted by present personalists is that of the
relationship between Personalism and theology." DeWolf awarded King a 93
for the examination and an A for the course.*

I. Relationship between Lotze and Bowne.[1]
1. Similarities:
(a) Both Lotze and Bowne held that personality was the clue to
the problems of philosophy. It can be explained (i.e. personality) by nothing else, but everything else can be explained
by it. They both agree that the antinomies of identity and
change, the One and the many can be solved in personality.
(b) Both Lotze and Bowne were theist. They held that theism was
the only metaphysical framework that could give epistemology a rational grounding. Moreover, theism for them is
the only theory that can account for interaction. We might
state at this point, however, that Lotze used an argument to
establish the existence of God which was never found in
Bowne. Lotze set forth a sort of revised ontological argument.
(c) Both Lotze and Bowne saw some validity in mechanism.
Bowne spoke of a mechanism expressive of purpose. However Lotze went beyond Bowne at this point. He held that all
life converges in mechanistic forces, and that the only difference in life matter and organtic was that of arrangement.
Lotze probably placed more emphasis on mechanism than
any other personalist.
2. Dissimilarities
(a) Bowne and Lotze were at somewhat opposing poles on the
doctrine of freedom. Lotze was quite vague at this point, and
certainly he never affirmed its validity emphatically. On the
other hand, however, Bowne was the forthright champion of
freedom. He affirmed that without it both kn reason and morality would go shipwreck. This was probably Bowne's most
characteristic emphasis. For him freedom had both metaphysical and epistemological significance.

---

1. King refers to Rudolf Hermann Lotze (1817–1881) and Borden Parker Bowne (1847–
1910).

(b) Lotze is also not as emphatic on the doctrine of immortality as is Bowne. He remains vague at this point, while Bowne is very explicit in affirming its reality.

(c) Bowne also deviated from the panpsychism which was set forth by Lotze. He was more of an occasionalist. Moreover, he placed more emphasis on pluralism, while Lotze was more of a radical monist because of his panpsychistic emphasis.[2]

II. The chief modification that Brightman has brought about to the personalistic philosoph of Bowne is that of method. Bowne's method adhered more or less to the Aristotelian-Kantian tradition of reason which defined reason as an ~~principle of~~ a priori principle. Brightman on the contrary falls in line with the Platonic-Hegelian tradition which defines reason as a principle of coherence. So that Brightman's method places more emphasis on coherence than did Bowne's. Brightman's method may be called rational empiricism. In this method emphasis is placed on analysis, but Brightman insist that there must be a post analytic synopsis.

Brightman is quite critical of Bowne's oft quoted phrase that "life is deeper than logic." On the one hand he admits that this is a superfluous truism in the sense that life is more than logic, but on the other hand he sees it as being an injurious philosophical emphasis. According to Brightman, if this view was followed to its logical conclusion there would be no way to distinguish between truth and a mere illusion. For Brightman "truth is the whole." He learned his logic from Hegel.

Brightman also modified Bowne's personalistic system by positing a finite God. Bowne was in every sense of the word a theistic absolutist. Brightman, on the other hand is a theistic finitist. For him God is a struggling God. His God is a conscious Person who eternally finds and controls "the Given" in every moment of his experience. His will didn't create this "Given" but it has to work with it. This fact accounts for God's limitation. His power is finite, and his goodness infinite.[3]

III. Personalism differs from absolute idealism in being a quantitative pluralism. Absolute idealism is monistic, both qualitatively and quantitatively. Closely related to this difference is the diffence in epistemology. Personalism stresses epistemological dualism while absolute idealism stresses epistemological monism. For the "typical" Personalist the thing series and the thought series are numerical two rather than one.

The relative strength of absolute idealism at this point is that it satisfies the mind's demand for unity. Moreover, it gives an easy explanation of interaction. But there is a point at which this relative strength becomes an absolute weakness, namely in explaining error and the problem of evil. Certain arguments have been set forth by this school of thought

---

2. King received 9 points for this answer.
3. King received 8+ points.

stating that evil is incomplete good and when seen in terms of the whole it is really good. The same would apply for error. But one could readily answer that the whole is never perceived by anyone at anytime, so how is it possible to know that evil is incomplete good. Someone could just as well say that good is incomplete evil.

Certainly Personalism has a much stronger ground to stand on at this point. With an epistemic dualism error and evil can be explained without attributing it to the Absolute. Moreover, creation can be a real factor with the personalist, but not so with the Absolute idealist.

If morality is to be rational and worship real there must be a separation between God and man. Metaphysical otherness is a necessity for God and man if morality, worship and reason are to be meaningful[4]

IV. I think that the most serious criticism of personalism is in the area of the mind-body problem. Personalism, according to many, has failed to give an adequate explanation of this important problem. There have been several explanation in the history of philosophy of this problem, among them being, illusionism, interactionism, and epiphenomenalism. Personalists, on the whole, have accepted the interaction explanation. Recently professor DeWolf has attempted to deal with the problem in terms of a double aspect theory. In this theory it is argued that the person as it is in and for itself is a conscious person, but the person as observed by others is system of orderly processes. Such a view might be a "Conciliation of Personalism and Behaviorism." Indeed it is an important and brillant attempt to solve this pressing problem.

Certainly Behaviorist and other physiological psychologist have revealed the profundity of this problem. It is now up to the personalist to confront it.[5]

V. To my mind one of the most important problems confronted by present personalists is that of the relationship between Personalism and theology. This problem grows up mainly because of the emphasis, by many personalist, on the method of coherence. The problem boils down to this: Can one hold to an empirical method of coherence and at the same time make absolute decisions? Certainly religion demands such absolute decisions.

As for me, I have found a solution of this problem in the thought of men like Karl Gross, Brightman and Hocking. Theoretically we can never make a claim to absolute certainty. This is certainly the emphasis of a method of coherence and that I accept. But while we cannot be theoretically certain about any issue, we are compelled to act. And certainly we have a right to act and accept any belief until one better is found if it does not contradict experience. So that along with a "theo-

---

4. King received 10 points.

5. King received 10 points.

retical relativism," we ~~are perfectly~~ have the perfect right to adopt a
"practical absolutism."[6]

AHDS. MLKP-MBU: Box 113.

---

6. King received 9 points.

"Contemporary Continental Theology"

[*13 September 1951–15 January 1952?*]
[*Boston, Mass.?*]

Probably written during the first term of DeWolf's Seminar in Systematic
Theology, this essay examines the theologies of Nicholas Berdyaev, Jacques
Maritain, Gustaf Aulén, and Karl Barth. King also examines Anders Nygren's
influential work on agape and eros. King's section on Maritain is similar to the
contents of "Jacques Maritain," a short essay he wrote earlier in 1951 while at
Crozer.[1] Although the essay is largely appropriated from Walter Marshall Horton's
Contemporary Continental Theology *and an article by George W. Davis, his*
former professor at Crozer, DeWolf judged it "Superior."

The field to be explored in a study of contemporary continental theological thought is much vaster
than I can even approximate in a paper of this length.
Perhaps it is folly to attempt even a bird's eye view of
Continental theology in so brief a compass. Conscious
of many inevitable omissions, I have nevertheless decided to use the method of selective sampling rather
than exhaustive portrayal.[2] I have not limited this
study to the well known Barthian thought, which is
so influential on the continent, but I have attempted
to set forth some light on all phases of continental
thought. It should be made clear that there is by no
means one theological system common to the whole

---

1. See King, "Jacques Maritain," in *Papers* 1:436–439.

2. Walter Marshall Horton, *Contemporary Continental Theology: An Interpretation for Anglo-Saxons*
(New York: Harper, 1938), p. xi: "Obviously, the field to be explored is much vaster than that
which I undertook to survey in my other book; and to explore it by the same method, the method
of selective sampling rather than exhaustive portrayal, will leave vast areas untouched. Perhaps
it is folly to attempt even a bird's-eye view of Continental theology in so brief a compass as four
chapters. Conscious of many inevitable omissions, I have nevertheless decided that the method
of sampling is the best way."

of continental thinking. No matter how influential Barthianism is on the continent, it is quite erroneous to think of all continental theologians as Barthians. In Norway, for example, which is split into a conservative pietistic and a liberal party, Barth is rejected with equal unanimity by both groups: by the liberals because of his reactionary tendencies, by the conservatives because of his freedom in Biblical criticism. In Sweden, Barth is sympathetically studied; but Swedish theology, having always held to the Lutheran ideas of the mysterious majesty of God, does not feel the need of reemphasizing it, and objects to Barth's stating it in a way that seems to obscure the other pole of Lutheran thought, the Fatherly love of God. In Finland, apparently, Barth's name is little known.[3] So that the catagorical assertion that Barthism covers the whole of continental thought is far from within the facts. But Barth is highly influential, no one can doubt that. For this reason we will deal more with his theology than that of any other continental theologian. No matter how much we disagree with Barth, we cannot dismiss him as "another fool", for he is by all standards of measurement on of the most influential Theologians in the world today and from an intellectual point of view he is well prepared. Before turning to Barth, however, we may delve into the thought of a few other continental theologians and see what essence can be brought forth.

A Lay Theologian:
Nicholas Berdyaev

It is not an easy job to set forth the theology of Nicholas Berdyaev mainly because of its abstruseness and obscurity. The average pragmatic-minded American looks askance at his speculative flights and his odd jargon. However when one reads Berdyaev seriously

---

3. Horton, *Contemporary Continental Theology*, pp. 150–151: "In Norway, which is split into a conservative pietistic and a liberal party, Barth is rejected with equal unanimity by both groups: by the liberals on account of his reactionary tendencies, by the conservatives because of his freedom in Biblical criticism! In Sweden, Barth is sympathetically studied; but Swedish theology, having always held to the Lutheran ideas of the mysterious majesty of God, does not feel the need of reemphasizing it, and objects to Barth's stating it in a way that seems to obscure the other pole of Lutheran thought, the Fatherly love of God. In Finland, apparently, Barth's name is little known."

and comes to grasp the essence of his thought, he finds a sincere Christian attempting to clarify the unsolved problem of conventional Christian thought. The basic philosophical and theological views of Berdyaev are set forth in his two most important works, The Destiny of Man and The Meaning of History. In the latter book the author looks backward over man's history toward its eternal source, in order to grasp the significance of the present crisis of modern humanistic culture; whereas in the former work he looks forward through the ethical duties and dangers of our era toward mankind's eternal end and goal.[4]

As Berdyaev ventures to set forth a philosophy of history we immediately see his religious views creeping out. In his diagnosis of our present transition from an age of true "culture" to an age of mere "civilization", concerned purely with power and technique, Berdyaev reminds us of Oswald Spengler—to whom, indeed, he makes explicit reference.* Like Spengler, he is convinced that civilizations pass through life-cycles. Unlike Spengler, however, he teaches that civilization does not fatally revert to barbarism once this process of degeneration has begun; instead, it may pass through "religious transfiguration" and be reborn as a new culture at the very moment when its death is imminent. History, in other words, is not purely the process of rigid necessity; it is "made up of the complex interaction of the three principles of necessity, freedom, and transfiguring Grace;"† and the deepest of these is Grace.[5]

According to Berdyaev the ultimate ground of the dialectic of history is to be found upon some divine or eternal plane. History begins with a mysterious "prologue in heaven," of which religion speaks in

* The Meaning of History, p. 207.

† Ibid., p. 61.

---

4. Horton, *Contemporary Continental Theology*, p. 14: "In this earlier book, the author looks backward over man's history toward its eternal *source*, in order to grasp the significance of the present crisis of modern humanistic culture; whereas in *The Destiny of Man* he looks *forward* through the ethical duties and dangers of our era toward mankind's eternal end and *goal*."

5. Horton, *Contemporary Continental Theology*, p. 15: "In his diagnosis of our present transition from an age of true 'culture' to an age of mere 'civilization,' concerned purely with power and technique, Berdyaev reminds us of Oswald Spengler—to whom, indeed, he makes explicit reference. Like Spengler, he is convinced that civilizations pass through life-cycles. . . . Unlike Spengler, however, he teaches that civilization does not fatally revert to barbarism once this process of degeneration has begun; instead, it may pass through 'religious transfiguration' and be reborn as a new culture at the very moment when its death is imminent. History, in other words, is not purely the product of rigid necessity; it is 'made up of the complex interaction of the three principles of necessity, freedom and transfiguring Grace'; and the deepest of these is Grace."

mythological symbols, vague but profoundly true. We can read these symbols because they correspond to something deep within us, the history they interpret is our own history. There is an inner tie between God, the world and ourselves, which is found in Christ, the God-man. The motion of human history toward God and eternity is a response to an eternal motion of God toward man; in Christ the two motions merge, and the divine love for man finds its perfect response in "freely given" human love for God.[6] Here we readily see that for Berdyaev Christ is the center of history.

Berdyaev talks a great deal about Jesus as the Messiah. He is convinced that both Judaism and Marxism contain a "false Messianism," which demands an abstract, universal justice on earth only to be realized by compulsion—and so, in practic, not realizable at all.* The true Messiah, when he came, delivered man not only from the pagan dominion of the cycle of nature, but also from the dominion of social compulsion, and from all-devouring time itself, by revealing the eternal worth and destiny of the individual soul.[7]

Berdyaev is a great critic of modern humanistic culture and he sees the collapse of humanistic culture in our day as the definitive disproof of the religion of progress, which for so many moderns has taken the place of Christianity—a rationalized, secularized version of the ancient Jewish hope of a Messianic Age. In all of its forms this hope assumes a false and illusory view of time, according to which the past and future have no inner, organic connection, and only at the end of the time-process is any meaning introduced. But thus to postpone meaning to the end of

* Ibid, p. 56 F.

---

6. Horton, *Contemporary Continental Theology*, pp. 15–16: "The ultimate ground of the dialectic of history is not, then, to be found upon the human or temporal plane, but upon the divine or eternal plane. History begins with a mysterious 'prologue in heaven,' of which religion speaks in mythological symbols, vague but profoundly true. We can read these symbols because they correspond to something deep within us; the history they interpret is *our own* history. There is an inner tie between God, the world and ourselves, which is found in Christ, the God-man. The motion of human history toward God and eternity is a response to an eternal motion of God toward man; in Christ, the two motions merge, and the divine love for man finds its perfect response in 'freely given' human love for God."

7. Horton, *Contemporary Continental Theology*, p. 17: "But he is now convinced that both Judaism and Marxism contain a 'false Messianism,' which demands an abstract, universal justice on earth only to be realized by compulsion—and so, in practice, not realizable at all. The true Messiah, when he came, delivered man not only from the pagan dominion of the cycle of nature, but also from the dominion of social compulsion, and from all-devouring time itself, by revealing the eternal worth and destiny of the individual soul."

history is to postpone it forever. A truer view of the time process finds eternity penetrating it at every moment, binding the present to the past and future in memory and hope; and time, conversely, penetrating eternity "as a moment in the everlasting mystery of Spirit."*[8]

In <u>The Destiny of Man</u>, Berdyaes's masterpiece, the scattered insights which gleam through these essays are gathered up into one comprehensive vision: first, of man's metaphysical origin and nature; second, of his present duty; third, of his final destiny.[9]

It will be recalled that history, for Berdyaev, is a product of three factors: human freedom, natural necessity and divine Grace. Now the usual teaching of "positive" Theology is that the first and second factors are derived from the {latter}; i.e., God made nature and man, giving to man the power to use nature's resources and his faculties well or ill, as he chose. This theology, thinks Berdyaev, is a prolific source of atheism, for freedom is admitted to lead to sin and, for at least a great proportion of mankind, to eternal punishment; and yet God, foreseeing these terrible consequences, bestowed this fatal gift upon his ignorant and unsuspecting creature! In contrast to this teaching of "positive" theology is the "negative" or mystical theology, according to which God the Creator himself is eternally born out of a dark Abyss of deity or divine Nothingness; and man and universe are then created by God out of the same ultimate, indeterminate metaphysical stuff from which he himself proceeds. Since non-being is of the very essence of this primal stuff, freedom is uncreated, coeternal with God, and man may be described as the child of two parents: God,

---

8. Horton, *Contemporary Continental Theology*, p. 20: "The collapse of humanistic culture in our day is the definitive disproof of the religion of progress, which for so many moderns has taken the place of Christianity—a rationalized, secularized version of the ancient Jewish hope of a Messianic Age. In all its forms, ancient or modern, this hope provides no solution of the problem of human destiny. It assumes a false and illusory view of time, according to which the past and future have no inner, organic connection, and only at the *end* of the time-process is any meaning introduced. But thus to postpone meaning to the end of history is to postpone it forever. A truer view of the time-process finds eternity penetrating it at every moment, binding the present to the past and future in memory and hope; and time, conversely, penetrating eternity 'as a moment in the everlasting mystery of the Spirit.'"

9. Horton, *Contemporary Continental Theology*, p. 23: "In *The Destiny of Man*, Berdyaev's masterpiece, the scattered insights which gleam through these essays are gathered up into one comprehensive vision: *first*, of man's metaphysical origin and nature; *second*, of his present duty; *third*, of his final destiny."

the formative agent in the process, and "meonic freedom," the passive stuff which simple "consented" to
God's creative act. The element of uncreated freedom
in man's nature is the source of his instinctive urges
and creative powers; it is also the source of his ability
to rebel against God and resolve himself back into the
chaos of non-being.[10]

The story of man's fall belongs to the dim border
between time and eternity, and can be narrated only
in mythological symbols. "Paradise" stands for the
original unconscious unity of God, man and nature
after the Creation—a blissful state, and yet an imperfect one, since God was then "merely a sustaining
power"* and his rich tri-unity was not yer revealed to
his creatures. It was, in one sense, an advance to pass
from this pre-concious state to one of conscious "division, reflection, valuation, freedom of choice;"† and
yet in the act of becoming conscious of his creative
powers, and the divisity of choices open to him, man
came under the sway of the chaotic element in his nature; indeed, it may have been the pain and loss of
this revolt that made him conscious in the first place.
After the Fall man's only way back to bliss was onward
through conscious struggle ans suffering, toward a
new and higher level of existence, super-conscious
and not merely pre-conscious. As man treads this
long and tragic road, he is not alone; for when man
falls away, God prepares a "second act" in the divine
drama of destiny: as God the Son, he decends into the
dark abyss of meonic freedom to struggle unarmed

* The Destiny of Man,
p. 48.

† Ibid., p. 51.

---

10. Horton, *Contemporary Continental Theology*, pp. 23–24: "It will be recalled that history, for
Berdyaev, is a product of three factors: human freedom, natural necessity and divine Grace.
Now, the usual teaching of rational or 'positive' theology is that the first and second factors are
ultimately derived from the third; i.e., God made nature and man, giving to man the power to
use nature's resources and his own faculties well or ill, as he chose. This theology, thinks Berdyaev, is a prolific source of atheism, for freedom is admitted to lead to sin and, for at least a
great proportion of mankind, to eternal punishment; and yet God, foreseeing these terrible consequences, bestowed this fatal gift upon his ignorant and unsuspecting creature! In contrast to
this teaching of 'positive' theology is the teaching of 'negative' or mystical theology (Boehme,
Eckhart), according to which God the Creator himself is eternally born out of a dark Abyss of
deity, the so-called *Ungrund*, or divine Nothingness; and man and universe are then created by
God out of the same ultimate, indeterminate metaphysical stuff from which he himself proceeds.
Since indeterminacy or non-being ($\mu\eta$ $o\nu$) are of the very essence of this primal stuff, freedom is
uncreated, coeternal with God, and man may be described as the child of two parents: God, the
formative agent in the process, and 'meonic freedom,' the passive stuff which simply 'consented'
to God's creative act. The element of uncreated freedom in man's nature is the source of his
instinctive urges and creative powers; it is also the source of his ability to rebel against God and
resolve himself back into the chaos of non-being."

(except by love and sacrifice) with his evil creation, to redeem it "by enlightening it from within without forcing."* Apart from such divine and gracious aid, man could never fulfil his destiny.[11] This is man's only way to salvation.

A Catholic Critic:
Jacques Maritain

Jacques Maritain stands out as the foremost Catholic philosopher on the Continent. From his chair in the Institut Catholique in Parid, Maritain views the whole modern age with a critical eye, diagnoses its diseases, and prescribes "Integral Thomism" as the infallible antidote for all its ills.[12]

Maritain is far from Catholic in many of his political views. He has no desire to see the mediaeval supremacy of Church over state restored; he only hopes for a day when "and entirely moral and spiritual activity of the Church shall preside over the temporal order of a multitude of politically and culturally heterogeneous nations, whose religious differences are still not likely to disappear."† He deplores the social inertia and reaction which beset so many Catholics. Some years back he incurred considerable criticism by many of his fellow Catholics because he refused to see

† Essays in Order, pp. 28–29.

---

11. Horton, *Contemporary Continental Theology*, pp. 24–25: "The story of man's Fall belongs to the dim borderland between time and eternity, and can be narrated only in mythological symbols. 'Paradise' stands for the original unconscious unity of God, man and nature after the Creation—a blissful state, and yet an imperfect one, since God was then 'merely a sustaining power' and his rich tri-unity was not yet revealed to his creatures. It was, in one sense, an advance to pass from this pre-conscious state to one of conscious 'division, reflection, valuation, freedom of choice'; and yet in the act of becoming conscious of his creative powers, and the diversity of choices open to him, man came under the sway of the chaotic element in his nature; indeed, it may have been the pain and loss of this revolt that *made* him conscious in the first place. Man having thus fallen away from his original unity with God, the world fell away from its original unity with man; the gates of the first paradise were closed to him forever, and the only way back to bliss was onward through conscious struggle and suffering, toward a new and higher level of existence, superconscious and not merely pre-conscious. As man treads this long and tragic road, he is not alone; for when man falls away, God prepares a 'second act' in the divine drama of destiny: as God the Son, he descends into the dark abyss of meonic freedom to struggle unarmed (except by love and sacrifice) with his evil creation, to redeem it 'by enlightening it from within without forcing.' Apart from such divine and gracious aid, man could not fulfil his destiny."

12. Horton, *Contemporary Continental Theology*, pp. 48–49: "Jacques Maritain, who from his chair in the *Institut Catholique* in Paris views the whole modern age with a critical eye, diagnoses its diseases, and prescribes 'Integral Thomism' as the infallible antidote for all its ills."

in General Franco the perfect Christian knight-errant that the Vatican saw him to be.[13]

If it be asked how a loyal Catholic can thus take sides against the interests of his own church, the answer is very clear. Maritain refuses to identify the interests of Catholics with the interest of the Church, or the Kingdom of God. The Invincible Armada was sent out by his Most Catholic Majesty, Philip II of Spain, with holy intent and with prayers upon the lips of the faithful; but in Maritain's candid opinion, God was against it.[14]

As we turn to Maritain's critique of modern culture, we find him diagnosing its ills in intellectual terms. The disease of modernity began, according to Maritain in the realm of the mind. When modern philosophy abandoned its dependence on theology, it started a process of dissociation which could not be checked short of the very verge of dissolution. The three great symptoms of this state of dissociation, in its last stages, are (1) agnosticism, or the complete separation of the knowing mind from the object of knowledge; (2) naturalism, or the complete separation of the world from its divine Source and Ground, and (3) individualism, or the complete separation of the rebellious human will from any object of trust and obedience. Maritain now goes on to show that Thomism is the specific antidote for these three alarming symptoms, and for the disease that underlies them.[15]

---

13. Horton, *Contemporary Continental Theology*, pp. 49–50: "He has no desire to see the mediaeval supremacy of Church over State restored; he only hopes for a day when 'an entirely moral and spiritual activity of the Church shall preside over the temporal order of a multitude of politically and culturally heterogeneous nations, whose religious differences are still not likely soon to disappear.' He deplores the social inertia and reaction which beset the Catholics. . . . He has lately incurred considerable opprobrium among his fellow Catholics by refusing to see in General Franco the perfect Christian knight-errant that the Spanish landed proprietors—yes, and the Vatican itself—seem to take him to be."

14. Horton, *Contemporary Continental Theology*, p. 50: "If it be asked how a loyal Catholic can thus take sides against the interests of his own church, the answer is very clear. Maritain refuses to identify the interests of Catholics with the interests of the Church, or the Kingdom of God. The Invincible Armada was sent out by his Most Catholic Majesty, Philip II of Spain, with holy intent and with prayers upon the lips of the faithful; but in Maritain's candid opinion, God was against it."

15. Horton, *Contemporary Continental Theology*, p. 55: "The disease of modernity began, according to Maritain, in the realm of the mind. When modern philosophy abandoned its dependence on theology, it started a process of dissociation which could not be checked short of the very verge of dissolution. . . . The three great symptoms of this state of dissociation, in its last stages,

In applying Thomism as the general solution to the various problems of the modern era, Maritain gives special attention to two closely related questions which we have seen to be central concerns of Berdyaev's system: the question of freedom, and the question of the destiny of man.[16]

In his book, <u>Freedom in the Modern World</u>, Maritain offers a rationalistic account of the origin of freedom. The world of freedom, he says, is not to be opposed to the world of nature, as in the Kantian philosophy; neither is it to be confused with it, as in the philosophy of Spinoza and Hegel; it is to be seen as grounded in the world of nature, but distinct from it. Maritain agrees with St. Thomas that "the whole root of freedom lies in reason." Freedom arises in nature precisely where reason arises. Inanimate and irrational beings have no freedom; in this part of nature, God rules without an adversary. Freedom of choice arises in man, a rational yet corporeal creature, because on the one hand he is capable of envisaging the universal Good, and tending toward it, while on the other hand his sensitive faculties present to him all manner of concrete "goods," which attract but do not permanently hold his will. The Infinite God is his chief end, and alone can satisfy him; but he is capable of being temporarily attracted by many specific ends that conflict with the chief end; and even when his speculative reason grasps the true good, his practical reason may fail to perform the act that chooses it. In this world of freedom, then, "God appears as legislator and as end of that special order which constitutes the moral order, and from this point of view He has adversaries, for He permits created spirits to resist His will, which is ideally manifest to them as the supreme rule or norm of Freedom . . . God has the power but does not will to prevent the creature (when

are (1) *agnosticism*, or the complete separation of the knowing mind from the object of knowledge; (2) *naturalism*, or the complete separation of the world from its divine Source and Ground, and (3) *individualism*, or the complete separation of the rebellious human will from any object of trust and obedience. Thomism is the specific antidote for these three alarming symptoms, and for the disease that underlies them."

16. Horton, *Contemporary Continental Theology*, pp. 56–57: "In applying this general solution to the various problems of the modern era, Maritain gives special attention to two closely related questions which we have already seen to be the central concerns of Berdyaev's system: the question of *freedom*, and the question of the *destiny of man*."

it is so inclined) from interposing its refusal. For the hands of God are tied by the inscrutable designs of His love as were those of the Son of Man upon the Cross."*[17]

* Maritain, Freedom in the Modern World, p. 27.

Although Maritain and Berdyaev differ on the origin of freedom, they substantially agree about the practical solution of the problem it presents. Freedom of choice is not true freedom. True freedom consists in choosing the Good. When a man chooses the Good, he participates in that "freedom of antonomy" which God possesses in its perfection. God is so fixed upon the Good that he cannot choose otherwise; and the saints, who participate in God's holiness, participate also in his fixity of character and will.[18]

Maritain's views on the destiny of man are quite fascinating, and in many instances they remind one of Berdyaev's historical writings. Like Berdyaev, Maritain feels that Christianity necessarily involves a very exalted view of man. The tragedy of modern humanism springs not from its having been "humanistic," but from its having been man centered. Anthropocentrism is fatal both to the idea of man itself and to

---

17. Horton, *Contemporary Continental Theology*, p. 57–58: "In *Freedom in the Modern World*, Maritain offers a more rationalistic account of the origin of freedom. The world of freedom, he says, is not to be *opposed* to the world of nature, as in Kant's philosophy; neither is it to be *confused* with it, as in the philosophy of Spinoza and Hegel; it is to be seen as *grounded* in the world of nature, but *distinct* from it. 'The whole root of freedom,' as St. Thomas says, 'lies in reason.' Freedom arises in nature precisely where reason arises. Inanimate and irrational beings have no freedom; in this part of nature, God rules without an adversary. Freedom of choice arises in man, a rational yet corporeal creature, because on the one hand he is capable of envisaging the universal Good, and tending toward it, while on the other hand his sensitive faculties present to him all manner of concrete 'goods,' which *attract* but do not permanently *hold* his will. The Infinite God is his chief end, and alone can satisfy him; but he is capable of being temporarily attracted by many specific ends that conflict with his chief end; and even when his speculative reason *grasps* the true good, his practical reason may fail to perform the act that *chooses* it. In this world of freedom, then, 'God appears as legislator and as end of that special order which constitutes the moral order, and from this point of view He has adversaries, for He permits created spirits to resist His will, which is ideally manifest to them as the supreme rule or norm of Freedom. . . . God has the power but does not will to prevent the creature (when it is so inclined) from interposing its refusal. For the hands of God are tied by the inscrutable designs of His love as were those of the Son of Man upon the Cross.'" Ellipses in original.

18. Horton, *Contemporary Continental Theology*, p. 58: "If Berdyaev and Maritain differ on the *origin* of freedom, they substantially agree about the practical solution of the problem it presents. Freedom of choice is not true freedom. True freedom consists in choosing the Good. When a man chooses the Good, he participates in that 'freedom of autonomy' which God possesses in its perfection. God is so fixed upon the Good that he cannot choose otherwise; and the saints, who participate in God's holiness, participate also in his fixity of character and will."

the ideas of culture and God ~~and God~~ that are linked with it.[19]

Humanistic culture, beginning with a noble heritage from the Christian Middle Ages, passed into a second phase in the eighteenth century, when it began consciously to turn against its own historic sources, and into a third phase with the Russian Revolution, when it replaced all ideal ends by purely material ones. In the first of these three phases, God is still believed in as a real power, but becomes the guarantor of man's success (Bacon, Descartes) in dominating nature; in the second phase, when man begins to trust in his ability to dominate nature single-handed, by his own science and technology, God becomes a mere idea (Kant) or, with Hegel, the "ideal limit of the development of the world of humanity;" in the third phase, with the disappearance of the divine image in man, the death of God is announced.[20]

The attempt to revive pure Christianity in our day has two principle forms, according to Maritain: the "reactionary" attempt to turn humanism upside down by the "annihilation of man before God" (Barth), and the "progressive" attitude of Neo-Thomism, which aims to preserve the dignity of man and rescue the valuable elements in humanistic culture by incorporating them in a new Christian civilization. Maritain is not too hopeful about the possibility of a new Christian civilization in the future. He rejects with equal decisiveness the view that this world is simply the kingdom of Satan, and the view that the Kingdom of

---

19. Horton, *Contemporary Continental Theology*, p. 59: "Maritain's views on the destiny of man are most clearly expressed in his *Humanisme intégral*, a book that reminds one frequently of Berdyaev's historical writings. . . . Like Berdyaev, Maritain feels that Christianity necessarily involves a very exalted view of man. The tragedy of modern humanism springs not from its having been 'humanistic,' but from its having been *man-centered*. Anthropocentrism is fatal both to the idea of *man* itself and to the ideas of *culture* and *God* that are linked with it."

20. Horton, *Contemporary Continental Theology*, pp. 59–60: "Humanistic *culture*, beginning with a noble heritage from the Christian Middle Ages, passed into a second phase in the eighteenth century, when it began consciously to turn against its own historic sources, and into a third phase with the Russian Revolution, when it replaced all ideal ends by purely material ones. In the first of these three phases, *God* is still believed in as a real power, but becomes the *guarantor of man's success* (Bacon, Descartes) in dominating nature; in the second phase, when man begins to trust in his ability to dominate nature single-handed, by his own science and technology, God becomes *a mere idea* (Kant), or, with Hegel, the 'ideal limit of the development of the world of humanity'; in the third phase, with the disappearance of the divine image in man, the *death of God* is announced."

God is ever fully to be realized in it. "The true Christian doctrine of the world and of the earthly city is that they are at once the kingdom of man, of God, and of the devil."* History is marching both toward the harvest of wheat and the harvest of tares. Just now, the age of humanism is marching toward its own "liquidation." The end of this age, however, does not mean the end of the world. History is not yet ripe to be swallowed up in eternity. God has yet to guild us through many acts of the human drama.[21] So much for Maritain.

* Quoted from Horton's, Contemporary Continental Theology, p. 60.

Scandinavian Theology: Nygren and Aulen

The prevailing trend of contemporary Swedish theology has been set by the "Ludensian" school, led by Gustof Aulen and his close associate, Anders Nygren.[22] The work of these men has proceeded on quite original lines, and constitutes one of the most distinctive schools of Protestant thought in the world today.[23]

It is interesting to note that the two books by which Aulen and Nygren are now known to the English-speaking world, Christus Victor (Aulen) and Agape and Eros (Nygren), are both historical studies. The history of doctrine has a special importance for them

---

21. Horton, *Contemporary Continental Theology*, pp. 60–61: "The attempt to revive pure Christianity in our day has two principle forms, according to Maritain: the 'reactionary' attempt to turn humanism upside down by the 'annihilation of man before God' (Karl Barth), and the 'integral' or 'progressive' attitude of Neo-Thomism, which aims to preserve the dignity of man and rescue the valuable elements in humanistic culture by incorporating them in a new Christian civilization. Maritain is not too hopeful about the possibility of a new Christian civilization in the near future. He rejects with equal decisiveness the view that this world is simply the kingdom of Satan, and the view that the kingdom of God is ever fully to be realized in it. 'The true Christian doctrine of the world and of the earthly city is that they are *at once* the kingdom of man, of God, and of the devil.' History is marching both toward the harvest of wheat and the harvest of tares. Just now, the age of humanism is marching toward its own 'liquidation.' . . . The end of this age, however, does not mean the end of the world. History is not yet ripe to be swallowed up in eternity. . . . The Providence of God has yet to guide us through many acts in the human drama."

22. Horton, *Contemporary Continental Theology*, pp. 154–155: "The prevailing trend of contemporary Swedish theology has been set by the 'Lundensian' school, led by Gustaf Aulén and his close associate, Anders Nygren."

23. Horton, *Contemporary Continental Theology*, p. 155: "The work of Aulén and his colleagues at Lund has proceeded on quite original lines, and constitutes one of the most distinctive schools of Protestant thought in the world today."

both. The task of theology, according to them is not
to prove the truth of Christian Faith, or engage in
metaphysical speculations, but rather to set forth this
faith in its simplicity and unity, clearing it of all alien
entanglements. The task of dogmatic theology is to
define the unique and determinative motives of the
Christian faith—which cannot be done in the abstract, without close attention to history.[24] In their historical method, Aulen and Nygren set out to distinguish between fundamental religious motives and the
concepts or figures of speech in which they are expressed. We may first turn to Aulen's <u>Christus Victor</u>
and see how he attempts to disentangle motives from
concepts.[25]

In the writings of the early Greek fathers, a view of
the Work of Christ finds frequent expression which is
usually dismissed by modern Western theologians as
unworthy of serious consideration. It is commonly
known as the "ransom to Satan theory;" and it makes
use of some strange figures of speech.[26] Aulen believes that this much maligned view, when stripped of
its mythological language, and its underlying "religious motive" has thus been revealed, will prove to
be far more than a historical curiosity. What are
the religious "values" or "motives" inbedded in this
theory.[27] Before answering this question the conten-

---

24. Horton, *Contemporary Continental Theology*, pp. 155–156: "It is no accident that the two
books by which Aulén and Nygren are now known to the English-speaking world, *Christus Victor*
(Aulén) and *Agape and Eros* (Nygren), are both *historical* studies. The history of doctrine has a
special importance for them both. The task of theology, according to Aulén's great work, *The
Common Christian Faith* (*Den allmänneliga Kristna tron*, 1920; 3rd edition 1931) is not to prove the
truth of Christian faith, or engage in metaphysical speculations, but rather to set forth this faith
in its simplicity and its unity, clearing it of all alien entanglements. According to Nygren, the task
of the philosophy of religion is to define the uniqueness of the religious experience, and that of
dogmatic theology is to define the unique and determinative motives of the Christian
faith—which cannot be done in the abstract, without close attention to *history*."

25. Horton, *Contemporary Continental Theology*, p. 157: "The historical method of . . . that of
the Lundensians . . . endeavors to distinguish between fundamental religious *motives* and the
concepts or figures of speech in which they are expressed. . . . The disentanglement of motives
from concepts is best seen in Aulén's *Christus Victor*."

26. Horton, *Contemporary Continental Theology*, p. 157: "In the writings of the early Greek fathers, a view of the Work of Christ finds frequent expression which is usually dismissed by modern Western theologians as unworthy of serious consideration. It is commonly known as 'the
ransom to Satan theory'; and it makes use of some very strange figures of speech."

27. Horton, *Contemporary Continental Theology*, p. 158: "Aulén believes that this much maligned
view, when the mythological language in which it is clothed has been properly interpreted, and
its underlying 'religious motive' has thus been revealed, will prove to be far more than a historical
curiosity. . . . What are these religious 'values' or 'motives'?"

tions of this theory must be set forth. The first contention is that the devil acquired rights over man when he fell into sin, and it is right that his Satanic Majesty should demand a "ransom" in exchange for man's deliverance. On the other hand it is contended that man belongs by nature to God, and the devil has brought him violently into captivity.[28]

The religious motive behind the first of these contentions is "the desire to assert the guilt of mankind, and the judgment of God on human sin."* The motive behind the second is the feeling that man's sin is only a part of a wider, cosmic apostasy from God's will, in which everything evil is included, and which forms a rival kingdom violently striving against God's.[29]

* Aulen, Christus Victor p. 64.

Aulen never doubts that this "classic" view of the Greek fathers is superior to the mediaeval and modern views; "Its central theme is the idea of Atonement as a Divine conflict and victory: Christ—Christus Victor—fights against and triumphs over the evil powers of the world, the tyrants under which mankind is in bondage and suffering, and in Him God reconciles the world to Himself." †[30] In comparison with all modern "subjective theories of the Atonement, from Abelard to Liberal Protestantism, the classic view is more truly "objective" than Anselm's, for "it describes a complete change in the relation between God and the world, and a change also in God's own attitude," ‡ due to the passing of a great crisis in the cosmic combet between the Creator and his apostate creation.[31]

† Ibid, p. 21.

‡ Ibid, p. 22.

---

28. Horton, *Contemporary Continental Theology*, p. 159: "The devil acquired rights over man when he fell into sin, and it is right that his Satanic Majesty should demand a 'ransom' in exchange for man's deliverance. On the other hand, it is protested . . . that man belongs by nature to God, and the devil has brought him violently into captivity."

29. Horton, *Contemporary Continental Theology*, p. 159: "The religious motive behind the first of these contentions is '*the desire to assert the guilt of mankind, and the judgment of God on human sin.*' The motive behind the second is the feeling that man's sin is only a part of a wider, cosmic apostasy from God's will, in which everything evil is included, and which forms a rival kingdom violently striving against God's."

30. Horton, *Contemporary Continental Theology*, p. 160: "He finds in this 'classic' view of the Greek fathers . . . a view of Christ's Work clearly distinguishable from the mediaeval and modern views, and much superior thereto. . . . 'Its central theme is the idea of Atonement as a Divine conflict and victory: Christ—Christus Victor—fights against and triumphs over the evil powers of the world, the "tyrants" under which mankind is in bondage and suffering, and in Him God reconciles the world to Himself.'"

31. Horton, *Contemporary Continental Theology*, pp. 160–161: "In comparison with all modern 'subjective' theories of the Atonement, from Abelard to Liberal Protestantism, the classic view is

When we turn to Professor Nygren we find him fol- 15 Jan
lowing Aulen in placing emphasis upon active, self 1952
imparting Divine love as the Ground-motive of Christian Faith. In his book, <u>Agape and Eros</u>, he is primarily concerned with the contrast between two kinds of
love, easily confused in modern languages, but clearly
distinguished in Greek: the "love" (Eros) of which
Plato speaks in his Symposium and the "love" (Agape)
of which St. Paul speaks in the 13th Chapter of I Corinthians. In these two words he finds the Ground-
motives of Greek religion and original Christianity
concretely expresses.[32]

As Nygren set out to contrast these two Greek
words he finds that Eros loves in proportion to the
value of the object. By the pursuit of value in its objects, Platonic love is led up and away from the world,
on wings of aspiration, beyond all transient things
and persons to the realm of the Ideas. Agape as described in the Gospels and Epsitles, is "spontaneous
and uncaused," indifferent to human merit," and creates value in those upon whom it is bestowed out of
pure generosity. It flows down from God into the
transient, sinful world; those whom it touches become
conscious of their own utter unworthiness; they are
impelled to forgive and love their enemies, because
the God of Grace imparts worth to them by the act of
* Nygren, <u>Agape and</u>   loving them.*[33]
<u>Eros</u>, pp. 52–56.   The union of Eros with Agape began with St. Au-

---

as truly, nay *more* truly, 'objective' than Anselm's, for 'it describes a complete change in the relation between God and the world, and a change also in God's own attitude,' due to the passing of
a great crisis in the cosmic combat between the Creator and his apostate creation."

32. Horton, *Contemporary Continental Theology*, p. 163: "For the English-speaking public, this
characteristic 'Lundensian' emphasis upon active, self-imparting Divine love as the Ground-
motive of Christian faith is best expressed in Professor Nygren's remarkable book, *Agape and
Eros*. It is primarily concerned with the contrast between two kinds of love, easily confused in
modern languages, but clearly distinguished in Greek: the 'love' (*Eros*) of which Plato speaks in
his *Symposium*, and the 'love' (*Agape*) of which St. Paul speaks in the 13th Chapter of I Corinthians.
In these two words he finds the Ground-motives of Greek religion and original Christianity concretely expressed."

33. Horton, *Contemporary Continental Theology*, p. 164: "It is Eros, not Agape, that loves in
proportion to the value of its object. By the pursuit of value in its object, Platonic love is led *up
and away* from the world, on wings of aspiration, beyond all transient things and persons to the
realm of the Ideas. Agape, as described in the Gospels and Epistles, is 'spontaneous and "uncaused,"' 'indifferent to human merit,' and 'creates' value in those upon whom it is bestowed out
of pure generosity. It flows *down from God* into this transient, sinful world; those whom it touches
become conscious of their own utter unworthiness; they are impelled to forgive and love their
enemies, not because they are inherently lovable, but because the God of grace imparts worth to
them by the act of loving them."

gustine. It was his Neo-Platonism, with its double motion, form God to man as well as from man to God
that made it possible to unite Platonic love with Christian love in the new composite idea of charity. The
union was carried to perfection in the teaching of St.
Thomas Aquinas; but his work was soon undone by
Luther (who went back to primitive Christian Agape)
and the Renaissance (which went back to Platonic
Eros). Liberal Protestantism is not the hier of Luther,
but of the Renaissance.[34]

The Crisis Theologians:
Barth, Brunner and Heim

The most striking feature of the situation in the
German world today is the almost complete collapse
of liberal Protestantism. Throughout the nineteenth
century, Protestant theological faculties in the German and Swiss universities enjoyed a degree of academic liberty (both from ecclesiastical and from political censorship) and a reputation for thorough
scholarship and bold speculation which made them the
world's greatest centers for theological study.[35] Where
we used to hear the liberal voices of Schleiermacher (1768–1834), Ritschl (1822–89), and Troeltsch
(1865–1923), we now hear the Nep-Supernaturalistic
voices of Barth, Brunner, and Heim. These men have
been called the crisis theologians because they see all
men under the judgment of God, and the beginning
of religion is when God presents himself to man in
the crisis situation. At this point we may turn to a discussion of God, Jesus, Man, and Revelation in crisis
theology.

---

34. Horton, *Contemporary Continental Theology*, p. 165: "The union of Eros with Agape began
with St. Augustine. It was his Neo-Platonism, with its double motion, from God to man as well as
from man to God . . . that made it possible to unite Platonic love with Christian love in the new
composite idea of *charity* (*caritas*). The union (or confusion!) was carried to perfection in the
teaching of St. Thomas Aquinas; but his work was soon undone by Luther (who went back to
primitive Christian Agape) and the Renaissance (which went back to Platonic Eros). Liberal Protestantism is not the heir of Luther, but of the Renaissance."

35. Horton, *Contemporary Continental Theology*, p. 85: "The most striking feature of the situation in the German Protestant world today is the almost complete collapse of liberal Protestantism. Throughout the nineteenth century, Protestant theological faculties in the German and
Swiss universities enjoyed a degree of academic liberty (both from ecclesiastical and from political
censorship) and a reputation for thorough scholarship and bold speculation which made them
the world's greatest centers for theological study."

Concerning God, the crisis theologians are always true to their conviction that the infinite God is forever unknowable and indescribable. Even when we say we know him our knowledge is of an incomprehensible Reality. He is the Wholly Other. Consider, for example, the personality of God. Barth writes: "God is personal, but persOnal in an incomprehensible way, in so far as the conception of His personality surpasses all our views of personality. This is so just because He and He alone is a true, real and genuine person." * [36]

Barth goes on to argue that even through the knowledge which comes by faith, than which "no more objective and strict form of knowledge can exist, and (that which) no type of knowledge can lay claim more definitely to universal validity," † no full knowledge of God comes to us. Even when God reveals himself to the man of faith, still that man with faith will confess God as the God of majesty and therefore as the God unknown to us." ‡ As Dr. Davis says, "In Barth's thought we have the majestic, hidden incomprehensible, though personal God, who is made know to us, mediated to us, in his Word made flesh in Jesus Christ." § [37]

† Ibid, p. 25.

‡ Ibid., p. 28.

§ George Davis, "Crisis Theology," Crozer Quarterly, July, 1950.

We immediately see the affinity of this view with the Greek philosophical conception of God. Influenced by the Platonic tradition of a transcendental deity lifted high above the corruptness of phenomenality, they introduced the same emphasis into the stream of Christian thought. Their God was also a high God, far removed from earth, transcendent, indescribable,

---

36. Davis, "Some Theological Continuities," pp. 208–209: "Concerning God, Barth is always true to his conviction that the infinite God is always unknowable and indescribable. . . . He is the Wholly Other. Even when we say we know him our knowledge is of an incomprehensible Reality. Consider, for instance, the personality of God. Barth writes: 'God is personal, but personal in an *incomprehensible* way, in so far as the conception of His personality surpasses all our views of personality. This is so, just because He and He alone is a true, real and genuine person.'"

37. Davis, "Some Theological Continuities," p. 209: "Barth also contends that even through the knowledge which comes by faith, than which 'no more objective and strict form of knowledge can exist, and [than which] no type of knowledge can lay claim more definitely to universal validity,' no full knowledge of God comes to us. Even when God reveals himself to the man of faith, . . . still that man with faith 'will confess God as the God of majesty and therefore as the God unknown to us.' To put it in brief conclusion, in Barth's thought we have the majestic, hidden, incomprehensible, though personal God, who is made known to us, mediated to us, in his Word made flesh in Jesus Christ."

unknowable, hidden, coming into touch with men only through an intermediary, who, for most of them, was found in the Logos who was Christ.[38] It is clear that in the early Christian centuries thinkers thought of God as the "Wholly Other," just as Rudolf Otto and Karl Barth are doing in contemporary times. As many of the early Christians proclaimed the utter separation of the high God and the world, so now does Barth. The two are totally unlike and exclusive. At no point does God touch the external world with its corrupted nature and evil matter. No part of the world is, therefore, a manifestation of God. Here "otherness" implies "exclusive separation." Through no experience of ours can we find God, now through and effort of our minds can we comprehend him. We are complete aliens until he wills to give himself {to} us. As Barth puts it: "If we do not wish to end by really defining ourselves, when we think that we are defining God, we can only take the second way and therefore hold fast to the incomprehensible majesty in which God meets us in His revelation, the majesty of His as Father, Son and Holy Spirit."*[39]

* Karl Barth, op. cit., p. 33

We find Karl Heim placing a great deal of emphasis on the Transcendence of God. In the preface to his book entitled, <u>God Transcendent</u>, Heim has this to say: "In the dispute concerning the relation between God and racial distinctions, the old question of the transcendence of God has again become prominent.

---

38. Davis, "Some Theological Continuities," p. 209: "To the student of Christian thought Barth's transcendentalism is essentially a philosophical conception of God. . . . Influenced by the Platonic tradition of a transcendental deity lifted high above the corruptness of phenomenality, they introduced this same emphasis into the stream of Christian thought. Their God was also a high God, far removed from earth, transcendent, indescribable, unknowable, hidden, coming into touch with men only through an intermediary, who, for most of them, was found in the Logos who was Christ."

39. Davis, "Some Theological Continuities," pp. 210–211: "Such statements from Origen, Clement, Minucius Felix, as well as Justin Martyr, make it clear that in the early Christian centuries thinkers thought of God as the 'Wholly Other,' just as Rudolph Otto and Karl Barth are doing in contemporary times. As many of the early Christians proclaimed the utter separation of the high God and the world, so now does Barth. The two are totally unlike and exclusive. At no point does God touch the external world with its corrupted nature and evil matter. No part of the world is, therefore, a manifestation or revelation of the infinite, majestic Deity. Here 'otherness' implies 'exclusive separation.' . . . Through no experience of ours can we find God, nor through any effort of our minds can we comprehend him. We are complete aliens until he wills to give himself to us. As Barth puts it pointedly: 'If we do not wish to end by really defining ourselves, when we think that we are defining God, we can only take the second way and therefore hold fast to the *incomprehensible* majesty in which God meets us in His revelation, the majesty of His person as Father, Son and Holy Spirit.'"

The question has emerged, This power enclosing me, this world of concrete reality, is it the Divine? Or is there, between the highest which this world can show and God Himself, always a deep gulf, across which we can throw no bridge from our side, which must be bridged, if at all, by God Himself, without our aid? . . . What is the truth about the transcendence of God, and how is this transcendence different from any transcendence within the sphere of this world?"*[40] Heim feels that God is so transcendent that no earthly analogy can adequately convey his being. Heim makes no attempt to prove that such a God exists; for he has demonstrated that such a procedure would be fruitless. A God so transcendent as the God of the Bible can only be known as he reveals himself, as he speaks his {Word.}[41]

15 Jan
1952

* Heim, God Transcendent, p. 185.

Jesus

Concerning Jesus, the crisis theologians are always true to the conviction that Jesus was God entering human flesh. Jesus is held to be the reconciler between God and man. Jesus id God steping in the place of mere man so that man can step in the place of God. He changes the majesty of the Godhead to come into human life. This is what Barth calls a change of parts between God and man. According to this view there is no salvation outside of Jesus Christ. The very title of Brunner's book, The Mediator, reveals the exalted position to which these men raise Jesus. He is the Mediator between God and man. As Brunner says, "Jesus was eternity entering into time in order that time may become eternal."†

When we turn to the positive teaching of Heim, we

† Brunner, The Mediator, p. 13

---

40. Horton, *Contemporary Continental Theology*, p. 130: "The connection of ideas is real, and is indicated in the author's preface: 'In the dispute concerning the relation between God and racial distinctions, the old question of the transcendence of God has again become prominent. The question has emerged, This power enclosing me, this world of concrete reality, is it the Divine? Or is there, between the highest which this world can show and God Himself, always a deep gulf, across which we can throw no bridge from our side, which must be bridged, if at all, by God Himself, without our aid? . . . What is the truth about the transcendence of God, and how is this transcendence different from any transcendence within the sphere of this world?'"

41. Horton, *Contemporary Continental Theology*, p. 133: "Heim makes no attempt to prove that such a God exists; for he has demonstrated that such a procedure would be fruitless. A God so transcendent as the God of the Bible can only be known as he reveals himself, as he speaks his Word."

find that his message centers in three epithets describing the work of Christ: Jesus as Lord and Leader (Fuehrer), Jesus as Savior from sin (Versohner), and Jesus as Deliverer of the world from the powers of darkness and death (Weltvollender).[42] Heim places a great deal of emphasis on these three aspects of the work of Christ, and like the other crisis theologians he sees Christ as the center of history.

Man

In the thinking of the crisis theologians there is a basic pessimism about man. They argue that man lost his likeness of God in the fall. In his present condition man is absolutely hopeless and helpless. Barth goes so far as to say that the image of God was totally effaced in the fall. Brunner, being less radical, sees a bit of the image of God left in man. But they both agree that man in his fallen state has had both his reason and will corrupted. He cannot will anything good without the help of God. All of his thinking ends in contradictions. So far is he in the valley of depravity that only God can pull him out. "Man is suspended between heaven and hell and can only wait on God to move him up or down."

Although reason may be helpful to man in his everyday round of existence, it is totally incapable of helping him reach ultimate reality. "The reason sees the small and the larger but not the large. It sees the preliminary but not the final, the derived but not the original, the complex but not the simple."* Christianity is a religion set apart from all other religions and rests upon what God does for man, including self-disclosure in a supernatural way and not upon man's searching. The anguish is still there until the complete surrender is made. The "Word of God" must take possession. The Word is in essence the same as Luther proclaimed in his Christological emphasis. Thus, again, the reaffirmation of a long tradition: man the sinner, man a derelict, who is bedeviled by his thoughts and ever helpless until he becomes pos-

* Barth, The Word of God and The Word of Man, p. 1.

---

42. Horton, *Contemporary Continental Theology*, p. 134: "The message centers in three epithets describing the work of Christ: Jesus as *Lord* and *Leader* (Fuehrer), Jesus as Savior from sin (*Versöhner*), and Jesus as *Deliverer* of the world from the powers of darkness and death (*Weltvollender*)."

sessed by a transrational experience of otherness. Here we can see the direct influence of existentialism on the thinking of the crisis theologians. It seems the Kierkegaard has arisen from the grave. For these men Biblicism takes the place of even the most exalted type of ordinary reason and experience. Philosophers and theologians are mere playboys sporting with the fad of reason. A Christian builds on faith not reason, faith is higher than reason. All of this is said to substantiate the view of the impotence of man. As Barth so often says: "God is in Heaven and man is on earth." As Kierkegaard said long before, "there is a qualitative difference between God and man."

Revelation

For the crisis theologians revelation is the elemental and indispensable condition of any saving work in man. Moreover it is the indispensable avenue of knowledge of God. Revelation for these thinkers means God himself coming to man. It is always a movement from God to man rather than from man to God. These thinkers place so much emphasis on revelation that their theology is often referred to as the "theology of the word of God." We only think, seek and know God by his word. The Word is directly God's work. In it "<u>Deus dixit</u>"; "God speaks." In it God gives or reveals himself to man.[43]

The Word of revelation, from the Barthian point of view has three principle forms: the spoken word of the preacher; the written word of the Scripture from which the preacher's word is derived and by which it is controlled; and finally, the revealed Word of God to which the spoken and written word are only human testimonies. Concretely, this revealed Word is Jesus Christ, the Word made flesh, in whom the majesty of God took on the form of a servant, and so remained veiled in the very act of revelation.

In his early days Brunner agreed absolutely with Barth on the question of revelation. But in a later

---

43. Davis, "Some Theological Continuities," p. 213: "Suffice it to say here that whatever else the Word of God is to him [Barth], it is the elemental and indispensable condition of any saving work in man. The Word is directly God's work. In it '*Deus dixit*'; 'God speaks.' In it God gives or reveals himself to man."

book he shows that it is at the point of natural revelation that he breaks with Barth. While passing we
may list the points at which Brunner breaks with
Barth. Brunner seeks to make it clear in his pamphlet, <u>Nature and Grace</u>, why he could no longer follow Barth all the way. It seemed to him that Barth was
drawing, from six fundamental truths a series of unwarranted logical deductions, which plunged him
into absurdity: (1) From the truth that man is a sinner, who can only be saved by divine grace, he was
deducing that the image of God in man is completely
obliterated by the Fall. (2) From the truth that Scriptural revelation is the sole norm of our knowledge of
God and the sole source of our salvation, he was deducing that there was no general revelation of God in
nature, conscience and history. (3) From the truth
that we must acknowledge the grace of the Lord Jesus
Christ as the only saving grace, he was deducing that
there was no expression of God's grace in the creation
and preservation of the world. From the same truth
he was deducing (4) that there was no expression of
the divine will in the so-called "law of nature" embodied in the basic social institutions; (5) no <u>Anknupf-
ungspunkt</u> (point of contact) or "divine image" in
human nature to which divine grace could make its
appeal; and (6) no developmental relations between
nature and grace, the natural man and the new man
in Christ, but only one of "substitution."[44]

More than anything else Brunner was pleading for
natural revelation, that which Barth was unwilling to
accept. He saw that without natural revelation there

---

44. Horton, *Contemporary Continental Theology*, p. 112: "Brunner then proceeded to make
clear, in the aforesaid pamphlet, *Nature and Grace*, why he could no longer follow Barth all the
way. It seemed to him that Barth was drawing, from six fundamental truths . . . a series of
unwarranted logical deductions, which plunged him into absurdity: (1) From the truth that man
is a sinner, who can only be saved by divine grace, he was deducing that the image of God in man
is completely obliterated by the Fall. (2) From the truth that Scriptural revelation is the sole norm
of our knowledge of God and the sole source of our salvation, he was deducing that there was no
general revelation of God in nature, conscience and history. (3) From the truth that we must
acknowledge the grace of the Lord Jesus Christ as the only saving grace, he was deducing that
there was no expression of God's grace in the creation and preservation of the world. From the
same truth he was deducing (4) that there was no expression of the divine will in the so-called
'law of nature' embodied in the basic social institutions; (5) no *Anknüpfungspunkt* (point of contact)
or 'divine image' in human nature to which divine grace could make its appeal; and (6) no developmental relations between nature and grace, the natural man and the new man in Christ, but
only one of 'substitution' (*Ersetzung*)."

could be no responsibility. Even the unbeliever has some connection with God, and is therefore responsible. In other words Brunner makes some room for the "I." There is something that man can do. However all crisis theologians agree that revelation is a movement from God to man and never man to God.

Conclusion

From our foregoing survey we have seen that there is no single continental theology. It would be as fallacious to set forth such an assumption as it would be to speak of a single political system on the continent. What is most commonly meant by the "Continental" point of view is the Barthian point of view; or else, more broadly, the new Protestant orthodoxy which Brunner, Heim, Aulen, and Lecerf all share with Barth in spite of their differences.[45] But if we take this new uncompromising Protestantism as the one clear expression of the "Continental" point of view, it becomes necessary to classify all Orthodox and Catholic theology as un-Continental. We must see that the Eastern Orthodox and Roman Catholic churches of the Continent have made sufficiently vital contributions to contemporary Christian thought to be included in any concept of "contemporary Continental theology."[46]

Let it be stated that there is a great deal that we a {as} westerners can learn through a sympathetic study of Continental theology. Experience has shown that some of the richest insights into religious truth came when two groups of Christians with contrasting backgrounds wrestle with one another over some funda-

---

45. Horton, *Contemporary Continental Theology*, p. 215: "It needs no argument, after our survey . . . to prove that there is no such thing as a single 'Continental theology.' . . . What is most commonly meant by the 'Continental' point of view is the Barthian point of view; or else, more broadly, the new Protestant orthodoxy which Brunner, Heim, Aulén, and Lecerf all share with Barth in spite of their differences."

46. Horton, *Contemporary Continental Theology*, pp. 216–217: "But if we take this new uncompromising Protestantism as the one clear expression of the 'Continental' point of view, it becomes necessary to classify all Orthodox and Catholic theology as un-Continental. . . . I believe that the Eastern Orthodox and Roman Catholic churches of the Continent have made sufficiently vital contributions to contemporary Christian thought so that our concept of 'contemporary Continental theology' should include Orthodox and Catholic theology."

mental issue, candidly but respectfully, listening for the word God may be seeking to convey to them through their theological adversaries. I am sure that Continental theology has something to contribute to Anglo-American theology, just because it cuts across our accustomed ways of thinking, and because it refuese to be drawn over into our system of thought of {or} comprehended in terms of our categories.[47] I am convinced, moreover, that the sympathetic study of Continental theology will tend to deepen, correct and steady our faith: At the point where we face the mystery of the future, the mystery of human destiny. We in the Anglo-Saxon world, securely relying upon our vast natural resources, our highly developed science and technology, and our fairly stable social institutions, have been thinking and talking far too glibly about the Kingdom of God as of something that we might hope to "bring in" by our own human efforts. Half unconsciously, we have been confusing the ancient hope of the coming of God's Kingdom with the modern doctrine of progess.[48] Have not we depended too much on man and too little on God?

On every hand our Continental brothers are calling up back to the depths of the Christian faith. They warn us that we too easily capitulated to modern culture. Is that not true? Somehow we must rethink many of our so-called liberal theological concepts. Take the doctrine of man. There is a strong tendency in liberal Protestantism toward sentimentality about man. Man who has come so far in wisdom and dencency may be expected to go much further as his methods of attaining and applying knowledge are im-

---

47. Horton, *Contemporary Continental Theology*, pp. xiv–xv: "Experience has shown that some of the richest insights into religious truth come when two groups of Christians with contrasting backgrounds wrestle with one another over some fundamental issue, candidly but respectfully, listening for the word that God may be seeking to convey to them through their theological adversaries. . . . I am sure that Continental theology has something to contribute to Anglo-American theology, just *because* it cuts across our accustomed ways of thinking, *because* it refuses to be drawn over into our system of thought or comprehended in terms of our categories."

48. Horton, *Contemporary Continental Theology*, pp. xv–xvi: "I am convinced that the sympathetic study of Continental theology will tend to deepen, correct and steady our faith: at the point where we face the mystery of the future, the mystery of human destiny. We in the Anglo-Saxon world, securely relying upon our vast natural resources, our highly developed science and technology, our relatively sheltered military situation, and our still fairly stable social institutions, have been thinking and talking far too glibly about the Kingdom of God as of something that we might hope to 'bring in' by our own human efforts. Half unconsciously, we have been confusing the ancient Christian hope of the coming of God's Kingdom with the modern doctrine of progress."

proved. This conviction was put into a phrase by an outstanding Humanist: "The supreme value and self perfectibility of man."* Although such ethical religion is humane and its vision a lofty one, it has obvious shortcomings. This particular sort of optimism has been discredited by the brutal logic of events. Instead of assured progress in wisdom and decency man faces the ever present possibility of swift relapse not merely to animalism but into such calculated cruelty as no other animal can practice.

Maybe man is more of a sinner than liberals are willing to admit. I realize that the sinfullness of man is often over-emphasized by some continental theologians, but at least we must admit that many of the ills of the world are due to plain sin. The tendency on the part of some liberal theologians to see sin as a mere "lay of nature" which will be progressively eliminated as man climbs the evolutionary ladder seems to me quite perilous. I will readily agree that many of man's shortcomings are due to natural necessities, but ignorance and finiteness and hampering circumstances, and the pressure of animal impulse, are all insufficient to account for many of man's shortcomings. We have to recognize that man has misused his kingly prerogative as a social animal by making others bear the burden of his selfishness. Only the one who sits on the peak of his intellectual ivory tower looking unrealisitically with his rosey colored glasses on the scene of life can fail to see this fact. The word sin must come back into our vocabulary.

Again the continental theologians call us back to the dimension of depth in the Bible. This {is} not to say that the critical approach to the study of Scripture must be disregarded. But it does mean that Biblical criticism must remain a means, not an end. Too many liberals have been so involved in "higher Criticism" that they failed to see the vital issues of the Christian faith. After one has gone through the whole process of Biblical criticism, he must be able to answer the question, "what then?" We must see the Bible as both the Word of God and the Word of Man. The Bible is more than a piece of historical literature, as many liberals would reduce it to; it is a personal word from a living God. We may wish to supplement Barth's exclusive emphasis upon God's self revelation in Scripture with a corrective emphasis upon tradition, reason or Christian experience, but we must agree that the Biblical revelation is classic and normative for Christian

* C. F. Potter, <u>Humanism A New Religion</u>, p. 14.

137

thought; it is the central pillar on which the whole structure of Christian theology must rest.

Does this mean that we must all go Barthian? No, no that. I have studied Barth quite sympathetically; but I am as far as ever from being a Barthian. What I wish to commend to you is that there is a great corrective and great challenge in this theology of crisis.[49] It calls us back to the depths of the Christian faith. Of course we are not to accept all of their conclusions, for many of them are one-sided generalizations, but at least we can accept the good that they have to offer. "They do insist that religion begins with God and that men cannot have faith apart from him. They do stress the fact that faith is not a rational achievement, but a passionate belief that divine Reality is such as we find in Jesus Christ. They do suggest that man is not sufficient into himself for life, but is dependent upon the proclamation of God's living Word, through which, by means of Bible, preacher, and revealed Word, God himself comes to the consciences of men. They do proclaim that apart from God our human efforts turn to ashes and our sunrises into darkest night."[50] Much of this is good, may we not not accept it.

Bibliography

1. Aubrey, E. E., Present Theological Tendencies. Harpers, 1936.
2. Aulen, G., Christus Victor. Macmillan, 1931.
3. Barth, K., The Word of God and The Word of Man. Pilgrim Press, 1928.
4. ———The Doctrine of the Word of God. T. and T. Clark, 1936.
5. Berdyaev, N., The Meaning of History. Scribners, 1936.
6. ———The Destiny of Man. Scribners, 1937.
7. Brunner, E., The Mediator. Macmillan, 1934.

---

49. Horton, *Contemporary Continental Theology*, p. xix: "'So you think we must all go Barthian, after all?' No, not that. I have met Karl Barth personally . . . but I am as far as ever from being a Barthian. What I wish to commend to the . . . Anglo-Saxon world is not just Barth's 'Theology of Crisis,' but the great, multiform movement of Christian thought which has emerged simultaneously within the various Continental churches . . . and which bears the general character of *a* theology of crisis."

50. This quotation is from Davis, "Some Theological Continuities," pp. 217–218.

8. ———Natur und Gnade. Tubingen, Mohr, 1935.   2 Apr
9. Heim, K., God Transcendent. Scribners, 1935.   1952
10. Mackintosh, H. R., Types of Modern Theology. Nisbet, 1937.
11. Maritain, J., Freedom in the Modern World. Scribners, 1936.
12. ———Humanisme Integral, Paris, Aubier, 1936.
13. Nygrene, A., Agape and Eros. Macmillan, 1932

THDS. MLKP-MBU: Box 112.

"Reinhold Niebuhr"

[*2 April 1952*]
[*Boston, Mass.*]

King prepared this outline for an oral report in DeWolf's Seminar in Systematic Theology. Although King agrees with Niebuhr's assessment of the "inevitable sterility of the humanistic emphasis," he criticizes Niebuhr's agnosticism as "unchristian."[1] King expanded these ideas in a later essay for the Dialectical Society.[2]

1. Biographical Sketch:
Born: June 21, 1892 in Wright City, Mo. Ed. Elmhurst (Ill.) coll., 1910; Eden Theo. Sem., 1912; Yale Divinity Sch., B.D. 1914, A.M. 1915. D.D. Ginwell coll. 1936, Weslyan coll., 1937, U. of Pa., 1938, Amherst, 1941, Yale, 1942, Oxford, 1943, Harvard, 1944, Hobart coll., 1948; LLD. Occidental coll., 1945; D.D. Princeton Univ., 1946, Glasgow Univ, 1947, New York Univ., 1947. Ordained ministry Evang. Synod of North America, 1915; pastor at Detroit, 1915–28; asso. prof. philos. of religion,

---

1. Reinhold Niebuhr (1892–1971) was one of the most influential figures in American religious and political thought in the twentieth century. He received his B.D. (1914) and M.A. (1915) from Yale Divinity School. After pastoring a church in a working-class section of Detroit for thirteen years, Niebuhr began teaching at Union Theological Seminary in 1928, where he remained for the rest of his life. A politically active socialist during the 1920s and 1930s, he was editor of *The World Tomorrow*, the journal of the Socialist party. As a founder of the journal *Christianity and Crisis* and of the political group Americans for Democratic Action, he was an influential proponent of Christian or liberal realism. Among his voluminous writings are *Does Civilization Need Religion?* (1927), *Moral Man and Immoral Society* (1932), *Reflections on the End of an Era* (1934), *An Interpretation of Christian Ethics* (1935), *The Nature and Destiny of Man* (1941–1943), and *Faith and History* (1949). For more information, see *Reinhold Niebuhr: His Religious, Social, and Political Thought*, ed. Charles W. Kegley and Robert W. Bretall (New York: Macmillan, 1956); and Richard Wrightman Fox, *Reinhold Niebuhr* (New York: Pantheon Books, 1985).

2. See King, "The Theology of Reinhold Niebuhr," April 1953–June 1954, pp. 269–279 in this volume.

Union Theo. Sem., 1928–30, prof. applied Christianity since 1930. In the early years of his training Niebuhr was greatly impressed with religious liberalism. Soon, however, he came to feel that the predominating theological liberalism of his time was not relevant to the concrete problems of life and daily experience.

2. Influences affecting his Thought:
Deeply influenced in his pastoral years by the plight of the worker in the Ford plant.[3] Theological influences; Luther, Calvin, Augustine. Philosophical influences: Hegel (dialectics); Marxism; Heidegger; Kierkegaard.[4]

3. Most Important Ideas:

(1) The Construction of Dialectical Theology: There is forever a dialectual tension between time and eternity. The whole of Christianity must be stated dialectically. The thesis of the Christian ethic is the endless possibilities for the fulfillment of brotherhood in history. This is the "wisdom of the cross". The antithesis is the "foolishness of the cross". Original sin makes the fulfillment of the rule of agape love impossible. The synthesis is "the power of the cross". Through faith and justification resources of grace are made accessible to the individual who remains within the pincers of the dialectic.

(2) Anthropology: There are three aspects of human experience which distinguish the Christian view of man from all other views. (1) "It emphasizes the height of self transcendence in man's spiritual stature in its doctrine of image of God". (2) It insists on man's weakness, dependence, and finiteness . . . . . regarding this finiteness, as, of itself a source of evil in man. (3) It affirms that the evil in man is a consequence of his inevitable, though not necesarry unwillingness, to acknowledge his dependence". (NDM, I, 150).[5]

(3) Sin: "Sin is occasioned precisely by the fact that man refuses to admit his creatureliness. . . . . He pretends to be more than he is". (NDM, I, 16). Both the fall of man and original sin are accepted by Niebuhr as mythological categories to explain the universality of sin.

---

3. King's earlier draft is more expansive: "As the result of his pastoral work among the workers in the Ford plant, and of his own social observation, Niebuhr came to comprehend the profoundly tragic and contradictory character of human nature as manifested in social and economic relationships. It was here that he developed his profound and personal interest and concern in the exploited classes of capitalist society" ("Draft, Reinhold Niebuhr," 2 April 1952, MLKP-MBU: Box 115).

4. After the word "Marxism" King wrote in the rough draft: "(Marx is wise in understanding that men always demand more than either security requires or justice permits, and so must be restrained by force or power.)"

5. King refers to Reinhold Niebuhr, *The Nature and Destiny of Man*, vol. 1 (New York: Scribner, 1941), p. 150.

(4) <u>Philosophy of History</u>: The final problem of history becomes the fact that "before God no man living is justified".[6] Since it is impossible to act in accord with the ethical ideals of Christianity in history, the problems of grace, judgement and redemption become crucial ones.

(5) <u>Christology</u>:[7] Christ is the moral absolute which stands outside of history to exhaust the freedom of man but sufficiently in history to clarify history's possibilities and limitations.

(6) <u>God</u>: God is Creator, Judge, and Redeemer. Yet God's existence and nature are inexplicable and incomprehensible to man. Because of his limitation man can never understand the ways of God.[8]

4. <u>Critical Evaluation</u>:

The merit of Niebuhr is that, seeing the problem of our age in its proper relations and dimensions, and laying firm hold on ultimate principles, he sets forth with rigour and profundity in analysis and criticism the fundamental weaknesses and inevitable sterility of the humanistic emphasis. Yet we may ask if Niebuhr's views are as orthodox and Biblical as he assumes them to be.[9] We may also question his agnosticism as to the nature of God as being unchristian.

THDS. MRP-GAMK.

---

6. There is an additional sentence in the draft: "Good can never triumph over evil in history, due to the limitations of human nature."

7. In the draft this section begins, "Christ is the moral solution to the predicament of man."

8. The citation in the draft is "NDM, I, 163, 170, 258–59."

9. Walter G. Muelder, "Reinhold Niebuhr's Conception of Man," *The Personalist* 26 (July 1945): 284: "In commenting on Niebuhr's claims it may be said at the outset that his views are probably less orthodox and certainly less Biblical than he assumes them to be."

"Reinhold Niebuhr's Ethical Dualism"

9 May 1952
[*Boston, Mass.*]

In this essay for DeWolf's Seminar in Systematic Theology, King examines Niebuhr's views both on the role of love and justice in society and on the tension between individual and corporate ethics. He agrees with Niebuhr's critique of the most idealistic forms of perfectionism but criticizes his pessimism about the transforming power of agape. "He is right," King wrote, "in insisting that we must be realistic regarding the relativity of every moral and ethical choice," but Niebuhr failed "to see that the availability of the divine <u>Agape</u> is an essential affirmati[on] of the Christian religion." DeWolf gave the essay an A − and commented: "Excellent interpretation and exposition. I wish the critical evaluation had been carried further. The beginning looked promising."

9 May
1952

One of the perennial problems facing the ethical theorist is to find the relation between individual and group ethics. Certainly there is no easy solution. However, a few thinkers have courageously faced this difficult problem. Among those in the modern world to face this problem is the brilliant and influential theologian, Reinhold Niebuhr. In partly solving this problem he resorts to a formula of "dualistic ethics." In the present paper, it is our purpose to discuss this ethical dualism in the thinking of Niebuhr.

Factors Leading to Ethical Dualism

For some years a minister in Detroit under the shadow of the Ford factories, Niebuhr was overwhelmed by the appalling injustices evident in modern industrial civilization, and particularly by the concentration of power and resources in the hands of a relatively small wealthy class. Economic power, he declared, in modern society has "become the source of more injustice than any other, because the private ownership of the productive processes and the increased centralization of the resultant power in the hands of a few, make inevitably for irresponsiblity."* Adequate housing for the poor "can never be initiated within the limits of private enterprise." Social work itself accepts "philanthropy as a substitute for real justice," and though it pretends to be scientific is little better than the "most sentimental religious generosity."† Irresponsible power leads inevitably to injustice "no matter how intelligent the person who wields it." Hence the real problem cannot be solved by increasing social intelligence and humanitarian sentiments, but "only by setting the power of the exploited against the exploiters."‡ In industrial society "equalitarianism becomes a more and more compelling social philosophy" because of inequality which periodically results in economic chaos. And though the workers may in due time "develop a social strategy which will horrify every middle-class indealist," it is to the modern proletarian that "the future in an industrial civilization undoubtedly belongs."§

Along with all of this Niebuhr noticed a terrible contrast between "moral man and immoral society." He observed a great distinction between the relatively decent, good behavior of man as an individual and

* CRSW, 77

† CRSW, 80

‡ Ibid, 82

§ Ibid, 83, 84, 87

man as society. His analysis of this contrast led him to the roots of the contradiction of human nature. He cogently states,

> Individual men may be moral in the sense that they are able to consider interests other than their own in determining problems of conduct, and are capable, on occasion, of preferring the advantages of others to their own . . . But all these achievements are more difficult, if not impossible, for human societies and social groups. In every human group there is less reason to guide and to check impulse, less capacity for self transcendence, less ability to comprehend the need of others and therefore more unrestrained egoism than the individuals, who compose the groups, reveal in their personal relationships.*

* MMIS, 11, 12

In these words, Nieburh stresses the fact of the morality of man the individual, and the immorality of man the collective. Man the individual is natively equipped with certain unselfish impulses.† He also has a conscience which is his sense of obligation to what he judges to be good. And yet, when men engage in collective activity they are overwhelmed by moral inability. The goodness of the individual man in his immediate relationships disappears when he acts as a member of a group.‡

† Ibid, 25 ff.

‡ Ibid, 14, 34 ff.

Niebuhr came to see that reason could never solve the problem. While he concludes that reason may restrain natural egoism,§ and guide the imagination cinto productive channels‖ and harmonize conflicting impulses;# he insists that it cannot compete in power with the impulses and that it must, therefore, be combined with emotion and will.** Furthermore, he thinks that reason is unconsciously the instrument of egoism.
It becomes the agent of egoism under the impression that it is transcending it.††

§ Ibid, 37
‖ Ibid, 27f; CRSW, 68ff.
Ibid, 28f

** REE, 264f

†† MMIS, 95

Niebuhr came to see that the complexity which results from this conflict between individual morality and societal morality is staggering, and all hope of finding a simple moral program to cover both the individual and collective mind vanishes. The group lacks the organs of sensitivity of the individual. It is at this point that Niebuhr turns to ethical dualism as a way out.

Agape, which remains a law for the individual as a vertical reference, must suffer in purity when taken into social relations. Agape is at best a regulative social norm.‡‡ It sets the outside definition of ideal jus-

‡‡ ICE, 149

tice as well as tempering whatever realistic means must be employed to dynamite recalcitrant centers of pride and injustice. Love remains a leaven in society, permeating the whole and giving texture and consistency to life. The balanced Christian, therefore, must be both loving and realistic. As an individual who in moments of prayerful self-transcendence has been justified by faith, he given final allegiance to Christ; but as an individual in complex social relations he must realistically meet mind with mind and power with power. In life two perspectives always vie for primacy.

One focus is in the inner life of the individual, and

> the other in the necessities of man's social life. From the perspective of the individual the highest ideal is unselfishmess. Society must strive for justice even if it is forced to use means, such as self-assertion, resistance, coercion and perhaps resentment, which cannot gain the moral sanction of the most sensitive moral spirit. The individual must strive to realize his life by losing and finding himself in something greater than himself.*

* MMIS, 257

The Christian, being in though not of this world, is never fully free from the complexities of acting as a vicar of Christ in his intentional life and a social and political agent in his actual life. The more aggressively one relates the gospel to life, the more sensitively he realizes that the social unit can accommodate only justice, not <u>agape</u>.†

† ICE, 144f

<u>Agape</u> is always a possibility/impossibility. It remains perennially relevant in society as the regulative principle of morals, but it is realized in society only through infinite degrees of justice. Niebuhr states:

> A rational analysis reveals both the ideal possibility and the actual situation from which one must begin. In that sense there are really two natural laws—that which reason commands ultimately and the compromise which reason makes with the contingent and arbitrary forces of human existence. The ideal possibility is really an impossibility, a fact to which both Stoic and Christian doctrine do justice by the myth of the Golden Age in Stoic doctrine and the age of perfection before the Fall in Christian doctrine. The ideal is an impossibility because both the contingencies of nature and the sin in the human heart prevent men from ever living in that perfect freedom and equality which the whole logic of the moral life demands. . . . yet this impossibility is not one which can be relegated

simply to the world of transcendence. It offers immediate possibilities of a higher good in every given situation.*

* Ibid, 147–148. "The Christian religion is thus an ethical religion in which the optimism, necessary for the ethical enterprise, and the pessimism, consequent upon profound religious insights, never achieve a perfect equilibrium or harmony." REE, 213

† ICE, 51

‡ MMIS, 48

Niebuhr freely admits that justice is morally inferior to equality in love, but one still has the moral responsibility to choose a "second best." One must realistically adjust himself to the fact that the ethic which controls the individual cannot inform the group. The individual ethic "is oriented by only one vertical religious reference, to the will of God; and the will of God is defined in terms of all-inclusive love."† Consequently, the group lacks the organs of self-transcendence to understand <u>agape</u>. And "the larger the group the more difficult it is to achieve a common mind and purpose and the more inevitably will it be unified by momentary impulses and immediate and unreflective purposes."‡ Justice is a this-worldly value; <u>agape</u> is an eternal value which only the initiated understand and strive for.

Niebuhr makes it quite clear, however, that justice is never discontinuously related to love. Justice is a negative application of love. Whereas love seeks out the needs of others, justice limits freedom to prevent its infringement upon the rights and privileges of others. Justice is a check (by force, if necessary) upon ambitions of individuals seeking to overcome their own insecurity at the expense of others. Justice is love's message for the collective mind.[1]

> In a struggle between those who enjoy inordinate privileges and those who lack the basic essentials of the good life it is fairly clear that a religion which holds love to be the final law of life stuptifies itself if it does not support equal justice as a political and economic approximation of the ideal of love . . . The relativity of all moral ideals cannot absolve us of the necessity and duty of choosing between relative values; and that the choice is sometimes so clear as to become an imperative one.§

Niebuhr senses that neither liberal nor orthodox Christianity has fully understood the relation between love, justice, and a dualistic theory of ethics. Orthodoxy, while properly sensing the inevitability of

---

1. DeWolf commented at the bottom of this paragraph, "Good, clear exposition."

sin in the world and the consequent defeat of pure love as a moral force, inclines to be pessimistic about the cultural possibilities of love. It tends to withdraw from the world in preference to interacting in it. Christian orthodoxy "failed to derive any significant politico-moral principles from the law of love . . . It therefore destroyed a dynamic relationship between the ideal of love and the principles of justice."* Orthodoxy has not yet found the exact relation of justice to love. Individual perfection is too often made an end in itself.

The liberal ethic, contends Niebuhr, is a religious expression of the Renaissance fallacy. Enlightened on the law of love, but insensitive to the inevitability of sin in history, liberalism vainly seeks to overcome justice though purely moral and rational suasions. "The unvarying refrain of the liberal church in its treatment of politics is that love and cooperation are superior to conflict and coercion, and that therefore they must be and will be established."† Liberalism confuses the ideal itself with the realistic means which must be employed to coerce society into an approximation of that ideal. Perfect justice will not come by a simple statement of the moral superiority of brotherhood in the world, for men are controlled by power, not mind alone. This liberalism failed to see. He states:

† ICE, 176

> If the liberal Church had had less moral idealism and more religious realism its approach to the political problem would have been less inept and fatuous. Liberal solutions of the social problem never take the permanent difference between man's collective behavior and the moral ideals of an individual life into consideration. Very few seem to recognize that even in the individual there is a law in his members which wars against the law that is in his mind.‡

‡ Ibid, 178–179

The Inevitability of Government

Just as the Christian must become realistic in ethics, so, Niebuhr contends, he must become realistic in his attitude toward the power which employs force to coerce justice. If <u>agape</u> were a historical reality in the lives of men, government, ideally, would be unnecessary, since forceful suasions are irrelevant wherever a love for God is perfected. The man who loves will

naturally prefer the needs and securities of his neigh-
bor. Actually, however, government is very necessary,
for men inevitably corrupt their potentialities of love
through a lust for self-security which outruns natural
needs. Men must be restrained by force, else they will
swallow up their neighbors in a desperate effort to
make themselves secure. In this sense government is
approved of God. "Government is divinely ordained
and morally justified because a sinful world would,
without the restraints of the state, be reduced to anarchy by its evil lusts."* The force of sinfulness is so
stubborn a characteristic of human nature that it can
only be restrained when the social unit is armed with
both moral and physical might.

* REE, 220

Niebuhr makes it quite clear that government, although holy as an instrument for restraining the sinful, must never be looked upon as divine. The individuals reverence for government extends only as far
as the purpose for which that unit was created. When
the government pretends to be divine, the Christian
serves God rather than man. The Christian must constantly maintain a "dialectical" attitude toward government while the collective ego remains within its
bounds, while being critical whenever these bounds
are overpassed.

While Niebuhr contends that the ambiguity of government is deeply embedded in every conceivable political form, he makes it clear that some political cohesions expose a greater surface of self-criticism than
others. Critical insight reveals, he affirms, that the
most desirable cohesion is democracy, even as the
least desirable is totalitarianism. "For certainly one
perennial justification for democracy is that it arms
the individual with political and constitutional power
to resist the inordinate ambition of rulers, and to
check the tendency of the community ot achieve order at the price of liberty."†

† CLCD, 46

Pragmatically, therefore, though not absolutely, democracy is the most satisfactory form of collective
rule. Its adequacy lies in the measure in which it realistically lends itself to the dialectical relation between time and eternity. "An adequate approach to
the social and moral problem must include a political
policy which will bring the most effective social check
upon conflicting egoistic impulses in society."‡ Democracy anticipates in its normal operation the right
of the individual to criticize the rules. Impeachment
is the final expression of this right.

‡ REE, 229

It is the highest achievement of democratic societies that they embody the principle of resistance to government within the principle of government itself. The citizen is thus armed with constitutional power to resist the unjust exaction of government. He can do this without creating anarchy within the community, if government has been so conceived that criticism of the rules becomes an instrument of better government and not a threat to government itself.*

* NDM, II, 268

Niebuhr admits that there is risk in arming men with the power of resistance, but he sees the alternative risk as worse. If society is not empowered with rights to free expression, it will explode from internal combustion.

Niebuhr makes it clear that a perfect democracy is just as impossible to reach as either a perfect society or a perfect individual. The evils of democracy are patent. The most self-evident is, according to Niebuhr, that democracy is founded on an initial deception. [*strikeout illegible*] {See paragraph at the end.}[2] Niebuhr sees the salvation of both democracy and capitalism in the continual reshuffling of its centers of power until a perceptible increase of justice and equality is evidenced.

Before closing this discussion, we might say just a word about Niebuhr's defense of the balance-of-power strategy. It might be remembered that Niebuhr's dialectic makes him unqualifiedly pessimistic about the future of things. "As long as the character and nature of man is not changed into something now quite unknown in human history, neither a new and more perfect social pedagogy nor a more perfect social organization will be able to eliminate all possibilities of injustice and conflict in human society."†

† REE, 243

But he is likewise unqualifiedly optimistic about our responsibility to maintain the best possible order as a "second best." This realistic compromise is the balance of power. Morally inferior to either a moral and rational form of collective cohesions or the community of love, it nevertheless is our only realistic expedient to promote justice. "The very essence of politics is the achievement of justice through equilibria of power. A balance of power is not conflict, but a tension between opposing forces underlies it. Where

2. King inserted this comment in the margin, drawing attention to it with an arrow.

* ICE, 189

there is tension there is potential conflict, and where there is conflict there is potential violence."*

The balance-of-power strategy turns on the inevitability of strife through a sinful assertion in both individual and collective minds. "The selfishness of human communities must be regarded as an inevitability. Where it is inordinate it can be checked only by competing assertions of interest."† Through the expedient of balancing power against power the pretensions of a collective ego are checked. One power is brought to bay through an equally ambitious power over against it. Balance of power "is in fact a kind of managed anarchy."‡

† MMIS, 272

‡ CLCD, 174

Since "no participant in a balance is ever quite satisfied with its own position,"§ the balance is always precarious. Niebuhr has no fond illusion either of the moral worth of this solution or of its resulting problems. The best he can proffer is a realistic approach to a wretchedly complex situation, believing only that within the terms of a dialectic balance of righteous and unrighteous insights can the probability of either anarchy or tyranny be lessened.

§ Ibid, 175

In the following remarkably concise way Hughley has charted Niebuhr's solution:‖

‖ Hughley, J. Neal, TPSI, 127

1. That the struggle for social justice is always involved in a contest of power. It is never a question or mere morality versus power

   (a) Because all contending groups lay claim to right; to morality, giving moral justification to their position or demands.

   (b) Because men are always power-seekers, even the most moral of them. Even their 'ideals' express themselves in a quest for power.

   (c) Because groups are even more concerned for power (less for morality) than individuals, and thus justice becomes a question of continual adjustment of group claims.

2. That the essence of social justice is a full consideration of the claims of all parties, with every system of justice resulting from compromise. No contending group can have all it wants or contends for, and hence must be restrained by force in its selfish aspiration.

3. That achievement of justice is dependent upon a relative equality of power (or balance of power), for

   (a) Where vast disproportions of power exist,

justice is a mockery—it becomes the will of the mighty. The system of order resulting is merely the law of the ruling power which never fully considers the claims of the weaker.

(b) Where equality of power exists all contenders get a hearing because the power of an opponent always tends to check one's pretensions and claims.

4. A structure of justice based on a balance of power is morally inferior to a community of love. But corrupt human nature will require a rough balance to the end of time. To imagine otherwise is to be victimized by illusions concerning man and social processes.

Conclusion

The strength of Dr. Niebuhr's position lies in its critique of the easy conscience and complacency of some forms of perfectionism.[3] He is right, it seems to me, in insisting that we must be realistic regarding the relativity of every moral and ethical choice. His analysis of the complexity of the social situation is profound indeed, and with it I would find very little to disagree. But there is one weakness in Niebuhr's ethical position which runs the whole gamut of his writings. This weakness lies in {the} inability of his system to deal adequately with the relative perfection which is the fact of the Christian life. How one can develop spiritually; by what powers Christian values are conceived in personality; and how the immanence of <u>Agape</u> is to be concretely conceived in human nature and history—all these problems are left unsolved by Niebuhr.[4] He fails to see that the availability of the divine <u>Agape</u> is an essential affirmatim of the Christian religion. In an article on Niebuhr's conception of

---

3. Walter G. Muelder, "Reinhold Niebuhr's Conception of Man," *The Personalist* 26 (July 1945): 291: "The strength of this position lies in its critique of the easy conscience and the complacency of some forms of perfectionism."

4. Muelder, "Reinhold Niebuhr's Conception of Man," pp. 291–292: "But its weakness resides in its inability to deal adequately with the relative perfection which is the fact of the Christian life. How there can be development in the spiritual life of the self; by what powers Christian values are conserved in personality; . . . and how the immanence of *Agape* in human nature and history is to be concretely conceived—all these issues are left unresolved."

man, Dean Muelder has made a statement that is well worth our quoting at this point.[5] He says:

> There is a Christian perfectionism which may be called a prophetic meliorism, which, while it does not presume to guarantee future willing, does not bog down in pessimistic imperfectionism. Niebuhr's treatment of much historical perfectionism is well-founded criticism from an abstract ethical viewpoint, but it hardly does justice to the constructive historical contributions of the perfectionist sects within the Christian fellowship and even within the secular order. There is a kind of Christian assurance which releases creative energy into the world and which in actual fellowship rises above the conflicts of individual and collective egoism.*

* Muelder, Art. (1945)

Despite this criticism, we must cordially thank Dr. Niebuhr for giving us a stimulating and profound ethical theory. It is an interpretation with which we must reckon, and contains much of permanent value.

BIBLIOGRAPHY

Hughley, J. Neal.—TPSI
Trends In Protestant Social Idealism.
New York: King's Crown Press, 1948.
Niebuhr, Reinhold.—CRSW
The Contribution of Religion to Social Work.
New York: Columbia University Press, 1930.
———. —MMIS
Moral Man and Immoral Society.
New York: Scribner's, 1933.
———. —REE
Reflections on the End of an Era.
New York: Scribner's, 1934.
———. —ICE
An Interpretation of Christian Ethics.
New York: Harpers, 1935.
———. —NDM
The Nature and Destiny of Man, 2 vols.
New York: Scribner's, 1941–1943.
———. —CLCD
The Children of Light and the Children of Darkness
New York: Scribners, 1944

---

5. At this time Walter G. Muelder was dean of Boston University's School of Theology.

Muelder, Walter.—Art(1945
"Reinhold Niebuhr's Conception of Man"
The Personalist, 36 (1945), 282–293.}[6]

THD. MLKP-MBU: Box 113.

---

6. The last two entries in the bibliography are in King's own hand.

Examination Answers,
History of Recent Philosophy

[*26 May–5 July 1952*]
[*Boston, Mass.*]

After finishing his first year at Boston University, King remained in Boston for a six-week summer session. In these answers for Richard M. Millard's course on the history of recent philosophy, King comments on an internal contradiction in Karl Marx's thought.[1] Marx, he writes, "starts with a high Kantian motivation which emphasizes the worth of the human personality as a means rather than an end" and concludes with a "rigid determinism" that eliminates freedom. This course work, one of King's few academic encounters with Marx, may have helped him prepare for a sermon he gave later in the summer at Ebenezer entitled "The Challenge of Communism to Christianity."[2] In his answers King also describes the philosophical ramifications of Charles Darwin's research, the topic of his term paper for the course.[3] Several words are missing because of torn pages in the manuscript. Millard gave the answers 94 points out of 100, an A.

---

1. Richard Marion Millard (1918–1992) received his A.B. in 1941 from DePauw University and his M.A. in 1942 and Ph.D. in 1950 from Boston University. He taught at Boston from 1949 to 1967, serving as chairman of the philosophy department, acting dean of the Graduate School, and dean of the College of Liberal Arts. He left Boston University for a career in public policy and postsecondary education, including a term as president of the Council on Postsecondary Accreditation from 1981 to 1987. His publications include *Personality and the Good: Psychological and Ethical Perspectives*, co-authored with Peter A. Bertocci (1963).

2. This sermon has not been located by the King Papers Project, but King published a version of it as "How Should a Christian View Communism?" in *Strength to Love* (New York: Harper & Row, 1963), pp. 93–100. For a reaction to King's Ebenezer sermon, see Melvin H. Watson to King, 14 August 1952, pp. 156–157 in this volume.

3. King, "The Influence of Darwinian Biology on Pragmatism with Special Emphasis on William James and John Dewey," 26 May–5 July 1952, MLKP-MBU: Box 115. In his analysis King appropriated extensively from Philip P. Wiener, *Evolution and the Founders of Pragmatism* (Cambridge, Mass.: Harvard University Press, 1949); and Morton Gabriel White, *The Origin of Dewey's Instrumentalism* (New York: Columbia University Press, 1943).

1. Herbert Spencer was a thoroughgoing agnostic when it came to knowledge of ultimate reality. For him all knowledge is finite. Only that which can be related and compared is knowable. The "Unknowable" being the totality cannot be known because there is nothing else with which it can be related or compared. Spencer made it clear that although we cant know the "Unknowable," we cant doubt its existence, for every judgment presuppose [*its*] existence. He use two [*word missing*] of evidence to establish [*word missing*] reality the "Unknowable" [*F*]irst there is the dialectical proof. It asserts that we must assume the existence of the unconditioned before we can talk about the conditioned. To say that something is knowable is to assume the existence of something unknowable. Second, there is the proof from experience. Experience itself affirms that there is something outside causing our sensation. Although the "Unknowable" cannot be known, its existence is the most familiar aspect of experience.

   It is interesting to note that Spencer's agnosticism was derived indirectly from Kant through the Scottish thinker Hamilton and Mansel.[4] Both of these men had taken the Kantian agnosticism and [*word missing*] to a justification of theology and [*word missing*] revelation. All knowledge is phenomen[*al*] and therefore metaphysical thinking is absurd and even impossible when it come to knowing ultimate reality. But if such a view denies the possibility of reason to meet ultimate question, it affirms the validity of revelation. As Hamilton affirmed, the limitation of philosophy is the justification of theology.

   Spencer's agnosticism differed from that of Mansel and Hamilton in the sense that it was not strictly theology. In other words he secularized the agnostic thinking of these two men.[5]

2. The internal contradiction in Marx thinking is found in the fact that he starts with a high Kantian motivation which emphasizes the worth of the human personality as a means rather than an end, and ends up with a thoroughgoing materialistic view which make mind only a by-product or an effect of matter (epiphenomenalism). Moreover, he ends up with a rigid determinism which destroys this validity of his initial Kantian motivation.

   The source of this contradiction in Marx' thought is found in the fact that he attempted to synthesis his Kantian motivation with a Hegelian methodology. At the same time he "turns Hegel upside down" by emphasizing the primacy of matter rather than spirit. So he was led to Dialectically materialism. He became a thoroughgoing economic determinist. History is moving inevitably toward the classless society. Nothing can stop its consumation. Such a view destroyes freedom, while the high Kantian motivation affirms it.

---

4. King refers to William Hamilton (1788–1856) and Henry Longueville Mansel (1820–1871), who were mentioned by Millard in a lecture on Herbert Spencer. See King, Class notes, History of Recent Philosophy, 26 May–5 July 1952, MLKP-MBU: Box 114.

5. Millard gave the answer 9 points and wrote: "However—did identify Unknowable as religious object. This asserted & even supports religion."

We may conclude then that Marx' attempt to combind the Hegelian methodology with his Kantian motivation caused the flagrant contradiction in his thinking.[6]

3. Metz statement that Darwin was no Darwinian is essentially true in the sense that Darwin never set out to establish any metaphysical or philosophical conclusions.[7] He wrote as a biologist and not as a metaphysician. The one exception of a deviation from his biological interest was his attempt to delve into ethical theory. But certainly Darwin never set forth many of the philosophical theories that later became attached to his system. A case in point is Herbert Spencer. After Darwin published his Origin of the Species Herbert Spencer welcomed it and proceeded to apply its underlying theories to the whole of society. We find Haelkel attempting to define everything in terms of the Darwinian theory of evolution along with the law of substance.[8] Many other examples could be cited. But these are adequate enough to show that many philosophical tenets developed from Darwins system that he never realized. So Metz is essentially right: "Darwin was no Darwinian.

There are mainly four reasons why Darwins evolutionary hypothesis raised such a furor.

(1) It seem to contradict the traditional view of the immutability of species.

(2) It contradicted those who accepted a literal account of the Bible.

(3) It seemed to take teleology from the universe. A first cause was also cast aside.

(4) It seemed to lessen man's status.

So we can see the Darwin's theory raised a deal of furor because it upset certan habits of mind. Of course most of the above accusation did not necessarily follow from the Darwinian hypothesis.[9]

4. There can be no gainsaying of the fact that Herbart's answer to the Kantian problem of the Ding an sich was the very antithesis of Hegel's answer.[10] Hegel solved the problem in terms of idealism, affirming that Reason was the thing in itself (the rational is the real and the real is the rational). Herbart, on the other hand, solved the problem in terms of realism. He was systematically opposed to Hegel's method, principles and conclusions. Things are not thoughts as the idealist Hegel would

---

6. Millard gave this answer 8.5 points and commented: "[word illegible] ideas (& ideals) have been used as instruments of exploitation too. Ideas are only reflections of economic material processes."

7. Millard mentioned this quotation from Rudolf Metz in his lecture on Darwin. See King, Class notes, History of Recent Philosophy; and Rudolf Metz, A Hundred Years of British Philosophy, trans. J. W. Harvey, T. E. Jessop, and Henry Sturt (New York: Macmillan, 1938), p. 95.

8. King refers to Ernst Heinrich Haeckel (1834–1919), who was mentioned by Millard in his lecture on Charles Darwin.

9. Millard gave this answer 10 points.

10. King refers to Johann Friedrich Herbart (1776–1841).

affirm. Things are independent of the mind that knows them. He agrees
with Kant that all knowledge must begin with experience. But he sees
that when we look at experience we find it filled with contradiction.
Therefore he would also affirm with Kant that experience is phenomenal. But we can get at the real by absolving the contradictions of our
general ideas. In doing this we must use the method of relation. From
this method Herbart comes to the conclusion the the real is unchang-
able, immovable, nonspacial and nontemporal.[11] We can immediately see
how this again contradicts Hegel who saw the real as process itself. Herbart goes further by saying that there are a number of independent
"reals" (reele) which are absolute. Again this pluralistic view is absolutely
opposed to Hegel monistic emphasis. Herbart, as we can see, is the very
antithesis of Hegel in every respect. For him the real is unchanging and
nontemporal. For Hegel the real is changing process.[12]

AHDS. MLKP-MBU: Box 115.

----

11. Millard commented: "[*plurality?*] of reals."
12. Millard gave this answer 10 points.

To Charles E. Batten

29 July 1952
Atlanta, Ga.

Through a cooperative relationship with Boston University, King took two
philosophy courses at Harvard University during the 1952–1953 school year. In
his reply to King's request for a Crozer transcript, Batten wrote, "On your way
north, why don't you stop here for a chat so that we can hear about what you are
doing. Your friends here at school join me in all good wishes."[1]

Dean Charles E. Batten,
Crozer Theological Seminary
Chester, Pa.

Dear Dean Batten:

I would like to have a transcript of my academic work at Crozer, sent to
Harvard University, as soon as possible. It should be addressed to the Dean
of Special Students, 11 Weld Hall, Harvard University, Cambridge 38, Mass.
If there is any charge for this, please forward the bill to me.

----

1. Charles E. Batten to King, 31 July 1952, CRO-NRCR.

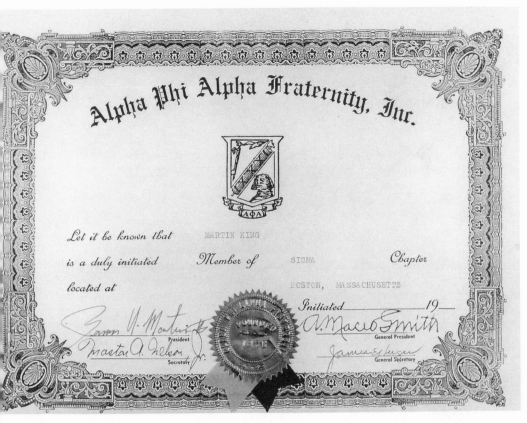

Alpha Phi Alpha Fraternity, Inc.

Let it be known that   MARTIN KING

is a duly initiated   Member of   SIGMA   Chapter

located at   BOSTON, MASSACHUSETTS

Initiated _____ 19__

President

Secretary

General President

General Secretary

On 22 June 1952, King was initiated into Boston's Sigma chapter of the Alpha Phi Alpha social fraternity.

I would appreciate it very much if you would notify the office that my Boston University address has been changed to 397 Massachusetts Ave.

Thank you for your cooperation.

Sincerely yours
[*signed*] M. L. King Jr.
Martin L. King, Jr.

MLK/w

THLS. CRO-NRCR.

From Melvin H. Watson

14 August 1952
Atlanta, Ga.

The son of P. O. Watson, longtime clerk of Ebenezer Baptist Church, Watson was dean of the Morehouse School of Religion.[1] Watson offers friendly criticisms of King, Jr.'s 10 August sermon at Ebenezer entitled "The Challenge of Communism to Christianity."[2] King served as Ebenezer's pastor in charge during the summer.

Dear Little In-Coming Doctor!

I thought I would take a few minutes and set down my reaction to your sermon on last Sunday: The Challenge of Communism to Christianity.

In spite of the fact that you announced that you were presenting a religious lecture, you did succeed very well indeed in sermonizing your theme. It was really not just a lecture. From where I sat it seemed to me that you should have been encouraged by the response. Some people did sleep, but some would have slept regardless of the theme.

Your major points seemed to me to be sound: (1) Social Justice (2) Dedication (3) Unite for Action.

There are one or two details that came out in your development that I would like to mention:

---

1. Watson (1908–) graduated in 1930 from Morehouse with King, Sr. After receiving the M.A., B.D., and S.T.M. at Oberlin he studied at the Pacific School of Religion in Berkeley, California, earning a doctorate in theology in 1948. Watson was dean of men and professor of religion at Shaw and Dillard universities before he returned to Morehouse as dean and professor of philosophy and religion in the School of Religion, where he remained for many years. While teaching at Morehouse he became pastor of Liberty Baptist Church in Atlanta, where he still serves. Watson's publications include "The Social Thought of Paul Tillich," *Journal of Religious Thought* 10, no. 1 (Autumn–Winter 1952–1953): 5–17.

2. In 1963 King published the similarly titled sermon "How Should a Christian View Communism?" in *Strength to Love* (New York: Harper & Row, 1963), pp. 93–100.

(1) In discussing Communist theory in the early part of the sermon it was not clear to me whether you understood Communist materialism. The Communist theorists were definitely not materialists after the fashion of the Greek atomists. Marx's position was that the culture, thoughts, in fact, the whole life of man is conditioned (seems to use the word, determine, at times by the means of production by his relationship to {the} instruments necessary to the making of a living. This variety of materialism is very difficult to refute and is a very disturbing phenomenon. Whether a man stands in relation to the means of production as an owner or a mere user does make a difference in the way he thinks, acts, etc. It is exceedingly difficult to deny this and make it stick!

(2) Most folk who speak of religion and the communist attitude toward it discuss the question out of context. What you said about the communist attitude toward religion was true. But you don't have a proper appreciation of the communist attitude toward religion until you read the history of the church in Russia. When you set Marx's attitude toward religion in the context of the history of the Christian church in Russia, the conclusion you reach is likely to be very sobering and will probably not make especially good sermonizing material.

(3) Stalin would certainly not make the question of race a sub-point as you did on Sunday. With him it is a major point. It was he who as Commissar of Nationalities ~~who~~ wrote into the Soviet Constitution the proposition which makes the treatment of persons on the basis of race a national offence in the Soviets and it was he who argued that the Soviet Union would make a strong appeal to nations of the East—India, Japan, China, et al., if she established the reputation of dealing with all races on the basis of equality. Ref. to Stalin's book: "Marxism and the National and Colonial Question." I think there can be no doubt about it that the appeal of communism to the Eastern nations today can be traceable to a large degree to the Soviet attitude toward race. This is a strategic policy with Russia.

I have made these observations, but they by no means indicate a lack of appreciation for the fine job you did on Sunday.

Every good wish.

Sincerely,
[*signed*] Melvin Watson

ALS. MLKP-MBU: Box 117.

Petition to the Boston University Faculty

18 September 1952
[*Boston, Mass.*]

Dean of the Graduate School Chester M. Alter granted King's petition to continue with course work although he had not yet taken the examination in German.

I am desirous of taking twelve hours toward the Ph D degree this semester in the Boston University Graduate School. My major field is Systematic Theology. At present I have completed twenty eight hours toward the degree, and passed the French examination. I plan to take the German examination in October, 1952. I would have taken the examination before now, but I wanted to make sure that I had an adequate background in German before taking it. For the past two years I have been a close student of German. In the light of this I am fairly certain that I can pass the examination in October.

[*signed*] Martin L. King Jr.

ATFmS. MLKP-MBU: Box 117.

From H. Edward Whitaker

31 October 1952
Niagara Falls, N.Y.

Whitaker, King's classmate at Crozer, writes about founding the first black church in Niagara Falls, New York.[1] He refers to Walter "Mac" McCall and Samuel Proctor, both graduates of Crozer.[2] Whitaker and his wife, Vivit, met King's parents at a meeting of the National Baptist Convention.

Dear Mike,

How does it feel to be in school this year? Pleasant I am sure. It was my intention to have scribble a note before now, but this changing from the Center here has just about knocked me out. Things are beginning to settle down

---

1. Horace Edward Whitaker (1918–) received his B.A. from Virginia Union University in 1948 after being employed as an insurance agent in Virginia and serving in the army during World War II. After receiving his B.D. from Crozer Theological Seminary in 1951 he served as pastor of New Hope Baptist Church in Niagara Falls, New York. In 1962 he returned to Virginia as pastor of Zion Baptist Church in Portsmouth, where he remained until 1968. He was later pastor of Emmanuel Baptist Church in Brooklyn and an area representative and minister for the American Baptist Churches. In 1971 Whitaker received his D.Min. from Andover-Newton Theological School. See Whitaker to King Papers Project, 13 April 1992.

2. McCall and King graduated from both Morehouse College and Crozer together, in 1948 and 1951, respectively. King met Samuel Dewitt Proctor (1921–) when Proctor visited Crozer to give a lecture. Proctor received his A.B. at Virginia Union University in 1942 and his B.D. at Crozer in 1945. In 1950 Proctor received his Th.D. from Boston University. After serving as pastor of Pond Street Baptist Church in Providence, Rhode Island, from 1945 to 1949 he became professor of religion and ethics at Virginia Union. He was promoted to vice-president in 1953 and president in 1955. In 1960 he became president of North Carolina A & T State University, where he remained until 1964. He then worked in the federal government and at several universities until, in 1972, he was called to the pastorate of Harlem's Abyssinian Baptist Church after the death of its pastor, Adam Clayton Powell, Jr. He has written several books, including *The Young Negro in America* (1966), *Sermons from the Black Pulpit* (1984), *Preaching About Crises in the Community* (1988), *My Moral Odyssey* (1989), and *How Shall They Hear?* (1992). See Proctor to King Papers Project, 18 November 1991.

now, and the response is so favorable to our ministry, I am not altogether certain as to what we are going to do to make it possible for our people to attend service. We simply don't have the room. Of course we don't have much to begin with. But we are going to be forced to build before we are altogether ready. We have already started our planning. If things continue favorably we will begin building in the spring.

I had a letter from Proctor a few days ago and he was telling me of your success. I am glad to hear it, although I would not expect to hear anything else

I saw your mother and father at the Convention. They look real well. Vivit was with me at the Convention. Your mother said you had taken all of her pots and pans and cut-out for Boston. I can imagine that it is some apartment you are keeping. You can't wash dishes or can you? I certainly would not like to stop by for a meal because I would probably take with acute indigestion and die—Well so much for the joke. I think that is fine. I hope everything goes well for you. Don't bring in any extra help—

By the way you told me two years ago you would be married by the next summer. Apparently you are still meeting these girls who are one-time wreckers. Watch the Doctor don't let one catch with your shoes off.

I was in Boston in August, visiting with my wife's sister. It is my hope to get back there again before you leave. We met this fellow who died a few weeks ago and had such large funeral. In fact we had dinner together. I was surprise to hear of his death. I think both he and his wife were students at the University (Boston). How long do you expect to be in Boston now? Will this year wind up your residence work? Remember I must have a copy of your Doctors dissertation.

Take it easy Mike and let me hear from you sometime. Vivit and Edward are well and things are going along normally. I wrote Mac today—

Sincerely
[*signed*] H. Edw Whitaker

ALS. MLKP-MBU: Box 117.

From William R. Strassner

6 November 1952
Raleigh, N.C.

Shaw University president Strassner sought someone to succeed him as dean of Shaw's School of Religion.[1] *Sankey Blanton recommended King to Strassner as*

---

1. William Russell Strassner (1901–) is a graduate of Arkansas Baptist College, Virginia Union University, and Andover-Newton Theological School. After serving Baptist congregations in Westmoreland County, Virginia, Charlottesville, Virginia, and Boston, Massachusetts, he became dean of religion at Bishop College in Marshall, Texas. He then was appointed dean of the School of Religion at Shaw University in Raleigh, North Carolina; in 1951, Strassner became president of that Baptist college. See Strassner to King Papers Project, 28 December 1991; and

someone who could assume these new responsibilities and still complete his degree,
but the president of Shaw sought confirmation from King.[2]

The Reverend M. L. King
397 Massachusetts Avenue
Boston, Massachusetts

Dear Reverend King:

We are in search of a good man for appointment as Dean of the School of Religion at Shaw University.

I asked Dr. Sankey Blanton, President, Crozer Theological Seminary, for a suggestion and he immediately recommended you in the highest terms. Dr. Blanton and I were schoolmates at Andover-Newton.

If you are interested in the position, kindly fill out the enclosed application form and return it to me at your earliest convenience.

I recall that I was guest minister at your father's church in Atlanta a year or two ago on the very fine occasion of Men's Day.

Sincerely yours,
[*signed*] Wm. R. Strassner
William R. Strassner
President

WRS:rfl

Enclosure 1 [3]

TLS. MLKP-MBU: Box 117.

Strassner, "My Ministerial Career in Retrospect," in *Voices of Experience*, ed. Michael A. Battle (New York: Martin Luther King Fellows Press, 1985), pp. 24–42.

2. See also Strassner to King, 2 January 1953, MLKP-MBU: Box 117. King's response, if any, has not been located.

3. A blank application was enclosed with this letter (see "Faculty Application, Shaw University," 6 November 1952, CSKC).

From W. T. Handy, Jr.

18 November 1952
Alexandria, La.

Handy was a student in Boston University's School of Religion during King's first
year in Boston.[1] *In this letter the Methodist preacher describes his experiences as a*

---

1. William Talbot Handy, Jr. (1924–), graduated from New Orleans's Dillard University in 1948 with a B.A. degree. He earned a B.D. at Atlanta's Gammon Theological Seminary and an

first-year pastor of a church in Louisiana and cautions King, "The only element to
restrain our expectations from bearing fruit will be M. L. himself." Handy refers
to Roland Haynes, Doug Moore, and Wayman "Mac" McLaughlin, three fellow
graduate students at Boston.[2]

18 Nov
1952

Dr. M. L. King, Jr. (Not the real Doctor)
745 Commonwealth Ave.
Boston 15, Mass.

Dear M. L.:

I imagine you were not expecting a letter from me at all, but I assure you that I have not forgotten you nor will I ever. The year we fellowshiped together has made a lasting imprint upon my heart and shall never be obliterated. Then too, if we did drift the relationship between Ruth and the other members of your family would always maintain some sort of tie.

How is old B.U.? I miss the gang in the room solving the problems of the world, politically, socially, and in the theological realm. If only the people of the world would listen to us, there would be no trouble. How is Mac? Has he decided to relieve himself of his many responsibilities? Does he still jump up in the air and kick his heels together? I certainly hope he does something before he has a nervous breakdown.

I am now pastor of a church. I have about 240 members on roll with approximately 160 adult ones I can place my hands on. I realize this is a remarkable percentage and am thankful that seemingly they are now rallying to the cause of the church. When I was appointed I found only 65 active, 31 out of town, 42 children, and 13 dead, all carried on the roll. Honestly one lady had been dead six years and they were still carrying her. To get improvements has meant hard work and I cannot understand how a man can pastor away from the people.

When you go to your church (if ever) please try not to get embroiled in a

---

S.T.M. at Boston University. Handy was pastor of Newman Methodist Church in Alexandria, Louisiana, from 1952 to 1959, when he was appointed pastor of St. Mark Methodist Church in Baton Rouge. After leaving St. Mark in 1968 he worked with the Methodist Publishing House in Nashville. He was later elected a bishop of the United Methodist Church. He has served as president of the board of trustees for the Interdenominational Theological Center and Gammon Theological Seminary in Atlanta, and as the secretary of the board of trustees of Southern Methodist University in Dallas. See Handy to King Papers Project, 21 November 1991; and Handy, telephone interview with Clayborne Carson, 1 July 1992.

2. Roland Emerson Haynes (1928–) received his A.B. in 1949 from Clark College in Atlanta and his S.T.B., S.T.M., and Ph.D. from Boston University in 1952, 1953, and 1961, respectively. He was college minister and professor of psychology at Clark College from 1957 until 1963. Thereafter he taught at several colleges in South Carolina before becoming professor of psychology at the University of South Carolina in 1972, where he still serves. See Haynes to King Papers Project, 16 May 1992.

Douglas Moore (1928–) received his A.B. from North Carolina College in Durham (1949). Although he never received his Ph.D., he did pursue graduate work at Boston University from 1950 to 1953. Moore was a founding member of the Southern Christian Leadership Conference.

building campaign in your first year. When I arrived here I realized that a new edifice would be needed but I had intentions of starting next year. But events took place over which I had no control.

About two months ago a realtor approached me concerning a plot of land half-a-square for $25,000.00. When he mentioned the price, he could just as well have mentioned 25 million. Yet the tract was ideal for our purposes. The location was fine, and their was enough land to erect a nice building, parsonage, and eventually an educational building or gymnasium. Since then I have scurried around and found interests to loan us the major portion of the sum. Last week we entered into the transaction, with the close of the deal and $24,000.00 more due on January 28, 1953. Pray for me.

On the other hand, the location of our church is in the business district of the city. We are isolated but yet the value of the property is of such a nature that when sold we could erect a modest building without too much debt. Therefore today we are negotiating with realtors to sell. Our minimum asking price is one thousand dollars per front foot and we have 106.66 feet. Therefore $106,660.00. Brother you see I am now talking in high finance. But do not think it is all smooth. It can certainly develop headaches when the pastor has to do so much of the work himself.

I cannot find time to do as much reading as I would like to. I do get some opportunities and it pays off in the pulpit. Last Sunday was one of my good days and I felt it myself. Still a preacher has his good days and his bad ones. I still am in a dither about my night sermons, and feel somewhat guilty about them. I do alright in the morning but flunk usually ascends the rostrum with me at night. I pray that when this business deal is completed I will do better.

Two weeks ago I was at Dillard to deliver the vesper message. It was quite an experience returning to the alma mater in such a position. Ten years ago there would have been prohibitive odds against such an occurrence. I used as a theme "Gaining God's Approval" with the text coming from the R.S.V. II Tim. 2:15. In the sermon I used the silent conclusion and it seemed to be quite effective. I used an illustration and when I concluded appeared as if I was to continue then abruptly, "Let us pray".

At my annual Conference I delivered one of the morning sermons. Man, there was pandemonium and the place was a wreck. At one point, the place got into such a tantrum that I just stopped until peace could be restored. Really though I did preach one of my best sermons and I cannot understand why. The Lord was evidently with me because I thought I was going to flunk. It was at this session that I met young Jamerson from Gardner Taylor's former church.[3] I saw him later and he is really doing a bang up job at Mt. Zion. He

---

3. Handy refers to Theodore Judson Jemison (1918–) and Gardner Calvin Taylor (1918–). Jemison succeeded Taylor as pastor of Mount Zion Baptist Church in Baton Rouge in 1947. Taylor received his A.B. from Leland College in 1937 and his B.D. from Oberlin in 1940. He led churches in Ohio and New Orleans before becoming pastor of Mount Zion in 1943. After leaving Mount Zion he became pastor of Concord Baptist Church in Brooklyn, where he still serves. Taylor served as president of the Protestant Council of New York City, and was also a member of the city's board of education. In 1961, after contesting the reelection of J. H. Jackson as president,

also is going to rebuild and get a new parsonage. The boy sounds like he can "tell the story". I heard him give a few remarks.

I know you are now married? Which one was it? No, I know you are still galivanting around Boston, the most eligible and popular bachelor in town. I wonder how you are progressing wih my steadying influence gone. Remember M. L., "we are expecting great things from you".[4] The only element to restrain our expectations from bearing fruit will be M. L. himself. However I know that he will not allow himself or influences to bring failure about him or embarrasment to his beloved Father and Mother.

I won't preach to you anymore. Let me know how Roland is faring. I was somewhat disturbed about his family when he left Atlanta. Is Doug Moore still up in the clouds? Tell him that it is a little different out here and that the world is not going to be converted overnight. However every now and then a little evidence will show you that it all is not in vain.

Ruth has been sick since you last saw her. About six weeks ago I had to rush her to the hospital where she lost her opportunity to have a baby at present. It was quite discouraging but she is fine and in good spirits now. I hope that she will be able to teach next semester. Eventually she is going to need an operation. She sends her regards and hears about you through Christine.

Tomorrow the ministers of the district will convene at our church so that means preparation for entertainment with wholly inadequate facilities. Somehow we will meet the responsibilities. Continue your good work. Keep your eye on the goal. Have you taken your German exam as yet?

Give my regards to Drs. Rowlingson, Booth, Chalmers, and DeWolf. When

---

he led a movement out of the National Baptist Convention to form the Progressive National Baptist Convention. His books include *How Shall They Preach* (1977) and *The Scarlet Thread* (1981).

Jemison was the youngest child of D. V. Jemison, president of the National Baptist Convention from 1941 until his retirement in 1953. T. J. Jemison received his B.S. from Alabama State College in 1940 and his M.Div. from Virginia Union University in 1945. As pastor of Mount Zion Baptist Church in Staunton, Virginia, Jemison organized the city's first local NAACP chapter. In 1949 he became pastor of Mount Zion Baptist Church in Baton Rouge, Louisiana, where he still serves. In June 1953, Jemison helped organize a ten-day bus boycott in Baton Rouge to protest segregated seating. The carpool system employed by Jemison and others in that city served as a model for the Montgomery Improvement Association's carpool during its boycott of city buses in 1955 and 1956. Also in 1953, Jemison was elected general secretary of the National Baptist Convention, in which capacity he served until his election to the presidency in 1982. Jemison was the founding secretary of the Southern Christian Leadership Conference in 1957, but resigned a year later. See Weptanomah W. Carter, *Born to Be President* (Baltimore: Gateway Press, 1984).

4. Handy later explained in a telephone interview that he was quoting a letter written to King, Jr., by Alberta Williams King the previous year. Handy had visited the senior Kings during one of his frequent trips to Atlanta to be with his wife, Ruth, who was teaching at an Atlanta school with Christine King. "We'd go by the [Kings'] house where they fed us and all that kind of thing. Once I went down there and said to Mrs. King how popular he was, how the girls were after him, how he wasn't doing anything wrong, but that he was very popular. . . . She wrote him very soberly and I remember that he shared the letter with me. She said I'd been there and that she'd heard some things about him and she just wanted to be sure that he gets there straight. And she wrote those words, 'Remember M. L., we're expecting great things from you'" (Handy, interview with Clayborne Carson, 1 July 1992). Alberta King's letter has not been located.

is DeWolf's book off the press?[5] Next week I will hear Gardner Taylor again, he'll be here for the Teacher's Convention. Bye now,

Your Friend,
[*signed*] Handy

TALS. MLKP-MBU: Box 117.

––––––––––

5. Donald Taggart Rowlingson (1907–) was professor of New Testament at Boston University from 1950 until his retirement in 1972; Edwin Prince Booth (1898–1969) was professor of church history at Boston from 1925 until his retirement in 1963; Allan Knight Chalmers (1897–1972) was professor of preaching and applied Christianity at Boston from 1948 to 1962. DeWolf's book *A Theology of the Living Church* was published by Harper in 1953.

Sankey L. Blanton to William R. Strassner

3 December 1952

President William R. Strassner
Shaw University
Raleigh, North Carolina

Dear President Strassner:

Thank you for your letter. I am emphatically of the opinion that King is eminently qualified to serve as Dean of your School of Religion.

I would hope that it would be possible for him to accept the appointment and continue work on his dissertation while in residence with you. I am sure he is capable of doing that provided the regulations of the institution in which he takes his degree would permit. In fact, I think Mr. King has great ability and that he would do more for you while finishing the dissertation than the average man would do without any other duties besides.

I am sorry I could not reach you while I was in Raleigh recently.

Yours cordially,
Sankey L. Blanton

SLB:LK

cc: Rev. Martin Luther King

TLc. MLKP-MBU: Box 117.

Notecards on Books of the Old Testament

[*22 September 1952–28 January 1953*]
[*Boston, Mass.*]

These six notecards were found among the hundreds that King wrote for DeWolf's
Religious Teachings of the Old Testament. In his informal exegesis of biblical

*passages—particularly those from the books of Psalms, Jeremiah, and Amos—
King reveals his views about human nature, personal immortality, the nature of
divinity, and social ethics. In his examination of a famous passage from Amos ("let
judgment run down as waters, and righteousness as a mighty stream"), King notes
that "unless a man's heart is right, . . . the external forms of worship mean
nothing." Worship and ritual, King writes, can never be "a substitute for ethical
living." He argues that Christians have a special duty to strive for social justice.
"Whenever Christianity has remained true to its prophetic mission, it has taken a
deep interest in social justice. Whenever it has fallen short at this point, it has
b[r]ought about disastrous consequences."*

God   (Amos)

5:21:24—This passage might be called the key passage of the entire book.[1]
It reveals the deep ethical nature of God. God is a God that demands justice
rather than sacrifice; righteousness rather than ritual. The most elaborate
worship is but an insult to God when offered by those who have no mind to
conform to his ethical demands. Certainly this is one of the most noble idea
ever uttered by the human mind.

One may raise the question as to whether Amos was against all ritual and
sacrifice, i.e. worship. I think not. It seems to me that Amos' concern is the
ever-present tendency to make ritual and sacrifice a substitute for ethical living. Unless a man's heart is right, Amos seems to be saying, the external forms
of worship mean nothing. God is a God that demands justice and sacrifice fo
can never be a substitute for it. Who can disagree with such a notion?

Social Ethics   (Amos)

Amos' emphasis throughout seems to be that justice between man and man
is one of the divine foundations of society. Such an ethical ideal is at the root
of all true religion. This high ethical notion conceived by Amos must alway
remain a challenge to the Christian church

Man   (Jer)

17:5.[2] "Cursed is the man who trusts in man . . ." For Jeremiah one of the
greatest of sins is the sin of trusting in man rather than God. He probably felt

---

1. Amos 5:21–24: "I hate, I despise your feast days, and I will not smell in your solemn
assemblies. Though ye offer me burnt offerings and your meat offerings, I will not accept them:
neither will I regard the peace offerings of your fat beasts. Take thou away from me the noise of
thy songs; for I will not hear the melody of thy viols. But let judgment run down as waters, and
righteousness as a mighty stream."

2. Jeremiah 17:5: "Thus saith the Lord; Cursed be the man that trusteth in man, and maketh
flesh his arm, and whose heart departeth from the Lord."

that man was to weak and to finite to even approximate the ~~infit~~ infinite power of God. So it is the man who trusts in the Lord that is on sound footing.

This passage makes it plain that Jeremiah was opposed to any form of humanism in the modern sense. It might be well that those of us who are opposed to humanism in the modern world would speak out against it as did Jeremiah and set out to give a rational defense of theism.

It seems to me that one of the great services of neo-orthodoxy, notwithstanding its exstremes, is its revolt against all forms of humanistic perfectionism. They call us back to a deeper faith in God. Is not this the need of the hour? ~~Did n~~ Has not modern man placed to much faith in himself and to little faith in God?

Sin   (Jer)

4:22.[3] Here it is implied that goodness is a foreign thing to human nature. In fact men dont even know how to do good. They are only skilled in doing evil.

We may question such a conclusion. Does man ever become so corrupt and wicked that he can have no conception of the good? I think not. It seems to be that no matter how low an individual sinks in sin, there is still a spark of good within him.

Evil   (Jer)

12:1—Here Jeremiah inquires of God why the wicked prosper.[4] This point disturbed Jeremiah greatly. Here we find a revolt against the Deuteronomic idea which asserted that prosperity always followed righteous and trouble or disaster followed wickedness.

Jeremiah was realistic enough to see that this didn't always follow, at least from a materialistic point of view. He saw that there were times when the wicked prospered and the righteous suffered.

We must admit that Jeremiah raises a significant question at this point. If God is justice there must somehow and ~~sometime~~ {somewhere} be a wedding of virtue and happiness. This doesn't always take place in life as Jeremiah so candidly points out. What then is the solution? It seems to me that the only solution to this problem is found in the doctrine of personal immortality. In another existence man will receive the benefits unattainable in this existence. Without immortality the universe is irrational and the justice and love of God are put in jeopardy.

---

3. Jeremiah 4:22: "For my people is foolish, they have not known me: they are sottish children, and they have none understanding: they are wise to do evil, but to do good they have no knowledge."

4. Jeremiah 12:1: "Righteous art thou, O Lord, when I plead with thee: yet let me talk with thee of thy judgments: Wherefore doth the way of the wicked prosper? Wherefore are all they happy that deal very treacherously?"

72—This whole psalm is a plea for social justice.[5] There is expressed a deep concern for the needy and the oppressed. The oppresor is looked upon with scorn. He is to be crushed.

This emphasis found its greatest expression, excluding the fine work of the prophets, in the teaching of Jesus. Throughout his ministry th he manifested a deep concern for the poor and oppressed people of his day. While somewhat extravagant, there is a healthy warning in the statement, Christianity was born among the poor and died among the rich. Whenever Christianity has remained true to its prophetic mission, it has taken a deep interest in social justice. Whenever it has fallen short at this point, it has bought about disastrous consequences. We must never forget that the success of communism in the world today is due to the failure of Christians to live to the highest ethical tenents inherent in its system.

AD. CSKC.

---

5. Among the relevant passages in Psalm 72 is the fourth verse: "He shall judge the poor of the people, he shall save the children of the needy, and shall break in pieces the oppressor."

Final Examination Answers, Religious Teachings of the Old Testament

[*22 September 1952–28 January 1953*]
[*Boston, Mass.*]

In three of the five examination questions for this course, DeWolf asked his students to discuss different conceptions of God in the Old Testament. Affirming that there is rational evidence in the Old Testament to sustain belief in God, King notes that the writer of the book of Job questions that faith. "Why do the righteous suffer? In other words, how can a good God allow so much evil to exist in the world?" For King, the prophets Amos and Hosea offer the "most illuminating conceptions of God." "For Amos God is a God of righteousness who demands ethical actions from his children. . . . For Hosea God is a God of love, and even his justice is but an expression of his love." DeWolf gave King 94 points for the examination and an A − for the semester.

1. Probably the most rational evidence presented for belief in God in the Old Testament is found in Deutero Isaiah. He sets forth arguments to establish the validity monotheism. First he argues that Yehweh is the only being that can adequately predict the future. Secondly, he turns to the testimony of creation. This he feels is a fit testimony to the existence of one God. Evidence for God's existence in creation is a constant argu-

ment in the Old Testament. The Psalmist could cry, "the heaven declare the glory of God and the firmament his handiwork."[1] Such evidence for belief in God the Old Testament writers felt was open to all. Thirdly, Deutero Isaiah turns to the absurdity of idolatry to establish the existence of God. Nothing can be compared to God.

There is also evidence for belief in God in history. The O. T. writers seem to say that ~~since God controls all nations~~ the rise and fall of nations establishes the existence of God.[2]

The most apparent difiance of evidence for God by faith is found in the book of Job. Job find himself confronted with the problem of evil. Why do the righteous suffer? In other words, how can a good God allow so much evil to exist in the world? Are not the goodness of good and the existence of evil incompatible ideas? These are the questions which baffle the writer of Job. The existence of evil calls his faith into question.[3]

Maybe I am not to clear on this question. I think not.[4]

2. It seems to me that the most untenable conceptions of God appear in the pre-prophetic period of the Old Testament. Here God is looked upon first as an anthropomorphic being. He walks in the garden in the cool of the evening. He comes down to the towel of Babal. He come down in the clouds to speak to Moses. (Ex. 19:11)[5]

Also in many of these writings the moral character of God is quite low. He comes down to the towel out of jealousy (Gen. 11:7)[6] He justifies Abraham in a lie. He commands an individual to do something and the scorns him for doing it. (Num 22:20–22)[7]

Also at this period we find Yahweh presented as a tribal deity. He is not a universal father whose love extends to all people. So we often find

---

1. King refers to Psalms 19:1: "The heavens declare the glory of God; and the firmament sheweth his handywork."

2. In the margin DeWolf wrote, "Good."

3. DeWolf commented, "Yes. Yet he affirms that faith. 'Though He slay me . . .'" DeWolf refers to Job 13:15: "Though he slay me, yet will I trust in him."

4. DeWolf commented, "You seem clear enough, though 'I' is not quite finished." King received 9 points for the answer.

5. King refers to Genesis 3:8 ("And they heard the voice of the Lord God walking in the garden in the cool of the day"), Genesis 11:5 ("And the Lord came down to see the city and the tower"), and Exodus 19:9 ("And the Lord said unto Moses, Lo, I come unto thee in a thick cloud, that the people may hear when I speak with thee, and believe thee forever").

6. Genesis 11:6–7: "And the Lord said, Behold, the people is one, and they have all one language; and this they begin to do: and now nothing will be restrained from them, which they have imagined to do. Go to, let us go down, and there confound their language, that they may not understand one another's speech."

7. King may be referring to Abram and Sarai entering Egypt as brother and sister rather than as husband and wife (Genesis 12:11–20). He also refers to Numbers 22:20–22: "And God came unto Balaam at night, and said unto him, If the men come to call thee, rise up, and go with them; but yet the word which I shall say unto thee, that shalt thou do. And Balaam rose up in the morning, and saddled his ass, and went with the princes of Moab. And God's anger was kindled because he went; and the angel of the Lord stood in the way for an adversary against him."

Yahweh justifying all types of immoral actions against non-Israelites.
Even Yahweh himself is often found using deceitful and ruthless methods against individuals outside of his tribal authority.

Finally at this period we find that God is only one among many gods. To be sure, he is the only one worthy of worship, but other gods still exist. At this period the Hebrews were Henotheist rather than monotheist.

Certainly these are the most untenable conceptions of God found in the Old Testament. It is probable that many factor accounted for their appearance at this ~~first~~ period. First there was no necessary relation between religion and ethics at this period. Moral values were still at a low ebb. For this reason it was not to difficult to attribute many immoral practices to Yahweh. Moreover the Hebrew had not reached national and international crises at this point which could cause them to rise above anthropomorphism and belief in many gods. Monotheism was a development from national disasters.

One point must be made in passing concerning the above. We must not conclude that all of the untenable conceptions of God are found in this period. Knudson has warned us against such an error in his book. It is certainly true that we find some low conceptions of God in late writings and some high conceptions of God in early writing. But it is certainly true to say that the most untenable conceptions of God on the whole are found in this period.[8]

3. Certainly the Old Testament rises to its most illuminating conceptions of God in the prophets. The greatest of these conceptions is the affirmation of monotheism. In all of the 8th century prophets we find it implied. For Amos God is a God of righteousness who demands ethical actions from his children. The most elaborate ritual is but an insult to God when offered by the hands of an unethical person. For Hosea God is a God of love, and even his justice is but an expression of his love.

This emphasis on ethical monotheism is found in Jeremiah, Isaiah, Amos, Hosea, Micah and a few others. It is probably true that you dont get an explicit monotheism in these writer, but it is implied throughtout. It becomes ~~explit~~ explicit in Deutero-Isaiah. So ~~tha~~ we might conclude that the most illuminating conceptions of God are found in the literary prophets. They stress One God, who is a God of righteousness and love, a God of holiness (meaning ethically pure) and eternality. He is a God "who inhabits eternity, and whose name is holy."[9]

The Hebrews were lead to this conception through divers experiences of national and international disaster. The prophets had predicted that because of disobedience the nation would fall. Finally this day came when both the northern and southern kingdoms fell. So they concluded that the prophets must have been right. God must be

---

8. King refers to Albert C. Knudson's book *The Doctrine of God* (New York: Abingdon Press, 1930). DeWolf gave King 10 points for the answer.

9. Isaiah 57:15.

a God who control all history and all nations. Unlike the Greek who came to monism through intellectualizing on the unity of the world, the Hebrew came to monotheism through the realistic experiences of history.[10]

4. The suffering servant passage in the 53rd chapter of Isaiah could well be applied to Jesus. In a real sense Jesus is the only one who fulfills this prophesy. Certainly Jesus was a lowly man. A man of sorrow and acquainted with ~~grift~~ grief.[11] Certainly the real meaning of the atonement is that Christ died in order that sinful men might be incited to rise out of their sinfullness and be reconciled to God. In other words through his suffering and moral influence men are reconciled to God.

There has been much debate as to whether this passage refers to the nation or to an individual. Jewish scholars have inclined toward the former while Christians scholars have inclined toward the latter. It is my opinion ~~with~~ that the passage refers to an individual, and, Jesus more than any other fulfills its descriptions. Jesus fulfills it in a way that Isaiah could never have conceived of.[12]

5. I would say that Old Testament religion is primarily social. We may point to at least three Old Testament doctrines which would support this conclusion. First we may cite the doctrine of sin. In most instances when individuals sin the whole nation or the family is held responsible. For an instance Achan's whole family is punished for his sin (Jud 7:10−26)[13] The idea ~~of individual~~ of individual responsibility is rather late in Hebrew thought. It is Ezekiel who says "the soul that sins it shall die."[14] Traces of this idea appeared earlier in Hebrew thought, but the idea as a whole was late getting hold of Old Testament religion.

Second we may take the idea of immortality. There is no explicit doctrine of personal immortality in the Old Testament. Indeed the doctrine is explicitly denied by many writers (cf Job, Ecclesiastes) If there is any immortality in Old Testament ~~it~~ religion it is social or national immortality. The individual survives only through the nation or the group.

The above in not to be interpreted as saying that the Old Testament has no personal religion. There can be no gainsaying of the fact that we find a great personal element in the writing of Jeremiah and Ezekiel. But withall the primary emphasis of Old Testament religion is social rather than personal.[15]

AHDS. MLKP-MBU: Box 112.

---

10. King received 10 points for the answer.

11. Isaiah 53:3: "He is despised and rejected of men; a man of sorrows, and acquainted with grief."

12. King received 10 points for the answer.

13. The story of Achan is told by Joshua (7:16−26).

14. Ezekiel 18:20: "The soul that sinneth, it shall die."

15. DeWolf underlined "three" in the second sentence of the first paragraph and marked King's first and second points. At the end of the answer he wrote "3. Covenant?" King received 8 points for the answer.

4 February 1953
[*Boston, Mass.*]

After postponing the examination in German until 10 October 1952, King failed
it on the first attempt. Chester M. Alter granted King's petition to continue his
coursework "subject to passing German examination in February." King passed the
examination on 18 February.

I am a graduate student in the field of Systematic Theology working toward
the PhD degree. At present I have completed thirty seven hours toward the
degree, and passed the French exmanination. I plan to take the German examination on February 18, 1953. I have had the examination once, but unfortunately I did not pass it. Now, however, I feel that I can pass it with little difficulty. For more than two years now I have been a very close student of German.

In the light of the above facts I petition the faculty for permission to take
eleven hours this semester. It so happens that most of the courses which I
took last semester are two semester courses, and to have to drop them at this
point would be a definite loss in my doctoral studies.

[*signed*] Martin Luther King Jr.

ATFmS. MLKP-MBU: Box 117.

From D. E. King

17 February 1953
Louisville, Ky.

D. E. King, pastor of Zion Baptist Church in Louisville, Kentucky, had met King
in 1949 at the National Baptist Sunday School and Baptist Training Union
Congress, which was associated with the National Baptist Convention.[1]

The Reverend M. L. King, Jr.
397 Massachusetts Avenue
Boston, Massachusetts

My dear Brother King:

We met in a casual way during the Congress session, in Memphis 1949.
However, because of my friendship with your Dad and Mother, I feel that I
am personally acquainted with you.

---

1. Dearine Edwin King (1910–) received his A.B. at LeMoyne College and his B.D. and M.A.
at the Howard University School of Religion. He was pastor of Zion Baptist Church in Louisville
from 1946 until 1963, when he became pastor of Friendship Baptist Church in New York. D. E.
King also served as secretary of the National Baptist Convention.

This letter is occasioned by the reply which your father made to an invitation for him to preach at our church. He could not come and recommended you. Because I had other plans in case he did not acacept, I found it inconvenient to invite you for this particular occasion. However, I thought we might work out an engagement with you for any regular Sunday morning and night as you return home from school this spring or summer. If this be possible please advise as to the time that you expect to return home. I am sure that your coming will be an inspiration to all of us, and especially the young people.

With anticipation for sharing your fellowship and services, and praying God's choicest blessing upon you, I am

Sincerely yours,
[*signed*]
D. E. King

DEK:arb

TLS. MLKP-MBU: Box 117.

To Otto R. Loverude

[*March 1953*]
[*Boston, Mass.*]

Loverude, the pastor of First United Baptist Church in Lowell, Massachusetts, had invited King to speak for the church's College of Missions on 12 April. In an 18 February letter Loverude asked King to "tell us something of what it means to be a member of the minority race in the South."[1] This draft of a reply to Loverude's letter and the following one to D. E. King were written on the same page. The final versions of both letters have not been found.

The Reverend Otto R. Loverude
First United Baptist Church
Church and George Streets
Lowell, Mass.

Dear Rev. Loverude:

This is to acknowledge your letter of February 18. Following your suggestion I will use as a subject at the 5:30 discussion group: "What it means to be

---

1. See Loverude to King, 18 February 1953, MLKP-MBU: Box 117. Loverude (1900–1973) received his B.D. from Northern Baptist Theological Seminary near Chicago and his M.A. from Colgate Rochester Divinity School. He served as pastor of First United Baptist Church in Lowell, Massachusetts, from 1940 until 1955.

a Negro in the South." My subject for the regular evening service will be: "What does it mean to believe in God?"

I am very happen to be able to serve you and your church and I will look forward to this occasion with great anticipation. Please feel free to contact me about any additional information. I would appreciate it very much if you would give me some directions as to getting to the church. I will be driving out.

Sincerely yours,
[*signed*] Martin L. King Jr.

ALdS. MLKP-MBU: Box 116.

To D. E. King

[*March 1953*]
[*Boston, Mass.*]

The Reverend D. E. King
2818 West Chestnut Street
Louisville, Kentucky

Dear Rev. King:

~~This is to acknowledge your letter of February 17. I was very pleased to hear from you.~~

I was very pleased to receive your letter of February 17. I shall be very happy to ~~accept~~ speak for you whenever I'm ~~passing~~ traveling that way. At present ~~I can't say when I shall be coming that way. It is still to early in the 2nd semester for me to have worked out my schedule so as to as to commit myself de definitely commit myself. However, as soon as I have done so, and know definitely when I shall be passing through your territory section of the country, I shall contact you immediately.~~

~~with every good wish for your success.~~

~~Sincerely yours,~~
however, my schedule is of such an uncertain nature that it would be impossible for me to make a definite committment. I had {originally} planned ~~planned~~ to go to Atlanta during the Spring holidays, but a very busy schedule seems to prevent it. This probably means that it will be sometime in mid summer before I will get down that way. As soon as ~~I'm~~ my plans are definite, I will let you.

Certainly I appreciate this invitation to the highest and look forward with great anticipation to serving you and your great church

~~Sorry~~ I have heard of the great revival you conducted at our church last year. It seems to be a generally accepted fact that you must be classed with the "great preachers" of our day.

You have my continual prayers in all of your endeavors.

Sincerely yours,

AHLd. MLKP-MBU: Box 116.

"A Comparison and Evaluation of the Theology of Luther with That of Calvin"

15 May 1953
[*Boston, Mass.*]

King submitted versions of this essay for two courses at Boston: Edwin Prince Booth's Seminar in Historical Theology and L. Harold DeWolf's History of Christian Doctrine.[1] In this version, written for DeWolf, King differs with Luther and Calvin's undue emphasis on the sovereignty of God, arguing that "God is first and foremost an all loving Father." DeWolf graded the paper "A. Very good" but added: "awkwardly worded title."

Within the brief compass of this paper it would be impossible to give an adequately comprehensive treatment of so extensive a theme as a comparison and evaluation of the theology of Luther with that of Calvin; however, the most salient feature of these systems of theology may at least be cursorily described.[2] Certainly the significance of these two great personalities cannot be exaggerated. Both historians and theologians would admit this fact. Even those of us who do not subscribe to many of their views are forced to

---

1. Edwin Prince Booth (1898–1969) received his A.B. in 1919 from Allegheny College and his S.T.B. in 1922 and his Ph.D. in 1929 from Boston University. He was ordained a Methodist minister in 1922 and thereafter served as pastor of the Community Church in Islington, Massachusetts. In 1924 Booth joined Boston University's faculty as an instructor in church history, becoming a professor the following year. He remained at Boston until his death. His publications included *Martin Luther: Oak of Saxony* (1933). King received an A from Booth for the earlier version of this essay (see "A Comparison of the Theology of Luther with that of Calvin," 26 May–5 July 1952, MLKP-MBU: Box 113) and a B+ for the course. King revised the essay for DeWolf by omitting several paragraphs and making several additions; the passages that did not appear in Booth's version of the essay are noted here.

2. Williston Walker, *John Calvin: The Organizer of Reformed Protestantism, 1509–1564* (New York: G. P. Putnam, 1906), p. 409: "Within the brief compass allotted to this volume no adequately comprehensive treatment can be given to so extensive a theme as Calvin's theology; but its salient features must at least be cursorily described."

admit that they stood out as great leaders, notwithstanding their mistakes, in the historical movement
which was moving toward individual responsibility
and freedom of thought. The reformation was inevitable and certainly we cannot point to any single individual as being responsible for its coming. It was a
development in the social order. But in all fairness,
we must give some credit to the individual. The significance of the individual in such a period of history
is that he stands in the midst of the ongoing social
movement and gives it guidance and direction. Such
credit must be given to men like Luther and Calvin.

The theology of these two great reformers and
the great churches that sprang from them are quite
different in temper and character. Philip Schaff, in
his Creeds of Christendom, lists nine distinctions between the two. However, Schaff goes on, and rightly
so, to emphasize the close affinity between these two
men and the churches that owe their existence to
them.[3] Certainly when one scrutinizingly compares
the writings of Luther and Calvin on great doctrinal
questions he is immediately struck with the amazing
similarities of the two, even more so than their disagreements. For example, we often distinguish between the two Reformers by saying that the regnant
principle of Luther's theology was justification by
faith, while for Calvin it was the sovereignty of God.
But this distinction is largely a matter of emphasis
and ought not leave the impression that Luther did
not speak of the sovereignty of God or that Calvin did
not speak of justification by faith. For Luther, as for
Calvin, God is the great sovereign power. For Calvin,
as for Luther, justification by faith is the heart of the
Christian faith.[4] In other particulars, the affinity between the two Reformers is so close that it would be
difficult to detect differences of any kind. They were

---

3. Hugh Thomson Kerr, Jr., ed., *A Compend of Luther's Theology* (Philadelphia: Westminster
Press, 1943), p. xii: "Something has already been said of the contrast that is often made between
Luther and Calvin, and certainly the two Reformers as well as the great Churches that sprang
from them are very different in temper and character. Philip Schaff, in his *Creeds of Christendom*,
lists nine distinctions between the two. . . . Surely Schaff is right in emphasizing the close affinity
between these two men and the Churches that owe their existence to them."

4. On the earlier version of this essay, Booth wrote in the margin: "But what was faith? and in
what? Faith for Luther is faith in an act done by God—Jesus on Cross—for me[.] Faith for Calvin
is faith in the sovereignty, wisdom etc. of God. Faith in his love of Justice in predestination to
heaven & hell. Trust God & accept his wisdom."

at one in their scorn of the Roman Church; they were at one in their stand upon Scripture as the final authority for the faith; they were at one in emphasizing the evangelical doctrines of the Gospel.[5] With these preliminary observations, we may now turn to a more detailed discussion of the theologies of Luther and Calvin.

God

Luther's view of God may be said to be threefold. First, for those outside of Christ, God is the great judge who passes penalty upon sinful men. He is the God of wrath, the stern judge who hates sin. Luther insisted that the very nature of God would be contradictory if he did not hate sin, therefore, his wrath is an inevitable corollary of his nature. But Luther does not stop here, he goes on to a second view of God, which to him is all important. For those in Christ, God is an all loving Father who is constantly revealing himself through his son Jesus Christ. Luther is well convinced that love is God's own proper work; wrath is his alien work. Actually, God does not want to be a wrathful God, but men with their sin make it so. Luther's view of a personal loving God grew primarily out of his experience. After his long struggle for ~~sahation~~ {salvation} he came to peace because of his vision of the forgiving love of God in Christ.[6] Moreover, Luther could not forget the advice of his

---

5. Kerr, *Luther's Theology*, p. xiii: "In a comparison of the writings of Luther and Calvin on the great doctrinal questions what strikes one with greater force than their disagreements is the amazing similarity of the two, even to the point of detail in many instances. For example, so far as the authors themselves are concerned, there would seem to be little reason for distinguishing between them by saying that the regnant principle of Luther's theology was justification by faith, while for Calvin it was the sovereignty of God. If there is any truth in such a distinction, it is largely a matter of emphasis and ought not to leave the impression that Luther did not speak of the sovereignty of God or that Calvin did not treat of justification by faith. . . . For [Calvin], as for Luther, justification by faith is the heart of the Christian faith. . . . In other particulars the harmony between the two Reformers is so close that it would be difficult to detect differences of any kind. They were at one in their scorn of the Roman Church; they were at one in their refusal to be led into subtleties and verbal casuistry; they were at one in their stand upon Scripture as the Word of God and the final authority for faith; they were at one in emphasizing the evangelical doctrines of the Gospel."

6. Arthur Cushman McGiffert, *Protestant Thought Before Kant* (London: Duckworth, 1919), p. 29: "Peace came to him, after his long struggle to appease the wrath of God by meritorious works, solely because of his vision of the forgiving love of God in Christ."

teacher, Staupitz, who pointed out to him that true penitence began not with fear of a punishing God, but with love of God. In emphasizing this primacy of a God of love, Luther was well in line with the true Christian view of God. But amid all of this emphasis on a God of love, Luther sets forth a third view of God which complicates his whole theology. He comes forth saying that God is an absolute sovereign power who predestines some men to eternal salvation and others to eternal damnation. God is responsible for everything that happens. Man is denied of free will when it comes to choosing ultimates. He is free, but not free to choose the good. How man could have any freedom at all in the face of an absolute sovereign God is a question which Luther never answers. He goes on insisting that man is free in a limited sense, and yet God is still absolute sovereign.

Calvin's view of God is quite similar to that of Luther. The difference between the two is primarily a matter of emphasis rather than a matter of content. For Calvin, God is strictly a personal being whose omnipotence controls everything. Like Luther, he held that God is absolute sovereign. However, Calvin goes a little beyond Luther in his emphasis on this point. This is the major premise of Calvin's theology, and from it flows logically the rest of his views. If one accepts Calvin's premise, he must inevitably accept the remainder of his theology. According to Calvin everything that happens is decreed by God. Such things as being shipwrecked on a stormy sea, or being robbed, or being killed by the fall of a tree must be attributed to God as causal agency rather than to fate.*[7] God is forever exercising his will; he willed everything in the past, present and future. Of course, God wills nothing but the right. This is how Calvin accounted for the problem of evil. If God wills a thing it is right, for everything that he wills is determined by his glory and honor.

As a logical corollary of his major premise, Calvin posits a view of absolute predestination. Like Luther, Calvin insisted that some men are elected for salvation and others for damnation. But Calvin goes beyond Luther in emphasizing this point. According to Calvin, God not only foresaw "the fall of the first man

* Insti., I. xvi. 3.

---

7. This sentence does not appear in the earlier version of this essay.

or in him the ruin of his posterity, but arranged all by the determination of His own will."*[8] In other words, God decreed the fall itself. This view is often spoken of as supralapsarianism in contrast to infralapsarianism, the view that God gave the decree of election after the fall of man.

* Insti., III. xxiii. 7.

From this brief summary, we can see a slight difference in Luther's view of God and Calvin's view of God. The former, although recognizing the wrath of God, placed emphasis on the love of God. Primarily, God is an all loving father. On the other hand, it is justice and power that are prominent in Calvin's God. To the Reformed Theologian, though he recognized the love of God, the power and will of God were fundamental. God the creator and ruler of the world was the God of Calvin.[9]

The Person of Jesus

The genius of the Christian religion for Luther, was to know God through Jesus Christ. Luther would say that we do not know God through intellectual speculation, nor through the mystic flight, but through Jesus alone. He makes it clear that "man will not find God outside of Christ, even should he mount up above the heavens or descend below hell inself, or go beyond the limits of the world."†

† Kerr, CLT, 49.

This Christocentric emphasis is a conspicuous part of Luther's theology. When he comes to the person of Jesus, Luther quite readily accepts the orthodox views of the councils. With Nicaea he sees Jesus as "Very God of Very God." With Chalcedon he sees Jesus as fully human and fully divine. However, Luther went beyond the councils by setting forth the views that the human nature of Jesus absorbs the divine nature and the divine nature of Jesus absorbs the human nature. This view of Luther's is called communicatic ideomatum, "The communication of attributes." Through the interchange of attributes, the divine nature of Jesus could experience birth, suffering and death, while the human nature of Jesus could experience eternity, omnipotence and ubiquity. It is probably that Luther

---

8. This sentence does not appear in the earlier version of this essay.

9. These two sentences do not appear in the earlier version of this essay.

posited this view in order to give logical validation to his view of consubstantiation.

Like Luther, Calvin accepts the orthodox views of the Church councils as to the person of Christ. In The Institutes, he states,

> Choosing from the womb of the Virgin a temple for his residence, he who was the Son of God, became also the Son of man, not by a confusion of substance, but by a unity of person. For we assert such a connection and union of the Divinity with the humanity, that each nature retains its properties entire, and yet both together constitute one Christ.*

* Insti., II. xiv. 2.

This immediately reveals that Calvin does not accept Luther's view of the communicatio ideomatum. He is quite convinced that "each nature retains its properties entire." Moreover, Calvin does not place as much emphasis on the revelation of God in Christ as does Luther. As stated above, Luther was insistent on the point that knowledge of God is only possible through Christ.

Man and Human Nature

When we turn to the reformer's view of man and human nature, we are immediately confronted with a stream of pessimism. First, we may turn to Luther. His view of man grows mainly out of two sources, viz., Augustinianism and his own personal experience. Luther became convinced with Augustine that God alone begins and ends the salvation process. There is no power in man's life to perform a saving good. Man's will is in moral bondage, leaving him free only to choose the evil. God alone has free will. Because of this, everything is from God to man. Man can never make a move toward God. Man, like a helpless creature in the bottom of a well, can do nothing until God reaches down and pulls him up.

Man finds himself in this condition because he misused his original freedom which resulted in the fall. After the fall, Adam's total nature was corrupted, and this corruption was passed on to all of his posterity. Luther's feeling of sinfullness in his own life convinced him of the logic of this view. He came to the conclusion that memory, understanding and will were totally corrupted by the fall. Before the fall, Adam was inclined only to the good. In this state of origi-

179

nal righteousness, man could know God, love God, and believe God, but the loss of original righteousness wrought man incapable of doing either of these. From this point on the human race became a mass of perdition.

With the exception of minor modifications, Calvin's view of man is well nigh identical with that of Luther. Like Luther, Calvin asserts that every man is evil from periphery to core and never can hope to be good unless God elects him to be so. The image of God, though not totally effaced from man, is in a terrible condition. Says Calvin: "Wherefore, although we allow that the divine image was not utterly annihilated and effaced in him, yet it was so corrupted that whatever remains is but horrible deformity."*[10] Guilt as well as corruption come to us from Adam. At birth, every man stands before God as a sinner. Calvin defines original sin as the "hereditary depravity and corruption of our own nature diffused through all the parts of the soul, rendering us obnoxious to the Dinne wrath."† With Luther, Calvin goes on to speak of the moral bondage of man's will. Says Calvin, "The will, therefore, is so bound by the slavery of sin, that it cannot excite itself, much less devote itself to anything good."‡ It is God, however, who wills the corruption of man. Every evil tendency in human nature is a decree by God. Even the fall itself was decreed by God. Luther never went to the extreme of Calvin at this point. He was content to see the fall as a result of man's free will. However, Calvin's conclusion at this point logically follows from his major premise.

* Insti., I. xv. 4.

† Insti., II. i. 8.

‡ Insti., II. iii. 2.

Views of Salvation

Luther contended that salvation is of God alone, independent of all human effort. Following Paul, Luther maintained constantly that man is saved by faith and not by works. His position at this point is most emphatic and probably the most familiar part of his teaching. But is not salvation thus made dependent on man's efforts? Is not the substitution of "faith alone" for the traditional formula "faith and works" simply the substitution of one form of human merit for an-

---

10. These two sentences do not appear in the earlier version of this essay.

other? This would be true if faith were man's work, but according to Luther even faith is bestowed upon man by God. God produces it, and so it is not in any sense a form of human merit.*[11]

* Kerr, CLT, 32.

Luther was thus a thoroughgoing predestinarian; this fact has been emphasized above. But Luther's predestinarianism was not a theological or metaphysical affiar. It is true that in his desire to show the sole activity of God in the salvation process, he was led to present his predestinarian views in theological form, but this was not the essence of the matter. Luther's belief in predestination was the fruit of experience rather than the results of speculation. This is made clear, for an instance, by the fact that while he frequently speaks of the absolute bondage of the human will, and declares that all of our deeds are caused by God, he yet recognizes man's freedom in matters which do not concern salvation. Evidently Luther's primary concern was not to safeguard the divine omnipotence, but to give expression to his own experience of God's divine power in saving him. He had attempted to find salvation through meritorious work and this was to no avail, but finally he was able to gain peace because of his vision of the forgiving love of God in Christ. This convinced him that peace came to him through God's work, and not his.[12] There could

---

11. McGiffert, *Protestant Thought*, p. 28: "Though Luther believed, as I have already said, that salvation is of God alone, independent of all human effort, he yet taught that it is conditioned upon faith. Following Paul, who became here the interpreter of the reformer's own experience, he maintained constantly that man is saved by faith and not by works. His position at this point is the most familiar part of his teaching. But is not salvation thus made dependent after all upon human activity? Is not the substitution of 'faith alone' for the traditional formula 'faith and works' simply the substitution of one form of human merit for another? This would be so if faith were man's own work, but, according to Luther, it is the work of God. He produces it, and so it is not in any sense a form of human merit."

12. McGiffert, *Protestant Thought*, p. 29: "Luther was thus a thoroughgoing predestinarian; but his predestinarianism was not a theological or metaphysical affair. It is true that in his desire to do away with all human merit, and show the sole activity of God in the salvation of man, he was led to present his predestinarian convictions in theological form. . . . But none of this is of the essence of the matter, and it should not be made the starting-point in interpreting his thought. His belief in predestination was the fruit of experience, not of speculation. This is made abundantly clear, for instance, by the fact that while he frequently asserts, in the most categorical fashion, the absolute bondage of the human will, and declares that all our deeds, evil as well as good, are directly caused by God, he yet recognizes man's freedom in matters which do not concern his salvation. Evidently his controlling interest was not to safeguard the divine omnipotence, but to give expression to his own experience of God's controlling power in saving him. Peace came to him, after his long struggle to appease the wrath of God by meritorious works, solely because of his vision of the forgiving love of God in Christ. The peace was God's work, not his own."

be no two agents in the salvation process. We may call this a monogistic view of salvation.

In dealing with Luther's view of salvation, we are inevitably led to a discussion of his view of the sacraments. It will be remembered that Luther reduced the sacraments to two in number, Baptism and the Lord's Supper. These sacraments could accomplish a deal of results in the lives of men, such as the forgiveness of sin, and the rendering of Grace, provided that the recipient was a believer. Luther could not accept the Roman Catholic view of <u>ex opere operato</u> (the view that the sacraments take effect in and of themselves without regards to the faith of the individual or the moral condition of the priest); instead he held the view of <u>nullum sacramentum sine fide</u> (no sacrament without faith). Luther would say that the sacraments depend basically on faith. If the recipient has not faith, the sacrament has no meaning.*

* Kerr, CLT, 164–170.

When he came to the interpretation of the Lord's Supper, Luther remained closer to Roman Catholicism than any of the {other} Reformers. To him Christ's words, "This is my body", were literally true.[13] "His deep religious feeling saw in an actual partaking of Christ the surest pledge of that union with Christ and forgiveness of sins of which the Supper was the divinely attested promise."† However, Luther's interpretation of the Lord's supper is not identical with the Roman Catholic view. The view held by the latter is known as transubstantiation (trans-change; substantia-substance). Here it is held that the bread and the wine change into the substance of the body and blood of Christ. On the other hand, Luther held a view known as consubstantiation (con-with; substantion-substance). Here it is held that the body and blood of Christ are along with the bread and wine rather than the latter changing into the former. The question arises, how can a physical body be in more than one place? Luther sought to explain this mystery by a scholastic assertion, derived largely from Occam, that the qualities of Christ's divine nature, including ubiquity, were communicated to His human nature.[14]

† Walker, HCC, 364.

---

13. Williston Walker, *A History of the Christian Church* (New York: Scribner, 1918), p. 364: "To Luther Christ's words, 'This is my body,' were literally true."

14. Walker, *History of the Christian Church*, p. 364: "A physical body could be only in one place. . . . [Luther] sought to explain the physical presence of Christ on ten thousand altars at

When we come to Calvin's view of salvation, we immediately notice the affinity between his view and that of Luther. Calvin, like Luther posits the view that salvation is by God alone. Since God determines everything he determines salvation. Man's position in determining his salvation is manifestly nil. In a profound sense, Calvin's view of salvation grows out of his view of human nature. Spiritually, the natural man is as dead as a stone. The result is for Calvin a one way traffic.

Obviously Calvin's view of salvation is grounded in a thoroughgoing predestinarianism. It must be noticed, however, that Calvin, in his theory of predestination was moved, not only by Luther's practical interest, but also by a theological motive which the Wittenberg reformer did not share, and he carried the theory further than Luther did, and gave it a more controlling place in his thinking. This doctrine for Calvin is a logical outgrowth of his view of the majesty and might of God. To reject or even to minimize predestination seemed to limit God and throw contempt upon him.[15] Again, we are reminded of the fact that if we grant Calvin his premise, viz., the absolute sovereignty of God, then his conclusion that salvation depends totally on God is quite logical.

Calvin was quite as convinced as Luther that salvation is by faith alone. "Man," he states, "being subject to the curse of the law, have no means left of attaining salvation but through faith alone."* Yet, the emphasis on the primacy of faith does not cause Calvin to minimize works, for he is convinced that

* Kerr, CCI, 108.

> We never dream either of a faith destitute of good works, or of a justification unattended by them; this is the sole difference, that while we acknowledge a necessary connection between faith and good works, we attribute justification, not to works, but to faith.†

† Kerr, CCI, 115.

Hence, faith is always accompanied by works. It seems at times that good works are stressed much {more} by Calvin than by Luther. The former seems to say trust

---

once by a scholastic assertion, derived largely from Occam, that the qualities of Christ's divine nature, including ubiquity, were communicated to His human nature."

15. McGiffert, *Protestant Thought*, p. 87: "But Calvin gave [predestination] an essential place in a system whose controlling principle was the majesty and might of God. As a result to reject or even to minimize it seemed to limit God and throw contempt upon Him."

God and do your duty. The latter seems to say trust God and do as you please.[16]

Calvin's view of the significance of the eucharist or Lord's Supper is somewhat opposed to the view held by Luther. Luther had taught the Real Presence in the emblems while Zwingli had taken the diametrically opposite position and declared for the unalloyed symbolism of the holy meal. Calvin mediated these two positions with a leaning toward the Swiss reformer in form, and to the German in spirit. With Zwingli, he denied any physical presence of Christ; yet he asserts in the clearest terms a real, though spiritual presence received by faith. "Christ, out of the substance of His flesh, breathes life into our souls, nay, diffuses His own life unto us, though the real flesh of Christ does not enter us."* Calvin stresses the view that the sacraments are only effective for the elect. The sacrament is a channel through which the divine grace enters the elect.

We cannot close this section without mentioning the two reformer's theory of atonement. It seems that Luther and Calvin were at one on this point. They shaped a theory of atonement with the analogies of criminal law. They agreed that the enormity of sin required an infinite satisfaction to God if he was to release the sinner.† This satisfaction that was due to God consisted in punishment. To meet this requirement Christ actually took the place of sinners in the sight of God, and as a substitute suffered the punishment that was due to men. Upon him fell all the punishment of all the sins of men for whom he died; against them, therefore, penal justice could have no further claim. Calvin continually emphasized the fact that this atonement was limited only to the elect. It seems that this whole theory of atonement grew out of the influence that legalistic training had had on these two reformers.

* Calvin, <u>Insti.</u>, IV. xvii. 2.

† See Kerr, CCI, 88;
Kerr, CLT, 52–53.

The Church

The reformer's doctrine of the Church was to a great extent an outgrowth of their overall theology. First of all, let us turn to Luther's view of the Church.

---

16. This paragraph does not appear in the earlier version of this essay.

He speaks of the Church in a twofold manner. On the one hand ~~action and clergyman~~ {there is the visible Church which is an outward reality with action and clergymen.} On the other hand there is the invisible Church which is composed of all in spiritual fellowship with Christ. Says Luther:

> For the sake of brevity and a better understanding, we shall call the two Churches by different names. The first which is the natural, essential, real and true one, let us call a spiritual, inner Christendom. The other, which is man-made and external, let us call a bodily, external Christendom; not as if we would part them asunder, but just as when I speak of a man, and call him, according to the soul, a spiritual, according to the body, a physical man; or as the Apostle is want to speak of the inner and of the outward man. Thus, also the Christian assembly, according to the soul, is a communion of one accord in one faith, although according to the body it cannot be assembled at one place, and yet every group is assembled in one place.*

* Kerr, CLT, 125–126.

It is quite possible, argues Luther, to be in the visible Church without being in the invisible Church. However, this assertion never caused Luther to think of the visible Church as being separated from the invisible Church; the two are together like body and soul. The invisible Church exists within the visible Church. Needless to say that Luther sees no earthly head of the Church. Christ alone is the head of the Church.

Calvin's doctrine of the Church is quite similar to that of Luther. According to Calvin the Church is the means by which we are nourished in the Christian life. "To those to whom God is Father, the Church must also be a mother."† Following the line already marked out by Wyclif, Huss, and Zwingli, Calvin defines the Church as "all the elect of God, including in the number even those who have departed this life."‡[17] Like Luther, he sees the Church as both visible and invisible, and its marks are the word and the sacrament. Where the word is truly taught and the sacrament rightly administered there is the Church, and

† Insti., IV. i. 1.

‡ Insti., IV. i. 2.

---

17. Walker, *Calvin*, pp. 418–419: "[The Church] is the means by which we are nourished in the Christian life. 'To those to whom [God] is a Father, the Church must also be a mother.' Following the line already marked out by Wyclif, Huss, and Zwingli, Calvin defines the Church in the last analysis as 'all the elect of God, including in the number even those who have departed this life.'"

outside of it there is no salvation. Calvin was very insistent upon this point. He says,

> As our present design is to treat of the visible Church, we may learn even from the title mother, how useful and even necessary it is for us to know her, since there is no other way of entrance into life, unless we are conceived by her, born of her, nourished at her breast, and continually preserved under her care and government till we are divested of this mortal flesh, and become like Angels. . . . It is also to be remarked that out of her bosom there can be no hope of remission of sins, or any salvation.*[18]

* Insti., IV. i. 4.

Whoever alienates himself from the Church is a "deserter of religion." Yet to leave the Papacy is in no sense to leave the Church, for "it is certain that there is no Church where lying and falsehood have usurped the ascendancy".†[19]

† Insti., IV. ii. 1.

The visible Church is properly governed only by officers of divine appointment made human in the New Testament. There are pastors, teachers, elders, and deacons,—partly clerical and partly lay office bearers, for in Calvin's system the recognition of the rights of the laymen, characteristic of the whole Reformation movement, comes to its completest development. This recognition received further illustration in that the officers of the Calvinistic Churches, unlike those of the Roman, Lutheran, and Anglican communions, enter their charges only by the consent of the people whom they serve. Their call is twofold,—the secret inclination which has God as its author, and the election "on the consent and approbation of the people."‡[20]

‡ Insti., IV. xi. 1.

---

18. McGiffert, *Protestant Thought*, pp. 93–94: "But the Church is visible as well as invisible, and its marks are the word and the sacraments. Where the word is truly taught and the sacraments rightly administered there is the Church, and outside of its pale there is ordinarily no salvation. Calvin was very insistent upon this point. 'What God has joined together,' he says, 'it is wrong to put asunder; for to those to whom God is a Father the Church also is a mother.' And again: 'As our present design is to treat of the visible Church, we may learn even from the title of mother how useful and even necessary it is for us to know her, since there is no other way of entrance into life unless we are conceived by her, born of her, nourished at her breast, and continually preserved under her care and government till we are divested of this mortal flesh and become like the angels. . . . It is also to be remarked that out of her bosom there can be no hope of remission of sins nor any salvation.'"

19. Walker, *Calvin*, p. 419: "Whoever alienates himself from it is a 'deserter of religion.' Yet to leave the Papacy is in no sense to leave the Church, for 'it is certain that there is no Church where lying and falsehood have usurped the ascendancy.'"

20. Walker, *Calvin*, pp. 419–420: "This visible Church is properly governed only by officers of divine appointment made known in the New Testament. These are pastors, teachers, elders,

This, in brief, is the doctrine of the Church held by Luther and Calvin. Although they consider the Church important and even necessary, they never give it the authoritarian position that it held in Roman Catholicism. It was Christ that was supreme for them, not the Church or the Pope.

The Scripture

A survey of the theology of Luther and Calvin would be quite inadequate without a discussion of their views of the Bible. Certainly most of the Reformers were united in seeing the scripture as the absolute word of God. In speaking of scripture as the absolute word of God, Luther could say,

> We must make a great difference between God's word and the word of man. A man's word is a little sound, that flies into the air, and soon vanishes; but the Word of God is greater than heaven and earth, yea, greater than death and hell, for it forms part of the power of God, and endures everlastingly; we should, therefore, diligently study God's Word, and know and assuredly believe that God himself speaks unto us.*

* Kerr, CLT, 10.

Calvin could say that "we are not established in the belief of the Bible till we are indubitably persuaded that God is its Author."† Calvin was convinced that the Scriptures were written by men who were "sure and authentic amanuenses of the Holy Spirit."‡ In brief, both Calvin and Luther merely substituted the authority of Scripture for that of Church and Pope. But in their respective doctrines of Scripture, when fully developed, Calvin was for more narrow the Luther. The latter's teaching may be summed up thus: All teaching not found to contradict scripture may be true, while the former (Calvin) would say, all teaching not found in the Scripture is false. For the German the Scriptures were a partial revelation of truth while

† Insti., I. vii. 4.

‡ Insti., I. vi. 2.

---

and deacons,—partly clerical and partly lay office-bearers, for in Calvin's system the recognition of the rights of the layman, characteristic of the whole Reformation movement, comes to its completest development. This recognition receives further illustration in that the officers of the Calvinistic churches, unlike those of the Roman, Anglican, Lutheran, and Zwinglian communions, properly enter on their charges only with the assent of the congregation that they serve. Their 'call' is twofold,—the secret inclination which has God as its author, and their election 'on the consent and approbation of the people.'"

for the Frenchmen the Scriptures were an unabridged compendium of all truth. The one gave opportunity for a living God while the other embalmed Him and mummified him in the pages of the book.

Critique

The leading ideas of Luther's and Calvin's theology have been presented in the preceding paragraphs: it remains for us, in this closing section, to indicate the main lines of criticism which they have called forth in my mind.

First, let us turn to their doctrine of God. It will be remembered that both Luther and Calvin placed a great deal of emphasis on the sovereignty of God. But there is always the danger that an undue emphasis on the sovereignty of God will lose sight of the divine love. God is first and foremost an all loving Father, and any theology which fails to recognize this, in an attempt to maintain the sovereignty of God, is betraying everything that is best in the Christian tradition. Luther dimly recognized this, and attempted, although often unsatisfactorily, to stress the love of God. But not so with Calvin. It is justice and power that are prominent in Calvin's God. The God of the Genevan reformer was a monster of iniquity. He was so bent on justice that he possessed no conscience. He was so concerned about being respected and glorified that He found in Himself neither glory nor respect for men. When men become servants of such a God, they may be expected to set flame to the faggots piled high about the body of a Servetus or preach the sermon of Jonathan Edwards, "Sinners in the Hands of an Angry God."[21]

We may now turn to a criticism of the reformer's views of the person and work of Christ. Concerning the Person of Christ, both Luther and Calvin affirmed the traditional Two-Nature Doctrine. Both were convinced that a perfect, divine, and a perfect human nature were united in the personality of Christ. This doctrine, however, calls for a reinterpretation and modification. It was based on a Platonic substance philosophy which has been largely replaced

---

21. The remainder of the essay does not appear in the previous version.

today by a philosophy which see reality as active or
dynamic on the one hand and as individual and concrete on the other. On the basis of such thinking it
is a mistake to look upon Christ as having two independently existing natures.[22] As Knudson has so well
put it,

> There were factors in his personality that may be dis-
> tinguished as human and divine. But they were not
> distinct substances. They were simply different as-
> pects of the one unique personality. And this person-
> ality is to be viewed, not as a substance, but as an
> agent.*

* Knudson, BICT, 137.

Hence, we must affirm that Christ is a unitary personality, and this unity we find in his own ego. There
is nothing in rational speculation nor New Testament
thought to warrant the view that Jesus had two personal centers. We must then think of Christ as a unitary being whose divinity consists not in any second
nature or in a substantial unity with God, but in a
unique and potent God consciousness. His unity of
{with} God was a unity of purpose rather than a unity
of substance.

Concerning the work of Christ the two reformers
stressed a substitutionary theory of atonement. They
maintained that Christ actually took the place of sinners in the sight of God, and as a substitutee suffered
the punishment that was due to men. But all of this is
based on a false view of personality. Merit and guilt
are not transferable from one person to another. They
are inalienable from personality. Moreover, on moral
grounds, a person cannot be punished in the place of
another.[23]

Another weakness in this theory of atonement is
that it is based on the assumption that the chief obstacle to man's redemption is in the nature of God.
But there was never any obstacle to man's redemption
in God himself. The real obstacle to man's redemption has always lain in man himself. It is from this
standpoint, therefore, that the death of Christ is to

22. Albert C. Knudson, *Basic Issues in Christian Thought* (New York: Abingdon-Cokesbury
Press, n.d.), p. 137: "It is therefore a mistake to think of Christ as having two independently
existing natures."

23. Knudson, *Basic Issues*, p. 144: "All this taken literally is fictitious. Merit and guilt are inalienable from personality. They cannot be detached from one person and transferred to another.
Nor can one person morally be punished in place of another."

be interpreted. Christ's death was not a ransom, or a penal substitute, or a penal example, rather it was a revelation of the sacrificial love of God intended to awaken an answering love in the hearts of men.

Another phase of thinking in which our two theologians went to an extreme was in the doctrine of man. Both affirm that man was originally righteous, but through some strange and striking accident he became hopelessly sinful. Yet it has become increasingly difficult to imagine any such original state of perfection for man as Luther and Calvin continually presupposed. It is not within the scope of this paper to enter into any argument concerning evolution. However, it is perfectly evident that its major contentions would refute such a view.[24] We are compelled, therefore, to reject the idea of a catastrophic fall and regard man's moral condition from another point of view. Man's fall is not due to some falling away from an original righteousness, but to a failure to rise to a higher level of his present existence.

In the same ~~view~~ {vein} we must reject Luther's and Calvin's view that man is incapable of performing any saving good, and that man can do nothing to save himself. Certainly we must agree that the image of God is terribly scared in man, but not to the degree that man cannot move toward God. As seen in the life and teaching of Jesus, humanity remains conscious of its humble dependence upon God, as the source of all being and all goodness. "There is none good save one, even God." Yet in dealing with even the worst of men, Christ constantly made appeal to a hidden goodness in their nature. We must somehow believe that the lives of men are changed when the potential good in man is believed in particularly, and when the potential bad in man is sought to be overwhelmed.

A final doctrine of Luther and Calvin which needs to be critized is the doctrine of predestination. Any form of mechanical determinism is far from adequate for lasting Christian doctrine. The Kantian "I ought therefore I can" should stand out as a prelude in any Christian conception of man. Any attempt to maintain a doctrine of man ~~denied~~ {devoid} of freedom

---

24. DeWolf commented in the margin, "But note that the original <u>innocence</u> could not be refuted."

leads us into needless paradoxes. How can there be responsibility with no freedom? Indeed, how can there
be reason with no freedom? Freedom ~~as~~ {is} both a
moral and metaphysical necessity. In the final analysis
any denial of freedom is an affirmation of it since its
denial presupposes a <u>decision</u> for what appears true
over against what appears false.

In spite of these somewhat severe criticisms of Luther and Calvin we must not in the least minimize the
importance of their message. Their cry does call attention to the desperateness of the human situation.
They do insist that religion begins with God and that
man cannot have faith apart from him. They do proclaim that apart from God our human efforts turn to
ashes and our sunrises into darkest night. Much of
this is good, and may it not be that its re-emphasi~~sed~~
by the neo-orthodox theologians of our day will serve
as a necessary corrective for a ~~liberation~~ {liberalism}
that at times becomes all to shallow?[25]

BIBLIOGRAPHY

Calvin, John—ICR
<u>The Institutes of The Christian Religion</u>
(tr. Henry Beveridge)
Edinburgh: 1845.
Kerr, H. T.—CLT
<u>A Compend of Luther's Theology</u>.
Philadelphia: Westminister Press, 1943.
Kerr, H. T.—CCR
<u>A Compend of the Institutes of the Christian
Religion</u>
Philadelphia: Westminster Press, 1939.
Knudson, Albert C.—BICT
<u>Basic Issues In Christian Thought</u>
New York: Abingdon-Cokesbury Press, 1950.
Walker, Williston,—JC
<u>John Calvin</u>
New York: G. P. Putnam's Sons, 1906.

THDS. MLKP-MBU: Box 112.

---

25. A version of this paragraph appears in several of King's essays. Cf. King, "Karl Barth's
Conception of God," p. 106 in this volume.

Final Examination Answers,
History of Christian Doctrine

19 May 1953
[*Boston, Mass.*]

In his examination answers for DeWolf's History of Christian Doctrine, King
succinctly sets forth some of the ideas that he expressed in more detail elsewhere.
The second question asked him to "compare Schleiermacher's and Ritschl's[1]
teachings on the person of Christ," a topic he had pursued the previous May in an
essay for DeWolf on the two theologians' Christology.[2] *King also briefly states his*
opinions of Karl Barth. DeWolf gave this examination 97 points and commented,
"Good!" King received an A for the semester.

[*1. Compare the theological methods of Thomas Aquinas, Wesley and Schleier-*
macher.][3]

1. Thomas Aquinas argues that there are two ways of gaining religious
truth. The first way is that of philosophy. Here inferences are made
from sense data. The movement is upward from particular things to
God. The second way is that of theology. Here everything is revealed.
The movement is downward from God to particular thing. In Thomas
we get a synthesis of revealed theology and natural theology.

Wesley starts out affirming with the general reformation teachers that
the Bible is authorative. Indeed he affirms that the Bible is a sufficient
source of religious truth. Yet he does not stop here. He makes it very
clear that reason has a place in theological construction. Althought reason is not the source of doctrine, it must be used to interpret doctrine.
We need reason to infere and judge. So he concludes that we must use
our finite reason as far as possible and then we must depend on revelation. Here we can see that Wesley has something in common with
Thomas. Both find reason {to be} a valid instrument in theological construction and yet both are equally insistent that reason must be supli-
mented by revelation. It is probably true to say that Wesley places more
emphasis on the authority of the Bible than Thomas. Thomas, following
the Catholic emphasis, places a deal of importance and authority in the
councils.

Schleiermacher starts out attempting to discover what is universal in
religion. He discovers that it is a feeling of absolute dependence, rather

---

1. DeWolf refers to Friedrich Schleiermacher (1768–1834) and Albrecht Ritschl (1822–
1889).

2. King, "A Comparison of Friedrich Schleiermacher's Christology with That of Albrecht
Ritschl," 9 May 1952, MLKP-MBU: Box 112.

3. DeWolf refers to John Wesley (1703–1791).

than dogmas or ethical teachings. All theology is an attempt to explicate the teachings implied in this feeling of absolute dependence. In other words Schleiermacher's method is to describe didactically the religious consciousness, and state its implications regarding the attributes of God, the nature of the world and the relation of God and man.

Herein we see the difference between Scheiermacher, Wesley and Thomas. Wherein Thomas would begin with reason and revelation, and Wesley would begin with the Scripture ~~and~~ reason and revelation, Schleiermacher begins with something totally subjective, viz., the feeling of absolute dependence.[4]

[2. *Compare Schleiermacher's and Ritschl's teachings on the person of Christ.*]

2. Both Schleiermacher and Ritschl opposed the orthodox doctrines concerning the person of Christ. Both doubted the orthodox doctrine of the trinity. Both rejected the two nature doctrine of Christ. Both insisted that if Christ was divine it was not due to any substantial unity with God. For Schleiermacher the essence of Christ person was found in his unique God consciousness. The feeling of absolute dependence ruled in Christ supreme. Every action and attitude in his life was determine by this absolute God consciousness. So dominant was this God consciousness that Christ had the slightest inclination for sin. He was never even tempted. Schleiermacher was convinced that Christ was unique and could be replaced by non other. But his uniqueness was found in the complete God consciousness that ruled in him rather than in any substantial unity with God.

Ritschl made it very clear that ~~that~~ Christianity was of such nature as to provide a necessary place for its historical founder. Ritschl affirmed that "Jesus is God." But this does not mean that Jesus is God in any ontological sense. Jesus is God in the sense the he has the worth of God to us. (This is in line with Ritschl general epistemological position, viz., that religious knowledge is composed of value judgements, in constrast to Scientific and philosophical knowledge which is composed of factual and causal judgements as well as value judgements.) Ritschl makes it clear that to affirm that Jesus is God is not to affirm that he has any substantial unity with God. He, like Schleiermacher, emphatically denies this. Jesus unity with God is a unity of will and purpose.

Ritschl, like Schleiermacher, affirmed that Jesus is unique and replacable by no other. God worked in him as he worked through no other human being. But this does not mean that Christ possesses a different nature from other men. Both Ritschl and Schleiermacher would affirm that Christ possessed the same nature as other men.[5]

---

4. DeWolf gave this answer 10 points.
5. DeWolf gave this answer 10 points.

[3. *Show the place of philosophy in relation to the theology of Duns Scotus, Edwards, Ritschl and Kierkegaard.*][6]

3. Duns Scotus used philosophy to some degree in his theological construction, accepting basically the Christian Aristoteleanism of Aquinas. But he restricted the domain of philosophy quite a ~~bit~~ bit in theological thinking. For an instance, he held that immortality couldn't be proved philosophically. Moreover, the existence of God could not be proved philosophical. At best philosophical arguments for God prove only a first cause, but not the Personal Father of Christianity.

Edwards found philosophy to be quite a useful tool in relation to theology. His whole doctrine of the world is ~~bassed~~ based on a personalistic metaphysics. When he comes to refute free will he uses all of the tools of philosophical naturalism. His argument for the existence is based on the philosophical view of the ideality of matter.

Ritschl excluded, or rather attempted to exclude, philosophy almost completely from theological construction. His watchword could have well been: theology without metaphysics. Following the Kantian epistemology, he insisted that all knowledge is of phenomena. One can never get to the Ding an sich through reason. He goes on to argue that all religious knowledge consist of independent value judgments, in constrast to scientific and philosophical knowledge which is based on causal and factual judgments. So religion does not have to wait on philosophical proof to operate.

Kierkegaard had no use for philosophy. System making was at best a game. Philosophy is based on the false premise that one can be objective. ·But in the realm of Christianity one is called upon to make a choice which has ultimate significance. To make such a choice the individual must give his whole self to God or reality rather than wait for all the answers. Knowledge of existence is individual subjective and [*strikeout illegible*] existential. Universals do not give us knowledge because universals do not exist. So Kierkegaard ends up affirming that the chief instrument of philosophy, viz., reason must be crucified.[7]

[4. *How appropriate is the designation of Barth's theology as a "new orthodoxy?" Discuss as fully as possible within the available time.*]

4. It seems that the designation of Barth's theology as the "new orthodoxy" is quite appropriate at some points and quite inappropriate at other point. It is appropriate in the sense that it calls us back to ~~make~~ many teachings which are basic in reformation teachings and in orthodoxy

---

6. DeWolf refers to John Duns Scotus (ca. 1265/1266–1308), Jonathan Edwards (1703–1758), and Søren Kierkegaard (1813–1855).

7. DeWolf gave this answer 9+ points.

generally viz., the centrality of the Bible, the importance of the divin‐
ity of Christ, the sovereignty of God, the sinfulness of man, and the
absolute necessity for faith. But there are other points in Barth which
are quite unorthodox. For an instance his insistence on the unknowabil‐
ity and the incomprehensibility of God is not only unorthodox, but also
unbiblical.[8] His affirmation that God is the "Wholly Other" is much more
Kierkegaardian that Biblical. His scorn for history seems to me to be also
a quite unorthodox position. In fact Barth whole doctrine of God is
much more unorthodox and radical that he thinks it is. His God who is
so transcendent that he can never come in touch with the [*strikeout illeg‐
ible*] without a mediator is much more Greek than Christian orthodox.[9]

[5. *Summarize the characteristic theological teachings of Channing.*][10]

5. <u>Theological teachings of Channing</u>
   I Concerning God
      (1) God is known through nature, the Bible and human experience.
         The supreme proof of God is human moral experience.
      (2) God is <u>One</u> person. The doctrine of the Trinity is affirmed no
         where in the scripture.
   II Concerning Man
      (1) Man is God's most noble creation. We can learn more about God
         by looking at ourselves than by looking at the stars.
      (2) Man is not totally depraved. Man and his institutions are quite
         effected[11] with sin, but not to the degree that man cant turn to
         God
      (3) Man is an immortal being. All of the traditional argument for
         hell are based on mistranslations of the Bible or misunderstand‐
         ings of the particular passages.
      (5) All persons are of infinite worth. For this reason slavery and war
         are supremely evil.
   III Concerning Christ
      (1) The life and teachings of Christ are to incongruous with his age
         as not to attest to his divine origin.
      (2) However Christ is not of the same substance as God.
      (3) Christ was preexistent (In this sense Channing is an Arian)
      (4) The scripture gives us accurate acconts of the life and teachings
         of Jesus.[12]

---

8. DeWolf commented in the margin, "yet cf. Luther."

9. DeWolf gave this answer 9 points.

10. DeWolf refers to William Ellery Channing (1780–1842).

11. DeWolf circled the *e*, inserted an *a*, and commented: "Be sure to know the two <u>verbs</u>,
affect and effect."

12. DeWolf gave this answer 10 points.

[6. *Being as specific as possible, evaluate the treatment of late medieval and modern Christian thought by Neve and Heick.*][13]

6. Fisher's treatment of late medieval and modern Christian thought is presented quite objectively and in a lucid style. He never seems to be bias toward a particular view because it isn't in line with his religious tradition. This is especially true of ~~Catholic~~ his analysis of Chatholic thought in the late medieval period. For an instance, his [*strikeout illegible*] {interpretation} of Thomas I think is as good as any and his thought is made very meaningful to any prostatant thinker. When Fisher come to his treatment of the early modern period he continues his objective treatment. His analysis of the theology of Luther and Calvin is very good. Other minor movement of the early modern period are discussed with clearness and vividness. Although the treatment is often condenced it [*strikeout illegible*] never fails to give the major points and teachings of these movements. His discussion of Schliermacher and Ritschl is good as far as it goes. But it seems that the importance of these two figures in the whole development of modern theology would command a little more extensive treatment. Again his treatment of Wesley is somewhat too brief.

His treatment of the influence of philosophy on Christian thought in this period is very good, and shows a real understanding of philosophical trends.[14]

AHDS. MLKP-MBU: Box 115.

---

13. DeWolf recommended that his students read, among other surveys of Christian doctrine, *A History of Christian Thought* (1943) by Jürgen Ludwig Neve and Otto William Heick and *History of Christian Doctrine* (1896) by George Park Fisher.

14. DeWolf gave this answer 9+ points.

"An Exposition of the First Triad of Categories of the Hegelian Logic—Being, Non-Being, Becoming"

[*4 February–22 May 1953*]
[*Boston, Mass.*]

This is the last of six essays that King wrote for a two-semester seminar on Hegel taught by Brightman and Peter A. Bertocci.[1] *Brightman became ill after the second*

---

1. For the other four extant essays, see King, "The Development of Hegel's Thought as Revealed in His Early Theological Writings," 1 October 1952; "The Transition from Sense-Certainty

meeting; he never recovered from his illness, and Bertocci replaced him.[2] *The seminar studied many of Hegel's major works in chronological order. During the second semester they concentrated on Hegel's* Encyclopedia of the Philosophical Sciences *and* Philosophy of Right, *although they may have read* The Philosophy of History *as well. In this essay, which is largely derived from W. T. Stace's* The Philosophy of Hegel, *King discusses a section of the* Lesser Logic *in the* Encyclopedia. *Bertocci commented at the end of the paper, "B +, despite a misunderstanding of logics—see above!"*

In this report it is our purpose to discuss the first triad of the Hegelian Logic—Being, Non-Being, Becoming. Before entering this discussion directly, however, it might be well to devote a few paragraphs to Hegel's conception of the categories and his divergence from the Kantian conception.

The categories began their history, so far as modern philosophy is concerned, in the system of Kant.[3] The categories were for Kant, like space and time, pure forms without content or matter, prior to all experience, and not given from any external source but contributed to cognition by the mind itself. These categories were also universal and necessary.[4] But with all their importance, Kant insisted that the categories were limited to phenomena. They did not apply to the thing-in-itself (<u>Ding an sich</u>). The thing-in-itself was not a cause, or a substance; it was neither

to Sense-Perception in Hegel's Analysis of Consciousness," 15 October 1952; "The Transition from Sense-Perception to Understanding," 29 October 1952; and "Objective Spirit," 4 February– 22 May 1953; all in MLKP-MBU: Box 115.

2. Peter A. Bertocci (1910–) studied with Brightman at Boston University and received his B.A. from Boston in 1931, his M.A. from Harvard University in 1932, and his Ph.D. from Boston University in 1935 (at the same time as his good friend L. Harold DeWolf). Bertocci taught at Bates College from 1935 to 1944 before returning to Boston University as a professor of philosophy. After Brightman's death in 1953 Bertocci became Borden Parker Bowne Professor of Philosophy. His publications include *The Empirical Argument for God in Late British Thought* (1938); *The Human Venture in Sex, Love, and Marriage* (1950); *Free Will, Responsibility, and Grace* (1957); *Personality and the Good: Psychological and Ethical Perspectives,* co-authored with Richard M. Millard (1963); *The Person God Is* (1970); and *The Goodness of God* (1981). See his autobiographical article, "Reflections on the Experience of 'Oughting,'" in *Boston Personalist Tradition in Philosophy, Social Ethics, and Theology,* ed. Paul Deats and Carol Robb (Macon, Ga.: Mercer University Press, 1986), pp. 209–219.

3. W. T. Stace, *The Philosophy of Hegel* (London: Macmillan, 1924), p. 69: "The categories began their history, so far as modern philosophy is concerned, in the system of Kant."

4. Stace, *Philosophy of Hegel,* p. 42: "They are, like space and time, (1) pure forms without content or matter, (2) prior to all experience, and (3) not given from any external source but contributed to cognition by the mind itself. These categories are also universal and necessary."

quality nor quantity.[5] These concepts applied only to phenomena, not to noumena. So for Kant the categories were mere subjective forms of thought, not objective ontological entities.[6] It was at this point that Hegel went beyond Kant. The categories for Hegel were more than epistemological principles of knowing; they were ontological principles of being.[7] They were not merely the necessary and universal conditions of the world as it appears to us, but they were the necessary and universal conditions of the world, as it is in itself.[8] Reason, the system of categories, is self-explained and self-determined, dependent only upon itself. This means that it is real. Therefore, "the rational is the real and the real is the rational."

The task which Hegel undertakes in the <u>Logic</u> is, therefore, this: to give an account of the first reason of the world; to show that every single category necessarily and logically involves every other single category; and finally to show that all the categories, regarded as a single whold, constitute a self-explained, self-determined, unity, such that it is capable of constituting the absolutely first principle of the world.[9] Kant had named twelve categories. But he made no effectual attempt to deduce them from one another. Actually there was no reason why he should do so, because the categories were for him only epistemological forms of the mind, not objective ontological entities. But the fact remains that he did not deduce them.[10] When we come to Hegel, however, the pic-

---

5. Stace, *Philosophy of Hegel*, p. 42: "The categories cannot apply to the thing-in-itself. The thing-in-itself is not a cause, or a substance; it is neither one nor many; it has neither quantity, quality, nor relation."

6. Bertocci placed a "¶" after this sentence to suggest that a new paragraph should begin.

7. Stace, *Philosophy of Hegel*, pp. 60–61: "They were not ontological principles of being, but only epistemological principles of knowing."

8. Bertocci circled "in itself" and wrote a question mark in the margin.

9. Stace, *Philosophy of Hegel*, p. 83: "The task which Hegel undertakes in the *Logic* is, therefore, this: to give an account of the first reason of the world; . . . and finally to show that all the categories, regarded as a single whole, constitute a self-explained, self-determined, unity, such that it is capable of constituting the absolutely *first* principle of the world." See also Stace, *Philosophy of Hegel*, p. 82: "He shows that every single category necessarily and logically involves every other single category."

10. Stace, *Philosophy of Hegel*, p. 82: "Kant had named twelve categories. But he made no effectual attempt to deduce them from one another. There was no reason why he should do so, because the categories were for him not an ontological principle of explanation of the universe, but merely subjective epistemological forms of our minds. But the fact remains that he did not deduce them."

ture is different. Just as in formal logic the conclusion flows necessarily from the premises, so in Hegelian logic the categories are logically deduced from each other.[11]

Now as we turn to a discussion of the first triad of the Hegelian Logic we see this principle at work. Hegel begins with the category of being. Being is not chosen as the first category merely by chance or caprice. It is chosen because it is the highest abstraction, that which is common to every conceivable object in the universe. There are many objects of which it would not be true to say that they are green, or that they are material, or that they are heavy. But whatever object in the universe we choose, it must always be true to say it <u>is</u>. Being, therefore, must be the first category.[12] This Being which Hegel is speaking of as the first category is the "Pure Being" that we have to think, not any particular sort of being, such as this desk, this book, that chair.[13] "Pure Being makes the beginning: because it is on one hand pure thought, and on the other immediacy itself, simple and indeterminate; and the first beginning cannot be mediated by anything, or be further determined"*. In a word we are dealing with being in general, stripped of all determination. To get a clearer view of what Hegel means we may use the example of any concrete object, say this table. This table is square, hard, brown, shiny. Abstract from all these qualities, and we are left with "This table is."[15] Such being is absolutely indeterminate and featureless, completely empty and vacant.[16]

* Wallace, LOH, 158.[14]

---

11. Bertocci underlined and questioned the phrases "necessarily," "from the premises," and "logically deduced from." He asked in the margin: "But what does <u>logic</u> mean to Hegel?"

12. Stace, *Philosophy of Hegel*, p. 87: "The highest possible abstraction, that which is common to every conceivable object in the universe, is the concept of being. . . . There are many objects of which it would not be true to say that they are green, or that they are material, or that they are heavy. But whatever object in the universe we choose, it must always be true to say of it that it *is*. Being, therefore, must be the first category."

13. Stace, *Philosophy of Hegel*, p. 90: "It is the pure category that we have to think, not any particular sort of being, such as this pen, that book, this table, that chair."

14. King incorrectly cites the translator as author. He in fact quotes G. W. F. Hegel, *The Logic of Hegel: Translated from the Encyclopedia of the Philosophical Sciences*, 2d ed., trans. William Wallace (London: Oxford University Press, 1892), p. 158.

15. Stace, *Philosophy of Hegel*, p. 87: "This table, for example, is square, hard, brown, shiny. . . . Abstract lastly from the hardness, and then from the squareness, and we are left with 'This table *is*.'"

16. Bertocci underlined the phrase "emptiness turns out to be" and asked, "Is this deduced?"

This vacuum, this utter emptiness turns out to be not anything. Thus we inevitably find ourselves in the antithesis, viz., Nothing. Emptiness and vacancy are the same as nothing.[17] "Being, as Being, is nothing fixed or ultimate: it yields to dialectic and sinks into its opposite, which, also taken immediately, is Nothing."* Being, therefore, is seen to contain the idea of nothing. But to show that one category contains another is to deduce that other from it.[18] Hence Hegel had deduced the category Nothing from the category Being.[19]

* Wallace, LOH, 161.

Now since Being and Nothing are identical the one passes into the other. Being passes into Nothing. And conversely, Nothing passes back into Being; for the thought of nothing is the thought of emptiness, and this emptiness is pure Being. In consequence of this disappearance of each category into the other we have a third thought involved, namely, the idea of the <u>passage</u> of Being and Nothing into each other. This is the category of Becoming.[20] "Nothing, if it be thus immediate and equal to itself, is also conversely the same as Being is. The truth of Being and of Nothing is accordingly the unity of the two: and this unity is Becoming."† Thus we have three categories. We began with Being. From that we deduced Nothing. And from the relation between the two we deduce Becoming.[21] Being is the thesis. Nothing is the antithesis, and Becoming is the synthesis. The synthesis of this triad, as in all other Hegelian triads, both abolishes and preserves the differences of the thesis and antithesis. This two-fold activity of the synthesis is expressed by Hegel by the word <u>aufheben</u>, which is

† Wallace, LOH, 163.

---

17. Stace, *Philosophy of Hegel*, p. 90: "This vacuum, this utter emptiness, is not anything. . . . Emptiness, vacancy, is the same as nothing."

18. Bertocci circled "category contains another" and wrote a question mark in the margin.

19. Stace, *Philosophy of Hegel*, pp. 90–91: "Being, therefore, is the same as nothing. And the pure concept of being is thus seen to *contain* the idea of nothing. But to show that one category contains another is to deduce that other from it. Hence we have deduced the category nothing from the category being."

20. Stace, *Philosophy of Hegel*, p. 91: "Since they are identical the one passes into the other. Being passes into nothing. And conversely, nothing passes back into being; for the thought of nothing is the thought of emptiness, and this emptiness is pure being. In consequence of this disappearance of each category into the other we have a third thought involved here, namely, the idea of the *passage* of being and nothing into each other. This is the category of becoming."

21. Stace, *Philosophy of Hegel*, p. 92: "Thus we have already three categories. We began with being. From that we deduced nothing. And from the relations between these two we deduce becoming."

sometimes translated "to sublate." The German word has two meanings. It means both to abolish and to preserve.[22] In short, the thesis and the antithesis both die and rise again in the synthesis.[23]

Herein we see one of Hegel's original contributions to philosophy. The older view was that opposites absolutely exclude each other. We could only say A = A (the canon of identity) and never that A = not A.[24] But Hegel came on the scene with an explanation of how it was logically possible for two opposites to be identical while yet retaining their opposition.[25]

THDS. MLKP-MBU: Box 115.

22. Stace, *Philosophy of Hegel*, p. 106: "The synthesis of a triad both abolishes and preserves the differences of the thesis and antithesis. This two-fold activity of the synthesis is expressed by Hegel by the word *aufheben*, which is sometimes translated 'to sublate.' The German word has two meanings. It means both to abolish and to preserve."

23. Bertocci marked these two sentences and commented, "This isn't deduced."

24. Stace, *Philosophy of Hegel*, p. 96: "Hitherto it had always been assumed that, logically speaking, a positive and its negative simply excluded each other. . . . It had always been assumed that we can only say A is A, and that we can never under any circumstances say A is not-A."

25. Bertocci questioned the phrase "was logically." Stace, *Philosophy of Hegel*, pp. 95–96: "He explained and showed in detail how it is logically possible for two opposites to be identical while yet retaining their opposition."

From Rosemary Murphy

2 June 1953
Boston, Mass.

Mr. Martin L. King, Jr.,
397 Massachusetts Avenue
Boston, Massachusetts

Dear Mr. King:

The following is a summary of your recent examination at the Lahey Clinic. Your weight was 166 1/2 pounds, height 66 1/2 inches, blood-pressure 134/64, and pulse 70 with irregular rhythm. The general examination was satisfactory.

I am enclosing a copy of the laboratory and x-ray studies which you had done, since you may like them for future reference.[1] The tests showed no

1. Murphy encloses the medical report with this letter.

evidence of any anemia nor infection. The x-ray of the heart and lungs was normal.

Very sincerely yours,
[*signed*]
Rosemary Murphy, M.D.

RM/meb
523761
BT447

TLS. MLKP-MBU: Box 117.

From Charles E. Batten

23 June 1953

Crozer dean Charles Batten responds to King's marriage announcement. King, Jr., and Coretta Scott were married on 18 June 1953 at the Scott family home outside Marion, Alabama. Martin Luther King, Sr., performed the ceremony.

Reverend Martin Luther King, Jr.
501 Auburn Avenue
Atlanta, Georgia

Dear Martin:

We were very happy to receive the announcement of your marriage. The faculty and your friends at Crozer join me in sending to you our very best wishes. We sincerely hope that you will have a very happy life.

If you had made it four days later it would have been the wedding anniversary of Mrs. Batten and myself. I suppose the best wish I can make for you is that you and Coretta will be as happy as we have been in our married life. Do come see us when you can.

With all good wishes to both of you, I am

Sincerely,
Charles E. Batten, Dean

CEB/bt

TLc. CRO-NRCR.

From Henry Nelson Wieman

14 August 1953
St. Louis, Mo.

In preparation for his dissertation, "A Comparison of the Conceptions of God in the Thinking of Paul Tillich and Henry Nelson Wieman," King wrote Tillich and

Mr. and Mrs. Obie Scott

have the honor of announcing the marriage

of their daughter

Coretta

to

The Reverend Martin Luther King, Jr.

Thursday, June the eighteenth

Nineteen hundred and fifty-three

Heiberger, Alabama

After June 20
501 Auburn, Avenue
Atlanta, Georgia

*Wieman to inquire about work that others had done on the subject. He would later
send similar inquiries to Reinhold Niebuhr and other American theologians.*[1]
*Wieman, a professor at Union Theological Seminary, was teaching at Washington
University at the time of his response.*

Dear Mr. King:

Thank you for the letter of August 5. It was delayed in reaching me because
it had to be forwarded. I am teaching summer session here.

I know of only two writings that compare Tillich's thought with my own.
W. M. Horton in the volume on Tillich edited by Kegley and published by
Macmillan, is one case. Also a few years ago a student at Union Theological
Seminary in New York wrote a thesis on my thology, but as I come to hink of
it he compared me with Brightman more than with Tillich.[2] I have heard
rumors of other such comparisons but cannot refer you to them.

I have a good deal of material not yet published but cannot send more than
two pieces, partly because my mss. are at home and not here. But I am sending under separate cover two lectures that have been mimeographed and so
are expendable.[3] You need not {return them}

[*signed*] Henry N. Wieman

TALS. CSKC.

---

1. See, for example, King to Reinhold Niebuhr, 1 December 1953, pp. 222–223 in this volume.

2. See Walter Marshall Horton, "Tillich's Role in Contemporary Theology," in *The Theology of
Paul Tillich*, ed. Charles W. Kegley and Robert W. Bretall (New York: Macmillan, 1952), pp. 26–
47; and Arthur Raymond McKay, "A Critical Appraisal of Scientific Theology in the Writings of
Henry N. Wieman" (S.T.M. thesis, Union Theological Seminary, 1946). This thesis does not appear in the bibliography for King's dissertation.

3. See Henry Nelson Wieman, "Moral and Spiritual Values in Education, Sections I and II:
'Spiritual Values Interpreted for Education' and 'The Problem of Religion in Education,'" 14 August 1953, CSKC.

From Paul Tillich

22 September 1953
Ascona, Switzerland

Dear Mr. King,

I have received your letter while travelling in Europe till Christmas. I don't
know anybody who has written about the subject you are interested in. But
maybe you should ask my former assistant Prof. John Dillenburger, Columbia
University, Department of Religion. The only unpublished material of which
I could think are the propositions for my lectures in Systematic Theology

a copy of which you could get from my assistant Mr. Werner Rode, Union Theological Seminary New York.[1]

Sincerely yours
[*signed*] Paul

PS. I am very much interested in your subject.

TLS. MLKP-MBU: Box 117.

---

1. King later wrote letters to Rode and Dillenberger. See King to Werner Rode, 1 December 1953, pp. 221–222 in this volume; and King to John Dillenberger, 1 December 1953, MLKP-MBU: Box 116.

Qualifying Examination Answers, Theology of the Bible

[*2 November 1953*]
[*Boston, Mass.*]

Before beginning work on their dissertations, doctoral candidates in systematic theology at Boston were required to take three-hour qualifying examinations in four of the following fields: "Systematic Theology, Philosophy of Religion, Theology of the Bible, History of Doctrine, History of Philosophy, [or] the thought of one great theologian or philosopher of religion."[1] When examined on the theology of the Bible, King answered three of the four questions, per instructions.[2] In his answer on Christian hope, King declares faith in immortality: "Man will live again because he is of value to God." DeWolf, as King's academic advisor, graded this examination, probably in consultation with other faculty members. King received an A.

[*1. What is the proper form of the Christian's hope? Relate your answer to the principal relevant New Testament teachings, taking into account interpretations by Paul S. Minear and Rudolf Bultmann.*][3]

---

1. Boston University, Special Regulations for the Ph.D. in Theological Studies with Concentration in Systematic Theology, September 1951–November 1953, CSKC.

2. For King's other examinations, see King, Qualifying examination answers, History of Doctrine, pp. 212–218 in this volume; Qualifying examination answers, Systematic Theology, pp. 228–233 in this volume; and Qualifying examination answers, History of Philosophy, pp. 242–247 in this volume.

3. Paul Minear's book *The Eyes of Faith* (1946) appeared on the list of "minimum requirements in reading" in the special regulations for doctoral students in systematic theology cited above. Rudolf Bultmann's *Theology of the Bible* (vol. 1, 1951) was not listed, but the regulations stated that "the examination covers the entire field and is not restricted to the books specified." In his answer King mentions Millar Burrows, whose book *An Outline of Biblical Theology* (1946) was also on the reading list.

1. The Christian hope hinges around at least three or four concepts, viz.,
the Second coming of Christ, the final judgment, the Kingdom of God,
and the immortality of the soul. The New Testament has something to
say about each of these.

First we may turn to the teaching concerning the Second coming of
Christ. There is no doubt concerning the fact that after his death and
resurrection Jesus was identified with the "Son of Man" who was to return on the clouds and judge the quick and the dead. This hope of
Christ' immediate return was the chief hope of the early Christians Indeed, as Rudolf Bultmann has said, the earliest church was an eschatological congregation. The whole life of the Church was guided by this
expectation. And even to this day many Christians hold fast to this belief
in the second coming.

Whether Jesus accepted the title of "Son of Man" or whether he
ever thought that he would return to establish the kingdom is very
difficult to determine. Scholars are still in debate over this question.
Millar Burrows holds the opinion that Jesus did look upon himself as
the "Son of Man." Bultmann on the other hand believes that we can
never know whether Jesus accepted such a view of himself. In fact
Bultmann would rather think that Jesus had no messianic consciousness at all. Minear deal with the question by saying the Jesus wasn't to
concerned about titles. He was more concerned {with} response to his
message.

Although this question has not been settled or, all would agree that
the Biblical writer (i.e. the New Testament writers) in general looked
upon Jesus as the "Son of Man."

One New Testament writer, viz. the writer of the Fourth gospel, gave a
new spiritual meaning to the traditional concept. He insisted that Christ,
rather than returning at some date in the future, had already returned
as an abiding inner presence.

Modern man finds it quite difficult to find any meaning in this traditional hope. Minear attributes this to a faulty orientation in interpreting
specific predications

He affirms that the Day of the Son of man is other than the day of
man's calendar. This day does not dawn for all men at the same instant by
the objective clocks of the world. This conception, says Minear, stemms
from the assumption of the interpreter that the coming of the Son of
Man is everywhere treated in the N. T. as a simple objective event like
the coming of a train. With one important qualification, he says, the son
of man does not come to all men and places at precisely the same instant.
Jesus, for example, pictures the future judgment as coming at different
times for different people, in accordance with their watchfulness. We
may conclude with Minear that whenever the proclamation of calvey,
with its representation of sacrificial love, is heard in its decisive form
there again the Son of Man comes among man revealing the power of
the new day over all darkness.

This leads us to say a few words concerning the judgment. It was believed that one of the duties of the coming "Son of Man" was to "judge

the quick and the dead."[4] On that final day he would separate the wheat from the tares; the righteous would be rewarded and the wicked would be punished. This belief runs the whole gamut of the New Testament. They all looked forward to this day of reckoning which would mean salvation for the righteous.

The writer of the Fourth gospel spiritualized this concept as he did to all traditional eschatology. For him the judgment was not far off future event, but it was the sentence that a man passes upon himself for refusing the "light."

It is very difficult for ~~Along with all of this we find the belief in the king~~ us in the modern world to believe in the final judgment with all its external and symbolic features that we find in the New Testament. However there is a sense in which every Christian much look upon the judgment as final, and that is in the sense that God has planted in the fiber of the universe certain eternal laws which forever confront every man. They are absolute and not relative. There is an eternal and absolute distinction between right and wrong.

Another very important part of the Christian hope is the hope in the kingdom of God. This is probably the greatest item in the Christian hope. The belief in the kingdom of God runs throughout the New Testament. It is often debated whether the idea of the kingdom in the New Testament is spiritual or apocalyptic. Bultmann holds that it is purely apocalyptic. He says there is nothing in the New Testament that could be interpreted to mean that the Kingdom is spiritual in form and gradual in development. Minear along with other scholars would affirm that there is a spiritual view of the Kingdom that runs side by side with the apocalyptic view. The Kingdom is both present and future.

It seems clear to me that the facts are on the side of Minear. Such passage as these, "thou are not far from the Kingdom," "the kingdom of God is in the midst of you" and such parables as the seed growing of itself and the mustard seed, all seem to point to to a spiritual view of the Kingdom.[5]

So we must conclude that the Kingdom can be a ~~future~~ present possession according to the N. T. It might be true that in its final and universal form it will be "post historical," but it can exist as an inner possession in history. Wherever the love of God is sovereign in a man life there is the kingdom of God.

We must also mention that there is no warrant in the N. T. for looking upon the kingdom as an "idealized social order" but we must say that whenever there are advances in that direction there is an expression of the power of the kingdom.

Like the writer of the Fourth gospel we must believe that the kingdom is already here in the ministry of Jesus and in his continual presence (realized eschatology).

---

4. Acts 10:42.

5. The quotations are from Mark 12:34 and Luke 17:21. One version of the parable of the mustard seed appears in Matthew 13:31–32.

A final element in the Christian hope is the belief in immortality. It is at this ~~port~~ point that the New Testament surpasses the Old. The doctrine of immortality was very late appearing in the O. T. The emphasis in the earlier days was on the immortality of the nation. But with the Christian the individual will live again. This view runs throughout the N. T. Jesus in his argument against the Saducees accepted the view and there can be little doubt that every N. T. writer accepted ~~bef~~ belief in some form of immortality. The dominate note in the N. T. is a bodily resurrection rather than a survival of the soul independent of the body, but there are some signs of the latter view appearing in the N. T.

In the final analysis this hope in immortality is for the Christian given by God, rather than due to some natural immortal state of the soul (the Greek view) Man will live again because he is of value to God.

[2. *Distinguish the principal Old Testament teachings on the problem of natural evil, relating as specifically as possible to particular times and authors. What has the New Testament to add on this subject?*]

2. The earliest Old Testament teaching concerning natural evil was that it was due to a punishment for evil, i.e. sin. In early period it implied punishment for disobedience of ceremonial laws. The prophets improved on this view by affirming that natural evil was due to punishment for disobedience to moral and ethical laws rather than ceremonial laws.

The Deutoromonic writers built a whole philosophy of history on this principle. They contended throughout that the wicked suffer and the righteous prosper.

It was not long before this general was questioned. Habakkuk was the first to question this principle as it related to the nation. He wondered why it was that his nation, a righteous nation, suffered at the hands of a wicked nation. The answer given Habakkuk is simply that the just shall live by faith.

Jeremiah was the first to question the old principle as it related to the individual. All around him he say the evil prospering and the righeous suffering. He knew in his own experience that he often suffered and was even scorned and ridiculed for his attempt to do right. And so there were times that he felt the God was as a deceitful watersbrook. Jeremiah's problem is never solved intellectually. However it is affirmed by Jeremiah that the richness and intimatcy of his fellowship with God caused him to transcend his suffering on many occasion.

When we come to the book of Job we find a clear and systematic attempt to refute the old view. Job wanted to make it clear that the righteous do suffer and the wicked do prosper. In this great work the author has Job in argument after argument prove against the arguments of those who held the traditional view that the wicked do prosper and many of them go to their graves prosperous. At points it seems that Job is so disturbed over the problem that his conclusion is that God is almighty, but not just.

However there is something of a solution to the problem found in the prologue of the book of Job. Here it is affirmed that in the council of God the suffering of Job had a purpose although Job didn't know it. May it not be true that the natural evil in the world has a purpose that our finite limited minds cannot comprehend at the moment?

Another answer to the problem is set forth in the teaching of Deutero Isaiah concerning the suffering servant. This is one of the most noble teaching of all the Old Testament. Whether the servant he referred to was an individual or the nation is not easy to determine. But it is clear what the servant does. His suffering is not ~~for~~ due to something that he has done, but it is <u>vicarious</u> and <u>redemptive</u>. Through his suffering knowledge of God is spead to the unbelieving Gentiles and those unbelievers seeing that this suffering servant is innocent will become conscious of their sins and repent and thereby be redeemed. The nation would be healed by his [*strikeout illegible*] wombs.

The New Testament faces this problem and adds new light on it. First it identifies Jesus with Isaiah's suffering servant and sees in the cross a symbol of the meaning of suffering and a clue to its solution.

Also the New Testament sets forth a doctrine of immortality which is lacking in the Old Testament on the whole (The only passages in which a view of life after death is clearly stated in the O. T. is in Dan. 12:2 and Isaiah 26:19).[6] Through this doctrine one comes to see that the injustices of this life are corrected in the life to come. This great immortal hope which runs throughout the N. T. has given consolation to many souls that have walked the paths of life.

We may say in conclusion that the Bible teaches that the ultimate solution to the problem of suffering is in faith and fellowship with God. In such a setting the individual does not necessarily have an intellectual solution, but he transcends the problem.

[*3. Review, with critical evaluation, the principal works in Biblical theology by Millar Burrows, A. B. Davidson and H. C. Sheldon.*]

[*4. Summarize the Old Testament and New Testament teachings on sin and salvation, relating as specifically as possible to the literature.*]

3. There are two conceptions concerning the nature of sin in the Bible. The first comes under the category of taboo or disobedience to ceremonial. This is an impersonal and objective view of sin. We find this view particularly prevalent in the early days of Hebrew history. Inner intention does not enter the picture. Uzzar is struck dead because out of good intention he was trying to save the Ark from falling.

The other conception of the nature of sin is that sin is disobedience to

---

6. Daniel 12:2: "And many of them that sleep in the dust of the earth shall awake, some to everlasting life, and some to shame and everlasting contempt." Isaiah 26:19: "Thy dead men shall live, together with my dead body shall they arise. Awake and sing, ye that dwell in dust; for thy dew is as the dew of herbs, and the earth shall cast out the dead."

God. Here sin takes on a personal and ethical or subjective meaning. This view of sin was especially set forth by the prophets. Sin for them was not diobedence to some ceremonial law, but it was diobedence to the ethical and moral law of God.

This personal and ethical meaning of sin runs throughout the New Testament. For Jesus not only is the outward deed important, but also the inner motive. For Paul sin is clearly revolt against God, it is worshipping the creation rather than the creator.

Concerning the origin of sin the Bible teaches many things. It must be stated at the outset that the Bible teaches no doctrine of original sin. It is true that Paul comes pretty near the doctrine in Rom. 5:12 in affirming that sin came into the world through Adam, but he never states how and why.[7] In a word, the doctrine of original sin as it was later formulated by Augustine is not found in the Bible.

Genesis teaches that the origin of sin was in pride and desire. The prophets taught that the origin of sin was in selfishness, materialism and secularism. Jeremiah taugh that the origin of sin was in a stubborn heart. Jesus also taught that sin stemmed from the heart. Paul, as we have seen, conceived of sin as originating with Adam.

Concerning the extent of sin the Bible is almost unanimous in affirming its universality. There are occasional acceptions such as Noah and Enoch, but these truly exceptions and not the rule. The rule is that "all we like sheep have gone astray." "No one is good, no not one"[8] The New Testament is explicit in affirming that only Jesus is sinless. So it is clear that the Bible teaches the universality of sin. This, as was stated above, does not imply that the Bible teaches a doctrine of original sin. It simply means that all men have sinned

Because man is a sinner, i.e. in bondage to sin, he needs to be saved. So it became clear that the biblical doctrine of sin is closely tired to the doctrine of salvation. The O. T. seems to teach that man is saved by work of the law. The doctrine of atonement in most of the O. T. is bult upon around the legalistic system of sacrifice. It is the priest who through sacrifice atones (literally [*strikeout illegible*] wipes away are covers) for the sins of the people. ~~This v~~

This idea of salvation by works, devoid of its ritualistic and ceremonial forms, is also found in the N. T. in the sermon on the mount and in the epistle of James.

It is Paul who comes on the scene affirming that salvation comes through faith. The law is only set forth to show men that they cant save themselves, and must therefore depend on the grace of God in Jesus Christ. For Paul salvation has an objective as well as a subjective side. The objective side is found in the idea of justification. The subjective

---

7. Romans 5:12: "Wherefore, as by one man sin entered the world, and death by sin; and so death passed upon all men, for that all have sinned."

8. The quotations are from Isaiah 53:6 and Matthew 19:17.

side is found in the idea of regeneration. To be justified does not mean that one is sinless, but it means that one is accepted as sinless. In other words, God does not hold his sin against him, but imputes his righteousness to him. So Paul concludes that through faith, (by which he means a total surrender to God) one is justified, and this justification means regeneration. Through this faith the individual dies to the flesh and rises anew with Christ in the spirit, and is thereby saved.

The New Testament makes it very explicit that Jesus is savior and redeemer. It is contendes that through his death and resurrection God has prepared the way to a release from the bondage of sin and thereby offering him salvation. "God was in Christ reconciling the world unto himself."[9]

AHDS. MLKP-MBU: Box 115.

---

9. The quotation is from 2 Corinthians 5:19.

J. Timothy Boddie to Martin Luther King, Sr.

3 November 1953
Baltimore, Md.

Boddie informs his old friend King, Sr., that King, Jr., will give a guest sermon at Boddie's New Shiloh Baptist Church in Baltimore.[1] Boddie refers to King, Sr.'s absence at the annual meeting of the National Baptist Convention in Miami, where J. H. Jackson was elected president to succeed the retiring D. V. Jemison.

Dr. M. L. King
194 Boulevard N.E.
Atlanta, Georgia

My dear friend, M. L.

You were missed at Miami. But knowing you as I do you would have burned up a lot of energy stating and taking your position according to your convictions. Things worked out as we wanted them anyhow.

---

1. James Timothy Boddie (1900–1963) graduated from Virginia Theological Seminary and College in 1926 and received his B.D. from Colgate-Rochester Divinity School in 1929. After serving as pastor of Baptist churches in Virginia, New York, Maryland, and Pennsylvania he became pastor of New Shiloh Baptist Church in Baltimore in 1942, where he remained until his death. He was president of the Maryland Baptist Convention and vice-president of the National Baptist Convention. His wife, Emery Mae Moore, was a close childhood friend of Alberta Williams King. See J. Timothy Boddie, Jr., to King Papers Project, 9 September 1990.

I am arranging for M. L. Jr. to preach for me Sunday morning November the 15th. Although I'll be out of my pulpit the Sunday before I will arrange anything for anybody related to King, my friend.

Remember me kindly to my girl Alberta, the others in your household and all inquiring friends. All on this end send their fondest regards. I am

Your friend and brother,
[*signed*]
J. Timothy Boddie
JTB:VN

TLS. MLKP-MBU: Box 117.

J. T. Brooks to Martin Luther King, Sr., and Alberta Williams King

16 November 1953
Montgomery, Ala.

Joseph T. Brooks, a deacon of Dexter Avenue Baptist Church, indicates to King's parents that Dexter was interested in King, Jr., for its pastorate. Joseph T. Brooks, Jr., who is mentioned in the letter, was a classmate of King's at Morehouse.

Dear Rev & Mrs King:

I am addressing this note to both of you for fear that Reverend King may be out of town and it may be held until he is in town. Some time ago, Charlie Dunn, secretary of the pulpit committee of Dexter Avenue Baptist Church here, called you with reference to M L., Jr. We are interested in having him in the consideration for the pastorate of our church. The condition of our church treasury at present, however, does not seem to justify or to make possible our bringing him down from Boston, where I understand he is continuing his study.

Please ascertain for me the earliest time that he does plan to come home. If we could locate him in this area, we would certainly want him to come down with us for a sermon. I have heard so many fine things about him and his ability and possibility, that I am intensely interesting in having him down. Please answer this note if you can. And if you can not, please rush it on to him for reply as we are now in process of hearing a series of prospects and would like if possible to make a decision sometime in the not too distant future.

Sadie and I are fine. Joe, Jr is getting married next month in N C—that will get the last one off our hands. Thank Goodness!!! Love.

Cordially yours,
[*signed*] Joe
J T Brooks

TLS. CSKC.

From Melvin H. Watson

19 November 1953
Atlanta, Ga.

Reverend M. L. King, Jr.
396 North Hampton Street
Apartment 5
Boston, Mass.

Dear Young In-Coming Doctor:

The First Baptist Church of Chattanooga, Tennessee, is without a pastor. It is a strong church and has promise of becoming a much stronger one. The church is now drawing up a careful list of ministers to be considered for its pastorate. Interest has been demonstrated mainly in mature men, but I have put in a plug for the consideration of at least one or two younger persons. Your name has been added to the list. Kindly indicate when you plan to come to Atlanta, so that if a committee desires to confer with you or the church desires to have you visit, plans can be made in keeping with your schedule. I would appreciate having your answer by return mail.

I hope your research is going well.

Kindest regards to you and Mrs. King.

Sincerely yours,
[*signed*] Melvin Watson

TLS. MLKP-MBU: Box 117.

Qualifying Examination Answers, History of Doctrine

[*20 November 1953*]
[*Boston, Mass.*]

In this examination King discusses the influence of Augustine on modern theology, asserting that Barth and Niebuhr drew "heavily from Augustinian anthropology." King was required to answer six of the seven questions. He received a grade of A −.

[*1. Discuss the major Augustinian influences discernible in present-day theology.*]

1. There can be no gainsaying of the fact that Augustine has greatly influenced present day theological thinking, particularly what is know as neo-Orthodoxy. These theologians (among the most outstanding are Barth,

Brunner and Niebuhr) in an attempt to speak to the crisis of our age and analyze the causes of the crisis have drawn heavily from Augustinian anthropology.

The first area of Augustinian influence is found in the modern emphasis on the sinfulness of man. It will be remembered that Augustine continually insisted that man after the fall became so corrupted that he could do no saving good without grace (both prevenient and cooperative). Now we find a man like Barth, for an instance, saying the same thing in substance. Barth is convinced that man is so sinful that he can do nothing toward bettering his condition without the aid of the divine. Man is like a desperate being in a deep well who must wait for God to come to him. Salvation is solely in the hands of God (monogism)[1] rather than being a result of the cooperative activity of man and God (synergism). Barth says explicitly that we can do nothing to get to ~~good~~ {God}. This same emphasis runs throughout neo-orthodoxy generally. All of these thinkers feel that liberalism has presented a too shallow view of man, often forgetting that man is basically a sinner.

It will also be remembered that Augustine insisted that sin stems from pride. For Augustine sin means revolting against God, or to put it otherwise, it means turning away from the creator to the creature. In other words sin is man's failure to accept his creatureliness and his finiteness.

We do not have to look far to see that this same emphasis runs throughout neo-orthodox thinking. Hardly a page of any of Niebuhr's books can be read without finding the assertion that pride is man's chief sin. Niebuhr finds this pride rising to both intellectual and spiritual propotions. Man refuses to accept his creatureliness, and thereby depends on some transitory mutable good rather than the One Immutable God, viz God. This {same} emphasis is found in Barth and Brunner. All of these men by pass Schleiermacher who would say that sin is a sort of lag of nature or a matter of the flesh, and find consolation in Augustine who makes sin a matter of the will.

Along with this these theologians have been greatly influenced by Augustine's conception of the fall of man and original sin. To be sure, they would not accept these doctrines in the same form as Augustine presented them, but they all accept that truth implicit in the doctrines. Man misused his freedom and therefore he fell and ever since Adam's fall this evil tendency has been propagated through the human race. Niebuhr would say that these doctrine are mythological categories to explain the universality of sin. Nevertheless there is believed to be a real truth in the myth. It is very interesting to notice how all of the outstanding Neo-orthodox theologians accept the latest f results of Biblical and historical criticism, and yet hold to the most orthodox and traditional theological view.

---

1. An unidentified grader corrected "monogism" to "monergism."

[2. *Identify each of the following by citing his period and listing some distinguishing
characteristic or contribution made by him to Christian thought:*

Paul of Samosata	*Ignatius*	*Peter Lombard*
Duns Scotus	*Socinus*	*Irenaeus*
Arius	*William of Occam*	*Bernard of Clairvaux*]

2. Identify:
(1) Paul of Samosta—He was a member of the early church (3ʳᵈ & 4ᵗʰ centuries) during the heat of the Christological controversy. His contribution
was Christ was a man who been <u>adopted</u> by God to reveal his divine plan
to man. Hence his view was known as dynamistic or adoptionistic mon-
ochianism. He was attempting to preserve the unity of God.

(2) Duns Scotus—He lived during the great days of Scholasticism. His
strong emphasis was that the primary faculty in God and man was will.
While Thomas could insist that God wills a thing because it is good, Duns
could insist that a thing is good because God will it. Hence Duns Scotus
view is usually called voluntaristic, while Thomas view is more intel-
lectualistic (for him God's will is inseparable from his understanding.)
From these two great Scholastics emerged two schools, viz. Scotism and
Thomism.

(3) Arius (256–336)—He was at the center of the Christological controversy. He conceived of Jesus as a sort of demi god somewhat similar to
the Gnostic <u>demiurge</u>. He was not co equal or co eternal with the father,
yet he was more than a mere man. He was a sort of half-God. This view
was eventually defeated by the Church because, as Athanasius contended, it lead to practical polytheism.

(4) Ignatius—He was one of the Apostolic Fathers. His chief contribution
to Christian thought was in his insistence on the supremacy of the
Church and the authority of the bishops. It is probable that he was the
first to use the th term "catholic" to designate the universal Church.

He was also greatly influenced by the Johannine view of a mystical
union with Christ.

(5) Socinus—He lived immediately after the reformation period. His chief
contribution to Christian thought lay in his revolt against trinitarianism
and the two nature doctrine of Christ' person. For him God was one.
Jesus was certainly a revelation of God, but he had no substantial unity
with him. From this it is clear that he anticipated modern unitarianism.

(6) William of Occam—He was one of the great Scholastic thinkers. His
chief contribution lay in his doctrine of norminalism. This was a live
issue during the middle ages. Occam' contention was that universal are
mere abstract names, and from this it is affirmed that only particulars
are real.

(7) Peter Lombard—He lived at the beginning of the period of Scholasticism. His chief contribution was not found in his creative thought, but it
his ability to systematize the thinking of other. His Four books of <u>Sen-
tences</u> remained a textbook for theological studies for sometimes during

the middle ages. It is probably true that through his thinking the seven sacraments were finally formulated.

(8) Irenaeus—He was one of the early Church fathers of Asia Minor. He placed little emphasis on reason in theological thinking. He emphasized a theology of Biblical fact. Moreover, his emphasis was Christocentric rather than Logos-centric. He made it clear that what Adam had failed to do through his diobedence, Christ, the second Adam, had done through his obedience. Irenaeus great work <u>Against Heresies</u> was quite influential in his age.

(9) Bernard of Clairvaus—He lived at the wake of Scholasticism. His emphasis was mystical rather than rational. For him the chief end of life was the love of God. Man, insist Bernard, is a sinner until he rises above the mere love of self to the great love of God.

[*3. Expound the major answers to the problem of the relation of the divine and the human in Christ offered in the 4th and 5th centuries, showing their relation to each other and linking ideas with thinkers.*]

3. In 325 at Nicea it had been affirmed that Jesus was divine. Now the question of his humanity stood before the Church. Appolonius came on the scene affirming that the Logos had united was a human body and soul to form the divine-human being Jesus. In this union the divine had so transformed the human as to leave one divine-human nature. This view was soon condemned because it tended toward docetism.

The greatest opponents of Apollonarianism were the Antiochans. They were determined to preserve the humanity of Jesus. Chief among the representatives of this school was Nestorius. On the one hand he was strongly opposed to the tendency to speak of Mary as the "Mother of God." Along with this went his contention that the Logos resided in the man Jesus as in a shrine. So that that divine human relation in Jesus was a relation of grace rather than of essence. The view presented a God-bearing man rather than a God-man. Because of this Nestorianism was soon condemned. He was accused of dividing the one person Jesus into two persons.

The Alexandrians, represented chiefly by Cyril, came nearer to a satisfactory view. Here it was insisted that the divine Logos had become man, and that ~~that~~ the divine had so united with the human as to leave one person with two nature.

Eutycles came on the scene arguing that after the incarnation Jesus had only one nature, viz., the divine nature. This view was soon ~~cod~~ condemned. It led to the affirmation at Chalcedon (351)[2] that Jesus is one person with a human and a divine nature.

---

2. The grader corrected the date to 451.

After the Chalcedonian creed there was still conflict. ~~Those who~~ There were still those who believed that Jesus had only one nature (Monophysites). Those who held these views split off from ~~that~~ the state church and formed churches of there own. Even to this day some of these churches still exist.

[*4. Discuss the relation (e.g., similarity, opposition, or some other) which you find between the following:*
Clement of Alexandria and Calvin;
Anselm and Hegel;
Pelagius and Arminius; and
Kantianism and Barthianism today.]

Relation between the following

4.

(1) Clement of Alexandria and Calvin. These two thinkers seem to stand on two different poles at many points. ~~F~~ First we notice that Clement has a very healthy respect for reason. Calvin on the other hand has very little use for reason in theological formulation. He is forever speaking out against idle speculation. Again Clement never shared the pessimism concerning the plight of man as we find in Calvin. There is no sign of original sin or predestination in Clement. Clement insist that man possess genuine free will. On the other hand Calvin speaks of the Fall of man and original sin with strong conviction. Also he believes in unconditional predestination. For Calvin man is free only to do evil.

(2) Anselm and Hegel—The relation between these thinkers is found chiefly in the ontological argument for the existence of God as set forth by Anselm. This argument is based on the view that there is a necessary relation between idea and being. The idea of a being thru which none greater can be conceived proves the existence of such a being. Now the whole Hegelian philosophy is based on this principle. Hegel deifies the idea. God, for Hegel, becomes the "Absolute Idea." So in a sense the whole Hegelian philosophy (it might be referred to as absolute idealism) is based on the ontological argument.

(3) Pelagius and Arminius—The relation between these two thinker is found chiefly in the doctrine of Grace. Arminius affirmed against Calvin that grace was not irresistable. But this affirmation did not cause him to lose sight of the necessity of grace in the salvation. He held that no man can turn toward the good without the grace of God. Grace for him was absolutely necessary. On the other hand Pelagius looked upon grace as only relatively necessary. He felt that man could lift himself by his own bootstraps.

Again Arminius accepted a view of original sin. Pelagius, on the other hand, totally rejected such a view. The only relation of Adam's sin to other men's sins was the presence of a bad example.

(4) Kantianism and Barthianism—The relation between these two schools of thought is quite striking. It is found in the anti-metaphysical bias

of the former. Kant held that theoretical knowledge is limited to phenomena. Such concepts as God, freedom and immortality are metaphysical and therefore out of the domain of pure reason. We cant gain
a theoretical knowledge of the <u>Ding an sich</u>. Any attempt to reach the
noumenal realm by reason leads to antinomies. Strangely enough we
find something of this in Barth. Barth sees man's reason as so defective
that he can never get to God. God is "wholly other" and an attempt to
reason about him leads to antinomies. The great metaphysical questions
are beyond the domain of man's reason.

[5. *Discuss the views of Augustine, Thomas Aquinas, and Tertullian on the relation
between revelation and reason.*]

5. Augustine places a great deal of emphasis on the place of revelation in
theology. After becoming converted he accepted without question the
revealed doctrines of the Church. Yet even though we start with that
which is revealed, we must suppliment the revelation with reason. Augustine is convinced that the great doctrines of the Church are rational
through and through. Therefore he can spend many pages showing the
rationality of the revealed doctrine of the trinity. So for Augustine reason and revelation can go hand and hand.

Thomas Aquinas is probably the first theologian to systematically state
the relationship between revelation and reason. For him there are two
ways of knowing. The first is philosophy or natural theology. Here knowledge comes from infrances from sense perception. The second way of
knowing is through theology or revealed theology as he calls it. Here
knowledge comes totally by revelation. In philosophy there is an ascent
upward from particular things to God. In theology there is a decent
downward from God to particular things.

Thomas held that many important doctrines can be demonstrated by
reason, e.g. the existence of God and the immortality of the soul. On the
other hand, there are doctrines which cant be rationally demonstrated,
e.g. the trinity and the incarnation. These doctrines come through revelation. Thomas makes it clear that because these doctrines are revealed
does not mean that they are irrational.

So we see in Thomas a harmonious relationship between reason and
revelation. Both must exist side by side. They do not conflict; rather they
aid each other.

Tertullian places most of his emphasis on revelation. The more impossible and absurd a doctrine is the more certain it is. Or to put it otherwise, the more irrational a doctrine is the more rational it is to him.
One is not to use reason to test the validity. Ones sole obligation is to
accept it.

Here we see very little relation between reason and revelation. Everything came through revelation. However we must admit that Tertullian
in his own thinking did not stick to this disdain for reason. We need only
notice that his <u>De Anima</u>, for an instance, draws very heavily from Stoic
philosophy.

[6. *Discuss in relation to each other the conceptions of Christianity uppermost in Justin Martyr, Gregory the Great, Eckhart, and Martin Luther.*]

[7. *Discuss the locus of religious authority as viewed by Calvin, George Fox, Schleiermacher, and the Oxford Movement.*]

6.[3] The Locus of religious authority as viewed by the following:

1) Calvin found the locus of religious authority in the Bible. He conceives of the Bible as being above the councils or any other external authority. For him the Bible is the sole religious authority. The complete revelation of God is in the Bible, and theology must begin and end with it. Wherein Catholic thought found the sole authority in the Church, Calvin, along with other reformers, found it in the ~~Church~~ Bible.

2) George Fox did not turn to the Bible for religious authority nor did he turn to the Church. He turned to something within. He found his locus of authority in the inner light. For him religion is an inner light illuminated by God to them that believe. It was through this thinker that Quakerism came into being. In this sect little or no emphasis is placed on sacrament, public ministry, liturgy and oaths. These things are eliminated because the Quaker {does not} finds his authority in an external institution nor in a revealed Book, but in the immediate experience of God, or in the inner light.

Schleiermacher, like George Fox, found the center of religious authority is something within. He defines religion as a feeling of absolute dependence. It is this feeling or this immediate religious experience that is the true religious authority for the individual. Doctrine and creed are only interpretation of this feeling, and are therefore relative and subject to change. But the experience is absolute.

It was this emphasis of Schleiermacher that gave rise to modern liberalism. Religion, says the liberal, begin with experience. So the ultimate authority in religion is not the Church, or the Bible, or the creeds; the ultimate authority is found in the religious experience that gave rise to the Church, the Bible, and the creed. Doctrine are only derivation says Schleiermacher, therefore they can never be absolute. They are derived from the feeling of absolute dependence and herein lies the locus of religious authority.

The locus of religious authority for the Oxford movement was found is the external creed of the Anglo Catholic doctos. The aim of these men grouped under the Oxford movement was not to get to far away for the Catholic Church. They could not find authority within some internal feeling or within reason itself, but only in the liturgy and teaching of the Catholic Church.

AHDS. MLKP-MBU: Box 115.

3. The grader corrected the number of this answer to 7.

To Melvin H. Watson

24 November 1953
Boston, Mass.

King accepts an invitation to preach at First Baptist Church in Chattanooga,
Tennessee. He gave a trial sermon at the church on 17 January 1954.

Dr. Melvin H. Watson
Morehouse College
Atlanta, Georgia

Dear Dr. Watson:

Your letter of November 19, 1953 was received and I was very happy to
hear from you.

After carefully checking my schedule, I find that I will be in Atlanta on or
before December 24, remaining through January 20, 1954. I will be available
for a visit to the First Baptist Church in Chattanooga on the 1st or 3rd Sunday
in January.

I want to express my highest appreciation to you for submitting my name
to the Pulpit Committee for consideration.

Coretta and I are fine. My work is progressing very well. Please extend my
best regards to Mrs. Watson and little Melvin.

Sincerely yours,
M. L. King, Jr.

P. S. You may contact me at the above address until December 18. After this
date, contact me at 193 Boulevard, N.E., Atlanta, Ga.

TLc. MLKP-MBU: Box 117.

To J. Timothy Boddie

24 November 1953
Boston, Mass.

At Boddie's request, King preached at New Shiloh Baptist Church in Baltimore on
15 November.

The Reverend J. T. Boddie
821 West Lanvale
Baltimore, Md.

Dear Reverend Boddie:

Words cannot express my appreciation to you and your family in particular
and your church in general for the kind hospitality shown me in my recent

219

visit to your church. The experience was indeed rich and one that I will remember for years to come.

I was happy to observe first hand the inimmitable work that you and your lovely wife are doing at Shiloh. I am sure the church will continue to grow even to higher heights under you dynamic leadership.

Please express my personal regards to Mrs. Boddie and your sons. Since leaving Baltimore, I have spoken of Mrs. Boddie several times to my parents and my wife. From every point of view she is the ideal minister's wife. With such a charming, intelligent and devoted helpmate, it is understanding why you have been so successful.

Mother, Dad and my wife send their highest regards to you and your family.

Sincerely yours,
M. L. King, Jr.

TLc. MLKP-MBU: Box 116.

To J. L. Henry

24 November 1953
Boston, Mass.

Earlier in November, King spoke at the Reverend J. L. Henry's Tenth Street Baptist Church in Washington, D.C. Henry was pastor of Tenth Street from 1949 until his death in 1969.

The Reverend J. L. Henry
745 Princeton Place N.W.
Washington, D.C.

Dear Reverend Henry:

My I express to you my highest appreciation for the kind hospitality shown me while visiting your church. The fellowship was rich indeed, and I hope it will continue to grow.

I would like to commend you for the fine work that you are doing at your church. I am sure that with your dynamic leadership ability your church will continue to grow and rise to even higher heights.

You have my deepest prayers and warmest personal regards. I remain

Sincerely yours,
M. L. King,, Jr.

TLc. MLKP-MBU: Box 116.

To J. T. Brooks

24 November 1953
Boston, Mass.

*Responding to Brooks's letter to his parents, King, Jr., accepts the offer to deliver a
trial sermon at Dexter Avenue Baptist Church in Montgomery, Alabama. He
preached at Dexter on 24 January 1954.*

Mr. J. T. Brooks
The Alabama State College for Negroes
Montgomery, Alabama

Dear Mr. Brooks:

Your letter of November 16, 1953 was forwarded to me by my parents.
After carefully checking my schedule, I find that I will be in Atlanta on or
before December 24, remaining through January 20, 1954. I will be available
to serve you on the 2nd or 3rd Sunday in January, preferably the 2nd Sunday.

Certainly I wish to express my appreciation to you for your kind consideration.

Please extend my regards to your family.

Sincerely yours,
M. L. King, Jr.

P. S. You may contact me at the above address until December 18. After this
date, contact me at 193 Boulevard, N.E., Atlanta, Georgia.

TLc. MLKP-MBU: Box 116.

To Werner Rode

1 December 1953
Boston, Mass.

*In his letter of 22 September, Paul Tillich told King that Werner Rode, Tillich's
assistant at Union Theological Seminary, would make several of Tillich's
unpublished lectures available to King.*

Mr. Werner Rode
Union Theological Seminary
New York, New York

Dear Mr. Rode:

I am a graduate student of Boston University pursuing work toward the
Ph.D. degree in philosophical theology. At present, I am in the process of

writing my Dissertation. I have chosen as a tentative topic, <u>A comparison of the conception of God in the thinking of Paul Tillich and Henry Nelson Wieman</u>.

I am interested in getting as many of Dr. Tillich's unpublished works as possible. In recent correspondence with Dr. Tillich, he indicated that I could obtain his "propositions" for his lectures in Systematic Theology from you. I would appreciate very much if you would send this work to me. If there are any charges, please forward the same to me C.O.D.

Sincerely yours,
Martin L. King, Jr.

MLK/tlc

TLc. MLKP-MBU: Box 117.

To Reinhold Niebuhr

1 December 1953
Boston, Mass.

In addition to Niebuhr, King sent a similar letter to Bernard M. Loomer of the University of Chicago's Divinity School, John Dillenberger of Columbia University's Department of Religion, and Edward H. Roberts at Princeton Theological Seminary.[1]

Dean Reinhold Niebuhr
Union Theological Seminary
Broadway at 120th Street
New York, New York

Dear Dean Niebuhr:

I am a graduate student of Boston University pursuing work toward the Ph.D. degree in philosophical theology. At present, I am in the process of writing my Dissertation. I have chosen as a tentative topic, <u>A comparison of the conception of God in the thinking of Paul Tillich and Henry Nelson Wieman</u>.

---

1. Nola E. Meade, Niebuhr's secretary, replied on 2 December 1953, informing King that Niebuhr "hasn't any knowledge of any thesis on the subject" (Nola E. Meade to King, 2 December 1953, MLKP-MBU: Box 117). See also letters to Bernard M. Loomer, John Dillenberger, and Edward H. Roberts, 1 December 1953, all in MLKP-MBU: Box 116. For their replies, see Bernard M. Loomer to King, 8 December 1953, p. 226 in this volume; and letters from John Dillenberger and Edward H. Roberts to King, both dated 11 December 1953 and in MLKP-MBU: Box 117.

If you know of any Dissertation that has been written or of one that is in process in this area, I would appreciate your calling it to my attention. Please feel free to offer any other suggestions.

Enclosed you will find a stamped self-addressed envelop for your convenience in replying.

Sincerely yours,
Martin L. King, Jr.

MLK/

Enc.:(1)

TLc. MLKP-MBU: Box 116.

To George W. Davis

1 December 1953
Boston, Mass.

Writing to his mentor at Crozer, King agrees with Davis's review of DeWolf's book, A Theology of the Living Church, *and stresses the similarity between DeWolf and Davis.[1] King affirms that he remains a theological liberal: "I have come to see more than ever before that there are certain enduring qualities in liberalism which all of the vociferous noises of fundamentalism and neo-orthodoxy can never destroy."*

Dear Dr. Davis,

I have just finished reading your review of Dr. DeWolf's A Theology of the Living Church in the "Journal of Bible and Religion" and thought it was an excellent review. It was quite interesting to get your reaction. It seems that my reaction to the book was well nigh identical to yours. As you probably know, Dr. DeWolf is my major professor and I have noticed all along that there is a great deal of similarity between your thought and his. Dr. DeWolf refers to himself as an evangelical liberal and as I remember, this is about the same position that you would hold. So you can see that it was not difficult at all for me to emerge from your classroom to Dr. DeWolf's. I found the atmosphere in both classrooms saturated with a warm evangelical liberalism.

Theologically speaking, I find myself still holding to the liberal position. I have come to see more than ever before that there are certain enduring qualities in liberalism which all of the vociferous noises of fundamentalism and

---

1. George W. Davis, "Reasonable Christianity," *Journal of Bible and Religion* 21, no. 4 (October 1953): 268–269. See L. Harold DeWolf, *A Theology of the Living Church* (New York: Harper, 1953).

neo-orthodoxy can never destroy. When Schleiermacher stressed the primacy of experience over any external authority he was sounding a note that continues to ring in my own thought.[2] However, I must admit that in the last two years, I have become much more sympathetic towards the neo-orthodox position than I was in previous years. By this I do not mean that I accept neo-orthodoxy as a set of doctrines, but I do find in it a necessary corrective for a liberalism that became all too shallow and too easily capitulated to modern culture. At this point I have found your article, "Liberalism and a Theology of Depth" quite influential in my own thinking. Neo-orthodoxy certainly has the merit of calling us back to the depths of the Christian faith.

My work here at Boston University is progressing very well. Both Dr. DeWolf and the late Dr. Brightman have been quite impressed with my work. I must admit that my theological and philosophical studies with you have been of tremendous help to me in my present studies. In the most decisive moments, I find your influence creeping forth.

I have completed my residence work, and at present I am in the process of writing my Dissertation. So far, my Dissertation title is: "A comparison of the conception of God in the thinking of Paul Tillich and Henry Nelson Wieman". I am finding the study quite fascinating. If there are no basic interruptions, I hope to complete it by the end of the coming summer.

I have been intending to write you ever since I left Crozer, but like so many, I fell victim of that great thief of time, procrastination. I do hope that this letter finds you well. Please give my best regards to Mrs. Davis and your sons, and to the Crozer family in general.

Your former student,
[*signed*]
Martin L. King, Jr.

TALS. IGZ.

---

2. See King's essay for DeWolf entitled "A Comparison of Friedrich Schleiermacher's Christology with That of Albrecht Ritschl," 9 May 1952, MLKP-MBU: Box 112.

From Ven and Joel Lawrence King

3 December 1953
Lansing, Mich.

King's uncle, the Reverend Joel King, invites King, Jr., to preach at his church in January 1954.[1]

---

1. Joel Lawrence King (1915–) was born in Stockbridge, Georgia. In 1927 he went to live with King, Sr., and Alberta Williams King in Atlanta to attend Bryant Preparatory School. He was

Dear M. L. and Coretta:

Planned to write long ago but kept putting it off. Trust you both are well, happy and getting along nicely, which leaves us the same. We are just beginning to have some winter weather here, the month of November was exceedingly nice.

Am sure Brother enjoyed his trip to Boston, saw by the Atlanta World where he was back in his pulpit last Sunday.

I am sure you two are planning to go home for Christmas—would like to know if you are all engaged for the <u>first Sunday in Jan.</u> {(3, 1954)}—if not, would like to have you for our guest speaker, morning and evening,—nothing so eventful on that day—other than the climax of a rally for beautifying the interior of the church. Would be happy to have you with us on that day if possible. And if you are on your way from the South, bring the wife along too—happy to have you both.

Let us hear from you as to your plans.

Love,
[*signed*] Aunt Ven & Uncle Joel

ALS. MLKP-MBU: Box 117.

---

married in their home and licensed to preach by King, Sr. Joel King graduated from Morehouse College and Gammon Theological Seminary in Atlanta. He pastored sixteen churches in Georgia, South Carolina, and Michigan before becoming pastor of Mount Hermon Baptist Church in Mansfield, Ohio, in 1961.

From George W. Davis

7 December 1953
Chester, Pa.

Dear Martin:—

I was delighted to have your letter last week, mentioning the review of DeWolf's book and telling me at some length about your work. I am very grateful for your kind words and your confidence in the work I am trying to do here. Sometimes one wonders whether one's efforts are appreciated and whether they bear fruit. So your letter has heartened me considerably.

You have chosen an excellent dissertation topic. It presents striking contrasts in method and content and I think you can do a good piece of work with it. May I call your attention to an article in <u>Theology Today</u> for July, 1953, which it will profit you to read it you have not done so already. It is an article by Robert C. Johnson entitled "The Jesus of History and the Christian

Faith." The reflections on the approach and conclusions of Tillich seem to me to be very important.[1]

Our life here goes on about as usual. Perhaps the student body is slightly larger than when you were here. We can find sixty odd B.D. Students with a springling of ten or so specials of one kind or another. There is a good spirit among the students. We are hopeful of the future.

I trust that you will have a pleasant Christmas season. Give my regards to your father when you see him or write to him. Best wishes for a distinguished conclusion to your dissertation plans.

Ever sincerely,
[*signed*] George W. Davis

TLS. MLKP-MBU: Box 117.

---

1. King did not cite this article in his dissertation.

From Bernard M. Loomer

8 December 1953
Chicago, Ill.

Loomer, dean of the University of Chicago Divinity School, wrote this letter in response to King's request for information on King's proposed dissertation topic.

Mr. Martin L. King, Jr.
395 Northampton Street
Apt. #5
Boston Massachusetts

Dear Mr. King:

I am replying to your December 1 letter. I do not know of any dissertation that has been written, or that is in process of being written in the area of your proposed thesis topic. Your topic sounds very interesting, and you should have a lot of fun with it.

Sincerely yours,
[*signed*]
Bernard M. Loomer

BML:DBL

TLS. MLKP-MBU: Box 117.

To Joel Lawrence King

9 December 1953
Boston, Mass.

Dear Uncle Joel,

I just received your letter and as usual was very happy to hear from you and Aunt Ven.

Coretta and I are getting along very well. At present I am in the process of finishing last minute examinations and preparing to go home for the Christmas holidays. We will be leaving Boston around the 21st of December.

Unfortunately I will not be able to speak for you on the 1st Sunday in January because of a previous engagement. I have been invited to speak at the First Baptist Church in Chattanooga on that Sunday, which is without a pastor.[1] I regret very much that I cannot be with you on that Sunday for I know that it would be a rich experience to be with you and your people on the 1st Sunday in the year. I might say, however, that I plan to be in Michigan the last week of February and the first week of March. So I would be available to preach for you either the 4th Sunday in February or the 1st Sunday in March. Please let me know as soon as possible if either of these dates is suitable to you so that I can arrange my schedule accordingly. I plan to preach in Detroit one of those Sundays.

All of the folks at home are doing fine. Mother and Dad spent a week with us during Thanksgiving and we were more than glad to have them. A. D. and Naomi are quite well and as you probably already know, are expecting another baby.

Coretta sends her highest regards. Be sure to give our love and best wishes to Aunt Ven.

Your Nephew,
M. L. Jr.

P. S. Be sure to let me know at your earliest convenience if either of the dates mentioned above is abailable so that I can arrange my schedule.

TLc. MLKP-MBU: Box 116.

---

1. King delivered a trial sermon at First Baptist Church on the third Sunday in January, the 17th. See G. A. Key to King, 12 January 1954, p. 234 in this volume.

Qualifying Examination Answers,
Systematic Theology

[17 December 1953?]
[Boston, Mass.]

*In these answers, which appear to have been written for the qualifying examination
in Systematic Theology, King reveals his preference for aspects of both liberal and
neo-orthodox thinking and explains his definitions of religious faith and
conversion. He also notes that "without immortality the universe would be
somewhat irrational." His faith in immortality "assured [him] that God will
vindicate the righteous." King received a B on the examination.*

1. I would begin my of view of the function and importance of revelation
and reason in the Christian religion by stating that both are important
and necessary. For me the question is not revelation or reason, but revelation and reason. The one must supplement the other.

In modern contemporary Protestant theology, particularly continental theology, there is a strong tendency to cast out reason altogether.
Indeed the distinctive feature of continental theology is to reassert the
conflict between reason and revelation. For then it is a matter of either/
or and not both/and. Barth is very emphatic at this point. He leaves no
room for natural theology. Brunner is somewhat more sympathic toward natural theology. He gives reason a sort of propaedeutic function,
however subordinating it to revelation. But it remains true that both
Barth and Brunner affirm that reason is impotant in ultimate matter of
faith. Man cannot know God by reason. In fact they would affirm that
man can do nothing to get to God. It is God who must come to man
through revelation. In these thinkers we find a sort of deification of
revelation.

One the other hand we find many contemporary liberal Protestant
theologians who would strongly disagree with the crisis theologians.
For them reason must always supplement revelation. These theologians
would not say that revelation is not important. They would say rather
that revelation isn't meaningful or knowable apart from reason.

This certainly seems to me the more logical view. Without revel reason
revelation remains meaningless and confused. Without reason it would
be impossible to distinguish between a false revelation claim and a true
revelation claim. Indeed reason is a presupposition for revelation. Revelation cant come to inanimate objects. It can only come to a rational
person.

And then again reason is necessary to communicate revelation. Before
it (ie. revelation) can be communicated it must be placed in words and
concepts which only a rational being can do.

If there is no rational being to interpret a revelation claim then it remains a bundle of nothing. It is certainly true to say that without reason

revelation is impossible. On every hand revelation presupposes reason. This is not to deify reason. It is merely to affirm that revelation is meaningless apart from reason. Reason is alway needed to suppliment revelation. Reason and revelation are not ultimately incompatible. On the contrary, the two presuppose each other. Without revelation there can be no reason, and without reason there can be no meaningful revelation. Revelation makes reason possible. Reason articulates and makes revelation intelligible.

It is quite interesting to note that all those theologians who spends hour after hour to prove that reason isn't valid in matters of faith must use reason to establish such a claim. How contradictory it is to use reason to prove that there can be no reason.

Those continental theologians who affirm that the scripture is the norm and standard of truth should reread Rom. 1:19.[1] The man who refuses to use reason in interpreting God's revelation is without excuse.

2. In dealing with a situation like this the temptation would be to elaborate the theory of a finite God and leave the it there. But the solution isn't that easy as far as I am concerned. I would much rather affirm the limitations of man's knowledge than the limitations of God's power.

So I would first tell this intelligent layman that there might be some hidden meaning and purpose in this tragedy that our finite minds cannot discern at the moment. I would assure {him} that there is always some mystery in God's ways. If there were no mystery in God's dealing, he would not be God. It is true that now we only "know in part."

All along I would be attempting to show him the value in believing in immortality in moments like these. It is true that without immortality the universe would be somewhat irrational. But by having faith in the immortal life we are assured that God will vindicate the righteous. I would assure that the Christian faith in its emphasis on immortality assures us that the ambiguities of this life will be meaningful in the life to come.

Then again I would attempt to show him that this tragedy might have some instrumental value for good. It can be a means of bringing the church member together in sympathy and love in a way that has never existed before. May it not be that there are no surd evils with devoid of instrumental value.

With all of this I would again stress the fact of mystery concerning God's ways. I would stress the fact that our knowledge is finite and limited. And that so long as we are on earth we will never understand all of God's way. "We only see through a glass darkly." Many of these problem will never be solved until we see God "face to face."[2]

And finally I would emphasis the fact that the solution to the problem surrounding any tragedy is ultimately practical, not theoretical. Al-

---

1. Romans 1:18–19: "For the wrath of God is revealed from heaven against all ungodliness and unrighteousness of men, who hold the truth in unrighteousness: because that which may be known of God is manifest in them; for God hath shewed it unto them."

thought we cannot answer the problem theoretically, through faith we can transcend it as Christ did on the cross.

3. Sin has an ethical as well as a religious connotation. It is living contrary to one's own ideals as well as contrary to God will. Man has a relation with himself, with other men, and with God. A perverted relationship with either of these is sin. A perverted relationship with oneself leads to the sin of disloyalty. A perverted relationship with other men leads to the sin of selfishness. A perverted relationship with God is the sin of unbelief. On each of these levels sin has a distinctive meaning.

Sin is also pride. It is not true that pride is the essence of sin as many neo-orthodox theologians would affirm. But it is true that the Bible presents pride as a real meaning of sin.

Sin is basically ~~und~~ disobedience to the will of God. This disobedience to the will of God may be intentional or it may stem from ignorance. DeWolf refers to this distinction as that between formal sin and material sin, the former being intentionally and knowingly disobeying God's will and the latter being unknowingly disobeying God's will. Both, however, come under the category of sin.

The question of the origin of sin raises many question. The Bible points to several things as accounted for the origin of sin. Among them are the devil, the law, bodily passion ~~and~~ etc. It was tradition for older theology under the influence of Augustine to the fall of man and original sin as the explanation for the origin of sin. This emphasis on original sin is being reaffirmed today on the part of many neo-orthodox theologians. These theologians do not accept the doctrine in the Augustinian sense, since most of them accept the findings of historical and Biblical criticism. But they accept it as a mythological category to explain the universality of sin.

This doctrine of original sin, both in its traditional and modern forms raise the inevitable question of how can one be responsible and evil guilty of something that he hasn't committed? And furthermore such things as guilt and punishment are not transferable from one person to another. Such difficulties have lead many to totally cast out the category of original sin, recognizing, however, that within it are implied some profound truths.

Now all of this strikes me as erroneous and unhistorical. So long as the church is an organized historical institution, it can never be infallible. Moreover, it must be affirmed that it is erroneous to think of Christ as deliberately organizing the Church. It might be true to say that he believced in organization, the mere fact that he organized his disciples, but to say the Christ consciously organized the Church and made Peter the first Pope is push the record to false propotions.

It seems much more logical to find the origin of sin in man's free will. Sin originats when man misuses his freedom. A few theologian have tried to show how sin originats in misunderstood freedom. The child

---

2. 1 Corinthians 13:12: "For now we see through a glass, darkly; but then face to face: now I know in part; but then shall I know even as also I am known."

emerging from nonmoral irresponsibility to the awareness of moral con- sciousness attempt to assert himself to prove his freedom And in so do-ing he feels a sort of false autonomy.

All of this further validates the fact that the origin of sin is found in man's free will.

4.[3] Meaning of the following

(1) Faith has often been looked upon as mere intellectual assent to a proposition or merely belief. But faith is more than either. Faith is fundamentally an act of commitment to that which is believe to be most valuable. Religiously speaking it is total surrender to God. Basically faith is not <u>belief</u>, (although belief is an element in faith) but an <u>act</u>.

For this reason faith is always significant. It is necessary for the very living of life. Even reason itself is a venture of faith. When faith is properly interpreted it is true that salvation is by faith.

(2) Grace has always been a significant concept in religious history. It is God free gift or free importation to man. It is ~~the~~ God giving ~~of~~ to man something that he can gain by his own powers.

In the history of theology this concept has usually been dis-cussed in reference to salvation. It has lead to a discussion of prevenient grace and cooperative grace. (Augustine). In the ref-ormation one of the characteristic utterances was, "salvation by grace." This emphasis on grace has often lead to a denial of man's freedom. If salvation is solely by grace, it is affirmed, man cannot be free.

However all of this isn't necessary. One can stress the necessity of grace in the salvation process and still affirm human freedom, ~~Grace~~ for it may well be that freedom is a gift of grace.

When grace is properly interpreted it is ~~abid~~ of abiding signifi-cance. We are all dependent on the grace of God for life and every worthwile goal that accompanies it. It is quite true that in Him we live and move and have our being.

(3) Conversion means a change of attitude or rather it means the ac-ceptance of a new standard of values under the influence of some external power. Indeed every man in need of coversion. We are all in need of a better relationship with ourselves, with our fellow men, and with God. In this sense conversion must be a continual process. No one is every converted <u>all at once</u>.

(4) Repentance means a feeling sorry for one's sins accompanied by a change of attitude. It is a right about face. The feeling sorry with-out the change is not repentance. The two must go together.

If sin is a reality, as we all must admit, then ~~con~~ the concept of repentance is eternally significant. All men are in continual need of repenting. We must repent both invidually and collectively.

(5) Regeneration mean a new life that results after conversion and

---

3. DeWolf wrote "(5)" in the margin.

repentance. It is a new set of values. It is a new adjustment to God, man, and self. It is what Jesus refered to in the Fourth gospel as the new birth.

Here again we find this an important and significant concept. In every age men are standing in the need of the new birth.

(6) sanctification means achievement of Christian perfection. It is that state in which the individual is free from sin and temptation. It is the ideal of all Christian development.

We must admit that if sanctification means freedom from sin and the doing of the ultimate will of God, man cannot be santified in this life. We may do the will of God in a particular situation, but the complexity of the social situation makes it almost impossible to do the ultimate will of God.

5. For me the church is both visible and invisible or to put it otherwise both organized and spiritual. The organized church is that fallible historic church filled with many of the evils of history. The spiritual church is the great fellowship of sharing under the guidance of the holy Spirit. It is the <u>koinonia</u>. It is in a sense the kingdom of God on earth.

The Roman Catholic view of the church hinges around the infallibility of the organized Church. It is held that this Church was organized by Christ, who in turn gave Peter the keys to the kingdom, making him the first pope.

Now all of this strikes me as erroneous and unhistorical. So long as the church is an organized historical institution, it can never be infallible. Moreover, it must be affirmed that it is erroneous to think of Christ as deliberately organizing the Church. It might be true to say that he believed in organization, the mere fact that he organized his disciples, but to say the Christ consciously organized the Church and made Peter the first Pope is push the record to false propotions.

So we must affirm that the organized church is fallible. This, however, does not mean that the organized Church isn't necessary. It is absolutely necessary. It primary purpose in history is to keep the fellowship of love alive in history, to exhort and teach doctrine, and to raise its voice against social evils wherever they may exist.

The true Church is the spiritual Church. If there are any claims to infallibility it is here. It is in the spiritual Church that we witness the kingdom of God on earth. It is the true body of Christ. The organized Church is divided. But the spiritual Church is united.

6. It is hardly true to say that the affirmation of a monistic psychology with its emphasis on the inseparable union of personality and body is a disproof of human immortality. It all depends on ones conception of the body. If one holds a materialistic metaphysics believing that matter is ultimately real, then the above assertion is true. But if one holds a personalistic metaphysics, as I do, then Lamont's assertion does not follow.[4]

---

4. King refers to Corliss Lamont, author of *The Illusion of Immortality* (1935).

Personalism affirms that the body, as well as all matter, is a phenomenal appearance of the divine activity. In other words, the body is an appears of God's activity, making communication between finite persons possible. It is not ontologically real, but only phenominally so. It is not intrinsic, but only instrumental.

Now with such an emphasis Lamont's difficulty is cast aside. If the body is only an appearance of God's activity it is still soul that is ultimately real.

Now Lamont may ask, if you say that the body is an instrument for communication between persons you are saying that the body is necessary? Certainly it is true that if immortality is real there must be some means of communication possible but one could answer that just as God provides a means of communication on earth through the body, he will provide a means of communication in an immortal state.

So after all Lamont's assertion that immortality is an illusion is not conclusively proved. The body which he is so concerned about as ultimately real may turn out to be mean a phenomenal appearance or occasion of the divine energizing

AHDS. MLKP-MBU: Box 115.

From L. Harold DeWolf

30 December 1953

DeWolf explains the delay in evaluating King's qualifying examinations.

Mr. King:

I am sorry you have had to wait so long. Dr. Schilling left town before he had time to read the examinations and after his return we had to get together for consultation since our evaluations were not identical.

Happy New Year!

[*signed*] L Harold DeWolf

ALS. MLKP-MBU: Box 115.

From G. A. Key

12 January 1954
Chattanooga, Tenn.

Key, chair of the deacon board of First Baptist Church in Chattanooga and principal of Orchard Knob School, confirms King's preaching engagement.

Rev. M. L. King Jr.
193 Bauboard N.E.
Atlanta, Georgia

Dear Rev. King:

We are extremely glad you could accept the invitation to preach for us January 17, 1954.

Your recommendation and every thing we have heard about you have been of the highest caliber. We want you to feel free and be assured that the membership shall appreciate you.

Unfortunately, I shall be out of town on Saturday, January 16, but will return for the services Sunday and a conference with you. However, other officers will be here to greet you.

Should you drive, go directly to 1700 Oak Street, to the home of Mrs. T. A. Key or phone 4-1795, should you have any difficulty in finding it. Or better yet, go to the James A. Henry Branch Y.M.C.A. on East 9th Street and you will be properly directed.

Should you come by train, get a taxi to Mrs. Key's home. We hope you can arrange to stay over through at least Monday night.

Sincerely yours,
[*signed*]
G. A. Key,
Chairman of Deacon Board
First Baptist Church

TLS. MLKP-MBU: Box 117.

From J. T. Brooks

16 January 1954
Montgomery, Ala.

*Brooks thanks King for agreeing to preach at Dexter Avenue Baptist Church on
24 January and suggests how he could best promote the event.*

Dear M L:

We are glad that you can come to us for the fourth Sunday. I am writing to ask that you send to me a mat or a cut or a photo for the newspaper, along with some factual information on yourself. I know some things about you, but I am sure there are some others which I do not know and which I shall need to know.

Meanwhile, I would like to suggest that you plan a sermon which will not require too much dependence on a manuscript. If you can send the subject of your message and the text, it will help build up the attendance for the service . . . you know how congregations often are when they do not have a regular pastor.

Wonder if Alberta would not like to come down with you. Tell her we would be very happy to have her if she can make it. Let me know when to expect you and whether or not your wife will accompany you. You probably understand that you will be our houseguest.

Tell Alberta and your Dad that I saw them in the newspaper and that someday I'll work up to them in all these good trips to Hot Springs, etc., etc.[1]

Cordially yours,
[*signed*] JTB
J T Brooks

TLI. MLKP-MBU: Box 117.

—————

1. Hot Springs, Arkansas, was a meeting place of the National Baptist Convention.

From Walter R. McCall

17 January 1954
Fort Valley, Ga.

King's friend from Morehouse and Crozer was also under consideration for the pastorate of Dexter Avenue Baptist Church. McCall had delivered a trial sermon several weeks earlier and reports in this letter that Dexter had invited him to return in February, two weeks after King's trial sermon of 24 January.

Reverend M. L. King, Jr.
193 Boulevard, N.E.
Atlanta, Georgia

Dear Mike,

Both of your letters reached me, and I was very sorry that you were taken ill. Such often happens without our control, you know. It's good that you were up in time to fulfill your preaching date. Hope things came out the way you wished them.

Nevertheless, I was hoping that you could get down before you leave because I have somethings I wanted to talk over with you, before I put them into operation. Perhaps you could give me some insights (into them).

Well, there is nothing happening down here so interesting. As expected, I have been working rather persistently especially since my secretary had to go to do practice teaching last qtr. Since I have a new one, many of my headaches are alleviated.

Drop me a line if perchance you do not get back this way before leaving.

Please tell Reverend King that I really appreciated what he did for me to cut down on my headaches resulting from closed businesses which prevented my shopping. Boy, your father is a man who will live as long as I live, and even as long as my sons and daughters, for I shall tell them of his kindness toward me.

Well, Doc., how the news reach other schools about my being here I know not. I have two very important preaching engagements: one at Talladega and Florida A&M, Tallahassee; in addition to these, I'm preaching at Dexter on the Firts Sunday, February. A special delivery was here waiting my return with the hope that I fill the pulpit on Ist. Sunday, January. But that was too late. If you are interested in getting that church, I would be glad to put in a plug for you. You may inform me. Take it from me, that is a Great Church, Mike. Much honor will go to the man who gets it. Frankly, I have fallen in love with those people. Don't let anybody tell you that that church is such a hell raiser! It has some laymen, men who are concerned about the future of our preaching ministry among young men. That is a healthy sign.

Do not forget me Doctor. Drop me a line every now and then. All my boys are gone from the "Fort", so I am the only guy left here. I am void of intellectual companionship. Gals are rushing me and I am staying clear of them down here. For I want no "mess" from here out.

Your Pal,
Mac.

TL. MLKP-MBU: Box 117.

A. A. Banks, Jr.,
to Martin Luther King, Sr.

25 January 1954
Detroit, Mich.

Banks, a friend of the King family and pastor of Second Baptist Church in Detroit, confirms King, Jr.'s preaching engagement at Second Baptist in February.[1] Banks refers to King, Sr.'s sister, Woodie Clara King Brown, who lived in Detroit at the time.

Dr. M. L. King,
193 Auburn Avenue, N.E.,
Atlanta, Georgia.

Dear Dr. King:

I received your letter of January 21, 1954 confirming the engagement of your son, Rev. M. L. King Jr., to preach for us on the fourth Sunday, February 28, 1954 at ten-thirty o'clock in the morning.

---

1. Allen A. Banks, Jr. (d. 1977), graduated from Bishop College with a B.A. and received an M.A. in economics from Howard University. He then received his B.D. in 1938 and his M.A. in 1943 from Howard University's School of Religion. From 1947 until his death he was pastor of Second Baptist Church in Detroit. In 1956, the congregation of Second Baptist would contribute over $2,600 to the Montgomery Improvement Association.

I will be out of the city. In fact, I will leave probably the previous Wednesday as I am to preach at Virginia Union University February 26th and at Virginia State on February 28th.

Since I am leaving then, I would like for him to contact me when he gets to Lansing. I understand that he will be in the state prior to preaching here. Our office is closed on Saturdays. However, if he can let the office have his subject by Monday, February 22nd, the same can be posted on bulletin board and listed in order of worship; also <u>suggested Scripture</u>.

I believe your sister's name is Brown; is that right? Things are moving nicely. Note 'I have a Sermon in "Pulpit Digest"' for February.[2]

Yours in Christ,
[*signed*]
A. A. Banks Jr., Pastor,
Second Baptist Church of Detroit.

AAB:ACW

TLS. MLKP-MBU: Box 117.

---

2. A. A. Banks, Jr., "Jonah's Folly: A Prerequisite to Our Fellowship with God Is Brotherly Love for All Men," *Pulpit Digest* 34, no. 190 (February 1954): 61–64.

From Alberta Williams King

[*25 January 1954*]

Alberta Williams King writes to her son on the other side of Reverend Banks's letter to her husband, whom she often referred to as "King." She sends regards to "Coco," the family's nickname for Coretta Scott King.

Daddy wishes you to answer this letter from Rev. Banks. Be sure to write him in time. (over)

Will try to write tonite We are all fine at present. A. D.[1] is off his crutches—using a stick. Church is still progressing—balcony half full each Sunday—Jeff & King organized Brotherhood last week—Men quite enthusiastic. Will write real soon.

Love to Coco—

[*signed*] Mother

ALS. MLKP-MBU: Box 117.

---

1. A. D. (Adam Daniel) Williams King (1930–1969) was Martin Luther King, Jr.'s younger brother.

From Joel Lawrence King

4 February 1954
Lansing, Mich.

King's trip to Michigan included sermons at Second Baptist Church in Detroit on
28 February 1954 and at his uncle's church in Lansing on the morning of
7 March. Joel King informs his nephew that King, Jr.'s sermon will be broadcast
on the "Hour of Faith" radio program, which will also broadcast his sermon at
Second Baptist.

Dear M. L.

Received your letter this morning and I am answering it immediately, First, we will be expecting you here on the first Sunday in March as stated. But I waunt you to know the line up of the program for that day.

You will be speaking morning, evening, and night. The morning service will be broadcast over all stations in Lansing and Vicinity. It is the "Hour of Faith" program, one which our church is Honored Guest once every two months. I want your Sermon Topic's and cut for the paper as soon as possible. Arranging in the afternoon for you to speak to the youth of the church, and that night will be our regular Communion service. So there you have it all lined out, I know you will be a "toughman" for the boys, but son, I waunt you to let them have it. (smiles)

I will be leaving for the South On the 15th of this month, and will be back in my pulpit for the Fourth Sunday. So come on over from Detroit any time leading up to the First Sunday.

If possible let me hear from you before I leave, so that I {may} get things well in hand.

Heard from your father last week, all well and I was in Detroit last week they were getting along nicely there.

Tell Coretta we're are sorry she will not be able to make "The Cross Country Trip" but perhaps the next time. Wife is fine and will be here while I am away. She joins me in best regards to all.

Your Uncle
[*signed*]
Joel

TALS. MLKP-MBU: Box 117.

8 February 1954
Lansing, Mich.

Dear M. L.:

I am writing you concerning a matter which has occured since our last communication, that is that our local branch of the N.A.A.C.P. which holds its monthly meeting the first Sunday in each month.

Dr. Jessie Mcneil of Detroit was our guest speaker on yesterday, he brought a very fine message.[1] He also asked about you. I told him that you would be in Detroit with Rev. Banks on the fourth Sunday, and with me the first Sunday in March.

I have asked our President for you to be our guest speaker for our branch, which will be the First Sunday afternoon in March at 4 P.M. You will also be receiving a letter from our publicity committee, a Mr. Lee. I am asking that you would accept the engagement, as it would mean much to you and me. Rember that this is a cross section of Negro and White. Usually the message is from one half hour to one hour long. Would like for you to bring them a burning message, centering around some of our present day problems.

If he use your Cut, well I will not use it. Remember if you speak at this meeting there will be no Youth speaking for my young people in the afternoon.

Please call me immediately Collect after receiving the letter from him so that you may have full understanding of the whole matter whether I am here or in Atlanta. Again may I say that I will be leaving on the 14 and will be back by the 28th.

Sincerely
[*signed*]
Joel

TLS. MLKP-MBU: Box 117.

---

1. Jesse Jai McNeil (1913–1965) studied at Shurtleff College before earning a B.D. at Virginia Union University and B.S., M.A., and Ed.D. degrees at Columbia University. In 1947 he was called to the pastorate of Detroit's Baptist Tabernacle, where he remained until 1961, when he became pastor of Metropolitan Baptist Church in Pasadena, California. In 1964 he joined the faculty of California Baptist Theological Seminary in Covina as its first African-American professor. In addition to serving as a director of the National Baptist Convention's Sunday School Publishing Board, McNeil wrote many books, including *Things That Matter Now* (1946), *A Present Help* (1958), *The Preacher-Prophet in Mass Society* (1961), and *Mission in Metropolis* (1965). See Charles Emerson Boddie, "Jesse Jai McNeil," in *God's Bad Boys* (Valley Forge, Pa.: Judson Press, 1972), pp. 93–102.

From R. D. Crockett

8 February 1954
Montgomery, Ala.

On 17 January 1954, King preached "The Three Dimensions of a Complete Life"
at Dexter Avenue Baptist Church. Crockett, a friend of King's from Boston, was
the chaplain at Alabama State College and a deacon of Dexter.[1]

The Rev. M. L. King, Jr.
396 Northampton Street
Apartment 5
Boston, Massachusetts

Dear Brother King:

We received your kind letter the other day. Mrs. Crockett and I enjoyed reading it very much. Especially did we enjoy the part where you mentioned that the fellowship that you had with us was "ontologically real." (smile)

Although I had really meant to write you earlier, an abundance of work prevented my doing so until today. I hope you will forgive my tardiness.

Thank you very much for serving as guest minister. In my estimation your sermon was great. A number of students liked your message so much that they have asked me to invite you back before the school year ends. If our budget could accommodate the invitation, I would certainly extend it to you.

The members of Dexter are still praising your name. Who knows but that you may come to us permanently in the future?

Mrs. Crockett joins me in saying that the fellowship we had with you enriched both of our lives. We hope you will come to see us again. Best of luck in the writing of the dissertation, and please give our regards to our friends in Boston.

Very cordially yours,
[*signed*]
R. D. Crockett,
Chaplain and Professor of Philosophy

RDC/ajm

TLS. MLKP-MBU: Box 117.

---

1. Roosevelt David Crockett (1917–1968) received his B.A. from Philander Smith College in Little Rock, Arkansas, his B.D. from Drew University in Madison, New Jersey, and his Ph.D. from Boston University. He served as assistant chaplain at Tuskegee Institute in Alabama, chaplain of Bennett College in Greensboro, North Carolina, and as chaplain and professor of philosophy at Alabama State College. He also was administrative assistant to the president of Alabama State, H. Councill Trenholm, for eleven years before being named president of Philander Smith College. He later left that position to work in the federal government for the Agency for International Development. Crockett was completing his work for the Ph.D. at Boston when King was beginning his graduate work, and they met and became friends. Crockett also served as president of the Alabama Council on Human Relations during the Montgomery bus boycott and thereafter. See Effie B. Crockett to King Papers Project, 25 May 1990.

From J. McKinley Lee, Sr.

13 February 1954
Lansing, Mich.

Dr. Martin Luther King, Jr.
396 Northampton Street
Apartment #5
Boston, Massachusetts

Dear Dr. King:

I have been informed by your uncle, Dr. Joel L. King, that you will be in this vicinity about March 7, 1954. We would like to have you address the local branch of the National Association for the Advancement of Colored People. If you can arrange this in your schedule, please send me at once a picture and information on yourself.

Very sincerely yours,
[*signed*]
J. McKinley Lee, Sr.
Chairman of Program and Publicity Comm.

JML/rbs

P. S. Please state honorarium.

TLS. MLKP-MBU: Box 117.

From A. A. Banks, Jr.

19 February 1954
Detroit, Mich.

Rev. M. L. King, Jr.
396 Northhampton Street, Apt. 5
Boston, Massachusetts

Dear Rev. King:

We are expecting you to preach on the fourth Sunday, February 28, 1954.
I will be out of the city as I explained to you before. Rev. Edward C. Simmons will be in charge of the service and will take care of you.
Please call the office when you are in the city so that they will be sure and know that you are here.

I will be away and it will be difficult to make any change. Let nothing happen to you. We are expecting you dead or alive.

Yours in Christ,
[*signed*]
A. A. Banks, Jr., Pastor
Second Baptist Church of Detroit

AAB:WC

TLS. MLKP-MBU: Box 117.

Qualifying Examination Answers,
History of Philosophy

24 February 1954
[*Boston, Mass.*]

Just before his visit to Detroit and Lansing, King took this qualifying examination. He answered six of the seven questions, per instructions. DeWolf wrote on the examination: "Graded independently by Dewolf & Schilling. When notes were compared it was found both had arrived at the mark of A −. Both regarded the work as very good to excellent, excepting only Question #3. Let's discuss that some time."

[*1.* State the <u>problems</u> which were central in the attention of the following schools of Greek philosophy and show how these problems were related to each other: *1) School of Miletus; 2) Pythagorean School; 3) Eleatic School; and 4) the Atomists.*]

1. In the School of Miletus the central problem was the problem of substance. This school was interested in discovering the one stuff which gave rise to all other stuff. In other words they were interested in knowing what is the one stuff which is dependent on nothing else, but upon which everything else is dependent.

The central problem in the Pythagorean school was the problem of number. The Pythagoreans noticed propotion, relation, order, and harmony in the world. They reasoned that none of these could not exist without number. So for them number became the ultimate reality in the universe. The clue to the meaning of all reality was found in number.

The central problem in the Eleatic School was the problem of Change and Identity. On the one hand they noticed that things seem to change. But how can a thing change into something else? How can a thing both be and not be at the same time? How can being come from non-being? Or how can thought even conceive of non-being? All of these questions grew out of the the underlying problem that confronted the Eleatics.

They answered the problem by affirming that only the One underived 24 Feb
Being exist. Change, motion, and the many are all illusions. 1954

The Atomists were also confronted with the problem of change and Identity. On the one hand they noticed with the Eleatics that ultimate reality must be unchangeable. But on the other hand, they noticed with Heraclitus the reality of change. So they were confronted with the problem of determining which is real, permanence or change. They end up affirming the reality of both. In a real sense the Atomists form the synthesis to the problem of change and identity. The <u>thesis</u> is set forth by the Eleatics who affirm that "All is One." The antithesis is set forth by Heraclitus who affirms that "All is change." The synthesis is set forth by the Atomists who affirm ~~that~~ with the Eleatics that there can be no <u>absolute</u> change, but agree with Heraclitus in declaring that there is relative change.

It is not difficult to see how each of these problems is related to each other. For an instance as soon as one solves the problem of substance, he is confronted with the Pythagorean problem of determining whether this underlying reality is form (number) or matter. In other words, he is confronted with the problem of whether quality can be reduced to quantity or quantity to quality.

We can also see how both of these problems are related to the problem of change and identity. After one has determined the essence of the underlying reality of the universe, he is confronted with the problem of explaining how the world of multiplicity arose from the One substance. And then the question arises, how is the one related to the many, and the further question, is reality One or many? If it is one, how explain the many? If it is many, how explain the mind's demand for unity.

All of the problem of early Greek philosophy are closely cemented together. It is when we come to the great systematizers, Plato and Aristotle, that we get a treatment of all of these problem in their relation to each other Plato, in his theory of ideas, for an instance brings these problems together. The ideas are substance, they are also forms and they are one amid the many.

[2. *What were Aristotle's chief criticisms of Plato's thought? Evaluate them.*]

2. Aristotle's chief criticisms of Plato's thought develope around the theory of Ideas. We many briefly list some of these criticisms:
    (1) the Ideas do not explain things. Granted, says Aristotle that whiteness exist; this still does explain white things.
    (2) The theory of Ideas does not explain the relation of the Ideas to particular things. It is true, says Aristotle, that Plato attempts to explain with such words as "participation" and imitation, but these are mere poetic metaphors
    (3) The Ideas do not explain motion in things. How can motionless unchangeable Ideas give motion to particular things.
    (4) The most emphatic argument that Aristotle give against Plato's 243

theory of Ideas is that they are set forth as the essence of things, and yet are separated from things. How can the essence of a thing be separated from the thing?

This forms the basis of Aristotle's philosophy. The universal does not exist, as Plato said, in some transcendent realm, but it exist in the particular. Matter and form, the universal and particular exist together. The universal in and of itself is not substance. Substance is the unity of both the universal and the particular. From this we can see that Plato adheres to a transcendental teleology and Aristotle adheres to an immanent teleology.

We can also see a great difference between the two men in the realm of psychology. Plato felt that the soul had a sort of unnatural union with the body. The body was the prison of the soul. Aristotle disagreed totally with Plato at this point. For him the body and the soul were joined indisoluably together. The soul, for Aristotle, is the form or actuality of a body with the potentiality for life.

Many of Aristotle's criticisms against Plato are warrented and they have meant much to the growth of philosophy. But on the other hand, Aristotle seems unfair to Plato. It seems that there are two Platonic dialogues that Aristotle completely ignored, viz., the <u>Parmenides</u> and the <u>Timaeus</u>. In the former Plato raises many of the same criticisms of himself that Aristotle raises against him later.

Aristotle [*strikeout illegible*] affirms that Plato only recognized two of the causes, viz., material and formal cause. But it seems certain to me that Plato recognized clearly final cause in his idea of the Good. Also it seems that in his positing of the Demiurge in the <u>Timaeus</u> he set forth efficient cause. In this dialogue Plato seems to affirm that there are three eternal and uncreated realities, (1) the Ideas, (2) the Demiurge (God), and the Recepticle. If this is the case the relation of Ideas to things and the problem of motion are explained by the work of the Demiurge. This Aristotle completely overlooked.

[*3.* *What was the main problem of the medieval Schoolmen? Evaluate its underlying presuppositions and purpose.*]

3. The most important problem confronting the medieval Schoolmen was the promlen of the universal and particular or the problem that developed as a result around norminalism and realism. The former affirmed that the universal is a mere name. The latter affirmed that the universal is real and exist independent of the particular. Some Schoolmen such as Roscellinus and William of Occam took sides with norminalism. Others, like Anselm and William of Chapeaux took the realistic position. The problem continued through the middle ages. A synthesis was reached in

the thinking of Abelard. According to Abelard universals cannot be things (realisms), but just as little can they be words (norminalism). The universal is a concept (conceptualism) (1) The generic term refers to a class of [*strikeout illegible*] resembling particulars. (2) The object of a concept is a universal essence pevading the particular.

It is not difficult to see why this problem was basic for the Schoolmen, particularly for the Church. Many of the dogma of the Church, such as transubstantiation and original sin were based on the validity of the doctrine of universalism. Also the whole idea of the Church universal was based on it.

The other main problem of the Schoolmen was that of reconciling element which had previously been in conflict, such as nature and grace, reason and revelation, philosophy and theology. This was the great medival synthesis. They wanted to prove that the doctrines of the Church were grounded in reason. So the Schoolmen used philosophy to validate or rather substantiate the doctrine of the Church. Philosophy became the handimaden of theology.

[4. *Trace the development of the doctrine concerning the object of knowledge from Locke to Berkeley to Hume to Kant.*]

4. Locke came on the scene rejecting innate ideas and affirming that the mind at birth is like a blank sheet of paper. How then does knowledge arise? It arises, Locke answers, through experience. Ideas come only through <u>sensation</u> and <u>reflection</u>. The ideas as they first enter the mind are <u>simple ideas</u>. The mind is passive in receiving simple ideas. On the other hand the mind through its powers to abstract, compare, and combind, forms simple ideas into complex ideas.

Now the external object has the power to produce certain ideas in us. This power Locke refers to as quality. Some of these qualities are inherent in the objects themselves. These are original or <u>primary qualities</u>. The include such things as extension, shape, and motion. Some of the other qualities do not exist in the object, but have the power to produce sensations in us through the primary qualities. Such qualities as color, smell and taste come under this class.

So we can see that for Locke the object of knowledge along with the primary qualities have objective existence outside of mind. Only the secondary qualities are subjective.

Berkeley comes on the scene affirming that we have no right to posit the existence of anything but ideas and minds that perceive them. We gain nothing else in experience. He goes on to argue that primary qualities are just as subjective as secondary qualities. The object of knowledge is only our idea and there is no experiential evidence for the existence of a material substrate in which qualities inhere. What then is the cause of our sensations? It is mind itself. So he came to his famous <u>Esse est percipi</u>

Hume came on the scene and came empiricism to its logical conclusion. Since we experience only ~~our~~ impressions and ideas we have no right to affirm the existence of anything besides that. No only is there no evidence for material substance, but there is no evidence for mental substance. Moreover there is no evidence in experience for cause and effect. All that we experience is a series of passing impressions. To affirm the existence of substance or causality is a mere fiction of the imagination. So Hume ends up rejecting alike the materialism of Hobbes, the dualism of Descarte and Locke, and the mentalism of Berkeley.

Kant comes on the scene attempting to save philosophy from the skepticism which Hume had left it in. He goes on to show that Hume's weakness was his failure to see the creative activity of mind. Kant agrees with the empiricist in affirming that all knowledge begins with experience. But he transcends them by affirming that all knowledge is not derived from experience. Experience only furnishes the bricks, but it is mind the furnishes the cement. Kant divides the faculty of knowing into three subordinate faculties, Sensibility, Understanding, and Reason. It is the first two, through the forms of time and space and the categories of thought, that constitute knowledge. So Kant would say that Hume is wrong for looking for causality and substance in the external world. The are categories of the understaning which are necessary presuppositions for experience.

So for Kant sensations come to us as a blind manifold. Sensibility then gives it meaning through the forms of time and space. But we still dont have knowledge. Percepts must be thought understood and conceived. So the categories enter to give percept meaning.

In this whole analysis Kant is stressing the creative activity of the mind. The phenomenal world is constructed by the a priori forms of the mind synthesizing or giving meaning to the disconnected fragments of sensations.

Kant ends up with a noble mediation between continental rationalism and Bristish empiricism

[5. *Summarize and criticize the ethics of Fichte.*]

5. Fichte found his theory of right upon the freedom of individuals in their external relations with one another. An individual can realize his freedom only in a world of material things and of persons. It follows that each individual must recognize the equal right of others

In contrast to the external relations between individuals, ethics for Fichte deals with the internal conflict which arises within each person between his natural impulse for self preservation and pleasure, and his rational impulse to secure freedom through conformity to the moral law. The two impulses must be reconciled in such a way that rational freedom will prevail and the individual will do his duty. Fichte affirms that this cannot be done in time. The duty confronting man is infinite. Therefore he needs infinite time or immortality to complete it.

Fichte goes on the affirm that every individual has been created for a special vocation. It is the job of every person to discover this vocation and set out to do it with his whole self. The Ego has posited the Non-ego in order that man might fulfill his duty.

Just as every individual has been called for some vocation, so have nations been called for certain vocations.

There is something quite sublime about this ethical system of Fichte. To see that the external world exist for persons and as an outlet for their fulfillment of duty is quite lofty. Also his stress on freedom is to be accepted, along with his emphasis on the value of persons. However there is a nationalistic emphasis in Fichte's system which can hardly be accepted. If persons are of supreme worth and the world is the material of duty, it must transcend all nationalistic bounderies.

[6. *What is the relation between the individual and the larger whole to which he belongs according to Hegel? Discuss critically.*]

[7. *What does Schopenhauer mean by will? By idea? How are will and idea related in his philosophy?*]

7. When Schopenhauer speaks of the world as will he is not speaking merely of conscious volitions, but he is also speaking of subconscious and unconscious volition. In other words, he is speaking of the whole striving and conative side of nature. This will is blind and purposeless. It is moving to no direct end.

Schopenhauer speaks of will as the thing in itself (Ding an Sich). This will that he speaks of as thing in itself is not each individual will, but the universal will before it becomes individuated into particular will. The universal will is free and underived. Individuals wills are determined and derived.

When Schopenhauer speaks of the world as Idea he is using idea in the same sense as Berkeley use it, i.e. as sensation. There is no underlying material substratum in the world. "The world is my idea" There is no object without a subject."

The idea for Schopenhauer represents the outer side of reality. Will represents the inner side. It is true that all the world is idea (idealism). But the idea is the manifestation of will. (voluntarism). So Schopenhauer is a Voluntaristic Idealist. The world is idea, but idea is in the final analysis a manifestation of will. Idea is only the outer side of reality. Will is the inner and basic side. The body and the whole external world, which are really ones ideas, are the objectification of will. The eye is an objectification of the desire to see. The foot is an objectification of the desire to walk. The whole universe, including ideas, can be explained in terms of the endless striving of blind will.

AHDS. MLKP-MBU: Box 115.

Rediscovering Lost Values

28 February 1954
Detroit, Mich.

*During the trip to Michigan that included an address to the Lansing NAACP and
a sermon at his uncle's church, King delivered this sermon at Detroit's Second
Baptist Church. The Reverend Edward C. Simmons, an assistant pastor,
introduced King, mentioning that "his father has preached for us several times."
In this sermon King declares, "The great problem facing modern man is that the
means by which we live have outdistanced the spiritual ends for which we live."
Citing the biblical story of how Joseph and Mary had to return to Jerusalem
because they left Jesus behind after the Passover feast, King tells the congregation:
"If we are to go forward, if we are to make this a better world in which to live,
we've got to go back. We've got to rediscover these precious values that we've left
behind." King urges them to rediscover the moral laws of the universe, to be
"honest and loving and just with all humanity." He warns them not to substitute
possessions for God, proclaiming: "I'm not going to put my ultimate faith in the
little gods that can be destroyed in an atomic age, but the God who has been our
help in the ages past, and our hope for years to come, and our shelter in the time of
storm, and our eternal home."*

Reverend Simmons, platform associates, members and friends of Second
Baptist Church, I need not pause to say how happy I am to be here this morning, and to be a part of this worship service. It's certainly with a deal of hu-
mility that I stand in this pulpit so rich in tradition and history. Second Baptist
Church, as you know, has the reputation of being one of the great churches
of our nation, and it is certainly a challenge that, for me to stand here this
morning, to be in the pulpit of Reverend Banks and of a people who are so
great and rich in tradition.

I'm not exactly a stranger in the city of Detroit, for I have been here several
times before. And I remember back in about nineteen forty-four or -five,
somewhere back in there, that I came to Second Baptist Church for the first
time—I think that was the year that the National Baptist Convention met
here. And of course I have a lot of relatives in this city, so that Detroit is really
something of a second home for me, and I don't feel too much a stranger
here this morning. So it is a, it is indeed a pleasure and a privilege for me to
be in this city this morning, and to be here to worship with you in the absence
of your very fine and noble pastor, Dr. Banks.

I want you to think with me this morning from the subject: rediscovering
lost values. Rediscovering lost values. There is something wrong with our
world, something fundamentally and basically wrong. I don't think we have
to look too far to see that. I'm sure that most of you would agree with me in
making that assertion. And when we stop to analyze the cause of our world's
ills, many things come to mind.

We begin to wonder if it is due to the fact that we don't know enough. But
it can't be that. Because in terms of accumulated knowledge we know more
today than men have known in any period of human history. We have the

facts at our disposal. We know more about mathematics, about science, about social science, and philosophy, than we've ever known in any period of the world's history. So it can't be because we don't know enough.

And then we wonder if it is due to the fact that our scientific genius lags behind. That is, if we have not made enough progress scientifically. Well then, it can't be that. For our scientific progress over the past years has been amazing. Man through his scientific genius has been able to warp distance and place time in chains, so that today it's possible to eat breakfast in New York City and supper in London, England. Back in about 1753 it took a letter three days to go from New York City to Washington, and today you can go from here to China in less time than that. It can't be because man is stagnant in his scientific progress. Man's scientific genius has been amazing.

I think we have to look much deeper than that if we are to find the real cause of man's problems and the real cause of the world's ills today. If we are to really find it I think we will have to look in the hearts and souls of men. [*Congregation:*] (*Lord help him*)

The trouble isn't so much that we don't know enough, but it's as if we aren't good enough. The trouble isn't so much that our scientific genius lags behind, but our moral genius lags behind. (*Well*) The great problem facing modern man is that, that the means *by* which we live, (*Help him God*) have outdistanced the spiritual ends *for* which we live. (*That's right*) So we find ourselves caught in a messed-up world. (*Well*) The problem is with man himself and man's soul. We haven't learned how to be just and honest and kind and true and loving. And that is the basis of our problem. The real problem is that through our scientific genius we've made of the world a neighborhood, but through our moral and spiritual genius we've failed to make of it a brotherhood. (*Lord have mercy*) And the great danger facing us today is not so much the atomic bomb that was created by physical science. Not so much that atomic bomb that you can put in an aeroplane and drop on the heads of hundreds and thousands of people—as dangerous as that is. But the real danger confronting civilization today is that atomic bomb which lies in the hearts and souls of men, (*Lord have mercy*) capable of exploding into the vilest of hate and into the most damaging selfishness. That's the atomic bomb that we've got to fear today. (*Lord help him*) Problem is with the men. (*Yes, Yes*) Within the heart and the souls of men. (*Lord*) That is the real basis of our problem. (*Well*)

My friends, all I'm trying to say is that if we are to go forward today, we've got to go back and rediscover some mighty precious values that we've left behind. (*Yes*) That's the only way that we would be able to make of our world a better world, and to make of this world what God wants it to be and the real purpose and meaning of it. The only way we can do it is to go back, (*Yes*) and rediscover some mighty precious values that we've left behind.

Our situation in the world today reminds me of a very popular situation that took place in the life of Jesus. It was read in the Scripture for the morning, found over in the second chapter of Luke's gospel.[1] The story is very

---

1. Luke 2:41–52.

familiar, very popular, we all know it. You remember when Jesus was about twelve years old, (*Well*) there was the custom of the feast. Jesus' parents took him up to Jerusalem. That was an annual occasion, the feast of the Passover, and they went up to Jerusalem and they took Jesus along with them. And they were there a few days, and then after being there they decided to go back home, to Nazareth. (*Lord help him*) And they started out, and I guess as it was the tradition in those days, the father probably traveled in front, and then the mother and the children behind. You see they didn't have the modern conveniences that we have today. They didn't have automobiles and subways and buses. They, they walked, and traveled on donkeys and camels and what have you. So they traveled very slow, but it was usually the tradition for the father to lead the way. (*Yeah*)

And they left Jerusalem going on back to Nazareth, and I imagine they walked a little while and they didn't look back to see if everybody was there. But then the Scripture says, they went about a day's journey and they stopped, I imagine to check up, to see if everything was all right, and they discovered that something mighty precious was missing. They discovered that Jesus wasn't with them. (*Yes*) Jesus wasn't in the midst. (*Come on*) And so they, they paused there, and, and looked and they didn't see him around, and they went on, and, and started looking among the kinsfolk, and they went on back to Jerusalem and found him there, in the temple with the doctors of the law. (*Yeah, That's right*)

Now, the real thing that is to be seen here is this, that the parents of Jesus realized that they had left, and that they had lost a mighty precious value. They had sense enough to know that before they could go forward to Nazareth, they had to go backward to Jerusalem to rediscover this value. (*That's right*) They knew that. They knew that they couldn't go home to Nazareth until they went back to Jerusalem. (*Come on*)

Sometimes, you know, it's necessary to go backward in order to go forward. (*Yes*) That's, that's, that's an analogy of life. I remember the other day I was driving out of New York City into Boston, and I stopped off in Bridgeport, Connecticut, to visit some friends. And I went out of New York on a highway that is known as the Merritt Parkway, it leads into Boston, a very fine parkway. And I stopped in Bridgeport, and after being there for two or three hours, I decided to go on to Boston, and I wanted to get back on the Merritt Parkway. And I went out thinking that I was going toward the Merritt Parkway. I started out, and, and I rode, and I kept riding, and I looked up and I saw a sign saying two miles to a little town that I knew I was to bypass—I wasn't to pass through that particular town. So, I, I thought I was on the wrong road. I stopped and I asked a gentleman on the road which way would I get to the Merritt Parkway. And he said, the Merritt Parkway is about twelve or fifteen miles back that way. You've got to turn around and go back to the Merritt Parkway, you are out of the way now. In other words, before I could go forward to Boston, I had to go back about twelve or fifteen miles to get to the Merritt Parkway. May it not be that, that modern man has gotten on the wrong parkway? (*Lord help him*) And if he is to go forward to the city of salvation, he's got to go back and get on the right parkway. (*Amen*)

And so that was the thing that Jesus' parents realized, that, that they had to go back and, and, and find this mighty precious value that they had left behind, in order to go forward. They realized that. And so they went back to Jerusalem and discovered Jesus, rediscovered him so to speak, in order to go forward to Nazareth. (*Lord help him*)

Now that's what we've got to do in our world today. We've left a lot of precious values behind; we've lost a lot of precious values. And if we are to go forward, if we are to make this a better world in which to live, we've got to go back. We've got to rediscover these precious values that we've left behind.

I want to deal with one or two of these mighty precious values that we've left behind, that if we're to go forward and to make this a better world, we must rediscover.

The first is this—the first principle of value that we need to rediscover is this—that *all* reality hinges on moral foundations. In other words, that this is a moral universe, and that there are moral laws of the universe, just as abiding as the physical laws. (*Lord help us*) I'm not so sure we all believe that. We, we never doubt that there are physical laws of the universe that we must obey. We never doubt that. And so we just don't jump out of airplanes or jump off of high buildings for the fun of it—we don't do that. Because we, we unconsciously know that there is a final law of gravitation, and if you disobey it you'll suffer the consequences—we know that. Even if we don't know it in its Newtonian formulation, we, we know it intuitively, and so we just don't jump off the highest building in Detroit for the fun of it—we, we, we don't do that. Because we *know* that there is a law of gravitation which is final in the universe. (*Lord*) If we disobey it, we'll suffer the consequences.

But I'm not so sure if we know that there are, are moral laws, just as abiding as the physical law. I'm not so sure about that. I'm not so sure we really believe that there is a law of love in this universe, and that if you disobey it you'll suffer the consequences. (*Yes*) I'm not so sure if we really believe that. Now, at least two things convince me that, that we don't believe that, that we have strayed away from the principle that this is a moral universe. (*Lord help him*)

The first thing is that we have adopted in the modern world a sort of a relativistic ethic. Now, I'm not trying to use a big word here. I'm trying to say something very concrete. And that is that, that we have accepted the attitude that right and wrong are merely relative to our. . . . [2]

Most people can't stand up for their, for their convictions, because the majority of people might not be doing it. (*Amen, Yes*) See, everybody's not doing it, so it must be wrong. And, and since everybody *is* doing it, it must be right. (*Yes, Lord help him*) So a sort of numerical interpretation of what's right.

But I'm here to say to you this morning that some things are right and some things are wrong. (*Yes*) Eternally so, absolutely so. It's *wrong* to hate. (*Yes, That's*

---

2. Remainder of sentence and an unknown number of additional sentences are missing from the audio tape.

right) It always has been wrong and it always will be wrong! (*Amen*) It's wrong in America, it's wrong in Germany, it's wrong in Russia, it's wrong in China! (*Lord help him*) It was wrong in two thousand B.C., and it's wrong in nineteen fifty-four A.D.! It always has been wrong, (*That's right*) and it always will be wrong! (*That's right*) It's wrong to throw our lives away in riotous living. (*Yeah*) No matter if everybody in Detroit is doing it. It's wrong! (*Yes*) It always will be wrong! And it always has been wrong. It's wrong in every age, and it's wrong in every nation. Some things are *right* and some things are wrong, no matter if everybody is doing the contrary. Some things in this universe are absolute. The God of the universe has made it so. And so long as we adopt this *relative* attitude toward right and wrong, we're revolting against the very laws of God himself. (*Amen*)

Now that isn't the only thing that convinces me that we've strayed away from this attitude, (*Go ahead*) this principle. The other thing is that we have adopted a sort of a pragmatic test for right and wrong—whatever works is right. (*Yes*) If it works, it's all right. Nothing is wrong but that which does not work. If you don't get caught, it's right. [*Laughter*] That's the attitude, isn't it? It's all right to disobey the Ten Commandments, but just don't disobey the Eleventh, Thou shall not get caught. [*Laughter*] That's the attitude. That's the prevailing attitude in, in our culture. (*Come on*) No matter what you do, just do it with a, with a bit of finesse. (*All right*) You know, a sort of attitude of the survival of the slickest. Not the Darwinian survival of the fittest, but the survival of the slickest—who, whoever can be the slickest is, is the one who right. It's all right to lie, but lie with dignity. [*Laughter*] It's all right to steal and to rob and extort, but do it with a bit of finesse. (*Yes*) It's even all right to hate, but just dress your hate up in the garments of love and make it appear that you are loving when you are actually hating. *Just get by!* That's the thing that's right according to this new ethic. (*Lord help him*)

My friends, that attitude is destroying the soul of our culture! (*You're right there*) It's destroying our nation! (*Oh yes*) The thing that we need in the world today, is a group of men and women who will stand up for right and be opposed to wrong, wherever it is. (*Lord have mercy*) A group of people who have come to see that some things are wrong, whether they're never caught up with. Some things are *right*, whether nobody sees you doing them or not.

All I'm trying to say is, (*Have mercy, my God*) our world hinges on moral foundations. God has made it so! God has made the universe to be based on a moral law. (*Lord help him*) So long as man disobeys it he is revolting against God. That's what we need in the world today—people who will stand for right and goodness. It's not enough to know the intricacies of zoology and biology. But we must know the intricacies of law. (*Well*) It is not enough to know that two and two makes four. But we've got to know somehow that it's right to be honest and just with our brothers. (*Yes*) It's not enough to know all about our philosophical and mathematical disciplines. (*Have mercy*) But we've got to know the simple disciplines, of being honest and loving and just with all humanity. (*Oh yes*) If we don't learn it, we will destroy ourselves, (*That's right*) by the misuse of our own powers. (*Amen*)

This universe hinges on moral foundations. (*Yeah*) There is something in this universe that justifies Carlyle in saying,

> No lie can live forever.[3]

There is something in this universe that justifies William Cullen Bryant in saying,

> Truth, crushed to earth, will rise again.[4] (*My Lord, Amen*)

There is something in this universe that justifies James Russell Lowell in saying,

> Truth forever on the scaffold,
> Wrong forever on the throne.
> With that scaffold sways the future. (*Lord help him*)
> Behind the dim unknown stands God,
> Within the shadow keeping watch above his own.[5] (*Amen*)

There is something in this universe that justifies the biblical writer in saying,

> You shall reap what you sow.[6] (*Amen*)

This is a law-abiding universe. (*Amen*) This is a moral universe. It hinges on moral foundations. (*Lord help him*) If we are to make of this a better world, we've got to go back and rediscover that precious value that we've left behind. (*Yes*)

And then there is a second thing, a second principle that we've got to go back and rediscover. (*Help him*) And that is that all reality has spiritual control. In other words, we've got to go back and rediscover the principle that there is a God behind the process. Well this you say, why is it that you raise that as a point in your sermon, in a church? The mere fact we are at church, we believe in God, we don't need to go back and rediscover that. The mere fact that we are here, and the mere fact that we sing and pray, and come to church—we believe in God. Well, there's some truth in that. But we must remember that it's possible to affirm the existence of God with your lips and deny his existence with your life. (*Amen, Preach*) The most dangerous type of atheism is not theoretical atheism, but practical atheism—(*Amen*) that's the most dangerous type. (*Lord have mercy*) And the world, even the church, is filled up with

---

3. King may have been paraphrasing Carlyle's *French Revolution* (1837), part 1, book 3, chapter 1: "No lie you can speak or act but it will come, after longer or shorter circulation, like a bill drawn on Nature's Reality, and be presented there for payments—with the answer, No effects."

4. *The Battlefield* (1839), stanza 9.

5. *The Present Crisis* (1844), stanza 8. The original lines from the poem, written as an antislavery statement at the time of the proposed annexation of Texas, read: "Truth forever on the scaffold, Wrong forever on the throne,— / Yet that scaffold sways the future, and, behind the dim unknown, / Standeth God within the shadow, keeping watch above his own."

6. Galatians 6:7.

people who pay lip service to God and not life service. (*That's right, Filled up with, Come on, Lord help him*) And there is always a danger that we will make it appear externally that we believe in God when internally we don't. (*Yes*) We say with our mouths that we believe in Him, but we live with our lives like He never existed. (*That's right*) That is the ever-present danger confronting religion. That's a dangerous type of atheism.

And I think, my friends, that that is the thing that has happened in America. That we have unconsciously left God behind. Now, we haven't consciously done it, we, we have unconsciously done it. You see, the text, you remember the text said, that Jesus' parents went a whole day's journey not knowing that he wasn't with them. They didn't consciously leave him behind. (*Well*) It was unconscious. Went a whole day and didn't even know it. It wasn't a conscious process. You see, we didn't grow up and say, now, good-bye God, we're going to leave you now. The materialism in America has been an unconscious thing. Since the rise of the Industrial Revolution in England, and then the invention of all of our gadgets and contrivances and all of the things and modern conveniences—we *unconsciously* left God behind. We didn't mean to do it.

We just became so involved in, in getting our big bank accounts that we unconsciously forgot about God—we didn't mean to do it.

We became so involved in getting our nice luxurious cars, and they're very nice, but we became so involved in it that it became much more convenient to ride out to the beach on Sunday afternoon than to, than to come to church that morning. (*Yes*) It, it was an unconscious thing—we didn't mean to do it.

We became so involved and fascinated by the intricacies of television that we found it a little more convenient to stay at home than to come to church. *It was an unconscious thing.* We didn't mean to do it. We didn't just go up and say, now God, you're gone. (*Lord help him*) We had gone a whole day's journey, (*Yes*) and then we came to see that we had unconsciously ushered God out of the universe. A whole day's journey—didn't mean to do it. We just became so involved in things that we forgot about God. (*Oh yes*)

And that is the danger confronting us, my friends. That in a nation as ours where we stress mass production, and that's mighty important, where we have so many conveniences and luxuries and all of that, there is the danger that we will unconsciously forget about God. I'm not saying that these things aren't important, we need them, we need cars, we need money, all of that's important to live. But whenever they become substitutes for God, (*Yes*) they become injurious. (*Amen*)

And may I say to you this morning, (*Lord help him*) that none of these things can ever be real substitutes for God. Automobiles and subways, televisions and radios, dollars and cents, can *never* be substitutes for God. (*Amen*) For long before any of these came into existence, we needed God. (*Amen, Yes*) And long after they will have passed away, we will still need God. (*Oh yeah*)

And I say to you this morning in conclusion (*Lord have mercy*) that I'm not going to put my ultimate faith in things. I'm not going to put my ultimate faith in gadgets and contrivances. As a young man with most of my life ahead of me, I decided early (*Oh yeah*) to give my life to something eternal and

absolute. (*All right*) Not to these little gods that are here today and gone to-
(*Amen, Amen*)

Not in the little gods that can be with us in a few moments of prosperity. (*Yes*) But in the God who walks with us through the valley of the shadow of death, (*That's right*) and causes us to fear no evil. (*All right*) That's the God. (*Come on*)

Not in the god that can give us a few Cadillac cars and Buick convertibles, as nice as they are, that are in style today and out of style three years from now. (*All right*) But the God who threw up the stars, (*Come on*) to bedeck the heavens like swinging lanterns of eternity. (*All right, Oh yes*)

Not in the god that can throw up a few skyscraping buildings, but the God who threw up the gigantic mountains, kissing the sky, (*Yes*) as if to bathe their peaks in the loftitudes. (*Yes*)

Not in the god that can give us a few televisions and radios, but the God who threw up that great cosmic light, that gets up early in the morning in the eastern horizon, (*Oh yes*) who paints its technicolor across the blue, (*Oh yes, Come on*) something that man could never make. (*All right, Yes*)

I'm not going to put my ultimate faith in the little gods that can be destroyed in an atomic age, (*Yes*) but the God who has been our help in ages past, (*Come on*) and our hope for years to come, (*All right*) and our shelter in the time of storm, (*Oh yes*) and our eternal home.[7] That's the God that I'm putting my ultimate faith in. (*Oh yes, Come on now*) That's the God that I call upon you to worship this morning. (*Yes*) Go out and be assured that that God is going to last forever. (*Yes*) Storms might come and go. (*Yes*) Our great skyscraping buildings will come and go. (*Yes*) Our beautiful automobiles will come and go, but God will be here. (*Amen*) Plants may wither, the flowers may fade away, but the Word of our God shall stand forever, and nothing can ever stop Him. (*Bring it down*) All of the P-38s in the world can never reach God. All of our atomic bombs can never reach Him. The God that I'm talking about this morning (*Come on*) is the God of the universe and the God that will last through the ages. (*All right*) If we are to go forward this morning, (*Well*) we've got to go back and find that God. (*All right*) That is the God that *demands* and *commands* our ultimate allegiance. (*Right*)

If we are to go forward, (*Oh yes*) we must go back and rediscover these precious values (*Well*)—that all reality hinges on moral foundations (*Lord have mercy*) and that all reality has spiritual control. (*Yes*) God bless you. (*Amen, Amen, Amen*)

[*Hymn and invitation to join church omitted*]

> The Lord bless thee and keep thee,
> The Lord make His face to shine upon thee and be gracious unto thee,
> The Lord lift up the light of his countenance unto thee,
> And be with thee in thy going out and thy coming in,
> In thy labor and in thy leisure,

---

7. King alludes to a familiar hymn, "O God, Our Help in Ages Past."

In thy moments of joy and in thy moments of sorrow,
Until the day when there shall be no sunset and no dawning.[8]

At. SdBCC.

---

8. King's benediction is a liturgical variant on an ancient Jewish benediction, the Mizpah. See Numbers 6:24–26.

From R. D. Nesbitt and T. H. Randall

7 March 1954
Montgomery, Ala.

REV M L KING JR =
396 NORTHAMPTON ST APT 5 BSN =

THIS WILL ADVISE THAT YOU HAVE BEEN EXTENDED BY UNANIMOUS VOTE A CALL TO THE PASTORATE OF THE DEXTER AVENUE BAPTIST CHURCH. THE CHURCH FELT IT FITTING AND PROPER TO WITH HOLD OTHER MATTERS PERTAINING TO SAME UNTIL ITS OFFICERS HAVE HAD OPPORTUNITY FOR PERSONAL CONFERENCE WITH YOU. WE WOULD LIKE FOR YOU TO MEET OUR OFFICERS ON THE SATURDAY PRE-CEEDING THE THIRD SUNDAY IN MARCH IF THIS IS NOT CONVENIENT ADVISE US AS TO WHEN. PLEASE REPLY SO NECESSARY ANNOUNCEMENTS CAN BE MADE FROM THE PULPIT SUNDAY =

DEXTER AVENUE BAPTIST CHURCH R D NESBITT
CHURCH CLERK AND T H RANDALL CHAIRMAN
DEACON BOARD = . .[1]

PWSr. MLKP-MBU: Box 117.

---

1. A native of Montgomery, Robert D. Nesbitt was a longtime employee of the Pilgrim Health and Life Insurance Company of Augusta, Georgia, serving first as an agent, then as auditor and executive manager. His civic activities included membership in the NAACP, serving as chair of the Cleveland Avenue branch of the Young Men's Christian Association (YMCA), secretary of the board of the Metropolitan YMCA, and president and treasurer of the Montgomery Area Mental Health Authority. He was clerk of Dexter Avenue Baptist Church for thirty-five years, also serving terms as chairman of the deacon board and treasurer of the church. See R. D. Nesbitt to King Papers Project, 22 November 1991.

WESTERN UNION

W. P. MARSHALL, PRESIDENT

FX-1201

1954 MAR 7 PM 9 48

The filing time shown in the date line on telegrams and day letters is STANDARD TIME at point of origin. Time of receipt is STANDARD TIME at point of destination

BA243 NSA077

NS.MYA194 LONG NL PD=MONTGOMERY ALA 7=

REV M L KING JR=

396 NORTHAMPTON ST APT 5 BSN=

THIS WILL ADVISE THAT YOU HAVE BEEN EXTENDED BY
UNANIMOUS VOTE A CALL TO THE PASTORATE OF THE DEXTER
AVENUE BAPTIST CHURCH. THE CHURCH FELT IT FITTING AND
PROPER TO WITH HOLD OTHER MATTERS PERTAINING TO SAME
UNTIL ITS OFFICERS HAVE HAD OPPORTUNITY FOR PERSONAL
CONFERENCE WITH YOU. WE WOULD LIKE FOR YOU TO MEET
OUR OFFICERS ON THE SATURDAY PRECEEDING THE THIRD
SUNDAY IN MARCH IF THIS IS NOT CONVENIENT ADVISE US

THE COMPANY WILL APPRECIATE SUGGESTIONS FROM ITS PATRONS CONCERNING ITS SERVICE

WESTERN UNION

W. P. MARSHALL, PRESIDENT

FX-1201

The filing time shown in the date line on telegrams and day letters is STANDARD TIME at point of origin. Time of receipt is STANDARD TIME at point of destination

AS TO WHEN. PLEASE REPLY SO NECESSARY ANNOUNCEMENTS
CAN BE MADE FROM THE PULPIT SUNDAY=

        DEXTER AVENUE BAPTIST CHURCH R D NESBITT CHURCH
CLERK AND T H RANDALL CHAIRMAN DEACON BOARD=..

THE COMPANY WILL APPRECIATE SUGGESTIONS FROM ITS PATRONS CONCERNING ITS SERVICE

THE INSTALLATION OF

Rev. Martin L. King, Jr.

As Pastor Of

DEXTER AVENUE BAPTIST CHURCH

SUNDAY, OCTOBER THIRTY-FIRST

3:30 P. M.

NINETEEN HUNDRED AND FIFTY-FOUR

MONTGOMERY,   ALABAMA

REV. MARTIN L. KING, JR.

Rev. Martin L. King, Jr.

The Reverend Martin L. King, Jr., was born in Atlanta, Ga., January 15, 1929, the second child of Rev. and Mrs. M. L. King, Sr. His elementary school training was received in the Public School system of Atlanta, and his high school training was received at the Atlanta University Laboratory High and the Booker Washington High Schools of Atlanta, Ga.

Rev. King entered Morehouse College in 1944 as a freshman, receiving the A.B. Degree from that institution in 1948. After finishing Morehouse, he entered Crozer Theological Seminary, Chester, Pennsylvania, f r o m which he graduated at the head of his class in 1951. While at Crozer he served as president of the student body and upon graduating received the coveted Pearl Plafker Award for being the most outstanding student in his class during his three year course at the seminary. He was also awarded the J. Lewis Crozer Fellowship to work toward the Ph.D. Degree at the university of his choice. While at Crozer he also enrolled as a graduate student in the Philosophy Department at the University of Pennsylvania.

Upon graduating from Crozer, he enrolled at Boston University graduate school to pursue work toward the Ph.D. Degree in the field of Philosophical Theology. He has completed all residence requirements for the Ph.D. Degree at Boston University and is at present in the process of completing his dissertation. While at Boston University, Rev. King was also enrolled as a special student for two years in the Philosophy Department at Harvard University.

Rev. King began his ministerial career in 1947. He was ordained in the Ebenezer Baptist Church, Atlanta, Ga., of which his father is pastor. He served as assistant pastor for two years and as co-pastor for four years of the Ebenezer Baptist Church. Since beginning his ministry Rev. King has traveled extensively delivering the message of God.

From Joseph C. Parker, Sr.

10 March 1954
Montgomery, Ala.

Parker, minister of Hall Street Baptist Church in Montgomery, counsels King to accept Dexter's call.[1] He confidentially informs King of Dexter's salary offer and McCall's second trial sermon.

Rev. M. L. King Jr.
396 Northampton St.
Apt. 5
Boston, Mass.

My dear King:

I am sure that you have been informed of your call to the pastorate of the Dexter Ave. Baptist Church. If you haven't been informed already you will in the very near future.

Any way, I certainly hope that you will accept this Church. I have told them all along that you were the man for them. I have told them further that I believed that you would accept them. Even though, I don't know how you are thinking, I believe it will be to your advantage to accept this church. Furthermore, I shall be very pleased to have you pastor in the city with me.

Now confidentially, I should like to give you a slight idea of what they agreed to offer you for a salary. Of course, they may have told you. Anyway, they voted to offer you anywhere from $4000.00 to $4800.00 per year salary. This is the highest salary of any minister in the city.

The members said that they wanted a minister who would stay with them a long time and not resort to teaching. Of course, I had them to know that no minister knew how long he would stay with a church. But, I told them that the type of salary they offered a minister would have a great deal to do with how long he stayed with them.

I should like to say that, they have installed their officers and adopted their

---

1. Joseph C. Parker, Sr. (1920–1987), served in the U.S. Army for several years before graduating in 1949 from Morehouse College, where his friendship with King began. He received his B.D. from Gammon Theological Seminary in Atlanta in 1958. He was pastor of New Hope Baptist Church in Jacksonville, Alabama, before serving as principal of a school in Childersburg, Alabama, and pastor of Pilgrim Baptist Church in Anniston. In 1953 he was called to Hall Street Baptist Church in Montgomery. He was active in the Montgomery bus boycott before moving to Birmingham in 1957, when he became pastor of Jackson Street Baptist Church. As pastor of Jackson Street, he was involved in the Birmingham movement and groups struggling for social justice, including the NAACP and the Southern Christian Leadership Conference. In 1971 he became the pastor of Mount Gilead Baptist Church in Fort Worth, Texas, and later served as director of church relations at Bishop College in Dallas. At the time of his death he was pastor of the Parker Memorial Missionary Baptist Church in Dallas. See Joseph C. Parker, Jr., to King Papers Project, 11 July 1990 and 18 August 1992.

program for this year. Thus far, I understand that they are planning to have men's day, women's day homecoming day and youth day. I felt that they should have waited before adopting this program. But, nevertheless you can master the situation.

By the way, McCall came and fell through. The people forgot all about him as a prospect.

But, the Church voted unanimously for you.

Please remember that, what I have told you is to be kept strictly confidentially. I just wanted you to have some idea about the Church in advance of your acceptance. But, please consider them.

Yours in Christ,
[*signed*] Rev. J. C. Parker

P.S. Give our regards to your wife.

ALS. MLKP-MBU: Box 117.

To Pulpit Committee,
Dexter Avenue Baptist Church

10 March 1954
Boston, Mass.

King expresses his appreciation for Dexter's call and schedules a meeting with the pulpit committee. One week later, a Montgomery newspaper reported: "A call has been extended to the Reverend M. L. King, Jr., to serve as the pastor of the church. He has indicated through correspondence that he will be in the city for the first Sunday in April and it is hoped that the call can be accepted." [1]

Pulpit Committee
Mr. R. D. Nesbitt, Chairman
Dexter Avenue Baptist Church
Montgomery, Alabama

Gentlemen:

This acknowledges receipt of your telegram stating that I have been called unanimously to the pastorate of your church. Knowing the outstanding history of your great church, I feel distinctly honored by your call. Please express my appreciation to the officers and members for extending to me this great honor.

Because of previous commitments, I will be unable to meet with you on the

---

1. *Montgomery Examiner*, 18 March 1954.

date requested. However, it will be convenient for me to meet with you on the first Sunday in April. If this meets with your approval, I shall arrange to arrive in your city Saturday before the first Sunday.

With best regards I remain,

Respectfully yours,
M. L. King, Jr.
396 Northampton Street
Apartment 5
Boston, Massachusetts

MLK: sj

TLc. MLKP-MBU: Box 116.

From R. D. Nesbitt

15 March 1954
Montgomery, Ala.

Reverend M L King, Jr
396 Northampton Street (Apt 5)
Boston, Massachusetts

Dear Reverend King:

We appreciated very much your letter of recent date indicating that you can be with us for the first Sunday in April. This is quite satisfactory, as we shall be happy to have you serve our Communion for us on that day. There is also a possibility that we may wish to have you baptize about five candidates either at the morning hour or at an evening service which we could plan. At present our pool is not in condition to be used, but it may be possible that it can be put into usable condition by that time; otherwise, we may plan to have the baptism in some other church's auditorium and pool. These details can be cleared between now and that time.

We are glad that you can come down on Saturday. We shall make plans to have a meeting with the officers on that night to try to clear some of the details respecting the call which we have extended to you and which we sincerely hope that you can accept.

Looking forward to seeing you within the next few weeks, I am

Cordially yours,
[*signed*]
R D Nesbitt, Church Clerk

CC: Brother T H Randall, Chr Deacons
Loveless School
Montgomery, Alabama

TLS. MLKP-MBU: Box 117.

To Dexter Avenue Baptist Church

14 April 1954
Boston, Mass.

*After meeting with the members of Dexter's pulpit committee on 4 April King
conditionally accepts the call to the pastorate, at a salary that will make him one
of the highest-paid black ministers in Montgomery.*

Dexter Avenue Baptist Church
R. D. Nesbitt, Clerk
Dexter Avenue
Montgomery, Alabama

Dear Officers and Members:

After giving your call the most serious and prayerful consideration, I am
very happy to say that I accept it. However, I find it necessary to predicate my
acceptance upon the following considerations:

(1) That the parsonage will be completely furnished.
(2) That I be granted an allowance of time to complete my work at Boston
University coming to you as full time pastor not later than September
1st, 1954. However in this interval I will be able to fill the pulpit at least
once or twice per month. In such a proposal, I would expect you to take
care of my expenses, including traveling expenses.
(3) With reference to salary, I will accept the proposed $4200.00 with the
expectation of this being increased as the Church progresses.

Other matters will be discussed on my next visit with you. Please let me
hear from you as soon as possible concerning your reaction to the above
considerations.

Again I want to express my deep gratitude and sincere appreciation to you
for extending me this great honor. It is my only hope that I will prove worthy
of the tremendous responsibility and profound challenge inherent in such an
honor.

You have my continual prayers and best wishes in all of your endeavors.

Sincerely yours,
Martin L. King, Jr.

TLc. MLKP-MBU: Box 116.

From J. T. Brooks

15 April 1954
Montgomery, Ala.

Dear Reverend King:

Brother Nesbitt asked me to write this note to you to say that it will be satisfactory for you to plan to come down for the first Sunday in May, in view of your conflicting engagements for the original proposal of the second Sunday. It may be even better for the first Sunday, since that will be Communion Day.

We can still make plans for the dedication of the organ on the second Sunday, thus giving us two good Sundays in succession. We had a letter on yesterday from the St Louis company indicating the fact that a man will be coming in from Atlanta on Monday to dismantle the old instrument—which means that the new one should be installed at least by the second Sunday, if not by the first.

Our Easter cantata last Sunday was the finest thing I have ever tried to do. We had a good crowd, and the singing was excellent. We have had many comments of favorable nature concerning it—which of course has made us quite happy.

Looking forward to having you again as our house guest, I am

Cordially yours,
[*signed*]
J T Brooks

P S: As soon as you know what your subject and text will be, I shall be pleased to have it for publicity. If you have a glossy print of yourself, I'd like to have it also.

TLS. MLKP-MBU: Box 117.

From Leonard G. Carr

16 April 1954
Philadelphia, Pa.

*Carr, the pastor of Vine Memorial Baptist Church in Philadelphia, confirms
King's upcoming guest sermon.*[1]

---

1. Leonard George Carr (1902–1976) graduated from Lincoln University in Pennsylvania in 1933 with A.B. and S.T.B. degrees. He founded Vine Memorial Baptist Church in 1933 and served as treasurer of the National Baptist Convention for twenty years.

Rev. M. L. King Jr.
396 North Hampton Street—Apt. 5
Boston, Massachusetts

Dear Brother King,

Just a note to say wherever the opportunity avails itself, it is with pleasure to have you in the pulpit of the Vine Memorial Baptist Church, therefore, we shall be looking forward to your being our guest speaker on Sunday April 25th at the 10:45 A.M. service.

Congradulations upon your call to the pastorate of the Dexter Avenue Baptist Church. My blessings go with you.

With Best wishes I remain,
Respectfully yours,
[*signed*]
Leonard Geo. Carr

LGC:eb

TLS. MLKP-MBU: Box 117.

From R. D. Nesbitt

19 April 1954
Montgomery, Ala.

Reverend M L King, Jr
396 Northampton Street
Boston, Massachussetts

Dear Reverend King:

We acknowledge receipt of your letter of April 14 in which you have outlined the conditions on which you are able to accept the call to the pastorate of the Dexter Avenue Baptist Church. In a church meeting on yesterday morning, the congregation agreed to the stipulations listed by you regarding the furnishing of the parsonage, the allowance of time to complete your studies at Boston University, and the salary of $4200.00 annually. We note that you can not come on full time basis prior to September 1 at the latest.

We are looking forward anxiously to your being with us again for the first Sunday in May to conduct our services and to hold whatever business meeting(s) may be necessary or expedient.

You will be interested to know that today we are beginning the dismantling of the old organ preparatory to the installation of the new one possibly by the end of next week. The Easter services were good on yesterday, and we are doing well. We would like as soon as possible to have a cut or a mat or a glossy print of you for our publicity purposes for our Communion service for May, along if possible, with the subject of the message.

With every kind personal regard, I am

Faithfully yours,
[*signed*]
R D Nesbitt, Church Clerk

TLS. MLKP-MBU: Box 117.

From H. Edward Whitaker

8 May 1954
Niagara Falls, N.Y.

Whitaker mentions two mutual acquaintances from Crozer, Dean Charles E. Batten and Walter "Mac" McCall. Vivit and Edward are Whitaker's wife and son.

Rev. Martin L. King Jr.
396 Northampton Street
Apt 5
Boston, Mass.

Dear Mike:

I suppose you have wondered as to what happened to me during this year. It is a long story, too long to put in a letter. But I can say that I have been struggling with the matter of trying to build a Church here in our city. It is a very slow process, but I am glad to say we are making progress. We expect to begin our construction in about two weeks now, and probably will ready to go in it around the end of the year or the first of next year. It will be a wonderful accomplishment for our people when it is completed, and I know they will be very happy.

How are you doing these days? You will probably be finishing your work there this summer. I am sure you have had a very busy and yet a most interesting stay in those parts. We are glad for you and hope for you much success in all of your endeavors. How is the Madam these days? And too how is the married man doing? It is a wonderful life.

It is interesting to note that Dean Batten is leaving the Seminary this summer. It came as somewhat a surprize to me, and yet I guess there are many changes taking place at the Seminary these days. I have not been back there but once since I left. The work here has been auful confining, but I think I can see the light and I will be moving around the country a little more after this year.

I had a letter from Mac sometime ago and he seems to be doing alright. He was here with us last summer and he met some friends of our in Buffalo, who

263

happened to be a student at one of our colleges in the South. She arranged to have him to speak to their assembly this winter, and they tell me he did a superb job.

We hope some day to have you to come and help us in our work here, but things being what they are, I suppose they have to wait a little while until we can improve our facilities. If however, you will be passing through this way sometime, we would certainly want you to stop by and spend a few days with us, and of course to preach I would like that very much, but if such isn't possible, when we finish with our building, we will extend a formal invitation for you to conduct a special week long preaching mission. I hope at that time you will be able to accept.

Vivit and Edward are doing quite well. Edward is now five years old, and I am beginning to be an old man. He will begin school next September. We are very proud at the way he is developing. We only hope and pray that he will continue in this way.

Let me hear from you sometimes. With kind regards and best wishes to your family in Atlanta and there, I remain

Sincerely,
[*signed*] Whit
H. Edward Whitaker

TLS. MLKP-MBU: Box 117.

From R. D. Nesbitt

13 May 1954
Montgomery, Ala.

My dear Pastor:

I too, am very sorry that I did not get a chance to see you again before leaving our city. Been looking everywhere for the ordination program and just got my hands on one to-day. This belongs to Brother McGhee so please return it when finished. This will let you see how it was done, however feel free to go about it as you desire as we have no set pattern for it to be done. I would like to suggest that you think inturns of Reverend Parker or Lamberth to deliver the ordination sermon.[1] This is only a suggestion.

The organ dedication was one swell affair. It was simply grand and everybody who was present said so. Had a nice crowd inspite of the threat of rain all day. In our financial effort that morning we raised $1,017.25, and at the

---

1. Joseph C. Parker, Sr., was pastor of Montgomery's Hall Street Baptist Church; B. D. Lambert was pastor of Maggie Street Baptist Church.

recital in the afternoon $46.00 which to me was not bad. After all there was very little work or effort put into it by any of us. We hope to still get some more on Sunday. They started painting on the inside Monday.

Trust everything goes well with you and the wife, and looking forward to two big Sunday's with you present on May 30th and June 6th.

Sincerely yours,
[*signed*] Bro. Nesbitt.

P.S.—Got the books for the deacons to be ordained to study.

ALS. MLKP-MBU: Box 117.

To L. Harold DeWolf

15 May 1954
Boston, Mass.

The Theology Club mentioned in this letter was also known as the Dialectical Society, a group of black graduate students who met to discuss philosophical and political issues. In this letter to DeWolf, King thanks him for lecturing on "How the Kingdom Will Come." According to another member's notes on the lecture, DeWolf presented two views of how Jesus expected the Kingdom to come: the apocalyptic view and the view that the Kingdom is already present. According to the report, DeWolf attempted to reconcile these two views, arguing that a solution "may lie in a synthesis of both views." [1]

Dr. L. Harold DeWolf
Boston University School of Theology
Boston, Massachusetts

Dear Dr. DeWolf:

Just a note to express again my appreciation to you for the interesting lecture that you gave to our Theology Club on last Monday evening. It was stimulating indeed, and I assure you that we all went away with a clearer insight into the meaning of the Kingdom and how it will come.

Cordially yours,
Martin L. King, Jr.

TLc. MLKP-MBU: Box 116.

---

1. Percy A. Carter, Jr., Notes, meeting of the Dialectical Society, 10 May 1954, PACC.

To Joseph C. Parker, Sr.

15 May 1954
Boston, Mass.

Reverend J. C. Parker
602 Shepard Street
Montgomery, Alabama

Dear Parker,

I think I mentioned to you that we were planning to ordain a group of deacons at Dexter. Well, I have decided to go through with it. I would like very much to have you preach the ordination sermon. It will be held at the church on the fifth Sunday, May 30, at 3:30 p.m. I would appreciate it if you would let me know immediately whether or not you can serve us on this occasion, so that I can proceed to plan the program. I certainly hope you can come.

I hope everything goes well with you and your family. We are doing quite well and stydying hard as usual.

As I remember, you were in the midst of your revival when I left. I am sure it went over in a big way.

I will look forward to hearing from you immediately.

Sincerely yours,
M. L. King, Jr.

TLc. MKLP-MBU: Box 116.

To Leonard G. Carr

15 May 1954
Boston, Mass.

King preached at Carr's Vine Memorial Baptist Church on 25 April.

Dr. Leonard G. Carr
5317 West Master Street
Philadelphia 31, Pennsylvania

Dear Dr. Carr:

Just a note to again express my appreciation to you for giving me the opportunity to preach in your great church. I will never forget the kindness that you have shown toward me in my ministry, and I only hope that I will be able to repay it someday in some little way.

I hope everything goes well with you and your family. Please remember me to your charming wife.

With best wishes. I remain,

Cordially yours,
M. L. King, Jr.

TLc. MLKP-MBU: Box 116.

To Montgomery Pastors

*In this form letter, King invites Montgomery pastors to the afternoon ordination
service on 30 May (King misdated it as 29 May) of a group of deacons at Dexter.
Among those ordained were H. Councill Trenholm, president of Alabama State
College, and Dr. W. D. Pettus, a physician. At the regular morning service King's
sermon was "Loving Your Enemies."*

Reverend [*blank*]
Montgomery, Alabama

Dear Reverend [*blank*]:

You and two of your deacons are invited to participate in the Ordination
Service of a group of deacons at the Dexter Avenue Baptist Church. Your
congregation is also invited to attend the service. The service will be held at
the church on the Fifth Sunday, May 29, at 3:30 p.m. We would like for you
along with your deacons to come about a half an hour before the service
begins (ca. 3:00 p.m.), in order to form an ordination council.

Will you kindly notify me by return mail whether or not you find it possible
to accept this invitation. You may address your letter to the church. I assure
you that your cooperation at this time will be highly appreciated. I am,

Cordially yours,
DEXTER AVENUE BAPTIST CHURCH
R. D. Nesbitt, Clerk

[*signed*] M. L. King, Jr. (n)
M. L. King, Jr., Pastor

TLSr. MLKP-MBU: Box 116.

From Thomas Kilgore, Jr.

24 June 1954
New York, N.Y.

Kilgore and King exchanged letters after King delivered a sermon at Kilgore's
Friendship Baptist Church in New York.[1]

The Reverend M. L. King
396 Northampton Street, Apt. 5
Boston, Massachusetts

Dear Rev. King:

Please accept this note as an expression of my great appreciation for the very unusual services which you rendered for us on the Second Sunday. You have no idea how much your messages meant to us.

I wish you much success in your new fields of labor in Montgomery.

With best wishes, I am

Sincerely yours,
[*signed*]
Thomas Kilgore, Jr.,
Pastor

TK:dl

TLS. MLKP-MBU: Box 117.

---

1. Thomas Kilgore, Jr. (1913–), received his A.B. from Morehouse in 1935 and his M.Div. from Union Theological Seminary in 1957. He was pastor at Friendship Baptist Church in Winston-Salem, North Carolina, from 1938 until 1947, when he became pastor at Friendship Baptist Church in New York. He left Friendship in 1963 to take over the pastorate at Second Baptist Church in Los Angeles, where he remained until his retirement in 1985. He served as executive secretary of the General Baptist State Convention of North Carolina from 1945 to 1947; director of the Prayer Pilgrimage for Freedom in 1957; member of the executive board of the Southern Christian Leadership Conference; president of the American Baptist Churches in 1969 and 1970; president of the Progressive National Baptist Convention from 1976 to 1978; and chair of the board of trustees of Morehouse College. See Thomas Kilgore to King Papers Project, 27 June 1990.

To Thomas Kilgore, Jr.

24 June 1954
Boston, Mass.

Dear Brother Kilgore,

Just a note to again express my appreciation to you and your wife for the kind hospitality shown toward me while visiting your city and your church. The fellowship was indeed rich and the whole experience is one that I will cherish for years to come.

May I compliment you on the great work that you are doing at Friendship. I have just finished reading your annual report and after reading it, I can readily see the secret of your success. You have a superb organization and I assure you that many of your ideas will be helpful to me at Dexter.

Please give my regards to Mrs. Kilgore and to your lovely daughters, Jini and Lynnelda.

You have my prayers and best wishes for continual success in the great work that you are doing at Friendship. I remain

Cordially yours,
M. L. King, Jr.

MLK/csk

TLc. MLKP-MBU: Box 116.

"The Theology of Reinhold Niebuhr"

[April 1953–June 1954]
[Boston, Mass.]

Expressing views similar to those in his earlier essays on Niebuhr, King presented this essay to the Dialectical Society after first giving a handwritten draft of the essay to DeWolf for his comments. King agrees with Niebuhr's rejection of the perfectibility of human nature but asks, "Within such a view is there no hope for man?" [1]

---

1. For the handwritten essay, see King, "Draft, The Theology of Reinhold Niebuhr," April 1953–June 1954, MLKP-MBU: Box 113. The transcription presented here is based on the most legible of the several extant copies of the typed essay. The title of the version is simply "Reinhold Niebuhr," but David W. Briddell, a member of the Dialectical Society, reported that during King's presentation he corrected it to "The Theology of Reinhold Niebuhr" (David W. Bridell to King Center, 3 May 1982).

We may best begin our study of Niebuhr's most important ideas by discussing his dialectically emphasis. Like other dialectical theologians he is forever insisting that there is a dialectical tension between time and eternity.[2] This theme runs the whole gamut of Niebuhr's writings. Eternity is always relevant to, and yet ever tensionally set against, earth at every moment of time. Eternity may never be identified with earth, but earth may never declare independence from eternity. Both ideal and achievement must be suspended in a dialectical relation: at every moment eternity must set the ideal of man, which judging the relativities of history as partial, yet inadequate. It is essentially at this point that Niebuhr differs from Barthianian. He accuses German dialectical theology of being nearer Greek Platonistic dualism than the Christian paradoxes when vindicating the absolute difference between eternity and time. History and nature became meaningless in Barthian theology, as Niebuhr sees it, and even the very fact of the Incarnation ceases to be a historical fact, i.e., the absolute never becomes incarnate in time. For Niebuhr, the only adequate religious expression of the human situation is a combination of this-worldly and other-worldly hopes.

It is interesting to notice how Niebuhr proceeds to state Christianity dialectically. The thesis of the Christian ethic is the absoluteness of the moral ideal and the endless possibilities for the fulfillment of brotherhood in history. "In the religion of Jesus, says Niebuhr, the perfection of God is consistently defined as an absolute love by comparison with which all altruistic achievements fall short."* This is the wisdom of   * DCR[3]
the cross. This is the Renaissance side of the Christian ethic. The antithesis is the foolishness of the cross. Original sin makes the fulfillment of the rule of Agape love impossible, for pride encourages man to pretend pretend far more for himself than the facts will justify.[4] This is the Reformation side of the Christian ethic. It contains a realistic pessimism which balances the initial Renaissance optimism. The synthesis

---

2. This sentence is also in an outline by King, "Reinhold Niebuhr," p. 140 in this volume.

3. The full citation should read Reinhold Niebuhr, *Does Civilization Need Religion? A Study in the Social Resources and Limitations of Religion in Modern Life* (New York: Macmillan, 1927), p. 54.

4. The word "pretend" appears as the last word on one page and the first word on the next.

is the power of the cross. Through faith and justification resources of grace are made accessible to the individual who remains within the pincers of the dialectic.[5]

At this point, we may turn to Niebuhr's anthropology which is certainly the cornerstone of his thought.

One of the first problems to oppress Niebuhr was the terrible contrast between "moral man and immoral society," between the relatively decent, good behavior of man as an individual, and man as society. His analysis of this contrast led him to the roots of the contradiction of human nature. He cogently states, "Individual men may be moral in the sense that they are able to consider interests of others than their own in determining problems of conduct, and are capable, on occasion, of preferring the advantages of others to their own. . . . But all these achievements are more difficult, if not impossible, for human societies and social groups. In every human group there is less reason to guide and to check impulse, less capacity for self transcendence, less ability to comprehend the need of others and therefore more unrestrained egoism than the individuals, who compare the groups, reveal in their personal relationships."*[6]

* MMIS

Again, Niebuhr was captured by the fact that the characteristics of the so-called Enlightenment of the 18th century, which had its roots in the Renaissance, had made a new appearance in the easy optimism of the first three decades of the twentieth century. Man was viewed as the measure of all things. History was to witness a quick and steady progress to Utopia. Man had only to be educated and put in agreeable environments in order that the kingdom of Heaven might be realized on earth. Modern liberal or "progressive" version of the Christian faith readily joined in to sing with the optimistic charms of modernity. The obvious refutations of this view of man, particularly in comtemporary history, has brought about a definite swing away from this pattern of thought. Says Niebuhr, "Since 1914 one tragic experience has followed an-

---

5. Much of this paragraph is also in "Reinhold Niebuhr," p. 140 in this volume.

6. Reinhold Niebuhr, *Moral Man and Immoral Society* (New York: Scribner, 1932), pp. xi, xii. This paragraph is similar to one in King, "Reinhold Niebuhr's Ethical Dualism," pp. 142–143 in this volume.

other, as if history has been designed to refute the vain delusions of modern man."*

The basal problem is how man shall think of himself. On the one hand hand, he is a child of nature, caught up in its conditions, on the other, he is a transcendent being standing outside of nature. Niebuhr contends that in the course of history, the tendency is to confuse or to disregard the synthesis, and to construct a view of human nature on the basis of one or the other aspect of his dual being. Platonism and Aristotelianism understood man primarily from the standpoint of his rational faculties. Over against this so-called classical view Democritus, Heraclitus, and Epicurus interpreted man as wholly part of nature. Such dichotonic views of man, says Niebuhr, can have no conception of meaning in history, and no solution of the element of tragedy in human affairs, because of the necessity of their own logic. The modern philosophic since the revival of classicism in the Renaissance fall into the same ancient errors. They are either idealistic or naturalistic. If the former, they tend to lose a sense of the finiteness of human nature, conceiving the self as identical with reason. If the latter modern man seeks to interpret himself wholly with reference to nature. This naturalism has in our times, taken concrete expression in Marxism and Fascism.

Over against these anthropologies which fail to do justice to the dimension of human nature, and which, in spite of the inner logic of their assumptions and of the refutations of history, persist in falsifying the human situation by false notions of progress and by false dogmas of human perfectibility, Niebuhr sets forth the biblical and Christian Anthropology. It takes issue with the utopian optimism of Modernism, but with equal emphasis it repudiates the cynical pessimism that lies at the heart of the age. It views man in terms of both nature and of spirit. He is both in the realm of necessity and in the realm of freedom. At one and the same time man is under the dominion of nature and also transcends nature. Man's self transcendence forbids him to identify meaning with causality in nature; his bodily and finite particularity equally forbids the loss of the self in a distinctionless absolute of

---

7. Reinhold Niebuhr, *Faith and History: A Comparison of Christian and Modern Views of History* (New York: Scribner, 1949), pp. 6–7.

mind or rationality. God as will and personality is, therefore, the only ground of individuality. As creature, man is made in the image of God. But along with this high measure of the human stature stands also the concomitant fact that man is a sinner. And so this leads us to another important point of Niebuhr's thought.

Niebuhr never wearies of pointing out that man is a sinner. He points out that such modern thinkers as Kierkegaard, Nietzsche, and Sigmund Freud, in their explorations of the dark depths of the human heart, confirm afresh the biblical doctrine of the sinfullness of man. Niebuhr sees sin as what results when man tries to find security for himself outside the tension of the dialectical relation between time and eternity. "Sin is, in short, the consequence of man's inclination to usurp the prerogatives of God, to think more highly of himself than he ought to observing the limits to which a creaturely freedom is bound."*[8]

* FH

This view does not look upon sin as the inevitable consequence of man's finiteness as the fruit of his involvement in the contingencies and necessities of nature. Rather it places evil at the very centre of human personality: in the will. "Sin is thus the unwillingness of man to acknowledge his creatureliness and dependence upon God and his effort to make his won life independent and secure."†

† NDM, I, 138.[9]

We readily see that for Niebuhr, pride is the basic sin and all other sins such as injustice and sensuality result from this pride. It is one of Niebuhr's great merits to show how the sin of pride develops into the pride of power, pride of intellect, moral pride and spiritual pride.

Niebuhr resorts to the formula of "original sin" to explain why evil in history belongs to man. "Man being both free and bound, both limited and limitless is anxious. Anxiety is the inevitable concomitant of the paradox of freedom and finiteness in which man is involved. Anxiety is the internal precondition of sin. It is the inevitable spiritual state of man, standing in

---

8. King omitted several words. The quotation should read: "Sin is, in short, the consequence of man's inclination to usurp the prerogatives of God, to think more highly of himself than he ought to think, thus making destructive use of his freedom by not observing the limits to which a creaturely freedom is bound" (Niebuhr, *Faith and History*, p. 121).

9. Reinhold Niebuhr, *The Nature and Destiny of Man*, 2 vols. (New York: Scribner, 1941–1943).

the paradoxical situation of freedom and finiteness.*   * NDM, I, 182.
Existentially, man sins inevitably, yet not by necessity. Since sin does not flow anxiety, man is responsible for his sin. If one answers that the doctrine is illogical, Niebuhr would retort that the doctrine may be logically absurd, but it is psychologically profound. Just as Hegel's "dialectic" is a logic invented for the purpose of doing justice to the fact of "becoming" as a phenomenan which belongs in the category of neither "being" nor "nonbeing," the doctrine of original sin, which is such a basic fact of experience, requires a provisional defiance of logic. He states, "the Christian doctrine of original sin with its seemingly contradictory assertions about the inevitability of sin and man's responsibility for sin is a dialectical truth which does justice to the fact that man's self love and self-centredness is inevitable, but not in such a way as to fit into the category of natural necessity."†   † NDM, I, 263.

The universal reaction of all who have made spiritual contact with the law which defines ideal selfhood, is what Niebuhr calls "the fall." The fall is localized in th[a]t moment in freedom where the free self, assenting to the law of <u>Agape</u>, peers down into the empirical self and discovers selfishness. For this reason "every man is Adam." The Fall is a mythological expression for what is psychologically true in each person. The fall, says Niebuhr, "is an inward conflict between the is and the ought of life, between the ideal possibilities to which freedom encourages man and the drive of egoism, which reason sharpens rather than assuages."‡[10]   ‡ BT, pp. 137–138.

By now we see that for Niebuhr, original sin and the fall are not literal events in history; they are rather symbolic or mythological categories to explain the universality of sin. While passing we might say just a word about Niebuhr's conception of symbol and myth since they are such basic ideas in his thought. Ethical fruitfulness is measured by the ability of norms to maintain a tension between what is and what ought to be, between the historical and the transcendental. This means that eternity is the absolute and history the relative, and anything in history which is a pointer to the eternal can be no more than a symbol

---

10. Reinhold Niebuhr, *Beyond Tragedy: Essays on the Christian Interpretation of History* (London: Nisbet, 1947). The quotation should read "a particular conflict" rather than "an inward conflict."

of the eternal. To identify anything in history with eternity is to break the dialectical relation between time and eternity. Symbols are rallying points for the religious myth. The myth is a story, the origin of which is generally forgotten, which serves to explain the basis of a religious practice or belief. The myth is an artistic attempt to give depth to history. Says Niebuhr, "Meaning can be attributed to history only by a mythology."* Orthodoxy has vitiated the usefullness of myth by trying to literalize it into a metaphysical truth, while liberalism has bypassed the symbols as prescientific nonsense.

We pass now to Niebuhr's philosophy of history. Niebuhr's most systematic treatments of this subject are found in the Second Volume of <u>The Nature and Destiny of Man</u> and <u>Faith and History</u>. The argument in the latter book turns, as the subtitle suggests, on the contrast between the Christian and th[e] modern view of history. The "modern view" is that history itself is the redeemer. This is Niebuhr's way of expressing the idea that man can help himself to progress, and unless he helps himself, he is helpless. The Christian view is that history is an inadequate Christ, that man's history is a history of guilt, and that meaning can be found only in repentance. Only after repentance, is man able to receive the Christian revelation.†

For Niebuhr the final problem of history becomes the fact that "before God no man living is justified."‡ Every individual "is a Moses who perishes outside the promised Land."§ The result of this view is that there can be no real moral progress in man's social, political, and religious life: for good can never triumph over evil in history, due to limitations of human nature— though there may be a parallel development of good and evil throughout history. Within such a view is there no hope for man? Is man consigned to remain suspended within this dialectical tension guilty when he performs and guilty when he fails to perform? It is at this point that the doctrine of Grace becomes all important in Niebuhr's theology. The moment a person assumes the posture of rependance before God and confesses helplessness in the inward man, that instant God injects power into his heart. These resources are at once recognized as vitalities which have

* REE, 123.[11]

† FH, 140.

‡ NDM, II, 292.

§ NDM, II, 310.

---

11. Reinhold Niebuhr, *Reflections on the End of an Era* (New York: Scribner, 1934).

come from beyond man. Since the divine Grace comes from beyond man, it operates not in history, but outside, beyond, and at the "edge" of history. Justification supplies man with a "new nature." Sanctification releases a flow of grace to empower one to complete heights of <u>Agape</u> normally impossible on one's own strength. Justification is a feeling in the free self of a spiritual relief following upon the occasion of conversion and repentance. This release cannot be accounted for on the ground that one has merited release himself, for he remains a sinner; therefore, it must be the imputed righteousness of Christ. God accepts the intention to live according to the rule of Christ as the very act itself. The possession is always a righteousness by faith. Man is free from guilt "in principle" only never "in fact." Our sinful nature remains, although we feel that we are sinless. If man ever achieved <u>Agape</u> in fact, then the dialectic would be spoiled by history containing its own ideal.

In Niebuhr's philosophy of history such orthodox Christian doctrines as the second coming of Christ and the resurrection of the body become important. We must hasten to say, however, that his statement of these doctrines are not at all orthodox. The second coming of Christ is the symbolic way faith declares its assurance that Christ, who has already overcome the world, as <u>Tetas</u>, will assuredly achieve that triumph at the end of history. The first coming—Christ after the flesh, is the disclosure, and the second coming is the fulfillment. The resurrection of the body is a symbol implying on the one hand that eternity will fulfill the richness and variety which the temperol process has elaborated. On the other hand, it implies that the condition of finiteness and freedom is a problem for which there is no solution by human power. Only God can solve this problem.

For a clearer understanding of Niebuhr Philosophy of history it is necessary at this point to discuss his Christology, since, for him Christ is the heaven-sent clue to clarify the meaning of history.

In briefest compass, Niebuhr's general argument for the Christ concept is as follows: Because a free man stands outside of history, his full explanation requires a pattern or mind which likewise stands outside of history. History is one-dimensional; it suggests, therefore, more than it can explain. If history is to have meaning, such a meaning must not be identified with the process itself; for that which exemplifies a pattern is numerically different from the pattern. If, e.g., an act has meaning, the act is one thing and the meaning which it exemplifies is another. There is numerical difference between the blueprints used in constructing a building and the finished building itself. Stated religiously, Christ is the mind or blueprint which gives moral finality to our ideals. Niebuhr states, "Christianity enters the world with the stupendous claim that in Christ . . . the expectations of the ages have been fulfilled."* In short, for Niebuhr, Christ is the eternal in time, a breaking through of the everlasting mind of God which gives both meaning and consummation to process.

This Christ just discussed is not the Jesus of history that walked in Jerusalem rather he is a pure abstraction. Christ is only a symbol. Niebuhr laconically states, "Christ is the symbol both of what man ought to be and of what God is beyond man."† As to the person of the Jesus of history, Niebuhr fails to pass beyond his erstwhile liberalism.

At this point we may turn to Niebuhr's God concept. Unfortunately Niebuhr never gives a systematic statement of his doctrine of God, it is only here and there that one can find his view of God. First, he accepts the traditional theistic view that God is creator. "To believe that God created the world, states Niebuhr, is to feel that the world is a realm of meaning and coherence without insisting that the world is totally good or that the totality of things must be identified with the Sacred."‡ As creator, God is both transcendent and free. His existence must be postulated if one is to give a satisfactory account of the world itself. Natural causation can never explain why there is this causal series rather than another.

Secondly, Niebuhr stresses that fact that God is Judge. General revelation which is "the testimony in the consciousness of every person that his life touches a reality beyond himself, a reality deeper and higher than the system of nature in which he stands, is powerful in its witness that man is morally related to God as Judge. "We have a deep and abiding awareness of being seen, commanded, jusged, and known from beyond ourselves."§

* NDM, II, 35.

† BT.[12]

‡ ICE.[13]

§ NDM, I, 128.

---

12. Niebuhr, *Beyond Tragedy*, p. 23.

13. Reinhold Niebuhr, *Interpretation of Christian Ethics* (New York: Harper, 1935), p. 26.

The final solution to the predicament of man, together with the completion of the dialectical relation between time and eternity, cannot be enjoyed until the knowledge of God as Judge passes to God as Redeemer. So Niebuhr is continually speaking of God as Redeemer. This redemptive work is accomplished through Christ, for in Christ God takes the sins of the world into himself, effecting a final forgiveness.

There are many points in his writings in which Niebuhr speaks of God's existence and nature as inexplicable and incomprehensible to man. Man is so limited as never to be able to transcend his limitations and understand the ways of God.*

* NDM, I, 163.

CRITICAL EVALUATION: The merit of Niebuhr is that, seeing the problem of our age in its proper relations and dimensions, and laying firm hold on ultimate principles, he sets forth with rigour and consistency in analysis and criticism the fundamental weaknesses and contradictions and the inevitable sterility of the humanistic emphasis.[14] Moreover, I think that Niebuhr's anthropology is the necessary corrective of a kind of liberalism that too easily capitulated to modern culture. Man who has come so far in wisdom and decency may be expected to go much further as his methods of attaining and applying knowledge are improved. Although such ethical religion is humane and its vision a lofty one, it has obvious shortcomings. This particular sort of optimism has been discredited by the brutal logic of events. Instead of assured progress in wisdom and decency, man faces the ever present possibility of swift relapse not merely to animalism but into such calculated cruelty as no other animal can practice. Niebuhr reminds us of this on every hand.[15]

Yet we may ask if Niebuhr's views are as orthodox and Biblical as he assumes them to be.[16] His conception of original sin, the fall of man, and original righteousness, is overhauled in terms of historical and lib-

---

14. This sentence repeats the first sentence of the concluding paragraph in "Reinhold Niebuhr," p. 141 in this volume.

15. These four sentences are part of King's draft report on *Crozer Quarterly*, p. 141 in this volume.

16. This sentence, a paraphrase from an article by Walter G. Muelder, appears in King's conclusion to "Reinhold Niebuhr," p. 141 in this volume. See Muelder, "Reinhold Niebuhr's Conception of Man," *The Personalist* 26 (July 1945): 284.

eral criticism. His Christology is so novel that he can make essentially symbolic the reality of Chris[t], the sinlessness of Jesus, and the resurrection. Indeed, his use of myth and symbolization to explain Christian doctrine is so thoroughgoing that hardly any denotative meaning is possible.[17]

In setting forth the Biblical view of man, Niebuhr attacks and seemingly rejects Greek and modern idealism. Yet Niebuhr fails to see that in his argument he uses concepts and categories of the very idealism he rejects. What more can we say for such ideas as: self, consciousness, transcendence, self-transcendence, freedom, will, and personality? Niebuhr does not recognize the presuppositions of the idealistic categories, but begs the metaphysical question by putting them at the disposal of so-called Biblical presuppositions.[18]

Again, it may be pointed out that Niebuhr's extreme agnosticism as to the God concept is far from Biblical religion. In asserting that God's nature and existence are inexplicable and incomprehensible to man, Niebuhr is asserting what is essential to Thomas Henry Huxley's definition of agnosticism, that reason cannot demonstrate the existence and nature of God. Niebuhr is quite dependent on the Epistle to the Romans for many of his views, but there is one passage in the Epistle that he almost completely overlooks. "For the invisible things of hom from the creation of the world are clearly seen, being understood by the things that are made, even his eternal power and Godhead; so that they are without excuse.*

* Rom. 1:20.

TADS. PACC.

---

17. Muelder, "Niebuhr's Conception of Man," p. 284: "In commenting on Niebuhr's claims it may be said at the outset that his views are probably less orthodox and certainly less Biblical than he assumes them to be. . . . He overhauls in terms of historical and liberal criticism such ideas as original sin, the fall of man, original righteousness, and guilt. He introduces into the old wineskins of Christology novel assumptions of fact and doctrine. Thus he makes essentially symbolical the reality of the Christ, the sinlessness of Jesus, and the resurrection. Indeed, the use of myth and symbolization with respect to Christian doctrine is so thoroughgoing that hardly any direct denotative meaning can be recognized."

18. Muelder, "Niebuhr's Conception of Man," p. 285: "In stressing the uniqueness of the Biblical view of man, Niebuhr attacks and seemingly rejects Greek and modern idealism. Yet, it is idealistic concepts and categories which carry the weight of his argument. Such ideas are: self, consciousness, transcendence, self-consciousness, self-transcendence, freedom, reason, will, universality, and personality. . . . Unfortunately, Niebuhr does not recognize or face squarely the presuppositions of the idealistic categories, but begs the metaphysical question by putting them at the disposal of so-called Biblical presuppositions."

To Francis E. Stewart

26 July 1954
Roxbury, Mass.

Writing to a fellow graduate of Crozer, King reports on the restructuring of the Crozer faculty initiated by Sankey Blanton.[1] Blanton became president of Crozer in 1951 during King's third and final year. He attempted, with some success, to alter the school's image as a bastion of liberal theology and was thus able to attract funds that kept the school alive. Some words are obscured by stains on the letter.

Dear Francis,

It was certainly a happy experience to hear your voice the other day after such a long time. I had a very fine trip back to Boston, and fortunately I stopped in Chester and got some idea of what is taking place at Crozer. I found all of the things that you [*had?*] told me quite authentic. It is definitely true than Enslin, Prichard and Batten are leaving. Prichard is going to some school in California. Enslin was retired, and Batten has gone over into the Episcopal Church.

I have not been able to get the exact causal factor that lead to [*this?*] great turnover in faculty, but [*I?*] think at bottom it grew out of conflict with Blanton. I think he was desirous of getting rid of these men from the very beginning. Now the whole faculty will consist of men that he hired directly. What the outcome will be I dont know [*word illegible*]. I do hope that it wont be disastrous. I understand that a man from Eastern will replace Enslin.[2]

As for me, I am doing fine, and working hard to complete this dissertation. Brother it really requires a lot of work.

As I said to you the other night [*I have?*] been called to a Church in Montgomery Alabama. My wife and I will be moving in around the first of September. It is a very fine church with even greater possibilities. I hope that we will be able to do a good job there. When you get settled and get the program [*ready?*], I will want to have you over to preach for us.

---

1. Francis E. Stewart (1923–) received his A.B. from Mercer University in Macon, Georgia, in 1949 and his B.D. from Crozer in 1952. As a Crozer student he served as associate pastor of the First Baptist Church in Chester. From 1952 to 1964 Stewart was the pastor of a rural county-seat church, Monticello Baptist, in Monticello, Georgia, where he encountered opposition for preaching about racial injustice. He later served as chaplain of a hospital and administrator of community service centers before working for the State of Georgia as an administrator. From 1972 until his retirement in 1988 Stewart was senior policy analyst in the Governor's Office of Planning and Budget. See Stewart to King Papers Project, April 1990.

2. Eastern Baptist Theological Seminary in Philadelphia was Crozer's more conservative rival among northern white Baptist seminaries.

Please give my best regards to your lovely wife and to the kids. I am looking forward to seeing them in the near future. I hope for your continual success in your pastorship. When you have time be sure to [*send?*] me a line.

Sincerely yours
[*signed*] Martin King

ALS. FESP.

From Francis E. Stewart

29 July 1954
Monticello, Ga.

In his reply Stewart expresses concern about George W. Davis, King's former professsor, under the Blanton administration. Clarice is Stewart's wife.

Dear Martin:

Thank you very much for your good letter of July 26 which arrived this afternoon. I had suspected that Blanton was at the bottom of this shift, although I hesitated to say so. When he was down here earlier in the year he expressed some feelings of conflict, but it was directed more at Keighton and Batten. I am wondering about Dr. Davis and Keighton now, what do you think they are going to do as a result of all this?

Personally, I feel that if Blanton can bring about a better relationship between Crozer and Eastern so that the best factors of each school will be represented it will be all for the good. To be ministers of the gospel I feel that we must have a profound concern for those we serve. On the other hand, I am equally concerned that we not sacrifice our reasoning powers for any cheap, shoddy sentimentalism.

I do not know what the trustees had in mind when they brought Sankey to the seminary, but from what Dr. Davis said he has the backing of the trustees now. However, he seemed quite disturbed about the whole business. Sankey, as you very well know, is not what is [*strikeout illegible*] known as a tactful man.

We had a very fine meeting at Emory and I enjoyed the fellowship ~~very~~ immensely. Unfortunately, Dr. Boyd wrecked his car coming over to the meeting and we did not get to hear him. I understand it was a pretty bad wreck, but I don't think he was hurt too much.

It would be a genuine pleasure to come over and preach for you in Montgomery sometime. Clarice's mother lives at Langdale, Alabama which is about half-way between here and Montgomery so we go over that way fairly regularly.

Let me know if you hear any more on the situation at Crozer.

I hope you finish your work on your dissertation without any trouble. I met a professor from Boston U. while I was at Emory. He is Dr. John T. Greene, Professor of Marriage and family counseling at your institution. He is a very fine fellow who loves to talk. I know you won't have any free time to visit, but if you should run into him, please give him my regards.

We are all doing fine. Now we are trying to get ready for a few days f vacation, as soon as we finish a revival meeting out in the country.

Kindest Regards,
[*signed*] Francis.

TLS. MLKP-MBU: Box 117.

From Nannie H. Burroughs

3 August 1954

The president of the Woman's Auxiliary, National Baptist Convention, invites
King to speak at the group's annual meeting in St. Louis.[1]

Rev M L King Jr
193 Boulevard N E
Atlanta, Georgia

Dear Rev King:

I am writing to invite you to be one of the Noonday speakers at our St Louis meeting.

The theme of the Convention is "The Vision of the World Made New". The time allotted for the message is twenty minutes.

---

1. Nannie Helen Burroughs (1879–1961) was an educator, religious leader, and social activist. Pivotal in the 1900 founding of the Woman's Convention Auxiliary (WC) to the National Baptist Convention, Burroughs served as the WC's corresponding secretary from 1900 to 1948 and as president from 1948 until her death. Under her leadership the organization, representing over one million black Baptist women, provided means through which women organized on state and local levels around religious, political, and social issues. In 1909 she founded the National Training School for Women and Girls in Washington, D. C., which prepared women for jobs both in and outside the sphere of traditional female employment. A member of the National Association of Colored Women, Burroughs cofounded the National League of Republican Colored Women (1924) and lectured as a member of the Republican Party's national speakers' bureau during the 1920s. In 1931 President Hoover appointed her to chair a special committee on housing for African Americans.

You are scheduled to speak on Thursday, September 9th, and I hope it will be possible for you to accept the invitation.

Sincerely yours
Nannie H Burroughs, President

NHB/b

TLc. NHBP-DLC.

From Walter R. McCall

5 August 1954
Fort Valley, Ga.

McCall congratulates King on his new position as pastor of Dexter Avenue Baptist Church, a pulpit McCall had pursued himself. McCall also mentions his impending marriage and the difficulties he is experiencing in breaking off an earlier relationship. The latter woman's name has been deleted for reasons of privacy. Dudley is George W. Dudley, pastor of Liberty Baptist Church in Atlanta.

Dear Mike,

It was good to hear from you the other day, and to know that all things seem to be going your way. I must admit, however, that I thought that you had forgotten the Ole Boy. Yet, I do understand what it means to keep busy. Last week, I called your home and was told that you would be in on Friday night, so I took for granted that you were not going to remain very long, as was pointed out in your letter.

So, you will take over your church on the first Sunday, September? Very good! Long delay in matters of that nature can, at times, work havoc upon one, I suppose. People can become very disgruntled. I was talking to a young lady from Montgomery week before last. She and her whole family are members of that Church. They do, I am told, think highly of you.

Well, as for me things are going very good for me, but I am working in very hot weather. Trying hard, however, to keep from over doing it. I am! During the past year, I worked rather hard, and now I find it inexpedient to drive during the summer months.

By the way, things here from the lady angle. I am going to get married on June 14, 1954.[1] I would like to have you serve as the best man. The young lady to whom I plan to be married is an Annabelle Spann, of Chester, S.C. She is a girl who has impressed me more than any girl I have ever gone with.

---

1. McCall meant 1955.

She has poise, culture and refinement, attractiveness and shapeliness, and versatility. Moreover, she has a very fine family background. Above all, however, she loves me, and I love her. Between us is a spirit of mutuality. Frankly, I believe she'll make me a good wife. She holds the A.B., and M.A. degrees from S.C. State and Cornell University respectively and has done further study at the latter. She teaches Home Economics at State College in Huntsville, Ala. By the way, I suppose Dudley told you about my other chick from N.C. who was down visiting me in Feb. She works in N.C. and holds residence in Albany, Ga. Doc., really she is beautiful, but she does not have what this girl has. I hate to break off from her, but I am ready to be married, so I am not willing to continue playing the field.

[*Name deleted*] has gone to California. I gave her fifty dollars with the idea of helping to support the child, but that support only gave [*Name deleted*] a ray of hope to win me over to marry her although I have told her again and again that I am not going to do that. She has already worried the very day light out of me by long dustance phone calls and a host of letters. So, instead of continuing that support, I have cut it off already. Never do I expect to help in any fashion. Man, [*Name deleted*] will harass me to death if I give her the least o' consideration. Hate to take that attitude, but I think I am wise in so doing.

Yes, you may inform me in plenty of time as to when I may render any deed of service for you in connection with your parish. I will gladly do so. I will not be back at Fort Valley until the third week of September. I shall vacate. Best wishes for a continued summer of felicitations. A hello to Coretta.

Your Pal,
[*signed*]
Mac.

{Mamie Thompson who received her M.A. from B.U. is on our summer school faculty. Tell me, what is it between you and her?}

TALS. MLKP-MBU: Box 117.

II

Montgomery, Alabama

"Recommendations to the Dexter Avenue Baptist Church for the Fiscal Year 1954–1955"

[5 September 1954]
[Montgomery, Ala.]

King presents his vision for the future growth of Dexter and his plans for accomplishing it. The first two paragraphs stress the importance of pastoral authority, particularly in his interactions with the deacon board: "It is therefore indispensable to the progress of the church that the official board and membership cooperate fully with the leadership of the pastor." King assigns to the Social and Political Action Committee—"established for the purpose of keeping the congregation intelligently informed concerning the social, political and economic situation"—several members of the congregation who, in 1955 and 1956, would be crucial in initiating and sustaining the Montgomery bus boycott: Jo Ann Robinson, Rufus Lewis, and Mary Fair Burks.

When a minister is called to the pastorate of a church, the main presupposition is that he is vested with a degree of authority. The source of this authority is twofold. First of all, his authority originates with God. Inherent in the call itself is the presupposition that God directed that such a call be made. This fact makes it crystal clear that the pastor's authority is not merely humanly conferred, but divinely sanctioned.

Secondly, the pastor's authority stems from the people themselves. Implied in the call is the unconditional willingness of the people to accept the pastor's leadership. This means that the leadership never ascends from the pew to the pulpit, but it invariably descends from the pulpit to the pew. This does not mean that the pastor is one before whom we must blindly and ignorantly genuflect, as if he were possessed of some infallible or superhuman attributes. Nor does it mean that the pastor should needlessly interfere with the deacons, trustees or workers of the various auxiliaries, assuming unnecessary dictatorial authority. But it does mean that the pastor is to be respected and accepted as the central figure around which the policies and programs of the church revolve. He must never be considered a mere puppet for the whimsical and capricious mistreatment of those who wish to show their independence, and "use their liberty for a cloak of maliciousness." It is therefore indispensable to the progress of the church that the official board and membership cooperate fully with the leadership of the pastor.

Pursuant of these underlying principles, I respectfully submit the following recommendations:

1. In order that every member of the church shall be identified with a smaller and more intimate fellowship of the church, clubs representing the twelve months of the year shall be organized. Each member of the church will automatically become a member of the club of the month in which he or she was born. Those born in January will be members of the 287

"January" Club. Those born in February will be members of the "February" Club, etc. Each month club shall choose its own officers. Each club shall meet once per month, with the exception of the month for which the club is named. In the month for which the club is named, each club shall meet weekly. So the December Club, for example, shall meet once monthly until December. In December it shall meet each week. Each club shall be asked to make a special contribution to the church on the last Sunday of the month for which it is named. Also, on the Church Anniversary each club shall be asked to contribute at least one hundred dollars ($100.00). All of the money raised by these clubs shall be placed in a fund known as the building fund. The work of these clubs shall be to supplement that of the Building Fund Committee. (This committee will be discussed subsequently).

2. That the church shall begin a four year renovation and expansion program. Immediate renovations for 1954–55 shall include: carpeting the main auditorium; public speaking system; electric cold water fountain; new pulpit furniture; Communion table; and painting the basement. Renovations for 1955–56 shall include: new pews; and a new heating and cooling system. Improvements for 1956–57 shall include: new baptistry, and a general improvement of the basement. The remaining year of this four year program shall be spent adding large sums of money to the Building Fund for the construction of a religious education building. It is hoped that by 1959 a religious education building will be under construction. Obviously many emergency renovations will arise which are not included in the present list.

3. That a Building Fund Committee be formed consisting of the following persons Mr. J. H. Gilchrist and Mr. M. F. Moore, co-chairmen; the chairman of both boards; the clerk of the church; the superintendent of the Sunday School; all members of the Finance Committee; Mrs. E. M. Arrington; Mrs. Thelma Anderson; Miss Verdie Davie; Mr. Roscoe Williams; Mr. R. W. Brown, Mr. J. T. Brooks, and Dr. W. D. Pettus. Dr. H. C. Trenholm shall serve as advisor to this committee. The responsibility of this committee shall be twofold: (1) To seek to determine the advisability of expanding on this particular spot; (2) To formulate a systematic approach to the problem of raising the necessary funds for expansion of the church plant. This committee shall be requested to report its results to the pastor within six months. After the findings of this committee shall have been reported, the trustees under the sanction of the church, will be on the lookout for the purchasing of property necessary for the expansion program.

4. That a New Member Committee be formed consisting of the following persons: Mrs. B. P. Brewer, chairman; Mr. Julius Alexander, co-chairman; Mrs. R. E. Harris, secretary; Mrs. Mary Morgan, Mrs. E. M. Arrington, Mr. Epreval Davie, Sr., and Mrs. J. T. Alexander. The following shall be the duties of this committee:

   a. To welcome all new members into the Church on the Sunday that they join.

b. To interview all new members concerning their particular areas of interest in the church. If they have no particular interest, be sure to give them one. Place them in the particular department or circle of the church where they can exercise their maximum spiritual and intellectual potentialities. Also ascertain the month of the new member's birth, and assign him to his proper Month Club.

c. Explain the financial system to each new member. See that each new member has a box of church envelopes.

d. All names and vital statistics should be written plainly and turned over to the office secretary the following week in order that she may make an orderly transfer of such information to the permanent files of the church.

e. Request the chairman of the deacon board to assign a sufficient number of deacons to visit all new members within a week after they have united with this church. The president of the Month Club receiving new members shall also be requested to make a visit of welcome or assign some qualified member of the club to do so.

5. In order that there may be a reliable and orderly record of the church's origin, growth and future development, a Committee on the History of Dexter shall be organized consisting of the following persons: Mrs. Leila Barlow, chairman; Mr. N. W. Walton, Mrs. Mary Moore, Mr. C. J. Dunn, Mr. John Fulgham. This committee shall be requested to present a summary of the history of Dexter each year at the church anniversary. This committee shall also be requested to keep on file at least three weekly church bulletins, and look into the possibility of having them bound at the end of each church year. These records shall be carefully preserved by members of the committee until it is possible to develop a church library.

6. A Scholarship Fund Committee shall be established consisting of the following persons: Mrs. Thelma Morris, chairman; Mr. P. M. Blair, co-chairman; Mrs. Ive Pettus, Dr. Edward Maxwell, and Dr. H. L. Van Dyke. It shall be the responsibility of this committee to choose each year for a scholarship award the high school graduate of Dexter possessing the highest scholastic rating as well as unusual possibilities for service to humanity; one who has been actively engaged in some phase of church life and one who plans to attend college. The scholarship award for this year shall be one hundred dollars ($100.00). The awards may be increased in proportion as the church may grow and prosper.

7. A Cultural Committee shall be established consisting of the following persons: Mr. J. T. Brooks, chairman; Mrs. Coretta King, co-chairman; Mrs. C. K. Taylor, Miss Agnes Jette, Mr. Cleveland Dennard, Miss Grace Jackson. This committee shall invite two big cultural events to Dexter per year, one in the spring and one in the fall. They should seek to make one a group event (a school or church chorus) and present an individual artist in the other. Such an undertaking will have a fourfold purpose:

a. To lift the general cultural appreciation of our church and community

       b. To give encouragement to our school groups

       c. To give encouragement to promising artists

       d. To give financial aid to the church

8. In order to coordinate the efforts and aims of the musical units of the church a <u>Department of Music</u> shall be established. Mr. J. T. Brooks will serve as head of this department. The directors of all musical units shall be members. Other members will include: Miss Grace Jackson, Mrs. Coretta S. King, and Mrs. Edna King. The members of this department shall meet with the pastor once quarterly to discuss ways to implement the technical, artistic, and worship aims of the master.

9. In order to implement the program of religious education, a <u>Board of Religious Education</u> shall be organized. This board shall consist of the following members: Mrs. E. M. Arrington, chairman; Dr. W. E. Anderson, co-chairman; Mr. C. C. Beverly, Mrs. JoAnn Robinson, Mrs. Sadie Brooks, Mrs. Queen Tarver, Miss Dean (Olivet), Mr. William Thompson, and Mr. Cleveland Dennard. The immediate work of this committee shall be to study the need for the revitalization and reorganization of the B.T.U. and the Sunday School. Findings of this study are to be submitted to the pastor. This board will also plan for a two or three week Daily Vacation Bible School next summer. Obviously this should be one of the strongest boards in the church.

10. A <u>Social Service Committee</u> shall be established consisting of the following persons: Miss Marguerite Moore, chairman; Mrs. Verdie Davie, co-chairman; Mrs. Sallie Madison, Mrs. J. H. Gilchrist, Mrs. R. E. Harris, Mr. S. W. Wilson, Mr. Julius Alexander, Mrs. Mary Moore, Mrs. S. S. Austin. The duties of this committee shall be as follows: The care and visitation of the sick and needy. All appeals for help will come before this committee. This does not mean that the missionaries and deacons will be freed of their responsibility to visit the sick. It simply means that <u>all financial aid to the sick and needy will be made through this committee by official checks of the Dexter Avenue Baptist Church</u>. This system of helping the needy will discourage unbusiness-like practices, and prevent much duplication.

11. Since the gospel of Jesus is a social gospel as well as a personal gospel seeking to save the whole man, a <u>Social and Political Action Committee</u> shall be established for the purpose of keeping the congregation intelligently informed concerning the social, political and economic situation. This committee shall keep before the congregation the importance of the N.A.A.C.P. The membership should unite with this great organization in a solid block. This committee shall also keep before the congregation the necessity of being registered voters. Every member of Dexter must be a registered voter. During elections, both state and national, this committee will sponsor forums and mass meetings to discuss the relative merits of candidates and the major issues involved. This committee shall consist of the following persons: Mrs. Mary Burks, chairman; Mrs. JoAnn Robinson, co-chairman; Dr. R. T. Adair, Mr. F. W. Taylor, Sr., Dr. W. D. Pettus, and Mr. Rufus Lewis

12. Mrs. W. E. Anderson and Mrs. Zelia Evans shall comprise a committee

to organize a strong and dynamic <u>Women's Council</u>. All the women in 5 Sept
the church will automatically become members of this organization. Al- 1954
though this organization will have the liberty to elect its own officers, the
pastor is recommending that Mrs. Anderson and Mrs. Evans become
President and Vice-president, respectively, for the first year. Literature
and suggestions for organization can be obtained from the pastor.

13. Mr. P. M. Blair and Mr. J. H. Gilchrist shall comprise a committee to
organize an active and dynamic <u>Brotherhood</u>. This organization will include every man in the church. Mr. Blair and Mr. Gilchrist shall serve
as President and Vice-president respectively for at least the first year.
Literature and suggestions for organization can be obtained from the
pastor.

14. Mr. Cleveland Dennard, Reverend Porter, and Mrs. Athalstein Adair
shall comprise a committee to organize a strong and functional <u>Youth
Council</u>. This Council will have three divisions: (1) Children, (2) Youth,
and (3) Young Adults. The organization of a <u>Young Married Couples
Club</u> shall grow out of this Council. The pastor will meet with this committee to make suggestions.

15. In order to increase the feeling of real fellowship in the church and
make the visitors feel a hearty welcome, a <u>Courtesy Committee</u> shall be
organized. It will be the purpose of this committee to make its way to the
visitors on Sunday and give them a sense of real welcome. Also, this
committee shall sponsor coffee hours <u>at least once monthly</u> immediately
after the morning service. At this time both visitors and members shall
be invited to the basement of the church for a moment of fellowship and
getting acquainted. This committee shall consist of the following persons: Mrs. C. K. Taylor, chairman; Mrs. Fressie Maxwell, co-chairman;
Mrs. C. D. Alexander, Mrs. L. H. Whitted, Mrs. Roscoe Williams, Mrs.
Verdie Davie, Mrs. Clarene Sankey, Mrs. Fannie Motley, Mrs. Thelma
Morris, Mrs. Fannie Doak, and Mrs. Rosa Dawson.

16. That a <u>Sunday Nursery</u> be established in the basement of the church,
which will take care of the children of parents who wish to worship in
the morning service. The following persons shall serve as a committee
to set up this nursery: Mrs. Fressie Maxwell, chairman; Mrs. Sadie
Brooks, co-chairman; Mrs. Rebecca Nesbitt, Mrs. Thelma Morris. This
committee should also pursue the possibility of opening a Day Nursery.

17. That the following annual special days and events be enacted in the
church calendar:
    a. Church Anniversary   Second Sunday in December
    b. Youth Day   Second Sunday in March
    c. Spring Lecture Series   Week after Fourth Sunday in April
    d. Men's Day   Second Sunday in July
    e. Women's Day   Fourth Sunday in September
    It is hoped that a week of activities shall lead to each of these spe-
cial days. Speakers for each of these events will be secured by the pastor. This, however, does not mean that suggestions cannot come from
members.

18. That at a very early date all officers of the <u>Missionary Society</u> will meet 291

with the pastor to discuss ways and means of revitalizing the Missionary Society.

19. The chairman of the <u>Deacon Board</u> shall call a meeting of the deacons once monthly. The purpose of this meeting will be to discuss and seek ways to help the pastor improve the spiritual life of the church. Also the chairman should lead the deacons in a course on the major doctrines of Christianity and the duties of deaconship. The Deacon Board shall not be a legislative body. All legislation shall come through the official body, composed of deacons and trustees, called only by the pastor.

20. That <u>all members and officers of the official board, and all officers of the various auxiliaries</u> of the church will be recommended annually by the pastor.

21. That the <u>Church Membership Roll shall be divided into an active and an inactive list</u>. Those members who fail to register for the year and who contribute nothing to the financial upkeep of the church, shall be placed on the roll as an inactive member, unless some satisfactory explanation be given to the officers. An inactive member shall have no voting privileges in the church.

22. The membership shall be divided into groups of twenty-five persons, and each deacon will be responsible for the spiritual care of one of these groups. As far as possible this division will be worked out on the basis of geographical convenience. It will be the duty of the deacons to constantly call and visit members in his group. Members that are slack in church attendance and general church responsibilities should be persuaded to improve. At the end of every two months each deacon shall receive from the office secretary the names of members in his group who might be behind in their pledges. It shall be the duty of the deacon to persuade the member to catch up his or her pledge.

23. In order to revamp the financial system of the church, a <u>Unified Budget Plan</u> shall be established. This plan will do away with all rallies. Instead of giving haphazardly to this or that collection and to this and that auxiliary the individual, through this method, pledges a simple weekly contribution to the Unified Budget of the church. At the beginning of the church year, each member will receive a pledge card on which he states the amount of his weekly pledge toward the overall budget of the church. Each registered member will in turn be given a box of envelopes covering the fifty-two Sundays in the year in which he will place his weekly contribution. With the enactment of this plan, only one collection will be taken in the church. This plan will be explained more fully when we come to a discussion of the budget.

24. In order to implement the above financial plan as well as any business like plan, it is imperative that we have a <u>Central Treasury</u>. Therefore, I recommend that all money in the treasury of each auxiliary be turned over to the general church treasurer by November 1, 1954. The budget for each of these auxiliaries will then be incorporated in the Unified Budget of the church.

25. All bills shall be paid in checks.

26. All checks will be made out by the Financial secretary.

27. No checks will be paid out without the O.K. of the pastor.

28. The honorarium for guest speakers will be left to the discretion of the pastor.

29. In addition to the two check signers, there shall be a third signer in the person of the chairman of the Finance Committee.

30. All money shall be deposited on the day that it is raised, and the deposit slip shall be returned to the church office on the following day so that an accurate record can be kept at all times of the money on hand.

31. All money will be counted in the secretary's office in the basement of the church.

32. An accurate record of receipts and disbursements as well as financial statement of each individual contributor shall be placed in the hands of every member at the end of each quarter of the church year.

33. That the fiscal year of Dexter Avenue Baptist Church shall be from October 1, to September 30. Although the present recommendations if accepted, will not be enacted until around November 1, 1954, this change in fiscal policy will be retroactive to October 1. Elections will be held as usual the last of December. But it means that those elected will occupy their offices only nine months or until September 30, 1955. Elections should be held sometime during the first two weeks in September and those elected shall assume their office on the first of October. The annual meeting shall be held on Wednesday Night before the First Sunday in October and the Installation of Officers shall take place on the First Sunday in October at 3:30 P.M.

34. In order to implement this overall program, a full time Office Secretary shall be hired. The job of this person would be: (1) to mimeograph all programs and bulletins for the church; (2) to keep an accurate record of the financial standing of each member and of all receipts and disbursements; (3) to make out all checks and mail them if necessary by the O.K. of the pastor; (4) to be responsible for all correspondence for the pastor and church, (5) to receive money from members who desire paying pledges during the week or desire mailing them in; (6) to present a quarterly statement to each member of the church concerning its financial status; (7) to be on hand for calls into the church and for the giving of information to all in need of such, etc. This person should be a member of Dexter, having a familiarity with the overall program of the church or willing to be trained in such. In order to have a stable and well organized church, this office is indispensable.

This ends my recommendations. If every member will assume an equal responsibility in the implementation of this program, success will be as inevitable as the rising sun. It is quite true that there can be no great followship without great leadership, but it is equally true that there can be no great leadership without great followship. There must be mutuality on every hand. With this persistent reciprocity and the determination to keep God in the forefront, Dexter will rise to such heights as will stagger the imagination of generations yet unborn, and which even God himself will smile upon. This is our profound challenge. This is our overwhelming responsibility.

TD. MLKP-MBU: Box 117.

Notes on Speech by Martin Luther King, Jr., at Woman's Auxiliary, National Baptist Convention on 9 September 1954

Sept.
1954

On 9 September 1954, King delivered the noonday message to the Woman's Auxiliary, National Baptist Convention. The brief minutes of the convention show that King, introduced as the "son of the organist of the Woman's Convention," exhorted his audience to do more than simply pay lip service to the spiritual life. The minutes included only these few lines from the speech.

We must rediscover that all reality has spiritual control. It is possible to affirm there is a God with our lips but deny it with our lives. Most of us unconsciously leave God behind. He admonished us to pick up these values so we can move forward to the New World.

Record of the 74th Annual Baptist Convention, 1954; copy in SBHL-TNSB.

From H. Edward Whitaker

15 September 1954
Niagara Falls, N.Y.

Whitaker inquires about King's assessment of the recently concluded National Baptist Convention's annual meeting.

Dear Mike,

For quite a little while I have been intending to write, but the work here has been most confining and trying. I now know what it is to be put through the mills. Things are, however working out to our favor after much effort. We have finally arranged for the financing of our Church, and the building of the same. Construction will begin in about another week. We had our ground-breaking ceremony on the 1st Sunday. This will be the first real Negro Church to be built in our city though attempts have been made since 1914. We feel very thankful to have a small part to do with the realization of this long delayed dream. The need for such facilities here are great and I am sure it will be well supported in years to come.

I regret so very much the fact that I was not home the other week when you called It would have been a great joy to have talked with you.

You have my hearty congratulations for allowing yourself to be called to the Dexter Street Baptist Church. From what you say and from what some of my members here who know the Church, it is really a wonderful Church. I am sure you will do a good job. We are praying for your success. I am sure I need not say be careful, be watchful in all things.

Tell me about the National Baptist Convention. Has Dr. Jackson been able to get any progressive program in operation. How were the sessions this year? Were they orderly? What improvement has been made in the organizational structure? Perhaps it is too early to get very much started. It does take time to lift people out of a rut. I suppose every one was there, as usual. I really hated to miss the session, but my need here was greater than there, I am sure

Have you seen McCall since going on your field there. I suppose he will go back to Fort Valley this year. Poor fellow he is still talking about getting married. One of these days he is going to fool himself and wake up married. But marriage is what he needs, and I hope he can find it convenient to do so before long.

How is your wife? Well I hope. How do you like your field of labor? I am sure it is a real challenge

If I am fortunate in my plans, I expect to make a tour through the southland either this winter or late spring. My wife has never been south of Virginia and I would like for her to see the real Negro Cultural Centers before she is too old to enjoy & appreciate it When we make the trip, you can be sure that we will let you know and plan to spend a day with you.

Well, ole timer, whatever you do, be sure to "preach the word," in season and out of season." Declare the "Thus saith the Lord" With kind regards & best wishes, I remain

Sincerely
[*signed*] Whit

ALS. MLKP-MBU: Box 117.

From Nannie H. Burroughs

21 September 1954
Washington, D.C.

Burroughs expresses appreciation for King's 9 September speech at the annual meeting of the Woman's Auxiliary, National Baptist Convention, in St. Louis.

Rev M L King Jr
93 Boulevard N E
Atlanta, Georgia

Dear Rev King:

I cannot forgo the pleasure of saying, again, THANK YOU from the bottom of my heart for your rich and challenging contribution to the program of our St Louis Meeting.

The delegates were profoundly impressed. What your message did to their thinking and to their faith is "bread cast upon the water" that will be seen day by day in their good works in their communities.

Letters are pouring in telling me how grateful they are for the greatest meeting they ever attended.

I agree with them. The St Louis Meeting was certainly the best we have ever held. The lift and the vision that the delegates got from the early morning classes, the glorious worship, the challenging messages, the rich special feature programs and the soul stirring music, seem to have sent them forth determined to attempt greater things for God and to expect greater things from Him.

As a result, we begin our 1954–55 Conventional year with every assurance that our entire constituency will join us in making the entire program of the Woman's Convention a glory to God on earth.

Thank you and God bless you.

Sincerely yours
[*signed*]
Nannie H Burroughs, President

NHB/b

TLS. MLKP-MBU: Box 117.

From Estelle Jackson

24 September 1954
Roxbury, Mass.

Jackson may have been the proprietor of Mrs. Jackson's Western Lunch Box, a restaurant where King and other black students often ate.

Hello Rev. King,

We thought that by this time we would at least get a card from you. The children misses you and there wondering if you got home safe to your wife after that awfull storm we had. But I explained to them that your very busy trying to get your church going. We pray for your success, and we just know you'll make cause your a sincere person. I just know your wife is happy to have you back home. We do hope to meet her someday. The Hurrican we had that day left us without lights for almost a week. The second storm we had the same thing happened. But we can thank God we're all safe. I'll have the children write to you. So far theres been two mails for you. We're in hopes to hear from both of you. Must come to an end. *God Bliss Both* {of} you. Love from the children

Sincerly
[*signed*] Mrs. Estelle Jackson

ALS. MLKP-MBU: Box 117.

To Samuel D. Proctor

[*October 1954*]
[*Montgomery, Ala.*]

King invites Proctor, a fellow graduate of Crozer and Boston, to speak at Dexter's Spring Lecture Series on the general theme "The Relevance of the New Testament to the Contemporary Situation." Proctor agreed to lecture on 27–29 April 1955.[1]

Dr. Samuel D. Proctor, Vice-President
Virginia Union University
Richmond, Virginia

Dear Proctor:

I am in the process of setting up my program for the coming church year. In my recommendations to the church, I suggested that we have a Spring Lecture Series. I am seeking to make this an annual event at which time I will attempt to bring some of our best minds to Dexter Avenue Baptist Church, to discuss some of the major doctrines and issues of the Christian Faith. I need not remind you that most church people are appallingly ignorant at this point. This will be the first time that such a series has been attempted at Dexter, but I am sure that with the right speaker, it can be worked into one of the most significant events of the church year.

I know of no one who is more qualified to initiate this series than you. So I am extending the invitation to you to serve as our lecturer for the series. The series will cover a period of three nights, April 27, 28, 29, 1955 (Wednesday, Thursday and Friday), and I would like for you to stay over and preach for the 11 o'clock service the lst Sunday in May. I would like to make the general theme for this series "The Relevance of the New Testament to the Contem-

---

1. See Proctor to King, 28 October 1954, MLKP-MBU: Box 117.

porary Situation." So that your three lectures would grow out of this general theme. However, if you are more disirous of lecutring in another area, that will be acceptable. The time limit for the lecture and discussion should not exceed one hour and fifteen minutes. Although this is referred to as a lecture series, it is hoped that the lectures will be inspirational as well as informative.

I am seeking to make this a "big event" for our church and the community at large. I sincerely hope that you can accept the invitation. Your presence as well as your message would mean so much to the success of the occasion. Please let me hear from you as soon as possible concerning this matter so that I can proceed in setting up my church calendar for the year.

I hope everything goes well with you. Give my regards to all my friends at Virginia Union.

With best wishes, I remain

Sincerely yours,
M. L. King, Jr.

MLK/csk

TLc. MLKP-MBU: Box 117.

From Harold Edward Pinkston

4 October 1954
Richmond, Va.

Pinkston, a student at Virginia Union University in Richmond, writes to his former Boston roommate and Alpha Phi Alpha brother about their mutual friends in the Boston area. Prior to entering Virginia Union in the fall of 1952, Pinkston was assistant pastor along with King of the Reverend William H. Hester's Twelfth Baptist Church in Roxbury, Massachusetts.[1] In 1937 the Reverend L. A. Pinkston, Harold Edward Pinkston's cousin, had defeated King, Sr., in a bid for the presidency of the General Missionary Baptist Convention of Georgia. The two remained close friends during Pinkston's long tenure as president, traveling together as delegates to the National Baptist Convention. The elder Pinkston served on King, Jr.'s ordination council in 1948.

---

1. Harold Edward Pinkston (1931–) received the B.A. and M.Div. degrees from Virginia Union in 1954 and 1957, respectively; the M.A. from Connecticut's Wesleyan University in 1969; the Ph.D. from Temple University in 1971; and the Th.D. from Indiana's Trinity Theological Seminary in 1979. He was pastor of Baptist churches in Virginia, New Jersey, and New York before becoming pastor in 1976 of the Good Shepherd Baptist Church in Columbus, Ohio. Since 1970 he has been professor of English at Ohio Wesleyan University. Pinkston also served as vice-president of the Southern Christian Leadership Conference's Virginia affiliate. See Harold Edward Pinkston to King Papers Project, 8 March 1992.

Dear Brother King, 9 Oct 1954

Greetings to you from Union, all the boys, and your admirer as well as "potentate brother of the Cloth." I trust that you have been well and all has been well with you and Mrs. King.

Say King, my main objective is this: During the summer just leaving, or rather just before, I have lost contact with Miss Rosetta Moore's address and I really would like very much to have it. Can you help me? I believe she has finished Harvard now and I don't know whether she has gone "home" (to Florida which address I don't know) or New Orleans to teach, or returned to Dillard Univ. to work in the seminars there.

If you can locate it for me Brother, I shall greatly appreciate your kindness. I'll await your response as soon as you can reply.

How are your studies coming, have you completed them as yet? What about Bob. Carter, I send my best regards to him and "Niel" Range. Best wishes also to Rev. Hester and Mrs and Mr. Johnson on Shawmut Ave.

Oh yes, I might add—Upon my completion of my college work in Feb. I plan to enter seminary either in Los Angeles, Calif., or Colgate-Rochester in Rochester, N.Y.

So-long Brother, I await "the good news" from you.

Fraternally yours, in Christ & ΑΦΑ
[*signed*] H. E. Pinkston

TALS. MLKP-MBU: Box 117.

From Clyde L. Reynolds

9 October 1954

In one of the few surviving letters from a member of Dexter during King's early years as pastor, Reynolds thanks King for the eulogy of his mother.

Dear Reverend King,

You could not have delivered a better eulogy for my mother if you had been her pastor for 50 years. Thank you very much for a brilliant and comforting message, and a beautiful Christian funeral service. Both will remain with me vividly as a fitting and sacred memorial.

May you continue to bring to "Dexter Avenue" dynamic and intelligent leadership. God bless you!

Sincerely,
[*signed*] Clyde L. Reynolds

ALS. MLKP-MBU: Box 117.

To Paul Tillich

19 October 1954
Montgomery, Ala.

King asks Tillich to meet him in Boston during King's November visit. Tillich,
however, was in Scotland and did not begin teaching at Harvard until fall 1955.[1]

Dr. Paul Tillich
Harvard University Divinity School
Cambridge, Massachusetts

Dear Dr. Tillich:

I am a non-resident graduate student of Boston University in process of writing a dissertation entitled, "A Comparison of the Conception of God in the Thinking of Paul Tillich and Henry Nelson Wieman." I have been away from Boston for the past four months. However, I plan to be in Boston for about a week in the month of November, from the 10th through the 17th. I would appreciate the privilege of having a personal interview with you at some time during this week to discuss some aspects of this dissertation.

Please let me know by return mail if it will be possible for me to see you within this week, also, on what day and at what hour.

Thanks in advance for your cooperation.

Sincerely yours,
Martin L. King, Jr.

MLK/csk

TLc. MLKP-MBU: Box 116.

---

1. See Paul Tillich to King, 3 November 1954, p. 310 in this volume.

To Ralph W. Riley

19 October 1954
Montgomery, Ala.

King answers Riley's inquiries about John Wesley Dobbs and invites Riley, a
former pastor of Dexter, to give the sermon for Dexter's anniversary.[1] *A week later,*

---

1. For Riley's request, see Riley to King, 29 September 1954, MLKP-MBU: Box 117. Ralph Waldo Riley (1900–1959) received his A.B. from Morehouse College and his B.D. from Gammon

Dr. R. W. Riley, President
American Baptist Theological Seminary
Nashville 7, Tennessee

Dear Dr. Riley:

I am very sorry that I am somewhat tardy in answering your last letter, but it so happened that I was out of the city on its arrival. I did, however, get the certificate off to Detroit. Mr. Nesbitt did not have a record of the exact date that Mr. Dobbs was baptized, so I had to use one of the dates that you suggested. I am sure that the certificate has been received by now.

I have been intending to write you for the past two weeks to extend an invitation to you to preach for our Church Anniversary at the 11 o'clock service on the 2nd Sunday in December, 1954. We are seeking to make this a significant event and your presence as well as your message would add so much to that occasion. I hope that you will be able to accept this invitation. Please let me hear from you at your earliest convenience concerning this matter.

Our work here is going very well. We are getting real cooperation from the entire membership. I only hope that it will last.

With best wishes, I remain

Sincerely yours,
M. L. King, Jr.

MLK/csk

TLc. MLKP-MBU: Box 116.

Theological Seminary. He did graduate work at the University of Pittsburgh and Atlanta University. He served as secretary of the Benefit Board of the National Baptist Convention from 1937 to 1939. He was pastor of Baptist churches in Florida and Georgia before becoming the seventeenth pastor of Dexter Avenue Baptist Church in the late 1930s, where he remained until 1944. Riley was then president of the American Baptist Theological Seminary in Nashville for twelve years before accepting his final pastorate in 1956 at Hopewell Baptist Church in Newark, New Jersey.

2. See Ralph W. Riley to King, 25 October 1954, MLKP-MBU: Box 117.

To Walter R. McCall

19 October 1954
Montgomery, Ala.

King invties McCall to preach at Dexter and urges his friend to attend the upcoming installation ceremony.

Dean Walter R. McCall
Fort Valley State College
Fort Valley, Georgia

Dear Mac,

I have been intending to write you for some time but a budy schedule has prevented it. At present I am in the process of making out my program for the coming church year. I would like to extend an invitation to you to preach the annual Youth Day sermon at the 11 o'clock service on the 2nd Sunday in March (13th) 1955. We are hoping that this will be a high day at Dexter and your presence as well as your message would add so much to the occasion.

As you have probably heard, my installation will be held on the 5th Sunday. Daddy is coming down to preach the sermon and will bring about 100 people. I was talking with T. W. Smith the other day and he wants you to come over that morning and preach for him and the two of you drive over for the afternoon service.[1] It will mean a great deal to me for you to come. So I hope that you will be able to do so.

Our work here is going very well. We are getting superb cooperation. Last Sunday we had our Women's Day and it was a tremendous success. Over $2100 was raised.

How are things going with you, and how is the marriage situation coming? Let me hear from you and be sure to let me know about this speaking invitation so I can proceed with my calendar.

Coretta is doing fine and sends her best regards.

Sincerely yours,
M. L. King, Jr.

MLK/csk

TLc. MLKP-MBU: Box 116.

---

1. T. W. Smith was pastor of a church in Columbus, Georgia.

From Melvin H. Watson

20 October 1954
Atlanta, Ga.

King had sent copies of "Recommendations to the Dexter Avenue Baptist Church for the Fiscal Year 1954–1955" to colleagues for comment.

Reverend M. L. King, Jr., Pastor   21 Oct
Dexter Avenue Baptist Church   1954
Montgomery, Alabama

Dear Young-in-coming Doctor:

Greetings and salutations!

I have read with more than usual interest and satisfaction the recommendations made by you to Dexter Avenue Baptist Church. Please allow me to
make one or two observations in regard to them. In the first place, the recommendations give clear evidence of careful thought. The manner in which
they are put together deserves praise. They are far-reaching in scope, and,
happily, at several points depart from the beaten path. Secondly, Dexter Avenue has displayed the depth of its yearning for a constructive program by the
mood in which it accepted the recommendations. Surely this is a favorable
omen for your ministry in the Montgomery Community. The third observation is in the form of an amber light. Organization is necessary for the ad-
vancing life of any institution. Religious institutions, however, have to be on
their guard always against over-organization. Hectic activity in the church in
not necessarily an indication that the cause of the Kingdom is being promoted. I am confident that I am not telling you something which you do not
already know full well. So this is written not in the spirit of accusing you of
anything, but in the spirit of a reminder.

When I reached nos. 12 and 13 on the list of recommendations, I found
myself pausing and reviewing hastily the types of organizations already called
for in the previous recommendations. When I completed the list I returned
to these same two items to examine them for purpose. I don't believe my
questions regarding these two arise out of any bias against them as legitimate
church activities.

Let me close by saying that your two introductory paragraphs were beautifully and appropriately formulated.

It is my hope and prayer that God will bless your ministry at Dexter Avenue
Baptist Church and in the whole city.

Sincerely yours,
[*signed*]
Melvin Watson

TLS. MLKP-MBU: Box 117.

From Walter R. McCall

21 October 1954
Fort Valley, Ga.

*McCall accepts King's invitation to speak at Dexter and asks King to be best man
at his wedding.*

Reverend M. L. King, Jr.
309 Jackson Street
Montgomery, Alabama

Dear Mike,

Thanks for the letter today. To know that you and family are well, and that you are getting on excellently in your work was good news indeed. I had been just [*insertion illegible*] wondering just waht had happened to you folk as I had written you before you left Boston, but upon second thought I discovered that work keeps one from writing leisure letters at times.

As for me, things are going well, but I have been a bit under the weather. As a matter of fact, I went to the Johns Hopkins hospital this post summer school year. Stayed for one week. Everything was perfect as the doctors said. I had taken the worst beating of life the year I was away from Fort Valley. Stress, strain, hustle and bustle coupled with other things put me in a bad state. I am alright now, as it is over.

About the wedding: It is progressing beautifully. My fiancee came down once to visit me as I have little time off. She is to be here on tomorrow. The wedding date is June, 1955. We will make definite plans at Christmas time. By the way, could you be my best man? If not, I will have Gunter if possible.

Yes, I will be glad to be guest Youth Day Speaker. So, I shall put that date on my calendar. About the fifth Sunday, I cannot say with any degree of certainty. If possible I shall gladly attend. Reverend Smith and I planned to do something like that as of last Spring.

Please give my best regards to Coretta. Be not deceived Mike, you are with a fine group of people. Therefore to know that they are cooperating is not surprising. Keep up your best, and you will find the best coming back. With all good wishes for a good year ahead, I am

A pal,
[*signed*]
Mack

{P.S. Enclosed is a snapshot of Annabelle in her summer attire here, send it back. Hello to Bob & Parker, Please.}[1]

TALS. MLKP-MBU: Box 117.

---

1. McCall refers to fellow Morehouse classmates, Robert Williams and J. C. Parker, Sr. Williams was professor of music at Alabama State College for Negroes, and Parker was pastor of Hall Street Baptist Church in Montgomery.

To William H. Hester

26 October 1954
[*Montgomery, Ala.*]

*At the annual September meeting of the National Baptist Convention in St. Louis
King had talked with Hester about preaching at his church near Boston. King and
other African-American students in the Boston area often preached at Hester's
Twelfth Baptist Church in nearby Roxbury.*

The Reverend W. H. Hester
37 Howland Street
Roxbury, Massachusetts

Dear Rev. Hester:

I remember saying to you in St. Louis that I would let you know when I
would be in Boston. As it stands now, I plan to be in Boston the week of the
2nd Sunday in November. I will be available to preach for you on the 2nd
Sunday. Please let me hear from you by return mail concerning this date.

Our work here is going very well. We are getting real cooperation from the
entire membership.

I hope everything goes well with you and Mrs. Hester. Please give the
family my best regards.

Coretta is doing fine and sends her best regards to you and the family.

With every good wish, I remain

Sincerely yours,
Martin L. King, Jr.

TLc. MLKP-MBU: Box 116.

To Benjamin Elijah Mays

[*October 1954*]
[*Montgomery, Ala.*]

*In a letter of 4 November, Mays accepted King's invitation to preach the Men's Day
sermon on 10 July 1955.[1]*

---

1. See Benjamin Elijah Mays to King, 4 November 1954, MLKP-MBU: Box 117.

Dr. B. E. Mays, President
Morehouse College
Atlanta, Georgia

Dear Dr. Mays:

I am in the process of setting up my program for the coming church year. The second Sunday in July has been set aside as the date for the annual Men's Day. I am seeking each year to bring some of the great preachers of our nation to Dexter Avenue Baptist Church for this occasion. I would like to extend to you an invitation to preach the Men's Day sermon on the 2nd Sunday in July (10th), 1955.

I am seeking to make this a big event for our church and the community at large. I sincerely hope that you can accept the invitation. Your presence as well as your message would mean so much to our church and to our community. Please let me hear from you as soon as possible concerning this matter so that I can proceed with setting up my church calendar.

Our work here is going very well. We are getting superb cooperation from the membership at large.

I hope everything goes well with you and I hope you continual success in the superb job you are doing at Morehouse.

With every good wish, I remain

Sincerely yours,
M. L. King, Jr.

MLK/csk

TLc. MLKP-MBU: Box 116.

From Major J. Jones

[*November 1954*]
Boston, Mass.

Jones, King's classmate at Boston University, praises King's "Recommendations,"
commenting specifically on his explanation of pastoral authority and the plan to
centralize Dexter's treasury.[1]

---

1. Major J. Jones (1919–) received his A.B. from Atlanta's Clark College in 1941, his B.D. from Gammon Theological Seminary in 1944, his S.T.M. from Oberlin Theological Seminary in 1950, and his Th.D. from Boston University in 1957. An ordained minister in the Methodist church, Jones served as a pastor and a district superintendent in eastern Tennessee from 1956 to 1967. He served on the General Board of Education of the Methodist church; and the boards of directors of the Committee of Southern Churchmen and the Southern Christian Leadership Conference. From 1967 to 1985, Jones was president of Gammon Theological Seminary. Since then he has been chaplain of the Atlanta University Center. His publications include *Black Awareness: A Theology of Hope* (1971) and *Christian Ethics for Black Theology* (1974).

Dear Martin,

Just a line to say how much I do appreciate your sending me your most interesting "Recommendations to the Dexter Avenue Baptist Church" which I read with much interest; as you had asked me, when I got the time, to say what I thought of them. After reading them over I do not feel that there anything I could say that you did not say in the act of speaking to the over all needs of the church. I feel that you did a very good job in pointing out the relationship which should exist between the pastor and the people of the church. Likewise I would have no questions to raise about methodology, which point you covered very well. I think some of the plans which you gave were very good, and I say some to speak of those which were new and which I am sure were new to the church. I put of this in the first section of the paper as it has to do with my reading and with what I thought after having read, with interest, the recommendations.

Now let me say this in the way of a suggestion which may or may not add anything to the overall recommendations of the church, but which would give more unity to the purpose for it all, and which will act as some sort of aims and objectives for the church at large. I find that when we organize any large group of people into many competing groups we have to be careful not to make each group the end unto itself; each forgetting the whole. I feel that you could have offset a lot of this by stating in the outset a gorup of aims and objective around which all of the other things which you said could have been integrated, not to say they are not implicit in each of the things which you mentioned. But this would have given a concept of the nature of the church as it becomes relative for this particular church. You can see that there are some people who want to know what the church's purpose is as it might be spelled out in concrete policy or aim. These aims and objective could have caught up in a collective statement what you said in each of the separate things which relate to each of the recommandations.

Now I was interested in another aspect of the recommendations, and that was the matter of the Unified Budget plan, and also the Central Treasury. In many cases the central treasury has made for less organizational ambition. I once tried a method like the bank, where each club or organization would hold its money in a central treasury, presenting a chech or draft as needed, and with the church unable to use the money only in a state of crises voted by the board. I feel that your way is better if it works with the people and will get activities desired without people, as groups having controll of Monies.

I am planning to come home for Xmas and will be staying at Ra. 0668, or 1003 Palmetto, I do hope that I have the chance to see you before I come back here. There is no other news other than that Rev. Gibson's wife died.[2]

Very truly yours,
[signed]
Major

---

2. Jones refers to W. Marvin Gibson, pastor of Cambridge's Union Baptist Church, where King had preached the previous summer.

{Give my regards to the wife and I do hope I will be able to see the two of you when I come home to talk some more about this most interesting paper-}

TALS. MLKP-MBU: Box 117.

From Sankey L. Blanton

1 November 1954
Chester, Pa.

King wrote Blanton on 26 October, providing his new address and informing Blanton of his work at Dexter.[1]

Rev. Martin L. King, Jr.
Dexter Avenue Baptist Church
Montgomery, Alabama

Dear Mr. King:

Thank you for your letter. I am delighted to know where you are, and that you are happy. I regard you as one of the most promising students that I have met, and will watch your career with a deep personal interest and some pride. I will be coming to Alabama in mid-winter. When I come, I will call you in the hope that I can drop by to see you for a little while.

Yours sincerely,
[*signed*]
Sankey L. Blanton

SLB/sr

TLS. MLKP-MBU: Box 117.

---

1. See King to Blanton, 26 October 1954, MLKP-MBU: Box 116. In the letter King reported that "we are getting off to a good start here. We are getting real cooperation from the entire membership. I am enjoying my work very much, however, it really keeps me busy."

From William H. Hester

2 November 1954
Roxbury, Mass.

The Reverend Martin L. King, Jr.
Dexter Avenue Baptist Church
Dexter Avenue at Decatur Street
Montgomery, Alabama

Dear Rev. King:

This is in reply to your letter dated, October 26. We shall be very happy to have you preach for us the Second Sunday in November.

We are glad to learn your work is going very well, and you have a cooperative congregation.

Trusting you and Mrs. King are enjoying the best of health, I am

Respectfully yours,
[*signed*]
Rev. William H. Hester

TLS. MLKP-MBU: Box 117.

To Melvin H. Watson

2 November 1954
[*Montgomery, Ala.*]

Writing two days after his installation as pastor, King thanks Watson for his comments on the "Recommendations" and invites him to preach Dexter's Seventy-eighth Anniversary sermon on 12 December. Watson accepted.[1]

Dr. Melvin Watson, Dean
School of Religion
Morehouse College
Atlanta, Georgia

Dear Dr. Watson:

Our Church Anniversary will be observed at the 11 o'clock service the 2nd Sunday in December, 1954. I would like to invite you to serve as our guest

---

1. See Watson to King, 12 November 1954, MLKP-MBU: Box 117.

preacher for that occasion. I am sorry that this invitation comes rather late, but there has been some question in my mind as to whether or not we would celebrate our anniversary this year. However, I have decided to go ahead with it.

Please let me hear from you as soon as possible concerning this matter so that we can proceed with our arrangements.

I received your most cordial letter concerning my recommendations. I assure you that all of your observations were well taken. The program has gotten off to a good start. The difficult task will come about in implementing the ideas that are now on paper.

I hope everything goes well with you. Give my best regards to the madam and the children. Coretta sends her regards.

With every good wish. I remain

Sincerely yours,
M. L. King, Jr.

MLK/csk

TLc. MLKP-MBU: Box 116.

From Paul Tillich

3 November 1954
Aberdeen, Scotland

Tillich and King were never able to meet to discuss King's dissertation.

Dear Mr. King,

Your letter has reached me at Aberdeen, Scotland where I am delivering the Gifford Lectures. I shall not be at Harvard before Fall, 1955, but I shall be in Chicago next January and in New York, Union Theological Seminary, from February to June, 1955.

I would, of course, to have a talk with you about your thesis.

Sincerely yours,
[*signed*]
Paul Tillich.

TLS. MLKP-MBU: Box 117.

From Benjamin Elijah Mays

4 November 1954
Atlanta, Ga.

Mays asks King to contribute $200 to Morehouse College through Dexter. King included a contribution of that amount in the church budget.

Reverend M. L. King, Jr.   4 Nov
Dexter Avenue Baptist Church   1954
Dexter Avenue at Decatur Street
Montgomery, Alabama

Dear Reverend King:

There are only two times a year we are permitted to solicit our alumni—
Founder's Day and Class Reunion at Commencement. The rest of the year we
work and give to the United Negro College Fund from which Morehouse
benefits mightily. This appeal is for Founder's Day, February 18, 1955.
THERE IS A GREAT SCANDAL AT MOREHOUSE. IT IS THE MORE-
HOUSE GYMNASIUM. IT'S A SHAME! IT'S A DISGRACE! IT'S EMBAR-
RASSING! IT NAUSEATES ME TO LOOK AT IT. IT OUGHT TO NAU-
SEATE YOU.
We are $200,000 short of what it takes to construct the New Physical Edu-
cation and Health Building. We have $300,000 toward the new building,
money we received from the United Negro College Fund. At best it will be
two years before we get another $200,000 from the fund. The building will
cost at least $500,000. If we can get $50,000 more the Trustees will let us
begin building this Spring. Here is what you can do to help eliminate the
Scandal and in addition help underwrite $10,000 of the $25,000 which we
give in scholarships each year.
You are very new at Dexter and you may not be able to contribute anything
by February 18, 1955. Look over the situation and see if you can contribute
through your church $200.00 toward this project. If you cannot do it I will
understand.
With kindest regards and best wishes, I am

Sincerely,
[*signed*]
Benjamin E. Mays
PRESIDENT

BEM:lec

TLS. MLKP-MBU: Box 117.

"Montgomery-Antioch Ass'n. Endorses
Wilson and Washington"

4 November 1954

*As reporter for the association, King filed this account of the annual meeting of the
Montgomery-Antioch District Association, the local affiliate of the Alabama Baptist
Missionary State Convention, which in turn was associated with the National
Baptist Convention. The district association elected King as reporter at the session.*   311

The Montgomer-Antioch District Association met in its Sixty-first annual session October 20–21, at the Hutchinson Street Baptist Church of Montgomery, the Rev. H. H. Johnson, pastor. The session was filled with spiritual fervor throughout. The general theme of the session was: "The Church in a Chainging World." All of the inspirational addresses grew out of this general theme. These addresses, delivered so ably by Rev. J. A. Turner, Dr. A. W. Wilson and Rev. R. J. Glasco, were both inspirational and informative.[1]

On Wednesday morning Dr. D. C. Washington of Seventeenth Street Baptist Church, Anniston, Alabama, gave a stirring message on behalf of the Minister's Benefit Board of the Alabama State Baptist Convention. His message was accepted with warm enthusiasm.[2]

Sermons for the association were preached by Rev. William McCloud, Rev. W. S. Briggs, and Rev. J. J. Rose. All of these men preached from their hearts, and left their hearers with a real spiritual experience.

The highlight of the association was the first Annual Address delivered by Moderator G. S. Jarett since he succeded the late Rev. J. H. McIntosh. In introducing Dr. Jarrett, Dr. D. C. Washington referred to him as a man of facts, faith and fire, and there can be no doubt that his message proved the validity of thsi characterization at every point. Dr. Jarrett chose as a subject for his address; "The duties and Responsibilities of the Gospel Ministry." He emphasized that "the duty of the Gospel Minister is to pursue his path of self sacrificing regardless of the danger of the task that may be just ahead of him." He admonished his hearers to take heed unto themselves, for "self heed is the secret of public power for preparation of yourself is the preparation of your message." Throughout his message Dr. Jarrett revealed a profound knowledge of the Bible. His message was delivered with force and power. After the address, the messengers voted unanimously to elect Moderator Jarrett for another term. All other officers were reelected with the exception of Rev. R. D. Abernathy who graciously resigned his position as statistician to devote his time to his newly elected post as Dean of the District Congress. Rev. J. C. Parker was elected to succeed Rev. Abernathy as statistician. The other officers elected to succeed themselves were: Dr. M. C. Cleveland, Vice-Moderator; Dr. H. H. Johnson, Recording Secretary; Dr. A. W. Wilson, Corresponding Secretary; Rev. W. E. Robinson, Treasurer.[3] The body appointed Rev. M. L. King, Jr., to serve as reporter for the Association and all of its Auxiliaries.

---

1. H. H. Johnson was pastor of Hutchinson Street Baptist Church from 1934 to 1971. A. W. Wilson (1902–1989) was pastor of Holt Street Baptist Church from 1939 until his death. R. J. Glasco, pastor of First Baptist Church in Jacksonville, Alabama, and director of the Baptist Center in Montgomery, later served as chair of the Montgomery Improvement Association's finance committee and secretary of its transportation committee during the bus boycott.

2. Dennis Comer Washington (1905–) was pastor of Seventeenth Street Baptist Church in Anniston, Alabama, from 1938 until 1959, when he became executive director of the Sunday School Publication Board of the National Baptist Convention.

3. After moving from Atlanta to Montgomery in 1950, Abernathy served as dean of men at Alabama State College and pastor of Eastern Star Baptist Church in Demopolis before taking

One of the most significant notes of the Association was its endorsement of   6 Nov
1954
Dr. D. C. Washington and Dr. A. W. Wilson for the President and Vice-President respectively of the Alabama State Baptist Convention.

The session ended with overwhelming success, and it was the sentiment of the entire body that the Hutchinson Street Baptist Church serving as host under the dynamic leadership of Dr. H. H. Johnson along with the cooperation from other churches of the city manifested a hospitality that can hardly be surpassed.

Respectively submitted,
Rev. M. L. King, Jr., Rep.

PD. *The Baptist Leader*, 4 November 1954. Also in A-Ar.

To Ebenezer Baptist Church Members

6 November 1954
[*Montgomery, Ala.*]

Members of Ebenezer Baptist Church participated extensively in King's installation as pastor at Dexter: King, Sr., gave the sermon, Alberta King played the organ, and the Ebenezer choir sang. "As I have said to you before," King tells the church members, "you can never know what your presence in such large numbers meant to me at the beginning of my pastorate."

The Ebenezer Baptist Church
The Rev. M. L. King, Sr., Pastor
Atlanta, Georgia

Dear Members:

I would like to take this way to express our deepest appreciation to you for the "big way" in which you helped to make our recent installation a great success. Words cannot adequately express my gratitude, and I assure you that your tremendous response to this occasion shall be remembered so long as the cords of memory shall linger. Both your presence and your financial con-

---

over Montgomery's First Baptist Church in 1952. A student activist during his undergraduate years at Alabama State, Abernathy shared Martin Luther King, Jr.'s social gospel outlook, and the two became close friends after King arrived in Montgomery in 1954. For biographical information on Abernathy, see note 142 in Introduction and Abernathy's autobiography, *And the Walls Came Tumbling Down* (New York: Harper and Row, 1989). Marshall Cleophus Cleveland, Sr. (1882–1978), was the pastor of Day Street Baptist Church and chair of the board of trustees of Selma University.

tributions were appreciated beyond expression. All of this continues to prove to me that there is but one Ebenezer. Your generosity and big heartedness will always keep you in the forefront, and you will always stand as a symbol of what other churches ought to be.

As I have said to you before, your prayers and words of encouragement have meant a great deal to me in my ministry; and you can never know what your presence in such large numbers meant to me at the beginning of my pastorate. I want you to know Ebenezer, that I feel greatly indebted to you; and that whatever success I might achieve in my life's work you will have helped to make it possible.

Mrs. King joins me in this expression of our appreciation to you. We pray God's blessings upon all of you as you go forward in trying to bring His Kingdon on earth.

With sincere affection,
M. L. King, Jr.

TLc. MLKP-MBU: Box 116.

From Samuel W. Williams

18 November 1954
Atlanta, Ga.

Williams, pastor of Friendship Baptist Church in Atlanta, was King's philosophy professor at Morehouse.[1] *Williams refers to Christine King, King's sister.*

The Reverend M. L. King, Jr.
309 South Jackson Street
Montgomery, Alabama

Dear M. L.:

I'm very happy that it was possible for you to accept our invitation to deliver the Mens' Day Sermon on November 28. The entire Church is delighted that you're coming.

Now Brother, we need to have the likeness of you in the newspaper. So if you have available a cut or a mat, would you please send the same to us for publicity purposes next week? We would like also a brief biographical sketch.

---

1. Samuel Woodrow Williams (1912–1970) received his A.B. from Morehouse in 1937 and his B.D. and M.A. from Howard University's School of Religion in 1941 and 1942, respectively. He completed his course work, though not the dissertation, for a Ph.D. in philosophy at the University of Chicago. After teaching at Alcorn College in Lorman, Mississippi, and Alabama A & M in Normal, he joined the Morehouse faculty in 1946. In addition to teaching at Morehouse, Williams also served as pastor of Friendship Baptist Church from 1954 until his death.

Christine told me this morning that you're likely to be in town Saturday. I hope I may see you, but in any case, call me.

Very fine reports are reaching Atlanta of your works at Dexter. Our prayer is that all will continue to go well.

Very sincerely yours,
[*signed*] Sam/s
Samuel W. Williams

SWW/japs

TLSr. MLKP-MBU: Box 117.

To Ralph Abernathy

24 November 1954
[*Montgomery, Ala.*]

King sent variations of this letter to Abernathy and other participants in his installation ceremony. King thanks his good friend Abernathy, pastor of First Baptist Church, for supporting his installation, even though Abernathy could not attend. The other recipients were T. M. Alexander, M. C. Cleveland, H. H. Johnson, B. D. Lambert, Joseph C. Parker, Sr., W. J. Powell, and G. Franklin Lewis.[1] At the ceremony Parker introduced the speaker, King, Sr.; Alexander provided the Charge to the Church; Cleveland presided over the Charge to the Minister; Johnson delivered the welcome from the community churches; Lambert led the Prayer of Installation; and Powell gave the Scripture reading. Abernathy and Lewis sent greetings in the official program.

The Reverend Ralph D. Abernathy
1327 South Hall Street
Montgomery, Alabama

Dear Ralph,

This is just a note to express my appreciation to you for the big part which you played in making my recent Installation a real success. Words cannot adequately express my deep gratitude to you.

---

1. See letters to T. M. Alexander, M. C. Cleveland, H. H. Johnson, B. D. Lambert, Joseph C. Parker, Sr., W. J. Powell, and G. Franklin Lewis; all dated 24 November 1954, in MLKP-MBU: Box 116. Alexander was an Atlanta investment broker, chair of the board of directors of the Butler Street YMCA, trustee of Morehouse College, and a former member of Dexter. The other six men were pastors in Montgomery: Cleveland, of Day Street Baptist Church; Johnson, of Hutchinson Street Baptist Church; Lambert, of Maggie Street Baptist Church; Parker, of Hall Street Baptist Church; Powell, of Old Ship AME Zion Church; and Lewis, of First Congregational Church.

Although you could not be present, your encouragement and financial con-tribution were appreciated beyond expression.

I intended writing you long before now, but as you know, I was absent from the city for more than two weeks which prevented my doing so.[2]

With every good wish, I am

Sincerely yours,
M. L. King, Jr.

MLK/csk

TLc. MLKP-MBU: Box 116.

---

2. King traveled to Boston immediately after his installation as pastor at Dexter.

To William H. Hester

24 November 1954
[*Montgomery, Ala.*]

During the two weeks King spent in Boston working on his dissertation he preached at Hester's Twelfth Baptist Church.

Reverend W. H. Hester
38 Howland Street
Roxbury, Massachusetts

Dear Rev. Hester:

This is just a note to again express my appreciation to you for the oppor-tunity to preach at your very fine church on last Sunday. I always feel a rich sense of fellowship whenever I come to your church and you are to be com-mended for keeping this fellowship alive.

Words cannot adequately express my appreciation to you for your kindness and big heartedness. I only hope that at some time and in some way I shall be able to return your kindness.

Give my best regards to Mrs. Hester and Mattie. With every good wish, I am

Sincerely yours,
Martin L. King, Jr.

MLK/csk

TLc. MLKP-MBU: Box 116.

To Benjamin Elijah Mays

24 November 1954
[*Montgomery, Ala.*]

King responds to Mays's request for contributions to Morehouse College.

Dr. Benjamin E. Mays, President
Morehouse College
Atlanta, Georgia

Dear Dr. Mays:

This is to acknowledge receipt of your letter of November 4, 1954. Absence from the city for some two weeks has delayed my reply.

I assure you that I am in sympathy with the great need at Morehouse for a Physical Education and Health building, and you can expect my full cooperation in contributing toward its construction. It might interest you to know that in making out the budget for the church year 1954–55, I included $200 for Morehouse College and $50 for the School of Religion. All of the items in this budget were unanimously accepted by the church.[1]

I will do my bery best to issue the check for $200 to Morehouse by Founder's Day.

We are very happy that you will be able to serve as our Men's Day speaker next July. I will keep you informed as things develop concerning it.

With every good wish, I am

Sincerely yours,
M. L. King, Jr.

MLK/csk

TLc. MLKP-MBU: Box 116.

---

1. The contribution was one-third of the budget for Dexter's Ministry of Christian Education and Missions. See King, "Annual Report, Dexter Avenue Baptist Church," 1 October 1954–31 October 1955, MLKP-MBU: Box 77.

From Melvin H. Watson

29 November 1954
Atlanta, Ga.

Watson forwards publicity information for his upcoming Dexter visit and comments on King's Men's Day sermon at Samuel W. Williams's Friendship Baptist Church in Atlanta.[1]

Reverend M. L. King, Jr., Pastor
Dexter Avenue Baptist Church
454 Dexter Avenue
Montgomery, Alabama

Dear M. L.:

Thank you for your recent letter. Under separate cover I am sending a cut. My wife says it makes me look like a thug, but for ordinary newspaper publicity it passes very well, I think.

Enclosed is a brief biographical statement.

I will need to indicate later my means of transportation.

If you have any information about the history of Dexter Avenue Baptist Church, I would be pleased to have it.

You did a very commendable service at Friendship Baptist Church yesterday. Your message was sound and impressively delivered. I heard many favorable comments about your performance, and all of them made me happy.

I am off this morning for Columbus, Georgia, to be with Brother T. W. Smith and the Minister's Institute for this week.

Best wishes.

Sincerely yours,
[*signed*]
Melvin Watson

TLS. MLKP-MBU: Box 117.

---

1. King had requested the materials for "publicity purposes." See King to Melvin H. Watson, 24 November 1954, MLKP-MBU: Box 116.

From Benjamin Elijah Mays

30 November 1954
Atlanta, Ga.

Rev. M. L. King, Jr.
309 S. Jackson Street
Montgomery, Alabama

Dear Rev. King:

Your letter came this morning. It had not come when I talked with you over the telephone yesterday. I thank you kindly for pledging $250 and if you do this it will be an excellent contribution for Dexter Avenue Baptist Church; and especially so since you are just taking charge.

I want to say again that I think you did a most acceptable job when you preached at Friendship last Sunday.

Sincerely yours,
[*signed*]
Benjamin E. Mays
President

BEM:H

TLS. MLKP-MBU: Box 117.

From Martin Luther King, Sr.

2 December 1954
Atlanta, Ga.

After hearing about his son's well-received sermon at Friendship Baptist Church, King, Sr., warns: "Persons like yourself are the ones the devil turns all of his forces aloose to destroy." T. M. Alexander was a trustee of Friendship Baptist Church. King, Sr., also refers to May Harper, the mother of Emmett Proctor and the daughter of C. L. Harper, who was the first principal of Booker T. Washington High School. The Harpers were neighbors of the Kings on Auburn Avenue in Atlanta.

Rev. M. L. King, Jr.
309 South Jackson
Montgomery, Alabama.

My dear M. L.:

I received your letter today, contents noted with care. Glad to know you and Coretta are doing fine. This leaves us all well.

Sister Luella Allen lost her husband yesterday. I am sure you remember her, she is the little Sister that usually sits on the left side of the church, shouts up against the wall. With the exception of that every thing seems to be moving on very well around the church.

Alexander called me yesterday just to tell me about how you swept them at Friendship Sunday. Every way I turned people are congradulating me for you. You see young man you are becoming very popular. As I told you you must be much in prayer. Persons like yourself are the ones the devil turns all of his forces aloose to destroy.

I will get the clergys to you as soon as they are released. I am enclosing your bank book as you will see it is marked up to date. Notice a $20.00 withdrawal which was not on the book. I am also enclosing May Harper's address.

Love to Coretta from us all.

Yours,
[*signed*] M. L. King, Sr.
Daddy

ENC2
MLK.w

TLS. MLKP-MBU: Box 117.

From Roland Smith

10 December 1954
Nashville, Tenn.

*King was appointed to an advisory council to the National Baptist Convention's
National Baptist Training Union Board, on which Smith served as secretary.*[1]

Rev. M. L. King Jr.
309 South Jackson St.
Montgomery, Alabama

My dear Rev. King:

Your letter of December 7, 1954, accepting the place as a member of the advisory counsil on curriculum and literature of the Baptist Training Union Board, received.

---

1. Roland Smith (1902–) graduated from Morehouse in 1929. He pastored churches in Georgia and Alabama before becoming pastor of Little Rock's First Baptist Church in 1947. He was statistician of the National Baptist Convention from 1932 until 1954, when he became secretary of the National Baptist Training Union Board; he served in that position until 1957.

We appreciated your acceptance and I will advise you with reference to our plans for the future.

With the best of wishes, I am

Sincerely Yours,
[*signed*]
Roland Smith, Secretary
National B.T.U. Board

TLS. MLKP-MBU: Box 117.

From Melvin H. Watson

15 December 1954
Atlanta, Ga.

*Watson thanks King for the opportunity to preach the anniversary sermon at
Dexter on 12 December.*

Reverend M. L. King, Jr., Pastor
Dexter Avenue Baptist Church
Dexter Avenue at Decatur Street
Montgomery, Alabama

Dear Young-In-Coming-Doctor:

My visit over the week-end in Montgomery convinced me (although further convincing was not needed) that Brother Milner's title is altogether appropriate. This note is merely to put into the record what has already been said to you in words. The visit to your home and the Church was a deeply gratifying experience. I enjoyed being in the home with you and Miss Coretta, and I was thrilled by the church experience. It meant so much to me to see you in the Church functioning and to see the grand response the congregation is giving you. You are definitely off to a promising start, and I believe the Lord is with you. You have my prayers and best wishes for continued growth in spiritual stature and in the capacity to serve the people.

Cordially yours,
[*signed*] Melvin Watson

TLS. MLKP-MBU: Box 117.

From J. Pius Barbour

21 December 1954
Chester, Pa.

Barbour was editor of the National Baptist Voice *and pastor of Calvary Baptist
Church in Chester, Pennsylvania, the home of Crozer Theological Seminary. After
King's installation as pastor at Dexter he wrote Barbour, enclosing the installation
program, which included photographs of the Kings.*

Dear Mike:

Let me congratulate you on those Photos: yours flatter you and Coretta's
does not quite give her justice. However this is typical of what her life will be
with you: you will always manage to keep her in second place by hook or
crook. If you can do that in the field of beauty the rest will be easy. McCall
wrote me about the Old Man's sermon, and what good he thought it did.[1]
After all a Man who can build a Church like Ebenezer ~~andrpor~~ and produce
young "Mike" is no fool. The trouble with you fellows from Universities is:
you think that there is only one type in the World . . the Socratic. But history
records ~~Attl~~ Attilla the Hun as well as Jesus; Stalin as well as Paul. And by the
way I never heard of Attilla drinking the Hemlock or Stalin going to the cross.
Dont believe that mess about the Pen is mightier than the sword. Give me the
Sword!

I am stiring up a rucus in two fields: (1) My new Church is half way up.
I am just doing it because you and McCall said I did nothing but sit on my
fat fanny and read. I want to {show} you Simon Magus's that I could out do
the most materialistic preacher if I wanted to. Now at sixty I am spending
$123,000.00 and PAYING AS I GO. The First Unit will be ready when you
come up out of the subway for air this summer on your way to Boston or
Phila. or some other Civilized place. Second: I have put out the doctrine that
the Age of the SPIRIT has closed. You will see it in the VOICE. I am going
to Baltimore this Spring to lecture to the Ministers on it and will do the
same at Louisville, Ky. on the Fourth Sunday in Jan. I just came back from
~~PittbbrgO~~ Pittsburg where I preached Men's day. I dont know what was the
matter with me. Only twenty people shouted; six joined the Church and {they}
gave me a collection of Two hundred dollars. I could not get myself together
and I guess that accounts for the results ~~faoll~~ falling so far below the average
{for} my presence.

Crozer is in a Mess. The boys say Bristol is just a Sunday School expounder.
No man in "O.T." yet. Cant find a Ph.D. in that field. That Aramaic and Syriac
beat the boys down and they wont tackle the field. Enslin has no job yet. I will

---

1. Walter R. McCall had written Barbour about King, Sr.'s sermon at the installation.

see him at "The Society of Biblical Lit. and Exegesis," a group of Savants, which meets in New York on the 28th. Proctor and I and a few other spooks are members. Do you know Greek or Hebrew? If so I will get you in. If you dont, then I cant reccomend an ignoramus. Littlejohn is doing nothing but sitting on his fat fanny expecting me to get him a Church like Concord. Like McCall, he thinks he can preach much better than he can. Proctor took him to his church in Providence but things have not worked out yet.[2] That is the Church for you and not down in those sticks. You need not tell me about Dexter; I know Montgomery and its superficial intellectuality. A plant-hand in the North has more *WORLD WISDOM* than a college Pres. in the SOUTH. Thats why Bennie Mays column in the Courier sounds like nothing.[3] Something wrong with SOUTHERN INTELLECUALITY. I know what it is: it does not have the atmosphere ~~thats~~ that breeds profundity. . . . all abstraction. My young people attacked me Sunday in the BTU ~~you~~ on the ground that preachers are always talking about Salvation and it means nothing in this day and time. No souhtern youths would raise such a question. The Purpose of all this is to keep you ~~andp~~ and Coretta from "letting that Triple Attendance and Triple collection" lull you to sleep down there. Son, hard liberty is to be prefered to servile pomp!

The Preachers of Phila. just laid $31,000.00 in cash on the table for the Xmas drive for Africa. The Mau Mau trouble stimulate them. Ask Johnson and Cleveland about the Mau Mau.[4]

I murdered them Sunday on this question. The wise men asked: Where is he that is born King of The Jews? Why did they not ask for a SAVIOR? Luke called him a Saviour and Math. a "King." WHY? Becauae Luke was interested in ECONOMICS and Math. in Legislation. Therefore these preachers who try to make Christianity STRICLY a religion of the Poor are all wet. There have taken a *PARTICULAR* viewpoint and tried to make it a *UNIVERSAL*. This was Nietzsche's trouble. This is the trouble with those who claim that the Church is recreant to its task. They really are backing ~~Ouke~~ Luke, a particular. *SALVATION IS FOR ALL* {—a universal}, not just a group. That was my subject; *SALVATION FOR ALL*. For unto you is born a Saviour, was the text. Then the Question. *WHAT YOU?* Dr., It was awful! Then with that Thesis I roamed over the world starting as I always do with the international, then

---

2. Barbour's son, Worth Littlejohn Barbour, asked King in October 1950 for a letter of recommendation in support of his application to Crozer. He graduated from Crozer in 1954, six months before J. Pius Barbour wrote this letter. Barbour mentions that Samuel D. Proctor took McCall to Pond Street Baptist Church in Providence, Rhode Island, where Proctor was pastor from 1945 to 1949. In an April 1956 letter, Littlejohn mentioned to King that both he and Walter McCall were candidates for a church in Rochester. He wrote, "I hope it's his call; for Mc really wants to be a pastor and I think he would fit in that church very nicely" (Worth Littlejohn Barbour to King, 2 April 1956, MLKP-MBU: Box 14). See Charles E. Batten to King, 11 October 1950, in *Papers* 1:332; and King to Charles E. Batten, 30 October 1950, in *Papers* 1:333.

3. Benjamin E. Mays wrote a weekly column for the *Pittsburgh Courier*.

4. Barbour refers to H. H. Johnson and M. C. Cleveland, two Montgomery ministers.

National, then Individual. From what young man ~~to~~ do you wished to be saved? Frustrated Ambition? ~~Broe~~ Human weakness? I went to town on Human weakness as I had just finished BULTMAN'S BOOK.[5]

Well it is seven oclock in the morning and that is why I am writing such a long letter. I hide out during holidays as Nigger mess about festivities worry me. I have been in the bed so much until I cant sleep as all I do is lie in bed and read while you are trying to save the world. I have only looked at the New work going on {at my church} once in a month. I dont want to get enraptured with the Temple. I have put a gallery in the Church and I am sorry as I see now that I have not got as many people in the Church as I thought. *IT WAS EMPTY SUNDAY*! Took out ten seats to make room for the gallery and then had PLENTY ROOM FOR THE CROWD. How we preachers deceive ourselves! Get BULTMAN'S "Theology of the New Testament" and digest it. Learn how to stir up the spooks on the end. Never mind Dexter. Stir up the spooks so you wont get in a pocket. You may have to try for a Mass Church some day. Love to Coretta. Dont invite me down because Montgomery always reminds me of my failure.[6]

Yours

[*signed*] J Pius Barbour

(1) YOUNG ARTHUR YOUNGER, COATSVILLE, GOT MCNIELS CHURCH AT DAYTON {OHIO}—A CHURCH LIKE DEXTER.

(2) GARDNER TAYLOR RAISED $40,000.00 CASH IN A RALLY.[7]

DONT BE A HYPOCRITE. PUT YOUR NAME AND <u>DEGREES</u> ON YOUR STATIONARY. I DID IT AND INCREASED MY INCOME $3,000 A YEAR!

TALS. MLKP-MBU: Box 63.

---

5. Barbour refers to Rudolf Bultmann, *Theology of the New Testament* (New York: Scribner, 1951). A second volume of this work was published in 1955. Bultmann was a "special lecturer" at Crozer during the 1952–1953 school year.

6. Barbour was pastor of Montgomery's Day Street Baptist Church from 1921 to 1931. M. C. Cleveland followed Barbour as pastor of the church in 1933. Despite Barbour's warning, King extended an invitation to Barbour to lecture at Dexter's Spring Lecture Series for a week in April 1956. Barbour accepted and gave a sermon and three lectures on 15–17 April 1956. See Barbour, "Religion in Montgomery, Alabama," *National Baptist Voice*, May 1956; J. Pius Barbour to King, 21 July 1955, pp. 564–566 in this volume; and King to J. Pius Barbour, 13 March 1956, DABCC.

7. Gardner Taylor was pastor of Concord Baptist Church in Brooklyn, New York.

From Percy A. Carter, Jr.

[1955?]
Dixon, Ill.

*Carter was a member of the Dialectical Society and pastor of Second Baptist
Church in Dixon, Illinois. He refers to Wayman McLaughlin, a fellow member of
the Dialectical Society.*

The Reverend M. L. King
Dexter Avenue Baptist Church
Montgomery, Alabama

Dear Martin:

Greetings to you and Coretta. We have been in constant remembrance of you and are yet mindful of the rich fellowship which was ours to share together in Christ. How is the work progressing at the church and how are you both enjoying it? We shall be most pleased to hear from you at anytime. I supposed you know that the McLaughlin's have a cute little girl. When we left Mass. the Dialectical Society was still in operation and enjoying good participation. I really miss the fellowship which was ours to enjoy in Boston. But sooner or later, we must leave the mountaintop experiences having received a breath of heaven to go down into the valley and sit where man sits.

We shall keep thinking of you and wish for you the keeping of the Master's love to guide you in all His paths.

Fraternally,
[*signed*] Percy

TLS. MLKP-MBU: Box 117.

"The Challenge of the Book of Jonah"

[1951–1955?]
[Boston, Mass.?]

*The following sermon outlines were found among the hundreds of notecards King
prepared for his courses at Boston. In the sermons King argues that God's love is
universal and inclusive of all faiths and races.*

No more delightful moments can be spent than those spent reading the book of Jonah. It is one of the greatest books of the Old Testament. Its themes is both arresting and electrifying. Its unknown author appears to have possessed the vision of a Saint Paul, the satiric power of a George Bernard Shaw, and the delicious humor of a G. K. Chesterton. This book does not represent an actual occurrence any more than the parable of the prodigal son. But who can doubt the accuracy of either as portraits of ~~of~~ multitude of human hearts. To often have we spent our time arguing over the historicity of Biblical stories, while failing to grasp the underlying truths.

Let us look at this story for a moment and see what it has to offer us. Recall the story

    I Tell the Story

   II This story has within it ~~two~~ {three} fundamental truth that I would like to set forth

       1. God's love is boundless and Universal

          (1) God loves the Ninevite

          (2) Deal with Jonah's failure to see this and the whole Jewish attitude.

          (3) Deal with Christian view. Love men because God loves them.

          (4) Story of the lost sheep.

          (5) There is no class system. Aunt June is just as significant as the Ph.D. The person who lives in the ally is just as worthful to God as the richest person in the community.

       2. All men are their brothers keepers and dependent on each other.

          (1) Deal with Jonah's failure to see this

          (2) We are all involved in a single process and whatever effects one directly effects the other indirectly. So long as there is slavery in the world I can never be totally free.

          (3) Science has made this obviously true. We must have one World or none.

          (4) Quote John Donne[1]

AD. CSKC.

---

1. The poem from John Donne favored by King was "No man is an Iland, intire of it selfe; every man is a peece of the Continent, a part of the maine; if a Clod bee washed away by the Sea, Europe is the lesse, as well as if a Promontorie were, as well as if a Mannor of thy friends or of thine owne were; any mans death diminishes me, because I am involved in Mankinde; And therefore never send to know for whom the bell tolls; it tolls for thee" ("Devotions upon Emergent Occasions," in John Donne, *Selected Prose*, comp. Evelyn Simpson and ed. Helen Gardner and Timothy Healy [Oxford: Clarendon Press, 1967], p. 101). See, for example, King, "Facing the Challenge of a New Age," 3 December 1956, MLKP-MBU: Box 83.

"The Bigness of God"

[1951–1955?]
[Boston, Mass.?]

Int—The great danger facing religion is not disbelief in God, but a too narrow estimate of the God believed in.

1. Conflict over dogmas
2. White man lyching negroes

1. ~~Deuto-Isaiah~~ Israel's early tribal God and its implications Deutero Isaiah's answer and text of the sermon
2. God greatness in nature
3. The bigness of his purpose which includes all mankind.
    1. Not a denominational God
    2. Not a racial God
    3. Might even reveal himself in other religion. "I have other sheep that are not of this fold.[1]
4. Step out in the bigness of God. Out of your narrowness to his bigness. You will begin to see life in a new light.

AD. MLKP-MBU: Box 118.

---

1. King refers to John 10:16: "And other sheep I have, which are not of this fold; them also I must bring, and they shall hear my voice; and there shall be one fold, and one shepherd."

"God's Love"

[1951–1955?]
[Boston, Mass.?]

I. God's love has breath (It is all inclusive) This is what distinguishes the New T from the Old. The God of the O.T. was only a tribal God. Moreover God's love is ~~spontaneous~~ impartial. He makes his sun to rise on the good and the evil. If God gave us what we deserve all of us would deserve condemnation.

II. God's love is self giving (ie spontaneous, autonomous) He loves because it is a part of his nature. No external force requires him to do his duty. Man's love is heteronomous. He loves and does his duty because he is commanded to do it. So God's gift to man was given not because God was asked to give it but because he wanted to give it. e.g. a gift that a man gives his wife which she doesn't ask for is more appreciated than one which is given which she ask for. So it is with God.

III. God's love is redemptive. "Whoever believest . . . shall live."[1] God live gives life and new light. It saves us from death.

AD. CSKC.

---

1. King may be referring to John 3:16: "For God so loved the world, that he gave his only begotten Son, that whosoever believeth in him should not perish, but have everlasting life."

From Emory O. Jackson

12 January 1955
Birmingham, Ala.

Jackson, managing editor of the Birmingham World, *asks King for a
biographical sketch and photo so that he can publicize King's upcoming speech
to a meeting of the Birmingham branch of the NAACP.*[1]

Rev. M. L. King, Jr., Pastor
Dexter Avenue Baptist Church
Montgomery, Alabama

Dear Rev. Mr. King:

Please be kind enough to forward to us a glossy-print photo of yourself and
a biographical sketch that we may use this material in connection with your
forthcoming appearance as feature speaker at the NAACP installation program here.

Your prompt attention to this matter would be most helpful inasmuch as
we are trying to give the best and widest possible news built-up to the NAACP
installation program.

Yours truly,
[*signed*] Emory O. Jackson/a
Emory O. Jackson, Managing Editor

Birmingham World
P. O. Box 1968
312 North 17th Street
Birmingham, Alabama

EOJ/w

TLSr. MLKP-MBU: Box 117.

---

1. Emory Overton Jackson (1908–1975) received an A.B. from Morehouse College in 1932
and studied at Atlanta University. He became managing editor of the *Birmingham World* in 1943.
Jackson was founder and first president of both the Alabama Newspaper Association and the
Alabama State Conference of the NAACP. A photograph of King and a short biography appeared a week later ("Rev. King to Deliver NAACP Officers' Installation Talk," *Birmingham World*,
21 January 1955). See also "NAACP to Install Officers; Rev. M. L. King Jr., Speaker," *Birmingham
World*, 14 January 1955.

14 January 1955
Savannah, Ga.

Law, a longtime NAACP activist, notes the announcement in the Birmingham
World *promoting King's scheduled speech to the organization's Birmingham
branch.*[1]

Rev. M. L. King, Jr.
Pastor,
Dexter Avenue Baptist Church
Montgomery, Alabama

Dear Mr. King:

Just read in the <u>Birmingham World</u>, the valiant Emory Jackson's fighting
newspaper, that you are the speaker for the installation of the officers for the
Birmingham (Ala.) Branch of the National Association for the Advancement
of Colored People.

I have followed with interest all of your activities and am very happy over
the very rapid strides you have made.

As I remember, you worked in the Morehouse College Chapter, NAACP,
and to see you continue interest in this very worthwhile organization (I like to
think of it as a movement) in Freedom's cause, now that you have assumed
community leadership, is heartwarming.

I wish, further, to congratulate you in your new post as pastor of the Dexter
Avenue Baptist Church and pray that you will continue to be successful in
every way.

Hoping that you will continue to find opportunity for service in the NAACP,
I remain

Very sincerely yours,
[*signed*]
W. W. Law

TLS. MLKP-MBU: Box 117.

---

1. Westley W. Law (1923–) earned his B.S. at Georgia State College (now Savannah State
College). Rejected for a teaching position because of his affiliation with the NAACP, Law became
a mail carrier for the U.S. Post Office. He was president of the Savannah branch of the NAACP,
a position he held for twenty-six years. Law also served as head of the Georgia State Conference
of the NAACP. He was a member of the national organization's board of directors for thirty years
beginning in 1950.

"Apathy Among Church Leaders
Hit in Talk by Rev. M. L. King"

25 January 1955
Birmingham, Ala.

This unsigned Birmingham World *article describes "A Realistic Approach to Progress in Race Relations," which King delivered to the Birmingham NAACP on 23 January.[1] In his speech King emphasized gaining the ballot as a step toward first-class citizenship, saying, "A voteless people is a powerless people." The article also reports his efforts to enlist all Dexter church members as "voters and members of the NAACP."*

Blasting away at apathy among church leaders in the field of civil rights, the Rev. Martin L. King, Jr., pastor Dexter Avenue Baptist Church of Montgomery, condemned racial segregation as "a wrong" in a speech made at an NAACP rally Sunday afternoon at Tabernacle Baptist Church.

Meantime he took a frowning view of the opinions expressed by Dr. Collier P. Clay, 68-year-old president of Union Theological Seminary here, made at Notasulga, Ala., Saturday, Jan. 22 on a program sponsored by the Southern Negro Improvement Association of Alabama, Inc., headed by Samuel H. Moore of Birmingham. Clay in his speech approved segregation.[2]

The youthful minister asserted that "segregation is a form of slavery" and denounced those Negro individuals who imply that they believed in as "mental slaves" which the speaker declared was one of the worst forms of slavery. He said that the group's true leadership must speaker out against those who advocate and condone segregation, discrimination and humiliation.

He used the subject, "A Realistic Approach to Progress in Race Relations." The Rev. King said there were two extreme approaches, neither which merited adoption. One was the extremely optimistic view that much progress has been made, therefore we should sit down. The other was the extremely pessimistic view that very little had been done, hence we should sit down and do nothing.

He recommended a third or realistic approach which took the best of both of the extreme views. "We have come a long long way but we have a long, long way to go," he expressed it. He recited the achievement of the group and then outlined the goals. This he called the "realistic" approach.

---

1. This version of the speech has not been located. For a later version, see "A Realistic Look at Race Relations," speech at the annual dinner of the NAACP Legal Defense and Educational Fund, 17 May 1956, MLKP-MBU, Box 5.

2. Clay reportedly endorsed segregation and denounced the NAACP and its "troublemakers." The Alabama NAACP executive committee issued a statement repudiating Clay's speech. After an investigation into the matter, the Birmingham Baptist Ministers Conference voted to exclude Clay and C. J. Glaze, president of the Southern Association for Improvement of Race Relations, from its membership. See "Barrage of Criticism Levelled at Dr. Clay," *Alabama Tribune*, 4 February 1955; and *Baptist Leader*, 3 and 24 February 1955.

Among the ways the group can help itself toward the goals of first-class citizenship he said was by getting the ballot. "A voteless people is a powerless people." A second method is to joining the NAACP and put some big money into the freedom fight. Thirdly, he recommended using the courts more to obtain unjustly denied rights. He called for an immediate start toward the implementation of the May 17 U.S. Supreme Court decision banning the segregated school system.

"You must do more than pray and read the Bible" to destroy segregation and second-class citizenship—"you must do something about it," the speaker counselled. He related how at fashionable Dexter Avenue Baptist Church he had set up a social and political action committee whose job it was to assist persons in the church in becoming qualified voters and in enrolling in the NAACP. He said that he wanted all of his members to be voters and members of the NAACP. He also told how from his pulpit he had denounced the "Negro Inaugural Ball" as a venture to extend dying segregation to an area where it could draw new breath.[3]

The Atlanta-born, Morehouse-trained, Ph.D.-level minister was introduced by the Rev. W. P. Vaughn, host pastor. The Rev. J. L. Ware, pastor of Trinity Baptist Church, who also said he had expressed disapproval of Dr. Clay's views during his services, introduced the Rev. Vaughn.

Music for the installation program was furnished by First Baptist Church of Ensley. The statement of occasion by Mrs. Osie Ware Mitchell, the appeal by Emory O. Jackson, solo by Miss Savannah Crews, and the installation of officers by the Rev. R. L. Alford, minister of the Sardis Baptist Church, rounded out the program.

W. C. Patton, retiring branch president who presided, offered a resolution which was unanimously adopted, rejecting the reported racial views of Dr. Clay as unrepresented and contrary to the position and sentiment of the recognized and authentic leadership of the Negro group. [. . .][4]

PD. *Birmingham World*, 25 January 1955.

---

3. The inaugural committee for newly elected governor James Folsom planned a segregated inaugural ball for African Americans. See "God and Supreme Court Against P. S. Segregation, Says Jemison," *Alabama Tribune*, 7 January 1955.

4. The remainder of the article, which lists those involved in the installation ceremony and those installed as officers, is omitted.

From William J. Cole

5 February 1955
Chicago, Ill.

A former member of Dexter, Cole donated a Communion table to the church in memory of his mother.

Rev. M. L. King Jr.

Dear Sir:-

Your kind letter received to day and very glad to hear from you. I am happy to know the Cummunion Table is in the process of making and will be delivered soon.

I am more than happy to know Dexter has a leader now and a good Pastor I pray for your continued success. I shall do {all} I can to help my church. I still consider Dexter my church as I can never forget my church. I believe the people of the South are beginning to be like the Northern people. No night service. We can hardly get enough people out in some churches to have a prayer meeting.

I have often wondered what could be done to stimulate the evening services. I hope to visit Montgomery this Spring & I hope to see the table.

May God's blessings be upon you and family.

Sincerely Yours
[*signed*] William J Cole.

ALS. MLKP-MBU: Box 117.

From Roland Smith

24 February 1955
Nashville, Tenn.

Smith writes concerning King's attendance at a meeting of the advisory council on literature and curriculum of the National Baptist Training Union Board.

Rev. M. L. King, Jr.
Pastor, Dexter Avenue Baptist Church
Montgomery, Alabama

Dear Rev. King:

I shall expect you to attend the meeting of the Advisory Council on literature and curriculum at the Sunday School Publishing Board Fourth Avenue and Charlotte on March 23rd and 24th, 1955. If you have written me that you cannot attend both days, then attend the day that's best for you.

Your expenses will be paid in the attendance of this meeting.

I should like for you to come prepared with ideas and plans as to the quality and critical analysis of our literature and plans as to our curriculum and leadership training.

Very truly yours,
[*signed*]
Roland Smith, Secretary
National Baptist Training Union Board

RS:e

TLS. MLKP-MBU: Box 117.

First Reader's Report, by L. Harold DeWolf

26 February 1955
Boston, Mass.

*DeWolf, King's advisor, filed this report as part of the official evaluation of the
first draft of King's dissertation, "A Comparison of the Conceptions of God in the
Thinking of Paul Tillich and Henry Nelson Wieman." In this report DeWolf
admits that "Mr. King's task is a difficult one," because he tries to compare "two
unusually influential theologians—the position of neither is simple and Tillich's
writing is sufficiently difficult so that there are wide differences of interpretation
among his foremost admirers and critics." He notes as the dissertation's "most
conspicuous weakness . . . the lack of an Abstract," which King later provided.[1]
DeWolf concludes that King's work demonstrated "broad learning, impressive
ability and convincing mastery of the works immediately involved," and approves
the draft of the dissertation "subject to revision as indicated."*

Mr. King's dissertation serves the purpose of showing many significant relations between two unusually influential theologians, each of whom maintains
a remarkably original and unique point of view. The position of neither is simple and Tillich's writing is sufficiently difficult so that there are wide differences of interpretation among his foremost admirers and critics. Hence Mr.
King's task is a difficult one. In general, he approaches it with broad learning,
impressive ability and convincing mastery of the works immediately involved.

The First Reader has read most of the chapters, one by one, and sent his
criticisms to the candidate. These criticisms, most of them formal or minor,
will not be repeated here. The whole dissertation must be gone over with care
for the correction of the form. Mr. King has shown himself well able to carry
out this assignment.

The most conspicuous weakness of the present draft is the lack of an Abstract. This is the most important part of a dissertation. It must be prepared
and presented sufficiently early so that it can be criticized and revised before
the Final Draft is due. The candidate is warned that often several revisions of
the Abstract are required. Ample time must be allowed.

Within the main body of the dissertation, my chief criticism is the lack of a
clear statement setting forth the presuppositions and norms employed in the
critical evaluation. Generally the main norm seems to be adequacy in expressing the historic Christian faith—or perhaps the religious *values* of historic
Christianity. Sometimes it is a more inclusive intellectual or philosophical adequacy. The norms should be more explicit in systematic statement. If it could
be shown that Tillich and Wieman themselves claim to measure up to the
standards by which they are here criticized, that demonstration would greatly
strengthen the criticism by showing it to be internal and not merely external.

Some further criticisms of specific passages follow, with page references.

---

1. See Abstract of "A Comparison of the Conceptions of God in the Thinking of Paul Tillich
and Henry Nelson Wieman," pp. 545–548 in this volume.

P. 219. Are these procedures of Tillich and Wieman actually parallel to Anselm's ontological argument? It should, at least, be pointed out that Anselm sought to prove the existence of the being with richest conceivable attributes, while Wieman and Tillich seek to prove by definition "a being of minimum specifications." In other words, Anselm sought to prove by a definition with maximum specification of attributes, while Tillich and Wieman seek to prove by definitions with minimum specifications.

P. 224, section 3. Do not most theologians think that God is ground or author of all being and source of all good? How does Tillich's dilemma regarding evil differ from the dilemma of other theists?

P. 226, section 5. Compare <u>The Christian Century</u> editorial review of Wieman, <u>The Source of Human Good</u>, characterizing his view as "cosmic behaviorism."[2]

P. 247, 8th to 6th line from the bottom. Relate to the doctrine of personal immortality?

When revised in response to these criticisms and to self-criticism, Mr. Martin's work promises to be an excellent and useful scholarly achievement.

TFmS. SPS.

---

2. DeWolf refers to Charles Clayton Morrison, "A Behavioristic Theology," *Christian Century* 63, no. 46 (13 November 1946): 1374–1376.

Second Reader's Report, by S. Paul Schilling

26 February 1955
Boston, Mass.

Schilling concludes that King's first draft is "competently done—carefully organized and systematically developed," showing "sound comprehension and critical capacity."[1] Schilling's criticisms emphasize "stylistic improvement," as well

---

1. Sylvester Paul Schilling (1904–) received his B.S. in 1923 from St. John's College in Annapolis, Maryland, and his M.A., S.T.B., and Ph.D. from Boston University in 1927, 1929, and 1934, respectively. His dissertation, entitled "The Empirical and the Rational in Hegel's Philosophy of Religion," was directed by Edgar S. Brightman. He served as pastor of several Methodist churches in the Washington, D.C., area from 1932 until 1945, when he joined the faculty of Westminster Theological Seminary in Baltimore. In 1953 he returned to Boston University as a professor of systematic theology, where he remained until his retirement in 1969. His publications include *Contemporary Continental Theologians* (1966), *God in an Age of Atheism* (1969), *God Incognito* (1973), *God and Human Anguish* (1977), and *The Faith We Sing* (1983). For his intellectual autobiography, see Schilling, "Developments in My Thought," in *The Boston Personalist Tradition in Philosophy, Social Ethics, and Theology*, ed. Paul Deats and Carol Robb (Macon, Ga.: Mercer University Press, 1986), pp. 187–207.

as the addition of "a discussion of Wieman's use of specifically Christian symbols in his conception of God." He approves the draft with the assumption that "the changes indicated will be made."

This piece of research has been competently done. It is carefully organized and systematically developed. The expository chapters are accurate, objective, and clear, presenting a true portrayal of the views of Tillich and Wieman. The writer seems to have made judicious use of all the available sources, which are considerable in extent. The comparisons and evaluations are fair-minded, balanced, and cogent. The author shows sound comprehension and critical capacity.

Stylistic improvement is needed at various points. Since the entire dissertation, except Chapter VI, has already been read chapter by chapter, the reader lists here only those items not previously listed or so far uncorrected (mostly because of lack of time). Particularly in Chapter IV the construction at various points is awkward, rough, or ungrammatical. Presumably these lacks will be corrected in the second draft.

Among various suggestions regarding content made previously to Mr. King, one may be mentioned here: the desirability of including in Chapter IV a discussion of Wieman's use of specifically Christian symbols in his conception of God. This aspect of his thought should be brought out clearly.

The reader is appending a list of needed corrections, to be added to those previously pointed out. The present list concerns mainly Chapter I, II, and VI.[2]

As a first draft, and assuming that the changes indicated will be made, the manuscript is approved.

TFmS. SPS.

---

2. This list has not been located.

To Julian O. Grayson

2 March 1955
Montgomery, Ala.

With this letter to Grayson, King enclosed the "Recommendations" and a program from his installation ceremony on 31 October 1954.[1]

---

1. Julian O. Grayson (1916–) received his M.Div. from Crozer in 1950, a year ahead of King.

Rev. Julian O. Grayson
4041 Clay Place, North East
Washington, D.C.

Dear Grayson,

I have been intending to write you for quite sometime but a busy schedule has prevented it. I have been through Washington several times within the last few months, but it was always passing through without any long stop. However, I plan to be in that section within the next six weeks and I will plan to stop over with you a day or two.

Things are going very well with me in my new church. The cooperation on the part of the membership is excellent. I will have to tell you all about it when I see you. Enclosed you will find some material concerning the church, and this will give you some idea of what we are doing. You will see the financial statement for the first three months of our church year. You will notice also my recommendations and a program of the Installation Ceremony. Look over these things and let me know what you think about them. Give my best regards to Erma and tell her that I will look forward to see you all very soon. Coretta is doing very well and making an excellent minister wife. I am

Sincerely yours,
[*signed*] King
M. L. King, Jr.

MLK:cpc
Enclosure:

TLS. JOG.

From Walter R. McCall

3 March 1955
Fort Valley, Ga.

A member of the Dexter congregation planned to attend Fort Valley State College, where McCall was now chaplain and dean of men. McCall promises to "take a personal interest in him" and "guide him aright to the best of my ability."

The Reverend Mr. M. L. King, Jr., Minister
The Dexter Avenue Baptist Church
309 Jackson Street
Montgomery, Alabama

Dear Mike:

Thanks for your letter of March 2, 1955. Its content was considered and has been acted upon in every way possible. Relative to Nesbitt, I called the

Registrar's Office this morning and have been informed that he has not sent in his application as yet, but I am certain that he will be accepted. We shall do all in our power to help him find his way. As a matter of fact, I shall follow your advice: take a personal interest in him, and shall guide him aright to the best of my ability. I would urge you to urge him to send in his application immediately as we have many applications this time of the year, that I may look out for him in regard to lodging quarters in the dormitory. The places in the city to live are poor. Personally, I do not advise students to seek lodging in the city in anywise.

Yes, you may look for me on Saturday, March 12th. I am not too sure that I will be able to get off on Friday, yet I do need to take such break as I have been working like mad! In the meantime, perchance I leave here on Friday (which is doubtful), I hope to bring my girl friend along. She teaches at Albany State College. She has been for two or more {yrs.} a great source of inspiration to me in my ministry.

Please convey my best wishes to all whom I may know, especially Bob Williams and my good friend and patriarch, Deacon Randall. He has done more to strengthen my interest in the preaching ministry than all persons I know.

Tell Coretta that I am hungry for good home cooked foods. Look out! Best wishes, I am

Sincerely yours,
[*signed*] Mac
Walter Raleigh McCall

TLS. MLKP-MBU: Box 117.

From Julius James

14 March 1955
Brunswick, Ga.

James, a classmate of King's at Morehouse and pastor of Shiloh Baptist Church in Brunswick, Georgia, sends his regrets for being unable to deliver the Anniversary sermon at Dexter.[1] In the fall of 1954 Coretta Scott King gave a recital at Shiloh.

---

1. Julius James (1918–) graduated from Morehouse College in 1952 and the Morehouse School of Religion in 1954. He pastored Zion Hill Baptist Church and Shiloh Baptist Church, both in Georgia, before being called to St. John Baptist Church in Gary, Indiana, a pastorate he has held since 1955. He served as president of the Baptist Minister's Conference of Gary from 1959 to 1960 and as president of the local branch of the NAACP in the late 1950s. He founded the Freedom Movement and Fair Share, two organizations dedicated to promoting fair housing and employment practices in Gary.

Dr. Martin Luther King, Jr.
309 South Jackson Street
Montgomery, Alabama

Dear Martin:

Your letter dated March 8, 1955 was received, and the contents therein was noted with particular care. I must say fist that you are a great "<u>DOCTOR</u>." I do appreciate the invitation extended to me by you inviting me to speak at your eleven o,clock services on your Anniversary ocassion. I consider it an honor as well as a great privilege. I regret very much that it comes on the second Sunday in December, because that is our Communion Sunday, and it is the closing of our fiscal year and wouldn't like to be away that Sunday. If it was any other Sunday I could make it, but I am afraid it will be impossible to be away at that time. However I hope that this will not be the last invitation. Let me say again, I regret that it comes on that Sunday.

I am very happy to know that your church program is going along so well there at Dexter, but there is no other way for it to go with a man of your ability and integrity, and with the beautiful Rose (Coretta) by your side. Tell Coretta that Brunswick is still talking, and that the city is looking forward to the time when we will present her again. Allow me to say that our church program here at Shiloh is going along fine also. We have recently purchased a new Balwin 5 Organ an we plan to finish paying for it the fifth Sunday in May. We are still baptising new souls into the church. I will have been here a year on the fifteenth of this month which is tomorrow, and we have taken in eighty members since I have been here it must be the hand of God. Gloria and the kids join me in sending their best regards to you and Coretta.

Best wishes, and I bid you God's speed.

Sincerely yours
[*signed*]
Julius James

jj/jj

TLS. MLKP-MBU: Box 117.

"A Comparison of the Conceptions of God in the Thinking of Paul Tillich and Henry Nelson Wieman"

[15 April 1955]
[Boston, Mass.]

In the winter of 1953 King chose his dissertation topic and enrolled in the required course Directed Study in Thesis and Dissertation Writing taught by Jannette E. Newhall.[1] Working with Newhall and DeWolf, King developed a bibliography, a preliminary organizational outline, and a short introduction.[2] During the summer of 1953 King contacted Wieman and Tillich to ask if they knew of any similar comparisons of their thought.[3] Beyond these exploratory letters, though, the newly married King did not work on the dissertation while serving as pastor in charge of Ebenezer during the summer. After studying during the fall and winter, King passed his final comprehensive examination in February 1954 and began working extensively on the dissertation.[4] On 9 April, just a few days after he accepted the call to Dexter, King's outline was approved by the Graduate School.

In the first chapter, after explaining his choice of the topic, King reviewed his sources. In the second chapter he explored the methodologies of the two theologians. By using a "method of correlation" Tillich sought first to describe the questions generated by the human condition and then to examine the specifically Christian symbols used to answer those questions. Wieman appealed to the scientific method, using "sensory observation, experimental behavior, and rational inference" to analyze Christian beliefs. In chapters 3 and 4 King described Tillich's and Wieman's conceptions of God. In the fifth chapter he compared and criticized their ideas.[5]

King's initial drafts of the dissertation were marked by the flawed citation practices that characterized his other academic essays and the final version of the dissertation. King appropriated virtually all of his first draft of the introduction

---

1. Jannette E. Newhall (1898–1979) studied at Radcliffe and Columbia and received her Ph.D. from Boston University in 1931. After teaching at Wheaton College in Norton, Massachusetts, she worked at Andover-Harvard Theological Library and other libraries in Massachusetts. Newhall was librarian and professor of research methods, as well as Brightman's longtime assistant, at Boston University's School of Theology from 1949 until her retirement in 1962. Her course on research methods covered, among other things, correct citation practices and ethical use of sources. See Newhall, Syllabus, Thesis and Dissertation Writing, 4 February–22 May 1953, MLKP-MBU: Box 115.

2. See King, Draft of table of contents, 4 February–22 May 1953, MLKP-MBU: Box 114; also drafts in MLKP-MBU: Boxes 96 and 107.

3. King's letters to Wieman and Tillich, probably written in early August, are not extant. For their replies, see Wieman to King, 14 August 1953, pp. 202–203 in this volume; and Tillich to King, 22 September 1953, pp. 203–204 in this volume.

4. See King, Qualifying examination answers, Theology of the Bible, 2 November 1953; History of Doctrine, 20 November 1953; Systematic Theology, 17 December 1953; and History of Philosophy, 24 February 1954; all published in this volume, pp. 204–210, 212–218, 228–233, and 242–247, respectively.

5. For a longer analysis of the dissertation's content, see the Introduction, pp. 23–26 in this volume.

verbatim from an article by Walter Marshall Horton.[6] *Newhall noted that in one of King's footnotes he cited a source not listed in the bibliography.*[7] *King corrected the error in later versions, but the introduction still contained several plagiarized passages.*

King's faulty citation practices were rooted in the notecards he created while conducting research on Tillich and Wieman.[8] *Large sections of the expository chapters are verbatim transcriptions of these notecards, in which errors he had made while creating his notes are perpetuated. In one case, although King properly quoted Tillich on the notecard, he used a section of the quotation in the dissertation without quotation marks.*[9] *Some of the notecards were adequately paraphrased from Tillich and Wieman, but many others were nearly identical to the source. King rarely noted down proper citations as he took notes, particularly from secondary sources. After reading an author's interpretation of a Tillich quotation, for example, King would transcribe the interpretation, the Tillich quotation, and the footnote to Tillich's writings but would neglect to mention the secondary source. One of his most important uncredited sources was a Boston University dissertation on Tillich that DeWolf had read just three years before. In the introduction King noted his reliance on "valuable secondary sources" and acknowledged Jack Boozer's "very fine" dissertation; thereafter, however, King obscured the extent to which he utilized this secondary source by citing it only twice.*[10] *He also relied heavily on a review of Tillich's* Systematic Theology *by Raphael Demos, King's professor at Harvard, and on several essays in a collection entitled* The Theology of Paul Tillich, *underreporting these sources in his citations.*[11]

King completed his draft of the dissertation while serving as the full-time pastor of Dexter. "I rose every morning at five-thirty and spent three hours writing the

---

6. Walter Marshall Horton, "Tillich's Role in Contemporary Theology," in *The Theology of Paul Tillich*, ed. Charles W. Kegley and Robert W. Bretall (New York: Macmillan, 1952), pp. 36–37.

7. King, "Draft of chapter 1," 4 February–22 May 1953, MLKP-MBU: Box 107.

8. It is unclear when King created these notecards. He probably wrote the bulk of them in Boston the summer of 1954 before moving to Montgomery, since many of his materials, particularly articles in scholarly journals, would not be available in Montgomery. He did, however, continue to check out library books from Boston University's library while in Montgomery. See Florence Mitchell to King, 15 October 1954, MLKP-MBU: Box 117.

9. See King, Notecard on "Freedom," 1948–1955, CSKC.

10. See Jack Stewart Boozer, "The Place of Reason in Paul Tillich's Concept of God" (Ph.D. diss., Boston University, 1952). Boozer (1918–1989) received both his bachelor's degree in philosophy (1940) and B.D. (1942) from Emory University. He entered graduate school at Boston University in 1942, but interrupted his studies to serve as an Army chaplain in Europe from 1944 to 1947. He returned to Boston in 1948 and received his Ph.D. in 1952. Boozer taught at Emory from 1950 until his retirement in 1987, serving as professor of religion and chair of the department of religion. His publications include *Faith to Act* (1967), coauthored with William Beardslee, and *Rudolf Otto. Aufsätze zur Ethik* (1981), which he edited.

11. Horton, "Tillich's Role in Contemporary Theology," pp. 26–47; George F. Thomas, "The Method and Structure of Tillich's Theology," pp. 86–105; David E. Roberts, "Tillich's Doctrine of Man," pp. 108–130; John Herman Randall, Jr., "The Ontology of Paul Tillich," pp. 132–161; all in Kegley and Bretall, eds., *Theology of Paul Tillich*. Although King's dissertation topic was similar to Charles Hartshorne's essay "Tillich's Doctrine of God" (in ibid., pp. 164–195), he did not utilize the essay extensively. See also Raphael Demos, Book Review of *Systematic Theology* by Paul Tillich, *Journal of Philosophy* 49 (23 October 1952): 692–708. A signed copy of this review with King's marginal comments is in MLKP-MBU: Box 107.

thesis," he later wrote, "returning to it late at night for another three hours."[12] In November 1954, several months after leaving Boston, King returned to that city for consultations with DeWolf and Schilling.

DeWolf and Schilling had mostly praise for King's draft, pointing out only minor changes necessary for their approval. In characteristically brief fashion, DeWolf returned King's draft with very few corrections or marginal comments, praising King for succeeding "with broad learning, impressive ability and convincing mastery of the works immediately involved." Schilling, evaluating one of his first dissertations as a professor, provided more extensive comments than DeWolf. In two instances Schilling noticed that King had improperly cited his sources by "inaccurately" quoting a Tillich text and omitting quotation marks around another paragraph. Acknowledging that the first draft was "competently done, . . . carefully organized and systematically developed," Schilling promised to approve the dissertation after the appropriate changes were made.[13] King incorporated many of these corrections, but made few other changes as he revised the dissertation.

After submitting the final draft sometime before the 15 April deadline, King returned to Boston to defend his work before an examining committee. Chaired by Schilling, the committee included DeWolf, Peter A. Bertocci, John H. Lavely, Richard M. Millard, and Newhall.[14] On 31 May the graduate school faculty of Boston University officially voted to confer the doctorate on King at the university's commencement on 5 June. Unable to be present for the service, King received the Ph.D. in systematic theology in absentia.

Table of Contents

I. INTRODUCTION
    1. Statement of problem
    2. Sources of data
    3. Review of the work of other investigators
    4. Methods of investigation
    5. The structure of the dissertation
II. THE METHODOLOGIES OF TILLICH AND WIEMAN
    1. Tillich's method of correlation
        i. The negative meaning of correlation
            (1) Supernaturalism
            (2) Naturalism
            (3) Dualism

---

12. King, *Stride Toward Freedom* (New York: Harper, 1958), p. 26.

13. See L. Harold DeWolf, First Reader's Report, 26 February 1955, p. 333–334 in this volume; King, Draft of chapter 3, 1954–1955, MLKP-MBU: Box 96A; and S. Paul Schilling, Second Reader's Report, 26 February 1955, pp. 334–335 in this volume.

14. Walter G. Muelder, dean of the School of Theology, was a member of the committee but did not attend the oral examination. See Boston University, Transcript of Record, 5 June 1955, BUR-MBU.

          ii. The positive meaning of correlation
- (1) The correspondence of data
- (2) Logical interdependence of concepts
- (3) Real interdependence of things or events
- (4) Correlation as existential questions and theological answers in mutual interdependence
- (5) The meaning of philosophy and its relation to theology

2. Wieman's scientific method
- i. Tests of truth which Wieman rejects
  - (1) Revelation
  - (2) Faith
  - (3) Authority
- ii. The positive meaning of the scientific method
- iii. Knowledge of God through the scientific method

3. A comparison and evaluation of the methodologies of Tillich and Wieman

III. TILLICH'S CONCEPTION OF GOD

1. The question of being
- i. The basic ontological structure
  - (1) Man, self, and world
  - (2) The logical and the ontological object
- ii. The ontological elements
  - (1) Individuality and participation
  - (2) Dynamics and form
  - (3) Freedom and destiny
- iii. Being and finitude
  - (1) Being and non-being
  - (2) The finite and the infinite
- iv. The categories of being and knowing
  - (1) Time
  - (2) Space
  - (3) Causality
  - (4) Substance

2. God as being itself
- i. God's transcendence of finite being
- ii. God's transcendence of the contrast of essential and existential being
- iii. The invalidity of all arguments for the existence of God
- iv. God as being and the knowledge of God

3. God as the unconditional

4. God as ground and abyss of power and meaning
- i. God as ground
- ii. God as abyss
- iii. Is the abyss irrational?

5. God as creator
- i. God's originating creativity
- ii. God's sustaining creativity
- iii. God's directing creativity

Chapter I

INTRODUCTION
1. Statement of problem

The problem of this dissertation is to compare and evaluate the conceptions of God in the thinking of Paul Tillich and Henry Nelson Wieman.

It was in the year of 1935, at a ten-day seminar on religion, that Paul Tillich and Henry Nelson Wieman, along with several other distinguished religious thinkers, gathered at Fletcher Farm, Proctorsville, Vermont, to discuss some of the vital problems of religion. One of the most heated discussions of the conference was a discussion on the nature of God, in which all lecturers took part.[1] In this particular discussion, Tillich and Wieman ended up in radically different positions. Wieman contended that Tillich "was at the same time more monistic and less realistic than he . . . pluralistic at the human level and monistic at the transcendent level." Against this monistic thinking, Wieman sought to maintain an "ultimate pluralism whereby God was in no way responsible for evil . . . with no statement as to the ultimate outcome of the struggle between it and good and as opposed to God, not merely an instrument of God for good."* Tillich in reply "commented upon Dr. Wieman's complete break with the Christian tradition and Greek philosophy, and characterized his position as in direct line with Zoroastrianism . . . the plurality of powers and the duality of good and evil. . . . God was a duality and at the same time ultimate, which was a contradiction in terms."†

It is probable that Wieman and Tillich went away from this conference not fully understanding each other's position. The controversy between Wieman and Tillich arose again a few years later when Wieman, in <u>The Growth of Religion</u>, grouped Tillich, Barth, Brunner, and Niebuhr together as "neo-supernaturalists." In a review of this book, Tillich sought to make it palpably clear that Wieman was erroneous in his grouping. Tillich writes:

> What we have in common is simply the attempt to affirm to explain the majesty of God in the sense of the prophets, apostles and reformers—a reality which we feel is challenged by naturalistic as well as the fundamentalistic theology.‡[2]

---

* Quoted from Horton, Art. (1952), 36.
† Ibid.
‡ Tillich, Rev. (1940), 70.

---

1. Horton, "Tillich's Role in Contemporary Theology," p. 36: "A high point in the conference was a three-cornered discussion on the nature of God, in which all the lecturers took part."

2. Horton, "Tillich's Role in Contemporary Theology," pp. 36–37: "It is probable that neither of the two understood the other very fully at this first meeting. . . . A few years later, in *The Growth of Religion* (1938), Wieman grouped Barth, Brunner, Niebuhr, and Tillich together as

Chapter I

Introduction

1. Statement of Problem

The problem of this dissertation is to compare and evaluate the conception of God in the thinking of Paul Tillich and Henry Nelson Wieman.

~~It was in the year of 1935~~ ~~at a less lay seminar on religion~~ that Paul Tillich and Henry Nelson Wieman, along with several other distinguished religious thinkers, gathered at Fletcher Farm, Proctorsville, Vermont, to discuss some of the vital problems of religion. One of the most heated discussions of the conference was a discussion on the nature of God, in which all lecturers took part. ~~In this particular discussion, Tillich and Wieman ended up in radically different positions.~~ Wieman contended that Tillich "was at the same time more monistic and less realistic than he ... pluralistic at the human level and monistic at the transcendent level." Against this monistic thinking, Wieman sought to maintain an ultimate pluralism whereby God was in no way responsible for evil ... with ~~and~~ no statement as

Chapter V

A Comparison *and Evaluation* Of The Conceptions of God in *the thinking* ~~Wieman~~ and Tillich

We turn now to a discussion
of the basic problem of this
~~dissertation~~ dissertation, viz.; comparing
and evaluating the conceptions of God in the
thinking of Wieman and Tillich.
Up to this point we have
attempted to interpret the conception
of God held by Wieman and
Tillich separately, without any
mention of their points of
agreement ~~or~~ disagreement. Now
we will ~~~~ look at their
conception ~~~~ ~~God~~ together, with a
view of determining their ~~~~
~~of similarity and dissimilarity~~
convergent and divergent points.

We shall see as the
discussion develops that Wieman
and Tillich have much more
in common than is ordinarily
supposed. It has been a not
~~too~~ infrequent tendency to group
Wieman with the naturalistic
thinkers and Tillich ~~with~~ the

This affirmation does not put God outside the natural world as Wieman claims. And so Tillich goes on to affirm:

> With respect to myself, I only need point to practically all my writings and their fight against the "side by side" theology even if it appears in the disguise of a "super." The Unconditioned is a qualification of the conditioned, of the world and the natural, by which the conditioned is affirmed and denied at the same time.*[3]

In other words, Tillich is seeking to make it clear that he cannot be labeled a supernaturalist. The Divine, as he sees it, is not a being that dwells in some transcendent realm; it is the "power of being" found in the "ecstatic" character of this world.[4]

It is clear that in neither of these debates has the real difference between Wieman and Tillich been defined. Yet there is a real difference which needs to be defined. This dissertation grows out of an attempt to meet just this need.

The concept of God has been chosen because of the central place which it occupies in any religion; and because of the ever present need to interpret and clarify the God-concept. And these men have been chosen because they are fountainhead personalities; and because each of them, in the last few years has had an increasing influence upon the climate of theological and philosophical thought.

2. Sources of data

The primary sources of data are those works of Tillich and Wieman in which the concept of God is treated. Prominent among Tillich's writings which contain discussions of the conception of God are the following in chronological order: The Religious Situation (1932), The Interpretation of

---

* Tillich, Rev. (1940), 70.

'neo-supernaturalists.' In his review of this book, Tillich rejected Wieman's interpretation of all four, while also objecting to the grouping. 'What we all have in common,' he says, 'is simply the attempt to affirm and to explain the majesty of God in the sense of the prophets, apostles and reformers—a reality which we feel is challenged by the naturalistic as well as the fundamentalistic theology.'"

3. Horton, "Tillich's Role in Contemporary Theology," p. 37: "This affirmation does not put God 'outside' the natural world, as Wieman claims, even in the case of Barth. . . . 'With respect to myself, I only need point to practically all my writings and their fight against the "side by side" theology even if it appears in the disguise of a "super." The Unconditioned is a qualification of the conditioned, of the world and the natural, by which the conditioned is affirmed and denied at the same time.'"

4. Horton, "Tillich's Role in Contemporary Theology," p. 37: "The Divine, as he sees it, does not inhabit a transcendent world above nature; it is found in the 'estatic' character of this world, as its transcendent Depth and Ground."

History (1936), The Protestant Era (1948), Systematic Theology I (1951), and The Courage to Be (1952).

The main works of Wieman which contain discussions of the conception of God are: Religious Experience and Scientific Method (1927), The Wrestle of Religion with Truth (1927), The Issues of Life (1930), Normative Psychology of Religion (1935), The Growth of Religion (1938), and The Source of Human Good (1946).

The writings of Tillich and Wieman relevant to our problem also include several articles found in various theological and philosophical journals. These articles may be found listed in the Bibliography.*

3. Review of the work of other investigators

Since the publication of his magnum opus, Systematic Theology, in 1951, there has been an upsurge in the number of investigators of Paul Tillich's thought. Prior to that time James Luther Adams of the Federated Faculty of the University of Chicago had been the chief interpreter of Tillich to American readers. Adams selected and translated the essays contained in The Protestant Era which was published in 1948. As a final chapter in this book Adams wrote an excellent interpretation of Tillich's thought entitled "Tillich's Concept of the Protestant Era." Adams had earlier translated a chapter of Tillich's Religiöse Verwirklichung and published it in the Journal of Liberal Religion.† W. M. Urban was asked to give a critique of this article which appeared in the same issue of the journal under the title, "A Critique of Professor Tillich's Theory of the Religious Symbol."‡[5]

In 1952 a very fine dissertation was done in this school by Jack Boozer entitled, The Place of Reason in Tillich's Conception of God.

Since the publication of his Systematic Theology, the investigators of Til-

---

* For a general account of all sources of data see the Bibliography. Writings of Tillich and Wieman will be designated by abbreviations. All other references will include the names of the authors and abbreviations of their works.
† "The Religious Symbol," Journal of Liberal Religion, 2 (Summer, 1940), 13–34.
‡ Journal of Liberal Religion, 2 (Summer, 1940), 34–36.

---

5. Boozer, "Place of Reason," pp. v–vi: "James Luther Adams of the Federated Faculty of the University of Chicago has been the chief interpreter of Tillich to American readers. Adams selected and translated the essays contained in The Protestant Era which was published in 1948. . . . In addition to selecting and translating the essays Adams writes as the final chapter in the book a splendid interpretation of Tillich's thought entitled 'Tillich's Concept of the Protestant Era.' . . . Adams translated a chapter of Tillich's Religiöse Verwirklichung and published it in the journal, asking W. M. Urban to write a critique which appeared in the same issue of the journal under the title, 'A Critique of Professor Tillich's Theory of the Religious Symbol.'"

lich's thought have almost tripled. Numerous articles have appeared in theological and philosophical journals dealing with some phase of his thought. The most obvious evidence for the growing interest in Tillich's thought is the fact that the editors of The Library of Living Theology chose him as the subject for the first volume.* This volume contains fourteen essays on various aspects of Tillich's thought by men like W. H. Horton, T. M. Greene, George F. Thomas, John Herman Randall, Jr., Charles Hartshorne, Reinhold Niebuhr and J. L. Adams. At the end of the volume Tillich himself gives a reply to the interpretations and criticisms of his thought. If the enthusiasm of the contributors to this volume is an index of what is to come, we may expect even more extensive investigations of Tillich's thought in the future.

Wieman's thought has also been investigated quite extensively. Ever since he published his first book in 1927, Wieman's thought has been interpreted and criticised by thinkers of all shades of opinion. Throughout the nineteen thirties and early forties theological and philosophical journals abounded with interpretations of Wieman's thought, and with the publication of his magnum opus, The Source of Human Good, in 1946, such interpretations and criticisms continued with tremendous strides. It is probably no exaggeration to say that hardly a volume has appeared in the last twenty years in the fields of philosophy of religion and systematic theology, which has not made some reference to Wieman's thought, particularly to his conception of God.

The present inquiry will utilize from these valuable secondary sources any results which bear directly on the problem, and will indicate such use by appropriate footnotes.

4. Methods of investigation

Several methods of procedure will be employed in the investigation of the problem stated for this dissertation. They are as follows:

---

* Kegley and Bretal (ed.), TPT. This series is consciously imitative of Paul A. Schilpp's, The Library of Living Philosophers. The editors admit that they are seeking to do for present-day theology what Schilpp has done and is continuing to do so well for philosophy. Each volume of The Library of Living Theology, like The Living Philosophers, will be devoted to the thinking of a single living theologian, and will include (1) an intellectual autobiography; (2) essays on different aspects of the man's work, written by leading scholars; (3) a "reply to his critic" by the theologian himself; and a complete bibliography of his writings to date.[6]

---

6. "Introduction" to Kegley and Bretall, eds., *Theology of Paul Tillich*, pp. vii–viii: "[Schilpp's] idea was original and unique: to devote each volume in the series to the thinking of a single living philosopher, and to include in each (1) an intellectual autobiography; (2) essays on different aspects of the man's work, written by leading scholars; (3) a 'reply to his critics' by the philosopher himself; and (4) a complete bibliography of his writings to date. . . . Our aim, quite simply, is to do for present-day theology what he has done and is continuing to do so well for philosophy."

(1) Expository.

We shall begin by looking at the thought of each man separately. In this
method we shall seek to give a comprehensive and sympathetic exposition of their conceptions of God.

(2) Comparative.

After looking at the thought of each man separately, we shall look at
their conceptions of God together with a view of determining their convergent and divergent points.

(3) Critical.

A critical evaluation of their conceptions of God will be given. In seeking to
give this critical evaluation two norms will be employed: (i) adequacy in expressing the religious values of historic Christianity; and (ii) adequacy in
meeting the philosophical requirements of consistency and coherence. We
shall also seek to discover the extent to which Tillich and Wieman claim to
measure up to the standards by which they are here criticized, thus making
the criticism internal as well as external. As a rule, critical appraisal will be
preserved until a thorough elaboration of Tillich's and Wieman's positions has
been made.[7]

Perhaps it is appropriate at this point to say a word concerning the general
philosophical and theological orientation of Wieman and Tillich. For Wieman, God, or "creativity," or "the creative event," is the producer, or the production of unexpected, unpredictable good. In specifying the nature of the
creative event Wieman is both eloquent and illuminating.

Throughout Wieman's thought it is very easy to see the influence of Whitehead and Dewey. His naturalism and empiricism are quite reminiscent of
Dewey. Like Dewey, he speaks of processes of creation, and also describes the
production of good as issuing from a context of events. On the other hand,
he goes beyond Dewey by insisting that the emergence of value is the work of
God. Wieman sees a great deal of value in Whitehead's "principle of concretion," but he is generally skeptical of his metaphysical speculations. Disagree-
ing both with Whiteheadian metaphysics and Dewey's humanistic naturalism,
Wieman's thought lies between these systems, containing a few features of
both, and some few emphases foreign to both.

The immediate background of Tillich's philosophy is the ontological and
historical strains of nineteenth century German speculation. The later, post-
Böhme philosophy of Schelling, the various mid-century reactions against the
panlogism of Hegel, like Feuerbach and the early Marx, Nietzsche and the
"philosophy of life," and the more recent existentialism, especially of Heidegger—all these have contributed to Tillich's formulation of philosophic
problems.[8]

---

7. Boozer, "Place of Reason," p. vii: "As a rule, critical appraisal has been reserved until a
thorough elaboration of his position has been made."

8. Randall, "Ontology," p. 132: "The immediate background of Tillich's philosophy is certain
of the more ontological and historical strains of nineteenth century German speculation. The
later, post-Böhme philosophy of Schelling, the various mid-century reactions against the panlog-

There is also a monistic strain in Tillich's thinking which is reminiscent of Plotinus, Hegel, Spinoza and Vedanta thought. In his conception of God he seems to be uniting a Spinozistic element, in which God is not a being, but the power of being, with a profound trinitarian interpretation of this, which allows for what is traditionally called transcendence.

5. The structure of the dissertation

The Introduction presents the main problem of this study and presents a brief summary of what other investigators have contributed to it. The materials on which this study is based and the methods which it follows are also set forth.

Since the question of method is of such vital importance in theological and philosophical construction, it will be necessary to discuss the methodologies of Tillich and Wieman. This will be done in Chapter II. In Chapter III an exposition of Tillich's conception of God is presented. In this Chapter it will be necessary to devote a few pages to a discussion of Tillich's ontology as a whole, since it is his ultimate conviction that God is "being-itself." In Chapter IV an exposition of Wieman's conception of God is given. In Chapter V the conceptions of God in the thinking of Wieman and Tillich will be compared and evaluated. Chapter VI will give the conclusions of the dissertation.

---

ism of Hegel, like Feuerbach and the early Marx, Nietzsche and the 'philosophy of life,' and the more recent existentialism, especially of Heidegger—all these have contributed to his formulation of philosophic issues and problems."

Chapter II

THE METHODOLOGIES OF
TILLICH AND WIEMAN

The question of theological method has been much discussed during the past century. Many hold that only as one settles this question can one expect to settle any other, for it underlies every other. Tillich and Wieman agree that the question of method is of fundamental importance, and both take pains to elaborate their methodologies.

Since the question of method is of such vital importance in theological construction, it is hardly possible to gain an adequate understanding of a theologian's basic thought without an understanding of his methodology. So we can best begin our study of the conceptions of God held by Tillich and Wieman by giving an exposition of their methodologies. We turn first to Tillich.

1. Tillich's method of correlation

Throughout his theology Tillich undertakes the difficult task of setting forth a systematic theology which is at the same time an apologetic. His aim is to show that the Christian message actually does answer the questions which modern man is being forced to ask about his existence, his salvation and his destiny.

Tillich's theology is quite frankly a dialogue between classical Christianity and modern man. In this it is analogous to the work of the second century apologists who mediated between Christianity and late classical culture.

The method used to effect this apologetic task is the "method of correlation." In Tillich's first book entitled, <u>Das System der Wissenschaften nach Gegenstanden und Methoden</u> ("The System of Knowledge: Its Contents and Its Methods"), theology is defined as "theonomous metaphysics." This definition was Tillich's first step toward what he now calls the method of correlation. In the method of correlation Tillich seeks to overcome the conflict between the naturalistic and supernaturalistic methods, a conflict which he thinks imperils real progress in the work of systematic theology and also imperils any possible effect of theology on the secular world. The method of correlation shows the interdependence between the ultimate questions to which philosophy is driven and the answers given in the Christian message.[1]

> Philosophy cannot answer ultimate or existential questions <u>qua</u> philosophy. If the philosopher tries to answer them . . . he becomes a theologian. And, con-

---

1. Paul Tillich, *The Protestant Era*, trans. James Luther Adams (Chicago: University of Chicago Press, 1948), p. xxvi: "The method of correlation shows, at every point of Christian thought, the interdependence between the ultimate questions to which philosophy (as well as pre-philosophical thinking) is driven and the answers given in the Christian message."

versely, theology cannot answer these questions without accepting their presuppositions and implications.*

In this method question and answer determine each other; if they are separated, the traditional answers become unintelligible, and the actual questions remain unanswered. Philosophy and theology are not separated, and they are not identical, but they are correlated.[2] Such a method seeks to be dialectical in the true sense of the word. In order to gain a clearer understanding of this method of correlation it is necessary to discuss its negative meaning.

i. The negative meaning of correlation

Tillich's method of correlation replaces three inadequate methods of relating the contents of the Christian faith to man's spiritual existence.[3] These inadequate methods are referred to as supranaturalistic, naturalistic or humanistic, and dualistic. We turn first to a discussion of the supranaturalistic method.

(1) Supranaturalism

The supranaturalistic method sees the Christian message as a "sum of revealed truths which have fallen into the human situation like strange bodies from a strange world."† The chief error in this method is found in its failure to place any emphasis on an analysis of the human situation. According to this method the truths of the Christian faith create a new situation before they can be received. At many points the supranaturalistic method has traits of the docetic-monophysitic heresy, expecially in its valuation of the Bible as a book of supranatural "oracles" in which human receptivity is completely overlooked.[4] This method finally ends up seeking to put man in the impossible position of receiving answers to questions he never has asked.

---

* Tillich, PE, xxvi.
† Tillich, ST, I, 64.

---

2. Tillich, *Protestant Era*, p. xxvi: "Question and answer determine each other; if they are separated, the traditional answers become unintelligible, and the actual questions remain unanswered. . . . Philosophy and theology are not separated, and they are not identical, but they are correlated, and their correlation is the methodological problem of a Protestant theology."

3. Paul Tillich, *Systematic Theology*, vol. 1 (Chicago: University of Chicago Press, 1951), p. 64: "The method of correlation replaces three inadequate methods of relating the contents of the Christian faith to man's spiritual existence."

4. Tillich, *Systematic Theology*, p. 65: "In terms of the classical heresies one could say that the supranaturalistic method has docetic-monophysitic traits, especially in its valuation of the Bible as a book of supranatural 'oracles' in which human receptivity is completely overlooked."

It is chiefly at this point that Tillich criticizes Barth. Tillich is strongly opposed to anything of a heteronomous character.*[5] A completely foreign substance or authority, suddenly thrown at man could have no meaning to him.[9]

> Revelation would not be even a divine possibility if it could not be received by means of forms of culture as human phenomena. It would be a destructive foreign substance in culture, a disruptive "non-human" entity within the human sphere, and could have had no power to shape and direct human history.†

Tillich says in an even sharper criticism of Barth:

> The "Grand Inquisitor" is about to enter the Confessional Church, and strictly speaking, with a strong but tightfitting armor of Barthian Supranaturalism. This very narrow attitude of the Barthians saved the German Protestant Church; but it created at the same time a new heteronomy, an anti-autonomous and anti-humanistic feeling, which I must regard as an abnegation of the Protestant principle.‡

In his <u>Systematic Theology</u> Tillich sets forth his criticism of Barth in still clearer terms. All theology as he sees it, has a dual function: to state the basic truth of the Christian faith and to interpret this truth in the existing cultural situation. In other words, theology has both a "kerygmatic" and an "apologetic" function. Barth's theology performs the first of these tasks admirably.

---

* Tillich uses the term heteronomous in relation to "autonomy" and "theonomy." Autonomy means the obedience of the individual to the law of reason, which he finds in himself as a rational being.[6] Heteronomy means imposing an alien law, religious or secular on man's mind.[7] Theonomy is a kind of higher autonomy. "It means autonomous reason united with its own depth . . . and actualized in obedience to its structural laws and in the power of its own inexhaustible ground." (ST, I, 85.)[8]

† Tillich, Art. (1935), 140.

‡ Tillich, IOH, 26.

---

5. Boozer, "Place of Reason," p. 97: "Tillich is strongly critical of anything of a heteronomous character."

6. Tillich, *Systematic Theology*, p. 84: "Autonomy means the obedience of the individual to the law of reason, which he finds in himself as a rational being." This sentence appears in Randall ("Ontology," p. 144) without quotation marks.

7. Tillich, *Protestant Era*, p. 46: "Heteronomy imposes an alien law, religious or secular, on man's mind."

8. Randall, "Ontology," p. 144: "'It means autonomous reason united with its own depth . . . and actualized in obedience to its structural laws and in the power of its own inexhaustible ground (85).' 'Theonomous reason' is thus for Tillich really a kind of higher autonomy." Ellipsis in original. Randall's quotation from Tillich is not accurate. Cf. Tillich, *Systematic Theology*, p. 85: "It means autonomous reason united with its own depth. In a theonomous situation reason actualizes itself in obedience to its structural laws and in the power of its own inexhaustible ground."

9. Boozer, "Place of Reason," p. 97: "A completely foreign substance or authority suddenly thrown at man could have no meaning to man." The two quotations from Tillich that follow this sentence also appear in Boozer's dissertation.

By lifting the message above any frozen formula from the past, and above the very words of the Scripture, Barth has been able to recover the great recurrent refrain that runs through all Scripture and Christian teaching. But he refuses, with the most persistent pertinacity, to undertake the apologetic task of interpreting the message in the contemporary situation. "The message must be thrown at those in the situation—thrown like a stone."* Tillich is convinced, on the contrary, that it is the unavoidable duty of the theologian to interpret the message in the cultural situation of his day. Barth persists in avoiding this function, thus falling into a dogmatic "supranaturalism".[10]

All of this makes it clear that Tillich is adverse to all supranaturalistic methods. His method of correlation, the basis of his whole theology, is expressly designed to avoid the pitfalls of supranaturalism without falling back into idealistic liberalism.[11]

(2) Naturalism

The method of naturalism is the second method that Tillich rejects as inadequate for relating the contents of the Christian faith to man's spiritual existence. Naturalism tends to affirm that the answers can be developed out of human existence itself. Tillich asserts that much of liberal theology fell victim to this type of naturalistic or humanistic thinking. The tendency was to put question and answer on the same level of creativity. "Everything was said by man, nothing to man."†

Naturalism teaches that there is only one dimension in life, the horizontal dimension. There is no God who speaks to man beyond human existence. There is no vertical relationship whatsoever. Whatever is is in man completely.[12]

---

* Tillich, ST, I, 7.
† Tillich, ST, I, 65.

---

10. Horton, "Tillich's Role in Contemporary Theology," pp. 30–31: "Barth's 'kerygmatic' theology performs the first of these tasks admirably. Without identifying the message with some frozen formula from the past, or with the very words of Scripture, Barth has been able to recover (for a generation that had lost it) the great recurrent refrain that runs through all Scripture and Christian teaching. . . . But he refuses, as though it were treason, the apologetic task of interpreting the message to the contemporary situation. 'The message must be thrown at those in the situation—thrown like a stone.' Tillich is convinced, on the contrary, that it is the unavoidable duty of the theologian to relate the Christian message to the cultural situation of his day. Barth persists in dodging this duty, thus falling into a 'supranaturalism' that 'takes the Christian message to be a sum of revealed truths which have fallen into the human situation like strange bodies from a strange world.'"

11. Horton, "Tillich's Role in Contemporary Theology," p. 31: "Tillich's method of correlation, the basis of his whole theology, is expressly designed to avoid this pitfall without falling back into idealistic liberalism."

12. Boozer, "Place of Reason," p. 262: "Humanism teaches that there is only one dimension in life, the horizontal dimension. . . . There are no absolute norms, there is no God who speaks

But this tendency to see everything in terms of the natural is as much an error as to see everything in terms of the supernatural.[13] The error that Tillich finds in naturalism generally is its failure to see that human existence itself is the question. It fails to see, moreover, that the "answers must come from beyond existence."* It is partially right in what it affirms; it is partially wrong in what it denies.[14]

(3) Dualism

The third method to be rejected by Tillich is called the "dualistic" method. Dualism seeks to build a supranatural structure on a natural substructure. It divides theology into natural theology and supranatural theology. Tillich admits that this method, more than any other, is aware of the problem which the method of correlation tries to meet. It realizes that in spite of the infinite gap between man's spirit and God's spirit, there must be a positive relation between them. It tries to express this relation by positing a body of theological truth which man can reach through so-called "natural revelation".[15] And herein lies the falsity of this method; it derives an answer from the form of the question. Like the naturalistic method, dualism fails to see that the answers must always come from something beyond existence.†

It is essentially at this point that Tillich criticises so-called natural revelation. There is revelation through nature, but there is no natural revelation. Natural revelation, if distinguished from revelation through nature, is a contradiction in terms, for if it is natural knowledge, it is not revelation. Natural knowledge cannot lead to the revelation of the ground of being. It can lead only to the question of the ground of being. But this question is asked neither by natural revelation nor by natural theology. It is the question raised by reason, but reason cannot answer it. Only revelation can answer it. And this answer is based on neither natural revelation nor natural theology, but on real revela-

---

* Tillich, ST, I, 65.
† Tillich, ST, I, 65.

---

to man from beyond man's existence. There is no vertical relationship whatsoever. Whatever is is in man completely."

13. Boozer, "Place of Reason," p. 263: "To see everything in terms of the natural is as much an error as to see everything in terms of the supernatural."

14. Boozer, "Place of Reason," p. 263: "Each is partially right in what it affirms, each is partially wrong in what it denies."

15. Tillich, *Systematic Theology*, p. 65: "The third method to be rejected can be called 'dualistic,' inasmuch as it builds a supranatural structure on a natural substructure. This method, more than others, is aware of the problem which the method of correlation tries to meet. It realizes that, in spite of the infinite gap between man's spirit and God's spirit, there must be a positive relation between them. It tries to express this relation by positing a body of theological truth which man can reach through his own efforts or, in terms of a self-contradictory expression, through 'natural revelation.'"

tion.[16] "Natural theology and, even more definitely, natural revelation are misnomers for the negative side of the revelation of the mystery, for an interpretation of the shock and stigma of nonbeing."*

Tillich is quite certain that the method of correlation solves the historical and systematic riddle that has been set forth by the method of dualism. It solves it by resolving so-called natural theology into the analysis of existence and by resolving so-called supranatural theology into the answers given to the questions implied in existence.[17]

ii. The positive meaning of correlation

We now turn to a discussion of the positive meaning of the method of correlation. The term "correlation" can be used in three ways. It can designate the correspondence of data; it can designate the logical interdependence of concepts, as in polar relations; and it can designate the real interdependence of things or events in structural wholes. In theological construction all three meanings have important implications.[18] We shall discuss each of these meanings respectively. Then, in order to gain a clearer understanding of the method of correlation, we may go on to discuss how systematic theology proceeds in using the method of correlation, and how theology is related to philosophy.

(1) The correspondence of data

Correlation means correspondence of data in the sense of a correspondence between religious symbols and that which is symbolized by them. It is

---

* Tillich, ST, I, 120.

---

16. Tillich, *Systematic Theology*, pp. 119–120: "'Natural revelation,' if distinguished from revelation through nature, is a contradiction in terms, for if it is natural knowledge it is not revelation, and if it is revelation it makes nature ecstatic and miraculous. Natural knowledge about self and world cannot lead to the revelation of the ground of being. It can lead to the question of the ground of being, and that is what so-called natural theology can do and must do. But this question is asked neither by natural revelation nor by natural theology. It is the question of reason about its own ground and abyss. It is asked by reason, but reason cannot answer it. Revelation can answer it. And this answer is based neither on a so-called natural revelation nor on a so-called natural theology. It is based on real revelation, on ecstasy and sign-events."

17. Tillich, *Systematic Theology*, pp. 65–66: "The method of correlation solves this historical and systematic riddle by resolving natural theology into the analysis of existence and by resolving supranatural theology into the answers given to the questions implied in existence."

18. Tillich, *Systematic Theology*, p. 60: "The term 'correlation' may be used in three ways. It can designate the correspondence of different series of data, as in statistical charts; it can designate the logical interdependence of concepts, as in polar relations; and it can designate the real interdependence of things or events in structural wholes. If the term is used in theology, all three meanings have important applications."

upon the assumption of this correspondence that all utterances about God's nature are made. This correspondence is actual in the <u>logos</u> nature of God and the <u>logos</u> nature of man. There is an understandable contact between God and man because of this common <u>logos</u> nature.[19]

But one cannot stop here because God is always more than ground or reason; God is also abyss. This abyss-nature of God makes it impossible for man ever to speak about God except in symbolic terms.[20] Since this idea of the symbol is such a basic facet of Tillich's thought, we must briefly discuss its meaning.

Tillich regards every theological expression as being a symbolic utterance. Since the unconditional is "forever hidden, transcendent and unknowable, it follows that all religious ideas are symbolical."* No finite word, form, person or deed can ever be identified with God. There is an infinite gap between man and God.†[21]

God, for Tillich, is not an object or being, not even the highest object or being; therefore, God cannot be approached directly as an object over against man as subject. The "really Real" grasps man into union with itself. Since for Tillich the really real transcends everything in the empirical order it is unconditionally beyond the conceptual sphere. Thus every form or word used to indicate this awareness must be in the form of myth or symbol. As Tillich succinctly states: "Offenbarung ist die Form, in welchem das religiöse Object dem religiösen Glauben theoretisch gegeben ist. Mythos ist die Ausdrucksform für den Offenbarungsinhalt."‡[22]

---

* Tillich, RS, X.
† Tillich, ST, I, 65.
‡ Tillich, Art. (1925), 820.

---

19. Boozer, "Place of Reason," pp. 265–266: "(1) Correspondence of data. Correlation means correspondence of data in the sense of a correspondence between religious symbols and that which is symbolized by them. It is upon the assumption of this correspondence that all utterances about God's nature are made. This correspondence is actual in the <u>logos</u>-nature of God and the <u>logos</u>-nature of man. . . . The fact that God and man have a common <u>logos</u>-nature makes possible an understandable contact between God and man."

20. Boozer, "Place of Reason," p. 266: "There is a problem here because God is always more than ground or reason, God is also abyss. The abyss-nature of God makes it impossible for man ever to speak about God except in symbolic terms."

21. Boozer, "Place of Reason," pp. 123–124: "Tillich regards every theological expression as being a symbolic utterance. For since the unconditional is 'forever hidden, transcendent and unknowable, it follows that all religious ideas are symbolical.' The spirit of the Protestant protest is that no finite form, word, person, or deed shall be identified with God. There is an infinite gap between man and God."

22. Boozer, "Place of Reason," pp. 124–125: "God is not an object, not even the highest object. . . . The really real cannot be approached directly as an object over against man as subject. The really real grasps man into union with itself. . . . Since for Tillich the really real transcends everything in the empirical order it is unconditionally beyond the conceptual sphere. Thus every word or form man uses to indicate this awareness of the really real is in the nature of a symbol

Tillich insists that a symbol is more than a merely technical sign.* The basic characteristic of the symbol is its innate power. A symbol possesses a necessary character. It cannot be exchanged. A sign, on the contrary, is impotent and can be exchanged at will. A religious symbol is not the creation of a subjective desire or work. If the symbol loses its ontological grounding, it declines and becomes a mere "thing," a sign impotent in itself. "Genuine symbols are not interchangeable at all, and real symbols provide no objective knowledge, but yet a true awareness."†[23] The criterion of a symbol is that through it the unconditioned is clearly grasped in its unconditionedness.[26]

Correlation as the correspondence of data means in this particular case that there is correspondence between religious symbols and that reality which

---

* Tillich, Art. (1940)[1], 14 ff.

† Tillich, Art. (1940)[1], 28. There seems to be a basic inconsistency in Tillich's thought at this point. The statements, "all knowledge of God has a symbolic character" and "symbols provide no objective knowledge, but yet true awareness" are difficult to reconcile with each other. This contradiction becomes even more pronounced in Tillich's discussion of the analogia entis between the finite and infinite. On the one hand he says, "Without such an analogy nothing could be said about God." On the other hand he says, "It is not a method (analogia entis) of discovering truth about God."[24] It is very difficult for one to make much out of such contradictions. W. M. Urban has expressed the dilemma in his effort to understand Tillich (Art. (1940), 34–36). Urban's position is that "unless there is 'analogy of being' between the 'Creator' and the 'created', between being in itself and being for us, it is perfectly futile to talk of either religious symbolism or religious knowledge." (Art. (1940), 35)[25]

---

or myth. 'Offenbarung ist die Form, in welchem das religiöse Object dem religiösen Glauben theoretisch gegeben ist. Mythos ist die Ausdrucksform fur den Offenbarungsinhalt.'"

23. Boozer, "Place of Reason," p. 125: "A characteristic of the symbol is its innate power. A symbol possesses a necessary character. It cannot be exchanged. On the other hand a sign is impotent in itself and can be exchanged at will. . . . The religious symbol is not the creation of a subjective desire or work. If the symbol loses its ontological grounding, it declines and becomes a mere 'thing,' a sign impotent in itself. 'Genuine symbols are not interchangeable at all, and real symbols provide no objective knowledge, but yet a true awareness.'"

24. Boozer, "Place of Reason," p. 126: "Even though Tillich is saying essentially that the analogia entis is a power of expression rather than knowledge, the statements, 'without such an analogy nothing could be said about God,' and 'it is not a method of discovering truth about God,' are difficult to reconcile with each other." Schilling wrote on a draft of this chapter that King's footnote was a "sound criticism, I believe" (King, Draft of chapter 2, 1954–1955, MLKP-MBU: Box 96).

25. Boozer, "Place of Reason," p. 128: "W. M. Urban has expressed the same dilemma in his effort to understand Tillich. Urban mentions two of Tillich's statements—'all knowledge of God has a symbolic character;' 'symbols provide no objective knowledge but yet a true awareness'—confessing that he cannot 'make much' out of such contradictions. Urban's position is that 'unless there is "analogy of being" between the "Creator" and the "created," between being in itself and being for us, it is perfectly futile to talk of either religious symbolism or religious knowledge.'"

26. Boozer, "Place of Reason," p. 125: "The criterion of a symbol is that through it the unconditioned is clearly grasped in its unconditionedness."

these symbolize. Once a true religious symbol is discovered one can be sure that here is an implicit indication of the nature of God.[27]

(2) Logical interdependence of concepts

A second meaning of correlation is the logical interdependence of concepts. It is polar relationships that fall chiefly under this meaning of correlation. Correlation, as used here, determines the statements about God and the world. The world does not stand by itself. Particular being is in correlation with being-itself. In this second meaning of correlation, then, Tillich moves beyond epistemological considerations to ontological considerations.[28]

Tillich develops a very elaborate system of ontological elements. These elements are individualization and participation,* dynamics and form,† and freedom and destiny.‡ Each of these stands in polar relationship with each other, neither pole existing apart from the other. This ontological polarity is seen further in being and nonbeing and the finite and infinite. In setting forth these polar relationships Tillich is attempting to overcome the basic weaknesses found in supranaturalism, humanism and dualism. He admits that dualism, more than either of the other methods, is aware of the two poles of reality, but dualism conceives these in a static complementary relationship. Tillich maintains that these poles are related in dynamic interaction, that one pole never exists out of relation to the other pole. Herein is one of Tillich's basic criticisms of Hegel. Hegel, according to Tillich, transcends the tension of existential involvement in the concept of a synthesis.§[29] He identifies exis-

---

* Tillich, ST, I, 174.
† Tillich, ST, I, 178.
‡ Tillich, ST, I, 182.
§ Tillich, IOH, 166.

---

27. Boozer, "Place of Reason," p. 267: "Correlation as the correspondence of data means in this particular case that there is correspondence between religious symbols and that reality which these symbolize. Once a true religious symbol has been discovered one can be sure that here is an implicit indication of the nature of God."

28. Boozer, "Place of Reason," pp. 267–268: "(2) Logical interdependence of concepts. A second meaning of correlation is the logical interdependence of concepts. Tillich regards polar relationships as falling under this meaning of correlation. . . . The world does not stand by itself. Particular being is in correlation with being-itself. In the second meaning of correlation, then, Tillich moves beyond an epistemological consideration to an ontological consideration."

29. Boozer, "Place of Reason," p. 268: "These elements are individualization and participation, dynamics and form, and freedom and destiny. These stand in polar relationship with each other, neither pole existing completely apart from the other. The ontological polarity is shown further in being and non-being and the finite and the infinite. . . . Tillich is trying to develop positively what he finds lacking in supranaturalism, humanism and dualism. Dualism is aware of the two poles of reality, but dualism conceives these in a static complementary relationship. Tillich maintains that they are related in a dynamic interaction, that one pole never exists out of relation

tential being with essential being. Tillich believes that no existing being can rise above ambiguity, tension, and <u>angst</u>.* Synthesis is reserved for God. Correlation, then, in the sense of logical interdependence of concepts, implies a polar structure of all existential reality.[30]

(3) Real interdependence of things
or events

The third meaning of correlation designates the real interdependence of things or events in structural wholes. The particular relationship which Tillich is alluding to under this meaning of correlation is the relationship between God and man, the divine-human relationship. The implication of this view is clear, viz., that if there is a divine-human correlation God must be partly dependent upon man.[31] Such a view has evoked strong protest from theologians such as Karl Barth. Tillich, in defending his position at this point, has this significant statement to make:

> But although God in his abysmal nature is in no way dependent on man, God in his self manifestation to man is dependent on the way man receives his manifestation.†

Here Tillich is apparently saying that God in his essence is to be distinguished from God revealing himself in existence.[32] God as abyss is unconditioned while God as self-manifesting is conditioned by man's receipt of the manifestation.

Tillich insists throughout that God and man are interdependent.

---

* Tillich, IOH, 137, 141.
† Tillich, ST, I, 61.

---

to the other pole. One feels here again that it is upon this issue that Tillich criticizes Hegel. For, according to Tillich, Hegel transcends the tension of existential involvement in the concept of a synthesis."

30. Boozer, "Place of Reason," pp. 268–269: "Tillich believes that no existing spirit has the perspective of God, the perspective of synthesis. All existing life is lived in ambiguity, tension, and <u>angst</u>. Correlation in the sense of the logical interdependence of concepts, then, implies a polar-structure of all existential reality."

31. Boozer, "Place of Reason," p. 269: "(3) Real interdependence of things and events. The third meaning of correlation is the real interdependence of things and events. The particular relationship about which Tillich speaks under this meaning of correlation is the relationship between God and man, the divine-human relation. The implication here is clear, that if there is a divine-human correlation God must be to some extent dependent upon man." The following quotation from Tillich appears in Boozer (p. 269).

32. Boozer, "Place of Reason," p. 269: "Tillich is apparently saying here, that God in his essence is to be distinguished from God revealing himself in existence." Boozer also quoted the following passage from Tillich (p. 270).

The divine-human relation, and therefore God as well as man within this relation, changes with the stages of the history of revelation and with the stages of
every personal development. There is a mutual interdependence between "God
for us" and "we for God". God's wrath and God's grace are not contrasts in the
'heart' of God (Luther), in the depth of his being; but they are contrasts in
the divine-human relationship. The divine-human relation is a correlation. The
"divine-human encounter" (Emil Brunner) means something real for both sides.
It is an actual correlation, in the third sense of the term.*

In a real sense, then, God manifests himself in history. This manifestation
is never complete because God as abyss is inexhaustible. But God as logos is
manifest in history and is in real interdependence with man. The method of
correlation seeks to express this relationship.[33]

(4) Correlation as existential questions
and theological answers in mutual
interdependence

"The method of correlation," says Tillich, "explains the contents of the
Christian faith through existential questions and theological answers in mutual interdependence."†[34] In using this method systematic theology first
makes an analysis of the human situation out of which the existential questions arise, and then proceeds to demonstrate that the symbols used in the
Christian message are the answers to these questions. The analysis of the human situation is done in terms of "existentialism." Here the individual becomes aware of the fact that he himself is the door to the deeper levels of
reality, and that his own existence reveals something of the nature of existence
generally. Whoever has immediately experienced his own finitude can find
the traces of finitude in everything that exists.[35]

---

* Tillich, ST, I, 61.
† Tillich, ST, I, 97.

---

33. Boozer, "Place of Reason," pp. 270–271: "In a real sense, then, God enters history, God
manifests himself in history. This manifestation is never complete because God as abyss is inexhaustible. But God as logos is manifest in history and is in real interdependence with man and
man's logos. . . . The method of correlation seeks to express this relationship."

34. Thomas, "Method and Structure," p. 98: "'The method of correlation,' says Tillich, 'explains the contents of the Christian faith through existential questions and theological answers in
mutual interdependence' (60)." King's citation to page 97 is incorrect; Thomas correctly cited the
quotation to Tillich, *Systematic Theology*, p. 60.

35. Tillich, *Systematic Theology*, pp. 62–63: "In using the method of correlation, systematic
theology proceeds in the following way: it makes an analysis of the human situation out of which
the existential questions arise, and it demonstrates that the symbols used in the Christian message
are the answers to these questions. The analysis of the human situation is done in terms which

The analysis of the human situation employs materials from all realms of culture. Philosophy, poetry, drama, the novel, therapeutic psychology, and sociology all contribute. The theologian organizes these materials in relation to the answers given by the Christian message. This analysis of existence may be more penetrating than that of most philosophers.[36] Nevertheless the analysis of the "situation" and the development of the "questions" constitute a "philosophical task." Though this task is carried out by the theologian, he does it as a philosopher, and what he sees is determined only by the object as it is given in his experience.[37]

After the questions have arisen from an analysis of the human situation, the Christian message provides the answers. These answers come from beyond existence and are taken by systematic theology "from the sources, through the medium, under the norm."* Although the answers are spoken to human existence from beyond it, there is a mutual dependence between question and answer. "In respect to content the Christian answers are dependent on the revelatory events in which they appear; in respect to form they are dependent on the structure of the questions which they answer."†

---

* Tillich, ST, I, 64. A word might be said concerning Tillich's conception of the sources, medium and norm of systematic theology. Tillich sharply rejects the neo-orthodox claim that the Bible is the only source of theology, on the ground that the Biblical message could not have been understood and cannot be received without the preparation for it in religion and culture. However, the Bible is the basic source, since "it is the original document about the events on which the Christian Church is founded" (ST, I, 35). In addition to the Bible, the sources are church history, including historical theology, and the history of religion and culture. Experience is the medium through which the sources come to us. On this point Tillich is closer to the Protestant Reformers than he is to the theological empiricists for whom experience is the main source of systematic theology. He holds that "Christian theology is based on the unique event Jesus the Christ," and that "this event is given to experience and not derived from it" (ST, I, 46). The norm of theology is "the 'new Being' in Jesus as the Christ." Here Tillich transcends the norm of both Roman Catholicism and traditional Protestantism.
† Tillich, ST, I, 64.

---

today are called 'existential.' . . . And then he has become aware of the fact that he himself is the door to the deeper levels of reality, that in his own existence he has the only possible approach to existence itself. . . . Whoever has penetrated into the nature of his own finitude can find the traces of finitude in everything that exists."

36. Tillich, *Systematic Theology*, p. 63: "The analysis of the human situation employs materials made available by man's creative self-interpretation in all realms of culture. Philosophy contributes, but so do poetry, drama, the novel, therapeutic psychology, and sociology. The theologian organizes these materials in relation to the answer given by the Christian message. In the light of this message he may make an analysis of existence which is more penetrating than that of most philosophers."

37. Thomas, "Method and Structure," p. 98, quoting Tillich, *Systematic Theology*, p. 64: "The analysis of the 'situation' and the development of the 'questions' constitute a 'philosophical task.'

We can better understand the method of correlation if we look at an example of its application: the "question" of Reason and the "answer" of Revelation.[38] After one analyzes man's rationality, especially his cognitive rationality, it is revealed that under the conditions of existence reason falls into
"self-destructive conflicts" with itself. The polarity of "structure" and "depth"
within reason produces a conflict between "autonomous" and "heteronomous" tendencies, and this conflict leads to "the quest for theonomy." The
polarity between "static" and "dynamic" elements within reason leads to a conflict between "absolutism" and "relativism." This leads to "the quest for the
concrete-absolute." The polarity between "formal" and "emotional" elements
produces a conflict between "formalism" and "irrationalism," and this conflict
leads to the "quest for the union of form and mystery." "In all three cases,"
says Tillich, "reason is driven to the quest for revelation."* Also a dilemma
arises between "controlling" knowledge and "receiving" knowledge. "Controlling knowledge is safe but not ultimately significant, while receiving knowledge can be ultimately significant, but it cannot give certainty."† This dilemma
leads to the quest for revelation which gives a truth which is both certain and
of ultimate concern. The "final revelation" in Jesus Christ, Tillich argues,
gives the answers to these questions implied in the existential conflicts of reason. It liberates and reintegrates reason and thus fulfills it.[39] It overcomes the
conflict between autonomy and heteronomy by re-establishing their essential
unity.[40] Says Tillich,

---

* Tillich, ST, I, 83.
† Tillich, ST, I, 105.

Though this task is carried out by the theologian, he does it as a philosopher, and what he sees
'is determined only by the object as it is given in his experience.'"

38. Thomas, "Method and Structure," p. 98: "We can understand better the 'method of correlation' if we look briefly at an example of its application: the 'question' of Reason and the
'answer' of Revelation."

39. Thomas, "Method and Structure," pp. 98–99, quoting Tillich, *Systematic Theology*: "Under
the conditions of existence, Tillich says, reason falls into 'self-destructive conflicts' with itself. The
polarity of 'structure' and 'depth' within reason produces a conflict between 'autonomous' and
'heteronomous' tendencies, and this conflict leads to 'the quest for theonomy.' The polarity between 'static' and 'dynamic' elements within reason leads to a conflict between 'absolutism' and
'relativism.' This leads to 'the quest for the concrete-absolute.' The polarity between 'formal' and
'emotional' elements produces a conflict between 'formalism' and 'irrationalism.' This leads to
'the quest for the union of form and mystery.' 'In all three cases,' Tillich remarks, 'reason is driven
to the quest for revelation' (83). Also a dilemma arises between 'controlling' knowledge and 'receiving' knowledge. 'Controlling knowledge is safe but not ultimately significant, while receiving
knowledge can be ultimately significant, but it cannot give certainty.' This 'dilemma' leads to the
quest for revelation which gives a truth which is both certain and of ultimate concern (105). The
'final revelation' in Jesus as the Christ, Tillich argues, gives the 'answers' to these 'questions' by
overcoming the conflicts within reason. It liberates and reintegrates reason and thus fulfills it
(150)."

40. Tillich, *Systematic Theology*, p. 147: "Revelation overcomes the conflict between autonomy
and heteronomy by re-establishing their essential unity."

Final revelation includes two elements which are decisive for the reunion of autonomy and heteronomy, the complete transparency of the ground of being in him who is the bearer of the final revelation, and the complete self-sacrifice of the medium to the content of revelation.*

Also the final revelation in Christ liberates reason from the conflict between absolutism and relativism by presenting a "concrete absolute." "In the New Being which is manifest in Jesus as the Christ," says Tillich, "the most concrete of all possible forms of concreteness, a personal life, is the bearer of that which is absolute, without condition and restriction."† Again, the final revelation in Christ overcomes the conflict between the formal and the emotional elements in reason through the participation of the whole of a person's life in it and the consequent bringing together of all the elements of reason.[41]

We have described the "method of correlation" and illustrated its application by reference to the correlation of the "question" of Reason with the "answer" of Revelation. This method determines the whole structure of Tillich's system.[42] He says,

> The method of correlation requires that every part of my system should include one section in which the question is developed by an analysis of human existence and existence generally, and one section in which the theological answer is given on the basis of the sources, the medium, and the norm of systematic theology.‡

Since the form of the "answers" is determined by the philosophical analysis of the situation, the way in which that analysis is conceived is important for an adequate understanding of the "method of correlation." So we turn to a discussion of Tillich's view of philosophy and its relation to theology.[43]

---

* Tillich, ST, I, 147.
† Tillich, ST, I, 150.
‡ Tillich, ST, I, 66.

---

41. Thomas, "Method and Structure," p. 99, quoting Tillich, *Systematic Theology*, p. 150: "For example, it liberates reason from the conflict between absolutism and relativism by presenting a 'concrete absolute.' 'In the New Being which is manifest in Jesus as the Christ,' says Tillich, 'the most *concrete* of all possible forms of concreteness, a personal life, is the bearer of that which is *absolute*, without condition and restriction.' . . . Again, the final revelation in Christ overcomes the conflict between the formal and the emotional elements in reason through the participation of the whole of a person's life in it and the consequent bringing together of all the elements of reason."

42. Thomas, "Method and Structure," p. 99: "We have described the 'method of correlation' and illustrated its application by reference to the correlation of the 'question' of Reason with the 'answer' of Revelation. The *structure* of Tillich's whole system is determined by his use of this method." The following quotation from Tillich also appears in Thomas (p. 99).

43. Thomas, "Method and Structure," pp. 99–100: "Since the form of the 'answers' is determined by the philosophical analysis of the situation, the way in which that analysis is conceived is crucial for any evaluation of the 'method of correlation.' What is Tillich's *view of philosophy* and its relation to theology?"

Tillich's conception of the nature of philosophy and its relation to theology is clearly set forth in the following paragraph:

> Philosophy asks the ultimate question that can be asked, namely, the question as to what being, simply being, means. . . . It arises out of the philosophical shock, the tremendous impetus of the questions: What is the meaning of being? Why is there being and not not-being? What is the character in which every being participates?. . . . Philosophy primarily does not ask about the special character of the beings, the things and events, the ideas and values, the souls and bodies which share being. Philosophy asks what about this being itself. Therefore, all philosophers have developed a "first philosophy", as Aristotle calls it, namely, an interpretation of being. . . . This makes the division between philosophy and theology impossible, for, whatever the relation of God, world, and man may be, it lies in the frame of being; and any interpretation of the meaning and structure of being as being unavoidably such has consequences for the interpretation of God, man, and the world in their interrelations.*[44]

This rather lengthy quotation reveals that Tillich conceives of philosophy as basically ontology.† He affirms that the Kantians are wrong in making epistemology the true first philosophy, for as later Neo-Kantians like Nicolai Hartmann have recognized, epistemology demands an ontological basis.[45] Since knowing is an act which participates in being, every act of knowing refers at the same time to an interpretation of being.

The attempt of logical positivism and related schools to reduce philosophy to logical calculus has also been unsuccessful. Logical positivism cannot avoid the ontological question.

> There is always at least one problem about which logical positivism, like all semantic philosophies, must make a decision. What is the relation of signs, symbols, or logical operations to reality? Every answer to this question says something about the structure of being. It is ontological.‡

---

* Tillich, PE, 85.
† Tillich regards the traditional term "metaphysics" as too abused and distorted to be longer of any service. This abuse came through a misuse of the syllable "meta" in metaphysics, which in spite of the testimony of all textbooks on philosophy that it means the book after the physics in the collection of Aristotelian writings has received the meaning of something beyond human experience, open to arbitrary imagination.
‡ Tillich, ST, I, 20.

---

44. This quotation also appears in Randall, "Ontology," p. 137.

45. Randall, "Ontology," p. 137: "The Kantians are wrong in making epistemology the true first philosophy, for as later Neo-Kantians like Nicolai Hartmann have recognized, epistemology demands an ontological basis."

Philosophy necessarily asks the question of reality as a whole; it asks the question of the structure of being.[46] Theology also asks the question of the structure of being. In this sense, theology and philosophy converge. Neither the theologian nor the philosopher can avoid the ontological question.[47]

Though both philosophy and theology deal with the structure of being, they deal with it from different perspectives. Philosophy asks the question of the structure of being in itself; theology deals with the meaning of being <u>for us</u>.[48] "Theology deals with what concerns us inescapably, ultimately, unconditionally."* There are two ways in which the ultimate concern can be considered. It can be looked at as an event beside other events to be described in detached objectivity; or it can be understood as an event in which he who considers it is existentially involved. In the first case the philosopher of religion is at work. In the second the theologian speaks. The philosopher of religion is only theoretically concerned with the ultimate concern, while the theologian's interpretation of the ultimate concern is itself a matter of ultimate concern.[49]

Theology at its best unites two elements, viz., the existential and the methodical. Theology is the existential and methodical interpretation of an ultimate concern. Theological propositions, therefore, are those which deal with an object in so far as it is related to an ultimate concern. On the basis of this criterion, no object is excluded from theology, not even a piece of stone; and no object is in itself a matter of theology, not even God.[50] Tillich is certain that this criterion "makes theology absolutely universal, on the one hand, and absolutely definite, on the other hand."†

So we can see that the first point of divergence between the philosopher and the theologian is found in their cognitive attitude. The philosopher seeks

---

* Tillich, PE, 87.
† Tillich, Art. (1947), 18.

---

46. Tillich, *Systematic Theology*, p. 20: "Philosophy asks the question of reality as a whole; it asks the question of the structure of being."

47. Tillich, *Systematic Theology*, p. 21: "Neither of them can avoid the ontological question."

48. Tillich, *Systematic Theology*, p. 22: "Philosophy deals with the structure of being in itself; theology deals with the meaning of being for us."

49. Paul Tillich, "The Problem of the Theological Method," *Journal of Religion* 27 (January 1947): 17: "It can be looked at as an event beside other events, to be observed and described in theoretical detachment; or it can be understood as an event in which he who considers it is 'existentially' involved. In the first case the philosopher of religion is at work, in the second the theologian speaks. . . . For the theologian the interpretation of the ultimate concern is itself a matter of ultimate concern."

50. Tillich, "Problem of Theological Method," p. 18: "Theology is the existential and, at the same time, methodical interpretation of an ultimate concern. . . . Theological propositions, therefore, are propositions which deal with an object in so far as it is related to an ultimate concern. No object is excluded from theology if this criterion is applied, not even a piece of stone; and no object is in itself a matter of theology, not even God as an object of inference."

to maintain a detached objectivity toward being.[51] He seeks to exclude all personal and historical conditions which might destroy his longing for objectivity.
So in this sense the philosopher is like the scientist.

The theologian, quite differently, does not seek to be detached from his object. He is involved in it. He seeks a personal relationship with it. In other words, the attitude of the theologian is commitment to its object.[52]

> He is involved—with the whole of his existence, with his finitude and his anxiety, with his self-contradiction and despair, with the healing forces in him and in his social situation. . . . Theology is necessarily existential, and no theology can escape the theological circle.*

Another point of divergence between the philosopher and the theologian is the difference in their sources. The philosopher looks at the whole of reality and seeks to discover within it the structure of reality. He assumes that there is an identity between the <u>logos</u> of reality as a whole and the <u>logos</u> working in him, so he looks to no particular place to discover the structure of being. The place to look is all places.[53]

The theologian, on the other hand, finds the source of his knowledge not in the universal <u>logos</u>, but in the <u>logos</u> "who became flesh," and the medium through which he receives knowledge of the logos is not common rationality, but the Church.

A third point of divergence which Tillich finds between philosophy and theology is a difference in their content. The philosopher deals with the categories of being in relation to the material which is structured by them, while the theologian relates the same categories to the quest for a "new being." The philosopher deals with causality as it appears in physics, while the theologian discusses causality in relation to a first cause, i.e. the ground of the whole series of causes. The philosopher analyzes biological or historical time and discusses astronomical as well as microcosmic space, but the theologian deals with time in relation to eternity and space in relation to man's existential

---

* Tillich, ST, I, 23.

---

51. Tillich, *Systematic Theology*, p. 22: "The first point of divergence is a difference in the cognitive attitude of the philosopher and the theologian. Although driven by the philosophical *erōs*, the philosopher tries to maintain a detached objectivity toward being and its structures."

52. Tillich, *Systematic Theology*, pp. 22–23: "The theologian, quite differently, is not detached from his object but is involved in it. . . . The basic attitude of the theologian is commitment to the content he expounds."

53. Tillich, *Systematic Theology*, p. 23: "The second point of divergence between the theologian and the philosopher is the difference in their sources. The philosopher looks at the whole of reality to discover within it the structure of reality as a whole. . . . He assumes—and science continuously confirms this assumption—that there is an identity, or at least an analogy, between objective and subjective reason, between the *logos* of reality as a whole and the *logos* working in him. . . . There is no particular place to discover the structure of being; . . . The place to look is all places."

homelessness.[54] Tillich uses several such examples to prove that the content of theology is different from that of philosophy.*

Just as there is a divergence between philosophy and theology, there is, insists Tillich, an equally obvious convergence. The philosopher like the theologian is caught in an existential situation and has an ultimate concern, whether he realizes it or not. Even the most scientific philosopher must admit this, for if an ultimate concern were lacking, his philosophy would be devoid of passion, seriousness, and creativity.[55] "Every creative philosopher," says Tillich, "is a hidden theologian."†

The theologian is also confronted with the same burden. In order to establish the universal validity of what concerns him ultimately, he like the philosopher must seek to be detached from his existential situation and seek obedience to the universal <u>logos</u>. He must take the risk of standing outside of the theological circle.‡

The conclusion that Tillich draws from the duality of divergence and convergence in the relation between theology and philosophy is that there is neither conflict nor synthesis between theology and philosophy.[56] A conflict presupposes a common basis on which to fight. But then there is no common basis between theology and philosophy.[57] When the theologian enters the philosophical arena, he must enter it as a philosopher; only as a philosopher can he be in conflict with another philosopher, that is, he must make his appeal to reason alone.§[58]

There can be no synthesis of philosophy and theology for the same reason: there is no "common basis" on which they can meet. Therefore, the ideal of

---

*   See ST, I, 24.
†   Tillich, ST, I, 25.
‡   Tillich, ST, I, 25.
§   Tillich, ST, I, 26.

---

54. Tillich, *Systematic Theology*, p. 24: "The philosopher deals with the categories of being in relation to the material which is structured by them. He deals with causality as it appears in physics or psychology; he analyzes biological or historical time; he discusses astronomical as well as microcosmic space. . . . The theologian, on the other hand, relates the same categories and concepts to the quest for a 'new being.' . . . He discusses causality in relation to a *prima causa*, the ground of the whole series of causes and effects; he deals with time in relation to eternity, with space in relation to man's existential homelessness."

55. Tillich, *Systematic Theology*, pp. 24–25: "There is no reason why even the most scientific philosopher should not admit it, for without an ultimate concern his philosophy would be lacking in passion, seriousness, and creativity."

56. Thomas, "Method and Structure," p. 100: "The conclusion Tillich draws from this divergence between philosophy and theology is that there can be neither conflict nor synthesis between them." Cf. Tillich, *Systematic Theology*, p. 26: "Neither is a conflict between theology and philosophy necessary, nor is a synthesis between them possible."

57. Tillich, *Systematic Theology*, p. 26: "A conflict presupposes a common basis on which to fight. But there is no common basis between theology and philosophy."

58. Thomas, "Method and Structure," p. 100: "When the theologian enters the philosophical arena, he must enter it as a philosopher; only as a philosopher can he be in conflict with another philosopher, that is, he must make his appeal to reason alone."

the "Christian philosophy" is both futile and self-contradictory, because it denotes "a philosophy which does not look at the universal <u>logos</u> but at the assumed or actual demands of a Christian theology."* Of course, any Western
thinker may be a "Christian philosopher" in the sense of one whose thinking
has been in some measure shaped by the Christian tradition, but an "intentionally" Christian philosopher is a contradiction in terms because the philosopher must "subject himself" to nothing but being as he experiences it.[59]

2. Wieman's scientific method

Throughout his writings Wieman contends that the only way to gain true
knowledge is through the scientific method. He is convinced that all knowledge must depend ultimately upon science, since "science is nothing else than
the refined process of knowing."† The scientific method is the very center of
Wieman's thought. As Van Dusen puts it:

> Scientific Method is more than a thread running through all Professor Wieman's
> writings; it is not too much to say that it is the central pivot around which every-
> thing else must revolve and in relation to which it must take its reference and
> obtain its validity.‡

In accepting the scientific method as the only way to distinguish between
truth and error, Wieman automatically rejects most traditional "ways of knowing." In order to gain a clearer understanding of Wieman's use of the scientific
method we may briefly discuss some tests of truth he rejects.

i. Tests of truth which Wieman rejects

It is often claimed that religious knowledge is peculiarly derived from revelation or faith or authority.[60] Wieman emphatically rejects each of these tests
of truth. We may discuss Wieman's view of them in order.

---

* Tillich, ST, I, 28.
† Wieman, RESM, 23.
‡ Van Dusen, Art. (1931), 711.

---

59. Thomas, "Method and Structure," pp. 100–101: "There can be no *synthesis* of philosophy
and theology for the same reason: there is no 'common basis' on which they could meet. Therefore there can be no such thing as a 'Christian philosophy.' Indeed, the ideal of a 'Christian
philosophy' is a self-contradictory one, because it denotes 'a philosophy which does not look at
the universal *logos* but at the assumed or actual demands of a Christian theology' (28). Of course,
any Western thinker may be a 'Christian philosopher' in the sense of one whose thinking has been
in some measure shaped by the Christian tradition, but an 'intentionally' Christian philosopher
is a contradiction in terms because the philosopher must 'subject himself' to nothing but being as
he experiences it."

60. Henry Nelson Wieman, *The Source of Human Good* (Chicago: University of Chicago Press,
1946), p. 214: "It is often claimed that religious knowledge is peculiarly derived from revelation

(1) Revelation

Some things are held to be true because it is claimed that they are revealed by God to man.[61] The Barthian theologians would insist, for instance, that the only avenue for religious truth is through revelation. Even Tillich, as we have seen, affirms that the final <u>revelation</u> in Jesus Christ gives answers to the questions implied in the existential conflicts of reason. Wieman, however, seeks to show that revelation provides no access to truth beyond the bounds of observation, agreement of observers, and coherence. Revelation in itself is not knowledge, notwithstanding the fact that revelation may be an avenue to knowledge.[62] Revelation for Wieman is "the lifting of the creative event to a place of domination in the devotion of a continuing fellowship to form one enduring strand of history."* This lifting to a place of domination was not done by man, but by such events as the life and teaching of Jesus, the Crucifixion; the Resurrection; and the forming of the fellowship. The chief consequence of this revelation is not an unveiling of knowledge, but the release of creative power to transform the world into richness of value. The immediate consequence of revelation is faith and salvation, rather than knowledge. In time, however, the religious man gains a knowledge from revelation that he could never have gained without. But this knowledge of revelation, if and when it is attained, demands the same tests of truth as any other knowledge.[63]

Wieman finds revelation to be an inadequate test of truth because it ultimately has to throw us back to some further test. Even if it be affirmed that truth is what God reveals, one must still ascertain what is revelation and what not. One may claim that the Holy Spirit shows what is truly revelation. But how can one know he has the Holy Spirit? In other words, one cannot know what is revelation by further revelation from the Holy Spirit. He must then

---

* Wieman, SHG, 214.

---

or faith or intuition or mystical experience or Bible or Jesus Christ or (more narrowly) the teachings of Jesus."

61. Henry Nelson Wieman and Regina Westcott-Wieman, *Normative Psychology of Religion* (New York: Thomas Y. Crowell, 1935), p. 118: "Some truths are held because it is claimed they were revealed by God to men."

62. Wieman, *Source of Human Good*, p. 214: "[Revelation] provides no access to truth beyond the bounds of observation, agreement of observers, and coherence. Revelation in itself is not knowledge at all, although it may open the way to knowledge."

63. Wieman, *Source of Human Good*, pp. 214–215: "This lifting to a place of domination was not done by man. It was accomplished by certain events which might be listed thus: the life and teachings of Jesus; the Crucifixion; the Resurrection; the forming of the fellowship. . . . The chief consequence of this revelation is not knowledge but the release of creative power to transform the world into richness of value and to save man from self-destruction and other evils which impoverish and break him. The first consequence of revelation for man is, therefore, faith and salvation. In time he gains knowledge from this revelation that he never could have gained without it. But this knowledge derived from revelation, when and if man attains it, demands the same tests of truth as any other knowledge."

prove not only the validity of the first revelation but also the second. Thus revelation demands some further test. It cannot itself be the test.[64]

(2) Faith

Faith is sometimes alleged to be a peculiar way of knowing that can cast off the ordinary tests of truth. For Wieman, however, faith is not knowledge primarily, but is a self-giving.[65] Faith is

> the act of deciding to live in a way required by the source of human good, to maintain association with a fellowship practicing that commitment, to follow the rituals designed to renew and deepen this commitment, to search one's self for hidden disloyalties to this devotion, to confess and repudiate these disloyalties.*

"Since faith is an act," says Wieman, "it is neither a belief going beyond the evidence nor knowledge."† It may be guided by the most thoroughly tested and accurate knowledge. But never does human knowledge plumb the full depths of the reality commanding religious commitment of faith. Even when the beliefs directing religious commitment become knowledge of the most precise and thoroughly tested sort, still the knowledge never exhausts the reality commanding faith.‡[66]

(3) Authority

Another test of truth which Wieman rejects is that of authority. He is quite aware that "authority is indispensable for any extensive accumulation of knowledge."§ Authority rightly used plays a large part in any form of knowl-

---

* Wieman, SHG, 46.
† Wieman, SHG, 47.
‡ Wieman, SHG, 47, 48.
§ Wieman, NPOR, 118.

---

64. Wieman and Westcott-Wieman, *Normative Psychology of Religion*, p. 118: "One must ascertain what revelation is and what not. One may claim that the Holy Spirit shows him what is truly revelation. But how can one know he has the Holy Spirit? One cannot know what is revelation by further revelation from the Holy Spirit. . . . He must then prove not only the validity of the first revelation but also the second. Thus revelation throws us back to some further test. It cannot itself be the test."

65. Wieman, *Source of Human Good*, p. 215: "Not only revelation but also faith is sometimes alleged to be a peculiar way of knowing that can cast off the ordinary tests of truth. We have tried to show that faith is not knowledge primarily but is a self-giving."

66. Wieman, *Source of Human Good*, pp. 47–48: "But, still again, faith may be guided by the most thoroughly tested and accurate knowledge. . . . Never does human knowledge plumb the full depths of the reality commanding religious commitment of faith. . . . Even when the beliefs directing religious commitment become knowledge of the most precise and thoroughly tested sort, still the knowledge never exhausts the reality commanding the faith."

edge.[67] The great insights of science could have never appeared without individual scientists depending on their associates and predecessors by accepting their findings. If they had to test everything for themselves, they would never catch up with what is already known, not to mention going on beyond to some further discovery. Moreover, there are many fields in which we are not equipped to test for ourselves the body of accepted knowledge. Thus authority is an indispensable labor-saving device in the acquisition of knowledge.[68]

But reliable authority simply conserves and hands on to others what has been found to be true by some other test than that of authority.[69] In other words, the trustworthiness of what is found in an authority does not depend upon the authority.[70] Says Wieman, "an authority is reliable in so far as it states accurately what has been discovered, and sets forth fully and correctly the evidence on which this discovery rests."* Thus authority like revelation depends on some further test of truth.[71]

We may now turn to a discussion of the positive meaning of the scientific method.

ii. The positive meaning of the scientific method

Wieman defines scientific method as the method in which sensory observation, experimental behavior, and rational inference are working together.[72]

> It becomes more fully scientific as (1) observation is made more accurate, selective, and refined; as (2) rational inference is made more pure and rigorous; as

---

* Wieman, NPOR, 119.

---

67. Wieman and Westcott-Wieman, *Normative Psychology of Religion*, p. 118: "Authority rightly used plays a large part in any form of knowledge."

68. Wieman and Westcott-Wieman, *Normative Psychology of Religion*, p. 118: "The scientist, for example, could not advance the frontiers of knowledge if he did not stand on the shoulders of his associates and predecessors by accepting their findings. If he had to test everything for himself he would never catch up with what is already known, not to mention going on beyond to some further discovery. Thus authority is a great labor-saving device in the acquisition of knowledge. Also there are many fields in which we are not equipped to test for ourselves the body of accepted knowledge."

69. Wieman and Westcott-Wieman, *Normative Psychology of Religion*, p. 118: "But reliable authority simply conserves and hands on to others what has been found to be true by some other test than that of authority."

70. Wieman and Westcott-Wieman, *Normative Psychology of Religion*, p. 119: "But the trustworthiness of what is found in an authority does not depend upon the authority."

71. Wieman and Westcott-Wieman, *Normative Psychology of Religion*, p. 118: "Thus authority, like revelation, depends on some further test of truth."

72. Henry Nelson Wieman, "Authority and the Normative Approach," *Journal of Religion* 16, no. 2 (1936): 184: "Scientific method is the method of sensory observation, experimental behavior, and rational inference, these three working together."

(3) experimental behavior is made to operate under controlled conditions and
(4) as these three are made to check one another more closely.*

This method repudiates pure rationalism, pure behaviorism and pure observation. It demands that all three enter into the forming, the correcting and the validating of any belief about any reality. These three tests of truth apply to every proposition alleged to be true, whether it is in the field of common sense, science, philosophy, or religion.

Wieman seeks to make it clear at every point that the scientific method is not to be confused with positivism, the view that we get our knowledge from sensation alone. Sensation alone can never give knowledge. Neither can abstract reason alone yield knowledge. First observation under the control of reason must discover some order in the field of sensuous experience. After discovering such an order, it becomes possible to follow it by pure reason beyond the reach of sensuous experience. But the starting point is what is sensible, and it is necessary to be able to come back to what is sensible for verification. So according to this method, knowledge is not limited to sensation, but neither can it dispense with sensation.

It might be well at this point to say a few words concerning Wieman's conception of observation, since it commands such a central position in Wieman's methodology. Observation is a series of perceptual events. The perceptual event is not merely sense data.[73] The perceptual event "includes everything within and without the biological organism, which experiment can demonstrate makes a difference to conscious awareness when the perceptual reaction occurs."† When the perceptual event is so interpreted it is clearly seen that is is only an infinitesimal part of the total universe. Innumerable happenings are constantly occurring in the wide reaches of the world which make no difference whatsoever to the conscious awareness accompanying the perceptual reaction of the organism.[74]

Many structures are present or ingredient in every perceptual event. Far fewer are common to a sequence of such events. From these that are common, selective attention picks out one, and that is what is perceived.[75]

---

* Wieman, Art. (1936)[1], 184.
† Wieman, SHG, 182.

---

73. Wieman, *Source of Human Good*, p. 181: "Observation, as here understood, is a series of perceptual events. The perceptual event is not merely sense data."

74. Wieman, *Source of Human Good*, p. 182: "Complex and intricate as the perceptual event is, when so interpreted, it is only an infinitesimal part of the total universe. Experiment easily shows that innumerable happenings can occur in the wide reaches of the world, and even in close proximity to the organism, perhaps also in it, which make no difference whatsoever to the conscious awareness accompanying the perceptual reaction of the organism."

75. Wieman, *Source of Human Good*, p. 182: "Innumerable structures are ingredient in every perceptual event. Far fewer are common to a sequence of such events. From these that are common, selective attention picks out one, and that is what we perceive."

Wieman is convinced that all knowledge is achieved by perception, even metaphysical knowledge. The only difference between metaphysical knowledge and other forms of knowledge is that the former is achieved "by a more elaborate analysis of perceptual events to the end of discovering structures not merely common to a selected series but those essential to all perceptual events whatsoever."* Time and space, for example, are essential ingredients in every perceptual event. This is discovered by an analysis of perceptual events. Wieman thinks that all categories sought by metaphysical or other philosophical inquiry can be uncovered by proper analysis of the perceptual event.†[76] As we shall see subsequently, even God is known by way of perception. So we can say that, for Wieman, observation enters into all cases of getting genuine knowledge.[77] Not even reason can gain knowledge without observation. There must be a working together of the two. In the final analysis the scientific method means "observation under control of reason, and reason under the control of observation."‡

Wieman also stresses the point that the scientific method requires the utmost use of imagination. Nothing of great importance can be discovered without the great power of imagination. The imagination is needed to construct a theoretical order. But all such imagination must be constantly under the control of reason and observation, else it will give us only the constructions of human fancy and build around us a wall of dreams to shut out objective reality.

In his book, <u>The Issues of Life</u>, Wieman analyzes the scientific method in four steps:

(1) Forming an idea of what course of action will produce specified consequences by observing various consequences that have issued from specified conditions.§

(2) Ascertain as accurately as possible just what are the conditions under which this course of action can be profitably followed to produce the desired and anticipated consequences.

(3) Find or create these conditions, perform the course of action, and observe what happens.

(4) Develop by logical inference what further to expect in the light of what

---

* Wieman, SHG, 182.
† Wieman, SHG, 183.
‡ Wieman, Art. (1932)², 109.

§ Wieman feels that this is the most difficult step of all. It is here that the greatest genius is displayed, in religion and science, and in every other branch of life where discovery is demanded.

---

76. Wieman, *Source of Human Good*, pp. 182–183: "Time and space, for example, are essential ingredients in every perceptual event. This we discover by analysis of perceptual events. . . . all the categories sought by metaphysics or other philosophical inquiry can be uncovered by proper analysis of the perceptual event."

77. Wieman, *Source of Human Good*, p. 187: "We have tried to show that observation enters into all cases of getting genuine knowledge."

has been observed to happen and test these inferences, just as the original idea was tested, namely by steps one, two, and three just described.*[78]

These, in short, are the steps of the scientific method. Here it is again made explicit that the only valid test of any belief is observation combined with reason. In order to gain a clearer understanding of Wieman's use of the scientific method, we turn to a discussion of the knowledge of God through the scientific method.

iii. Knowledge of God through the scientific method

Wieman rejects the view that knowledge of God is a special kind of knowledge which comes through special faculties like feeling, intuition, faith, and moral will. It is true that all of these designate a kind of immediate experience which provides the data that may lead to the knowledge of God. But it is erroneous to identify knowledge with immediate experience. "Immediate experience never yields knowledge, althought it is one indispensable ingredient in knowledge inasmuch as it provides the data from which knowledge may be derived."†

All of this leads Wieman to affirm emphatically that we know God just as we know any other object; that there are no other faculties of knowledge except those by which we know ordinary objects.

The method by which Wieman seeks to gain knowledge of God is the same as that used to gain knowledge of any other object, viz., the scientific method. As we have seen above, Wieman is quite certain that without this scientific method we have no accurate method of verifying our ideas or of distinguishing between truth and error.[79]

Wieman admits that because of the exceeding complexity of the data of

---

* Weiman, IOL, 187–188.
† Wieman, RESM, 22.

---

78. Henry Nelson Wieman, *The Issues of Life* (New York: Abingdon Press, 1930), pp. 187–188: "(1) Forming an idea of what course of action will produce specified consequences by observing various consequences that have issued from specified conditions. This first step is the most difficult of all. It is here that the greatest genius is displayed, not only in religion, but in the sciences and in every branch of life where discovery is demanded. . . . (2) Ascertain as accurately as possible just what are the conditions under which this course of action can be profitably followed to produce the desired and anticipated consequences. (3) Find or create these conditions, perform the course of action, and observe what happens. (4) Develop by logical inference what further to expect in the light of what has been observed to happen and test these inferences just as the original idea was tested, namely, by steps one, two, and three just described."

79. Henry Nelson Wieman, *Religious Experience and Scientific Method* (Carbondale: Southern Illinois University Press, 1926), p. 46: "Without a science we have no accurate method of verifying our ideas and certainly distinguishing between truth and error."

religious experience no method has yet been devised which can treat them scientifically. But all effort on the part of religious thinkers must be in that direction.

> Only by developing a scientific technique which is fit and able to interpret correctly the significance of that which is given in immediate experience when immediate experience is at that flood-tide called mysticism can God be known. It is probable He can never be known completely; but we can increase our knowledge of Him by contemplation which draws on mysticism from one side and from scientific method on the other.*

Wieman proceeds to formulate the requirements for a scientific knowledge of God in the following manner:

> In moving toward a more adequate, i.e., a more scientific knowledge of God, even though we approach from afar off, three things are required: (1) a clarification of the type of experience which can be called distinctively religious; (2) an analysis or elucidation of that datum in this experience which signifies the object being experienced and (3) inference concerning the nature of this object.†

In order to assure the success of the scientific method in obtaining knowledge of God men will have to relinquish all claim to knowledge of God except that obtainable by the combination of observation and reason. Sense experience of God is the first indispensable step in acquisition of knowledge of God through the scientific method. But the element of sense experience is only one side of the pole. The data of sense must be subjected to the scrutiny of reflection.

For Wieman, the adequacy of one's concept of God must ultimately be tested by three questions: 1. Does the concept designate that something in all being upon which human life must depend and to which humans must adjust, in order to attain the greatest possibilities of good? 2. Does it deal adequately with the problem of evil? 3. Is it true to religious experience.‡

There can be no doubt, asserts Wieman, that men are persistently meeting a reality like this. This reality must be God. When men come to the point of living the contemplative life, they know more about this God.§

Wieman continually affirms that God is an object of perception. He is just as capable of being perceived as any other object in the physical world.# Per-

---

* Wieman, RESM, 84–85.
† Wieman, RESM, 33.
‡ Wieman, WRT, 198.
§ By the contemplative life Wieman does not mean a life of passive reflection, but a life which includes both maximum awareness and appreciation of sense experience.
# Wieman admits that the perception by which God is known is "perception wherein the analysis and the search are carried much further than the automatic and habitual analysis and selection made by automatic reactions of the organism." (SHG, 183) These are sufficient for perceiving hills and houses, but not for perceiving God, "the everlasting creative event."[80]

---

80. Wieman, *Source of Human Good*, p. 183: "These suffice for perceiving hills and houses and spoons, but not for perceiving God (the everlasting creative event)."

ception of God is possible because God reveals himself. Through revelation God provides the preliminary conditions for perception of himself.

> Revelation is the development in some strand of history and in some community, of those meanings, of those perceptual events, and of that structured interrelation of events whereby God can be known. The development of meanings and perceptual events pertaining to God is the work of that creativity which generated all meanings.*

But even after these meanings, perceptual events, and structures have been provided, men do not necessarily perceive God.

> There are special commitments, discipline, and practices, as well as the general procedures of all empirical inquiry, to which men must subject themselves to perceive God after revelation is accomplished, just as they must do this to attain knowledge of any other complex object of cognition.†

From this interpretation of revelation Wieman seeks to explain why God is hidden. He sets forth the following four explanations for God's hiddenness. (1) God is hidden where and when he has not revealed himself. (2) He is hidden where and when men will not follow the methods and submit to the disciplines necessary to achieve true perception. (3) He is hidden when men hold to myth and revelation as a kind of knowledge. (4) He is hidden when men's appreciations and evaluations are so formed and directed that they cannot appreciate the divine significance of that creativity which generates all real value.‡[81] When the idea of the hiddenness of God is so interpreted, Wieman is certain that a major stumbling block to the perception of God is removed.

Another misunderstanding which must be removed if God is to be perceived is that concerning the nature and function of myth. "Myth," says Wieman, "is a statement, rather complex as a rule by which conduct, attitude, and devotion are directed to deal religiously with important reality without intellectual understanding of what they really mean."§ Wieman admits that myth, while lacking cognitive proficiency, possesses pragmatic efficacy. It may even be indispensable in dealing with some of the most important and complex realities because of the limitations of man's intellectual understanding. The

---

* Wieman, Art. (1943)[1], 28.
† Wieman, Art. (1943)[1], 28.
‡ Wieman, Art. (1943)[1], 29.
§ Wieman, Art. (1943)[1], 30.

---

81. Henry Nelson Wieman, "Can God Be Perceived?" *Journal of Religion* 23 (1943): 29: "This interpretation of revelation explains why God is hidden. God is hidden, first of all, where and when he has not revealed himself. He is hidden, in the second place, where and when men will not follow the methods, submit to the disciplines, and use the categories required to achieve true perception. He is hidden, in the third place, when men hold to myth and revelation as to a kind of knowledge. He is hidden, fourth (and this is the most tragic cause of his hiddenness), when men's appreciations and evaluations are so formed and directed that they cannot appreciate the divine significance of that creativity which generates all real value."

central Christian myth of the crucified and yet living Christ, for instance, is a way of saying

> that the reality with which we deal through the myth of Christ is so deep and so high, so intimate and so complex, that our intellectual understanding is inadequate.*

Myths are not false; but neither are they true. The pragmatic efficacy of the myth in directing one to important reality is simply a fact. It simply happens when and if it does happen. These happenings either occur or do not. When they occur, they are neither true nor false. Only propositions about them can be true or false.[82]

The myth when rightly interpreted is seen to be a valuable way of directing conduct and devotion to important reality. But when myth is thought to be knowledge it confuses the mind and makes impossible perceptual knowledge of God.

A final confusion which Wieman seeks to dissipate in order to make perceptual knowledge of God possible pertains to the work of theology.[83] He thinks that the work of theology should be limited to the job of

> criticizing and revising the myths so that they will continue to be efficacious and reliable guides to God within the changing context of the prevailing culture.†

Since myths will always be there, some field of expert scholarship must be devoted to the task. When theology goes beyond this and pursues the cognitive job of getting knowledge of God, it ends in a morass of confusion and futility.[84]

---

* Wieman, Art. (1943)[1], 30.
† Wieman, Art. (1943)[1], 31–32. It is difficult to follow Wieman at this point. In most instances he contends that theology should give us knowledge of God. But here he is contending that theology should only criticize and revise religious myths so as to nurture experience of creativity. It is hard to make much of this contradiction.

---

82. Wieman, "Can God Be Perceived?" p. 30: "Myths are not false; neither are they true. . . . But the pragmatic efficacy of the myth in directing us to the uncomprehended reality of God is simply a fact. It happens, when and if it does happen, as thunder and winter and tides happen. These happenings either occur or do not. When they do not, they are not false, and when they do, they are not true. Only propositions about them can be false or true."

83. Wieman, "Can God Be Perceived?" p. 31: "But when myth is thought to be knowledge it confuses the mind and diverts it from those procedures by which alone knowledge can be achieved. . . . The last confusion that must be dissipated, if we are to have the perceptual knowledge of God that we need, pertains to the work of theology."

84. Wieman, "Can God Be Perceived?" p. 32: "Since we must always have myths, no matter how much more knowledge is now required to supplement them, some field of expert scholarship must be devoted to this task. . . . If we follow that trail with that intent, we end in a morass of confusion and futility."

Wieman is quite certain that once these misunderstandings concerning revelation, myth and theology are removed one can move toward perception of God. This point of the perception of God is so important to Wieman because he is seeking to be a thoroughgoing empiricist at every point. That which cannot be observed does not exist.

3. A comparison and evaluation of the methodologies of Tillich and Wieman

The methodologies of Tillich and Wieman are quite divergent at many points. As we have seen, Wieman contends that one only gains true knowledge through the scientific method. All knowledge, whether it is knowledge of God or knowledge of a stick or stone, is obtained through the scientific method. With this contention, Tillich is in strong disagreement. He looks upon this "methodological imperialism" as being as dangerous as political imperialism, for, like the latter, "it breaks down when the independent elements of reality revolt against it."* It is Tillich's conviction that the adequacy of a method cannot be decided <u>a priori</u>; rather it is continually being decided in the cognitive process itself. For Tillich, method and system determine each other, making it absolutely erroneous for any method to claim to be adequate for every subject.[85]

Another point of disagreement between Tillich and Wieman is on the question of existential participation. Wieman's attempt to be a thoroughgoing empiricist causes him to look askance upon anything that smacks of existentialism. He seeks to deal with the data of theology through detached objectivity. Tillich, on the other hand, is convinced that the existential factor cannot be eliminated from theology. And so he contends, contrary to Wieman, that theology can never be an "empirical science." The object of theology, asserts Tillich, is not an object within the whole of scientific experience. Theology does not deal with objects that can be "discovered by detached observation," or "tested by scientific methods of verification." In these methods the testing subject is always outside the test situation. But the object of theology, says Tillich, can be verified only by a participation in which the testing theologian risks himself in the ultimate sense of "to be or not to be."[86] Tillich contends

---

* Tillich, ST, I, 60.

---

85. Tillich, *Systematic Theology*, p. 60: "Whether or not a method is adequate cannot be decided a priori; it is continually being decided in the cognitive process itself. Method and system determine each other. Therefore, no method can claim to be adequate for every subject."

86. Horton, "Tillich's Role in Contemporary Theology," p. 39: "Macintosh and Wieman have claimed that theology is an 'empirical science' in this sense; Tillich finds the claim entirely groundless. Theology does not deal with objects that can be 'discovered by detached observation' or 'tested by scientific methods of verification,' which always eliminate the personal equation. 'The

that "this test is never finished not even in a complete life of experience. An element of risk remains and makes an experimental verification in time and space impossible."*

Tillich thinks that the demand for existential participation is confirmed by the results of scientific-experiential theology itself. Without such an existential participation Wieman's "creative process," for instance, is a nonreligious concept: with it, it is no longer a scientific concept.[87] Tillich is certain that "in no case can scientific experience as such produce a foundation and source of systematic theology."†[88]

Tillich does not totally eliminate the empirical factor from his theological method. Like Wieman, he sees the importance of the empirical factor in theology. But he is not willing to carry it as far as Wieman. Tillich prefers to stand "on the boundary" between Barth and Wieman on the issue of theological empiricism.[89]

When it comes to the question of the rational factor in theological methodology, both Tillich and Wieman concur on its importance. We have seen how Wieman applies rational inference to sensory observation and experimental behavior to achieve the proper results of the scientific method. We have also seen how Tillich employs semantic, logical, and methodological rationality in his theological system. Tillich insists that the dialetical character of his method of correlation does not mean that it is opposed to logic and rationality; for "dialectics follows the movement of thought or movement of reality through yes and no, but it describes it in logically correct terms."‡ So for Tillich and Wieman reason plays an important part in methodological construction.

Tillich goes beyond Wieman, however, by insisting that reason needs revelation. Therefore revelation receives a very prominent place in the methodology of Tillich. He holds that the final revelation in Jesus Christ gives answers to the questions implied in the existential conflicts of reason. Wieman seeks to

---

* Tillich, ST, I, 44.
† Tillich, ST, I, 44.
‡ Tillich, ST, I, 56.

---

object of theology can be verified only by a participation in which the testing theologian risks himself in the ultimate sense of "to be or not to be."'"

87. Horton, "Tillich's Role in Contemporary Theology," p. 39: "Without such an existential participation Wieman's 'creative process' and Brightman's 'cosmic person' are nonreligious concepts; with it, they are no longer 'scientific' concepts."

88. King submitted a draft of this chapter that ended with this paragraph. Schilling commented: "Here you should go on to show what you think of W's criticism. I believe also that a brief Section 3 in Chap. II. summarizing the main points of similarity & difference betw. T. & W. would greatly increase the value of the chapter" (King, Draft of chapter 2).

89. Horton, "Tillich's Role in Contemporary Theology," p. 39: "Tillich's place in American Protestant theology might be briefly summarized by saying that he stands 'on the boundary' between Barth and Wieman on the issue of theological empiricism."

show that revelation provides no access to truth beyond the bounds of obser-

vation and agreement of observers.[90] His theory of revelation abjures any attempt to make revelation a part of supernaturally mediated knowledge. Tillich would agree that revelation adds nothing to the totality of our ordinary knowledge, i.e., to our knowledge about the subject-object structure of reality.[91] But he would disagree with Wieman's assertion that revelation mediates no form of knowledge. Tillich affirms that revelation mediates knowledge about the mystery of being to us, not about beings and their relation to one another. There is one other qualification that Tillich makes concerning knowledge of revelation, namely, that it can be received only in the situation of revelation, and it can be communicated—in contrast to ordinary knowledge—only to those who participate in this situation. According to this view, revelation cannot interfere with knowledge that is ordinary. Likewise, ordinary knowledge cannot interfere with knowledge of revelation.[92]

Several points concerning Wieman's scientific method and Tillich's method of correlation require comment.

1. Wieman insists that the religious inquirer seeking knowledge of God must stick to what is immediately given within the fluid process of "sensory experience, experimental behavior and rational inference."[93] This is what Wieman means by the requirements of thoroughgoing empiricism. Such a method seeks to eliminate faith and analogical reference from the quest for knowledge of God.

But is it possible to eliminate faith and analogical reference from genuine knowledge of God, or from any knowledge for that matter? The outcome of such an elimination would be, as Santayana has shown, a "solipsism of the present moment."* Without faith and recourse to analogy it is impossible to develop a working knowledge of the actual world.

Certainly Wieman is not consistent in his attempt to eliminate faith and analogical reference from the quest for knowledge of God. He says, for instance, that "the terms 'process' and 'interaction' apply to everything that ex-

---

* Santayana, SAF, 14–18.

---

90. King used the previous two sentences earlier in this chapter; see p. 370 in this volume.

91. Tillich, *Systematic Theology*, p. 109: "Nor does [revelation] add anything directly to the totality of our ordinary knowledge, namely, to our knowledge about the subject-object structure of reality."

92. Tillich, *Systematic Theology*,.pp. 129–130: "Knowledge of revelation is knowledge about the revelation of the mystery of being to us, not information about the nature of beings and their relation to one another. Therefore, the knowledge of revelation can be received only in the situation of revelation, and it can be communicated—in contrast to ordinary knowledge—only to those who participate in this situation. . . . Knowledge of revelation cannot interfere with ordinary knowledge. Likewise, ordinary knowledge cannot interfere with knowledge of revelation."

93. This quotation is from Wieman, "Authority and the Normative Approach," p. 184.

ists because everything in existence is a process and interacts with other things."* But how is this known? Certainly not by direct observation. In such affirmations one must assume that what lies beyond observation is analogous to what is observed. Since it is possible to observe only an infinitesimal portion of all that has been, is, and will be, it can be truly said that any assertion made about anything that exists will involve a bold use of analogy.

2. One of the weak points of the scientific method in religion is that this method omits so much valid experience. Science must inevitably be selective and exclusive. In a world of such infinite variety and richness, science by the nature of its instruments and procedures must limit itself to a few items or elements within that richness. Thus a vast wealth of potential experience is always deliberately ignored in any scientific endeavor. Whatever may be the merit of the foregoing, the surprising thing is that Wieman states categorically: "We do not yet have any knowledge of God that we can call scientific." This would seem to mean that the purely scientific methodology is a hope and not a fact.

3. Even if the scientific method were a fact it would hardly be adequate for religion. The scientific method requires that the investigator maintain a detached objectivity toward his object. He must seek to exclude all personal and historical conditions which might destroy his longing for objectivity. The theologian, on the other hand, does not seek to be detached from his object. He seeks a personal relationship with it. In other words, the attitude of the theologian is commitment to his object. Tillich's criticism of Wieman's method at this point is quite sound.

4. It seems that Tillich begs the question as to the relation between philosophy and theology in his contention that the philosopher seeks the truth only in the whole of reality, and never looks for it in any particular place. There is nothing to prevent a philosopher from finding the key to the nature of reality in a particular part of reality. Indeed this is what the creative philosopher has done all along. He takes as his starting point some particular aspect of reality which seems to him to provide the clue to an understanding of reality as a whole.[94]

Now the philosopher who is a Christian does not differ from other philosophers in starting with a belief which he takes as the key to reality. He finds the key to reality in the event of God's revelation in Jesus the Christ. This does

---

* Wieman, Art. (1936)², 430.

---

94. Thomas, "Method and Structure," p. 101: "But Tillich begs the question as to the relation between philosophy and theology when he asserts that the philosopher seeks the truth only in 'the whole of reality,' 'the universal *logos* of being,' and never looks for it in any particular place. For there is nothing to prevent a philosopher from finding the key to the nature of reality in a concrete manifestation, a particular part of reality. Indeed, every creative philosopher must take as his starting point some part or aspect of reality which seems to him to provide the clue to an understanding of reality as a whole."

not mean that having found the key in a particular event, he should cease to look at the universal structure of being. The fact that he has found the key enables him to look at the structure of being with a clearer understanding of it.[95]

So it seems that Tillich's contention that there can be no Christian philosophy is somewhat exaggerated. He thinks that the ideal of a Christian philosophy is impossible because philosophy must approach the structure of being with detachment and without reference to its meaning for us. Yet Tillich himself, admits that every great philosopher has an ultimate concern, and has been in a sense a theologian. If this is so the distinction between philosophy and theology is relative, not absolute. Therefore Tillich's effort to distinguish between theology and philosophy in the last analysis breaks down.*[96]

5. In seeking to distinguish between philosophy and theology it seems that Tillich leaves a too sharp dualism between the theoretical and existentialism or "practical." This is one of the things that both existentialism and American instrumentalism have sought to break down. As J. H. Randall, Jr. puts it, "The theoretical interest or 'pure reason,' . . . is not something opposed to the practical and existential. Rather, theory and detached objectivity are moments or stages in a broader context or matrix of 'practice'."† Tillich is quite aware of this, but he still does not entirely free himself of the old Kantian dualism in which "pure reason" is set over against "practical reason." Tillich fails to take the existential character of theory seriously enough.[97]

---

* For a further elabora- † Randall, Art. (1952),
tion of this criticism see 141.
G. F. Thomas, Art. (1952),
101–104.

---

95. Thomas, "Method and Structure," p. 101: "Now the philosopher who is a Christian does not differ from other philosophers in starting with a belief which he takes as the key to reality. . . . This does not mean that, having found the key in a *particular* place, he should cease to look at the *universal* structure of being. . . . But the fact that he has found the key enables him to look at the structure of being with a clearer understanding of it."

96. Thomas, "Method and Structure," p. 102: "The main reason Tillich rejects the possibility of such a Christian philosophy is that he thinks philosophy must approach the structure of being with detachment and without existential concern. For it is only on this supposition that philosophy has to be restricted to the purely 'critical' task of analyzing the structure of being without reference to its meaning for us. Yet Tillich himself admits that the creative philosophers have been moved by an ultimate concern, and hence have been in a sense theologians. If so, the distinction between philosophy and theology is relative, not absolute." In the margin on a draft of this chapter Schilling wrote that King's "criticism [was] well-grounded & developed." He asked next to the last sentence: "What about his 3rd point of divergence?" (King, Draft of chapter 2).

97. Randall, "Ontology," p. 141: "It clearly does not take the 'existential' character of theory seriously enough."

Chapter III

TILLICH'S CONCEPTION OF GOD

1. The question of being

It is impossible to understand Tillich's conception of God without a prior knowledge of his ontology as a whole, since it is his ultimate position that "God is being-iteelf." To attempt to understand Tillich's conception of God without an understanding of his conception of being is like trying to understand the humanistic conception of God without understanding its conception of man. So we may well begin our study with a discussion of Tillich's ontological position.

Tillich insists that the core of philosophy is the ontological question, and this ontological question is logically prior to every other. Thought must start with being; it cannot go behind it. Ontology is possible because there are concepts less universal than "being," but more universal than the concepts that designate a particular realm of beings. Such ontological concepts have been called "principles," "categories" or ultimate notions.* Tillich's analysis of these concepts is the very heart of his philosophy.[1]

These concepts, he holds, are strictly <u>a priori</u>. They are necessary conditions for experience itself. They are present whenever something is experienced, and hence constitute the very structure of experience. Tillich makes it emphatically clear that this does not mean that the concepts are known prior to experience; on the contrary, "they are products of a critical analysis of experience."†[2]

Taken seriously this Kantian language implies that the "being" to be analyzed is to be found only in the knower, and not, except derivatively, in the known.[3] But this is exactly what Tillich seems to be denying, for he says that

---

* Tillich, ST, I, 166.
† Tillich, ST, I, 165.

---

1. Randall, "Ontology," p. 151: "Ontology is the core of philosophy, and the ontological question of the nature of being is logically prior to all others. Ontology is possible because there are concepts less universal than 'being,' but more universal than the concepts that designate a particular realm of beings. Such ontological concepts have been called 'principles,' 'categories,' or 'ultimate notions.' Tillich's analysis of these concepts is the heart of his philosophy."

2. Randall, "Ontology," p. 151: "Such concepts, he holds, are strictly '*a priori*': they are present whenever something is experienced, and determine the nature of experience itself. . . . This does not mean that they can be known prior to experience: they are known rather through the critical analysis of actual instances of experience."

3. Randall, "Ontology," p. 151: "Taken seriously, such language implies that the 'being' to be analyzed is to be found only in the knower, and not, except derivatively, in the known; and this is the essence of an idealistic epistemology."

the structure of experience is discovered in experience, by analysis. In other
words Tillich's language implies the Kantian critical philosophy, while his
analysis implies an epistemological realism.*

Tillich distinguishes four levels of ontological concepts: (1) the basic ontological structure; (2) the "elements" constituting that structure; (3) the characteristics or being which are the conditions of existence, or "existential being;" and (4) the categories of being and knowing.[4] We shall discuss each of
these in order.

i. The basic ontological structure

The basic starting point for ontology, in Tillich's thought, is the self-world
correlation. The ontological question, "what is being?" presupposes an asking
"subject" and an object about which the question is asked; it presupposes the
subject-object structure of being. This in turn presupposes the self-world
structure as the basic articulation of being; being is man encountering the
world. This logically and experientially precedes all other structure.[5]

(1) Man, self and world

Man experiences himself as having a world to which he belongs, and it is
from the analysis of this polar relationship between man and the world that
the basic ontological structure is derived. Since man is estranged from nature,
and is unable to understand it in the way he understands man—he does not
know what men's behavior means to men—the principles which constitute the
universe must be sought in man himself. Following Heidegger's <u>Sein und Zeit</u>,
Tillich finds "being there" (<u>Dasein</u>)—the place where the structure of being is
manifest—given to man within himself. "Man is able to answer the ontological

---

* In criticizing Tillich at
this point Randall has
said: "The Kantian lan-
guage hardly seems essen-
tial to Tillich's position, or
even indeed, ultimately
compatible with it. The
structure of experience is
discovered in experience,
by analysis; it is recog-
nized within the process
of experiencing. Why
then call it a presupposition, which suggests that it
is brought to experience
from elsewhere?" (Ran-
dall, Art. (1952), 151).

---

4. Randall, "Ontology," p. 152: "Tillich distinguishes four levels of ontological concepts:
(1) the basic ontological structure; (2) the 'elements' constituting that structure; (3) the characteristics of being which are the conditions of existence, or 'existential being'; and (4) the categories
of being and knowing."

5. Randall, "Ontology," p. 152: "The ontological question, 'What is being?' presupposes an
asking 'subject' and an 'object' about which the question is asked; it presupposes the subject-object
structure of being. This in turn presupposes the self-world structure as the basic articulation of
being: being is man encountering the world. This logically and experientially precedes all other
structures."

question himself because he experiences directly and immediately the structure of being and its elements."* Tillich makes it palpably clear that this approach does not mean that it is easier to get a knowledge of man "sufficient for our purposes" than a knowledge of nonhuman objects. It means rather that man is aware of the structures which make cognition possible. Being is revealed not in objects, but in "the conditions necessary for knowing." "The truth of all ontological concepts is their power of expressing that which makes the subject-object structure possible. They constitute this structure."†[6]

Being a self means that man is both subject and object. He is a subject in the sense that he is so separated from everything as to be able to look at it and act upon it. He is object in the sense that he so belongs to the world, that he is an intimate part of the process. But each factor determines the other. It is wrong to assume that the environment wholly explains behavior.[7]

> The mistake of all theories which explain the behavior of a being in terms of environment alone is that they fail to explain the special character of the environment in terms of the special character of the being which has such an environment. Self and environment determine each other.‡

Moreover, because man has an ego-self,§ he transcends every possible spatio-temporal environment. His "world" cannot be thought of simply as an aggre-

---

* Tillich, ST, I, 169.
† Tillich, ST, I, 169.
‡ Tillich, ST, I, 170.
§ In speaking of man as an ego-self Tillich means that man possesses self-consciousness, in contrast to other beings who are not fully developed selves. He writes, "selfhood or self-centeredness must be attributed in some measure to all living beings, and in terms of analogy, to all individual Gestalten even in the inorganic realm. . . . Man is a fully developed and completely centered self. He 'possesses' himself in the form of self-consciousness. He has an ego-self." (ST, I, 169, 170).

---

6. Randall, "Ontology," p. 152: "Man experiences himself as having a world to which he belongs, and it is from the analysis of this polar relationship between man and the world that the basic ontological structure is derived. Since man is estranged from nature, and is unable to understand it in the way he understands man—he does not know what the behavior of things means to them, as he does know what men's behavior means to men—the principles which constitute the universe must be sought in man himself. Following Heidegger's Sein und Zeit, Tillich finds 'being there' (Dasein)—the place where the structure of being is manifest—given to man within himself. 'Man is able to answer the ontological question himself because he experiences directly and immediately the structure of being and its elements' within himself. This does not mean that it is easier to get a knowledge of man 'sufficient for our purposes' than a knowledge of nonhuman objects. . . . It means that man is aware of 'the structure that makes cognition possible,' the conditions of knowing. Being is revealed, not in objects, but in 'the conditions necessary for knowing.' 'The truth of all ontological concepts is their power of expressing that which makes the subject-object structure possible. They constitute this structure' (169)."

7. Roberts, "Tillich's Doctrine of Man," p. 115: "Being a self means that man is both over against the world, as a subject, and in the world, as an object. He is so separated from everything as to be able to look at it and act upon it; he so belongs to the world that he is an episode in the process. But each factor determines the other. It is wrong to assume that the environment wholly explains behavior."

gate containing everything that exists; it is an organized structure, and the organizing reflects the self. In short the self-world correlation includes not only the environment in which man lives, but the universal norms and ideas by means of which man apprehends and interprets. Every content, psychic as well as bodily, is within the world, otherwise the self would be an empty form. But man is so differentiated from the world that he can look at it as an organized whole; otherwise he would be completely immersed in the flux.*[8]

Tillich is convinced that this starting point avoids the notorious pitfalls of those philosophical systems which attempt to generate the world from the ego, or the ego from the world; it also avoids, he contends, the dilemma of Cartesian dualism which has to try to unite an empty <u>res cogitans</u> with a mechanistically conceived <u>res extensa</u>. In so far as it is thought about, everything (including even God) is an object; but in so far as everything involves individual self-relatedness, nothing (not even an atom) is merely an object.†[9]

(2) The logical and the
ontological object

Within the self-world polarity are to be found the derivative polarities of objective and subjective reason, of logical object and subject. Pure objects, "things," are completely conditioned or <u>bedingt</u> by the scheme of knowing. But man himself is not a "thing" or merely an object. He is a self and therefore a bearer of subjectivity. He is never bound completely to an environment.[10]

---

* Tillich, ST, I, 170.
† Tillich, ST, I, 170, 173–174.

---

8. Roberts, "Tillich's Doctrine of Man," pp. 115–116: "Moreover, because of self-consciousness man transcends every possible spatiotemporal environment. His 'world' cannot be thought of simply as an aggregate containing everything that exists; it is an organized structure, and the organizing reflects the self. In short, the self-world correlation includes not only the environment in which man lives, but the universal norms and ideas by means of which man apprehends and interprets. Every content, psychic as well as bodily, is within the world; otherwise the self would be an empty form. But man is so differentiated from the world that he can look at it as an organized whole, otherwise he would be completely immersed in the flux."

9. Roberts, "Tillich's Doctrine of Man," p. 116: "This starting-point avoids the notorious pitfalls involved in trying to generate the world from the *ego*, or the *ego* from the world; it also avoids the dilemma of Cartesian dualism which has to try to unite an empty *res cogitans* with a mechanistically conceived *res extensa*. In so far as it is thought about, everything (including even God) is an object; but in so far as everything involves individual self-relatedness, nothing (not even an atom) is *merely* an object."

10. Randall, "Ontology," p. 153: "It is within this polarity that are to be found the derivative polarities of objective and subjective reason, of logical object and subject. Pure objects, 'things,' are completely conditioned or *bedingt* by the scheme of knowing. But man himself is not a 'thing' or object: he is never bound completely to an environment." The following quotation appears verbatim in Randall, "Ontology," p. 153.

He always transcends it by grasping and shaping it according to universal norms and ideas. . . . This is the reason why ontology cannot begin with things and try to derive the structure of reality from them. That which is completely conditioned, which has no selfhood and subjectivity, cannot explain self and subject. . . . It is just as impossible to derive the subject from the object. . . . This trick of deductive idealism is the precise counterpart of the trick of reductive naturalism. . . . The relation is one of polarity. The basic ontological structure cannot be derived. It must be accepted.*

This analysis of the "basic ontological structure," in which Tillich is following Heidegger, assumes without question that the epistemological "subject-object distinction" is absolutely ultimate, not only for knowledge, but for being: It is not only "prior to us," but also "prior in nature," as Aristotle puts it.†[11]

ii. The ontological elements

The second level of ontological analysis deals with those "ontological elements" which constitute the basic structure of being. Unlike the categories, these elements are polar: each is meaningful only in relation to its opposite pole.[13] "One can imagine a realm of nature beside or outside the realm of history, but there is no realm of dynamics without form or of individuality without universality."‡ There are three outstanding pairs which constitute the basic ontological structure; individuality and universality, dynamics and form, freedom and destiny. Each of these distinctions is discovered in the self's ex-

---

* Tillich, ST, I, 170, 173–174.
† Randall has made a very sound criticism of Tillich's analysis of the basic ontological structure. He argues that there are two conflicting strands running through Tillich's thought at this point. At times, Randall affirms, Tillich follows Heidegger's idealistic ontology in looking for the structure of being in man. At other times he holds that the structure of being is found by man in his encounters with the world.[12] This, Randall contends, is a quite different ontology from that of idealism it is something of an empirical naturalism. And so Randall concludes that "it would be clarifying to have Tillich decide which position he is really maintaining—idealism; or an experiential and functional realism."
‡ Tillich, ST, I, 165.

---

11. Randall, "Ontology," p. 153: "This analysis of 'the basic ontological structure,' in which Tillich is following Heidegger, assumes without question that the epistemological 'subject-object distinction' is absolutely ultimate, not only for knowledge, but for all being: It is not only 'prior for us,' but also 'prior in nature,' as Aristotle puts it."

12. Randall, "Ontology," p. 154: "At times he follows Heidegger in looking for the structure of being 'in man.' . . . But at other times Tillich, following his own insights rather than another's thought, holds that the structure of being is found *by* man *in* his encounters with the world."

13. Randall, "Ontology," p. 154: "The second level of ontological analysis deals with those 'ontological elements' which constitute the basic structure of being. Unlike the categories, these elements are polar: each is meaningful only in relation to its opposite pole."

perience of the world, and then generalized for all interactions within being.[14]
The first element in each of these polarities expresses the "self-relatedness of being," i.e., its power of being something for itself. The second element expresses the "belongingness of being," i.e., its character of being a part of a universe of being.*[15]

(1) Individuality and participation

Individualization is a quality of everything that exists; "it is implied in and constitutive of every self, which means that at least in an analogous way it is implied in and constitutive of every being."†[16] To be a self is to be an individual. Selfhood and individualization may be different conceptually, but they are inseparable actually.‡[17] To be is to be an individual. But man's individualization is not absolute or complete. It gains meaning only in its polar relation with participation. Leibniz emphasizes this point when he speaks of the microcosmic structure of the monad.§ Whitehead sets it forth when he speaks of the "prehension" of the whole by the actual occasion.‖ Martin Buber emphasizes this role of participation in the process of individualization when he sets forth the role of the "thou" in the development of the "I".[18] Each of these thinkers gives backing to what Tillich is attempting to say, namely, that individuation implies participation. Man participates in the universe through the rational structure of mind and reality. When individualization reaches the perfect form we call a "person," participation reaches the perfect form we call

---

* Tillich, ST, I, 165.   par. 62.
† Tillich, ST, I, 175.   ‖ Whitehead, AOI, 300.
‡ Tillich, ST, I, 175.
§ Leibniz, <u>Monadology</u>,

---

14. Randall, "Ontology," p. 154: "There are three outstanding pairs: individuality and universality or participation, dynamics and form, and freedom and destiny. These distinctions are discovered in the self's experience of the world, and then generalized for all interactions within being."

15. Tillich, *Systematic Theology*, p. 165: "In these three polarities the first element expresses the self-relatedness of being, its power of being something for itself, while the second element expresses the belongingness of being, its character of being a part of a universe of being."

16. Randall, "Ontology," p. 154: "Individualization is a quality of everything: 'it is implied in and constitutive of every self, which means that at least in an analogous way it is implied in and constitutive of every being.'"

17. Tillich, *Systematic Theology*, p. 175: "Selfhood and individualization are different conceptually, but actually they are inseparable."

18. Boozer, "Place of Reason," p. 244: "But man's individualization is not absolute or complete. The element of participation is in polar relation with individualization. Leibniz speaks of the microcosmic structure of the monad. Whitehead speaks of the 'prehension' of the whole by the actual occasion. Both indicate the element of participation. Martin Buber emphasizes the role of the 'thou' in the development of the 'I.'"

"communion." Persons become persons only by participating in society. It is only in the communion of personal encounter that persons can grow. Participation is essential for the individual.[19] "Without individualization nothing would exist to be related. Without participation the category of relation would have no basis in reality."*[20]

It is clear from the foregoing that Tillich is not interested in slanting such statements either in the idealistic or in the naturalistic direction. But it is especially important to recognize that he does not regard them as being derived from empirical observation concerning contingent facts. Rather, he conceives of individualization and participation as ontological elements which, in the course of a critical analysis of experience, reveal themselves to be a priori in the sense that experience could not be what it is unless it occurred within them. The reciprocal relationship between "personal" and "communal"—for example, one cannot become fully a self except in relation with other selves— is a structural characteristic of being. In the polarity of individualization and participation Tillich finds a solution to the endless problem of nominalism and realism.[21] Individuals are real, but they participate in the universal structure, which, however, is not some sort of second reality lying behind empirical reality.†

(2) Dynamics and form

Being something means having a form. Whatever loses its form loses its being. But every form forms something, and this something Tillich calls "dynamics." The concept of dynamics is a very complex one with many connotations. Its complexity is due to the fact that it cannot be thought of as something that is; and yet it cannot be thought of as something that is not.

---

* Tillich, ST, I, 177.
† Tillich, ST, I, 178.

---

19. Tillich, *Systematic Theology*, pp. 176–177: "Man participates in the universe through the rational structure of mind and reality. . . . When individualization reaches the perfect form which we call a 'person,' participation reaches the perfect form which we call 'communion.' . . . Participation is essential for the individual, not accidental. . . . Persons can grow only in the communion of personal encounter."

20. Boozer quoted this passage from Tillich ("Place of Reason," p. 244).

21. Roberts, "Tillich's Doctrine of Man," p. 116: "It is clear from the foregoing that Tillich is not interested in slanting such statements either in an idealistic or in a naturalistic direction. But it is especially important to recognize that he does not regard them as deriving from empirical observation concerning contingent facts. Rather, he conceives of individualization and participation as ontological elements which, in the course of a critical analysis of experience, reveal themselves to be a priori in the sense that experience could not be what it is unless it occurred within them. The reciprocal relationship between 'personal' and 'communal'—for example, one cannot become fully a self except in relation with other selves—is a structural characteristic of *being*. The polarity between individualization and participation also solves the problem of nominalism and realism."

Dynamics is the "me on," the potentiality of being, which is nonbeing in contrast to pure nonbeing.* This polar element to form appears as the <u>Urgrund</u> of Böhme, the will of Schopenhauer, the "will to power" of Nietzsche, the "unconscious" of Hartmann and Freud, the <u>elan vital</u> of Bergson. Each of these concepts points symbolically to what cannot be named literally. "If it could be named properly it would be a formed being beside others instead of an ontological element in contrast with the element of pure form."†[22]

The polarity of dynamics and form appears in man as vitality and intentionality. "Vitality is the power which keeps a living being alive and growing."‡ It is not an existing something such as "will" or the "unconscious;" it is rather the power of being. By intentionality, on the other hand, Tillich does not necessarily mean consciously conceived purpose; but he does mean structures that can be grasped as universals. In other words, when vitality becomes human it cannot be thought of as operating by necessity, or chaotically, or without reference to objective structures.§[23]

The inclusion of dynamism within the ontological structure of human nature is Tillich's answer to historical relativism, which denies the possibility of an ontological or a theological doctrine of man because "human nature" connotes to them something static. Tillich willingly admits with process philosophy that human nature changes in history, but he insists that one structural characteristic underlies all these changes; namely, "being one who has a history."[24]

---

* Tillich, ST, I, 179.
† Tillich, ST, I, 179.
‡ Tillich, ST, I, 180.
§ Tillich, ST, I, 181.

---

22. Randall, "Ontology," pp. 154–155: "Being something means having a form. But every form forms something, and this something Tillich calls 'dynamics'—a rather unfortunate term. 'Dynamics' is the '*me on*, the potentiality of being, which is nonbeing in contrast to things that have a form, and the power of being in contrast to pure nonbeing' (179). This element polar to form appears as the *Urgrund* of Böhme, the 'will' of Schopenhauer, the 'will to power' of Nietzsche, the 'unconscious' of Hartmann and Freud, the *élan vital* of Bergson. Each of these concepts points symbolically to what cannot be named literally. 'If it could be named properly, it would be a formed being beside others instead of an ontological element in contrast with the element of pure form' (179)."

23. Roberts, "Tillich's Doctrine of Man," p. 117: "Another polarity, that of dynamics and form, appears in man as vitality and intentionality. . . . 'Potentiality,' in this sense, is not an existing something, such as 'will' or 'the unconscious'; it is rather the *power* of being. By 'intentionality,' on the other hand, Tillich does not necessarily mean consciously conceived purpose; but he does mean structures that can be grasped as universals. In other words, when vitality becomes human it cannot be thought of as operating by necessity, or chaotically, or without reference to objective structures."

24. Roberts, "Tillich's Doctrine of Man," p. 117: "The inclusion of dynamism within the ontological structure of human nature is Tillich's answer to those who eschew all talk about human 'nature' because it connotes to them something static. He willingly admits that human nature changes in history, but he insists that one structural characteristic underlies all these changes; namely, 'being one who has a history.'"

This structure is the subject of an ontological and theological doctrine of man. Historical man is a descendant of beings who had no history, and perhaps there will be beings who are descendants of historical man who have no history, But neither animals nor supermen are the objects of a doctrine of man.*[25]

Change is just as real as structure; but it is absurd to regard the latter as process, because this would mean that there could be no continuity, within the life of man, between antecedent and subsequent conditions. Consequently, man can develop indefinitely beyond any given physical and biological situation, transforming both nature and himself through applied science and cultural growth; but he cannot slough off the structure which makes intentionality and historicity possible.†[26]

(3) Freedom and destiny

The third ontological polarity which Tillich discusses is that of freedom and destiny. Here the description of the basic ontological structure and its elements reaches both its fulfilment and its turning point. Ordinarily one thinks of necessity as the correlate of freedom. However, necessity is a category and not an element. Its contrast is possibility, not freedom.[27]

> Whenever freedom and necessity are set over against each other, necessity is understood in terms of mechanistic determinacy and freedom is thought of in terms of indeterministic contingency. Neither of these interpretations grasps the structure of being as it is experienced immediately in the one being who has the possibility of experiencing because he is free, that is, in man.‡

The problem of freedom is traditionally posed in terms of mechanistic determinism versus indeterminism. But Tillich asserts that neither of these theo-

---

* Tillich, ST, I, 181, 182.
† Tillich, ST, I, 181, 182.
‡ Tillich, ST, I, 182.

---

25. The citation and text are inaccurate. The last sentence begins, "This simply means that neither animals nor supermen" (Tillich, *Systematic Theology*, p. 167). The inaccurate quotation appears verbatim in Randall ("Ontology," p. 151).

26. Roberts, "Tillich's Doctrine of Man," p. 117: "Change is just as real as structure; but it is absurd to regard the latter as process, because this would mean that there could be no continuity, within the life of a man, between antecedent and subsequent conditions. Consequently, man can develop indefinitely beyond any given physical and biological situation, transforming both nature and himself through applied science and cultural growth; but he cannot slough off the structure which makes intentionality and historicity possible."

27. Tillich, *Systematic Theology*, p. 182: "The third ontological polarity is that of freedom and destiny, in which the description of the basic ontological structure and its elements reaches both its fulfilment and its turning point. . . . Ordinarily one speaks of freedom and necessity. However, necessity is a category and not an element. Its contrast is possibility, not freedom."

ries does justice to the way in which man grasps his own ontological structure. Both of these conflicting parties presuppose that there is a thing called "will" which possesses a certain quality, namely freedom. So long as the problem is posed in this manner, determinism always wins; for by definition a <u>thing</u> is always completely determined.[28] "The freedom of a thing is a contradiction in terms."* Thus indeterminism, in a blundering attempt to defend man's moral and cognitive capacities, is forced to postulate decision without motivation; for at the level of things a break in the causal nexus can occur only as something uncaused. Needless to say, when the indeterminist holds out for the latter his defense of man's moral and cognitive capacities is not convincing; for he rests his case upon the occurrence of unintelligible accident, which is at the opposite pole from the "responsibility" he is trying to characterize. However, both theories fall into contraction when they claim to be true, for the grasping of truth presupposes an intelligible decision against the false as a possibility. Mechanistic determinism cannot make room for decision, and indeterminism cannot make room for intelligibility.†[29]

Freedom must be approached, therefore, not as a quality of a faculty called the will, but as an element in man's ontological structure.[30] We must not speak of the freedom of a function (the "will"), but of man.[31] This means that every part and every function which constitutes man a personal self participates in his freedom.[32]

---

* Tillich, ST, I, 183.
† Tillich, ST, I, 183.

---

28. Roberts, "Tillich's Doctrine of Man," p. 117: "The problem of freedom is often posed in terms of mechanistic determinism versus indeterminism. But Tillich asserts that neither of these theories does justice to the way in which man grasps his own ontological structure. Both of them treat the will as though it were a thing, and then disagree about whether it possesses a certain quality; namely, freedom. So long as the problem is posed in this manner, determinism always wins; by definition, a thing is completely determined."

29. Roberts, "Tillich's Doctrine of Man," pp. 117–118: "Thus indeterminism, in a blundering attempt to defend man's moral and cognitive capacities, is forced to postulate decision without motivation; for at the level of things a break in the causal nexus can occur only as something uncaused. Needless to say, when the indeterminist holds out for the latter his defense of man's moral and cognitive capacities is not convincing; for he rests his case upon the occurrence of unintelligible accident, which is at the opposite pole from the 'responsibility' he is trying to characterize. However, both theories fall into contradiction when they claim to be true, for the grasping of truth presupposes an intelligible decision against the false as a possibility. Mechanistic determinism cannot make room for decision, and indeterminism cannot make room for intelligibility."

30. Roberts, "Tillich's Doctrine of Man," p. 118: "Freedom should be approached, therefore, not as the quality of a faculty (the will), but as an element in man's ontological structure."

31. Tillich, *Systematic Theology*, p. 183: "Freedom is not the freedom of a function (the 'will') but of man."

32. Roberts, "Tillich's Doctrine of Man," p. 118: "This means that every function which plays a part in constituting man as personal also participates in his freedom."

Freedom is experienced as deliberation, decision, and responsibility. Deliberation points to an act of weighing motives. The person doing the weighing is always above the motives that are weighed.[33] "To say that the stronger motive always prevails is an empty tautology, since the test by which a motive is proved stronger is simply that it prevails."* The self-centered person does the weighting and then reacts with his whole self. This reaction is called decision. Etymologically the word "decision" like the word "incision" involves the image of cutting. In this context decision means cutting off possibilities. The person who does the cutting is always beyond what he cuts off.[34] Responsibility is the obligation that every individual has to give an answer for the decision he has made. Hence the self is responsible in so far as its acts are determined, not by something external or by some dissociated segment or function, but by the centered totality of the person's being.

Freedom, as thus defined, goes hand and hand with destiny.[35] Destiny is the basis of freedom and freedom participates in destiny.† The concrete self out of which decisions arise must not be thought of merely as a center of self-consciousness. Decisions issue from a self which has been formed by nature and history; the self includes bodily structures, psychic strivings, moral and spiritual character, communal relations, past experiences, (both remembered and forgotten), and the total impact of environment. Yet having a destiny does not contradict freedom, as "fate" does, because persons can realize their destinies. If man were subject to fate, there would be no point in talking about accepting or rejecting it, inasmuch as the alternative would disappear.‡

The polarity between freedom and destiny distinguishes man from all other levels of existence, yet this distinction arises within continuity.[37]

---

* Tillich, ST, I, 184.
† Destiny for Tillich is not some strange power that determines us. "It is myself as given, formed by nature, history and myself." (ST, I, 195).[36]
‡ Tillich, ST, I, 185.

---

33. Tillich, *Systematic Theology*, p. 184: "Freedom is experienced as deliberation, decision, and responsibility. . . . Deliberation points to an act of weighing (*librare*) arguments and motives. The person who does the weighing is above the motives."

34. Tillich, *Systematic Theology*, p. 184: "The self-centered person does the weighing and reacts as a whole, through his personal center, to the struggle of the motives. This reaction is called 'decision.' The word 'decision,' like the word 'incision,' involves the image of cutting. A decision cuts off possibilities. . . . The person who does the 'cutting' or the 'excluding' must be beyond what he cuts off or excludes."

35. Roberts, "Tillich's Doctrine of Man," p. 118: "Hence the self is responsible in so far as its acts are determined, not by something external or by some dissociated segment or function, but by the centered totality of the person's being. Freedom, as thus defined, goes hand in hand with destiny."

36. The correct citation is Tillich, *Systematic Theology*, p. 185.

37. Roberts, "Tillich's Doctrine of Man," pp. 118–119: "The concrete self out of which decisions arise must not be thought of merely as a center of self-consciousness. Decisions issue from a self which has been formed by nature and history; the self includes bodily structure, psychic

Since freedom and destiny constitute an ontological polarity, everything that
participates in being must participate in this polarity. But man, who has a complete self and a world, is the only being who is free in the sense of deliberation, and decision, and responsibility. Therefore, freedom and destiny can be applied to subhuman nature only by way of analogy; this parallels the situation with respect to the basic ontological structure and the other ontological polarities.*[38]

iii. Being and finitude

The third level of ontological concepts expresses the characteristics of being which are conditions of existence, and the difference between "existential being" and "essential being." This duality of essential and existential being is found both in experience and in analysis.[39]

There is no ontology which can disregard these two aspects, whether they are hypostasized into two realms (Plato), or combined in the polar relation of potentiality and actuality (Aristotle), or contrasted with each other (Schelling II, Kierkegaard, Heidegger), or derived from each other, either existence from essence (Spinoza, Hegel), or essence from existence (Dewey, Sartre).†[40]

Freedom as such is not the basis of existence, but rather freedom is unity with finitude. "Finite freedom is the turning point from being to existence." ‡ Finitude is hence the center of Tillich's analysis, for it is the finitude of existent being which drives men to the question of God.[41]

---

* Tillich, ST, I, 185.
† Tillich, ST, I, 165.
‡ Tillich, ST, I, 165.

---

strivings, moral and spiritual character, communal relations, past experiences (both remembered and forgotten), and the total impact of the environment. Yet having a destiny does not contradict freedom, as 'fate' does, because persons can realize their destinies. If man were subject to fate, there would be no point in talking about accepting or rejecting it, inasmuch as the *alternative* would disappear. The polarity between freedom and destiny distinguishes man from all other levels of existence, yet this distinction arises within continuity."

38. On a draft of this chapter, Schilling noted: "Inaccurately quoted. This passage varies considerably from the actual text" (King, Draft of chapter 3, 1954–1955, MLKP-MBU: Box 96A; see Calendar of Documents, no. 550000-096). King corrected the quotation.

39. Tillich, *Systematic Theology*, p. 165: "The third level of ontological concepts expresses the power of being to exist and the difference between essential and existential being. Both in experience and in analysis being manifests the duality of essential and existential being."

40. Randall quoted this passage from Tillich ("Ontology," p. 156).

41. Randall, "Ontology," p. 156: "Freedom as such is not the basis of existence, but rather freedom in unity with finitude. Finite freedom is the turning point from being to existence. Finitude is hence the center of Tillich's analysis, for it is the finitude of existent being which drives men to the question of God."

(1) Being and nonbeing

The problem of nonbeing brings us face to face with one of the most diffi-cult aspects of Tillich's thought. He agrees with Heidegger that the logical act of negating presupposes an ontological basis.[42] Man

> must be separated from his being in a way which enables him to look at it as something strange and questionable. And such a separation is actual because man participates not only in being but also in nonbeing. . . . It is not by chance that historically the recent discovery on the ontological question has been guided by pre-Socratic philosophy and that systematically there has been an overwhelm-ing emphasis on the problem of nonbeing.*

The problem cannot be solved simply by excluding nonbeing. For, as Par-menides' efforts show, this means that not only "nothing," but also the totality of finite existence, is excluded, leaving only static Being.†[43] The Platonists distinguished between the ouk on which means "nothing at all," and the me on which meant for them that which does not yet have being but can become being if united with ideas.[44] The mystery of nonbeing was not, however, re-moved, for in spite of its nothingness it had a positive power of resisting the ideas.‡[45] The Christian doctrine of creatio ex nihilo attempts to solve the problem by denying that there is a second principle coeternal with God; but it affirms that there is an element of nonbeing in all finite existence. Tillich denies that when Augustine attributes sin to nonbeing he is following a purely privative theory; rather Augustine is asserting that although sin has no posi-tive ontological status it nevertheless actively resists and perverts being. In-deed, since anything created originated out of nothing, it must return to noth-ing. This is why any view which regards the Son as a creature (Arianism) had to be rejected by the church on the ground that a creature cannot bring eter-

---

* Tillich, ST, I, 187.
† Tillich, ST, I, 186.
‡ Tillich, ST, I, 188.

---

42. Roberts, "Tillich's Doctrine of Man," p. 119: "He agrees with Heidegger that the logical act of negating presupposes an ontological basis."

43. Roberts, "Tillich's Doctrine of Man," p. 119: "The problem cannot be solved simply by excluding nonbeing. For, as Parmenides' efforts show, this means that not only 'nothing,' but also the totality of finite existence, is excluded, leaving only static Being."

44. Randall, "Ontology," p. 156: "The Platonists distinguished between the ουκ ον which means 'nothing at all,' and the μη ον which meant for them that which does not yet have being but can become being if united with ideas."

45. Tillich, Systematic Theology, p. 188: "The mystery of nonbeing was not, however, removed, for in spite of its 'nothingness' nonbeing was credited with having the power of resisting a com-plete union with the ideas."

nal life. And this is why Christianity rejects the doctrine of natural immortality in favor of the belief that eternal life is given by God alone.*[46]

Tillich concludes that the dialectical problem of nonbeing is inescapable. It is a problem of finitude. Finitude involves a mixture of being and nonbeing.[47] "Man's finitude, or creatureliness, is unintelligible without the concept of dialectical nonbeing."†

(2) The finite and the infinite

Now, being when limited by nonbeing is finitude. Finitude is "the 'not yet' and 'no more' of being."‡ Everything which participates in the power of being is mixed with nonbeing. It is finite. The basic ontological structure and the elements constituting that structure all imply finitude.[48] "To be something is not to be something else. To be here and now in the process of becoming is not to be there and then. . . . To be something is to be finite."§ Experienced on the human level, finitude is nonbeing as the threat to being, ultimately the threat of death.[49] Yet in order to experience his finitude, man must look at himself as a potential infinity.[50] In grasping his life as a whole as moving toward death, he transcends temporal immediacy. He sees his world in the setting of potential infinity, his participation in the setting of potential univer-

---

* Tillich, ST, I, 188.
† Tillich, ST, I, 189.
‡ Tillich, ST, I, 189.
§ Tillich, ST, I, 190.

---

46. Roberts, "Tillich's Doctrine of Man," pp. 119–120: "The Christian doctrine of *creatio ex nihilo* attempts to solve the problem by denying that there is a second principle co-eternal with God; but it affirms that there is an element of nonbeing in all finite existence. Tillich denies that when Augustine attributes sin to nonbeing he is following a purely privative theory; rather, Augustine is asserting that although sin has no positive ontological status it nevertheless *actively* resists and perverts being. Indeed, since anything created originates out of nothing, it must return to nothing. This is why any view which regards the Son as a creature (Arianism) had to be rejected by the Church on the ground that a creature cannot bring eternal life. And this is why Christianity rejects the doctrine of natural immortality in favor of the belief that eternal life is given by God alone."

47. Tillich, *Systematic Theology*, p. 189: "The dialectical problem of nonbeing is inescapable. It is the problem of finitude. Finitude unites being with dialectical nonbeing."

48. Tillich, *Systematic Theology*, pp. 189–190: "Being, limited by nonbeing, is finitude. Nonbeing appears as the 'not yet' of being and as the 'no more' of being. . . . However, everything which participates in the power of being is 'mixed' with nonbeing. . . . It is finite. Both the basic ontological structure and the ontological elements imply finitude."

49. Randall, "Ontology," p. 157: "Experienced on the human level, finitude is nonbeing as the threat to being, ultimately the threat of death."

50. Tillich, *Systematic Theology*, p. 190: "In order to experience his finitude, man must look at himself from the point of view of a potential infinity."

sality, his destiny in the setting of potential all-inclusiveness. This power of transcending makes man aware of his own finitude, and at the same time marks him as belonging to Being itself. The latter kinship is shown by the fact that man is never satisfied with any stage of his development; nothing finite can hold him.*[51]

From the foregoing it is clearly seen that infinity is related to finitude in a different way than the other polar elements are related to one another. Infinitude is defined by the dynamic and free self-transcendence of finite being.[52] "Infinity is a directing concept, not a constituting concept. It directs the mind to experience its own unlimited potentialities, but it does not establish the existence of an infinite being."†

Finitude is the ontological basis of human anxiety. Therefore anxiety is as omnipresent as is finitude. As such it must be distinguished from fear which is directed toward definite objects and can be removed by action.‡[53] Anxiety cannot be overcome by action, for no finite being can conquer its finitude. Anxiety is ontological; fear is psychological.[55] Like Kierkegaard and Heidegger, Tillich regards anxiety as directed toward "nothingness." Though ineradicable, it can be accepted and used creatively as a part of what it means to be human.[56]

---

* Tillich, ST, I, 191.
† Tillich, ST, I, 190.
‡ Tillich stresses the point that psychotheraphy has the power of removing compulsory forms of anxiety and can reduce the frequency and intensity of fears, but never can it remove ontological anxiety, because it cannot change the structure of finitude.[54]

---

51. Roberts, "Tillich's Doctrine of Man," p. 120: "In grasping his life as a whole as moving toward death, he transcends temporal immediacy. He sees his world in the setting of potential infinity, his participation in the setting of potential universality, his destiny in the setting of potential all-inclusiveness. This power of transcending makes man aware of his own finitude, and at the same time marks him as belonging to Being itself. The latter kinship is shown by the fact that man is never satisfied with any stage of his development; nothing finite can hold him."

52. Tillich, *Systematic Theology*, p. 190: "According to this analysis, infinity is related to finitude in a different way than the other polar elements are related to one another. As the negative character of the word indicates, it is defined by the dynamic and free self-transcendence of finite being."

53. Roberts, "Tillich's Doctrine of Man," p. 120: "Finitude is the ontological basis of human anxiety. . . . As such it must be distinguished, of course, from fear, which is directed toward definite objects and can be overcome by action."

54. Tillich, *Systematic Theology*, p. 191n.7: "Psychotherapy cannot remove ontological anxiety, because it cannot change the structure of finitude. But it can remove compulsory forms of anxiety and can reduce the frequency and intensity of fears."

55. Tillich, *Systematic Theology*, p. 191: "Fear can be conquered by action. Anxiety cannot, for no finite being can conquer its finitude. . . . Anxiety is ontological; fear, psychological."

56. Roberts, "Tillich's Doctrine of Man," pp. 120–121: "Like Kierkegaard and Heidegger, Tillich regards *Urangst* as directed toward 'nothingness.' Though ineradicable, it can be accepted and used creatively as a part of what it means to be human."

The fourth level of ontological concepts consists of the categories. They "are the forms in which the mind grasps and shapes reality."* But they are not mere logical forms, related only indirectly to reality; they are ontological, and therefore present in everything.[57] "They appear implicitly or explicitly in every thought concerning God and the world, man and nature. They are omnipresent, even in the realm from which they are excluded by definition, that is, in the realm of the 'unconditional.'"†

For theological purposes Tillich finds four main categories that must be analyzed: time, space, causality, and substance. The traditional categories of quantity and quality have no direct theological significance, and therefore are not discussed. Categories (or rather concepts which have been called categories) like movement and rest or unity and manifoldness were treated implicitly in connection with the ontological elements, movement and rest in connection with dynamics and form, unity and manifoldness in connection with individuality and universality.‡[58]

The four categories are analyzed in the light of human finitude. Externally regarded, these categories express the union of being and nonbeing. Internally regarded, they express the union of anxiety and courage.§ The latter aspect of the interpretation must not be misunderstood as psychological. In accordance with the self-world correlation, the subjective side of the analysis is just as much a piece of ontology as is the objective.[60]

---

* Tillich, ST, I, 192.
† Tillich, ST, I, 191.
‡ Tillich argues that it is inaccurate to speak of concepts like unity and manifoldness, movement and rest as categories. Their polar character, he contends, puts them on the level of the elements of the basic ontological structure and not on the level of the categories.[59]
§ Anxiety, as we have seen, has no object, or rather, in a paradoxical phrase, its object is the negation of every object. "Anxiety is the existential awareness of nonbeing." (CTB, 33). Courage, for Tillich, is self-affirmation in spite of that which tends to hinder the self from affirming itself.

---

57. Randall, "Ontology," p. 157: "The fourth level of ontological concepts consists of the categories. They are 'the forms in which the mind grasps and shapes reality.' But they are not mere logical forms, only indirectly related to reality itself; they are ontological, present in everything."

58. Tillich, Systematic Theology, pp. 165–166: "From the theological point of view four main categories must be analyzed: time, space, causality, and substance. Categories like quantity and quality have no direct theological significance and are not especially discussed. Other concepts which often have been called 'categories,' like movement and rest, or unity and manifoldness, are treated implicitly on the second level of analysis, movement and rest in connection with dynamics and form, unity and manifoldness in connection with individuality and universality."

59. Tillich, Systematic Theology, p. 166: "The polar character of these concepts puts them on the level of the elements of the basic ontological structure and not on the level of the categories."

60. Roberts, "Tillich's Doctrine of Man," p. 121: "Externally regarded, these categories express the union of being and nonbeing. Internally regarded, they express the union of anxiety

The discussion of each category leads to an antinomy where a decision concerning the meaning involved cannot be derived from an analysis of the category itself. This method has obvious similarities to Kant's, and it leads to a point at which, since metaphysics cannot solve the problem, an existential attitude (positive or negative) is unavoidable.[61]

(1) Time

Time is the central category of finitude. Like other categories time unites an affirmative and a negative element. Those philosophers who emphasize the negative element

> point to the movement of time from a past that is no more toward a future that is not yet through a present which is nothing more than the moving boundary line between past and present.*

Those who emphasize the positive element in time "have pointed to the creative character of the temporal process, to its directness and irreversibility, to the new produced within it."† Yet neither side of the analysis is entirely satisfactory. Time cannot be illusory because only if the present is real can past and future be linked together. But neither is it simply creative, inasmuch as it carries all things toward disintegration and obliteration.[62]

To this objective antinomy there corresponds an inward polarity between anxiety and courage. Temporality means, for man, the anxiety of having to die; this anxiety is potentially present in every moment and permeates the whole of man's being. Yet anxiety of this sort comes from the structure of being and is not due to sin. The anxieties due to sin are, in principle, remediable; but as we have already seen, the anxiety of finitude is ineradicable. It

---

* Tillich, ST, I, 193.
† Tillich, ST, I, 193.

---

and courage. The latter aspect of the interpretation must not be misunderstood as psychological. In accordance with the self-world correlation, the subjective side of the analysis is just as much a piece of ontology as is the objective."

61. Roberts, "Tillich's Doctrine of Man," p. 121: "The discussion of each category leads to an antinomy where a decision concerning the meaning involved cannot be derived from an analysis of the category itself. This method has obvious similarities to Kant's, and it leads to a point at which, since metaphysics cannot solve the problem, an existential attitude (positive or negative) is unavoidable."

62. Roberts, "Tillich's Doctrine of Man," p. 121: "Yet neither side of the analysis is entirely satisfactory. Time cannot be illusory because only if the present is real can past and future be linked together. But neither is it simply creative, inasmuch as it carries all things toward disintegration and obliteration."

is balanced, however, by a courage which affirms temporality.[63] "Without this courage man would surrender to the annihilating character of time; he would resign from having a present."*

(2) Space

The present implies space; time creates the present through its union with space. Space like time is subject to contradictory valuations, being a category of finitude. Moreover, space like time unites being with nonbeing, anxiety with courage. To be means to have space.[64] Space is interpreted, on the positive side, in terms of the fact that every being strives to maintain a "place" for himself.[65]

> This means above all a physical location—the body, a piece of soil, a home, a city, a country, the world. It also means a social "space"—a vocation, a sphere of influence, a group, a historical period, a place in rememberance and anticipation, a place within a structure of values and meanings.†

Not to have a place is not to be. Thus the continual striving for spatiality is an ontological necessity.[66]

On the negative side, however, it must be observed that no place is definitely one's own.[67] "No finite being can rely on space, for not only must it face losing this or that space because it is a 'pilgrim on earth,' but eventually it must face losing every place it has had or might have had."‡ This awareness of

---

* Tillich, ST, I, 194.
† Tillich, ST, I, 194.
‡ Tillich, ST, I, 195.

---

63. Roberts, "Tillich's Doctrine of Man," p. 121: "To this objective antinomy there corresponds an inward polarity between anxiety and courage. Temporality means, for man, the anxiety of having to die; this hangs over every moment and characterizes the whole of human existence. Yet anxiety of this sort comes from the structure of being and is not due to sin. . . . The anxieties due to sin are, in principle, remediable; but as we have already seen, the anxiety of finitude is ineradicable. It is balanced, however, by a courage which affirms temporality."

64. Tillich, *Systematic Theology*, p. 194: "The present implies space. Time creates the present through its union with space. . . . Like time, space unites being with nonbeing, anxiety with courage. Like time, space is subject to contradictory valuations, for it is a category of finitude. To be means to have space."

65. Roberts, "Tillich's Doctrine of Man," p. 122: "Space is interpreted, on the positive side, in terms of the fact that every being strives to maintain a 'place' for itself."

66. Tillich, *Systematic Theology*, p. 194: "Not to have space is not to be. Thus in all realms of life striving for space is an ontological necessity." Cf. Randall, "Ontology," p. 157.

67. Roberts, "Tillich's Doctrine of Man," p. 122: "But on the negative side it must be observed that no place is definitely one's own."

ultimate loss of spatiality means insecurity which goes hand and hand with finitude.[68] However this anxiety is balanced by the courage which affirms the present and space.[69] "Everything affirms the space which it has within the universe. . . . It accepts its ontological insecurity and reaches a security in this acceptance.*

(3) Causality

The affirmative interpretation of causality points to the power from which things proceed, the power which can produce and maintain realities despite the resistance of nonbeing. The negative interpretation notes, however, that finite things do not possess their own power of coming into being. They are contingent: as Heidegger says, they have been "thrown" into being.[70]

> The question, "Where from?" is universal. Children as well as philosophers ask it. But it cannot be answered, for every answer, every statement, about the cause of something is open to the same question in infinite regression. It cannot be stopped even by a god who is supposed to be the answer to the entire series. For this god must ask himself, "Where have I come from?"†

So it turns out that causality and contingent being are the same thing.[71] The anxiety in which man is aware of this situation is anxiety about his lack of aseity (the self-sufficiency possessed by God alone). Tillich's discussion of causality supports the thesis that human existence is not necessitated. If the latter were the case, man would be incapable of anxiety, and he could not ask questions based upon awareness of the fact that he "might not" be. So far as the present category is concerned, the answer to anxiety is a kind of courage

---

* Tillich, ST, I, 195.
† Tillich, ST, I, 196. Note that at this point Tillich is anticipating his main argument that God must be considered as Being-itself. If God is considered as a being then infinite regress cannot be avoided.

---

68. Roberts, "Tillich's Doctrine of Man," p. 122: "This means insecurity which goes hand in hand with finitude."

69. Tillich, *Systematic Theology*, p. 195: "On the other hand, man's anxiety about having to lose his space is balanced by the courage with which he affirms the present and, with it, space."

70. Roberts, "Tillich's Doctrine of Man," p. 122: "The affirmative interpretation of causality points to the power from which things proceed, the power which can produce and maintain realities despite the resistance of nonbeing. The negative interpretation notes, however, that finite things do not possess their own power of coming into being; they are 'thrown' into existence."

71. Tillich, *Systematic Theology*, p. 196: "In this respect causality and contingent being are the same thing."

which achieves self-reliance despite the inescapable facts of contingency and dependence.*[72]

(4) Substance

The category of substance, in its connection with human nature, has to do mainly with self-identity.[73] It points to something underlying the flux, something relatively static and self contained. But it is nothing beyond the accidents in which it expresses itself—it is no "I-Know-not-what."[74]

> The problem of substance is not avoided by philosophers of function or process, because questions about that which <u>has</u> functions or about that which <u>is</u> in process cannot be silenced. The replacement of static notions by dynamic ones does not remove the question of that which makes change possible by not (relatively) changing itself.†

Therefore all change threatens the ground on which one stands, and the radical change from life to death threatens an ultimate loss of self-identity. We cannot solve the problem by trying to attribute permanence to a creative work, a love relationship, and the like. Courage can match anxiety only by being able to affirm the significance of the finite despite the fact that it can lose its substance.[75]

Thus all four categories express the union of being (the positive) and nonbeing (the negative) in everything finite. But the ontological analysis can-

---

* Tillich, ST, I, 196, 197.
† Tillich, ST, I, 197.

---

72. Roberts, "Tillich's Doctrine of Man," pp. 122–123: "For our purposes the most important point is that human anxiety is here associated with lack of aseity (the self-sufficiency possessed by God alone). We should also note that Tillich's discussion of causality supports the thesis that human existence is not necessitated. If the latter were the case, man would be incapable of anxiety, and he could not ask questions based upon awareness of the fact that he 'might not' be. So far as the present category is concerned, the answer to anxiety means a kind of courage which achieves self-reliance despite the inescapable facts of contingency and dependence."

73. Roberts, "Tillich's Doctrine of Man," p. 123: "The category of substance, in its connection with human nature, has to do mainly with self-identity."

74. Tillich, *Systematic Theology*, p. 197: "In contrast to causality, substance points to something underlying the flux of appearances, something which is relatively static and self-contained. . . . But the substance is nothing beyond the accidents in which it expresses itself."

75. Roberts, "Tillich's Doctrine of Man," p. 123: "Therefore all change threatens the ground on which one stands, and the radical change from life to death threatens an ultimate loss of self-identity. We cannot solve the problem by trying to attribute permanence to creative work, a love relationship, and the like. Courage can match anxiety only by being able to affirm the significance of the finite despite the fact that it *can* lose its substance."

not answer the question as to how courage is possible in the face of ineradicable anxiety. The answer to this question is furnished by revelation and by the existential decision which enters into faith in God.[76]

2. God as being itself

Tillich defines God in diverse ways. God is spoken of as "the name of this infinite and inexhaustible depth and ground of all being,"[*] as the name of the ground of history,"[†] as "the answer to the question implied in being,"[‡] as "the power of being in which every-being participates,"[§] as "the power in everything that has power,"[||] as "the name for that which concerns us ultimately,"[#] and as "being itself."[**][77] Out of all of these definitions, it seems that Tillich's most persistent definition of God is "being-itself," esse ipsum. Let us therefore turn to a discussion of Tillich's meaning of being-itself.

i. God's transcendence of finite being

In affirming that God is being-itself, Tillich is denying that God is a being besides other beings. He is also denying that God is a "highest being" in the sense of the "most perfect" and "most powerful" being. If God were a being He would be subject to the categories of finitude, especially to the categories of space and substance. Therefore if such confusions are to be avoided, says Tillich, God must be understood as being-itself or as the ground of being.[78]

---

[*] Tillich, SOF, 57.
[†] Tillich, SOF, 59.
[‡] Tillich, ST, I, 163.
[§] Tillich, Art. (1946)²,

11.
[||] Tillich, Art. (1946)²,
11.
[#] Tillich, ST, I, 211.

[**] Tillich, ST, I, 189,
205, 230, 235, 237, 243;
PE, 63.

---

76. Roberts, "Tillich's Doctrine of Man," p. 123: "Thus all four categories express the union of being (the positive) and nonbeing (the negative) in everything finite. But the ontological analysis cannot answer the question as to how courage is possible in the face of ineradicable anxiety. The answer to this question is furnished by revelation and by the existential decision which enters into faith in God."

77. Boozer, "Place of Reason," p. 151: "Though [Tillich] speaks of God in such diverse ways as 'the answer to the question implied in being,' 'the name of this infinite and inexhaustible depth and ground of all being,' as 'the name of the ground of history,' 'the basis and abyss of all meaning which surpasses all that is conceivable,' 'the power of being in which every being participates,' 'the power in everything that has power,' 'the name for that which concerns man ultimately,' as 'being itself,' and as 'Lord' and 'Father,' he is jealous to safeguard the non-existential status of God." King's footnotes are similar to Boozer's. In another section of his dissertation Boozer also wrote about God as being-itself (p. 256) and included a footnote listing the additional page numbers from Systematic Theology and The Protestant Era that King cites here.

78. Tillich, Systematic Theology, p. 235: "If God is a being, he is subject to the categories of finitude, especially to space and substance. Even if he is called the 'highest being' in the sense of

Tillich often speaks as though "absolute," "unconditional," "infinite," "eternal" were synonyms for "being-itself"; but he insists that being-itself, or God, is "beyond finitude and infinity," "relative" and "absolute,"* "temporal" and "eternal," and even "spatial" and "spaceless."†[79]

In saying that God is being-itself Tillich intends to convey the idea of power of being. God is the power of being in everything and above everything.‡ Tillich is convinced that any theology which does not dare to identify God and the power of being as the first step in its doctrine of God relapses into monarchic monotheism.[80]

The traditional category of omnipotence is included in the concept of God as being-itself. God as power of being resists and conquers nonbeing.§ In the Christian belief of an "almighty God," there is the assurance of the inexhaustible power of being to resist nonbeing. This is why God warrants man's ultimate concern. The omnipotence of God does not mean that God has the power to do anything he wishes.[81] Nor does it mean omni-activity in terms of physical causality. Such conceptions of omnipotence, asserts Tillich, are absurd and irreligious. Tillich uses the symbol of omnipotence to express the religious experience "that no structure in reality and no event in nature and history has the power of preventing us from communion with the infinite and inexhaustible ground of meaning and being."‖ This idea of omnipotence is expressed in the Pauline assertion that neither natural nor political powers, neither heavenly nor earthly forces can separate us from the love of God.[82]

---

* Tillich, ST, I, 144.
† Tillich, ST, I, 138.
‡ Tillich, ST, I, 236. This passage suggest an impersonal monism of power.
§ Tillich, ST, I, 272.
‖ Tillich, Art. (1940)[2], 8.

---

the 'most perfect' and the 'most powerful' being, this situation is not changed. . . . Many confusions in the doctrine of God and many apologetic weaknesses could be avoided if God were understood first of all as being-itself or as the ground of being."

79. Charles Hartshorne, "Tillich's Doctrine of God," in Kegley and Bretall, eds., *Theology of Paul Tillich*, pp. 164–165: "Professor Tillich often speaks, indeed, almost as though 'absolute,' 'unconditioned,' 'infinite,' 'eternal,' were synonyms for 'being-itself,' and equally literal in application to deity; but he also insists that being-itself, or God, is 'beyond finitude and infinity' (144), and implies the same with respect to 'relative' and 'absolute' (cf. 138), 'temporal' and 'eternal,' and even 'spatial' and 'spaceless' (184, 186)."

80. Tillich, *Systematic Theology*, p. 236: "He is the power of being in everything and above everything, the infinite power of being. A theology which does not dare to identify God and the power of being as the first step toward a doctrine of God relapses into monarchic monotheism."

81. Boozer, "Place of Reason," p. 189: "The traditional category of omnipotence is included in the concept of God as being-itself. God as power of being resists and conquers non-being. In the Christian belief in an 'almighty God,' Tillich sees a confidence in the inexhaustible power of being to resist nonbeing. Only the 'almighty' God can warrant man's ultimate concern. . . . The omnipotence of God does not mean that God is able to do whatever he wishes."

82. Paul Tillich, "The Idea of the Personal God," *Union Review* 2 (1940): 9: "Or what 'omnipotence' means must be found in the words Paul (Rom. 8) speaks to the few Christians in the slums

All of this leads Tillich to the conclusion that omnipotence means "the power of being which resists nonbeing in all its expressions."*

In this conception of God as being-itself or power of being, Tillich seeks to solve the problems of the immanence and the transcendence of God. God is transcendent in the sense that he, as the power of being, transcends every being and also the totality of beings—the world. God is beyond finitude and infinity; otherwise he would be conditioned by something other than himself.[83] Tillich makes it palpably clear that "being itself infinitely transcends every finite being. There is no proportion or gradation between the finite and the infinite. There is an absolute break, an infinite 'jump'."†

On the other hand God's immanence is expressed in the fact that everything finite participates in being itself and in infinity. If this were not the case everything finite would be swallowed by nonbeing, or it never would have emerged out of nonbeing.‡[84]

So we can see that all beings have a double relation to being-itself. This double relation that all beings have to being-itself gives being-itself a double characteristic.[85] Being-itself is both creative and abysmal. Its creative character is found in the fact that all beings participate in the infinite power of being. Its abysmal character is found in the fact that all beings are infinitely transcended by their creative ground.§

ii. God's transcendence of the contrast
of essential and existential being

As being-itself God is beyond the contrast of essential and existential being. The transition of being into existence which involves the possibility that being will contradict and lose itself, is excluded from being-itself.‖ Logically being-itself is prior to the split which characterizes finite being.[86]

---

* Tillich, ST, I, 273.
† Tillich, ST, I, 237. This reminds one of the Barthian "Wholly Other."

‡ Tillich, ST, I, 237.
§ Tillich, ST, I, 237.
‖ Tillich makes one exception to this statement,

viz., the christological paradox.

---

of the big cities when he pronounces that neither natural nor political powers, neither earthly nor heavenly forces can separate us from the 'Love of God.'"

83. Tillich, *Systematic Theology*, p. 237: "As the power of being, God transcends every being and also the totality of beings—the world. Being-itself is beyond finitude and infinity; otherwise it would be conditioned by something other than itself, and the real power of being would lie beyond both it and that which conditioned it."

84. Tillich, *Systematic Theology*, p. 237: "On the other hand, everything finite participates in being-itself and in its infinity. . . . It would be swallowed by nonbeing, or it never would have emerged out of nonbeing."

85. Tillich, *Systematic Theology*, p. 237: "This double relation of all beings to being-itself gives being-itself a double characteristic."

86. Tillich, *Systematic Theology*, p. 236: "As being-itself God is beyond the contrast of essential and existential being. We have spoken of the transition of being into existence, which involves

The ground of being cannot be found within the totality of beings, nor can the
ground of essence and existence participate in the tensions and disruptions characteristic of the transition from essence to existence.*

Therefore it is wrong to speak of God as universal essence, for if God is so
understood, he is identified with the unity and totality of finite potentialities,
thereby ceasing to be the power of the ground in all of them. "He has poured
all his creative power into a system of forms, and he is bound to these forms.
This is what pantheism means."†

On the other hand, it is a grave error to speak of God as existing.[87] Tillich
affirms that the Scholastics were right in their claim that in God there is no
difference between essence and existence. But they perverted this whole truth
by proceeding to talk of the existence of God and even attempting to prove
such existence.[88] "It is as atheistic to affirm the existence of God," asserts Tillich, "as it is to deny it. God is being-itself, not a being."‡ Again Tillich writes:

> It would be a great victory for Christian apologetics if the words "God" and
> "existence" were very definitely separated except in the paradox of God becom-
> ing manifest under the conditions of existence, that is in the Christological para-
> dox. God does not exist. He is being-itself, beyond essence and existence. There-
> fore, to argue that God exists is to deny him.§

Tillich is convinced that the usual discussions of the existence of God completely miss the essential nature of God. Such discussions start out with the
assumption that God is <u>something</u> or <u>someone</u>.[89] But God is not a being, not
even the most powerful or the most perfect being. The objectification or the
"thingification" (to use J. L. Adams' term) of God is blasphemy.[90] Whenever
God is made an object besides other objects, the existence of which is a matter

---

* Tillich, ST, I, 205.
† Tillich, ST, I, 236.
‡ Tillich, ST, I, 237.
§ Tillich, ST, I, 205.

---

the possibility that being will contradict and lose itself. This transition is excluded from being-
itself (except in terms of the christological paradox), for being-itself does not participate in
nonbeing. . . . Logically, being-itself is 'before,' 'prior to,' the split which characterizes finite
being."

87. Tillich, *Systematic Theology*, p. 236: "On the other hand, grave difficulties attend the attempt to speak of God as existing."

88. Tillich, *Systematic Theology*, p. 205: "The scholastics were right when they asserted that in
God there is no difference between essence and existence. But they perverted their insight when
in spite of this assertion they spoke of the existence of God and tried to argue in favor of it."

89. Boozer, "Place of Reason," p. 151: "Therefore the usual discussion of the existence of
God, as if God were som<u>ething</u> or som<u>eone</u> completely misses the essential nature of God."

90. Boozer, "Place of Reason," p. 159: "The objectification, or the 'thingification' (to use J. L.
Adams' term) of God is demonry."

of argument, theology becomes the greatest supporter of atheism.[91] "The first step to atheism is always a theology which drags God down to the level of doubtful things."*

iii. The invalidity of all arguments for the existence of God

Since God does not exist, Tillich finds the various arguments for the existence of God both futile and invalid. Theologians and philosophers, contends Tillich, should have said something about the ontological implications of finitude rather than present elaborate arguments for the existence of God. The analysis of finitude shows that finitude witnesses to something beyond the finite.[92] "The arguments for the existence of God neither are arguments nor are they proof of the existence of God. They are expressions of the question of God which is implied in human finitude."† It is in this sense that Tillich seeks to interpret the traditional arguments for the existence of God.

The so-called ontological argument points to the ontological structure of finitude.[93] The marks of man's existence are separation, self-contradiction and estrangement. Man is aware of that from which he is separated, else he could not feel separated at all. He is aware of what he ought to be as well as what he actually is. "Man knows that he is finite, that he is excluded from an infinity which nevertheless belongs to him. He is aware of his potential infinity while being aware of his actual finitude."‡ It is in the light of this religious a priori that Tillich would have us understand the ontological argument; not as a proposition which gives the result of God, but as an indication of the ontological structure of finitude.[94]

---

* Tillich, SOF, 45.
† Tillich, ST, I, 205.
‡ Tillich, ST, I, 206.

---

91. Paul Tillich, *The Shaking of the Foundations* (New York: Scribner, 1948), p. 45: "In making God an object besides other objects, the existence and nature of which are matters of argument, theology supports the escape to atheism."

92. Boozer, "Place of Reason," p. 152: "What the theologians and philosophers should have said rather than arguments for the existence of God was something about the ontological implications of finitude. The analysis of finitude shows that finitude witnesses to something beyond the finite."

93. Tillich, *Systematic Theology*, p. 206: "The so-called ontological argument points to the ontological structure of finitude."

94. Boozer, "Place of Reason," pp. 27–28: "The marks of man's existence are separation, self-contradiction and estrangement. . . . Man is aware of that from which he is separated as well as his actual state, else he could not feel separated at all. He is aware of the essence of what he is (what he ought to be) as well as what he actually is. . . . 'Man knows that he is finite, that he is excluded from an infinity which nevertheless belongs to him. He is aware of his potential infinity

The Anselmic statement that God is a necessary thought and that therefore this idea must have objective as well as subjective reality is valid in so far as thinking implies an unconditional element which transcends subjectivity and objectivity. However, the statement is not valid if this unconditional element is considered as a highest being called God.*[95]

The so-called cosmological and teleological arguments for the existence of God are valid in so far as they give an analysis of reality which indicates that the cosmological question of God is unavoidable. But they are not valid when they claim that the existence of a highest being is the logical conclusion of their analysis.†[96]

The cosmological argument moves from the finitude of being to an infinite being. From the endless chain of causes and effects it arrives at the conclusion that there is a first cause. But cause, affirms Tillich, is a category of finitude.[97] "The 'first cause' is a hypostasized question, not a statement about a being which initiates the causal chain. Such a being would itself be a part of the causal chain and would again raise the question of cause."‡ First cause is a symbol which expresses the question implied in finite being, the question of God.[98]

The teleological argument in the traditional sense moves from the finitude of meaning to a bearer of infinite meaning. It arrives at the conclusion that finite _teloi_ imply an infinite cause of teleology. But this conclusion, contends Tillich, is just as invalid as the other cosmological arguments. As the statement of a question, however, this conclusion is not only valid but inescapable.[99]

---

* Tillich, ST, I, 207.
† Tillich, ST, I, 208.
‡ Tillich, ST, I, 209.

---

while being aware of his actual finitude.' It is in the light of this religious a priori that Tillich would have us understand the ontological argument for God, not as a proposition which gives the result as God, but as an indication of the ontological structure of finitude."

95. Tillich, _Systematic Theology_, p. 207: "The Anselmian statement that God is a necessary thought and that therefore this idea must have objective as well as subjective reality is valid in so far as thinking, by its very nature, implies an unconditional element which transcends subjectivity and objectivity, that is, a point of identity which makes the idea of truth possible." In the margins of King's draft Schilling noted that this sentence was "almost exactly quoted" (King, draft of chapter 3).

96. Tillich, _Systematic Theology_, p. 208: "The so-called cosmological and teleological arguments for the existence of God are the traditional and inadequate form of this question. . . . They are valid in so far as they give an analysis of reality which indicates that the cosmological question of God is unavoidable. They are not valid in so far as they claim that the existence of a highest being is the logical conclusion of their analysis."

97. Tillich, _Systematic Theology_, p. 209: "[The cosmological argument] has moved from the finitude of being to an infinite being. . . . From the endless chain of causes and effects it arrives at the conclusion that there is a first cause. . . . But cause and substance are categories of finitude."

98. Tillich, _Systematic Theology_, p. 209: "First cause and necessary substance are symbols which express the question implied in finite being, . . . the question of God."

99. Tillich, _Systematic Theology_, p. 210: "This structure is used as a springboard to the conclusion that finite _teloi_ imply an infinite cause of teleology. . . . In terms of logical argument this

Tillich concludes that the task of a theological treatment of the traditional arguments is "to develop the question of God which they express and to expose the impotency of their 'arguments,' their inability to answer the question of God."*

Tillich's rejection of all arguments for the existence of God should not leave the impression that he is an irrationalist. What Tillich is really seeking to say is that God is presupposed in the question of God. Even to deny God is to affirm him. Says Tillich:

> Die Frage nach der Wahrheit der Religion ist beantwortet durch die metalogisch Erfassung des Wesens der Religion als Richtung auf den unbedingten Sinn. Es ist sinnlos, ausserdem zu fragen, ob das Unbedingte "ist," ob also der religiöse Akt sich auf Wirkliches richtet und insofern wahr ist oder nicht.†[100]

Tillich, like Augustine, is convinced that God neither needs nor can receive "proof." He is that ultimate—Tillich's term is das Unbedingte—which is a certain quality of the world man encounters and which analysis reveals as "presupposed" in all his encountering. Whereas Augustine's Platonism led him to an intellectual emphasis on the truth or Logos implied in all knowledge, Tillich has expanded it to the "power of being" implied in all men's varied participation in the world in which they are grasped by an ultimate concern.

God as the "power of being," as Seinsmachigkeit, is the source of all power. Thus the power of thought is derived from the Ground of power, yet that Ground is not accessible to thought.[101]

So far as one has power he cannot escape God. To doubt, to feel, to think, to know, indeed to exist affirms God. For God as "power of being" is that power by which one doubts, feels, thinks, knows, exists.

> Being itself, as present in the ontological awareness, is power of Being but not the most powerful being: it is neither ens realissimum nor ens singularissimum. It is the power in everything that has power, be it a universal or an individual, a thing or an experience.‡[102]

---

* Tillich, ST, I, 210.

† Tillich, Art. (1925), 798.

‡ Tillich, Art. (1946)², 11.

---

conclusion is as invalid as the other cosmological 'arguments.' As the statement of a question it is not only valid but inescapable and, as history shows, most impressive."

100. Boozer quoted this passage from Tillich ("Place of Reason," pp. 73–74).

101. Boozer, "Place of Reason," p. 74: "God as the 'power of being,' as ousia, as Seinsmächtigkeit, is the source of all power. . . . The power of thought is derived from the Ground of power, yet that Ground is not accessible to thought."

102. Boozer, "Place of Reason," p. 105: "To doubt, to feel, to think, to know; indeed, to exist affirms God. For God as 'power of Being' is the power by which one doubts, feels, thinks, knows, exists. 'Being itself, as present in the ontological awareness, is power of Being but not the most

iv. God as being and the
knowledge of God

15 Apr
1955

As we have already seen, God as being-itself is the ground of the ontological structure of being, without being subject to the structure himself. Therefore, if anything beyond this bare assertion is said about God, it no longer is a direct and proper statement. It is indirect and points to something beyond itself. The statement that God is being-itself is the only literal statement that can be made concerning God. It does not point beyond itself. It means what it says directly and properly. God is not God if he is not being-itself.

However after this has been said, nothing else can be said about God which is not symbolic.[103] All knowledge of God is expressed in terms of symbols.

> Glaube ist Richtung auf das Unbedingte als solchen Gegenstand sein, sondern nur das Symbol, in dem das Unbedingte anschaut und gewallt wird. Glaube ist Richtung auf das Unbedingte durch Symbole aus den Bedingten hindurch.*

He continues,

> Aber das Unbedingte ist kein gegenständlicher objekt. Es kann durch objekts nur symbolisiert, nicht erfasst werden.†

God as being-itself cannot be an object of thought or language.[104] All references to God must be expressed in terms of symbols. These symbols indicate something about the nature of God, but that indication is never precise, unambiguous, literal.‡

The general character of the symbol has been described.§ We must reiterate the fact that symbol and sign are different. The distinct characteristic of a

---

* Tillich, Art. (1925), 802.
† Tillich, Art. (1925), 804.
‡ With the possible exception of the affirmation that God is love and God is spirit. "But God is love. And since God is being-itself, one must say that being-itself is love." (ST, I, 279). "God is spirit. That is the most embracing, direct and unrestricted symbol for the divine life." (ST, I, 249).
§ See Chapter II, ii, (1).

---

powerful being. . . . It is the power in everything that has power, be it a universal or an individual, a thing or an experience.'"

103. Tillich, *Systematic Theology*, pp. 238–239: "The statement that God is being-itself is a nonsymbolic statement. It does not point beyond itself. It means what it says directly and properly. . . . However, after this has been said, nothing else can be said about God as God which is not symbolic. As we already have seen, God as being-itself is the ground of the ontological structure of being without being subject to this structure himself. . . . Therefore, if anything beyond this bare assertion is said about God, it no longer is a direct and proper statement, no longer a concept. It is indirect, and it points to something beyond itself."

104. Boozer also quoted the previous two passages from Tillich. He introduced them with the sentence, "God as ground and abyss cannot be an object of thought or language" ("Place of Reason," p. 160).

symbol is its innate power. A sign is impotent in itself. Because the sign has no inner power, it does not arise from necessity. It is interchangeable at will. The symbol, however, does possess a necessary character. It cannot be exchanged.*[105]

But the question arises, can a segment of finite reality become the basis for an assertion about that which is infinite? Tillich's answer is that it can, because that which is infinite is being-itself, and because everything participates in being-itself.

> Religious symbols use a finite reality in order to express our relation to the infinite. But the finite reality they use is not an arbitrary means for an end, something strange to it; it participates in the power of the ultimate for which it stands.†

This leads Tillich to affirm that religious symbols are doubled-edged. They express not only what is symbolized but also that through which it is symbolized.[106] They are directed toward the infinite which they symbolize and toward the finite through which they symbolize it. They open the finite and the human for the infinite and divine, and the infinite and divine for the finite and human. The symbol "Father," for instance, when applied to God, brings God down to the human relationship of father and child. But at the same time it lifts the human relationship up to its theonomous sacramental depth. If God is called king, something is said not only about God but also about the sacredness of kinghood. If the work of God is spoken of as "making whole" or "healing," something is said not only about God but about the holiness of all healing. Any segment of reality that is used as a symbol for God is at that moment elevated to the realm of the sacred. It becomes theonomous.‡[107]

---

* Tillich, Art. (1940), 14.
† Tillich, PE, 61.
‡ Tillich, ST, I, 240, 241.

---

105. Paul Tillich, "The Religious Symbol," *Journal of Liberal Religion* 2 (1940): 13–14: "The third characteristic of the symbol is its innate power. This implies that the symbol has a power inherent within it that distinguishes it from the mere sign which is impotent in itself. This characteristic is decisive for the distinction between a sign and a symbol. The sign is interchangeable at will. It does not arise from necessity, for it has no inner power. The symbol, however, does possess a necessary character. It cannot be exchanged."

106. Tillich, *Protestant Era*, p. 61: "A religious symbol is double edged. It expresses not only what is symbolized but also that through which it is symbolized."

107. Tillich, *Systematic Theology*, pp. 240–241: "Religious symbols are double-edged. They are directed toward the infinite which they symbolize *and* toward the finite through which they symbolize it. . . . They open the divine for the human and the human for the divine. For instance, if God is symbolized as 'Father,' he is brought down to the human relationship of father and child. But at the same time this human relationship is consecrated into a pattern of the divine-human relationship. If 'Father' is employed as a symbol for God, fatherhood is seen in its theonomous, sacramental depth. . . . If a segment of reality is used as a symbol for God, the realm of reality from which it is taken is, so to speak, elevated into the realm of the holy. . . . It is theonomous. If

Tillich asserts that theology has neither the duty nor the power to confirm or to negate religious symbols. Its task is to interpret the symbols according to theological principles and methods. But in the process of interpretation at least two things may happen: on the one hand, theology may discover contradictions between symbols within the theological circle; on the other hand, theology may speak not only as theology but also as religion. In the first case, theology can point out the religious and theological errors embedded in certain symbols; in the second case, theology can become prophecy, contributing to a change in the revelatory situation.*[108]

Tillich revolts vehemently against the idea that the symbol is nonreal. He contends that this erroneous idea stems partly from the confusion between sign and symbol, and partly from the identification of reality with empirical reality. He sees an even greater source of the confusion stemming from the tendency of some theological movements, such as Protestant Hegelianism and Catholic modernism, to interpret religious language symbolically in order to dissolve its realistic meaning and to weaken its seriousness, its power, and its spiritual impact. Such a view fails to see that the intention of most theologians who have spoken of God in symbolic terms has been to give to God more reality and power than a nonsymbolic and therefore easily superstitious interpretation could give them.† In this sense, asserts Tillich, symbolic interpretation is proper and necessary.[109]

3. God as the Unconditional

We have seen that Tillich is insistent on the point that God is not an object for us as subjects. He is not any particular meaning to be placed besides other

---

* Tillich, ST, I, 240.
† Tillich, ST, I, 241.

God is called the 'king,' something is said not only about God but also about the holy character of kinghood. If God's work is called 'making whole' or 'healing,' this not only says something about God but also emphasizes the theonomous character of all healing."

108. Tillich, *Systematic Theology*, p. 240: "Theology as such has neither the duty nor the power to confirm or to negate religious symbols. Its task is to interpret them according to theological principles and methods. In the process of interpretation, however, two things may happen: theology may discover contradictions between symbols within the theological circle and theology may speak not only as theology but also as religion. In the first case, theology can point out the religious dangers and the theological errors which follow from the use of certain symbols; in the second case, theology can become prophecy, and in this role it may contribute to a change in the revelatory situation."

109. Tillich, *Systematic Theology*, p. 241: "This is partially the result of confusion between sign and symbol and partially due to the identification of reality with empirical reality, with the entire realm of objective things and events. . . . But one reason remains, namely, the fact that some theological movements, such as Protestant Hegelianism and Catholic modernism, have interpreted religious language symbolically in order to dissolve its realistic meaning and to weaken its

meanings, not even the highest meaning.* He is not any particular value beside other values, not even the highest value.† He is not any particular being beside other beings, not even the highest being.‡ This complete lack of particularity in God is expressed in Tillich's idea of God as <u>das Unbedingte</u>, the Unconditioned or the Unconditional.§ Since Tillich has written at length about the unconditioned the idea may profitably be considered.[110]

Tillich's thought concerning the Unconditioned is not at all clearly stated. At times Tillich speaks of the unconditional as a quality; at other times he speaks as if the unconditioned were being-itself, i.e. God.[111]

In a very interesting lecture on "Kairos," Tillich speaks of the unconditional as a quality.[112]

> In every symbol of the divine an unconditional claim is expressed, most powerfully in the command: "Thou shalt love the Lord thy God with all thy soul and with all thy mind." No partial, restricted, conditioned love of God is admitted. The term "unconditioned" or the adjective made into the substantive, "the unconditional," is an abstraction from such sayings which abound in the Bible and in great religious literature. The unconditional is a <u>quality</u>, not a being. It characterizes that which is our ultimate and, consequently unconditional concern, whether we call it "God" or "Being as such," or the "God as such" or the "true as such," or whether we give it any other name. It would be a complete mistake to understand the unconditional as a being the existence of which can be discussed. He who speaks of the "existence of the unconditional" has thoroughly misunderstood the meaning of the term. Unconditional is a <u>quality</u> which we experi-

---

* Tillich, IOH, 222; PE, 163.
† Tillich, IOH, 223.
‡ Tillich, PE, 163.
§ J. L. Adams, one of the leadeng interpreters of

Tillich's thought, says that <u>das Unbedingte</u> should be translated "the unconditional" and never "the unconditioned." (Adams, Art. (1949),

300). But Tillich himself speaks of God as being "the unconditioned." (Art. (1946), 11).

---

seriousness, its power, and its spiritual impact. . . . Their intention and their result was to give to God and to all his relations to man more reality and power than a nonsymbolic and therefore easily superstitious interpretation could give them. In this sense symbolic interpretation is proper and necessary."

110. Boozer, "Place of Reason," pp. 154–155: "A persistent idea in Tillich's writing about God is that God is not an object for us as subjects. God is not any particular meaning to be placed <u>beside</u> other meanings, not even the highest meaning. God is not any particular value <u>beside</u> other values, not even the highest value. God is not any particular being <u>beside</u> other beings, not even the highest being. The complete lack of particularity in God led Dr. Harkness to write: 'The one element in our knowledge of God which is literal fact, and not symbol, is God's character as the Unconditioned.' As Tillich has written at length about the unconditioned, though without consistent clarity, the idea may profitably be considered." The quotation is from Georgia Harkness, "The Abyss and the Given," *Christendom* 3 (1938): 512.

111. Boozer, "Place of Reason," p. 155: "At times Tillich speaks of the unconditional as a quality of the encounter; at other times he speaks of the unconditional as if it were being-itself; indeed, as if it were God."

112. Boozer, "Place of Reason," p. 155: "In a footnote to a lecture on 'Kairos' Tillich speaks of the unconditional as a quality."

ence in encountering reality, for instance, in the unconditional character of the voice of the conscience, the logical as well as the moral.*[113]

In this lengthy passage Tillich is explicit in asserting that the unconditional is not a being but a quality. But even here the issue is clouded when Tillich says that the unconditional "characterizes that which is our ultimate and, consequently, unconditional concern, whether we call it 'God' or 'Being as such.'"[114] This seems to contradict the insistence in the immediately preceding passage that the unconditional is a quality.

There are passages in which Tillich seems to identify the unconditional with being-itself. For instance, Tillich writes:

> The unconditional meaning . . . toward which every act of meaning is directed is implicit faith, and which supports the whole, which protects it from a plunge into a nothingness void of meaning, itself has two aspects: it bears the meaning of each single meaning as well as the meaning of the whole. That is, it is the basis of meaning.†[115]

Tillich goes on in the same book to speak of the unconditional simultaneously as basis of meaning and abyss of meaning.‡[116] Both of these passages seem to set forth the unconditional as identical with being-itself. Again Tillich writes: "But the really real is not reached until the unconditional ground of everything real, or the unconditioned power in every power of being, is reached." Here again, unconditional seems to refer to the ground of being or being-itself. Other passages could be added to these to indicate Tillich's tendency to speak of the unconditional as being-itself, in spite of his insistence that the unconditional is a quality of being-itself.[117] However despite these ambiguities it seems to be consistent with Tillich's intention to say that the unconditional is a quality of being-itself; which quality man experiences in the encounter

---

* Tillich, PE, 32n. Italics
mine.
† Tillich, IOH, 222.
‡ Tillich, IOH, 222.

---

113. Boozer quoted this passage from Tillich ("Place of Reason," p. 155).

114. Boozer, "Place of Reason," p. 156: "Tillich is clear in asserting that the unconditional is not a being but a quality. Yet the issue is clouded in the next sentence when he says that the unconditional characterizes that which is our ultimate concern, whether we call that God or Being as such." King's quotation is from Tillich, *Protestant Era*, p. 32n.

115. Boozer quoted this passage from Tillich ("Place of Reason," p. 157).

116. Boozer, "Place of Reason," p. 157: "Again in the Interpretation of History Tillich says that we can speak of the unconditional simultaneously as basis of meaning and abyss of meaning."

117. Boozer, "Place of Reason," p. 158: "Again Tillich writes: 'But the really real is not reached until the unconditional ground of everything real, or the unconditioned power in every power of being, is reached.' Here again, unconditional refers to the ground of being or being-itself. Other passages could be added to these to indicate that in spite of Tillich's assertion that the unconditional is a quality and not a being." The quotation is from Paul Tillich, *The Protestant Era*, trans. J. L. Adams (Chicago: University of Chicago Press, 1948), p. 76.

with being-itself.[118] J. L. Adams also interprets Tillich's idea of the unconditional as a quality of being-itself. Of Tillich's unconditional he writes:

> Hence, as the depth or the infinity of things, it is both the ground and abyss of being. It is that quality in being and truth, in goodness and beauty, that elicits man's ultimate concern; thus it is the absolute <u>quality</u> of all being and meaning and value, the power and vitality of the real as it fulfills itself in meaningful creativity.*[119]

In his idea of God as the unconditional, Tillich is attempting to impress the point that God is not an object which we as subjects perceive or think about.[120] He insists that the term unconditional is not to be confused with the Absolute of German idealism, with the eternal essence of Platonism, with the superessential One of mysticism, with the Supreme Being of rational deduction, or with the "Wholly Other" of Barthian theology.† In all these terms that which should be thought of as Being itself tends to be looked upon as a particular being about whose existence there might be an argument. One can argue neither for nor against the existence of the unconditional. To argue about it is to presuppose it, for the very argument presupposes some unconditional demand and reality. The unconditional is not a section of reality; it is not an object among objects, not even the highest "object." The unconditional transcends the distinction between subject and object. The unconditional is not a being.[121] "Neither 'the Unconditioned' nor 'something unconditioned,' is meant as a being, not even the highest being, not even God. God is unconditional, that makes him God: but the 'unconditional' is not God."‡ To draw God down into the world of objects and beings is to indulge in the basest idolatry. And atheism is justified when it protests against the existence of a being.

---

* Adams, Art. (1948), 300, 301.   ‡ Tillich, Art. (1946)², 11.
Italics mine.
† Tillich, Art. (1946), 2, 10.

---

118. Boozer, "Place of Reason," p. 156: "It seems to be quite consistent with Tillich's intention to say that unconditionality is a quality of being itself; not of a being, but of being itself, which quality man experiences in the encounter with being itself."

119. Boozer, "Place of Reason," p. 158: "J. L. Adams also interprets Tillich's idea of the unconditional as a quality of being-itself. Of Tillich's unconditional he writes: 'Hence, as the depth or the infinity of things, it is both the ground and abyss of being. It is that quality in being and truth, in goodness and beauty, that elicits man's ultimate concern; thus it is the absolute quality of all being and meaning and value, the power and vitality of the real as it fulfills itself in meaningful creativity.'"

120. Boozer, "Place of Reason," p. 102: "God is not an object which we as subjects perceive or think about."

121. James Luther Adams, "Tillich's Concept of the Protestant Era," in Tillich, *Protestant Era*, p. 300: "One misunderstands the term 'the unconditional' if one confuses it with the Absolute of German idealism, with the eternal essences of Platonism, with the superessential One of mysticism, with the mathematically calculated laws of nature, with the Supreme Being of rational deduction, or with the 'Wholly Other' (as characterized by Rudolph Otto or Karl Barth). . . . In all these terms that which should be thought of as Being itself tends to be conceived as a particular

So for Tillich, "God is no object for us as subjects."* God is rather the prius of the separation into subject and object, that which precedes this division. As we shall see later in the discussion, this prius of separation is not a person. It is power, power of being. Tillich is greatly influenced by existential philosophy at this point. He interprets existential philosophy as an attempt to find a level which precedes the contrast between subject and object. "It aims to cut under the 'subject-object distinction' and to reach that stratum of Being which Jaspers, for instance, calls the 'Ursprung' or Source,"†[122]

Tillich's existential leaning leads him to affirm that one has awareness of the unconditional. The term "awareness" is used because it is a neutral term and may be distinguished from knowledge and experience. The term "experience" should not be used because it ordinarily describes the observed presence of one reality to another reality, and because the unconditioned is not a matter of experiential observation. The term "knowledge" presupposes the separation of subject and object, and implies a discrete theoretical act, which is just the opposite of awareness of the unconditioned.[123] Schleiermacher recognized the inappropriateness of "knowledge" as the basis of religious consciousness, but he conditioned the awareness by assigning it to "feeling." The awareness of the unconditional involves the whole being. "Man, not his cognitive function alone, is aware of the Unconditioned."‡ It is therefore possible to call this awareness existential in the sense that man as a whole participates in the cognitive act.[124]

---

* Tillich, Art. (1946)², 11.
† Tillich, Art. (1944)², 56.
‡ Tillich, Art. (1946)², 10.

---

being about whose 'existence' there might be an argument. . . . To argue about it is to presuppose it, for the very argument must itself presuppose some unconditional demand and reality. . . . The unconditional is not a section of reality; it is not a thing or an 'existing' entity; it is not an object among objects, not even the highest 'object.' . . . The unconditional transcends the distinction between subject and object. . . . The unconditional is not *a* being."

122. Boozer, "Place of Reason," pp. 102–104: "Believing that God 'is no object for us as subjects,' Tillich moves behind the separation to the prius of the separation into subject and object, to that which precedes this division. . . . But Tillich does not think of God as a person. . . . The prius of separation, then, is power, power of being. Tillich follows existential philosophy at this point. For he interprets existential philosophy as an attempt to find a level which precedes the contrast between subject and object. 'It aims to cut under the "subject-object distinction" and to reach that stratum of Being which Jaspers, for instance, calls the "Ursprung" or "Source."'"

123. Paul Tillich, "The Two Types of Philosophy of Religion," *Union Seminary Quarterly Review* 1, no. 4 (May 1946): 10: "Neither should the word 'experience' be used, because it ordinarily describes the observed presence of one reality to another reality, and because the Unconditioned is not a matter of experiential observation. 'Knowledge' finally presupposes the separation of subject and object, and implies an isolated theoretical act, which is just the opposite of awareness of the Unconditioned."

124. Tillich, "Two Types of Philosophy," p. 10: "It would, therefore, be possible to call this awareness 'existential' in the sense in which the Existential philosophy has used the word, namely the participation of man as a whole in the cognitive act."

From the above we can see that there is a close relationship between the unconditional and man's ultimate concern. This passage, in which Tillich defines "ultimate concern," clearly expresses the similarity:

> Ultimate concern is the abstract translation of the great commandment: "The Lord, our God, the Lord is one; and you shall love the Lord your God with all your heart, and with all your soul and with all your mind, and with all your strength." The religious concern is ultimate; it excludes all other concerns from ultimate significance; it makes them preliminary. The ultimate concern is unconditional, independent of any conditions of character, desire, or circumstance. The unconditional concern is total: no part of ourselves or of our world is excluded from it; there is no "place" to flee from it. The total concern is infinite: no moment of relaxation and rest is possible in the face of a religious concern which is ultimate, unconditional, total, and infinite.*

In an even clearer analysis of the nature of the ultimate concern, Tillich says: "Our ultimate concern is that which determines our being or not-being."† That which does not have the power of threatening or saving our being‡ cannot be of ultimate concern for us. Man is ultimately concerned about his being and meaning, about that which conditions his being beyond all the conditions in him and around him, about that which determines his ultimate destiny beyond all preliminary necessities and accidents.§[126]

So in Tillich's usage the unconditional is a philosophical symbol for the ultimate concern of man. God is the name for that which concerns man unconditionally or ultimately.

4. God as ground and abyss of power and meaning

We have seen that, according to Tillich, all beings have a double relation to being-itself. This double relation of all beings to being-itself gives being-itself

---

* Tillich, ST, I, 11, 12.
† Tillich, ST, I, 14.
‡ Tillich does not use being in this context to designate existence in time and space. He is aware of the fact that existence is continuously threatened and saved by things and events which have no ultimate concern for us. The term "being" means the whole of human reality, the structure, the meaning, and aim of existence.[125]
§ Tillich, ST, I, 14.

---

125. Tillich, *Systematic Theology*, p. 14: "The term 'being' in this context does not designate existence in time and space. Existence is continuously threatened and saved by things and events which have no ultimate concern for us. But the term 'being' means the whole of human reality, the structure, the meaning, and the aim of existence."

126. Tillich, *Systematic Theology*, p. 14: "Nothing can be of ultimate concern for us which does not have the power of threatening and saving our being. . . . Man is ultimately concerned about his being and meaning. . . . Man is unconditionally concerned about that which conditions his being beyond all the conditions in him and around him. Man is ultimately concerned about that which determines his ultimate destiny beyond all preliminary necessities and accidents."

a double characteristic. It is creative in the sense that everything participates in the infinite power of being. It is abysmal in the sense that all beings are infinitely transcended by their creative ground.*[127] This conception finds powerful expression in Tillich's assertion that God is ground and abyss of power and meaning.† In this definition Tillich is seeking to establish two polar concepts ontologically. "The divine life," says Tillich, "is the dynamic unity of depth and form."‡[128]

In a passage in his <u>Interpretation of History</u>, Tillich writes:

> The unconditional meaning . . . is the basis of meaning. Yet it is never to be grasped as such in any one act of meaning. It is transcendent in regard to every individual meaning. We can therefore speak of the unconditional simultaneously as basis of meaning and abyss of meaning (<u>Sinngrund und abgrund</u>). We call this object of the silent belief in the ultimate meaninglessness, this basis and abyss of all meaning which surpasses all that is conceivable, God. . . . Unconditional meaning has the quality of inexhaustibility. . . . The concept "meaning" is supposed to express all aspects of the human mind and therefore is just as valid in application to the practical as to the theoretical. The basis of meaning is just as much the basis of personality and community as of being and significance; and it is simultaneously the abyss of all. . . . The unconditioned appears as that which does not admit any conditioned fulfillment of its commandments, as that which is able to destroy every personality and community which tries to escape the unconditioned demand. We miss the quality of the unconditioned meaning, of being basis and abyss, if we interpret it either from an intellectual point of view or from a moral point of view alone. Only in the duality of both does the unconditioned meaning manifest itself.§[129]

This rather lengthy passage sets forth the two ideas that God is basis (ground) of being and meaning, and that God is the depth (abyss) of being and meaning. Here we see correlation lifted to the very nature of God. Moreover, we see that the tensions in existence between form and formlessness find their basis in the nature of God.[130] In order to get a clearer conception of these two aspects of the divine life, we shall discuss them separately.

---

* Tillich, ST, I, 237.
† Tillich, ST, I, 21, 250; IOH, 222.
‡ Tillich, ST, I, 156.
§ Tillich, IOH, 222, 223, 224.

---

127. Tillich, *Systematic Theology*, p. 237: "This double relation of all beings to being-itself gives being-itself a double characteristic. In calling it creative, we point to the fact that everything participates in the infinite power of being. In calling it abysmal, we point to the fact that . . . all beings are infinitely transcended by their creative ground."

128. Boozer, "Place of Reason," pp. 168, 170: "Tillich's basic definition of God is that God is ground and abyss of power and meaning. . . . Tillich here wishes to establish two polar concepts ontologically." In his footnote to the last sentence Boozer quoted page 156 of *Systematic Theology*: "The divine life is the dynamic unity of depth and form."

129. This quotation appears verbatim in Boozer, "Place of Reason," p. 169.

130. Boozer, "Place of Reason," pp. 170–171: "The two persistent ideas here are that God is basis (ground) of being and meaning, and that God is the depth (abyss) of being and mean-

i. God as ground

Tillich has a twofold purpose for emphasizing God as the ground of all being and reality. On the one hand, the concept establishes the dependence of "being" upon the source of being, all meaning upon the source of meaning. This emphasis saves man from the arrogance of thinking he is an autonomous being with no dependence on God, the source of being. On the other hand, the concept of ground is a basis of continuity between God and the world, of man and nature. This is the creativity of God.[131]

In the idea of ground, Tillich seems to be setting forth the idea of the rationality of God. Concerning the ground, Tillich writes:

> The ground is not only an abyss in which every form disappears; it also is the source from which every form emerges. The ground of being has the character of self-manifestation; it has <u>logos</u> character. This is not something added to the divine life; it is the divine life itself. In spite of its abysmal character the ground of being is "logical"; it includes its own <u>logos</u>.*[132]

In this passage Tillich seems to be saying that the ground of being has a <u>logos</u> character. Tillich's usual assertion is that God is ground of being and meaning. But here he says that ground has a <u>logos</u> character. In other words the ground is logical and rational. Here it seems that the ground takes on character and meaning, and God becomes more than the amorphous "being-itself" which is the ground of everything, without itself being anything. The nature of God as ground implies the rationality of God.[133]

But the issue is not totally clear. As one continues to read Tillich he discovers that it is difficult to determine whether Tillich's God is <u>logos</u> or the ground of <u>logos</u>. In the paragraph following the difficulty is set forth clearly:

---

* Tillich, ST, I, 157, 158.

---

ing. . . . The tensions in existence between form and the formless, good and evil, the sacred and the secular, find their basis in the nature of God."

131. Boozer, "Place of Reason," p. 171: "In emphasizing God as the ground of all being and meaning, Tillich wishes to establish the dependence of all 'beings' upon the source of being, all meanings upon the source of meaning. . . . But the major idea which Tillich strives to express in the concept of 'Ground' is a basis of continuity between God and the world of man and nature. This is the creativity of God."

132. Boozer quoted this passage from Tillich ("Place of Reason," p. 172).

133. Boozer, "Place of Reason," p. 174: "Tillich's basic and usual assertion is that God is the ground of being and meaning. But here he says that the ground has a <u>logos</u> character, that the ground is therefore logical and rational. . . . In this case the ground itself takes on character and meaning, and it supersedes the amorphous 'being itself' which is the ground of everything that is, without itself being anything. If this statement of Tillich's may be taken seriously the nature of God as ground seems to mean the rationality of God."

Since God is the ground of being, he is the ground of the structure of being. He is not subject to this structure; the structure is grounded in him. He is this structure, and it is impossible to speak about him except in terms of this structure.*[134]

Here Tillich inconsistently maintains that God is the ground of the structure, of <u>logos</u>, and that God is the structure. This is one of the difficulties that the interpreter of Tillich continually confronts. Is God a ground somehow behind every form and structure or is he a ground which has a form?[135]

It seems that Tillich comes to realize the difficulties of his indeterminant "being itself" which is the ground of everything, without itself being anything. And so he emerges to the point of emphasizing God as not only the ground of structure, but as structure; not only as the ground of reason, but as reason.[136] God is no longer merely that from which reason proceeds, but he himself is rational.

But this is not all of God. God is not only the source from which every form emerges, but also the abyss in which every form disappears.†[137] If one says that God is rational he must also say that God is abysmal.‡

ii. God as abyss

In the concept of the abyss Tillich is endeavoring to protect the inexhaustibility of God. God as ground forms creation. But God as abyss connotes the fact that no creation can fully express the richness of God. Abyss means for Tillich the depth of the divine life, its inexhaustible and ineffable character.

---

* Tillich, ST, I, 238.
† ST, I, 157.
‡ "Human intuition of the divine always has distinguished between the abyss of the divine (the element of power) and the fullness of its content (the element of meaning), between the divine depth and the divine logos." (ST, I, 250).[138]

---

134. Boozer, "Place of Reason," pp. 183–184: "The inconsistency about whether God is <u>logos</u> or ground of <u>logos</u> is still a point at issue. . . . In the concise paragraph following the difficulty is clearly put." Boozer then quoted a long passage from Tillich that includes the three sentences King quoted.

135. Boozer, "Place of Reason," p. 184: "Here Tillich maintains both that God is the ground of structure, of <u>logos</u>, and that God <u>is</u> the structure. . . . Is God a ground somehow behind and under every form and structure, or is God a ground which has a form and structure?"

136. Boozer, "Place of Reason," p. 185: "He emphasizes God not only as ground of reason, but as reason; not only as ground of structure, but as structure."

137. Tillich, *Systematic Theology*, pp. 157–158: "The ground is not only an abyss in which every form disappears; it also is the source from which every form emerges."

138. Boozer quoted this passage from Tillich in a footnote ("Place of Reason," p. 186).

The abysmal aspect of God represents the depth in God which man's reason cannot fathom. "That depth is what the word God means."*[139]

The holiness of God is included in the concept of God as abyss. The holiness of God expresses the unapproachable character of God, or the impossibility of having a relation with him in the proper sense of the word. God cannot become an object of knowledge or a partner in action. To speak of God as we do of objects whose existence or non-existence can be discussed is to insult the divine holiness. God's holiness makes it impossible to draw him into the context of the ego-world and subject-object correlation. He is the ground of this correlation, not an element in it.† The holiness of God requires that in relation to him we leave behind all finite relations and enter into a relation which is not a relation at all.[140] "God is essentially holy, and every relation with him involves the consciousness that it is paradoxical to be related to that which is holy."‡

In his conception of abyss, Tillich is seeking to maintain the uniqueness of God; that God cannot be exhausted by any creation or by any totality of creation. In a word, Tillich is seeking to protect the majesty of God.[141]

iii. Is the abyss irrational?

In discussing the abyss one is almost inevitably led to ask whether the abyss of being-itself is an abyss of inexhaustible meanings with which man's "meanings" are analogous? Or whether the abyss of being-itself is an irrational abyss which swallows up all finite meaning? Although Tillich does not set forth a series of unambigious passages at this point, it seems that the abyss is not

---

* Tillich, SOF, 57.
† Tillich, ST, I, 272.
‡ Tillich, ST, I, 271.

---

139. Boozer, "Place of Reason," p. 187: "Through the concept of the abyss Tillich wants to protect the inexhaustibility of God. God as ground of <u>logos</u> forms creation. But no creation can express fully the richness of God. . . . Abyss means for Tillich the 'depth of the divine life, its inexhaustible and ineffable character.' . . . There is always a depth in God which man's reason cannot fathom. 'That depth is what the word <u>God</u> means.'"

140. Tillich, *Systematic Theology*, pp. 271–272: "The unapproachable character of God, or the impossibility of having a relation with him in the proper sense of the word, is expressed in the word 'holiness.' . . . God cannot become an object of knowledge or a partner in action. . . . Ultimately, it is an insult to the divine holiness to talk about God as we do of objects whose existence or nonexistence can be discussed. . . . The holiness of God makes it impossible to draw him into the context of the ego-world and the subject-object correlation. . . . The holiness of God requires that in relation to him we leave behind the totality of finite relations and enter into a relation which, in the categorical sense of the word, is not a relation at all."

141. Boozer, "Place of Reason," p. 191: "What Tillich is trying to maintain through the concepts of abyss and being-itself is the infinity, the uniqueness of God; that God cannot be exhausted by any creation or by any totality of them. The majesty of God is the issue here for Tillich."

irrational.*[145] Tillich explicitly states that the abyss manifests itself in logical forms. "The depth of reason is the expression of something that is not reason but which precedes reason and is manifest through it."†[146]

Now it is clear that the depth is non-rational, but it is equally clear that the depth must be manifest through reason. In spite of Tillich's assertion that the abyss is what makes God God, he finds it difficult to rest with merely an abysmal God. He must stress more and more the rational nature of God as "ground." The abyss is not irrational; rather it is non-rational. Its irrationality is denied by the fact that in manifesting itself it must do so through reason.[147]

---

* There is quite a similarity between Tillich's abyss and E. S. Brightman's "Given" in God. The abyss for Tillich is inexhaustible power, infinite vitality.[142] The "Given" of Brightman consists of the eternal uncreated laws of reason, including logic, mathematical relations, and Platonic Ideas, and also of equally eternal uncreated nonrational aspects, "which exhibit all the ultimate qualities of sense objects, disorderly impulses and desires, such experiences as pain and suffering, the forms of space and time, and whatever in God is the source of surd evil." (POR, 337).[143] For Brightman God not only eternally finds "the Given" in his experience, but he also eternally controls it. Tillich asserts that God as form is always in control of the abyss so far as God's relation with existential man is concerned. Yet he nevertheless emphasizes the abyss as the primary essence of God. The abyss is "that which makes God God" (ST, I, 250). For Brightman God's essence is meaning, will, value and rationality. God's reason controls the "given" at every point.[144] There is a very interesting comparison of Brightman's "Given" with Tillich's "abyss" written by Georgia Harkness (Harkness, Art. (1938)).
† Tillich, ST, I, 79.

---

142. Boozer, "Place of Reason," pp. 193–194: "There are similarities between Tillich's 'abyss' and E. S. Brightman's 'given' in God. . . . The abyss for Tillich is inexhaustible power, infinite vitality."

143. Brightman, *Philosophy of Religion*, p. 337: "The Given consists of the eternal, uncreated laws of reason including logic, mathematical relations, and Platonic ideas, and also of equally eternal and uncreated processes of nonrational consciousness which exhibit all the ultimate qualities of sense objects . . ." The rest of the quotation from Brightman is accurate.

144. Boozer, "Place of Reason," pp. 193–194: "So far as God's revealing activity is concerned, that is God's relation with existential man, God as form is always in control of the abyss. As there are similarities between Tillich's 'abyss' and E. S. Brightman's 'given' in God, there is also a similarity between Tillich's idea that God's form controls his power and Brightman's idea that God's reason controls the given. . . . For Brightman God in his essence is meaning, will, purpose, value and rationality."

145. Boozer, "Place of Reason," p. 192: "Is the abyss of being-itself an abyss of inexhaustible meaning (the richness of God's personality) with which man's 'meanings' are analogous? Or is the abyss of being-itself an irrational abyss which swallows up all finite meanings? It seems that in spite of contrary passages, the abyss is not irrational."

146. Boozer, "Place of Reason," p. 192: "The abyss manifests itself in logical forms, meaningful structures. 'The depth of reason is the expression of something that is not reason but which precedes reason and is manifest through it.'"

147. Boozer, "Place of Reason," p. 192: "One cannot deny the non-rationality of the depth here, but neither can one deny the reason through which the depth is manifest. . . . But Tillich himself cannot rest with an abysmal God. He must emphasize more and more the rational nature

So we may conclude that by abyss Tillich means the <u>mysterium tremendum</u>, the inexhaustible depth of God's nature.[148] God as abyss is negative in content and form. In so far as God is <u>Sinnabgrund</u> he is unapproachably holy, infinitely distant from man.* The abyss is not irrational. "It is more a nonrational, unformed dimension of incalculable power."†

By the ground Tillich means the logical, orderly, knowable side of God.[150] The ground of meaning is that in God which supports the rational <u>logos</u> type of manifestation. This manifestation is positive in content and form. In so far as God is <u>Sinngrund</u> man can approach God through his own rational nature.[151] In a word, Tillich is saying something positive about the nature of God in the concept of God as "ground," viz., that God is rational. It is true that Tillich looks upon the abyss as the primary essence of God.‡ But he is confident that the "abysmal quality cannot swallow the rational quality of the divine life."§[152]

5. God as creator

Tillich sees creation as the proper activity of God; it is God's nature to create. Creation is identical with God's life.‖[153] For this reason it is meaningless to ask whether creation is a necessary or a contigent act of God. God's aseity implies that nothing is necessary for him in the sense that he is dependent on a necessity above him. Paradoxically speaking, he eternally "creates himself."

---

* Tillich, ST, I, 287.
† Boozer, PRTCG, 209.[149]
‡ Tillich asserts that the

abyss is what makes God God. (ST, I, 250).
§ Tillich, ST, I, 252.
‖ Tillich, ST, I, 279.

---

of God as 'ground.' The abyss is non-rational; but it is not irrational. And in manifesting itself it must do so through reason."

148. Boozer, "Place of Reason," p. 193: "Tillich means by the abyss the <u>mysterium tremendum</u>, the inexhaustible depth of God's nature."

149. King's source is Boozer, "Place of Reason," p. 193, not p. 209: "This abysmal nature of God is not irrational."

150. Boozer, "Place of Reason," p. 193: "Tillich means by the ground, on the other hand, the logical, orderly, calculable, revealing, knowable side of God."

151. Boozer, "Place of Reason," p. 153: "In general the ground of meaning is that in God which supports the rational, <u>logos</u> type of manifestation. This manifestation is positive in content and form. In so far as God is <u>Sinngrund</u> man can approach God through his own rational nature."

152. Boozer, "Place of Reason," p. 193: "For Tillich says that the abyss is what makes God God. Yet Tillich is confident that 'the abysmal quality cannot swallow the rational quality of the divine life.'"

153. Boozer, "Place of Reason," p. 45: "Creation is the proper activity of God; it is God's nature to create. Creation is identical with God's life."

This is the meaning of God's freedom.[154] But it must be affirmed with equal force that creation is not a contigent act of God. "It does not 'happen' to God, for it is identical with his life. Creation is not only God's freedom but also his destiny."*

But Tillich does not mean by creation an event which took place "once upon a time." Creation does not refer to an event, it rather indicates a condition, a relationship between God and the world. "It is the correlate to the analysis of man's finitude, it answers the question implied in man's finitude and infinitude generally."† Man asks a question which, in existence, he cannot answer. But the question is answered by man's essential nature, his unity with God. Creation is the word given to the process which actualizes man in existence. To indicate the gap between his essential nature and his existential nature man speaks of creation.‡[155]

Since the divine life is essentially creative, avers Tillich, it is necessary to use all three modes of time in symbolizing it. God <u>has</u> created the world. God <u>is</u> creative in the present moment. And God will creatively fulfill his <u>telos</u>. Therefore Tillich speaks of originating creation, sustaining creation, and directing creation.[156]

i. God's originating creativity

Classical Christian doctrine expresses God's originating creativity in the phrase <u>creation ex nihilo</u>. The obvious meaning of the words of this phrase is

---

* Tillich, ST, I, 252.
† Tillich, ST, I, 252.
‡ Tillich, ST, I, 253.

---

154. Tillich, *Systematic Theology*, p. 252: "Therefore, it is meaningless to ask whether creation is a necessary or a contigent act of God. Nothing is necessary for God in the sense that he is dependent on a necessity above him. . . . He eternally 'creates himself,' a paradoxical phrase which states God's freedom."

155. Boozer, "Place of Reason," pp. 45–46: "But Tillich does not mean by creation an event which took place 'once upon a time.' Creation does not describe an event, it rather indicates a condition, a relationship between God and the world. 'It is the correlate to the analysis of man's finitude, it answers the question implied in man's finitude and in finitude generally.' Man asks a question which, in existence, he cannot answer. But the question is answered by man's essential nature, his unity with God. Creation is the word given to the process which actualizes man in existence. To indicate the gap between his essential nature and his existential nature man speaks of 'creation.'" The quotation that Boozer and King attributed to Tillich is inaccurate. It should read: "It is the correlate to the analysis of man's finitude. It answers the question implied in man's finitude and in finitude generally" (Tillich, *Systematic Theology*, p. 252).

156. Tillich, *Systematic Theology*, p. 253: "Since the divine life is essentially creative, all three modes of time must be used in symbolizing it. God *has* created the world, he *is* creative in the present moment, and he *will* creatively fulfil his *telos*. Therefore, we must speak of originating creation, sustaining creation, and directing creation."

a critical negation. They express the fact that God finds nothing "given" to him which influences him in his creativity or resist his creative telos.* This doctrine of creatio ex nihilo protects Christianity from any type of ultimate dualism. Tillich is convinced that this negative meaning of creatio ex nihilo is decisive for every Christian experience and assertion.[157]

However the term ex nihilo seems to denote more than the rejection of dualism. The ex seems to refer to the origin of the creature. "Nothing" is what it comes from.† Now nothing can have two meanings. It can mean "nothing at all," i.e. the absolute negation of being (ouk on), or it can mean the relative negation of being (me on). If it means me on, it cannot be the origin of the creature. The term ex nihilo, nevertheless says something fundamentally important about the creature, namely, that it must take over "the heritage of nonbeing."‡ Creatureliness implies both the heritage of nonbeing and the heritage of being.[158] Its heritage of being stems from its participation in being-itself, in the creative ground of being.§

God's originating creativity is also expressed in the Nicene Creed which states that God is creator of "everything visible and invisible." Like the formula just discussed, this phrase also has a protective function. It is directed against the Platonic view that the Creator-God is dependent on the eternal essences or ideas. The essences are not independent of God, standing in some transcendent realm as models for his creative activity. They are, as Neo-Platonism taught, in the divine mind. They are themselves dependent on God's eternal creativity.[159] "The essential powers of being," affirms Tillich,

---

* Tillich, I, 252.
† Tillich, I, 252.
‡ Tillich, ST, I, 254.
§ Tillich, ST, I, 254.

---

157. Tillich, *Systematic Theology*, p. 253: "The classical Christian doctrine of creation uses the phrase *creatio ex nihilo*. . . . Their obvious meaning is a critical negation. God finds nothing 'given' to him which influences him in his creativity or which resists his creative *telos*. The doctrine of *creatio ex nihilo* is Christianity's protection against any type of ultimate dualism. . . . This negative meaning of *creatio ex nihilo* is clear and decisive for every Christian experience and assertion."

158. Tillich, *Systematic Theology*, p. 253: "The question arises, however, whether the term *ex nihilo* points to more than the rejection of dualism. The word *ex* seems to refer to the origin of the creature. 'Nothing' is what (or where) it comes from. Now 'nothing' can mean two things. It can mean the absolute negation of being (*ouk on*), or it can mean the relative negation of being (*me on*). . . . If *ex nihilo* meant the absolute negation of being, it could not be the origin of the creature. Nevertheless, the term *ex nihilo* says something fundamentally important about the creature, namely, that it must take over what might be called 'the heritage of nonbeing.' . . . [Creature-liness] includes both the heritage of nonbeing (anxiety) and the heritage of being (courage)."

159. Tillich, *Systematic Theology*, p. 254: "In the Nicene Creed, God is called the creator of 'everything visible and invisible.' Like the formula just discussed, this phrase also has, first of all, a protective function. It is directed against the Platonic doctrine that the creator-god is dependent on the eternal essences or ideas, the powers of being which make a thing what it is. . . . Neo-Platonism, and with it much Christian theology, taught that the essences are ideas in the divine

"belong to the divine life in which they are rooted, created by him who is everything he is 'through himself.'"*

Tillich goes on to affirm that originating creativity means that the creature is rooted in the creative ground of the divine life. But it also means that "man has left the ground in order to 'stand upon' himself, to actualize what he essentially is in order to be finite freedom."† This is the point at which creation and the fall join.‡ Tillich admits that this is the most difficult and the most dialectical point in the doctrine of creation. It says that fully developed creatureliness is fallen creatureliness. Man is not only "inside" the divine life, but also "outside" it. Being outside the divine life means to stand in actualized freedom, in an existence which is no longer united with essence. Seen from one side, this is creation. Seen from the other side, this is the fall.§[161] Creation is fulfilled in the creaturely self-realization which simultaneously is freedom and destiny.‖[162]

From this background we gain the meaning of what is called "human creativity." Man is creative in the sense of "bringing the new into being." But this human creativity differs sharply from God's creativity which consists of "bringing into being that which had no being." Man creates new syntheses out of given material.# But God creates the material out of which the new syntheses

---

* Tillich, ST, I, 254.
† Tillich, ST, I, 255.
‡ In identifying creation with the fall, Tillich seems to be implying, against his own intentions, that there is a destructive principle within God. He contends that creation has no ulterior purpose (ST, I, 263); it occurs as the exercise of divine creativity. In other words, God creates because he must, because that is how he is. (Tillich alludes to both freedom and destiny in this connection). Now, if creation is inevitable, and if the result is inevitably bad (a "fall"), then it follows that God contains a destructive principle.[160]
§ Tillich, ST, I, 255.
‖ Tillich, ST, I, 256.
Tillich says that man's creativity is really transformation.

---

mind. . . . They are themselves dependent on God's eternal creativity; they are not independent of him, standing in some heavenly niche as models for his creative activity."

160. Demos, Review of *Systematic Theology*, p. 701: "The author identifies creation (of finite being) with the fall (p. 257) and here the thoughtful reader is perplexed. Creation, says the author, has no ulterior purpose; it occurs as the exercise of divine creativity. In other words, God creates because he must, because that is how he is. (The author alludes to both destiny and freedom in this connection.) Now, if creation is inevitable, and if the result is inevitably bad (a 'fall'), then it follows that God contains a destructive principle."

161. Tillich, *Systematic Theology*, p. 255: "This is the point at which the doctrine of creation and the doctrine of the fall join. It is the most difficult and the most dialectical point in the doctrine of creation. . . . Fully developed creatureliness is fallen creatureliness. . . . To be outside the divine life means to stand in actualized freedom, in an existence which is no longer united with essence. Seen from one side, this is the end of creation. Seen from the other side, it is the beginning of the fall."

162. Tillich, *Systematic Theology*, p. 256: "Creation is fulfilled in the creaturely self-realization which simultaneously is freedom and destiny."

can be developed. God creates man, giving him the power of transforming himself and the world. Man can only transform that which is given.*[163] "God is primarily and essentially creative; man is secondarily and existentially creative."†

ii. God's sustaining creativity

We have seen that man has left the ground of his being in order to stand upon himself, to actualize what he essentially is.[164] But this actualized freedom remains continuously dependent on its creative ground. It is only in the power of being-itself that the creature is able to resist nonbeing. Creaturely existence includes a double resistence, that is, resistence against nonbeing as well as resistence against the ground of being upon which it is dependent.‡ This relation of God to the creature is called in traditional terms the preservation of the world.[165]

Tillich rejects those theories of preservation which affirm that after God created the world he either does not interfere at all (consistent deism) or interferes occasionally through miracles and revelation (theistic deism), or he acts in a continual interrelationship (consistent theism). In none of these cases, asserts Tillich, would it be proper to speak of sustaining creation.§ Tillich finds a more adequate interpretation of preservation in the Augustinian Theory that preservation is continuous creativity, in that God out of eternity creates things and time together. Tillich contends that since God is essentially creative, he is creative in every moment of temporal existence,[166] "giving the

---

* Tillich, ST, I, 256.
† Tillich, ST, I, 256.
‡ Tillich, ST, I, 261.
§ Tillich, ST, I, 262.

---

163. Tillich, *Systematic Theology*, p. 256: "Man creates new syntheses out of given material. This creation really is transformation. God creates the material out of which the new syntheses can be developed. God creates man; he gives man the power of transforming himself and his world. Man can transform only what is given to him."

164. Tillich, *Systematic Theology*, p. 255: "Man has left the ground in order to 'stand upon' himself, to actualize what he essentially is."

165. Tillich, *Systematic Theology*, p. 261: "At the same time, actualized freedom remains continuously dependent on its creative ground. Only in the power of being-itself is the creature able to resist nonbeing. Creaturely existence includes a double resistance, that is, resistance against nonbeing as well as resistance against the ground of being in which it is rooted and upon which it is dependent. Traditionally the relation of God to the creature in its actualized freedom is called the preservation of the world."

166. Tillich, *Systematic Theology*, p. 262: "But after its beginning he either does not interfere at all (consistent deism) or only occasionally through miracles and revelation (theistic deism), or he acts in a continual interrelationship (consistent theism). In these three cases, it would not be proper to speak of sustaining creation. . . . Preservation is continuous creativity, in that God out

power of being to everything that has being out of the creative ground of life."*

Sustaining creativity differs from originating creativity in that the former refers to the given structures of reality, to that which continues in change, to the regular and calculable in things. Without this static element neither action for the future nor a place to stand upon would be possible; and therefore being would not be possible. So Tillich concludes that faith in God's sustaining creativity is faith in the continuity of the structure of reality as the basis for being and acting.†[167]

iii. God's directing creativity

When one thinks of God's directing creativity, he usually thinks of the purpose of creation. But Tillich finds that the concept of "the purpose of creation" is at best an ambiguous concept. Creation, contends Tillich, has no purpose beyond itself. Looked at from the point of view of the creature, the purpose of creation is the creature itself, the actualization of its potentialities.[168] Looked at from the point of view of the creator, "the purpose of creation is the exercise of his creativity, which has no purpose beyond itself because the divine life is essentially creative."‡ Tillich rejects both the Calvinistic doctrine, which designates the purpose of creation as "the glory of God," and the Lutheran doctrine, which affirms that God creates the world in order to have a communion of love with his creatures. In both of these theologies God needs something that he could not have without creation.§ Such an idea Tillich rejects as pagan.

So the ambiguity of the concept "the purpose of creation" leads Tillich to replace the concept by "the telos of creativity"—the inner aim of fulfilling in actuality what is beyond potentiality and actuality in the divine life. One of

---

* Tillich, ST, I, 262.
† Tillich, ST, I, 262.
‡ Tillich, ST, 263, 264.
§ Tillich, ST, I, 264.

---

of eternity creates things and time together. . . . God is essentially creative, and therefore he is creative in every moment of temporal existence."

167. Tillich, *Systematic Theology*, p. 262: "The latter refers to the given structures of reality, to that which continues within the change, to the regular and calculable in things. Without the static element, finite being would not be able to identify itself with itself or anything with anything. Without it, neither expectation, nor action for the future, nor a place to stand upon would be possible; and therefore being would not be possible. The faith in God's sustaining creativity is the faith in the continuity of the structure of reality as the basis for being and acting."

168. Tillich, *Systematic Theology*, p. 263: "Creation has no purpose beyond itself. From the point of view of the creature, the purpose of creation is the creature itself and the actualization of its potentialities."

the basic functions of the divine creativity is to drive every creature toward such a fulfillment. This is the directing creativity of God in addition to his originating and sustaining creativity. This is the side of the divine life which is directed toward the future. The traditional term for God's directing creativity is "providence."*[169]

The term providence means a fore-seeing (<u>pro-videre</u>) which is a fore-ordering ("seeing to it"). Different interpretations of the concept of providence have resulted from this definition. There are those who have emphasized the element of foreseeing, making God an omniscient spectator who knows what will happen but who does not interfere with the freedom of his creatures. On the other hand there are those who have emphasized foreordering, making God a planner who has ordered everything that will happen "before the foundation of the world." In the first interpretation the creatures make their world, while God is a distant spectator. In the second interpretation, God is the only active agent, making the creatures mere cogs in a universal mechanism.†[170]

Tillich is emphatic in affirming that both of these interpretations of providence must be rejected. He sees providence as a permanent activity of God. God is never a spectator; he is forever directing everything toward its fulfillment.[171] "Yet God's directing creativity always creates through the freedom of man and through the spontaneity and structural wholeness of all creatures."‡ Providence works through the polar elements of being, through conditions of individual, social and universal existence, and through finitude, nonbeing, and anxiety. All existential conditions are included in God's directing creativity.[172] "Providence," says Tillich, "is not interference; it is creation. It uses all factors, both those given by freedom and those given by destiny, in cre-

---

* Tillich, ST, I, 264.
† Tillich, ST, I, 266.
‡ Tillich, ST, I, 266.

---

169. Tillich, *Systematic Theology*, p. 264: "The concept 'the purpose of creation' should be replaced by 'the *telos* of creativity'—the inner aim of fulfilling in actuality what is beyond potentiality and actuality in the divine life. One function of the divine creativity is to drive every creature toward such a fulfilment. Thus directing creativity must be added to originating and sustaining creation. It is the side of the divine creativity which is related to the future. The traditional term for directing creativity is 'providence.'"

170. Tillich, *Systematic Theology*, p. 266: "Providence means a fore-seeing (*pro-videre*) which is a fore-ordering ('seeing to it'). . . . If the element of foreseeing is emphasized, God becomes the omniscient spectator who knows what will happen but who does not interfere with the freedom of his creatures. If the element of foreordering is emphasized, God becomes a planner who has ordered everything that will happen 'before the foundations of the world.' . . . In the first interpretation the creatures make their world, and God remains a spectator; in the second interpretation the creatures are cogs in a universal mechanism, and God is the only active agent."

171. Tillich, *Systematic Theology*, p. 266: "Both interpretations of providence must be rejected. Providence is a permanent activity of God. He never is a spectator; he always directs everything toward its fulfilment."

172. Tillich, *Systematic Theology*, p. 266: "Providence works through the polar elements of being. It works through the conditions of individual, social, and universal existence, through fini-

atively directing everything toward its fulfillment."* The man who believes in providence does not believe that a special divine activity will alter man's existential conditions. He believes with the courage of faith that no condition whatsoever can frustrate the fulfillment of his ultimate destiny.† In Pauline terms it means that nothing can separate him from the love of God which is in Christ Jesus.‡[173]

Tillich discusses the question of theodicy under the concept of the directing creativity of God. Faith in God's directing creativity is continually challenged by the presence of meaninglessness and futility in the universe. The question forever arises, how can an almighty God be justified (theos-dike) in view of realities in which no meaning whatsoever can be discovered?[174]

In his discussion of the question of theodicy, Tillich divides evil into three classes. First there is physical evil, pain and death—which, according to him, offer no real problem because they are natural implications of creaturely finitude.§ Secondly, there is moral evil which is the tragic implication of creaturely freedom. Tillich contends that as creator, God cannot create what is opposite to himself; he must create creative beings, beings which are free, and in so far as they are free, independent and therefore estranged from the ground of being.‖ Finally, there is the (apparent) fact of meaninglessness and futility. This, according to Tillich, is the sort of evil which offers genuine difficulties for theological belief. Examples cited by Tillich are "early death, destructive social conditions, feeble-mindedness and insanity, the undiminished horrors of historical existence"—all of these being cases of entities which "are excluded from any kind of fulfillment, even from free resistance against their fulfillment."# Tillich's solution of the problem of evil of this third sort is very difficult to understand, partly because of its excessive conciseness. Such evils are described as "the negativities of creaturely existence." But God himself may be said to participate in the negativities of creaturely existence. God includes within himself "the finite and, with it, non-being." "Nonbeing is eternally conquered and the finite is eternally reunited within the infinity of the

---

* Tillich, ST, I, 267.
† Tillich, ST, I, 267.
‡ Romans, 8:38–39.
§ Here again it is very difficult to follow Tillich, Surely physical evil, pain, and death are evils, and the fact that they are implicated in the finitude of all creaturely being does not help at all. For if creation is of finitude, and finitude is evil, then God is the creator of evil.
‖ Tillich, ST, I, 269.
Tillich, ST, I, 269.

---

tude, nonbeing, and anxiety. . . . All existential conditions are included in God's directing creativity."

173. Tillich, *Systematic Theology*, p. 267: "The man who believes in providence does not believe that a special divine activity will alter the conditions of finitude and estrangement. He believes, and asserts with the courage of faith, that no situation whatsoever can frustrate the fulfilment of his ultimate destiny, that nothing can separate him from the love of God which is in Christ Jesus (Romans, chap. 8)."

174. Tillich, *Systematic Theology*, p. 269: "How can an almighty God be justified (*theos-dikē*) in view of realities in which no meaning whatsoever can be discovered?"

divine life."*[175] This is the ultimate answer to the question of theodicy.[176] "The certainty of God's directing creativity is based on the certainty of God as the ground of being and meaning. The confidence of every creature, its courage to be, is rooted in faith in God as its creative ground."†

6. The ontological elements applied to God

How are the polar elements of everything that has being related in being-itself? Tillich answers this question by asserting that the proper sense of the concepts must be distinguished from their symbolic sense. The symbols taken from finite relationships must be qualified when applied to God. In order to symbolize divine life, the concepts must be stripped of certain existential connotations.[177] This is what Tillich proceeds to do in applying each of the ontological elements to God.

i. Individualization and participation

Individualization is that self-centered character of everything in the light of which a thing is a definite thing. In the case of man individualization means

---

* Tillich, ST, I, 270.
† Tillich, ST, I, 270.

---

175. Demos, Review of *Systematic Theology*, p. 702: "In these two pages the author divides evil into three classes: (a) Physical evil, pain, and death—which, according to him, offer no real problem because they are natural implications of creaturely finitude. Yet surely they are evils, and the fact that they are implicated in the finitude of all creaturely being does not help at all. For if creation is of finitude, and finitude be evil, then God is the creator of evil. (b) Then there is *moral* evil which is the tragic implication of creaturely freedom. Professor Tillich makes what seems to me a wholly valid point, that, as a creator, God cannot create what is opposite to himself; he must create creative beings, beings which are free, and in so far as they are free, independent and therefore estranged from the ground of being. . . . (c) Finally, there is the (apparent) fact of meaninglessness and futility—and this, according to the author, is the only sort of evil which offers genuine difficulties for theological belief. Examples cited by the author are 'early death, destructive social conditions, feeble-mindedness and insanity, the undiminished horrors of historical existence'—all of these being cases of entities which 'are excluded from any kind of fulfilment, even from free resistance against their fulfilment.' The author's solution of the problem of evil of this third sort is very difficult to understand, partly because of its excessive conciseness. Such evils are described as 'the negativities of creaturely existence.' . . . God himself may be said to participate in the negativities of creaturely existence. God includes within himself 'the finite and, with it, non-being.' . . . 'Non-being is eternally conquered and the finite is eternally reunited within the infinity of the divine life.'"

176. Tillich, *Systematic Theology*, p. 270: "This is the ultimate answer to the question of theodicy."

177. Boozer, "Place of Reason," pp. 244, 246: "But how are these polar elements of everything that has being related in being-itself? . . . The proper sense of the concepts must be distinguished

unity of consciousness, selfhood. But man's individualization is not complete or absolute. The element of participation is in polar relation with individualization.[178]

When applied to God, these elements must be qualified. God is the "principle" of individualization and participation; God as being-itself is the ground of both. This does not mean that there is something alongside God in which he participates. God's participation and individualization are symbolical. God is not subject to the polarities of the ontological elements.[179]

If one asks the question, in what sense can God be called an individual, Tillich would answer that this question is only meaningful in the sense that God be called the "absolute participant."[180] And, according to Tillich, "this can only mean that both individualization and participation are rooted in the ground of the divine life and that God is equally "near" to each of them while transcending them both."*

ii. Dynamics and form

The dynamic-form polarity gives rise to several symbols which are central for any present day doctrine of God. Terms such as potentiality, vitality, and self-transcendence are indicated in the term "dynamics," while the term "form" embraces actuality, intentionality, and self-preservation.[181]

Potentiality and actuality appear in the famous Aristotelian-Thomistic formula that God is <u>actus-purus</u>. Tillich rejects this formula as inadequate because it allows the dynamic side in the dynamics-form polarity to be swallowed

---

* Tillich, ST, I, 245.

---

from their symbolic sense, Tillich maintains. The symbols taken from finite relationships must be qualified when applied to God. . . . But to symbolize the divine life, they must be stripped of certain existential connotations."

178. Boozer, "Place of Reason," pp. 243–244: "Individualization is that self-centered character of everything in the light of which a thing is a definite thing. In the case of man individualization means the indivisible unity of consciousness, selfhood. But man's individualization is not absolute or complete. The element of participation is in polar relation with individualization."

179. Boozer, "Place of Reason," p. 245: "God is the 'principle' of individualization and participation; God as being-itself is the ground of both. This does not mean that there is something alongside God in which God participates. . . . God's participation and his individualization are symbolical. . . . God is not subject to the polarity of the ontological elements."

180. Tillich, *Systematic Theology*, p. 244: "The question arises in what sense God can be called an individual. Is it meaningful to call him the 'absolute individual'? The answer must be that it is meaningful only in the sense that he can be called the 'absolute participant.'"

181. Tillich, *Systematic Theology*, pp. 245–246: "The polarity of dynamics and form supplies the material basis for a group of symbols which are central for any present-day doctrine of God. Potentiality, vitality, and self-transcendence are indicated in the term 'dynamics,' while the term 'form' embraces actuality, intentionality, and self-preservation."

by the form side. Actuality free from any element of potentiality is not alive. The God who is <u>actus-purus</u>, affirms Tillich, is not the living God.*[182]

This situation has induced many thinkers to emphasize the dynamics in God "and to depreciate the stabilization of dynamics in pure actuality." This first element is called the <u>Ungrund</u> by Böhme, the first potency by Schelling, the "given" in God by Brightman, <u>me-onic</u> freedom in Berdyaev, and the contingent in Hartshorne.† Each of these cases points symbolically to a quality of the divine life which is analogous to what appears as dynamics in the ontological structure.[183]

Tillich's symbolic application of the dynamics-form polarity to the divine life causes him to reject a nonsymbolic, ontological doctrine of God as becoming. Being, contends Tillich, is not in balance with becoming.[184]

> Being comprises becoming and rest, becoming as an implication of dynamics and rest as an implication of form. If we say that God is being-itself, this includes both rest and becoming, both the static and the dynamic elements. However, to speak of a "becoming" God disrupts the balance between dynamics and form and subjects God to a process which has the character of a fate or which is completely open to the future and has the character of an absolute accident.‡

What Tillich is getting at is now clear. In man there is a tension between dynamics and form. Vitality or dynamics is the power of life, open in all directions toward channels of expression. But man's vitality is conditioned by his form.[185]

The dynamics-form polarity, when applied to God, takes on a different

---

* Tillich, ST, I, 246.
† Tillich, ST, I, 246.
‡ Tillich, ST, I, 247.

---

182. Tillich, *Systematic Theology*, p. 246: "Potentiality and actuality appear in classical theology in the famous formula that God is *actus purus*. . . . In this formula the dynamic side in the dynamics-form polarity is swallowed by the form side. Pure actuality, that is, actuality free from any element of potentiality, is a fixed result; it is not alive. . . . The God who is *actus purus* is not the living God."

183. Tillich, *Systematic Theology*, p. 246: "This situation has induced some thinkers . . . to emphasize the dynamics in God and to depreciate the stabilization of dynamics in pure actuality. . . . The first element is called the *Ungrund* or the 'nature in God' (Böhme), or the first potency (Schelling), or the will (Schopenhauer), or the 'given' in God (Brightman), or *me-onic* freedom (Berdyaev), or the contingent (Hartshorne). . . . They point symbolically to a quality of the divine life which is analogous to what appears as dynamics in the ontological structure."

184. Tillich, *Systematic Theology*, p. 247: "These assertions include a rejection of a nonsymbolic, ontological doctrine of God as becoming. . . . Being is not in balance with becoming."

185. Boozer, "Place of Reason," pp. 246–247: "In man there is a tension between dynamics and form as well as between dynamic form and being-itself. Vitality or dynamics is the power of life, open in all directions toward channels of expression. But man's vitality is conditioned by his form."

meaning. It does not mean that there is tension in the divine life. The dynamics-form polarity applied to God means rather that in God possibility is united with fulfillment. "Neither side threatens the other, nor is there a threat of disruption."* God is dynamic in absolute unity with form.†[186]

iii. Freedom and destiny

In finite life freedom and destiny are in a polar relation of interdependence. In finite life destiny is the basis of freedom and freedom participates in shaping destiny. But when the elements of freedom and destiny are applied to divine life their meaning is altered.[187] Tillich affirms that if we speak of God as free in a non-symbolic sense, we are confronted with the unanswerable question of whether the structure of freedom is not itself something given in relation to which God has no freedom. Because of this difficulty, Tillich asserts that freedom in God, like the other ontological concepts must be understood symbolically.[188] When it is so understood,

> freedom means that that which is man's ultimate concern is in no way dependent on man or on any finite concern. Only that which is unconditional can be the expression of unconditional concern. A conditional God is no God.‡

Likewise, the term destiny cannot be applied to God if the connotation of a "destiny-determining" power above God is given. But both freedom and destiny can be applied symbolically to the divine life if one affirms that in God freedom and destiny are identical. God is his destiny. God's freedom does not shape his destiny. There is an absolute unity and identity of freedom and destiny in God.§

---

* Tillich, ST, I, 247.
† Tillich, ST, I, 244.
‡ Tillich, ST, I, 248.
§ Tillich, ST, I, 248.

---

186. Boozer, "Place of Reason," p. 247: "If one applies the dynamics-form polarity to God, he does not mean thereby that there is tension within the divine life. He rather means that in God possibility is united with fulfillment. 'Neither side threatens the other, nor is there a threat of disruption.' . . . God is dynamic in absolute unity with form."

187. Boozer, "Place of Reason," pp. 247–248: "In finite life freedom and destiny are in a polar relation of interdependence. In finite life destiny is the basis of freedom and freedom participates in shaping destiny. . . . But when the elements of freedom and destiny are applied to the divine life their meaning is altered somewhat."

188. Tillich, *Systematic Theology*, p. 248: "If taken nonsymbolically, this naturally leads to an unanswerable question, whether the structure of freedom, because it constitutes his freedom, is

One of the most illuminating sections in Tillich's discussion of the question of God is his analysis of the traditional attributes of God. Tillich feels that theologians have too long interpreted the attributes of God quantitatively. This type of interpretation has led to both illogical and irrational ideas about the nature of God. So Tillich proceeds to give a qualitative interpretation to the attributes of God rather than a quantitative one. We have already discussed Tillich's interpretation of the omnipotence of God. Now we may turn to a discussion of the eternity, the omnipresence, and the omniscience of God.

i. God is eternal

The concept of eternity is a genuine religious concept. It takes the place of something like omnitemporality, which would be the analogy to omnipotence and omnipresence. In his interpretation of the concept of eternity, Tillich contends that the concept must be protected against two misinterpretations. The first misinterpretation is the tendency to look upon eternity as timelessness. The meaning of olim in Hebrew and of aiones in Greek does not indicate timelessness. Rather than meaning timelessness, eternity means "the power of embracing all periods of time."* If God is a living God, asserts Tillich, he must include temporality and with this a relation to the modes of time. Philosophers throughout the ages have realized that eternity includes temporality. Plato, for instance, called time the moving image of eternity. For Plato eternity included time, even though it was the time of circular movement. Hegel pointed to a temporality within the absolute. These theories, says Tillich, point to the fact that eternity is not timelessness.[189]

Another misinterpretation that Tillich finds surrounding the concept of eternity is the tendency to look upon it as the endlessness of time. The concept of endless time, called "bad infinity" by Hegel, means the endless reiteration of temporality. Tillich looks upon this tendency to elevate the dissected mo-

---

* Tillich, ST, I, 274.

---

not itself something given in relation to which God has no freedom. The answer can only be that freedom, like the other ontological concepts, must be understood symbolically."

189. Tillich, *Systematic Theology*, pp. 274–275: "'Eternity' is a genuine religious word. It takes the place of something like omni- or all-temporality, which would be the analogy to omnipotence, omnipresence, etc. . . . The concept of eternity must be protected against two misinterpretations. Eternity is neither timelessness nor the endlessness of time. The meaning of *olim* in Hebrew and of *aiones* in Greek does not indicate timelessness. . . . If we call God a living God, we affirm that he includes temporality and with this a relation to the modes of time. Even Plato could not exclude temporality from eternity; he called time the moving image of eternity. . . . For Plato eternity included time, even though it was the time of circular movement. . . . Hegel pointed to a temporality within the Absolute. . . . Eternity is not timelessness."

ments of time to infinite significance as idolatry in the most refined sense. Eternity in this sense would mean that God is subjected to a superior power, namely, to the structure of dissected temporality.[190] "It would deprive him of his eternity and make him an everliving entity of subdivine character."*

So, for Tillich, eternity is neither timelessness nor the endlessness of time. Now the question arises: "What is the relation of eternity to the modes of time?" Tillich answers this question in terms of an analogy which is found in human experience, that is, the unity of remembered past and anticipated future in an experienced present. This analogy implies a symbolic approach to the meaning of eternity. Eternity is symbolized as an eternal present (<u>nunc eternum</u>).† But this <u>nunc eternum</u> is not simultaneity. Simultaneity would erase the different modes of time. The eternal present is moving from past to future but without ceasing to be present.[191]

It is through faith in the eternity of God that one finds the courage to conquer the negativities of the temporal process. Both the anxiety of the past and that of the future pass away. The dissected moments of time are united in eternity. Here, and not in the doctrine of the human soul, Tillich finds the certainty of man's participation in eternal life.[192] "The hope of eternal life," asserts Tillich, "is based not on a substantial quality of man's soul but on his participation in the eternity of the divine life."‡

ii. God is omnipresent

God's relation to space, as his relation to time, is interpreted by Tillich in qualitative terms. God, avers Tillich, is neither endlessly extended in space, as

---

* Tillich, ST, I, 275.
† Tillich, ST, I, 275.
‡ Tillich, ST, I, 276.

---

190. Tillich, *Systematic Theology*, p. 275: "Endless time, correctly called 'bad infinity' by Hegel, is the endless reiteration of temporality. To elevate the dissected moments of time to infinite significance by demanding their endless reduplication is idolatry in the most refined sense. . . . For God it would mean his subjection to a superior power, namely, to the structure of dissected temporality."

191. Tillich, *Systematic Theology*, p. 275: "'What is the relation of eternity to the modes of time?' An answer demands use of the only analogy to eternity found in human experience, that is, the unity of remembered past and anticipated future in an experienced present. Such an analogy implies a symbolic approach to the meaning of eternity. . . . Eternity must first be symbolized as an eternal present (*nunc eternum*). But this *nunc eternum* is not simultaneity or the negation of an independent meaning of past and future. The eternal present is moving from past to future but without ceasing to be present."

192. Tillich, *Systematic Theology*, p. 276: "Faith in the eternal God is the basis for a courage which conquers the negativities of the temporal process. Neither the anxiety of the past nor that of the future remains. . . . The dissected moments of time are united in eternity. Here, and not in a doctrine of the human soul, is rooted the certainty of man's participation in eternal life."

a theology inclined toward pantheist formulation would assert, nor limited to a definite space, as a theology of deistic tendencies would assert. The tendency to interpret omnipresence as an extension of the divine substance through all space subjects God to dissected spatiality and puts him alongside himself sacrificing the personal centers of the divine life.* The tendency to interpret omnipresence as meaning that God is present "personally" in a circumscribed place is equally inadequate. The spatial symbols of above and below should never be taken literally. The statement "God is in heaven," for instance, does not mean that he "lives in" or "descends from" a special place; it means, rather, that his life is qualitatively different from creaturely existence.†[193]

It is also improper to interpret omnipresence as spacelessness. Tillich holds that punctuality in the divine life must be rejected as much as simultaneity and timelessness. Extension is found in the ground of the divine life in which everything spatial is rooted. But God is not subject to this spatial existence; he transcends it and participates in it.[194] "God's omnipresence is his creative participation in the spatial existence of his creatures."‡

The religious value of God's omnipresence is immense. It overcomes the anxiety of not having a space for one's self. It means that wherever man is he is "at home" in the ground of God. One is always "in the sanctuary" when he experiences God's omnipresence. In such a presence of God every place is a "holy place." There is in that situation no difference between the sacred and the secular.§[195]

---

* Tillich, ST, I, 277.
† Tillich, ST, I, 277.
‡ Tillich, ST, I, 277.
§ Tillich, ST, I, 278.

---

193. Tillich, *Systematic Theology*, pp. 276–277: "God's relation to space, as his relation to time, must be interpreted in qualitative terms. God is neither endlessly extended in space nor limited to a definite space; nor is he spaceless. A theology inclined toward pantheist formulation prefers the first alternative, while a theology with deistic tendencies chooses the second alternative. Omnipresence can be interpreted as an extension of the divine substance through all spaces. This, however, subjects God to dissected spatiality and puts him, so to speak, alongside himself sacrificing the personal center of the divine life. . . . Further, omnipresence can be interpreted to mean that God is present 'personally' in a circumscribed place (in heaven above) but also simultaneously present with his power every place (in the earth beneath). But this is equally inadequate. The spatial symbols of above and below should not be taken literally in any respect. . . . 'God is in heaven'; this means that his life is qualitatively different from creaturely existence. But it does not mean that he 'lives in' or 'descends from' a special place."

194. Tillich, *Systematic Theology*, p. 277: "We must reject punctuality in the divine life as much as simultaneity and timelessness. God creates extension in the ground of his life, in which everything spatial is rooted. But God is not subject to it; he transcends it and participates in it."

195. Boozer, "Place of Reason," p. 198: "The religious value of the concept is immense. Wherever man is he is 'at home' in the ground of God. One is always 'in his sanctuary' when he experiences God's omnipresence. When the sacramental presence of God is felt, every place is a 'holy place.' There is in that situation no difference between the sacred and the secular."

In traditional theology omniscience is the faculty of a highest being who is supposed to know all objects, past, present, and future, and beyond this, everything that might have happened if what has happened had not happened. But Tillich looks upon this interpretation of omniscience as illogical and absurd. The absurdity of such an interpretation is due to the impossibility of subsuming God under the subject-object scheme. If one speaks of the unconditional character of divine knowledge, therefore, one must speak symbolically, indicating that God is not present in an all-permeating manner but that he is present spiritually.[196] It means that

> nothing is outside the centered unity of his life; nothing is strange, dark, hidden, isolated, unapproachable. Nothing falls outside the <u>logos</u> structure of being. The dynamic element cannot break the unity of the form; the abysmal quality cannot swallow the rational quality of the divine life.*

This has tremendous implications for man's personal and cultural existence. In personal life it means that there is no absolute darkness in one's being. Faith in God's omniscience overcomes the anxiety of the dark and the hidden. The divine omniscience is ultimately the logical foundation of the belief in the openness of reality to human knowledge. We are able to gain knowledge because we participate in divine knowledge. We are able to reach truth because the divine life in which we are rooted embodies all truth.[197]

8. Divine love and divine justice

Love and justice have often been looked upon as two distinct attributes of God. But Tillich feels that such a position is due to a misconception of the

---

* Tillich, ST, I, 279.

---

196. Tillich, *Systematic Theology*, pp. 278–279: "Omniscience is not the faculty of a highest being who is supposed to know all objects, past, present, and future, and, beyond this, everything that might have happened if what has happened had not happened. The absurdity of such an image is due to the impossibility of subsuming God under the subject-object scheme, although this structure is grounded in the divine life. If one speaks, therefore, of divine knowledge and of the unconditional character of the divine knowledge, one speaks symbolically, indicating that God is not present in an all-permeating manner but that he is present spiritually."

197. Tillich, *Systematic Theology*, p. 279: "This certainty has implications for man's personal and cultural existence. In personal life it means that there is no absolute darkness in one's being. . . . And, on the other hand, the anxiety of the dark and the hidden is overcome in the faith of the divine omniscience. . . . Therefore, the divine omniscience is the logical (though not always conscious) foundation of the belief in the openness of reality to human knowledge. We *know* because we participate in the divine knowledge. Truth is not absolutely removed from the outreach of our finite minds, since the divine life in which we are rooted embodies all truth."

nature of love and justice. Justice, contends Tillich, is a part of love. Love is the ontological concept. Justice has no independent ontological standing. Justice is dependent on love. It is a part of love's activity. With this statement of the complementary nature of love and justice we may examine them separately.[198]

i. The divine love

Love, for Tillich, is an ontological concept. He finds the ontological nature of love expressed in the tendency of every life-process to unite a trend toward separation with a trend toward reunion. Such a tendency is based on the polarity of individualization and participation. Love is absent where there is no individualization, and love can be fully realized only where there is full individualization, in man. But the individual also longs to return to the unity to which he belongs, in which he participates by his ontological nature.*[199] This is what Tillich means when he says that love is not the union of the strange but the reunion of the estranged.†

To say that God is love literally is to apply the experience of separation and reunion to the divine life. This, however, is impossible since God is not subject to the ontological elements. Therefore one must speak symbolically of God as love. When God is spoken of as love, the meaning is that the divine life has the character of love but beyond the distinction between potentiality and actuality.‡[200]

In order to gain a clearer meaning of the divine love, Tillich distinguishes between several different types of love.§ In each type of love there is a quest

---

* Tillich, ST, I, 279.
† Tillich, LPJ, 25.
‡ Tillich, ST, I, 280.
§ In his Systematic Theology Tillich refers to types of love. But in a more recent work Tillich affirms that it is improper to speak of types of love. There are not types of love, but qualities of love. "But I have learned, while elaborating these lectures, that there are not types but qualifications of love." (LPJ, 5).

---

198. Boozer, "Place of Reason," pp. 201–202: "iii. Divine love and divine justice. . . . Justice is part of love. Love is the ontological concept. Justice has no independent ontological standing. It is in a sense parasitic, a part of love's activity. . . . Recognizing the complementary nature of [love and justice] we may examine them separately."

199. Tillich, *Systematic Theology*, pp. 279–280: "Love is an ontological concept. . . . According to the ontological polarity of individualization and participation, every life-process unites a trend toward separation with a trend toward reunion. . . . Love is absent where there is no individualization, and love can be fully realized only where there is full individualization, in man. But the individual also longs to return to the unity to which he belongs, in which he participates by his ontological nature."

200. Tillich, *Systematic Theology*, p. 280: "If we say that God *is* love, we apply the experience of separation and reunion to the divine life. As in the case of life and spirit, one speaks symbolically of God as love. He *is* love; this means that the divine life has the character of love but beyond the distinction between potentiality and actuality."

for reunion. There is love as <u>libido</u> which is the movement of the needy toward that which fulfills the need. There is love as <u>philia</u> which is movement of the equal toward union with the equal. There is love as <u>eros</u> which is the movement of that which is lower in power and meaning to that which is higher. In all three of these forms of love the element of desire is present. But there is a from of love which transcends these, namely, the desire to fulfill the longing of the other being. This is love as <u>agape</u>. All love, except <u>agape</u>, is dependent on contingent characteristics which change and are partial, such as repulsion and attraction, passion and sympathy.* <u>Agape</u> is independent of these states. It affirms the other unconditionally. It is <u>agape</u> that suffers and forgives. It seeks the personal fulfillment of the other.

It is this type of love that is the basis for the assertion that God is love.[201] "God works toward the fulfillment of every creature and toward the bringing-together into the unity of his life all who are separated and disrupted."† It is in this sense, and in this sense only that God is called love. None of the other types of love can be applied to God. Certainly not <u>libido</u>, because God is not in need of anything. <u>Philia</u> cannot properly symbolize God's love, because there is no equality between man and God. Moreover, <u>eros</u> cannot properly synbolize God's love, because God in his eternity transcends the fulfillment and non-fulfillment of reality. The basic and only adequate symbol for God's love is <u>agape</u>.‡

We may raise the question of the possibility of divine self love at this point. Tillich is reluctant to speak of self-love on the human level, since he sees love as the drive towards the reunion of the separated. He contends that within the unity of self-consciousness there is no real separation, comparable to the separation of self-centered being from all other being.§ But although Tillich is reluctant to speak of self-love on the human level, he is quite willing to speak of divine self-love. He says in one instance that "man's love of God is the love with which God loves himself."‖ This is an expression of the truth that God is a subject even when he seems to be an object. It is a statement

---

* Tillich, ST, I, 280.
† Tillich, ST, I, 281.
‡ Tillich, ST, I, 281.
§ Tillich, LPJ, 33.

‖ Tillich, ST, I, 282. This passage is definitely suggestive of absolute quantitative monism.

---

201. Tillich, *Systematic Theology*, pp. 280–281: "Love as *libido* is the movement of the needy toward that which fulfils the need. Love as *philia* is the movement of the equal toward union with the equal. Love as *erōs* is the movement of that which is lower in power and meaning to that which is higher. It is obvious that in all three the element of desire is present. . . . But there is a form of love which transcends these, namely, the desire for the fulfilment of the longing of the other being, the longing for *his* ultimate fulfilment. All love, except *agapē*, is dependent on contingent characteristics which change and are partial. It is dependent on repulsion and attraction, on passion and sympathy. *Agapē* is independent of these states. It affirms the other unconditionally. . . . It suffers and forgives. It seeks the personal fulfilment of the other. . . . This type of love is the basis for the assertion that God is love."

about God loving himself. As we shall see subsequently, the trinitarian distinctions (separation and reunion) make it possible to speak of divine self-love.[202]

> Without separation from one's self, self-love is impossible. . . . Through the separation <u>within</u> himself God loves himself and through separation <u>from</u> himself (in creaturely freedom) God fulfills his love of himself—primarily because he loves that which is estranged from himself.*

ii. The divine justice

As we have seen, justice has no independent ontological standing. Justice is dependent on love. Justice is really an act of love protesting against that which violates love. Whenever an individual violates the structure of love, judgment and condemnation follow. But they do not follow by an act of divine retribution; they follow by the reaction of God's loving power against that which violates love.[203] "Condemnation is not the negation of love but the negation of the negation of love."† It is the way in which that which resists love, i.e. that which resists being reunited to that from which it is separated, is left to separation, with an implied and inescapable self-destruction.[204]

Tillich feels that the ontological character of love not only solves the problem of the relation of love and retributive justice, but also provides theology with the possibility of using the symbol "the wrath of God." The wrath of God is not an affect alongside God's love nor is it a motive for action alongside his providence;[205] "it is the emotional symbol for the work of love which rejects and leaves to self-destruction what resists it."‡ In this sense the metaphorical symbol "the wrath of God" is necessary and unavoidable.[206]

Tillich finds the final expression of the unity of love and justice in the sym-

---

* Tillich, ST, I, 282.
Here again we can see
Tillich's absolute monism.
† Tillich, ST, I, 284.
‡ Tillich, ST, I, 284.

---

202. Tillich, *Systematic Theology*, p. 282: "This is an expression of the truth that God is a subject even where he seems to be an object. . . . The trinitarian distinctions (separation and reunion) make it possible to speak of divine self-love."

203. Tillich, *Systematic Theology*, p. 283: "But they do not follow by a special act of divine wrath or retribution; they follow by the reaction of God's loving power against that which violates love."

204. Tillich, *Systematic Theology*, p. 283: "It is the way in which that which resists love, namely, the reunion of the separated in the divine life, is left to separation, with an implied and inescapable self-destruction."

205. Tillich, *Systematic Theology*, pp. 283–284: "The ontological character of love solves the problem of the relation of love and retributive justice. . . . This again provides theology with the possibility of using the symbol 'the wrath of God.' . . . The wrath of God is neither a divine affect alongside his love nor a motive for action alongside providence."

bol of justification. Justification points to the divine act in which love conquers the immanent consequences of the violation of justice. This divine love in relation to the unjust creature is grace.*[207]

9. The trinity

For Tillich the trinity is not the illogical and irrational assertion that three are one and one is three. It is a qualitative rather than a quantitative characterization of God. It is an attempt to express the richness and complexity of the divine life.[208]

The first person of the trinity is abyss. It is the abysmal character of God, the element of power which is the basis of the Godhead, "which makes God God."†[209] As we have seen, this first principle is the root of God's majesty, the unapproachable intensity of his being. It is the power of being infinitely resisting nonbeing.[210] God as Father is power.

The second person‡ of the Trunity is the <u>logos</u>, the element of meaning, the element of structure.[211] "The <u>logos</u> opens the divine ground, its infinity and its darkness, and it makes its fullness distinguishable, definite, finite."§ Without this second principle the first principle would be chaos, and God would be demonic.[212]

As we have seen in the earlier part of the discussion, these two poles in God's nature are indicated in the definition of God as abyss and ground of

---

* Tillich, ST, I, 285.
† Tillich, ST, I, 250; ST, I, 156.
‡ Tillich prefers to say

principle instead of person.
§ Tillich, ST, I, 251.

---

206. Tillich, *Systematic Theology*, p. 284: "The metaphorical symbol 'the wrath of God' is unavoidable."

207. Tillich, *Systematic Theology*, pp. 284–285: "The final expression of the unity of love and justice in God is the symbol of justification. It points to the unconditional validity of the structures of justice but at the same time to the divine act in which love conquers the immanent consequences of the violation of justice. . . . The divine love in relation to the unjust creature is grace."

208. Boozer, "Place of Reason," p. 214: "The doctrine of the trinity is not the illogical assertion that three are one. Rather it is a qualitative characterization of God. It is an effort to express the richness of the divine life."

209. Boozer, "Place of Reason," p. 214: "It is the abysmal character of God, the element of power, which is the basis of the Godhead, 'which makes God God.'"

210. Tillich, *Systematic Theology*, pp. 250–251: "It is the root of his majesty, the unapproachable intensity of his being, the inexhaustible ground of being in which everything has its origin. It is the power of being infinitely resisting nonbeing."

211. Boozer, "Place of Reason," p. 215: "The second person (or principle, as Tillich prefers) is the <u>logos</u>, the element of meaning, the element of structure, fullness, content."

212. Tillich, *Systematic Theology*, p. 251: "Without the second principle the first principle would be chaos. . . . Without the second principle God is demonic."

being and meaning. But Tillich does not stop with this polar concept of God's nature. There is a third principle, that of spirit.[213]

Spirit is that principle in which power and meaning, abyss and ground are united. Spirit stands for the unity of all the polar opposites: of power with meaning, of the static with the dynamic, even of mind with body.* God is no nearer one "part" of being than he is to another. He is as near the creative darkness of the unconscious as he is to the critical light of cognitive reason.[215] "Spirit is the power through which meaning lives, and it is the meaning which gives direction to power."†

It is through the concept of the Spirit that Tillich explains the self-separating and self-returning activity of God. Through the Spirit God goes out of himself, the Spirit proceeds from the divine ground. He gives actuality to that which is potential in the divine ground.[216] "Through the Spirit the divine fullness is posited in the divine life as something definite, and at the same time it is reunited in the divine ground."‡

Tillich emphasizes the point that a consideration of the trinitarian principles is not the Christian doctrine of the Trinity. It is preparation for it. The doctrinal formulation of the Trinity can be discussed only after the Christological dogma has been elaborated.§ But in order to speak meaningfully of the living God it is necessary to discuss the trinitarian principles.[217]

---

* Tillich seems to be abusing language here, for if religious common sense means anything in saying that God is a spirit, it means that God is immaterial. Probably the responsibility for such unnatural changes of meaning must be charged to the dialectical principle, which necessitates that a given meaning should embrace its opposite. Certainly no precision of meaning is possible under such conditions.[214]

† Tillich, ST, I, 250.
‡ Tillich, ST, I, 251.
§ Tillich's Christology will be presented in the second volume of his Systematic Theology.

---

213. Boozer, "Place of Reason," p. 215: "These poles within God's nature have been indicated in the basic definition of God as abyss and ground of being and meaning. But Tillich is not at ease in this polar concept of the nature of God. There is a third principle, that of spirit."

214. Demos, Review of Systematic Theology, p. 700: "Spirit, he says, stands for the unity of all the polar opposites: of power with meaning, of the static with the dynamic, even of mind with body (pp. 249–251). Surely he is abusing language here, for if religious common sense means anything in saying that God is a spirit, it means that God is immaterial. I think that the responsibility for such unnatural changes of meaning must be charged to the dialectical principle, which necessitates that a given meaning should embrace its opposite. I doubt that any precision of meaning—indeed any meaning—is possible under such conditions."

215. Tillich, Systematic Theology, p. 250: "God is not nearer to one 'part' of being or to a special function of being than he is to another. As Spirit he is as near to the creative darkness of the unconscious as he is to the critical light of cognitive reason."

216. Tillich, Systematic Theology, p. 251: "It is the Spirit in whom God 'goes out from' himself, the Spirit proceeds from the divine ground. He gives actuality to that which is potential in the divine ground and 'outspoken' in the divine logos."

217. Tillich, Systematic Theology, p. 251: "The consideration of the trinitarian principles is not the Christian doctrine of the Trinity. It is a preparation for it, nothing more. The dogma of the

10. The question of the personality of God

We have seen throughout the discussion that Tillich continually talks of God in terms of power. Now the question arises whether Tillich's God is an unconscious reservoir of power or whether he is a conscious person. An answer to this question is crucial for any adequate interpretation of Tillich's God-concept.

We have seen that Tillich considers all statements about God as being of a symbolic nature, except the statement that God is being-itself. We cannot say, for instance, that God is living in the literal sense of the word because life is literally "the process in which potential being becomes actual being," and God "transcends" the distinction between potential and actual. But God does live in the sense that He is the ground of life. Tillich carries this same method of thinking over into the question of the personality of God. He insists that the symbol, "personal God," does not mean that God is a person. "It means that God is the ground of everything personal and that he carries within himself the ontological power of personality."*[218] Tillich thinks that the tendency to speak of God as "a person" was a nineteenth century creation, brought into being through the Kantian separation of nature ruled by physical law from personality ruled by moral law.[219] Under this influence theism made God "a heavenly, completely perfect person who resides above the world and mankind."† But there is no evidence for the existence of such a highest person. At best Tillich finds the symbol "personal God" quite confusing.

In answering a criticism which Einstein raised against the idea of a personal God, Tillich admitted that most concepts of a personal God contradicted the scientific interpretation of nature. He writes:

> The concept of a "Personal God," interfering with natural events or being an independent cause of natural events makes God a natural object besides others, an object amongst objects, a being amongst beings, maybe the highest, but anyhow a being. This, indeed, is the destruction, not only of the physical system, but even more the destruction of any meaningful ideas of God.‡

---

* Tillich, ST, I, 245.

† Tillich, ST, I, 245.

‡ Tillich, Art. (1940)², 9.

Trinity can be discussed only after the christological dogma has been elaborated. But the trinitarian principles appear whenever one speaks meaningfully of the living God."

218. Schilling wrote on an early draft of this chapter: "On this basis, might we not just as well speak of a material, animal, or impersonal God, since G. for T. is the ground of all being?" (King, Draft of chapter 3).

219. Tillich, *Systematic Theology*, p. 245: "God became 'a person' only in the nineteenth century, in connection with the Kantian separation of nature ruled by physical law from personality ruled by moral law."

Yet in spite of the confusing nature of the idea of a "personal God," Tillich finds it indispensable for living religion, if for no other reason than, as the philosopher Schelling says, "only a person can heal a person."[220] God cannot be considered less than personal, although he can and must be more than personality.

In a sense God is the supra-personal.

> The supra-personal is not an "It," or more exactly, it is a "He" as much as it is an "It," and it is above both of them. But if the "He" element is left out, the "It" element transforms the alleged supra-personal into sub-personal, as it usually happens in monism and pantheism.*

Now we can clearly see that there is a basic inconsistency in Tillich's thought at this point. On the one hand Tillich's thought suggests the sub-personalism of Oriental Vedantism. On the other hand Tillich recognizes personality as a precious symbol denoting the unconditional, the ground and abyss of all being. He contends that this kind of symbolsim is indispensable and must be maintained against pantheistic and naturalistic criticism, lest religion fall back to the level of a primitive-demonic pre-personalism.†[221] Certainly this is a flagrant contradiction. It seems that Tillich both wants a personal God and does not want a personal God.[222]

At any rate, all of Tillich's conclusions tend to point to an impersonal God. Despite his warning that God is not less than personal, we see traits throughout Tillich's thinking that point to a God that is less than personal. Even those things which Tillich says about God with personalistic implications are finally given impersonal explanations. For instance, Tillich speaks of God as love. But on closer scrutiny we discover that love, for Tillich, is just the dialectical principle of the union of opposites. Tillich's use of the word love inevitable reminds one of the love (and strife) of Empodocles, who meant by "love" no more than the attraction of the elements for one another.[223] At one point

---

* Tillich, Art. (1940)[2],
10.

† Tillich, PE, 119.

---

220. Tillich, "Idea of the Personal God," p. 10: "For as the philosopher Schelling says: 'Only a person can heal a person.' This is the reason that the symbol of the Personal God is indispensable for living religion."

221. Tillich, *Protestant Era*, p. 119: "This kind of symbolism is indispensable and must be maintained against pantheistic, mystical, or naturalistic criticism, lest religion and with it our attitude toward nature, man, and society fall back to the level of a primitive-demonic pre-personalism."

222. DeWolf wrote "Good" next to this sentence on a draft of this chapter (King, Draft of chapter 3).

223. Demos, Review of *Systematic Theology*, p. 701: "Love is just the dialectical principle of the union of opposites. . . . The author's use of the word love in this connection inevitably reminds one of the love (and strife) of Empedocles, who meant by 'love' no more than the attraction of the elements for one another."

Tillich stresses the <u>logos</u> character of God, which would certainly give personalistic tones. But even this is distorted through Tillich's insistence that the
abyss is what makes God God.

So Tillich ends with a God who is a sub-personal reservoir of power, somewhat akin to the impersonalism of Hindu Vedantism. He chooses the less than
personal to explain personality, purpose, and meaning.

11. Is Tillich an absolute quantitative monist?

We come to a question at this point which has been cropping up throughout
our discussion of Tillich's God-concept, viz., the question of whether Tillich
holds to an absolute quantitative monism. Certainly there is much in Tillich's
conception of God which suggest that he does. For instance, his emphasis on
God's participation in every life as its ground and aim is monistic.* Also he
can talk of God's going out of himself and resting in himself. "The finite is
posited as finite within the process of divine life, but it is reunited with the
infinite within the same process."† Again he says: "God is infinite because he
has the finite within himself united with his infinity."‡ Still again he says: "The
divine life is creative, actualizing itself in inexhaustible abundance."§ The
similarity of Tillich's view at this point to Hegel's philosophy of spirit and
Plotinus' philosophy of the One inclines one to interpret Tillich as an absolute
monist.[224]

Perhaps Tillich's most explicit statement of monism is his contention that
"man's love of God is the love with which God loves himself. . . . The divine
life is the divine self-love."‖ Tillich makes the same assertion about divine
knowledge. "If there is knowledge of God, it is God who knows himself
through man."# Passages such as these cited indicate an absolute monism.[225]

There are some passages, on the other hand, which imply a quantitative

---

* Tillich, ST, I, 245.   § Tillich, ST, I, 282.
† Tillich, ST, I, 251.   ‖ Tillich, ST, I, 282.
‡ Tillich, ST, I, 282.   # Tillich, ST, I, 172.

---

224. Boozer, "Place of Reason," p. 61: "The similarity of Tillich's theology with Hegel's philosophy of spirit and Plotinus' philosophy of the One inclines one to interpret Tillich as an
absolute monist. God goes out from himself. He rests in himself. 'The finite is posited as finite
within the process of the divine life, but it is reunited with the infinite within the same process.'
'God is infinite because he has the finite within himself united with his infinity.' 'The divine life is
creative, actualizing itself in inexhaustible abundance.'"

225. Boozer, "Place of Reason," p. 62: "But perhaps the most convincing statement of monism
is in terms of love, that 'man's love of God is the love with which God loves himself. . . . The
divine life is the divine self-love.' . . . Passages such as these certainly indicate an absolute monism." Ellipsis in quotation from Tillich is in the original text of Boozer's dissertation. Boozer's
footnote to the quotation reads: "Actually Tillich makes the same assertion about divine knowledge. 'If there is a knowledge of God, it is God who knows himself through man.'"

pluralism. Tillich insists, for instance, that man is free. In fact he defines the nature of man as "finite freedom."* Tillich affirms that there would be no history unless man were to some degree free; that is, to some extent, independent from God. Tillich goes on to insist that one of the basic characteristics of existence is a separation of man and God. Man in existence is conscious of being separated from what he ought to be. He is to some extent "outside" the divine life.[226] This means that he stands "in actualized freedom, in an existence which is no longer united with essence."†[227]

It is obvious that this represents a basic contradiction in Tillich's thought, and he nowhere seeks explicitly to resolve the contradiction. Is any resolution of these seeming contradictions possible?[228] Boozer, in interpreting Tillich's thought at this point, thinks that the contradiction can be resolved on the basis of Tillich's distinction between essence and existence. Boozer writes:

> Essentially God is all in all; God is one, and man is not actual as a separate being. Man is a part of God. But in existence, in the realm of God's creation there is a partial separation of man from God through the actualization of man's finite freedom. The sustaining structure of existence is still unity with God. But the unity is not complete in existence. In existence, then, God and man are separate to an extent, and there is pluralism.‡

It is probably an oversimplification to say that this resolves the contradiction completely, for a contradiction cannot be resolved merely by denying one term of it (in this case pluralism), Moreover, even if it is gratned that Tillich holds to an ultimate ontological monism there is the further contradiction of how man can be free in such a monistic system. Freedom implies metaphysical otherness, and it is hardly possible to hold to an ultimate ontological monism and the freedom of man simultaneously. This is a contradiction that Tillich never seems to resolve.

In spite of the foregoing, however, Boozer is basically sound in his interpretation of Tillich's God as the only metaphysical reality; a God who goes out of himself into existence and returns to himself. At least three quotations from Tillich give weight to this conclusion.

---

* Tillich, Art. (1939),
202.

† Tillich, ST, I, 255.

‡ Boozer, PRTCG, 62.

---

226. Boozer, "Place of Reason," p. 62: "There would be no history unless man were to some degree free; that is, to some degree independent from God. . . . The basic characteristic of existence is a separation of man from God. . . . Man in existence is conscious of an absolute demand, an unconditional demand to become what he is not. . . . He is to some extent 'outside' the divine life."

227. Boozer quoted this passage from Tillich ("Place of Reason," pp. 62–63).

228. Boozer, "Place of Reason," p. 63: "What sort of resolution of these seeming contradictions is possible?"

The dialectical method attempts to mirror the movement of reality. It is the logical expression of a philosophy of life, for life moves through self-affirmation, going out of itself and returning to itself.*[229]

Speaking of God, Tillich writes: "We assert that he is the eternal process in which separation is posited and is overcome by reunion."†[230] Again he writes:

> The ground of Being of which every being takes its power of being has the character of selfseparating and selfreturning life. Selfseparating is the abbreviation for separating itself from itself towards the complete individualization of the self having itself. Selfreturning is the abbreviation of the return of life to itself in the power of returning love.‡[231]

In a very informative article on the nature of man, Tillich asserts that man has a threefold nature, viz., an essential nature, an existential nature, and an eschatological nature. It becomes clear now that Tillich applies this same threefold nature to God. It is through such an interpretation that we can understand Tillich's statement that God "is the eternal process in which separation is posited and is overcome by reunion." When one considers the fullness of God in the three natures, many contradictions are reconciled.

The conclusion is that Tillich holds to an ultimate ontological monism both qualitative and quantitative. God is ultimately the only metaphysical reality. The life of man is a phase of the actualization of God and not a separate metaphysical reality.[232]

---

* Tillich, ST, I, 234.
† Tillich, ST, I, 242.
‡ Tillich, Art. (1949)²,
15.

---

229. Boozer quoted this passage from Tillich ("Place of Reason," pp. 63–64).

230. Boozer, "Place of Reason," p. 64: "Speaking of God, Tillich writes: 'We assert that he is the eternal process in which separation is posited and is overcome by reunion.'"

231. Boozer quoted this passage from Tillich ("Place of Reason," p. 64).

232. Boozer, "Place of Reason," pp. 44, 45, 64: "Man for Tillich is not real as an individual metaphysical entity, the creation of God. Man is a phase of the objectification of God, the actualization of God. . . . The basic position around which Tillich's thought is oriented is that of an ultimate ontological monism, both quantitative and qualitative. . . . For Tillich, then, there is ultimately only one metaphysical reality, God." On a draft of this chapter, Schilling wrote: "A sound conclusion. But does this resolve the contradiction? It does, if a contradiction can be resolved, denying one term of it, in this case, personalism! Should you not point this out?" (King, Draft of chapter 3).

Chapter IV

WIEMAN'S CONCEPTION OF GOD

One of the most important phases of Wieman's thought is his concept of God. His emphasis is theocentric throughout. He never wearies of pointing out that God (creative good) must be dominant over all created good in the devotion of man. Wieman plainly states that his purpose in the field of religion is to promote a theocentric religion over against the prevalent anthropocentrism. In this endeavor he stresses the fact that men must worship the actuality of God and not their ideas about God. Further, it is imperative that men not allow their wishes and needs to shape their ideas of God but rather that the ideas of God be shaped solely in the light of objective evidence.

It is the success of this approach that constitutes the significance of Wieman. "One of the most persuasive reconstructed forms of theism that has appeared in this country," says Bernard Meland, "is the philosophy of religion developed by Henry Nelson Wieman."* D. C. Macintosh in a more definite but no less laudatory statement says:

> No one has gone as far as Professor Henry N. Wieman in suggesting a variety of ways in which the divinely functioning reality may be characterized and defined and at the same time known, strictly speaking, to exist. His definitions of God, insofar as God may be undeniably affirmed to exist, have a more curious interest, aiming to formulate the irreducible minimum of religious knowledge, they generally succeed sufficiently to have positive value for reasonable reassurance in religion.†

As we shall see throughout this chapter, Wieman's conception of God is quite different from that of traditional theism. He has classified his view as "theistic naturalism." This means that he would avoid any ultimate separation of God from nature; that he views God as one natural process or structure of processes among others which can be apprehended in clearly defined ways with predictable results. Such a process or structure of processes may be superhuman but cannot be "supernatural," because nature is defined by him as "what we know through the interaction between the physiological organism and its environment," while the supernatural is unknowable by definition.[1]

---

* Meland, MMW, 139.
† Macintosh, PRK, 165.

---

1. James Alfred Martin, Jr., *Empirical Philosophies of Religion: With Special Reference to Boodin, Brightman, Hocking, Macintosh, and Wieman* (Morningside Heights, N.Y.: King's Crown Press, 1945), pp. 87–88: "Wieman has classified his view as 'theistic naturalism'. This means that he

With these introductory remarks we turn now to a discussion of the nature of God.

1. The nature of God

Wieman contends that it has been his purpose "so to formulate the idea of God that the question of God's existence becomes a dead issue."* To accomplish this he has offered as a "minimal" definition of God the following: "God is that something upon which human life is most dependent for its security, welfare, and increasing abundance . . . that something of supreme value which constitutes the most important condition."†[2] But Wieman has developed this minimal definition in various ways. At one point in his intellectual pilgrimage he suggested that God as so defined is "that interaction between individuals, groups, and ages which generates and promotes the greatest mutuality of good . . . the richest possible body of shared experience."‡ In another volume he speaks of God as "that interaction which sustains and magnifies personality . . . the process of progressive integration";§ while in another place he undertakes to defend Whitehead's view of God as "the principle of concretion."‖[3] In his most mature work, The Source of Human Good, Wieman defines God as the "creative event." He feels that this latter definition most adequately expresses the nature of God.

---

* Wieman, Art. (1932)[3], 276.

† Wieman, RESM, 9

‡ This definition suggests Dewey's "religion of shared experience."

§ Wieman, Art. (1932)[1], 351.

‖ Wieman, WTR, 179–212.

---

would avoid any ultimate separation of God from nature; that he views God as one natural process or structure of processes among others which can be apprehended in clearly defined ways with predictible results. . . . Such a process or structure of processes may be superhuman but cannot be 'supernatural', because nature is defined by him as 'what we know through the interaction between the physiological organism and its environment' and the supernatural is unknowable by definition."

2. Martin, *Empirical Philosophies of Religion*, p. 87: "It has been his purpose, he says, 'so to formulate the idea of God that the question of God's existence becomes a dead issue'. To accomplish this he has offered as a 'minimal' definition of God the following: 'God is that something upon which human life is most dependent for its security, welfare, and increasing abundance . . . that something of supreme value which constitutes the most important conditions'."

3. Martin, *Empirical Philosophies of Religion*, p. 102: "But he has developed these 'minimal' definitions in various ways. At one point in his intellectual pilgrimage he suggested that God as so defined is 'that interaction between individuals, groups, and ages which generates and promotes the greatest mutuality of good . . . the richest possible body of shared experience', a definition suggesting Dewey's 'religion of shared experience'. In another volume he speaks of God as 'that interaction which sustains and magnifies personality . . . the process of progressive integration'; while in another place he undertook to defend Whitehead's view of God as 'the principle of concretion'."

i. God as the creative event

True to his naturalistic predilections Wieman defines God as the "creative event."[4] God as creative event is that process of reorganization which generates new meanings, integrates them with the old, and endows each event as it occurs with a wider range of reference.* God as creative event is actually creative good, standing in contrast to both kinds of created good, one of which is instrumental and the other intrinsic. It is by means of this creative good that systems of meaning having intrinsic value, previously so disconnected that the qualities of the one could not get across to the other, become so united that each is enriched by qualities derived from the other.[6]

The total creative event is made up of four subevents. This does not mean that there are four distinct subevents working apart from each other which constitutes the creative event. Wieman makes it clear that the distinctions are made only for the purpose of analysis, and must never obscure the unitary character of the creative event.[7]

The four subevents are: emerging awareness of qualitative meaning through communication with other persons; integrating new meanings with ones previously acquired; expanding and enriching the appreciable world by a new structure of interrelatedness; a widening and deepening of community.[8] We shall examine each of these separately.

---

* This is quite reminiscent of the thought of a long line of naturalistic thinkers. Some call it "the progression of emergents" (Morgan, Alexander); "holistic evolution" (Smuts); "a thrust toward concentration, organization, and life" (Montague); "the value-actualizing function of human imagination within the total cosmic-social matrix that sustains it." (Dewey).[5]

---

4. On a draft of the dissertation Schilling suggested that King "avoid repetition" of Wieman's definition of God as the creative event (King, Draft of chapter 4, 1954–1955, MLKP-MBU: Box 97).

5. Wieman, "Authority and the Normative Approach," p. 190: "Some call it the 'principle of concretion' (Whitehead); 'the progression of emergents' (Morgan, Alexander, Calhoun); 'holistic evolution' (Smuts); . . . 'a thrust toward concentration, organization, and life' (Montague); . . . 'the value-actualizing function of human imagination within the total cosmic-social matrix that sustains it' (Dewey)."

6. Wieman, *Source of Human Good*, p. 56: "When good increases, a process of reorganization is going on, generating new meanings, integrating them with the old, endowing each event as it occurs with a wider range of reference. . . . It is creative good, standing in contrast to both kinds of created good we have been considering. By means of this creative good, systems of meaning having intrinsic value, previously disconnected so that the qualities of the one could not get across to the other, are so unified that each is enriched by qualities derived from the other."

7. Wieman, *Source of Human Good*, p. 58: "It is made up of four subevents; and the four working together and not any one of them working apart from the other constitute the creative event. . . . We have to describe them separately, but distinctions made for the purpose of analysis must not obscure the unitary, four-fold combination necessary to the creativity."

8. Wieman, *Source of Human Good*, p. 58: "The four subevents are: emerging awareness of qualitative meaning derived from other persons through communication; integrating these new

(1) The first subevent

The first subevent is emerging awareness of qualitative meaning derived from other persons through communication. Qualitative meaning consists of actual events so related that each acquires qualities from the other. Every living organism so reacts as to break the passage of existence into units called "events" and to relate these to one another in the manner called "qualitative meaning."* This may be done by the organism without the aid of linguistic communication. In such a case the range and richness of qualitative meaning is very limited. But the world of meaning and quality expands to its greatest compass when the single organism is able to acquire the qualitative meanings developed by other organisms and add them to its own. Therefore the first subevent in the total creative event is this emerging awareness in the individual of qualitative meaning communicated to it from some other organism. Wieman admits that interaction between the organism and its surroundings, by which new qualitative meaning is created without communication, is certainly creative.[9] But it is the creative event as it works through intercommunication in human society and history that the miracle happens and "creativity breaks free from obstacles which elsewhere imprison its power."†[10]

(2) The second subevent

One of the chief sources of the growth of personality appears when these new meanings derived from others are integrated with meanings previously

---

* Wieman, SHG, 58
† Wieman, SHG, 59.

---

meanings with others previously acquired; expanding the richness of quality in the appreciable world by enlarging its meaning; deepening the community among those who participate in this total creative event of intercommunication."

9. Wieman, *Source of Human Good*, p. 58: "Let us remember that qualitative meaning consists of actual events so related that each acquires qualities from the others. Every living organism so reacts as to break the passage of existence into units or intervals called 'events' and to relate these to one another in the manner here called 'qualitative meaning.' So long as this is done by the organism without the aid of linguistic communication, the range and richness of qualitative meaning is very limited. Not until the single organism is able to acquire the qualitative meanings developed by other organisms and add them to its own can the world of meaning and quality expand to any great compass. Therefore the first subevent in the total creative event producing value distinctively human is this emerging awareness in the individual of qualitative meaning communicated to it from some other organism. Interaction between the organism and its surroundings, by which new qualitative meaning is created without communication or prior to communication, is certainly creative."

10. On a draft of the dissertation Schilling underlined "it is the creative event" and "that the miracle happens" and wrote in the margin, "Revise faulty construction" (King, Draft of chapter 4). King did not correct the error.

acquired. These new meanings integrated with the old both deepen and enrich the thoughts and feelings of the individual. Wieman emphasizes the point
that this integration does not occur in every case of communicated meaning,
since there is much noncreative communication in our modern world by way
of radio, newspapers, and casual interchange between individuals.[11] "The
mere passage through the mind of innumerable meanings," says Wieman, "is
not the creative event."[*] Before the creative event can occur the newly communicated meanings must be integrated with meanings previously acquired.
To make sure that this integrating is not the work of the individual, Wieman contends that it is largely subconscious, unplanned and uncontrolled
by the individual, save only as he may provide conditions favorable to its
occurrence.[13]

The supreme achievement of this second subevent seems to occur in solitude, sometimes quite prolonged. After the many meanings have been acquired through communication, there must be time for them to be assimilated. If one does not for a time withdraw himself from the material world
and cease to communicate with others, the constant stream of new meanings
will prevent the deeper integration.[14] "A period of loneliness and quiet provides for incubation and creative transformation by novel unification. If new
meanings are coming in all the time, the integration is hindered by the new
impressions.[†]

Examples of creative integration in solitude are Jesus in the wilderness of
temptation and in Gethsemene, Buddha alone under the Bo tree, Paul in the
desert on the way to Damascus, and Augustine at the time of his conversion.
It seems that the individuals through whom the creative event has done most
to transform and enrich the world with meaning have spent more time in
lonely struggles.[15]

---

* Wieman, SHG, 50.[12]
† Wieman, SHG, 60.

---

11. Wieman, *Source of Human Good*, p. 59: "This integrating does not occur in every case of
communicated meaning, since there is much noncreative communication in our modern world
by way of radio, television, movies, newspapers, and casual interchange between individuals."

12. The citation should read Wieman, *Source of Human Good*, p. 59.

13. Wieman, *Source of Human Good*, p. 59: "These newly communicated meanings must be
integrated with meanings previously acquired or natively developed if the creative event is to
occur. This integrating is largely subconscious, unplanned and uncontrolled by the individual,
save only as he may provide conditions favorable to its occurrence."

14. Wieman, *Source of Human Good*, p. 60: "The supreme achievements of this internally creative integration seem to occur in solitude, sometimes quite prolonged. When many meanings
have been acquired from communication and through much action on the material world,
there must be time for these to be assimilated. If one does not for a time draw apart and cease to
act on the material world and communicate with others, the constant stream of new meanings
will prevent the deeper integration."

15. Wieman, *Source of Human Good*, p. 60: "Jesus in the wilderness of 'temptation' and in
Gethsemane, Buddha alone under the Bo tree, Paul in the desert on the way to Damascus, Au-

In spite of this emphasis on solitude, however, Wieman makes it clear that mere solitude is not enough. Nothing can be more dangerous to the human spirit than solitude. Solitude ceases to be creative if the mind degenerates into a state of torpor in its moments of being isolated from communication with others. One of the major problems confronting man is to learn how to make solitude creative instead of degenerative.*[16]

(3) The third subevent

The expanding and enriching of the appreciable world by a new structure of interrelatedness is the third subevent. This subevent necessarily follows from the first two subevents. After there has been intercommunication of meanings and after these meanings have been creatively integrated, the individual sees what he could not see before. Events as they happen to him now are so connected with other events that his appreciable world takes on an expanded meaning unimaginable before. There is now a richness of quality and a reach of ideal possibility which were not there prior to this transformation.†[17]

Wieman asserts that this expanding of the appreciable world may actually make a man more lonely than he was before; for now he knows that there is a greatness of good which might be the possession of man but is not actually achieved. Such a profound sense of loneliness is difficult for any man to bear, and yet it is the hope of the world.[18]

---

* Wieman, SHG, 61.
† Wieman, SHG, 62.

---

gustine at the time of his conversion—all these exemplify creative integration in solitude. . . . It seems that the individuals through whom the creative event has done most to transform and enrich the world with meaning have been more lonely than other men and have spent more time in lonely struggles."

16. Wieman, *Source of Human Good*, pp. 60–61: "But mere solitude is not enough. Nothing can be more deadening and dangerous to the human spirit than solitude. If the mind degenerates into a state of torpor, as it generally does when isolated from communication with others, solitude is not creative. . . . One of the major unsolved problems of our existence is to learn how to make solitude creative instead of degenerative."

17. Wieman, *Source of Human Good*, pp. 61–62: "The expanding and enriching of the appreciable world by a new structure of interrelatedness pertaining to events necessarily follow from the first two subevents. It is the consequence of both the first two, not of either one by itself. If there has been intercommunication of meanings and if they have been creatively integrated, the individual sees what he could not see before; he feels what he could not feel. Events as they happen to him are now so connected with other events that his appreciable world has an amplitude unimaginable before. There is a range and variety of events, a richness of quality, and a reach of ideal possibility which were not there prior to this transformation."

18. Wieman, *Source of Human Good*, pp. 62–63: "One important thing to note is that this expanding of the appreciable world may make a man more unhappy and more lonely than he was before; for now he knows that there is a greatness of good which might be the possession of

This expanding of the appreciable world is not only the actual achievement of an increase of value in this world; it is also an expansion of the individual's capacity to appreciate and his apprehension of a good that might be, but is not fulfilled.*[19]

(4) The fourth subevent

The fourth subevent is a widening and deepening community between those who participate in the creative event. This new structure of interrelatedness, brought about by communication and integration of meanings, transforms not only the mind of the individual and his appreciable world but also his relations with those who have participated with him in this occurrence.[20] "Since the meanings communicated to him from them have now become integrated into his own mentality, he feels something of what they feel, sees something of what they see, thinks some of their thoughts."†

This deepening community includes intellectual understanding of one another. This means having the ability to correct and critize one another understandingly and constructively.‡[21]

So for Wieman, these are the four subevents which together compose the creative event. They are so intertwined as to make a single, total event continuously recurrent in human existence.[22]

A vivid example of the fourfold nature of the creative event is found in the

---

* Wieman, SHG, 63.
† Wieman, SHG, 64.
‡ Wieman, SHG, 65.

---

man but is not actually achieved. . . . Such a profound sense of loneliness is difficult for any man to bear, and yet it is the hope of the world."

19. Wieman, *Source of Human Good*, p. 63: "This expanding of the appreciable world, accomplished by the third subevent, is not, then, in its entirety the actual achievement of an increase of value in this world, although it will include that. But it is also, perhaps even more, an expansion of the individual's capacity to appreciate and his apprehension of a good that might be, but is not, fulfilled."

20. Wieman, *Source of Human Good*, p. 64: "Widening and deepening community between those who participate in the total creative event is the final stage in creative good. The new structure of interrelatedness pertaining to events, resulting from communication and integration of meanings, transforms not only the mind of the individual and his appreciable world but also his relations with those who have participated with him in this occurrence."

21. Wieman, *Source of Human Good*, p. 64: "This community includes both intellectual understanding of one another and the feeling of one another's feelings, the ability to correct and criticize one another understandingly and constructively."

22. Wieman, *Source of Human Good*, p. 65: "These are the four subevents which together compose the creative event. They are locked together in such an intimate manner as to make a single, total event continuously recurrent in human existence."

originating events of the Christian faith. It began with Jesus engaging in intercommunication with a little group of disciples. This intercommunication
took place with such depth and potency that the organization of the disciples'
personalities were broken down and they were remade.[23] "They became new
men, and the thoughts and feelings of each got across to the other. . . . There
arose in this group of disciples a miraculous awareness and responsiveness
toward the needs and interests of one another.*

But this intercommunication was not all; something else followed. The
meanings that each disciple derived from the other were integrated with
meanings that each had previously acquired. This led to a new transformation
and each disciple was lifted to a higher level of human fulfillment.[24]

A third consequence that followed necessarily from these first two was the
expansion of the appreciable world round about these men. They could now
see through the eyes of others and feel through their sensitivities. The world
was now more ample with meaning and quality.†[25]

Finally there was more depth and breadth of community between them as
individuals with one another and between them and all other men. This followed from their enlarged capacity to get the perspectives of one another.‡[26]

So we can see that the creative event is one that brings forth in the human
mind, in society and history, and in the appreciable world a new structure of
interrelatedness, whereby events are discriminated and related in a manner
not possible before. It is a structure whereby some events derive from other
events, through meaningful connection with them, and abundance of quality
that events could not have had without this connection.§[27]

---

*   Wieman, SHG, 39, 40.
†   Wieman, SHG, 40.
‡   Wieman, SHG, 41.
§   Wieman, SHG, 65.

---

23. Wieman, *Source of Human Good*, p. 39: "Jesus engaged in intercommunication with a little
group of disciples with such depth and potency that the organization of their several personalities
was broken down and they were remade."

24. Wieman, *Source of Human Good*, p. 40: "But this was not all; something else followed from
it. The thought and feeling, let us say the meanings, thus derived by each from the other, were
integrated with what each had previously acquired. Thus each was transformed, lifted to a higher
level of human fulfilment."

25. Wieman, *Source of Human Good*, p. 40: "A third consequence followed necessarily from
these first two. The appreciable world expanded round about these men, thus interacting in this
fellowship. Since they could now see through the eyes of others, feel through their sensitivities,
and discern the secrets of many hearts, the world was more rich and ample with meaning and
quality."

26. Wieman, *Source of Human Good*, pp. 40–41: "There was more depth and breadth of community between them as individuals with one another and between them and all other men. This
followed from their enlarged capacity to get the perspectives of one another."

27. Wieman, *Source of Human Good*, p. 65: "The creative event is one that brings forth in the
human mind, in society and history, and in the appreciable world a new structure of interrelat-

ii. God as growth

In his earlier works Wieman sought to define the nature of God under the concept of growth. He says:

> God is the growth of meaning and value in the world. This growth consists of increase in those connections between activities which make the activities mutually sustaining, mutually enhancing, and mutually meaningful.*

He goes on to affirm that "growth is creative synthesis. It is the union of diverse elements in such a way that the new relation transforms them into a whole that is very different from the mere sum of the original factors."† Chemical elements unite in this way. Flowers grow by absorbing such elements as sunshine, air, water, and minerals, however, these are transformed in the new synthesis so that the original elements are no longer recognizable. The human mind grows by absorbing ideas and sentiments from the social environment, which are in turn transformed in the new synthesis. The culture of a community grows by absorbing the ideas, techniques, sentiments of the past and adding to these the newer developments of the present, but the gifts from the past and the present transform one another into a new kind of whole.‡ [28] This is what Wieman means by growth.

Wieman makes it clear that this process of growth is not evolution as science uses the term. Growth is only one form of evolution. Much of the decomposition, conflict, and mutual destruction going on throughout nature science would call evolution. But through it all we also find the formation of connections of mutual support, mutual control, and mutual fulfillment between diverse activities forming new systems in which each part supports the whole and the whole operated to conserve the parts.§ [29] This is growth.

---

* Wieman, NPOR, 137. Wieman's definition of God as "growth of meaning and value" is generalized after the manners of "experience" in Dewey's familiar use of the word. (see Dewey's Experiences and Nature, p. 8.)

† Wieman, GOR, 325.

‡ Wieman, GOR, 325, 326.

§ Wieman, GOR, 367.

---

edness, whereby events are discriminated and related in a manner not before possible. It is a structure whereby some events derive from other events, through meaningful connection with them, an abundance of quality that events could not have had without this new creation."

28. Henry Nelson Wieman and Walter Marshall Horton, *The Growth of Religion* (Chicago: Willett, Clark, 1938), pp. 325–326: "Chemical elements unite in this way and it may be that all growth is a chemical process. A flower grows by absorbing such elements as sunshine, air, water, and minerals, but these are transformed in the new synthesis so that the orginial elements are no longer recognizable. The mind of a human being grows by absorbing ideas, sentiments, attitudes from the social environment, but these are transformed in the new synthesis. The culture of a community grows by absorbing the ideas, techniques, skills, sentiments of the past and adding to these the newer developments of the present. But the gifts from the past and the present . . . transform one another into a new kind of whole."

29. Wieman, *Growth of Religion*, pp. 326–327: "What we have described is not evolution as science uses that term. Growth is only one form of evolution. A great deal of decomposition,

We can see now that in the concept of growth Wieman is saying essentially the same thing he is saying in the concept of "creative event." In both cases God is an actual, existing operative reality in our midst bringing forth all that is highest and best in existence. He is the creative synthesis at work in the immediate concrete situation. In both cases God is that something that brings about a new structure of interrelatedness whereby events are related in a manner not possible before.

iii. God as supra-human

One of the persistent notes that runs the whole gamut of Wieman's writing is the affirmation that God is supra-human. Wieman is adverse to anything that smacks of humanism. His emphasis is theocentric through and through. He never wearies of pointing out that it is not the intelligence and purpose of man that is responsible for the creation and increase of good. "God," he contends, "is that which sustains, promotes and constitutes the greatest good, operating with men and in men, but also over and above the conscious and intelligent purpose of men."* Again he says:

> When men try to construct an order of good and superimpose it upon existence, they will fail. But when they seek out in existence the growing good with all its possibilities, near and remote, so far as they can, and minister to it with every ability, love it, give their lives to it, their living will be effective. But when they do this they are depending upon God, living for God and with God.†

Still again Wieman writes:

> We feel there is no more dangerous misinterpretation of religious experience than to represent it as "subjective." Our whole point has been to show that it is an experience of something not ourselves.‡

Wieman is convinced that the chief tragedies that befall man and his historic existence stem from man's tendency to elevate created good to the rank of creative good (God). The best in Christianity, contends Wieman, is the reversing of the order of domination in the life of man from domination of human concern by created good over to domination by creative good (God).§[30]

---

* Wieman, Art. (1932)[3], 320.
† Wieman, ITG, 324.

Art. (1932)[3], 324.
‡ Wieman, RESM, 209.
§ Wieman, SHG, 269.

---

conflict, and mutual destruction is going on throughout nature. Much of this would be called evolution by science. But through it all we also find the formation of connections of mutual support, mutual control, and mutual fulfillment between diverse activities forming new systems in which each part supports the whole and the whole operates to conserve the parts."

30. Wieman, *Source of Human Good*, pp. 268–269: "The best in Christianity . . . is revelation of God, forgiveness of sin, and salvation of man. . . . These three are different strands woven

(1) God and man

Wieman's aversion to humanism is clearly expressed in his affirmation that the work of God is totally different from the work of man. The difference is not merely of degree or magnitude. It is a difference of kind.[31] For Wieman there is a qualitative difference between God and man.

Wieman contends that the work of God is the growth of organism, while the work of man is the construction of mechanism.[32] In setting forth an example of this distinction, Wieman says:

> God rears a tree by growth of organic connections. Man constructs a house by putting the parts together mechanically. Man can choose the place for the tree to grow. But the actual growing he cannot do.*

The same applies to all growth, of flowers, friendships, cultures, self-development, and meanings.

Wieman looks upon mechanisms and organisms as two different kinds of systems which enter into the existence of almost everything.[34] "A mechanism is a system of external relations. An organism is a system of internal relations or, as I prefer to say, of organic connection."† Internal relations are creative. Therefore, when things are internally related, they undergo transformation and mutually control one another. All through the world is found organism, that is, systems of internal relations. But we also find mechanism. Organism cannot develop without mechanism to support it.

God's work is the growth of organic connections, that is, "the growth of meaning and value." This is not and can never be the work of man. However,

---

* Wieman, Art. (1932)², 441.[33]
† Wieman, Art. (1936)², 442.

---

together into a single complex event, the character of which can be simply stated: the reversing of the order of domination in the life of man *from* domination of human concern by created good *over to* domination by creative good."

31. Henry Nelson Wieman, "God Is More than We Can Think," *Christendom* 1 (1936): 441: "Man's work can be clearly distinguished from that of God. . . . The difference is not merely a matter of magnitude and power. It is a difference in kind."

32. Wieman, "God Is More," p. 441: "The work of God, which man never does, is the growth of organism. The work of man is the construction of mechanism."

33. The correct citation should read Wieman, Art. (1936)², 441. There are two additional sentences in the original before "Man can choose the place for the tree to grow" (Wieman, "God Is More," p. 441).

34. Wieman, "God Is More," pp. 441–442: "The same applies to all growth, to growth of flowers, friendships, cultures, self-development, meanings. Mechanisms and organisms are not two different kinds of things. Rather, they are two different kinds of systems which enter into the existence of almost everything."

man can serve it devotedly.[35] Man can provide some of the needed mechanism which enables the organism to develop.[36] Man can do innumerable things to remove obstacles and provide sustaining conditions which release the power of God to produce value. But it is only God that produces a structure which could not be intended by the human mind before it emerges, either in imagination or in the order of actual events. The structure of value produced by the creative event (God) cannot be caused by human intention and effort, because it can by produced only by a transformation of human intention and effort.*[37]

So God is superhuman because he operates without the conscious intent of man. God is superhuman, furthermore, because he generates personality. Wieman seeks to explain how this takes place. He begins with the theory of social psychology that personality can exist only in society. Personality is something that develops only when there is some interaction between individuals. Therefore, human personality does not create this kind of interaction. Rather this interaction creates personality.[38] This interaction is the God of the universe.†

Even God's purpose is different from purpose as found in man. Wieman writes:

> But we must understand purpose in two different senses. First, the kind of purpose which we see in minds, namely, the purpose involved in constructing mechanisms. Secondly, the kind of purpose we see in God, namely, the purpose in-

15 Apr
1955

---

* Wieman, SHG, 42.
† Wieman, Art. (1931)², 1209.

---

35. Wieman, "God Is More," p. 442: "Internal relations are peculiar. They are creative. That means that when things or parts of things are internally related, they undergo transformation and mutually control one another. . . . All through the world . . . we find organism, that is, systems of internal relations. But we also find mechanism. . . . The work of God is the growth of organic connections, that is, the growth of all meaning and value. Man cannot do that. But he can serve it devotedly."

36. Wieman, "God Is More," p. 441: "The work of man is to provide some of the needed mechanism which enables the organism to develop."

37. Wieman, *Source of Human Good*, pp. 74–75: "Innumerable things can be done by men to remove obstacles and provide sustaining conditions which release the power of creative good to produce value. . . . The creative event produces a structure which could not be intended by the human mind before it emerges, either in imagination or in the order of actual events. . . . The structure of value produced by the creative event cannot be caused by human intention and effort, because it can be produced only by a transformation of human intention and effort."

38. Henry Nelson Wieman, "God, the Inescapable, Part II," *Christian Century* 48 (30 September 1931): 1209: "It is superhuman because it operates without the conscious intent of man. . . . It is superhuman, furthermore, because it generates personality. It is a commonplace of social psychology that personality can exist only in a society. Personality is something that develops only when there is some intereaction of the sort we have described. Therefore, human personality does not create this kind of interaction. Rather this interaction creates personality."

volved in generating and promoting the growth of organic connections directly. This last we call simply by the name of growth.*

In an even more emphatic passage, Wieman declares:

> God, I have come to see with increasing clarity, is not merely man lifted to the nth dimension of perfection, any more than he is horse or any other animal so glorified. God is different from man. God works concretely. Man cannot possibly do that. Man must work abstractly . . . That is to say, man's plans, his ideals, his purposes, are necessarily abstractions by reason of the very nature of the human mind. God alone is concrete in his workings. God is creator. Man cannot be creator. The production of unpredictable consequences through the forming of "internal relations" is creation. A common word for it is growth. It is God's working not man's.†

These rather lengthy passages are rich in ideas. They express in no uncertain terms Wieman's strong conviction that there is a qualitative difference between God and man. God operates in ways over and above the plans and purposes of man, and often develops connections of mutual support and mutual meaning in spite of, or contrary to, the efforts of men.

In stressing the fact that God is supra-human, Wieman does not mean that God works outside of human life. Rather he means that God creates the good of the world in a way that man can never do. Man cannot even approximate the work of the creative event.‡ [39]

(2) God not supernatural

Wieman's persistent affirmation that God is supra-human might easily give the impression that he also holds that God is supernatural. But nothing is farther from Wieman's intention. He is as opposed to supernaturalism as he is to humanism. Both humanism and supernaturalism fail to get at the true nature of the universe.

As we have seen, Wieman's position is naturalistic. This means that he sees nothing in reality accessible to the human mind more basic than events and their qualities and relations.§ [40] The basic things in the world are events, hap-

---

* Wieman, Art. (1937), 212.
† Wieman, Art. (1939), 118.

‡ Wieman, SHG, 76.
§ Relations is another word for "structure."

---

39. Wieman, *Source of Human Good*, p. 76: "The creative event is supra-human, not in the sense that it works outside of human life, but in the sense that it creates the good of the world in a way that man cannot do. Man cannot even approximate the work of the creative event."

40. Wieman, *Source of Human Good*, p. 6: "There is nothing in reality accessible to the human mind more basic than events and their qualities and relations. ('Relations' is another word for 'structure.')"

penings, or processes. They are the "stuff" or substance of experience. There is nothing more fundamental or elemental than events. There is nothing transcending or undergirding events. Events do not happen to something which or someone who is not an event. Everything that exists is either an event, an aspect of an event, or a relation between or within events. Therefore, Wieman's naturalistic philosophy is opposed to substance philosophy. All philosophical categories are descriptive of events, and events of various kinds are the primary data for all inquiry.*

Wieman's naturalistic position also leads him to affirm that all things are "somewhere," and "somewhere" refers to events. There are no events without structures, and there are no structures or forms existing or subsisting apart from events.† There is no disembodied or nonincarnate order as <u>Logos</u>.

This principle also means that the world of our experience is self-explanatory. There are no floating transcendental principles which explain the world in terms of something outside the world. As we shall see subsequently, Wieman totally denies the traditional doctrine of creation. Principles, descriptions, and explanations refer to events and their relations (structures). Therefore, the ultimate in explanation is simply the most general concrete description possible.‡

Wieman is quite emphatic on the point that the limits of knowledge are defined by the limits of the experienceable, and the limits of the experienceable are defined by the limits of relationships. What we are not related to we cannot experience. What is unrelated to us is unknowable, and the unknowable is unknown. "Nature" comprises the experienceable. Therefore, in this case by definition, a purely transcendental or noumenal realm is regarded as unknown and superfluous. Everything that exists has the power either to affect other things or to be affected by them.§

All of this leads to the principle that God must be found within the natural order. Like everything else that exists, God is a material being, a process with an enduring structure which distinguishes his character from that of other processes. Whatever may be his several other attributes, his transcendence is not of the noumenal or completely independent variety. Whatever transcendence he has will be seen to arise out of his very immanence in the world of events.‖

Wieman contends further that God is directly experienceable, and experienceable in the same basic way that other processes are directly perceivable. Contrary to most schools of thought, Wieman holds that the God he is talking about is observable, and observable in a fundamentally physical manner. From this point of view the meaning of "revelation" is to be understood as a disclosure of one process to another resulting from their relationship or confrontation. So all theology is natural theology for Wieman.

Although God is not supernatural for Wieman, he insists that God is hidden. God's hiddenness derives from three factors: (a) man's sin makes him

---

* Wieman, SHG, 6.
† Whitehead calls this the "ontological principle."
‡ Wieman, SHG, 7.

§ Wieman is following Whitehead at this point. In Whitehead's system, every event is first of all af-

fected by past events and then, subsequently, affects other future events.
‖ Wieman, SHG, 33, 35.

blind to that upon which he is most dependent; (b) God's inexhaustible richness of creative power and goodness is such that man's appreciative awareness
is only dimly alive to the creative and dynamic depth that confronts him; (3)
man's consciousness appears to be such that it does not easily perceive those
elements of our experience which are always present. We more easily observe
those factors which are sometimes absent. Thus it is exceedingly difficult to
analyze and describe what we mean by "time." At a deeper level it is still more
difficult to perceive God because it is by the working of that very process in
us that our minds are recreated.

However, in spite of God's "hiddenness," Wieman insists that God's standard of value is compatible with ours. So when Wieman says that God is the
creative source of all value, he means that the source of all value must have a
structure or character that is compatible with, or supportive of, the structure
which characterizes values in general. The notion that God is the "wholly
other" needs to be qualified by this general consideration.

So for Wieman, nature includes all that is knowable, actually or potentially,
by normal processes of knowing. Nature includes mind, personality, and
value. According to this view, the "supernatural" is the semantically meaningless. Wieman sees the idea of the "supernatural" as not only unnecessary to
religion but confusing and frustrating in any genuine attempt to achieve adjustment to the word of God in the world.

So Wieman would answer the question, Where is God found? by saying that
God is within the cosmic whole. He is one aspect of it. He is here in nature,
present, potent, and widely operative. Wieman says further that God is not
the pervading purpose of the cosmic whole, as Protestant liberalism would
say. God is not to be identified with the cosmic whole in any way. Neither is
he the creator of the cosmic whole as the supernaturalists say. God is found
in nature all about us; he must be known by the same cognitive procedure by
which other realities in nature are known.

(3) The functional transcendence of God

Wieman's naturalistic position leads him to the conclusion that nothing can
make the slightest difference in our lives unless it be an event or some possibility carried by an event. This means that that which is considered metaphysically transcendent literally has nothing to do, since all value, all meaning,
and all causal efficacy are to be found in the world of events and their possibilities. So Wieman finds it necessary to deny the metaphysical transcedn-
ence of God as set forth by traditional Christianity. But there is a sense in
which God is transcendent, viz., functionally. Concerning God's transcendence Wieman says:

> Since creativity is not readily accessible to awareness, we can speak of creativity as
> transcendent. But it is not transcendent in the sense of being nontemporal, non-
> spatial, and immaterial. It can be discovered in the world by proper analysis.*

---

* Wieman, SHG, 77.

Although Wieman rejects the metaphysical transcendence of God, he is quite certain that God's functional transcendence serves all of the vital and saving functions performed by the "myth" of a metaphysically transcendental reality.[41] He lists six saving functions of the metaphysical myth of transcendence and seeks to demonstrate how a functionally transcendent God meets all these conditions.

The six saving functions of the "metaphysical myth of supernaturalism" are as follows: (1) The Christian myth has directed the absolute commitment of faith away from all created good and thus delivered man from bondage to any relative value. (2) It has established a demand for righteousness far beyond the socially accepted standards of a given time and place. (3) It has established a bond between men vastly deeper and more important than personal affection, mutual interest, and racial identity. (4) It has revealed that evil is deeper than any wrong done to society, or to any person, because in the last analysis evil is against the transcendental reality. (5) It has revealed any obligation laid upon man which overrides an obligation derived from society, tradition, ideal, or loyalty to persons. (6) It has opened the possibility for creative transformation beyond anything that could be accomplished by human effort.*[42]

God as creative event fulfills every one of these functions. However, the creative event (God) cannot accomplish these services unless men by faith give themselves to its control and transforming power.[43] Wieman also contends that God is functionally transcendent in the sense that he is the uncomprehended totality of all that is best. "God is both immanent and transcendent. Consider first the transcendence, meaning by transcendence not necessarily what is far away but what is too loftily good to be comprehended by us."†

---

* Wieman, SHG, 264, 265.
† Wieman, Art. (1932)³, 237.

---

41. Wieman, *Source of Human Good*, p. 264: "This source is not metaphysically transcendental, but it is functionally transcendental. It serves everyone of the vital and saving functions performed by the myth of a metaphysically transcendental reality."

42. Wieman, *Source of Human Good*, pp. 264–265: "The Christian myth has directed the absolute commitment of faith away from all created good and thus delivered man from bondage to any relative value and has thus saved him from good become demonic. It has established a demand for righteouness far beyond the socially accepted standards of a given time and place.... It has established a bond between men vastly deeper and more important than personal affection or kinship, mutual interest or shared ideal, institution or race. Moreover, it has shown evil to be deeper and darker than any wrong done to society, to any group, or to any person, because in the last analysis evil is against the transcendental reality. It has revealed an obligation laid upon man which overrides any obligation derived from society, tradition, ideal, or loyalty to persons. Finally, it has opened possibilities of creative transformation beyond anything that could be expected from human effort, idealism, or any other such power."

43. Wieman, *Source of Human Good*, p. 265: "But [the creative event] can accomplish these services only when men by faith give themselves to its control and transforming power."

Wieman further asserts that God is transcendent, "not in the sense of being wholly unknown, but in the sense of being unknown with respect to his detailed and specific nature."* At times Wieman comes close to saying that we can know that God is, but not what he is. What else can be inferred from the following passages?

> We are inert and unresponsive to the specific forms of God's presence. We cannot know save to an infinitesimal degree, these specific forms. But we can know that the reality is there, even when the specific forms of that reality are unknown.†

> But the fullness of God's being, and the richness of value in God, are immeasurable beyond the weak little fluttering attempts of human imagination to comprehend.‡

Here Wieman is saying that God can never be known in his fullness and richness. In this sense God is transcendent. He is more than we can think.

iv. God as absolute good

Wieman contends that creative good (God) is the only absolute good. He seeks to defend this claim by defining absolute in a fivefold sense. First of all, absolute good refers to that which is good under all circumstances and conditions. It is a good that is not relative to time or place or race or class or need or desire. It is good that remains changelessly and identically the same. It is good that remains even if it runs counter to human desire. It is a good that continues to be identically the same good even when it works with microscopic cells prior to the emergence of any higher organism.[44]

Creative good meets all these requirements. Its goodness is not relative to time or place or desire or even human existence.[45] It is good that would continue even if human existence ceased to be.

---

* Wieman, Art. (1936)[2], 437.
† Wieman, Art. (1937), 206, 207. This passage seems to contradict Wieman's assertion that God is the unknown rather than the unknowable. This statement implies that we can never know certain aspects of God.
‡ Wieman, Art. (1937), 207. Here again Wieman is saying that the fullness of God's being can never be known.

---

44. Wieman, *Source of Human Good*, p. 79: "When we speak of 'absolute good' we shall mean, first of all, what is good under all conditions and circumstances. It is a good that is not relative to time or place or person or race or class or need or hope or desire or belief. It is a good that remains changelessly and identically the same. . . . It is a good that retains its character even when it runs counter to all human desire. It is good that continues to be identically the same good even when it works with microscopic cells prior to the emergence of any higher organism."

45. Wieman, *Source of Human Good*, p. 79: "Creative good meets all these requirements pertaining to absolute good. Its goodness is not relative to human desire, or even to human existence."

This is what distinguished God's goodness from all types of created good. Created good is relative in all the senses that stand in contrast to the absolute as just described. Created good does not retain the same character of goodness under all circumstances and conditions. The creative good, however, does retain its character of goodness under all circumstances and is therefore the only absolute good.*[46]

A second mark of absolute good is that its demands are unlimited. A good is absolute if it is always good to give oneself, all that one is, possesses, and desires into its control to be transformed in any way that it may require.[47] Creative good is absolute in this sense because it demands wholehearted surrender.†

A third mark of absolute good is its infinite value. This mark is somewhat inseparable from the second. Absolute good is unlimited in its demands because it is infinite in value.[48]

> Its worth is incommensurable by any finite quantity of created good. No additive sum of good produced in the past can be any compensation for the blockage of that creativity which is our only hope for the future.‡

Fourth, absolute good is unqualified good. There must be no perspective from which its goodness can be modified. Always and from every standpoint its good must remain unchanged and self-identical, whether under the aspect of eternity or under the aspect of time, whether viewed as means or an end.§[49]

Finally, creative good is absolute because it is entirely trustworthy. Wieman is certain that the outcome of the working of the creative event will always be

---

* Wieman rejects the view that absolute means out of relation. "Instead of being out of all relations, it is rather the one kind of goodness that, without losing its identity, can enter into all relations. It is good always and everywhere, therefore relative to everything." (SHG, 80 n.)
† Wieman, SHG, 80.
‡ Wieman, SHG, 80.
§ Wieman, SHG, 81.

---

46. Wieman, *Source of Human Good*, pp. 79–80: "On the other hand, created good—the structure of meaning connecting past and future that we feel and appreciate—is relative value in all the senses that stand in contrast to the absolute as just described. . . . Thus created good does not retain the same character of goodness under all circumstances and conditions. . . . The creative good which does retain its character of goodness under all these changing conditions is, then, the only absolute good."

47. Wieman, *Source of Human Good*, p. 80: "A second mark of absolute good is that its demands are unlimited. A good is absolute if it is always good to give myself, all that I am and all that I desire, all that I possess and all that is dear to me, into its control to be transformed in any way that it may require."

48. Wieman, *Source of Human Good*, p. 80: "Thus in a third way, inseparable from the second, creative good is absolute. It is unlimited in its demands because it is infinite in value."

49. Wieman, *Source of Human Good*, pp. 80–81: "Fourth, absolute good is unqualified good. There must be no perspective from which its goodness can be modified in any way. Always, from every standpoint, its good must remain unchanged and self-identical, whether from the worm's view or the man's view, whether under the aspect of eternity or under the aspect of time, . . . whether viewed as means or as end."

the best possible under the conditions, even when it may seem to be otherwise.[50] Concerning the trustworthiness of the creative event, Wieman says:

> Even when it so transforms us and our world that we come to love what now we hate, to serve what now we fight, to seek what now we shun, still we can be sure that what it does is good. Even when its working re-creates our minds and personalities, we can trust it.*

Creative good will always be with us, even when other good is destroyed. So in this dual sense creative good is absolutely trustworthy: it always produces good; it never fails.†[51]

Wieman makes it clear that his claim that God is absolute good does not imply that absolute good means all powerful good. Such a view would conflict with Wieman's empiricistic position. He insists that the claim that any kind of good is almighty cannot be defended.‡[52]

We see here an emphasis in Wieman's thought concerning God which is found throughout his writings. Most thinkers are impressed with the power of God. Wieman, on the contrary, is more impressed with the goodness of God. His interest concerning God is axiological rather than ontological. The ever-recurring words in Wieman's concept of God are goodness and value. He says: "I maintain . . . that the basic category for God must be goodness or value."§

2. God and value

The one word that appears throughout Wieman's discussion of God is the word value. Indeed he defines God as "growth of living connections of value in the universe,"‖ and as "the growth of meaning and value in the world." He feels that values are the "primary data for religious inquiry," including inquiry concerning God. So we can see that his theory of value is all-important for an understanding of his conception of God. A summary of his value-theory is thus in order at this point.

---

* Wieman, SHG, 81. § Wieman, Art. (1943)[3],
† Wieman, SHG, 81. 267.
‡ Wieman, SHG, 82. ‖ Wieman, GOR, 363.

---

50. Wieman, *Source of Human Good*, p. 81: "Finally, creative good is absolute in that it is entirely trustworthy. We can be sure that the outcome of its working will always be the best possible under the conditions, even when it may seem to us to be otherwise."

51. Wieman, *Source of Human Good*, p. 81: "We can also be sure that creative good will always be with us. When all other good is destroyed, it springs anew; it will keep going when all else fails. In this dual sense creative good is absolutely trustworthy: it always produces good; it never fails."

52. Wieman, *Source of Human Good*, p. 82: "The claim that any kind of good is almighty cannot be defended."

Wieman holds that values are perceptible facts and that they constitute the primary data for religious inquiry, since religion is concerned with loyalty to supreme value.* Any distinction between value and fact in this realm is confusing. He says:

> We believe a great deal of confusion in religious thought may go back to the assumption that values are not facts. If value is a fact, just as truly as anything else, then many of the difficulties in the search for God would fade away as dreams. If values are in nature and are facts, God can be found as readily and naturally as other persistent and pervasive realities.†[53]

Wieman gratefully recognizes his indebtedness to Dewey in his theory of value. His refusal to separate values from nature is clearly in line with Dewey's position. And this refusal to make a sharp ontological distinction between the realms of value and of fact leads him also to reject the preferential treatment given to "ideals" in metaphysics by Brightman and other ethical idealists.‡ If one defies conceptual ideals, he says, then all concepts must share this status indiscriminately, and the resulting chaos can only be overcome through a further appeal to experience; ideals, in other words, are functional guides in the interpretation of experience but are not "transcendental."§[54]

---

* Wieman, NPOR, 137. For similar statements cf. RR, 155; Art. (1932)³, 13, 158–163.
† Wieman, Art. (1934), 117–118.
‡ Brightman defines value as "whatever is actually liked, prized, esteemed, desired, approved, or enjoyed by anyone at any time. It is the actual experience of enjoying a desired object or activity. Hence, value is an existing realization of desire." (POR, 88). Concerning ideals Brightman writes: "Ideals constitute a special class of instrumental values. An ideal is a general concept of a type of experience which we value." (POR, 90).
§ Wieman, RESM, 272–278.

---

53. Martin, *Empirical Philosophies of Religion*, p. 95: "For he, like Macintosh, holds that values are perceptible facts and that they constitute the primary data for religious inquiry, since religion is concerned with loyalty to supreme value. Any distinction between value and fact in this realm is confusing, he says: 'We believe a great deal of confusion in religious thought may go back to the [assumption] that values are not facts. If value is a fact, just as truly as anything else, then many of the difficulties in the search for God would fade away as dreams. If values are in nature and are facts, God can be found as readily and naturally as other persistent and pervasive realities.'"

54. Martin, *Empirical Philosophies of Religion*, p. 96: "Wieman's indebtedness to Dewey in this theory is gratefully recognized by him. . . . His refusal to separate values from nature is clearly in line with Dewey's position. And this refusal to make a sharp ontological distinction between the realms of value and of fact leads him also to reject the preferential treatment given to 'ideals' in metaphysics by Brightman and other ethical idealists. If one reifies conceptual ideals, he says, then all concepts must share this status indiscriminately, and the resulting chaos can only be overcome through a further appeal to experience; ideals, in other words, are functional guides in the interpretation of experience but are not 'transcendental'."

In order to get a clearer understanding of Wieman's value-theory we shall discuss it both in its negative and positive aspects. We shall begin by glancing at some of the value-theories that he rejects. Then we will turn to a discussion of Wieman's positive theory of value.

(1) Value theories rejected by Wieman

Wieman holds that any substantial theory of value must be based on something that transcends the subjective. He finds that most value-theories are lacking at this very point. Thus he finds it necessary to reject most theories of value. Most of these theories that Wieman rejects are quite familiar.

Emotion or feeling has been selected by some as giving the essence of value. Also specific emotions like love, satisfaction, liking, pleasure and happiness have been taken as guiding threads. But no amount of observation and analysis and interrelating of subjective emotions, cut off from the personalities having them and from the situation calling them forth, can be made to yield a rational structure or principle helpful in solving the important practical problems of life. Emotions are certainly involved in all experiences. But one could scarcely bring all values into the category of either of the above-mentioned emotions.[55]

Love, for instance, is a very vague term. It must be analyzed into forms that can give us some guidance. Satisfaction of desire, or liking, does enter into any direct experience of value, but it is precisely when we mistrust our own likings and satisfactions that we need and want a guiding theory. Happiness has in it all the ambiguities of liking and satisfaction.[56]

A second theory that Wieman rejects is the contention that intelligence is the substance of all value. Such a contention seems to overlook the fact that there are flagrant cases of evil intelligence. If it is admitted that evil is negative value, that is the criterion which distinguishes the positive from the negative value of intelligence.[57]

---

55. Henry Nelson Wieman, "Values: Primary Data for Religious Inquiry," *Journal of Religion* 16, no. 4 (October 1936): 381: "Emotion, or that more general term, feeling, has been selected by some as giving us the essence of value. Emotions and feelings are certainly involved in all experiences of value. But no amount of observation and analysis and interrelating of feelings, cut off from the personalities having them and from the situations calling them forth, can be made to yield a rational structure or principle helpful in solving the important practical problems of life. . . . Love is certainly one kind of value, but one could scarcely bring all values into this category."

56. Wieman, "Values," p. 382: "Love is a very vague term. It must be analyzed into forms or relations that can give us some guidance and light. . . . Satisfaction of desire, or liking, does enter into any direct and appreciative experience of value. But is is precisely when we mistrust our own likings and satisfactions that we need and want a guiding theory. . . . Happiness has in it all the ambiguity of liking and satisfaction."

57. Wieman, "Values," p. 382: "Intelligence has sometimes been honored as the substance of all value. . . . Apparently that is meant, and yet there seem to be flagrant cases of evil intelligence. If one says evil is negative value, then what is the criterion which distinguishes the positive from the negative value of intelligence?"

A third theory that Wieman rejects is the assertion that biological patterns, such as survival or adjustment or life, determine the mark of value. It is easy, says Wieman, to find instances of evil that has survived and good that has perished. The same general principle applies to adjustment and life. There is good adjustment and bad, and good life and bad. Hence these terms give us no guidance.[58]

A fourth theory that Wieman dismisses as false is the contention that personality is the distinctive mark of value. Sheer observation reveals that personalities are good and bad to the extreme. Hence it is not mere personality, but something about personality which is the value.[59]

A fifth theory that Wieman rejects is the assertion that the criterion of value is found in patterns in the physical world, such as order and purpose. It is true that value implies order of a kind. But what kind of order is better and what kind worse? More order is not necessarily more value unless it is the right kind of order. The same is true of purpose. Neither order nor purpose in itself gives us a clear distinction between better and worse.[60]

All of these theories are emphatically rejected by Wieman. They are not rejected because they are alien to value, for he quite readily admits that all of these elements enter into any experience of value. They are rejected as constructive theories of value. For such a theory one must go to something else.

(2) Value as appreciable activity

Wieman thinks that the factor in value which lends itself most readily to a guiding pattern by which to formulate a value theory is appreciable activity. He is determined to base his theory of value on something that transcends the shaky foundations of subjectivity. So it is in activity that he find something objective. It can be observed, computed, foreseen. Activities can be connected in meaningful and supporting ways.[61]

Since the words, activity and meaning, are of first importance in Wieman's

---

58. Wieman, "Values," p. 383: "Biological patterns have been said to be the determining mark of value, such as survival or adjustment or life. But it is easy to find instances of evil that have survived and good that has perished. . . . The same general principle applies to adjustment and life. There is good adjustment and bad, and good life and bad. Hence these terms give us no guidance at all."

59. Wieman, "Values," p. 383: "Personalities are good and bad to all extremes. Hence it is not mere personality, but something about personality which is the value."

60. Wieman, "Values," p. 384: "Patterns in the physical world, such as order and purpose, have been selected as criteria of value. Doubtless value implies order of a kind, but what kind of order is better and what kind worse? More order is not necessarily more value unless it is the right kind of order. The same is true of purpose. . . . At any rate, purpose of itself does not give us a clear distinction between better and worse."

61. Wieman, "Values," p. 385: "We believe the factor in value which lends itself most readily to a guiding pattern or principle by which to discover, appraise, and appreciate values is appreciable activity. Activity is objective. It can be observed, computed, foreseen. . . . Activities can be connected in meaningful and supporting ways."

theory of value, we may profitably pursue their meaning. An activity is first of all a change. But not all changes are activities. A change is an activity only when it is so related to other changes that they mutually modify one another in such a way as to meet the requirements of a system to which they belong. For instance, many of the changes that transpire in a cell are so related to many other changes of the physiological organism that they all mutually modify one another to the end of meeting the requirements of the living system. Or, again, gravitational changes mutually modify one another in such a way as to meet the requirements of the gravitational system.*[62]

It is possible for a change to be an activity with respect to one system and not in relation to another. As was stated above, gravitational changes are activities with respect to the gravitational system, but they are not necessarily activities with respect to the system of a living organism. Actually changes which sustain one system may be destructive of others.[63]

Wieman stresses the fact that an activity is a value only when it is appreciable. If it is not appreciable activity, it is not the datum in which value can be found.[64] "Activity may be a mechanical routine or a spasmodic impulse or a dizzy whirl."† To be appreciable means that some living consciousness may be affected by it with joy or suffering. But this does not mean that the consciousness must have some knowledge of this activity. Many activities qualify consciousness without being objects of consciousness. Oxidation of the blood in one's lungs, for instance, qualifies one's consciousness when one is not at all conscious of what is going on. These changes pertain, however, if their removal or cessation would destroy the system which yields the experience of value.‡[65]

---

* Wieman, Art. (1936)⁴, 388.
† Wieman, Art. (1936)⁴, 386.
‡ Wieman, Art. (1936)⁴, 387.

---

62. Wieman, "Values," p. 387: "Since these two, activity and meaning, are of first importance in our interpretation of value, we must try to make plain the idea we wish to express by each. An activity is, first of all, a change. But it is not every change. A change is an activity when it is so related to other changes that they mutually modify one another to the end of meeting the requirements of a system to which they belong. For example, gravitational changes mutually modify one another in such a way as to meet the requirements of the gravitational system. . . . Or, again, many of the changes that transpire in a cell are so related to many other changes in the physiological organism that they all mutually modify one another to the end of meeting the requirements of the living system."

63. Wieman, "Values," p. 388: "We have shown that gravitational changes are activities with respect to the gravitational system. But they are not activities, necessarily, with respect to the system of a living organism. . . . It is plain that a change may be an activity with respect to one system and not in relation to another. . . . Changes which sustain one system are often destructive of others."

64. Wieman, "Values," pp. 386, 388: "The activity must be appreciable. Otherwise it is not the datum in which value can be found. . . . An activity is a value only when it is appreciable."

65. Wieman, "Values," pp. 388–389: "To be appreciable means that some living consciousness sometime, somewhere, some way, may be affected by it with joy or suffering. This does not re-

With this explanation of activity let us now turn to a discussion of Wieman's view of meaning. He affirms that activity and meaning are closely related but not identical.[66]

> One change means another change when the first represents the second to an actual or possible experiencing mind. One change can mean another most effectively if the two changes so connected that, when certain modification occur in the one, certain other correlative modifications occur in the other.*

So the connection between changes which makes them to be activities within a system in a connection which is best fitted to make them carriers of meaning by virtue of the fact that they can represent one another to a mind that understands the connection between them. A throbbing pulse, for instance, means the presence of life to a mind that is able to understand the connection between these throbs and that system of co-ordinated changes in the organism which makes it a living thing. Rising smoke in the distance means the presence of fire to the mind that understands the connection between smoky changes in the atmosphere and correlative changes called combustion.†[67] This leads Wieman to say:

> Meaning is that connection between the here-and-now and the far-away which enables a mind that understands the connection to experience the far-away through the mediation of the here-and-now. This ability to transmit the far-away to the experience of a mind by way of representation is what we call meaning. This ability depends on two things: (1) The right connections and (2) the mind's understanding of these connections.‡

Wieman insists that meaning as set forth in his philosophy is not subjective. The experience of the meaning is subjective, but the meaning which is expe-

---

* Wieman, Art. (1936)⁴, 389.
† Wieman, Art. (1936)⁴, 390.
‡ Wieman, Art. (1936)⁴, 391.

---

quire that the consciousness have any knowledge of this activity. . . . They qualify consciousness without being objects of consciousness. Oxidation of the blood in my lungs qualifies my consciousness when I am not at all conscious of what is going on. These changes pertain to value, however, if their removal or cessation would destroy the system which yields the experience of value."

66. Wieman, "Values," p. 389: "With this understanding of activity let us now turn to the interpretation of meaning. Activity and meaning are closely related but not identical."

67. Wieman, "Values," pp. 389–390: "So we see that the connection between changes which makes them to be activities within a system is a connection which is best fitted to make them carriers of meaning by virtue of the fact that they can represent one another to a mind that understands the connection between them. A throbbing pulse means the presence of life to a mind that is able to understand the connection between these throbs and that system of co-ordinated changes in the organism which makes it a living thing. Rising smoke in the distance means the presence of fire to a mind that understands the connection between smoky changes in the atmosphere and correlative changes called combustion."

rienced, namely, the connection of mutual control or correlation between changes is not subjective. It is true, moreover, that meaning is dependent on understanding and appreciation which are themselves subjective, but that which is understood and appreciated is no more subjective than a mountain or a city.*[68] Now that we have discussed Wieman's "meaning of meaning" we can move on to his contention that value is a kind of connection.

It was stated above that value is not enjoyment. Enjoyment is too subjective to constitute the essence of value. What is enjoyable for one person may not be for another. What one person enjoys at one time is something loathsome to him under other conditions. But no matter how diverse may be the enjoyments of different people, one thing seems plain.[69] "The enjoyable activities, utterly different thought they may be, can be had only when they are so connected that they do not destroy one another."† Therefore, when we have any enjoyment, what we are actually experiencing is a great system of activities all connected in such a way as to yield that sort of enjoyment.[70]

Now since value is what makes an experience enjoyable, this analysis seems to indicate that value consists of the way activities are connected with one another.

All of this leads Wieman to the conclusion that value is not enjoyment, but it is that connection between activities which makes them enjoyable. In moments when we experience enjoyment, it is not merely our enjoyment that we enjoy; rather it is a certain connection between activities that we enjoy.[71] Out of this grows Wieman's definition of value. He says:

> Value is that connection between appreciable activities which makes them mutually sustaining, mutually enhancing, mutually diversifying, and mutually meaningful.‡

---

* Wieman, Art. (1936)[4], 392.

† Wieman, Art. (1934)[4], 392.

‡ Wieman, Art. (1936)[4], 394; For a similar definition see Wieman's NPOR, 48.

---

68. Wieman, "Values," pp. 391–392: "Meaning, as here set forth, is not subjective. The experience of the meaning is subjective if you equate experience with subjectivity. But the meaning which is experienced, namely, the connection of mutual control or correlation between changes, is no more subjective than a mountain or a city. . . . Meaning is dependent on understanding and appreciation, but that which is understood and appreciated is not subjective."

69. Wieman, "Values," p. 392: "What is enjoyable for one person is not for another. . . . What one person enjoys at one time is sometimes loathsome to him under other conditions. . . . But no matter how diverse may be the enjoyments of different people, or of the same person at different times in his development, one thing seems to be plain."

70. Wieman, "Values," p. 393: "Therefore, when we have any enjoyment, what we are actually experiencing is a great system of activities all connected in such way as to yield that sort of enjoyment."

71. Wieman, "Values," pp. 393–394: "If value is what makes an experience enjoyable, then our analysis would seem to indicate that value consists of the way activities are connected with

Wieman prefers the term appreciable over the terms enjoyed and enjoyable
because the latter may blind us to the fact that there are high austere values
which can be experienced at times only through great pain and suffering.[72]

Wieman makes it clear that his doctrine of value is not a hedonism which
identifies value with any sort of enjoyment.[73] Increase of value is not the mere
"additive sum of disconnected enjoyment."* Rather it is connection between
activities which makes them enjoyable by reason of their mutual support, mutual enhancement and mutual meaning.[74]

The first principle of value is mutual support. Eating wholesome food is
more valuable than eating unwholesome food because it is an activity which
supports many other appreciable activities. The same is true of honesty over
against dishonesty, good music over against bad, and the like.[75]

The second principle of value is mutual enhancement. Wholesome food not
only supports other enjoyable activities, but it makes those others more appreciable. Honesty not only supports but may enhance the value of many
other activities.[76]

Mutual diversification is a third characteristic of that connection between
activities which makes them appreciable and gives them value. "Activities
must be connected in such a way as to permit increase in their diversification
and number without permanently destroying their mutual support."† It is
quite possible, for instance, to have a system of mutual support which is
achieved and maintained by excluding all other activities and fixating the sys-

---

* Wieman, NPOR, 48.
† Wieman, Art. (1936)[4], 396.

---

one another. . . . All this points to the conclusion that value is not enjoyment, but it is that
connection between activities which makes them enjoyable. When we experience enjoyment, it is
not merely our enjoyment that we enjoy; what we enjoy is a certain connection between activities."

72. Wieman, "Values," pp. 394–395: "There is a further reason for speaking of appreciable
rather than of enjoyed or even enjoyable connections. . . . Such terms as enjoyed, enjoyment, and
enjoyable may blind us to the fact that there are high austere values which can be experienced at
times only through great pain and suffering."

73. Wieman and Westcott-Wieman, *Normative Psychology of Religion*, p. 48: "Thus the doctrine
of value we are here presenting is not a hedonism which identifies value with any sort of
enjoyment."

74. Wieman and Westcott-Wieman, *Normative Psychology of Religion*, p. 48: "Rather it represents value as that connection between activities which makes them enjoyable by reason of their
mutual support, mutual enhancement and mutual meaning."

75. Wieman, "Values," p. 395: "Thus eating wholesome food is an activity which supports
many other appreciable activities, while eating unwholesome food is an activity which does
not. . . . The same is true of honesty as over against dishonesty, good music as over against bad."

76. Wieman, "Values," p. 395: "Thus wholesome food not only supports other enjoyable activities, but it makes those others more appreciable. . . . Honesty not only supports but may
enhance the value of many other activities."

tem, as is found in political dictatorships in contrast with democracy.[77] "Connections of value must provide for increasing diversification on the part of the activities which are connected."*

A fifth characteristic of this connection between enjoyable activities deals with that activity which is exceedingly painful in itself, and yet is enjoyable by virtue of the meaning it carries. One chooses this painful but meaningful activity because of the enjoyableness of its meaning, not because of the enjoyableness of its pain.†[78]

We can now summarize the fivefold principle which Wieman sets forth as a way of distinguishing activities which are better from those that are worse. It is the principle of mutual support, mutual enhancement, mutual diversification, mutual meaning, and transformation of suffering into an experience which is positively appreciated. This fivefold principle is the principle of value, lifting it above the immediate subjective feeling of enjoyment. One activity is better when it is more appreciable by virtue of its connection with other activities. The connection is that of support, enhancement, diversification, meaning, and transmutation.[79]

ii. God as supreme value

In one of his writings Wieman defines God as "that structure which sustains, promotes and constitutes supreme value."‡ This structure of supreme value enters into existence, and it also extends far beyond existence into the realm of possibility. The terrible magnitude of evil makes it plain that the whole of existence is by no means conformant to this structure of God.[80]

---

* Wieman, Art. (1936)[4], 396.
† Wieman, Art. (1936)[4], 397.
‡ Wieman, Art. (1931)[3], 155.

---

77. Wieman, "Values," p. 396: "It is quite possible to have a system of mutual support which is achieved and maintained by excluding all other activities and fixating the system. In political order this is dictatorship as contrasted with democracy."

78. Wieman, "Values," p. 397: "There is still a fifth characteristic of this connection between enjoyable activities. . . . An activity may even be exceedingly painful, and yet be enjoyable by virtue of the meaning it carries. . . . We choose this painful but meaningful activity because of the enjoyableness of its meaning, not because of the enjoyableness of its pain."

79. Wieman, "Values," pp. 398–399: "We can now summarize the fivefold principle by which to distinguish activities which are better from those which are worse. It is the principle of mutual support, mutual enhancement, mutual diversification, mutual meaning, and transformation of suffering into an experience which is positively appreciated. This fivefold principle is the principle of value. . . . But one activity is better when it is more appreciable by virtue of its connection with other activities. This connection is that of support, enhancement, diversification, meaning, and transmutation."

80. Henry Nelson Wieman, "God and Value," in *Religious Realism*, ed. D. C. Macintosh (New York: Macmillan, 1931), p. 155: "In so far as this structure of supreme value enters into existence,

Supreme value is defined as that "system or structure which brings lesser values into relations of maximum mutual support and mutual enhancement."* This mutual support and enhancement is not only between contemporaries but also between successive generations, ages and culture.[81] This system or process which constitutes supreme value is variously called by Wieman "progressive integration,"† "creative event,"‡ and "principle of concretion."§ All of these are names for what we traditionally call God.

(1) God as more than possibility

One of Wieman's important contentions is that that to which all human life should be dedicated by reason of its supreme value is not merely some possibility or system of possibilities, but is rather the process which carries these possibilities. God is not merely the possibility of highest value, but he is actuality which carries those possibilities.[82] "He is present, potent, operative, existing actuality."‖ In this claim Wieman is seeking to refute outright the theory that the most important reality which can concern human life is not anything that exists, but rather some non-existent possibility. Wieman emphatically states:

> When we cut off the possibility from the process which makes it a possibility, and prize the possibility as more important than the process that carries it, we are assuming a self-defeating and self-contradictory attitude . . . To say that the process is mere means and therefore of less value than the possibility which is the end, is to set up a wholly vicious dichotomy between means and ends. The highest possibilities of value can never be attained except by way of process which leads to them.#

Again he writes:

> God is not merely possibility to be achieved. That is the ideal. But God is that order of existence and possibility by virtue of which the greatest possible good is truly a possibility and can be achieved by human effort.**

---

* Wieman, Art. (1931), 156. § Wieman, WRT, 179–212.
† Wieman, IOL, Art. (1931), ‖ Wieman, Art. (1932)[2], 110.
156. # Wieman, Art. (1931), 158.
‡ Wieman, SHG, 56. ** Wieman, IOL, 162.

---

we can speak of God as a process. But it extends far beyond existence, into the realm of possibility. And the whole of existence is by no means conformant to this structure of God. The terrible magnitude of evil makes this plain."

81. Wieman, "God and Value," p. 156: "This mutual support and enhancement must be not only between contemporaries but also between successive generations, ages, and cultures."

82. Henry Nelson Wieman, "Theocentric Religion," *Religion in Life* 1 (1932): 110: "God must be conceived not merely as the possibilities of highest value. God is the actuality which carries those possibilities."

Wieman also rejects the theory that the best is an impossibility. Such men as R. B. Perry, Bertrand Russell, Herman Randall, and George Santayana have affirmed that if men are to be faithful to the best, they must not supinely yield to the vulgarity of existence, either actual or possible, but must give their highest devotion to that nonexistent impossibility that never can be. But for one to adore the impossible, affirms Wieman, implies that his adoring of it is of great value. This adoring is itself a process of existence because he who adores is an existing personality. Therefore, if the value be a value, even when impossible of existence, that process of existence which enables one to value it as such, cannot be ignored or excluded from the high esteem we give to the impossibility of itself. Thus, some process of existence must be combined with some possibility (or impossibility) to make up the object of one's supreme devotion.* Since God is the name given to such an object, God must be identified with that process of existence which carries the possibilities of greatest value.[83]

Now we can see that, for Wieman, supreme value is always a combination of actuality and possibility. When these two are combined we have what is called growth. Growth is a kind of change which increases what is, so as to approximate what might be.

From this Wieman is led to affirm that supreme value is growth of meaning in the world. Why is this growth supreme value? It is supreme value for the following reasons:[84]

(1) In it the greatest value that can ever be experienced at any time is always to be found.

(2) It carries the highest possibilities of value, possibilities reaching far beyond the specific meanings we now know.

(3) All increase of value is found in it.

---

* Wieman, Art. (1931),
159.

---

83. Wieman, "God and Value," pp. 158–159: "Some hold that the best is not a possibility at all, but an impossibility. Therefore, if we are to be faithful to the best, we must not supinely yield to the vulgarity of existence, either actual or possible, but must give our highest devotion to that non-existent impossibility that never can be. R. B. Perry, Bertrand Russell, Herman Randall, Joseph Wood Krutch, George Santayana, . . . have been eloquent on this point. But he who adores the impossible, implies that his adoring of it is of great value. . . . But this adoring is itself a process of existence because he who adores is an existing personality. . . . Second, if the value be a value even when impossible of existence, then that process of existence which enables us to value it as such, cannot be ignored or excluded from the high esteem we give to the impossibility itself. Thus in any case some process of existence must be combined with some possibility (or impossibility) to make up the object of our supreme devotion. Since God is the name we give to such an object, God must be identified with that process of existence which carries the possibilities of greatest value."

84. Wieman and Westcott-Wieman, *Normative Psychology of Religion*, p. 51: "[Supreme value] is always a combination of actuality and possibility. When these two are combined we have what is called growth. Growth . . . is that kind of change which increases what is, so as to approximate what might be. . . . [Supreme value] is growth of meaning in the world. This is the supreme value for the following reasons."

(4) The best conceivable world can be approximated in existence to some
degree through this growth, and in no other way.*

As we have seen above, this growth of meaning and value in the world is God.[85] Wieman seeks to justify the claim that this supreme value is God on five grounds:

(1) Growth of meaning commands our supreme devotion and highest loyalty by right of its worthfulness.
(2) It creates and sustains human personality.
(3) It carries human personality to whatsoever highest fulfillments are possible to it.
(4) It has more worth than personality, hence human personality finds its highest destiny in giving itself to this growth to be mastered, used, and transformed by it into the fabric of emerging values.
(5) The greatest value can be poured into human life only as we yield ourselves to the domination and control of this growth. When we try to dominate and use it, we lose these values.†

All of this gives weight to Wieman's basic contention that God is the supreme value of the universe. He is certain that God is that order of structures of value, actual and possible, which will ultimately issue in the realization of the greatest value when we rightly conform to its requirements.‡[86]

(2) God as the unlimited growth of the connection of value

One of the main bases of Wieman's interpretation of God as supreme value is God's work as the unlimited growth of the connection of value. Every specific system of value is definitely limited, whether it be a living organism or a society of organisms, or a community of minds with the institutional structure called a culture. Each of these must perish. They are capable of carrying the growth of connections of value only to a certain limit, and then must stop. In order for values and meanings to grow indefinitely, it is necessary for each of these limited systems of value to pass away in time and give place to some

---

* Wieman, NPOR, 50.
† Wieman, NPOR, 51, 52.
‡ Wieman, IOL, 221, 222.

---

85. Wieman and Westcott-Wieman, *Normative Psychology of Religion*, pp. 51–52: "This growth of meaning and value in the world is God."

86. Wieman, *Issues of Life*, pp. 221–222: "It is that order of structures of value, actual and possible, which will ultimately issue in the realization of the greatest value when we rightly conform to its requirements."

other orders of existence and value.[87] Therefore, God cannot be identified with any of these limited systems of value. God is the growth which has no limit.

> God is the growth which goes on through the successions of these limited systems of value. God is the growth which exfoliates in all manner of value . . . God is the growth which springs anew when old forms perish. When one organism dies, others spring up. When one society perishes, others arise. When one epoch of culture declines, others in time come forth. This unlimited growth of connections is God.*

iii. God as creative source of value

Wieman defines God not only in terms of the maximum achievement of value, analogous to an ideal of perfection, but also in terms of those natural conditions which underlie the achievement of value. God, in other words, is not simply the greatest possible value or the process by which such value is achieved; he is also the sum-total of all the natural conditions of such value-achievement. Thus in a very interesting article Wieman says that "the value of God . . . is that of creative source . . . that particular sort which pertains to creator of all created values. The value of god is the value of creativity."†[88] Again he says:

> The value of God is the value not of the gifts but of the giver. Not the goal but the source, not the golden eggs but the goose that lays them, not the grains and fruit but the creative earth, not the products of love but the loving, not beauty but the generator of beauty, not truth but the source of truth, not moral righteousness but the creator and transformer of righteousness, not the profits of industry but the ultimate producer, not the goods but the creativity, must be given priority over all else if we would escape destruction, have salvation, and know the true and living God.‡

---

* Wieman, Art. (1936)[4], 404.
† Wieman, Art. (1943)[1], 25.
‡ Wieman, Art. (1943)[1], 25.

---

87. Wieman, "Values," pp. 403–404: "The most important reality which can command the loyalties of men is the unlimited growth of the connections of value. . . . Every specific system of activities having value is definitely limited, whether it be a living organism with its sustaining environment, or a society of organisms, or a community of minds with all their meanings and with a historic development and institutional structure called a culture. Each of these must perish. . . . If values and meanings are to grow indefinitely, each of these limited systems of value must pass away in time and give place to some other order of existence and value."

88. Martin, *Empirical Philosophies of Religion*, p. 104: "But we have noted that Wieman defines God not simply in terms of the maximum achievement of value, analagous to an ideal of perfection, but also in terms of those natural conditions which underlie the achievement of value. God, in other words, in not simply the greatest possible value or the process by which such value is achieved; he is also the sum-total of all the natural *conditions* of such value-achievement. Thus in

This rather lengthy pasage is an eloquent expression of Wieman's conviction that God is underlying "ground" or the "power" behind the creation of value.

Now it must be emphasized that when Wieman uses the term "create" he does not mean what traditional Christianity means by the term. Historically creation first referred to the act whereby the underived self-existent God brought into being what had no form of independent existence hitherto. This Christian notion contrasted radically with the Greek concept of "creation" as an "informing" or reshaping of pre-existent entity. So strong was the Christian, theistic belief in an absolute, transcendent God who worked under no external limitations, that creation was said to be ex nihilo, i.e. generation out of nothing. With this concept, however, Wieman is in total disagreement. He contends that the doctrine of creation ex nihilo is self-contradictory. Moreover, it would be impossible for Wieman on the basis of his method to get any knowledge of such an initial generation, supposing it ever occurred. By "create" Wieman means to produce what never was before, either in existence or in the imagination of man, to produce that which exposes to appreciative awareness more of the qualities of reality, or builds in that direction.*[89]

Another point that Wieman emphasizes is that God as creative source is not "the source of everything". He is only "the generative source of all other value." Wieman writes:

> God is not the creator, meaning the mysterious source of everything; he is only the source of the good, or rather is himself the good. The source of all good is simply the cosmic growing roots of all good, and these roots are themselves good.†

It is clear that Wieman is seeking to avoid pantheism by identifying God with only the good in the universe. Wieman is emphatic in affirming that "all is not God and God is not all. All is not good and good is not all." There are many disintegrating processes at work. There is death, futility and ruin. There is evil in the world vast and devastating. These facts Wieman never overlooks. What he is anxious to make plain is that there is also good, and that this good is derived from the process of integration.[90] "It is derived from God, the integrating behavior of the universe."‡

---

* Wieman, DIH, 61.
† Wieman, GOR, 267.
‡ Wieman, MPRL, 58.

---

a recent article he says that 'the value of God . . . is that of creative source . . . that peculiar sort which pertains to the creator of all created values. The value of God is the value of creativity'."

89. Henry Nelson Wieman, *The Directive in History* (Boston: Beacon Press, 1949), p. 61: "It would be impossible for us to get any knowledge of such an initial generation, supposing it ever occurred. . . . By *create* we mean to produce what never was before, either in existence or in the imagination of man, to produce that which exposes to appreciative awareness more of the qualities of reality, or builds in that direction."

90. Henry Nelson Wieman, *Methods of Private Religious Living* (New York: Macmillan, 1929), pp. 57–58: "There are many disintegrating processes at work. . . . All is not God and God is not

It is now clear what Wieman is seeking to say concerning the creative activity of God. God is not only supreme fulfillment or ideal perfection, but also creative source of value. This does not mean that God creates and sustains the universe as a whole. As we shall see in the discussion of "God and evil," such an assumption generates the "false problem" of evil. It is a flagrant contradiction to affirm the goodness of God's unlimited power in the face of the evil in the world of which he is creator.* So in order to escape this contradiction Wieman denies that God is author of the universe. Instead of being the creator and sustainer of the universe, God is the creator and sustainer of all that is good in the universe. Such a creator and sustainer is not of the universe as a whole, but only of the good that is in it.[91]

We may ask at this point whether it is justifiable for Wieman, on the basis of his empirical point of view, to speak of a creative source of value. If he means to refer to the natural conditions or forces which underlie value achievement, than it must be pointed out that empirically there is a plurality of such conditions, and the notion of a "creative source" is at best figurative and imaginative.

It is interesting to note that Dewey has discovered the same ambiguity in Wieman's concept of God.[92] Dewey grants "that there are in existence conditions and forces which, apart from human desire and intent, bring about enjoyed and enjoyable goods, and that the security and extension of goods are promoted by attention to and service of these conditions."† But these conditions and forces, contends Dewey, do not have enough unity to constitute a unitary object of devotion and so cannot be considered God. So Dewey concludes that Wieman reaches his view of God through the hypostatization of

---

* Wieman, GOR, 353,
354.
† Dewey, Rev. (1933),
196.

---

all. All is not good and good is not all. . . . There is death, disintegration, futility and ruin. . . . There is evil in the world vast and devastating. But there is also good. . . . All good is derived from the process of integration."

91. Wieman and Horton, *Growth of Religion*, pp. 353–354: "The assumption which generates the false problem of evil is this: A perfectly good God creates and sustains the universe and all that is in it. . . . The contradiction is between the goodness of God's unlimited power and the evil in the world of which he is creator and sustainer. . . . One who denies that God is the creator and sustainer of the universe, simply does not have the contradiction on his hands. . . . There is a creator and sustainer of all that is good in the universe. . . . Such a creator and sustainer, however, is not of the universe as a whole, but only of the good that is in it."

92. Martin, *Empirical Philosophies of Religion*, pp. 104–105: "If he means to refer to the natural conditions which may be utilized in the achievement of value, then once again we must point out that empirically there is a *plurality* of such conditions, and the notion of 'a' creative 'source' is at most imaginative and figurative. . . . It is interesting to note, in this connection, that Dewey has pointed to some of these ambiguities in objecting to Wieman's claim that his idea of God is a faithful theistic formulation of the religious faith implicit in Dewey's philosophy."

an undeniable fact, experience of things, persons, causes, found to be good and worth cherishings, into a single objective existence, a God.*[93]

From a more consistent empirical point of view, Dewey's criticisms seem justified; indeed he has pointed out a difficulty that appears over and over again in Wieman's whole system. When Wieman speaks of God there seem to be at least three different meanings. When he characterizes God as "supreme value" he seems to mean the ideal of perfection or of the achievement of maximum value. When he speaks of God as the "the unlimited connective growth of value-connections" he seems to mean the human and social processes which aim at the achievement of value. When he described God as the process of progressive integration and as the creative event he seems to mean the natural forces underlying the achievement of value. Certainly these three meanings cannot be viewed as constituting a unity except in a highly figurative and imaginative sense, and positively not for a religious philosophy which would be consistently empirical. We must conclude that at this point Wieman has failed to be consistently empirical.[94]

3. God and evil

Wieman holds that from a consistently empirical point of view the problem of evil, which has troubled so many thinkers, is a false problem. It arises only when one departs from the empirical evidence for God as "the good" or the chief factor for good in nature, and begins to speculate about God as somehow being the creator and sustainer of the universe. As we have seen, Wieman totally denies the view that God is creator of the universe. God is only the creator and sustainer of the good in the universe, namely the power of

---

* Dewey, Rev. (1933), 196, 196.

---

93. John Dewey, Review of *Is There a God?* ed. C. C. Morrison, *Christian Century* 40 (8 February 1933): 196: "I can but think that Mr. Wieman's God rests upon hypostatization of an undeniable fact, experience of things, persons, causes, found to be good and worth cherishing, into a single objective existence, *a* God."

94. Martin, *Empirical Philosophies of Religion*, p. 105: "Now it seems to us that, from a more consistently empirical point of view, Dewey's criticisms are justified; indeed, it seems that he has pointed clearly to the chief sources of difficulty in Wieman's total view. When Wieman speaks of God there seem to be at least three different meanings. He seems to mean the ideal of perfection or of the achievement of maximum value; the human and social processes which aim at the achievement of value; and the natural forces underlying or utilized in these processes. He does not realize that these three meanings may be viewed as constituting a unity (or a Trinity!) only in a highly imaginative and figurative sense, a sense appropriate to the life of faith and devotion, perhaps, but not to a religious philosophy which would be consistently empirical in this connection. We believe that it is his failure to be consistently empirical in this connection which is largely responsible for the confusions which we have found in his views of religious perception and method."

growth. Wieman feels that one must either deny the reality of evil, which is clearly unempirical, or give up the idea of God as Creator of all.* He chooses the latter. Wieman contends that the more empirical problem is to define the actual nature and scope of evil, and not indulge in unempirical speculation concerning its origin.[95] At this point we turn to a discussion of his view of the nature and scope of evil.

i. Evil as destructive of good

We have seen that Wieman follows Whitehead in defining God as "the principle of concretion."† On the basis of this definition evil is that which is destructive of concrete existence. It is anything that hinders the prehensive‡ capacity of any particular thing.[96]

The more fully any object prehends the rest of being, the more it is subject to the destructive works of evil. The higher we rise in the levels of prehension, the greater place there is for the destructive works of evil.[97]

Since evil is destructive of good there can be no evil unless there is first good. Evil is thus parasitic.§ It is dependent on the good. It cannot stand on its own feet. Evil can thrive and develop only when there is good to sustain it.[98] "The world is based on the good. The concrete world would have no

---

* Wieman feels that Brightman's idea of a finite deity only reformulates the false problem, which is stated as truly "insoluble."

† Wieman, WRT, 182.

‡ In the terminology of A. N. Whitehead, prehension is the process of feeling whereby data are grasped or prehended by a subject. See Process and Reality, Part III.

§ Wieman, WRT, 201.

---

95. Martin, *Empirical Philosophies of Religion*, p. 108: "From a consistently empirical point of view, he holds, [the problem of evil] is really a false problem; it arises only when one departs from the empirical evidence for God as 'the good', or the chief factor for good in nature, and begins to speculate about God as also somehow the creator of all existence. That is, one must either deny the reality of evil, which is clearly empirical, or give up the idea of God as Creator of all. . . . Brightman's idea of a finite deity only reformulates the false problem, which as stated is truly 'insoluble'. The more empirical problem is to define the actual nature and scope of evil, and not to indulge in unempirical speculation as to its 'origin'."

96. Henry Nelson Wieman, *The Wrestle of Religion with Truth* (New York: Macmillan, 1927), p. 200: "Evil is anything which hinders the prehensive capacity of any particular thing. . . . It is destructive of concrete existence."

97. Wieman, *Wrestle of Religion with Truth*, pp. 200–201: "The more fully any object prehends the rest of being, the more complicated and delicately balanced must all its adjustments be. . . . The higher we rise in the levels of prehension, the greater place there is for the destructive works of evil."

98. Wieman, *Wrestle of Religion with Truth*, p. 201: "Since evil is the destruction of good there can be no evil unless there is first the good. . . . Evil, then, is parasitic. It cannot stand on its own feet. It can thrive and flourish only when there is good to sustain it."

existence were it not for the principle of concretion which constitutes the good. Good and concrete existence are identical."* The concrete order of the world is good. Evil tends to destroy the order of concreteness,† and therefore the whole order of existence.

Evil is not merely a principle of nonbeing or an absence of something. It is both positive and aggressive.‡ But God is not evil, nor can evil and good be confused. Insofar as the existing world is concrete, it is due to the work of God, the principle of concretion and order.[99] But evil is destructive of all levels of concreteness. So Wieman concludes:

> God excludes evil, evil excludes God. God does not create evil nor sustain evil, except as a parasite is sustained. Evil could not exist without God's good to provide a standing ground; but the good alone is of God.§

ii. Kinds of evil

Wieman distinguishes between those evils rooted in the nature of things not caused by man and those that originate in human life. Evils rooted in the nature of things are called "inertias" and "protective hierarchies." Evils that originate in human life are called sin and demonry.[100]

By inertia Wieman means more than simply the opposite of change. It is first "lack of the sensitivity and responsiveness necessary to get the thought and feeling of another or to participate appreciatively in a more complex community."‖ Secondly, it is resistance to that kind of transformation whereby the individual organism, the world relative to that organism, and the associated community are all re-created so as to increase qualitative meaning.# In short, inertia is insensitivity and resistance to creativity. This kind of inertia is due

---

* Wieman, WRT, 201.
† The meaning of "concreteness", for Wieman, is contrasted with the meaning of "abstraction." By "concrete" he has reference to events in their wholeness, their individualized totality, their unique and full particularity. Anything less than this concrete wholeness or unique particularity is an abstraction. The being and therefore the power of causal efficacy of events refers to their concreteness.
‡ Wieman, GR, 358.
§ Wieman, WRT, 202.
‖ Wieman, SHG, 105.
Wieman, SHG, 105.

---

99. Wieman, *Wrestle of Religion with Truth*, p. 202: "Evil is something positive and aggressive, not merely the lack or absence of something. But God is not evil and there is no confusion of good and evil. Insofar as the concrete world exists at all, it is due to God, the principle of concretion and order." Cf. Wieman and Horton, *Growth of Religion*, p. 358: "We do not mean to say that evil is negative in the sense of being merely the absence of something. Particular evils are destructive and positive."

100. Wieman, *Source of Human Good*, p. 105: "The most general classification of evils distinguishes between those rooted in the nature of things not caused by man and those that originate in human life. . . . Evils that originate in human life we shall call 'sin,' 'immorality,' and 'demonry.'"

to at least three things: the lack of vital energy, the running down of energy, and the cancelling-out of conflicting energies.*[101] This threat of inertia and loss of meaning is not peculiar to human life. It hangs over all the world. It seems to be a cosmic drift and threat. But Wieman is certain that it can be conquered. He contends that there is a power more than human which works against it.† Wieman sees several times since this planet cooled when it seemed that power reached a level when defeat was imminent.[102] But this threatening defeat was avoided. "The transition from inanimate matter to the living cell may have been such a time. The transition from lower animal existence to man may have been another such dangerous and difficult passage."‡

Another evil, derivative from this of inertia, is the evil of protective hierarchy. Wieman contends that there are many kinds of hierarchy, but his concern is only with what he calls the "hierarchy of sensitivity." When he speaks of the "hierarchy of sensitivity," Wieman means that the graded capacity to undergo creative transformation and the graduated levels of sensitivity impose a hierarchy on existence in which only the few at the top can be the medium through which the creative event works most fully. This order of life is a hard necessity, contends Wieman, but it is evil because not all forms of life, not even all human organisms, can share equally the supreme fulfillments of qualitative meaning;[103] moreover "it is evil because some forms of life must support other forms by enduring hardships or other stultifying effects that

---

* Wieman, SHG, 105.
† When Wieman contends that there is a power more than human which works against inertia, one is reminded of Bright- man's view that God eternally controls the "given". However there is one distinct difference. For Brightman the "given" is within God. For Wieman inertia is outside of God.
‡ Wieman, SHG, 117.

---

101. Wieman, *Source of Human Good*, p. 105: "By 'inertia' we mean . . . resistance to that kind of transformation whereby the individual organism, the world relative to that organism, and the associated community are all re-created so as to increase qualitative meaning. . . . We shall discuss this kind of inertia—insensitivity and resistance to creativity—in three rough categories, according to its causes: inertia due to lack of vital energy, inertia due to the running-down of energy, and inertia due to the canceling-out of conflicting energies."

102. Wieman, *Source of Human Good*, pp. 116–117: "This threat of inertia and loss of meaning is not peculiar to human life. It hangs over all the world. It seems to be a cosmic drift and threat, but it can be conquered. There is a power more than human which works against it. Several times since this planet cooled, it seems, this power reached a level where further advance was precarious, where defeat was imminent."

103. Wieman, *Source of Human Good*, pp. 117–118: "Another evil, derivative from this of inertia, is the evil of protective hierarchy. There are many kinds of hierarchy, but here we are concerned only with what could be called the 'hierarchy of sensitivity.' The graduated levels of sensitivity and the graded capacity to undergo creative transformation impose a hierarchy on existence in which only the few at the top can be the medium through which the creative event works most fully. This ordering of life is a hard necessity, but it is evil. It is evil because not all forms of life, not even all human organisms, can share equally the supreme fulfilments of qualitative meaning."

render them less responsive and less sensitive."* Concerning the necessity and evil of the hierarchy, Wieman says:

> The hierarchy is both necessity and an evil: It is necessary to enable the creative event to produce the richest fulfillment of value with those most capable of engaging in that kind of communication. It is evil because it imposes upon many an undue protection from pain and discomfort; upon some an undue fatigue from hard labor; upon others impoverished organisms; upon still others the irresponsible existence which puts on the throne of life what they happen to like, without demonstrating by any reliable method that it is truly most important.†

Wieman concludes that the high peak of creative transformation will continue to soar far above the mass of people, with only a very few finding a place there. This is a hard necessity, an evil inherent in the cosmic situation. But it is a fact that we must face, ordering our lives accordingly.‡ [104]

The evils thus far treated are thrust upon man from sources outside of human living, and are somewhat inherent in the nature of things. Wieman admits that there are times when these evils pass over from the external source to the internal affairs of man, making it hard to draw the line precisely determining the place where human responsibility begins. Moreover, we unquestionably have responsibility for many of the inertias and hierarchies. Nevertheless, they are, by and large, thrust upon us from sources external to human life.§ [105]

Sin and demonry are the two kinds of evil originating with man. Sin is any resistance to creativity for which man is responsible. Man's responsibility is not limited to instances in which he is consciously aware of obstructing creativity or deliberately intending to do so. Unintended and unconscious resistance is sin, too, because it is the consequence of many past decisions for which the man is responsible.‖ Most sin is unconscious and unintended. To be uncon-

---

* Wieman, SHG, 118.
† Wieman, SHG, 119, 120.

‡ Wieman, SHG, 124.
§ Wieman, SHG, 125.
‖ Wieman, SHG, 126.

---

104. Wieman, *Source of Human Good*, p. 124: "The high peak of creative transformation will continue to soar far above the mass of people, with only a very few finding a place there. This a hard necessity, an evil inherent in the cosmic situation, so it seems. If this claim should be mistaken, none would be more happy than we; but if it is true, we must face the fact and order our lives accordingly."

105. Wieman, *Source of Human Good*, pp. 125–126: "The evils thus far treated are thrust upon man from sources outside of human living, and they seem to reside in the nature of things. . . . It is true that these evils pass over from the external source to the internal affairs of man, and it is hard to draw the line precisely determining the place where human responsibility begins. We unquestionably do have responsibility for many of the inertias. . . . Nevertheless, the inertias and the hierarchies are, primarily and in the large, thrust upon us from sources external to human life."

scious of one's sin when he could be conscious of it is itself a darker sin. Man can, if he will, be far more fully conscious of his sin than he generally is.[106] "To be conscious of one's sin is to be that far in the direction of deliverance from it; for the deeper enslavement to sin is the state in which one is not conscious of it."*

When Wieman says that sin is man's resistance to the creative event, he refers to what was meant by the theological statement: "Sin is man's rebellion against the will of God."[107] Another way that Wieman describes sin is to say that it is the creature turning against the creator—it is created good turning against creativity.† Man's personality, for instance, is a created good, and so also are his society, his culture, and his ideals. He, with his society and ideals, is forever refusing to surrender himself to the transforming power of the creative event. This is sin. He refuses to provide the conditions which he could provide and which are necessary for the freer working of creativity. This is rebellion against God. The "will of God is the demand of creative power that man provide conditions most favorable to its working."‡[108] When man fails to remove or fight the conditions obstructing creativity he is failing to do the will of God, and is thereby sinning.

The evil of demonry is another evil which Wieman refers to as originating within human nature. Demonry is the evil of resisting creative transformation

---

* Wieman, SHG, 127.
† For Wieman the terms "creativity" and "creative event" are inseparable, but the two words carry an important distinction in meaning. "Creativity is the character, the structure, or form which the event must have to be creative. Creativity is therefore an abstraction. The concrete reality is the creative event." (SHG, 299).
‡ Wieman, SHG, 127.

---

106. Wieman, *Source of Human Good*, pp. 126, 127: "Sin is any resistance to creativity for which man is responsible. . . . What is important, however, is that man recognize that his responsibility is not limited to instances in which he is consciously aware of obstructing creativity or deliberately intending to do so. Unintended and unconscious resistance is sin, too, because it is the consequence of many past decisions for which the man is responsible. . . . Most sin is unconscious and unintended. To be unconscious of one's sin when he could be conscious of it is itself a darker sin. . . . We here point only to the fact that man can, if he will, be far more fully conscious of his sin than he generally is."

107. Wieman, *Source of Human Good*, p. 126: "When we say that sin is man's resistance to the creative event, we refer to what was meant by the theological statement: 'Sin is man's rebellion against the will of God.'"

108. Wieman, *Source of Human Good*, p. 127: "Another way of describing sin is to say that it is the creature turning against the creator—it is created good turning against creativity. Man's personality is a created good, and so also are his society, his culture, his ideals. He, with his society, culture, and ideals, is forever refusing to meet the demands which must be met if the creative event is to rule in his life. This is sin. He refuses to provide the conditions which he could provide and which are necessary to release the freer working of creativity. . . . All this is rebellion against God. The 'will of God,' so far as it prescribes what man should do, is the demand of creative power that man provide conditions most favorable to its working."

for the sake of a vision of human good. In traditional usage the term devil
means the archtempter. The devil is what tempts man to sin in the most dangerous and evil way; and the devil is also one of the most glorious sons of God.[109] The devil is, symbolically speaking, "the most glorious vision of good that our minds can achieve at any one time when that vision refuses to hold itself subject to creativity."* Wieman contends that this is the most subtle and dangerous sin that man can commit. No vision of any race or culture at any time may be listed up and made supreme against the creative event.[110]

In the midst of the tremendous increase of power, due to the intensive industrialization of the planet, some group will surely rise to the height of power that no men ever before enjoyed. Such a group will be tempted to use its power to achieve what seems to it good and refuse to use it to serve the creative event.[111] To yield to such a temptation would mean that one is yielding to the worse form of demonry.†

So we now see the distinction which Wieman makes between evils rooted in the nature of things and those that originate in human life. Both types are mutually destructive. However, it is those evils rooted in the nature of things that we can do least about.

Traditional views have affirmed that evil will ultimately be overcome by the workings of an almighty God. Wieman's naturalism prevents him from accepting such a view. However, he does find some ground of hope from empirical sources. First, there are the empirical facts of the increase of good through millions of centuries. No one can doubt that qualitative meaning has increased over the years. The second ground of hope is the fact that evil cannot destroy creativity. It can only obstruct it.

Wieman finds an ultimate dualism more empirical than either a monistic idealism which would deny the existence of evil, or a quasi-monistic idealism which would seem to equivocate the issue.[112]

---

* Wieman, SHG, 128.

† Wieman, SHG, 129.

---

109. Wieman, *Source of Human Good*, p. 128: "The evil of resisting creative transformation for the sake of a vision of human good remains. . . . The devil is what tempts man to sin in the most dangerous and evil way; also the devil is the most glorious of the sons of God."

110. Wieman, *Source of Human Good*, p. 129: "This is the most subtle and dangerous and obstructive sin that man can sin. No vision of any man, race, or culture at any time can be lifted up and made supreme against creativity."

111. Wieman, *Source of Human Good*, p. 129: "When the power of man increases by leaps and bounds, as it is doing today with the intensive industrialization of the planet, . . . some group will surely rise to a height of power that no men ever before enjoyed. It will be tempted to use its power to achieve what seems to it good and refuse to use it to serve the creative event."

112. Martin, *Empirical Philosophies of Religion*, p. 108: "Thus Wieman, like Boodin, finds an ultimate dualism more empirical than either a monistic idealism which would deny the existence of evil, [or] a quasi-monistic idealism which would seem to equivocate the issue."

iii. God's finiteness

Wieman's conclusions on the whole problem of evil reveal that he is a theistic finitist. A theistic finitist is one who holds that the eternal will of God faces given conditions which that will did not create, whether those conditions are ultimately within the personality of God or external to God. All theistic finitists agree that there is something in the universe not created by God and not a result of voluntary divine self-limitation, which God finds as either obstacle or instrument to his will. Now it is clear that Wieman fits into this category. He does not hesitate to affirm that God's power is limited by evil. As we have already seen, "inertias" and "hierarchies," which are basic evils, originate in sources external to God, the creative event. Wieman's idea of a finite God clearly comes out in his affirmation that "the problem of evil arises only when you claim there is an almighty and perfectly good power that controls everything. I make no such claim."* God is only the source of the good and not of the universe as a whole. Wieman is thus content with an ultimate dualism.†

He is confident, however, that although God is finite his purpose and work cannot be defeated. In fact God tends to gain ground over the forces of evils as time goes on. Wieman writes:

> Our point is that the universe seems to be so constituted that this movement toward higher integration springs up again and again under all manner of conditions, places and times. Sometimes it mounts high, sometimes not so high. Again and again it may be beaten back or overwhelmed. But on the whole it seems to gain ground as ages pass.‡

There is a striking parallel between Wieman's thought at this point and Brightman's idea of God as "Controller of the Given." Brightman contends that God controls the Given in the sense that he never allows The Given to run wild. "God's control means that no defeat or frustration is final; that the will of God, partially thwarted by obstacles in the chaotic Given, finds new avenues of advance, and forever moves on in the cosmic creation of new values."§

---

* Wieman, Art. (1932)³, 201.

† Wieman's finite God may be compared with Brightman's finite God at many points. Brightman holds to the idea of a personal finite God whose finiteness consists in his own internal structure: An eternal unitary personal consciousness whose creative will is limited both by external necessities of reason and by eternal experiences of brute fact. These limits Brightman calls "the Given." The Given is an aspect of God's consciousness which eternally enters into every moment of the divine experience and into everything that is, either as obstacle or as instrument to the will of God. Wieman denies that God is a person. Also Wieman insists that that which limits God is outside of his nature. In a word, Wieman's finite God is a "process of integration" which is continually confronted with external conditions working against integration. Brightman's finite God is a personal being who is continually confronted with obstacles inside his own nature.

‡ Wieman, MPRL, 55.

§ Brightman, POR, 338.

4. The question of the existence of God

As we have seen, one of Wieman's chief aims is that of making the question of God's existence a dead issue. To this end he sets forth the following definitions of God: "God is that actuality which sustains, promotes and constitutes the supreme good."* "God is that something upon which human life is most dependent for its security, welfare, and increasing abundance. . . . , that something of supreme value which constitutes the most important conditions."† "God is that structure of existence and possibility which is supremely worthful."‡ If God be defined as supreme value or as that process which underlies and makes possible the maximum achievement of value, then the fact of his existence, if not full knowledge of his specific nature, is "inescapable." "The best there is and can be. . . . is a self-proving proposition."§ [113]

Wieman's interest in seeing a curtailment to the debate on the question of God's existence stems from his broader theocentric concern. He is deeply concerned in seeing men turn all their energies to living for God and seeking better knowledge about God. "Dispute about the existence of God," says Wieman, "is blocking and diverting that outpouring of constructive energy which religious devotion ought properly to release for the tasks that confront us.‖

So Wieman looks upon all arguments for the existence of God as futile and invalid. Just as it is folly to attempt to prove the existence of nature to natural creatures, or the United States to its citizens, it is equal folly to try to prove to humans, whose essential nature consists in seeking, adoring, and serving whatever has greatest value, that there is something which has greatest value.# [114] So Wieman is led to say:

> All the traditional arguments to prove the existence of God are as much out of place in religion as arguments to prove the existence of nature would be in science. Never in any of my writings have I tried to prove the existence of God except by "definition," which means to state the problem in such a way as to lift it out of the arena of debate.**

---

* Wieman, Art. (1932)³, 276.
† Wieman, RESM, 9.
‡ Wieman, Art. (1932)³, 276.

§ Wieman, Art. (1931)², 1171.
‖ Wieman, Art. (1932)³, 283.
Wieman, Art. (1932)³,

82.
** Wieman, Art. (1932)³, 284.

---

113. Martin, *Empirical Philosophies of Religion*, p. 87: "If God be defined as supreme value or as that process which underlies and makes possible the maximum achievement of value then the fact of his existence, if not full knowledge of his specific nature, is 'inescapable,' he feels. 'The best there is and can be . . . is a self-proving proposition.'"

114. Henry Nelson Wieman, "Is There a God?" in *Is There a God?* ed. C. C. Morrison (Chicago: Willett, Clark, 1932), p. 82: "In fact, anyone who started out to prove the existence of nature to natural creatures like ourselves, or of United States to its citizens, would be a fool. It is equal folly to try to prove to animals like ourselves, whose essential nature consists in seeking, adoring, and serving whatever has greatest value, that there is something which has greatest value."

Again he writes: "No one has less interest than I in trying to prove the existence of God. As already stated, I hold such procedure folly."*

Despite his insistence that he has made the existence of God so certain that all arguments for his existence are unnecessary, Wieman at times uses the argument of the gradation of being, an argument quite prevalent in Thomistic thinking. Wieman says, for example:

> There are a number of general truths about reality which we know with a very high degree of certainty, and these general truths are of utmost importance. We have mentioned a few of them, such as the truth that I exists, that other people exist, <u>that there is better and worse and that, therefore, there is the inevitable implication of better and worse, which is the Best</u>, or God.†

In a more concise passage he says:

> Since I know there is better and worse, I know there is the Best; for the best is the inevitable implication of the reality of better and worse. When I say 'God', I mean the best there is. Therefore I know God is.‡

In both of these passages Wieman is explicitly seeking to prove the existence of God through the argument of the gradation of being. This certainly conflicts with his persistent claim that all arguments for God's existence are invalid. We must conclude, therefore, that Wieman fails to achieve one of his basic objectives, viz., making the question of God's existence a dead issue. Against his fundamental intentions, he ends up seeking to prove (whether consciously or unconsciously) the existence of God.

5. The question of the personality in God

One of the most controversial phases of Wieman's thought hinges around the question of personality of God. In his earlier works Wieman granted the possibility that God might be mental or personal. "Nature," he says, "may very well be moved and sustained by the operation of a supreme mind or personality."§ Again he says: "It may be that what gives the character and creative advance to the whole of nature and every part of nature is that there is operative throughout the whole of nature a mind."‖

Despite this earlier willingness to grant the possibility of personality in God, Wieman, in his later works, emphatically denies that God can be a person. He is convinced that "God towers in unique majesty infinitely above the little hills which we call minds and personalities."# In order to get a better understanding of Wieman's thought at this point, we turn to a discussion of the objections

---

* Wieman, Art. (1932)³, 84.

† Wieman, Art. (1937), 207. Italics mine.

‡ Wieman, Art. (1937), 204.

§ Wieman, RESM, 180.

‖ Wieman, RESM, 181.

Wieman, Art. (1936)², 432.

which he raises to the idea of a personal God, and then to a consideration of his view that God is process.

i. Objections to the idea of a personal God

One of the basic reasons why Wieman objects to the idea of a personal God is his contention that personality is inconceivable apart from a society of persons. Personality is generated by interaction between individuals. If this is the case then God cannot be a personality. The only ground on which the theory can be defended is on the basis of the doctrine of the trinity. But there is not the slightest empirical evidence, contends Wieman, of such an ontological trinity.*

Another reason why Wieman denies that God is mental or personal is found in the essential limitations of personality. Something infinitely richer and more pervasive and precious than personality produces and constitutes the value of the world. Indeed it is this something which generates personality. Wieman turns to the sciences of personality, psychology, social psychology, and anthropology to gain validation for his contention that it is something more than a personality which generates personality, sustains and promotes its growth, and brings it to highest fulfillment. The reality which does all this, according to these disciplines, is a very complex and delicate system of connections of mutual control which grows up between the individual psycho-physical organism and its physical and social environment.[115]

For similar reasons Wieman cannot conceive of God as "mind." Mind and personality are "summit characters" in nature, but they are not universal features of nature as are process and interaction. To possess mind would automatically limit God. In discussing God in relation to prayer, Wieman says:

> To be conscious as we know consciousness is to have focus of attention. But to have focus of attention is to be able to attend to a few things in a certain area and not to attend to anything beyond. Can God function as God must, if he is so limited? . . . To have human mentality God must see things from a viewpoint that is localized at a certain time and place.†

As we have seen, Wieman holds that the work of God is clearly distinguished from that of man. The difference is not merely of degree or magnitude. It is a difference of kind. An understanding of this distinction is all-

---

* Wieman, SHG, 266.
† Wieman, NPOR, 133.

---

115. Wieman and Horton, *Growth of Religion*, p. 361: "What generates personality, sustains and promotes its growth, and brings it to highest fulfillment? The reality which does all this is a very complex and delicate system of connections of mutual control which grows up between the individual psycho-physical organism and its physical and social environment."

important for an understanding of Wieman's view that God is more than mind.

Wieman contends that the work of God is the growth of organism, while the work of man is the construction of mechanism. He looks upon mechanisms and organisms as two different kinds of systems which enter into the existence of almost everything.[116] "A mechanism is a system of external relations. An organism is a system of internal relations or, as I prefer to say, of organic connections."* Therefore when things are internally related, they undergo transformation and mutually control one another.[117]

So God's work is the growth of organic connections, i.e., "the growth of meaning and value." This is not and can never be the work of man. Since God's way of working is so different from that of mind as seen in man, Wieman concludes that God is more than mind.[118] "Mind," Wieman writes, "is just exactly what God is not. God is not intelligence, for what God does is. . . . exactly the opposite of what intelligence does."†

Another basic reason why Wieman rejects the claim of a personal God is to be found in his general naturalistic and empiricistic positions. As we have seen, he is determined to confine God to nature. God is the "creative event" <u>within</u> nature rather than the "creative event" <u>above</u> nature. There is not the slightest empirical evidence that God as the creative event within nature is personal in character. Empirical observation points more to process and interaction than to personality as the basic character of the "creative event."

Although Wieman denies the personality of God, he is quite certain that he preserves in God those things which the religious man is demanding when he asserts that God must be a person. God does respond to the intimate needs and attitudes of the individual personality.‡ Moreover, human personality and fellowship find in God the source of their origin, the continuous source of their enrichment, and the condition of their most abundant flowering.§[119]

---

* Wieman, Art. (1936)², 442.
† Wieman, Art. (1936)², 441.
‡ Wieman insists that God answers prayer. "Prayer," he says, "is a reverent, appealing attitude toward the process of interaction which makes for greatest mutuality." (Art. (1932)³, 89). The answer to prayer comes through this interaction producing precious blessings of mutuality which were only possibilities prior to one's taking this attitude.
§ Wieman, GOR, 363.

---

116. Wieman, "God Is More," p. 442: "Mechanisms and organisms are not two different kinds of things. Rather, they are two different kinds of systems which enter into the existence of almost everything."

117. Wieman, "God Is More," p. 442: "That means that when things or parts of things are internally related, they undergo transformation and mutually control one another."

118. Wieman, "God Is More," p. 442: "The work of God is the growth of organic connections, that is, the growth of all meaning and value. Man cannot do that. . . . Since God's way of working is so different from that of mind, as we see it in man, we feel that God is not only more than mind, he is more than we can think."

119. Wieman and Horton, *Growth of Religion*, p. 361: "Do human personality and fellowship find in God the source of their origin, the continuous source of their enrichment, and the con-

Wieman also quite readily sees the value of personality applied to God as a symbol for religious purposes:

> From all this we conclude that the mythical symbol of person or personality may be indispensable for the practice of worship and personal devotion to the creative power, this need arising out of the very nature of creative interaction and so demonstrating that the creative event is the actual reality when this symbol is used most effectively in personal commitment of faith. This symbol may be required even by those who know through intellectual analysis that a person is always a creature and that therefore personality cannot characterize the nature of the creator.*

However, this need of religious devotion to think of God as a person must not blind our minds to the fact that God cannot be a person.

The fact that God is not personal does not mean that he is <u>impersonal</u>. Wieman insists that God responds to personal adjustments in a "personal" manner, and that his nature must be so conceived that it accounts for the existence of personality. Because of this God cannot be <u>impersonal</u>. Actually, God is not sub-personal but supra-personal. Therefore, Wieman uses the personal pronoun in referring to God, though at the same time conscious of its inadequacy.†[120]

ii. God as process

One of the first things that the interpreter of Wieman discovers is his persistent affirmation that God belongs to the category of process. This appears throughout all his definitions of God. In one book Wieman refers to God as

> that <u>integrating process</u> which works through all the world not only to bring human lives into fellowship with one another but also to maintain and develop organic interdependence and mutual support between all parts and aspects of the cosmos.‡

Again he says:

> God is that <u>integrating process</u> at work in the universe. It is that which makes for increasing interdependence and cooperation in the world.§

---

* Wieman, SHG, 267–268.
† Wieman, IOL, 219–230; GOR, 359–362.

‡ Wieman, MPRL, 22. Italics mine.
§ Wieman, MPRL, 46, 47. Italics mine

---

dition of their most abundant flowering? . . . Now the religious naturalist says that God does respond to the intimate needs and attitudes of each individual personality."

120. Martin, *Empirical Philosophies of Religion*, p. 107: "It is true that God responds to personal adjustments in a 'personal' manner, and that his nature must be so conceived that it accounts for the existence of personality; that, in brief, God is not *impersonal*. Therefore Wieman uses the personal pronoun in referring to God, being at the same time conscious of its inadequacy."

Elsewhere he declares: "God is that interaction between things which generates and magnifies personality and all its highest values."* Now an interaction
is not a thing or a concrete object;† it is a process in which concrete objects
affect one another; it is an event, not a continuing entity. Interactions are not
"persistent realities."‡

When Wieman speaks of God as integrating process at the level of human
society he means the process by which men are made increasingly interdependent and their behavior is so changed as to make them more cooperative
and mutually helpful one to the other. Because this process goes on independently of human purpose Wieman calls it superhuman. But while it is more
than human it will not lift humanity to the great goods of life unless men
make right adaptation to it. "The process goes on whether we will or no, but
we must 'get right with it' if we would escape catastrophe." § 121

Wieman makes it clear that this process of progressive integration which is
seen at work in human society is cosmic in scope. It can be seen in electrons
interacting in such a way as to make atoms, atoms to make molecules, molecules to make cells, cells to make living organisms, living organisms to make
individual minds and human society. This process of progressive integration
is quite similar to what Smuts calls Holism, Whitehead the principle of concretion, S. Alexander and Loyd Morgan the nisus toward ever higher creative
syntheses, and Hocking the Whole Idea.122

Another way in which Wieman expresses the idea that God belongs to the
category of process is that of referring to God as the pattern of behavior. He
notices that the universe is not a passive state of being; it is rather a total event
which is continually transpiring. It is a total event made up of an infinite
number of subordinate events. In other words, the universe is continually
behaving.

Now this behavior of the universe, which is infinitely complex and varied,

---

* Wieman, ITG, 13.
† Wieman, WRT, 193.
‡ Wieman, Art. (1932)³,

45.
§ Wieman, WRT, 62.

---

121. Wieman, *Methods of Private Religious Living*, pp. 51–52: "When we speak of the integrating process at the level of human society we mean the process by which (1) we are made increasingly interdependent and (2) our behavior is so changed as to make us more coöperative and
mutually helpful one to the other. . . . But while it is more than human it will not lift humanity
to the great goods of life unless men make right adaptation to it. . . . The process goes on whether
we will or no, but we must 'get right with it' if we would escape catastrophe." Note that King's
reference to *Wrestle of Religion with Truth* is inaccurate.

122. Wieman, *Methods of Private Religious Living*, pp. 52–53: "This process of progressive integration which we see at work in human society is cosmic in its scope. Electrons interact in such
a way as to make atoms, atoms to make molecules, molecules to make cells, cells to make living
organisms, living organisms to make individual minds and human society. It is what Smuts calls
Holism, . . . Whitehead the principle of concretion, . . . S. Alexander and Lloyd Morgan the nisus
toward ever higher creative syntheses, Hocking the Whole Idea."

has a certain pattern and structure. This pattern of behavior upon which man is dependent for maximum security and increase of good, is the God of the universe. "God is the behavior of the universe which has thus nurtured human life and which continues to keep it going and growing."[123]

As we have seen above, Wieman makes it clear that God is not to be identified with all patterns of behavior or with the universe in its entirety (pantheism). Only that pattern of behavior can be called God "which preserves and increases to the maximum the total good of all human living where right adjustment is made."*

From the above we may conclude that Wieman's God is a process, an order of events, a system or patten of behavior. All of this is consistent with his naturalistic leanings. Traditional theism tends to see God as an all-powerful person who is the shaper of events, or the overruler of them, or somehow the generator of them. Wieman however, following his naturalistic learnings, sees God as a process within nature, a process which is the structure or order of events.

6. Wieman's use of specifically Christian symbols in his conception of God

No exposition of Wieman's mature view of God is complete without a discussion of the rather illuminating way in which he reinterprets many of the traditional Christian concepts concerning God. Wieman seeks to preserve and interpret everything which has given power to the life and worship of the Christian religion. As we have seen, this interpretation is made in the frame of his own naturalistic processes of thought. "Nothing has value except material events. . . ."† This means that most of the terms of classical Christianity must be used with a new and different meaning. These subtle changes in meaning must always be kept in the mind of the interpreter of Wieman because of Wieman's constant tendency of using historical phrases in a sense other than that which has been carried by them in the past.

Wieman's whole life's work represents the most valiant attempt to keep the values of evangelical Christianity while discarding its philosophy and thelogy. He looks upon the literal interpretation of most Christian doctrines as absurd and unscientific. But when these literal interpretations are removed, Christian doctrines are found to have a symbolic value that is indispensable for living religion. In an article which appeared in a series entitled, "How My Mind Has Changed in the Last Decade," Wieman writes:

---

* Wieman, WRT, 62.

† Wieman, SHG, 8.

---

123. The quotation is from Wieman, *Wrestle of Religion with Truth*, p. 62.

I use traditional Christian symbols much more than I did ten years ago. I do not think that this indicates any access to orthodoxy. But I find that when the ambiguities and superstitions and superficialities have been cleared away from these ancient forms of expressions, they carry a depth and scope of meaning which no other words can convey, because the same history which has made them has made us.*

With these propaedeutic remarks we turn now to a discussion of the basic Christian symbols which receive fruitful treatment in Wieman's conception of God.

i. The grace of God

Wieman agrees with the view that man can never achieve the good by his own power. Whenever man uses his power to serve the good that is discerned by his own appreciative consciousness rather than serve the good that is determined by the creative power of God, his efforts are doomed to defeat.† The structure of man's appreciative consciousness is too limited in scope and distorted in form ever to become an independent guide for human life. Man's awareness of this inadequacy leads to despair. But the despair which arises at this point is not totally destructive; it really opens the way to salvation; for despair concerning the adequacy of his own appraisal of value may lead man to give himself to the guiding grace of God.‡ [124]

Despair for its own sake has no value. But when it turns man from trust in his own reason or sense of value to absolute trust in the grace of God, it opens the way to salvation. "As a gateway into this transformed way of living, where security is found in the power and goodness of God, despair is the highest wisdom."§

Now what is this "grace of God" upon which man is so dependent. The grace of God is "creative transformation become dominant in the life of man."‖ Every individual has the important task of searching out the nature of creativity and seeking to live in accord with its demands. But the actual directing toward the good and the actual achievement of it cannot be exercised by the ability of man; this can be done only by the creative event when ac-

---

* Wieman, Art. (1939), 116.

† Wieman, SHG, 49.

‡ Wieman, SHG, 49.

§ Wieman, SHG, 49.

‖ Wieman, SHG, 49.

---

124. Wieman, *Source of Human Good*, p. 49: "Man uses his power and prosperity to serve the good as discerned by his own appreciative consciousness rather than the good as determined by the creative power of God. . . . This judgment of God and the despair it brings are not merely condemnation; they really open the way of salvation and fulfilment; for despair concerning the reliability of his own appraisal of value may lead man to commit himself to the healing and guiding grace of God."

cepted as sovereign over life.[125] This creative event operating in its sovereignty is what Wieman means by the "grace of God."*

ii. Divine love and justice

Wieman's interpretation of the love of God grows out of his doctrine of the creativity of God. As we have seen, God is the growth of connection between sensitive organisms, all the way from cells and plant spores to human personalities and groups. He is that creative interaction from which originates all the richness of experience, as well as personality and society. So as human personalities we are both originally and continuously generated by God's creativity. God's love is this creativity.† [126]

God's "judgment" is inseparable from his love. It is the same thing working under different conditions. God's love is the growth of connections whereby individuals and groups are brought closer together in mutual interaction. It is what we have just described as creativity. God's judgment is the "mutual destructiveness" which comes to individuals and groups as a result of their resistance to the transformtion which is required by the new life of interdependence. The closer drawn the cords of love, the more destructive of one another do men become when they resist the transformation brought forth by these closer connections.‡ [127]

iii. Divine forgiveness

The forgiveness of God is an expression of his love. It is accomplished by God setting up conditions whereby it is possible to transform sinners despite

---

* Wieman, SHG, 50.
† Wieman, Art. (1940)², 155.
‡ Wieman, Art. (1940)², 156.

---

125. Wieman, *Source of Human Good*, p. 50: "But the actual directing toward the good and the actual achievement of it can be exercised not by any ability of man but only by the creative event when accepted as sovereign over life."

126. Henry Nelson Wieman, "What Is Most Important in Christianity?" *Religion in the Making* 1 (1940): 153–155: "It is the growth of connections between sensitive organisms, all the way from cells and plant spores to human personalities and groups. . . . [Creative interaction] is the creative origin of all richness of experience as well as of personality and society. . . . As human personalities we are both originally and continuously generated by God's creativity. . . . God's love is this creativity."

127. Wieman, "What Is Most Important?" p. 155: "God's 'judgment' or 'wrath' is inseparable from his love. It is, indeed, the same thing, but working under different conditions. God's love is the growth of connections whereby individuals and groups become mutually enriching members of a shared life. It is what we have just been describing as creativity. God's wrath is the mutual

their resistance to his love. Sin is clinging to anything, or the striving after anything, when such clinging or striving is obstructive to creative transformation.*[128] Sin is anything in one's personality which resists the creativity of God. When sin is unforgiven, God cannot overcome this resistance except by destroying the individual or group which does the resisting. When sin is forgiven the resistance is still present but God can overcome it without destroying the persons who do the resisting.†[129]

Before this forgiveness of sin can be accomplished at least three things are required. First, creative interaction must be released from the coercive and absolute control of any one order of life or set of structures. Wieman holds that this first condition for the forgiveness of sin was partially met in the Roman Empire by the intermingling of races and the interpenetration of cultures.‡[130]

The second condition which has to be met in order that sins be forgiven is

> that a psychological, social historical process get under way which would make creativity potent and sovereign over the lives of a few (at least) so that no hope or dream, no ideal or order of existence could exercise equal control over them.§

This was accomplished by the life, crucifixion and resurrection of Jesus Christ.[131] We shall discuss Wieman's conception of the death and resurrection of Christ subsequently.

---

* Wieman, SHG, 278.
† Wieman, Art. (1940)², 150.
‡ Wieman, Art. (1940)², 160.
§ Wieman, Art. (1940)², 159.

---

destructiveness of such individuals and groups when they are drawn closer together by these connections but resist the transformation which is required by the life of mutual enrichment within these closer bonds of interdependence. . . . The closer draw the cords of love, the more destructive of one another do men become when they resist the transformation imposed by these closer connections."

128. Wieman, "What Is Most Important?" p. 156: "God's forgiveness is accomplished by setting up conditions whereby it is possible to . . . transform sinners despite their resistance to God's love. . . . Sin is the clinging to anything, or the striving after anything, when such clinging and striving prevents one from undergoing the transformations involved in creative interaction."

129. Wieman, "What Is Most Important?" p. 150: "Sin is anything in the conduct of human living which resists the creativity of God. When sin is unforgiven, God cannot overcome this resistance except by destroying the individual or group which does the resisting. When sin is forgiven the resistance is still present but God can overcome it without destroying the individuals or groups concerned."

130. Wieman, "What Is Most Important?" p. 159: "Creative interaction between persons must be released from confinement to any one set of structures or order of life. . . . This first condition for the forgiveness of sin was partially met in the Roman Empire by the intermingling of races, the interpenetration of cultures. . . . In this way the individual and the group was somewhat released from the coercive and absolute control of any one order of life."

131. Wieman, "What Is Most Important?" p. 160: "This was accomplished by the life, crucifixion and resurrection of Jesus Christ."

A third condition which must be met before the power of God unto salvation is free to deliver men from sin is repentance. The confession and repentance of sin means three things. It means, first, to recognize that there is something deep in one's personality which does resist the transformation required for that fullness of creative interaction demanded by the connections one has with other people.*[132]

Confession and repentance of sin mean, in the second place, that one shall resolve repeatedly to hold oneself subject to every transformation required by creative interaction, no matter what pain or loss such changes may involve.†[133]

Confession and repentance of sin mean in the third place that one must search out every habit, every object of desire, fear, hope, and dread which seems to be recalcitrant to creative interaction, and resolve that each of these shall be taken from or given to one only as creative interaction may require.[134] "Nothing shall be mine except as I receive it from the creativity of God. Nothing shall be held back by me when the creativity of God would take it away."‡

Whenever the three conditions stated above are met, Wieman is certain that God's forgiving power will be at work. God's forgiveness is not some static decree. Rather it is a dynamic reality working in history, in society and in each personality who meets the necessary conditions.

iv. The crucifixion and resurrection of Christ

Wieman looks upon the death and resurrection of Christ as indispensable events for the salvation of man. Jesus during his life developed in a small group of men a richness of creative interaction that was unique and sublime.

---

* Wieman, Art. (1940)², 164.
† Wieman, Art. (1940)², 164.
‡ Wieman, Art. (1940)², 165.

---

132. Wieman, "What Is Most Important?" p. 164: "There is, however, a third condition which must be met before the power of God unto salvation is free to work without limit in delivering men from that sin which is unto death. . . . The confession and repentance of sin means three things. It means, first, to recognize that my personality at depths far below the reach of consciousness at any given time is patterned and structured by an organization which does resist the transformations required for that fullness of creative interaction demanded by the connections I have with other people."

133. Wieman, "What Is Most Important?" p. 164: "Confession and repentance of sin mean, in the second place, that I shall resolve repeatedly, and with all the depths of sincerity that is in me, to hold myself subject to every transformation creative interaction may require, no matter what pain, death or loss such changes may involve."

134. Wieman, "What Is Most Important?" p. 165: "Confession and repentance of sin mean in the third place that I shall search out every habit, every object of desire, fear, hope and dread, that I can at all suspect to be recalcitrant to creative interaction, and resolve that each one shall be taken from me or given to me, according as creative interaction may require."

So long as Jesus lived, however, this creative interaction never broke free of the established patterns of the Hebrew traditon. The followers of Jesus continued to dream and hope that he would establish an earthly kingdom as Hebrew tradition prescribed.[135]

The crucifixion cracked this structure of existence and possibility. It did this by destroying the hope of the disciples, and even temporarily destroying the creative interaction which they had had in fellowship with one another when Jesus was with them. With the crucifixion Jesus failed them utterly. They had hoped that he was the messiah. But he died miserably upon a cross and was wholly unable to do what their Hebrew way of life prescribed for him. The hopes and dreams of the disciples all disappeared in the black-out of the crucifixion.[136]

But after the despair had lasted for about three days, something miraculous happened. The life-transforming creativity which Jesus had engendered among them came back.[137] It had risen from the dead.

> But what rose from the dead was not the man Jesus; it was creative power. It was the living God that works in time. It was the Second Person of the Trinity. It was Christ the God, not Jesus the man.*

Who is this Christ that rose from the dead? As we have seen, he is not merely the man Jesus. "Christ is the domination by the creative event over the life of man in a fellowship made continuous in history."† Through this domination Christ is the revelation of God to man, and the salvation of the world.‡[138]

---

* Wieman, SHG, 44.
† Wieman, SHG, 269.
‡ Wieman, SHG, 269.

---

135. Wieman, "What Is Most Important?" p. 160: "Jesus during his life developed in a small group a height and depth and richness of creative interaction that was unique. . . . It never broke free of the established patterns of their Hebrew heritage as long as Jesus lived. They continued to dream and hope that Jesus would establish a kingdom . . . as Hebrew tradition prescribed."

136. Wieman, "What Is Most Important?" pp. 160–161: "The crucifixion cracked this structure of existence and possibility. . . . It did this by destroying their hope and even, for a little while, the creative interaction which they had had in fellowship with one another when Jesus was with them. With the crucifixion Jesus failed them utterly. They had hoped that he was the messiah. But he died miserably upon a cross and was wholly unable to be or to do what their Hebrew way of life prescribed for him. . . . The hope of Israel . . . all disappeared in the black-out of the crucifixion."

137. Wieman, "What Is Most Important?" p. 161: "But after the numbness and the despair had lasted for about three days, a miracle happened. That kind of interaction which Jesus had engendered among them came back."

138. Wieman, Source of Human Good, p. 269: "Through this domination Christ is the revelation of God to man, the forgiveness of sin extended to all men, and the salvation of the world."

Chapter V

A COMPARISON AND EVALUATION OF THE CONCEPTIONS OF GOD IN THE THINKING OF WIEMAN AND TILLICH

We turn now to a discussion of the basic problem of this dissertation, viz., comparing and evaluating the conceptions of God in the thinking of Wieman and Tillich. Up to this point we have attempted to interpret the conceptions of God held by Wieman and Tillich separately, without any mention of their points of agreement or disagreement. Now we will look at their conceptions of God together, with a view of determining their convergent and divergent points.

We shall see as the discussion develops that Wieman and Tillich have much more in common than is ordinarily supposed. It has been a not too infrequent tendency to group Wieman with the naturalistic thinkers and Tillich with the neo-supernaturalistic thinkers. As we have seen, even Wieman himself attaches the neo-supernaturalist tag to Tillich. In The Growth of Religion, Wieman grouped Barth, Brunner, Niebuhr, and Tillich together as neo-supernaturalists. A close analysis of Tillich, however, will reveal that he cannot so easily be grouped with the neo-supernaturalists. There is much in his thinking that smacks of religious naturalism. His opposition to supernaturalism is much more pronounced than his opposition to naturalism. He is forever revolting against the view that there is a world behind the world.

Yet despite these similarities between Wieman and Tillich which are often overlooked, we must recognize that there are important differences between the two. Any adequate comparison of Wieman and Tillich will recognize their differences along with their points of concurrence.

1. God's existence

One of the basic points at which Tillich and Wieman concur is in affirming that God is an undeniable reality. Both are so convinced of the reality of God that they would dismiss all arguments for the existence of God as futile and invalid. As we have seen, Tillich contends that theologians and philosophers should have said something about the ontological implications of finitude rather than present elaborate arguments for the existence of God. "The arguments for the existence of God," contends Tillich, "neither are arguments nor are they proof of the existence of God. They are expressions of the question of God which is implied in human finitude."* In a similar vein Wieman affirms the futility of the traditional arguments. He says: "No one has less

---

* Tillich, ST, I, 205.

interest than I in trying to prove the existence of God. . . . I hold such proce-dure folly."*

Although Tillich and Wieman agree in the assertion that all arguments for the existence of God are invalid, they differ in reasons given for the invalidity of these arguments. Wieman thinks that the existence of God is as certain as any reality in the physical world; this God is capable of being perceived through the senses. Hence any attempt to prove the existence of God is as futile as attempting to prove the existence of the physical world or the people about us. Wieman laconically states: "All the traditional arguments to prove the existence of God are as much out of place in religion as arguments to prove the existence of nature would be in science."†

On the other hand, Tillich finds the traditional arguments invalid because of his contention that God transcends the category of existence. To say "God exists" is, for Tillich, the basest blasphemy. "It is as atheistic to affirm the existence of God," asserts Tillich, "as it is to deny it."‡ Tillich feels that it would be a great victory for Christian apologetics if the words "God" and "existence" were very definitely separated. God does not exist. He transcends the categories of essence and existence. Therefore, to argue that God exists, affirms Tillich, is to deny him.§[1]

Wieman is far more willing to apply the term existence to God than Tillich. Wieman never wearies of pointing out that God exists. Tillich's insistence that God transcends the category of existence grows out of his basic conviction that God is being-itself. This means that God is not a being, not even the most powerful or most perfect being. All discussions of the existence of God start out with the assumption that God is something or someone, i.e. a being. But this objectification or "thingification" of God, asserts Tillich, is blasphemy.[2]

So Tillich finds it necessary to say "God does not exist" because his onto-logical analysis leads him to define God as being-itself. Wieman, on the other hand, finds it necessary to say "God exists" because his naturalistic position leads him to define God as the creative event within nature. However, at bot-tom Tillich and Wieman are seeking to convey the same idea, viz., that the reality of God is an indubitable certainty. They are seeking to lift the question of God out of the arena of debate.

There is a further point at which Tillich and Wieman seem to be in agree-

---

* Wieman, Art. (1932)[3], 84.
† Wieman, Art. (1932)[3], 284.

‡ Tillich, ST, I, 237.
§ Tillich, ST, I, 205.

---

1. King used the quotation from *Systematic Theology*, p. 237 in chapter 3. The next four sen-tences also appear in chapter 3, but as part of a larger quotation from Tillich. Cf. Tillich, *Systematic Theology*, p. 205: "It would be a great victory for Christian apologetics if the words 'God' and 'existence' were very definitely separated except in the paradox of God becoming manifest under the conditions of existence, that is, in the christological paradox. God does not exist. He is being-itself beyond essence and existence. Therefore, to argue that God exists is to deny him."

2. This paragraph is similar to a passage in chapter 3; see p. 407 in this volume.

ment on the question of God's existence. Both seek to assure the reality of God through the definition of God. As we have seen, Wieman seeks "so to formulate the idea of God that the question of God's existence becomes a dead issue, like the question of the other inescapable forms of initial existence."* To accomplish this he has offered as a "minimal" definition of God the following: "God is that something upon which human life is most dependent for its security, welfare, and increasing abundance . . . that something of supreme value which constitutes the most important conditions."† If God be defined as supreme value or as that process which underlies and makes possible the maximum achievement of value, then the fact of his existence is "inescapable," he feels. "The best there is and can be . . . is a self-proving proposition."‡ So Wieman feels that just as it is folly to attempt to prove the existence of nature to natural creatures, or the United States to its citizens, it is equal folly to try to prove to human beings, whose essential nature consists in seeking, adoring, and serving whatever has greatest value, that there is something which has greatest value. He says: "Never in any of my writings have I tried to prove the existence of God except by definition."§ So Wieman is confident that he has solved the problem of proving God's existence by a definition.

Like Wieman, Tillich seeks through his definition of God to assure the reality of God and make it virtually impossible to deny him. Tillich's position at this point is clearly set forth in the following statement:

> The name of this infinite and inexhaustible depth and ground of all being is God. This is what the word God means. . . . If you know that God means depth then you know much about him. You cannot then call yourselves atheists or unbelievers. For you cannot think and say: "There is no depth in life! Life itself is shallow. Being itself is surface." Only if you could say this in complete seriousness you would be atheists—otherwise not.‖

Thus Tillich, like Wieman, is seeking so to formulate the idea of God that the question of God's existence becomes a dead issue.# As we have seen, Tillich's basic definition of God is "being-itself" or "power of being." God as being-itself neither needs nor can receive proof. He is that ultimate—Tillich's term is das Unbedingte—which is a certain quality of the world man encounters and which analysis reveals as "presupposed" in all his encountering. In other words, Tillich is seeking to say that God is presupposed in the question

---

* Wieman, Art. (1932)³, 276.
† Wieman, RESM, 9.
‡ Wieman, Art. (1931)², 171.
§ Wieman, Art. (1932)³, 284.
‖ Tillich, Art. (1944)⁴, 320.
In a very interesting article Tillich expresses definite agreement with Wieman's attempt to make the question of God's existence a dead issue. Tillich feels that such an approach is in line with the ontological method of the philosophy of religion, the method which he (Tillich) feels is most adequate. Tillich states: "If the idea of God is to be formulated in such a way that the question of God's existence becomes a dead issue" (Wieman), . . . we are in an ontological atmosphere, although the ontological approach is not clearly stated and its relation to the cosmological approach and to faith is not adequately explained." (Art. (1946)², 9).

of God. One cannot deny him without affirming him. God as the "power of being," as <u>Seinsmachtigkeit</u> is the source of all power. Thus the power of thought is derived from the ground of power. So far as one has power, contends Tillich, he cannot escape God. For God as "power of being" is that power by which one doubts, feels, thinks, knows, exists.

So by defining God as "being-itself" or "power of being," Tillich has made it virtually impossible for one to deny the reality of God. Even to deny him is to affirm him, because he is the power by which the denial is made.

Wieman and Tillich are at one in seeking to define God in such a way that even the sceptic and atheist cannot deny his existence. They believe they have solved the problem of proving the reality of God by a definition.

We may raise the question at this point whether Wieman and Tillich have been successful in their endeavors to make the question of God's existence a dead issue. In criticising Wieman's general procedure at this point, Macintosh suggests that an easy way to prove the existence of God to the satisfaction of everyone, is to reduce the definition of the term until everyone, even the confessed atheist will have to admit his existence. Macintosh questions this procedure on the ground that it gains assurance <u>that God is</u> by drastically subtracting from what God means.*[3]

This criticism is basically sound, and it applies to Tillich's procedure as well as Wieman's. Both Wieman and Tillich, in their attempt to formulate the idea of God so as to make the question of God's existence a dead issue, have given up much that is most essential from the religious point of view in the idea of God. As we shall see subsequently, both Tillich and Wieman reject the conception of a personal God, and with this goes a rejection of the rationality, goodness and love of God in the full sense of the words. An impersonal "being-itself" or "creative event" cannot be rational or good, for these are attributes of personality.

It seems that in the Christian message, "God" means "a being," not "being-itself." He is of course, not a being "alongside" others, but He is a being "above others." Therefore "existence" can be predicated of Him, though not the contingent finite existence of His creatures. He is not merely "the ground of everything personal"; He is personal Himself.[4]

---

* Macintosh, Art. (1932), 24.

---

3. D. C. Macintosh, "Is There a God?" in Morrison, ed., *Is There a God?* pp. 22–23: "Eager to demonstrate the existence of God to the satisfaction of everybody, one might begin by reducing the definition of God until the term means no more, to begin with, than everyone, even the confessed atheist, will have to admit to exist. . . . What I question . . . is his adding to the assurance *that God is* by subtracting so drastically and, it would seem, so permanently, from *what God means.*"

4. Thomas, "Method and Structure," p. 104: "It seems to me that in the Christian message, 'God' means '*a* being,' not 'being-itself.' He is, of course, not a being 'alongside' others, but He *is* a being 'above others.' Therefore 'existence' *can* be predicated of Him, though not the contingent finite existence of His creatures. . . . He is not merely 'the ground of everything personal'; He *is* personal Himself."

Moreover, the Christian God is not merely an impersonal process within nature. He is a personal being above nature, forever giving meaning and direction to process. If this is the Christian view, it is clear that Tillich's and Wieman's statement of it has been weakened at points by their attempt to make the question of God's existence a dead issue. Both Wieman and Tillich sacrifice too much for the sake of getting rid of a troublesome question.

Another question that we must raise at this point is the accuracy of making the question of "proof" of God's existence irrelevant <u>by definition</u>. In this procedure both Wieman and Tillich, whether they realize it or not, are employing a version of the ontological argument. This raises the perennial question whether the being of anything can be "proved" by definition, by the refinement of a concept.

It must be pointed out that the versions of the ontological argument set forth by Tillich and Wieman are quite different from the Anselmic version of the ontological argument. Anselm sought to prove the existence of the being with the richest conceivable attributes, while Wieman and Tillich seek to prove by definition "a being of minimum specifications." In other words, Anselm sought to prove the existence of God by a definition with maximum specification of attributes, while Tillich and Wieman seek to prove the reality of God by definitions with minimum specifications. In all three cases, however, the reality of God is involved in the definition of God, and hence is a necessary truth of reason. So Tillich's and Wieman's versions of the ontological argument present some of the same difficulties that men like Thomas Aquinas and Immanuel Kant found in the Anselmic version.

2. The personality of God

Tillich and Wieman are in one accord in denying the category of personality to God. They feel that to refer to God as a person is to limit him. Both would agree that "God towers in unique majesty infinitely above the little hills which we call minds and personalities."*

They differ somewhat, however, in the reasons given for objecting to the claim of a personal God. The basic reason for Wieman's objection is to found in his general naturalistic and empiricistic positions. We have seen that, for Wieman, the basic things in the world are events, happenings, or processes. There is nothing transcending or undergirding events. Everything that exists is either an event, an aspect of an event, or a relation between or within events. This means that God must be found in the natural order. Like everything else that exists, God is a material being, a process with an enduring structure which distinguishes his character from that of other processes.[5] God

---

* Wieman, Art. (1936)[2], 432.

5. The previous five sentences also appear in chapter 4; see pp. 462–463 in this volume.

is the "creative event" <u>within</u> nature rather than the "creative event" <u>above</u> nature. There is not the slightest empirical evidence, contends Wieman, that God as the creative event within nature is personal in character. Empirical observation reveals that personality is limited to creatures.

Wieman feels that it is much more empirical to refer to God as process than as personality. Throughout his definitions of God there is the persistent affirmation that God belongs to the category of process. He refers to God as an "integrating process,"* an "interaction,"† a "pattern of behavior,"‡ and the "creative event."§ In each of these definitions, Wieman is seeking to say that God is not a concrete object; he is a process in which concrete objects affect one another; he is an event, not a continuing entity. So Wieman is certain that empirical observation points more to process and interaction as the basic character of the "creative event" than to personality.

Tillich's objection to the claim of a personal God, unlike Wieman's, grows out of his general ontological analysis. This leads him to affirm that personality is a characteristic of beings, not of being-itself. Personality might be applied to being-itself in a symbolic sense, meaning that God is the ground of everything personal, but never can it be applied to him in a literal sense. Being-itself transcends the categories of finitude, and is prior to the split of subject and object. To speak of God as a person would mean making him an object besides other objects, a being among beings, maybe the highest, but anyhow a being.[6] But to objectify God in such a sense is, for Tillich, the basest blasphemy.

Tillich's objection to the conception of a personal God does not lead him to affirm with Wieman that God is process. Tillich feels that a God who is merely process is as limited as a God who is merely a person. God as being-itself is infinitely more than process or interaction.

It is interesting to note that Wieman and Tillich concur on the point that God is not impersonal. The fact that they deny that God is personal does not mean, for them, that God is impersonal. Wieman insists that God responds to personal adjustments in a "personal" manner, and that his nature must be so conceived that it accounts for the existence of personality.‖ Tillich, in a similar vein, insists that God is the ground of everything personal and that he carries within himself the ontological power of personality.#[7] Because of this, God can-

---

* Wieman, MPRL, 22, 46, 47.
† Wieman, Art. (1932)[3],

13.
‡ Wieman, WRT, 62.
§ Wieman, SHG, 58f.

‖ Wieman, GOR, 359–362.
Tillich, ST, I, 245.

---

6. This sentence also appears in chapter 3, but as part of a quotation from Tillich. Cf. Tillich, "Idea of the Personal God," p. 9: "The concept of a 'Personal God,' . . . makes God a natural object besides others, an object amongst objects, a being amongst beings, maybe the highest, but anyhow *a* being."

7. This sentence also appears in chapter 3, but as part of a quotation from Tillich. Cf. Tillich, *Systematic Theology*, p. 245: "It means that God is the ground of everything personal and that he carries within himself the ontological power of personality."

not be impersonal. In brief, Wieman and Tillich are certain that God is not sub-personal but supra-personal. Therefore they use the personal pronoun in referring to God, being at the same time conscious of its inadequacy.*[8]

In spite of their insistence that the idea of a personal God is confusing, Tillich and Wieman agree that the symbol is of vital importance for religious worship. Wieman says that "the mythical symbol of person or personality may be indispensable for the practice of worship and personal devotion to the creative power, this need arising out of the very nature of creative interaction. . . ."† Tillich finds the symbol of a personal God indispensable for living religion, if for no other reason than that, as the philosopher Schelling says, "only a person can heal a person."[9] He further contends that this kind of symbolism must be maintained against pantheistic and naturalistic criticism, lest religion fall back to the level of a primitive-demonic pre-personalism.‡

It must be pointed out that Tillich and Wieman use the word "symbol" in a somewhat different sense. Wieman uses symbol to mean little more than a sign. It is the creation of a subjective desire. Tillich, on the other hand, insists that a symbol is more than a technical sign. The basic characteristic of the symbol is its innate power. The genuine symbol participates in the reality of that which it symbolizes. Moreover, true symbols indicate something about the nature of God, but that indication is never precise, unambiguous, literal. So when Tillich speaks of personality as a symbolic expression of God's nature, he is sure that here is an implicit indication of the nature of God.

Several points require comment.

1. How sound is Wieman's view that God is process instead of personality? Wieman sees God as unifying activity seeking to bring about an organic unity as yet very incompletely actualized. This means that there is a gap between actual existence and unrealized possibility, between timeless forms and fluent process. Now this gap must be filled by God if he is properly performing his unifying activity. But in order to fill the gap, God must transcend the process and yet be active and actual. In other words, in order for God to perform his unifying activity, he must be more than process. He must have some unwav-

---

* Wieman, IOL, 219–230. Tillich's position at this point is clearly set forth in the following statement: "The supra-personal is not an 'It,' or more exactly, it is a 'He' as much as it is an 'It,' and it is above both of them. But if the 'He' element is left out, the 'It,' element transforms the alleged supra-personal into a sub-personal, as it usually happens in monism and pantheism." (Art. (1940)[2], 10).

† Wieman, SHG, 267–268.

‡ See Chap. III, sec. 10.[10]

---

8. This paragraph is similar to a passage in chapter 4; see p. 495 in this volume.

9. Tillich, "Idea of the Personal God," p. 10: "For as the philosopher Schelling says: 'Only a person can heal a person.' This is the reason that the symbol of the Personal God is indispensable for living religion."

10. See p. 445 in this volume.

ering grasp or vision of forms not yet actualized. This means that he must transcend the flux of events.

2. Wieman speaks of God as a system of events. The question still remains, however, what it is that generates the system. What is it that stands behind the system to account for its systematic character? Wieman leaves this problem unsolved because he refuses to see God as a concrete object or entity. He has tried to get away from metaphysics by defining God as a system of interactions, but he has merely succeeded in posing the problem of accounting for the system.[11]

3. Tillich affirms that God is personal in the sense that he is the ground of personality. God lives in that he is the ground of life. God is good in that he is the ground of goodness. Now since it is Tillich's conviction that God as "being-itself" is the ground of all being, it logically follows from this type of thinking that God is also evil and impersonal since he is the ground of these.

4. Both Tillich and Wieman contend that God is "supra-personal." Now if this means that Deity represents a higher type of consciousness and will than that represented by human personality, it simply states what has been maintained by almost every theistic personalist. As Thomas Aquinas says: "The name <u>person</u> is fittingly applied to God; not, however, as it is applied to creatures, but in a more excellent way (<u>via eminentiae</u>)."*

But it is one thing to say that personality which is in part known includes experiences which we do not yet know; and it is quite another thing to say that there is an entity of some sort which is lacking in consciousness and rationality. It is in the latter sense that Wieman and Tillich seem to speak. Such a position never reveals to us whether an unconscious "supra-personality" is better or worse than personality.

Certainly it seems more empirical to ascribe personality to God than to ascribe "supra-personality" to him. In the world of experiences the basic source of personality production and sustenance has been personality. Now when we are confronted with the fact of personality production and sustenance on a cosmic scale, why not ascribe the source to cosmic personality? It would be better by far to admit that there are difficulties with an idea we know—such as personality—than to employ a term which is practically unknown to us in our experience.

The "supra-personal" is a term without any concrete content; it is at best but a label for the unknown, and not a definable hypothesis. If we are, there-

---

* Quoted from Knudson,
DOG, 300.

---

11. Homer H. Dubs, "Religious Naturalism—An Evaluation," *Journal of Religion* 23, no. 4 (1943): 260: "If God is a system of events, we must still inquire what it is that generates this system; what it is that stands behind the system to account for its systematic character. But Wieman conceives of no such concrete object or entity. . . . He has tried to get away from metaphysics by defining God as a system of interactions; he has merely succeeded in posing the problem of accounting for that system."

fore, to think of God, it must be either under the personal or some impersonal form. There is no third alternative. But even though this be admitted, Wieman and Tillich would still insist that personality involves limitation and so is inapplicable to God. This idea, however, rests upon a false conception of the nature of personality. It is certainly true that human personality is limited, but personality as such involves no necessary limitation. It means simply self-consciousness and self-direction. The idea of personality is so consistent with the notion of the absolute that we must say with Bowne "that complete and perfect personality can be found only in the Infinite and Absolute Being, as only in him can we find that complete and perfect selfhood and self-expression which is necessary to the fullness of personality."* The conception of God as personal, therefore, does not imply limitation of any kind.

5. All the conclusions of Tillich and Wieman seem to point to an impersonal God. Despite their warnings that God is not less than personal, we see traits throughout their thinking that point to a God that is less than personal. Wieman's God, for instance, is an interaction, that is, a behavior process. Just as the psychological behaviorist takes man's behavior as man himself, Wieman takes God's behavior as God himself.† Thus God is not a concrete object or a continuing entity. He is a process. In short, Wieman's God is an unconscious process devoid of any true purpose.

Tillich's God is "being-itself" or the "power of being." But "being-itself," as we have seen, is little more than a sub-personal reservoir of power, somewhat akin to the impersonalism of Oriental Vedantism.‡ "Being-itself" suggests a pure absolute devoid of consciousness and life. Even Tillich himself unconsciously recognizes that "being-itself" is such an absolute. Concerning a living God he says:

> Most of the so-called anthropomorphisms of the biblical picture of God are expressions of his character as living. His actions, his passions, his remembrances and anticipations, his suffering and joy, his personal relations and his plans—all these make him a living God and distinguish him from the pure absolute, from being-itself.§

Here Tillich is saying what we have been implying all along, viz., that "being-itself" is an impersonal absolute devoid of life.

So Wieman and Tillich conclude by choosing the less-than-personal to explain personality, purpose and meaning.

6. What can be said concerning the positive religious value of the concep-

---

* Bowne, PER, 266f.
† Cf. Morrison, Rev.
(1946), 1374–1376.
‡ See Chap. III, sec. 10.[12]
§ Tillich, ST, I, 242.

---

12. See p. 445 in this volume.

tions of God held by Wieman and Tillich? Is it possible to worship a behavior process or an impersonal absolute? It hardly seems so. The impersonal may be an object of thought. But before thought, which is subjective activity, can pass into worship, which is a process of communion and intercourse between living minds, the impersonal must be personalized.[13]

The religious man has always recognized two fundamental religious values. One is fellowship with God, the other is trust in his goodness.* Both of these imply the personality of God. No fellowship is possible without freedom and intelligence. There may be interactions between impersonal beings, but not fellowship. True fellowship and communion can exist only between beings who know each other and take a volitional attitude toward each other. If God is a mere "interaction" or "process" as Wieman would say, or merely "being-itself" as Tillich would say, no communion with him would be possible. Fellowship requires an outgoing of will and feeling. This is what the Scripture means when it refers to God as the "living" God. Life as applied to God means that in God there is feeling and will, responsive to the deepest yearnings of the human heart; this God both evokes and answers prayer.[14]

It may be true that on the impersonal plane religion seeks union with the Divine Being.[15] But this type of union is vastly different from that of personal beings. As Knudson has so well put it:

---

* See Knudson, DOG,
304–308.

---

13. Andrew Martin Fairbairn, *The Philosophy of the Christian Religion* (New York: Macmillan, 1902), p. 241: "No impersonal Being whether named fate or chance, necessity or existence, the soul or the whole, can be an object of worship, though it may be an object of thought. . . . The impersonal must be personalized before thought, which is a subjective activity, can pass into worship, which is a reciprocal action, or a process of converse and intercourse between living minds."

14. Albert C. Knudson, *The Doctrine of God* (New York: Abingdon Press, 1930), pp. 305–306: "There are two fundamental religious values. One is fellowship with God, the other is trust in his goodness; and both of these imply his personality. No fellowship is possible without freedom and intelligence. There may be interactions between impersonal beings, both organic and inorganic. But true communion can exist only between beings who know each other and take an emotional and volitional attitude toward each other. If God were pure intellect, as Aristotle conceived him to be, no communion with him would be possible. . . . Fellowship . . . requires an outgoing of feeling and will. This it is that underlies the moving word of Scripture, the '*living*' God. Life, as applied to God, . . . means that in God there are a heart and will, responsive to human need, an attitude of mind that both evokes and answers prayer." In the early 1960s King used similar language in describing how his religious beliefs had changed during his years of civil rights activism; see King, *Strength to Love* (New York: Harper, 1963), pp. 141–142: "In the past the idea of a personal God was little more than a metaphysical category that I found theologically and philosophically satisfying. Now it is a living reality that has been validated in the experiences of everyday life. God has been profoundly real to me in recent years. . . . So in the truest sense of the Word, God is a living God. In him there is feeling and will, responsive to the deepest yearnings of the human heart: *this* God both evokes and answers prayer."

15. Knudson, *Doctrine of God*, p. 307: "Even on the impersonal plane religion seeks union with the Divine Being."

There is a vast difference between a mystical, metaphysical union with an impersonal Being and the kind of union with the Divine taught us in Scripture. Here we have to do not with the union of absorption, but with a union that grows out of reciprocal intercourse, a union of heart and will and intellect; and such a union is possible only between personal beings. Only the personality of God makes possible the union of communion with him.*

God's personality is also the presupposition of his goodness. There can be no goodness in the true ethical sense without freedom and intelligence. Only a personal being can be good. Wieman talks a great deal about the goodness of God and so does Tillich to a lesser extent; but this is goodness in an abstract impersonal sense, not in a genuine ethical sense. Goodness in the true sense of the word is an attribute of personality.[16]

The same is true of love. Outside of personality loves loses its meaning. Tillich speaks of God as being love. But it is not love in the full sense of the word. Love, for Tillich, is just the dialectical union of opposites. Tillich's use of the word love is hardly different from the meaning given it by Empedocles, who meant by "love" no more than the attraction of the elements for one another.†

Wieman writes a great deal about the need for loving God. But we may ask, How can one truly love an interaction? Wieman would reply that it is always an interaction that we love. He affirms: "When I love Mr. Jones it is not Mr. Jones in the abstract, but the fellowship of Mr. Jones. Fellowship is a kind of interaction. . . . It is the interaction which generates love and is the real object of love."‡ Now it is certainly true that the interaction generates the love, but it does not follow from this that we love interactions. What we love deeply is persons—we love concrete objects, persistent realities, not mere interactions. A process may generate love, but the love is directed primarily not toward the process, but toward the continuing persons who generate that process.[18] In the words of H. H. Dubbs,

> If God is to really be worthy of love, he must be more than a system of interactions—he must be an object, an enduring object, who can enter into interactions. A God who is merely interactions cannot really be love, so that religious devotion cannot attach to him.§

---

* Knudson, DOG, 307.   17, 18.
† See Chap. III, sec. 10.[17]   § Dubbs, Art. (1943),
‡ Wieman, Art. (1932)[3],   260.

---

16. Knudson, *Doctrine of God*, p. 307: "His personality is also the presupposition of his goodness. There can be no goodness in the ethical sense of the term without freedom and intelligence. In other words, only a personal being can be good. . . . Goodness is an attribute of personality."

17. See p. 445 in this volume.

18. Dubs, "Religious Naturalism—An Evaluation," p. 260: "[According to Wieman] we can deal only with interactions or systems of interactions: 'When I love Mr. Jones, it is not Mr. Jones in the abstract, but the fellowship of Mr. Jones. Fellowship is a kind of interaction. . . . It is the interaction which generates love and is the real object of love.' Of course, the interaction gener-

So we must conclude that Tillich's "being-itself" and Wieman's "creative event" are lacking in positive religious value. Both concepts are too impersonal to express adequately the Christian conception of God. They provide neither the conditions for true fellowship with God nor the assurance of his goodness.

3. The transcendence and immanence of God

In a very real sense Wieman may be referred to as a prophet of God's immanence. He never wearies of pointing out that God is within nature. This emphasis grows out of his basic naturalistic position. As we have seen, Wieman holds that there is nothing more fundamental or elemental than events. Everything that exists is either an event, an aspect of an event, or a relation between or within events. This means that there are no floating transcendental principles which explain the world in terms of something outside the world. Principles, descriptions, and explanations refer to events and their relations (structures).*

Like everything else that exists, God is found within the natural order. Whatever may be his several other attributes, his transcendence is not of the noumenal or completely independent variety. Whatever transcendence he has will be seen to arise out of his very immanence in the world of events.[20]

Tillich's thought at this point has often been considered the direct antithesis of Wieman's. He has been interpreted as a neo-supernaturalist, who affirms that God is above, before, and behind nature. As we have seen, Wieman himself so interprets Tillich's thought. But a close scrutiny of Tillich's view in this respect reveals that he is probably as near the naturalistic position as he is to the supernaturalistic. Tillich is forever revolting against the view that there is a world behind the world. His aversion for supernaturalism is clearly brought out in the following passage in which he answers Wieman's claim that he is a supernaturalist:

> With respect to myself, I only need point to practically all my writings and their fight against the "side by side" theology even if it appears in the disguise of a "super." The Unconditioned is a qualification of the conditioned, of the world

---

* See Chap. IV, sec. 1.[19]

---

ates the love, but I am afraid Wieman errs when he asserts that we always love interactions. . . . No, what we love deeply is not these memories or expectations, it is the person who brings them about—we love concrete objects, persistent realities, not mere interactions. . . . A process may generate love, but the love is directed primarily not toward the process, but toward the continuing persons (concrete objects) who generate that process." First set of ellipses in original.

19. See p. 451 in this volume.

20. This paragraph also appears in chapter 4; see p. 463 in this volume.

and the natural, by which the conditioned is affirmed and denied at the same time.*

In other words, Tillich is saying that in no sense can he be labeled a supernaturalist. He is convinced that the Divine does not inhabit a transcendent world <u>above nature</u>; it is found in the "ecstatic" character of <u>this</u> world as its transcendent depth and ground.[21]

God's immanence is also expressed in the fact that everything finite participates in being itself and in infinity. If this were not the case, everything finite would be swallowed by non-being, or it never would have emerged out of non-being. So in a sense Tillich is as zealous to preserve the immanence of God as Wieman.

But this is only one side of Tillich's thought at this point. His desire to protect the majesty of God and his complex ontological analysis cause him to stress the transcendence of God as much as his immanence. Indeed, at times Tillich seems to stress the transcendence more than the immanence. It is at this point that Tillich goes beyond Wieman, for Wieman is more impressed with the immanence of God than the transcendence.

Tillich finds a basis for God's transcendence in the conecption of God as abyss. God is transcendent in the sense that he, as the abyss of being, transcends every being and also the totality of beings—the world. God is beyond finitude and infinity, insists Tillich. "There is no proportion or gradation between the finite and the infinite. There is an absolute break, an infinite 'jump'."† As we have seen, the abyss is the inexhaustible depth of God's nature. This is the unknowable side of God. In so far as God is abyss he is unapproachably holy, infinitely distant from man.[22]

Interestingly enough, Wieman agrees with Tillich that there is an uncomprehended element in God's nature. Wieman speaks of "the uncomprehended reality of God's total being."‡ Despite his insistence that God is a knowable entity within nature, Wieman affirms that God is transcendent, "not in the sense of being wholly unknown, but in the sense of being unknown with respect to his detailed and specific nature."§ In other words, Wieman seems to be saying that although we have some knowledge of God, we can never know his ultimate nature, i.e., his "detailed and specific nature." Wieman is attempting to stress a functional transcendence rather than a metaphysical one.

---

* Tillich, Rev. (1940)[3], 70.

† Tillich, ST, I, 237.

‡ Wieman, Art. (1936)[2], 436.

§ Wieman, Art. (1936)[2], 437.

---

21. The quotation and the sentences following it also appear in chapter 1; see p. 346 in this volume.

22. This paragraph is similar to passages in chapter 3; see pp. 406 and 424 in this volume.

So we see that Tillich and Wieman have quite a bit in common on the question of the immanence and transcendence of God. But there is a distinct difference in emphasis. Wieman's attempt to be a thoroughgoing empiricist and naturalist causes him to stress the immanence of God much more than the transcendence. On the other hand, Tillich's desire to protect the majesty of God causes him to stress the transcendence of God much more than his immanence. This emphsis is so strong in Tillich's thinking that he goes to the extreme of saying that it is the abyss that makes God God. This is his way of saying that it is God's transcendence rather than his immanence that makes him God.

Whenever Wieman and Tillich stress the immanence of God, they must be commended. Such an emphasis sounds a much needed note in the face of a supernaturalism that finds nature so irrational that the order of creation can no longer be discerned in it, and history so meaningless that it all bears the "minus sign" of alienation from God.[23] The emphasis comes as a necessary corrective to a supernaturalism that has overstressed the transcendence of God.

However, there is always the danger that in revolting against any extreme view one will go the opposite extreme, failing to see the partial value inherent in the former. It is possible, for instance, so to stress the immanence of God that the truth in the doctrine of the divine transcendence will be completely overlooked. This is what happens in the case of Wieman. In his attempt to confront modern skepticism with a God who is immanent in nature, Wieman leaves out many basic Christian principles that are preserved in the doctrine of transcendence. God cannot be reduced to natural processes, because he is the ground and creator of the natural order. To make God merely a process in nature is to rob him of his divinity. If God is to be truly God, he must be more than a behavior process; he must, in some sense, be above and before nature. Wieman fails to affirm this because of his bias toward a naturalistic philosophy which is alien to the spirit of Christianity.

There is an unnecessary ambiguity in Tillich's thought concerning the transcendence and immanence of God. On the one hand he speaks as a religious naturalist making God wholly immanent in nature. On the other hand he speaks as an extreme supernaturalist making God almost comparable to the Barthian "wholly other." In other words Tillich seems to stress the absolute immanence of God on the one hand and the absolute transcendence of God on the other. But it is hardly possible to reconcile these two views. If God is absolutely immanent he cannot be absolutely transcendent, and conversely, if he is absolutely transcendent he cannot be absolutely immanent. Even Tillich's dialectical principle cannot come to his aid at this point because the presupposition of the dialectical principle is that there is a point of contact between the "yes" and "no." Tillich himself realizes this. In one of his most succinct criticisms of Barth, Tillich writes: "A dialectic theology is one in which 'yes'

---

23. Horton, "Tillich's Role in Contemporary Theology," p. 30: "[Barth and Gogarten] find nature so irrational that the order of creation can no longer be discerned in it, man's spirit so perverted that the image of God is lost, history so meaningless that it all bears the 'minus sign' of alienation from God."

and 'no' belong inseparably together. In the so-called 'dialectic' theology they are irreconcilably separated, and that is why this theology is not dialectic."*[24] 15 Apr 1955The dialectical principle, which balances the "yes" of God's immanence with the "no" of his transcendence, is totally disrupted when either the "yes" or the "no" is considered exclusive or absolute.

The basic weakness of Tillich at this point is that he fails to maintain the tension between the transcendence and immanence of God which is necessary for a meaningful theistic position. God must be both "in" and "beyond" the world. If he is absolutely beyond, then he is not in; if absolutely in, then not beyond; but remove the absolutely, and he may be both. The doctrines of transcendence and immanence are both half-truths in need of the tension of each other to give the more inclusive truth.

4. The super-human character of God

Tillich and Wieman have at the forefront of their thinking a deep theocentric concern. Both are convinced that God is the most significant Fact in the universe. However much they disagree on the nature of God, they are at one in affirming the significance of God. Both are convinced that man's ultimate devotion is due to God and God alone. Tillich expresses this idea in the assertion that God is what ultimately concerns us. This ultimate concern is the abstract translation of the great commandment: "The Lord, our God, the Lord is one; and you shall love the Lord your God with all your heart, and with all your soul and with all your mind, and with all your strength."† This ultimate concern is unconditional, total and infinite. For any preliminary concern to be elevated to ultimacy, is for Tillich, the height of idolatry. It is also the source of many tragedies. When something essentially partial is boosted into universality, and something essentially finite is given infinite significance, almost anything can occur.‡[25] Only God warrants man's ultimate concern.

Like Tillich, Wieman feels that nothing should be placed before God. He contends that man should give himself, all that he is and all that he desires, all that he possesses and all that is dear to him, into the control of creative good to be transformed in any way that it may require.§ He is convinced that

---

* Tillich, Art. (1935)¹, 127.
† Tillich, ST, I, 11.
‡ Tillich uses the contemporary idolatry of religious nationalism as an example.
§ Wieman, SHG, 80.

---

24. Horton introduced this quotation with the phrase "Tillich's most succinct criticism of Barth runs as follows" ("Tillich's Role in Contemporary Theology," p. 29).

25. Tillich, *Systematic Theology*, p. 13: "Idolatry is the elevation of a preliminary concern to ultimacy. Something essentially conditioned is taken as unconditional, something essentially partial is boosted into universality, and something essentially finite is given infinite significance (the best example is the contemporary idolatry of religious nationalism)."

the chief tragedies that befall man and his historic existence stem from man's tendency to elevate created good to the rank of creative good (God). Just as Tillich sees the elevation of preliminary concerns to the status of ultimacy as idolatrous, Wieman sees the elevation of created good to the rank of creative good as idolatrous. Wieman feels that the best in Christianity is the reversing of the order of domination in the life of man from domination of human concern by created good over to domination by creative good (God).*[26] So Wieman's emphasis, like Tillich's, is theocentric throughout.

This theocentric concern leads Tillich and Wieman to the further assertion that God is not man. Both are averse to anything that smacks of humanism. As we have seen, Tillich's ontological analysis leads him to affirm that God must not be confused with man in any sense. God as being-itself infinitely transcends all beings. He is not a being, not even a "highest being" or a "most perfect" being. He is the power of being in everything that has being.†

This idea is more concisely expressed in the assertion that God is the unconditional. The unconditional is not a section of reality; it is not an object among objects. The unconditional transcends the distinction between subject and object. Instead of God being an object for us as subjects, he is the <u>prius</u> of the separation into subject and object, that which precedes the division. As we have seen in the earlier part of the discussion, this <u>prius</u> of separation is not a person. It is power, power of being.[28]

All of this is Tillich's way of saying that God infinitely transcends human existence. He is convinced that there is a qualitative distinction between God and man.

Wieman, like Tillich, never wearies of pointing out that God is super-human. It is probably no exaggeration to say that Wieman's objectivistic, realistic, theocentric trend developed in opposition to religious humanism. He feels that the deification of man is the pitiable absurdity man has ever perpetrated. He is convinced that the work of God is totally difference from the work of man. The difference is not merely of degree or magnitude. It is a difference of kind.‡ So Wieman, like Tillich, sees a qualitative difference be-

---

* Wieman, SHG, 25, 26.
† See Chap. III, sec. 2.[27]
‡ This is one of the points at which Wieman is unalterably opposed to Dewey. Man is regarded by Wieman as a passive factor in the event from which good emerges, so that it is not really man who clarifies and carries forward the ideal. It is God, the creative event. Dewey, on the other hand, attributes the emergence of value to the co-working of men plus more general factors.[29]

---

26. Parts of this paragraph also appear in chapter 4; see pp. 459 and 467 in this volume.

27. See p. 404 in this volume.

28. This paragraph also appears in chapter 3; see pp. 416–417 in this volume.

29. Charles Hartshorne and William L. Reese, *Philosophers Speak of God* (Chicago: University of Chicago Press, 1953), p. 396: "Man is regarded by Wieman as a passive factor in the event from which good emerges so that it is not really man who clarifies, carries forward, and implements the ideal; this is the function of God or creativity. Where Dewey would attribute the emergence of value to the co-working of men plus more general factors, Wieman would say that this emergence is the work of God."

tween God and man. God operates in ways over and above the plans and purposes of man, and often develops connections of mutual support and mutual meaning in spite of or contrary to the efforts of men.[30]

For all that Wieman and Tillich have said about the primacy of God over everything else in the universe, we have nothing but praise. In spite of the fact that we have found it necessary to raise some questions as to the adequacy of their conceptions of God to speak to the deepest yearnings of the religious soul, we do not in the least want to minimize the importance of their messages as a cry against the humanism of our generation. They do insist that religion begins with God and that man cannot have faith apart from him. They do proclaim that apart from God our human efforts turn to ashes and our sunrises into darkest night. They do suggest that man is not sufficient to himself for life, but is dependent upon God. All of this is good, and it may be a necessary corrective to a generation that has had all too much faith in man and all too little faith in God.[31]

5. The power and knowledge of God.

Tillich places a great deal of emphasis on the omnipotence of God. He continually speaks of God as the power of being. The one word that stands in the forefront of Tillich's God-concept is the word power. Power is that which makes God God. God is the underlying "ground" or "power" behind everything that exists. God as power of being resists and conquers non-being. It is because of this power to resist non-being that God warrants man's ultimate concern. As we have seen, Tillich does not mean by omnipotence that God has the power to do anything he wishes. Nor does it mean omni-activity in terms of causality. Omnipotence means, rather, "the power of being which resists nonbeing in all its expressions."*[32]

Unlike Tillich, Wieman places little emphasis on the power of God. As we

---

* Tillich, ST, I, 273. In spite of his persistent stress on the power of God, Tillich places considerable limitation on God's power in his conception of God as "abyss". There is a basic ambiguity in Tillich's thought at this point. This ambiguity is found in the fact that Tillich's language and method suggest an extreme absolutistic theism, while his conception of God as "abyss" suggests finitistic theism. This phase of Tillich's thought will be discussed and evaluated in the section on God and evil.

---

30. Parts of this paragraph also appear in chapter 4; see pp. 459–460 and 462 in this volume.

31. A version of this paragraph appears in several other essays that King wrote at Boston University. See "Karl Barth's Conception of God," 2 January 1952, p. 106 in this volume; "Contemporary Continental Theology," 13 September 1951–15 January 1952, p. 138; and "A Comparison and Evaluation of the Theology of Luther with That of Calvin," 15 May 1953, p. 191. Cf. George W. Davis, "Some Theological Continuities in the Crisis Theology," *Crozer Quarterly* 27, no. 3 (July 1950): 217–218.

32. The preceding five sentences also appear in chapter 3; see p. 405 in this volume.

shall see subsequently, Wieman is much more impressed with the goodness of
God than the power of God. He emphatically denies that God is omnipotent.
If God has any power, it is the power of process or growth. Wieman writes:

> Process is power. Activity is power. I do not know of any kind of power except
> that of process, activity, movement, growth, fulfillment, on-going. The power of
> God is the power of this growth.*

Wieman considers it quite erroneous to look upon power as "back of" the
process or growth, making it go from the outside. Power is one essential constituent of the process of growth, which is God.[33]

So Wieman would totally disagree with Tillich's assertion that God is a sort
of reservoir of power that empowers every being that comes into existence.
Wieman, contrary to Tillich, emphatically denies that God is the underlying
"ground" or "power" behind everything that exists. For Wieman, God is only
the source of the good.

When it comes to the question of the omniscience of God, both Wieman
and Tillich are at one in refuting its traditional formulation. In traditional
theology omniscience is the faculty of a highest being who is supposed to
know all objects, past, present and future, and beyond this, everything that
might have happened if what has happened had not happened. Tillich looks
upon this interpretation of omniscience as absurd because of the impossibility
of subsuming God under the subject-object scheme. Wieman sees it as absurd
because there is not the slightest empirical evidence for the existence of such
a "highest being" who knows all objects, past, present, and future. It is Tillich's
attempt to remain true to his ontological assertion that God is being-itself that
causes him to deny the omniscience of God. It is Wieman's attempt to be a
thoroughgoing empiricist that causes him to deny the omniscience of God.

Despite his concurrence with Wieman on the absurdity of the traditional
doctrine of the omniscience of God, Tillich goes beyond Wieman by seeking
to set forth the qualitative and symbolic meaning of the doctrine. Herein lies
a great distinction between Wieman and Tillich on the attributes of God generally. Tillich, while rejecting the traditional meaning of attributes, seeks to
give them a qualitative interpretation and thereby to accept them—at least
symbolically. Wieman, on the other hand, finds the attributes out of harmony
with his naturalistic and empiricistic views, and therefore rejects them outright. This accounts for the fact that he nowhere gives a systematic treatment
to the attributes of God.

---

* Wieman, Art. (1936)[2], 429.

---

33. Wieman, "God Is More," p. 429: "To speak of power as 'back of' the process or growth or
activity, making it go from the outside, is an error, I think. . . . Power is one essential constituent
of the process of growth, which is God."

The omniscience of God means, for Tillich, that

> nothing is outside the centered unity of his life; nothing is strange, dark, hidden, isolated, unapproachable. Nothing falls outside the <u>logos</u> structure of being. The dynamic element cannot break the unity of the form; the abysmal quality cannot swallow the rational quality of the divine life.*

This has tremendous implications for man's personal and cultural existence. In personal life it means that there is no absolute darkness in one's being. The divine omniscience is ultimately the logical foundation of the belief in the openness of reality to human knowledge. We are able to reach truth because the divine life in which we are rooted embodies all truth.†

We shall reserve critical comment on this phase of Wieman's and Tillich's thinking until the section on the goodness of God.

6. The eternity and omnipresence of God

On the questions of the eternity and omnipresence of God, Tillich again gives clearer expression than does Wieman. Here, as in other instances, Wieman's naturalism prevents him from going all of the way with Tillich. As we have seen, Tillich affirms that two interpretations of eternity must be rejected, that of timelessness, and that of endlessness of time. Rather than meaning timelessness, eternity means "the power of embracing all periods of time."‡ The eternal keeps the temporal within itself by maintaining "the transcendent unity of the dissected moments of existential time."§ There is a similarity between the eternality of God and the eternality of a mathematical proposition.

A symbolic indication of the meaning of the eternity of God may be found in human experience, in the unity of remembered past and anticipated future in an experienced present. As the present is predominant in human experience, eternity is symbolized as an eternal present. But this present is not simultaneity. Simultaneity would erase the different modes of time. The eternal present is moving from past to future but without ceasing to be present.[35] In this sense God is eternal in such a way that the distinctions within the flow of time are preserved. So Tillich includes within the divine life both temporality and eternality.

---

* Tillich, ST, I, 279.
† See Chap. II, sec. 8.[34]
‡ Tillich, ST, I, 274.
§ Tillich, ST, I, 274.

---

34. Chapter II, section 8 does not exist.
35. This paragraph is similar to a paragraph in chapter 3; see p. 437 in this volume.

Wieman's stress is on the temporality of God rather than the eternality. Indeed his idea of God has been referred to as "extreme temporalistic theism."* His very definitions of God—"growth," "creative event" and "process"—point to something that is temporal and passing rather than eternal. An event or a process of growth is neither a continuing entity nor a persistent reality. It is something forever in a state of becoming. It is quite apparent that Wieman's characterization of God as "process" or "creative event" is due to his desire to abandon the scholastic notion of substantial being. Like Whitehead, he has preference for dynamic terminology. He seeks to stress the activity of God as against a static <u>ens necessarium</u>, absolute Being.[36] So, unlike Tillich, Wieman is so determined to make God a temporal reality that he almost completely overlooks his eternity.

When it comes to the question of God's omnipresence, both Tillich and Wieman are at one in denying its traditional meaning. However, Tillich goes beyond Wieman in seeking to interpret the attribute of omnipresence in qualitative terms. God is omnipresent in the sense that he creates extension out of his nature as ground and that he is the ground in which all space is rooted. Space is in God, not God in space. So Tillich concludes that God cannot be spatial, although he must be temporal.

Now a word of critical comment. Certainly Wieman and Tillich are on sound ground in affirming the temporality of God. It is often supposed that if God is nonspatial, he must be nontemporal. But this does not necessarily follows. The two categories are sufficiently different to stand on their individual footing. If God is a living God he must include temporality, and with this a relation to the modes of time.

This stress on the temporality of God, however, must not obscure the fact that there is some permanence in God's nature. Herein lies the weakness of Wieman. He stresses the temporality of God to the point of minimizing his eternity. As stated above, Wieman's characterization of God as "process" or "creative event" is due to his desire to abandon the scholastic notion of substantial being. He seeks to stress the activity of God as against a static absolute being. But this attempt to avoid one sort of abstraction, namely, one which leaves out becoming, leads directly into another, namely, one that

---

* See Hartshorne's and Reese's chapter on Wieman in PSG, 395–408.

---

36. Robert Lowry Calhoun, "God as More than Mind," *Christendom* 1, no. 2 (Winter 1936): 344–345: "I welcome the evident values of this preference for 'dynamic' terminology which Wieman shares with Mead, Dewey, and Whitehead. . . . But with whatever gain there may be in their declaration of independence from the scholastic notion of substantial being, there is danger of a serious loss of precision. . . . These are terms which Wieman employs to signalize the *actuality* of God as against abstract form or ideal, and the *activity* of God as against a static *ens necessarium*, absolute Being."

leaves out that which becomes.[37] Tillich sees this and therefore attempts to preserve in God, at least symbolically, both dynamics and form, temporality and eternality.*

Wieman's temporalistic view of God comes as a proper revolt against a misconceived and one-sided substance philosophy. But his whole doctrine of God is weakened by his failure to emphasize the factor of permanence in the idea of God. The religious worshiper is in quest of a God who is not only the increaser of value, but also the conserver of value. We have seen how Wieman continually identifies God with the production or emergence of values. Production of value, we are told, is also destruction of value. New values displace old. But what happens to these displaced values? Are they simply destroyed as though they never existed? In this case all of man's objectives must in the long run prove futile.[38]

Wieman would probably retort that values are conserved in works of art and in many forms of conscious and unconscious memory. But what happens when human life no longer inhabits the earth? Even if we concede that the earth will be inhabitable forever—an astronomical impossibility—we still have to confront the fact that the human attention span is too limited to house, at any given human present, any appreciable proportion of the values of past generations. So without an eternal conserver of values our efforts are worthless, and no act can in the long run have better consequences than any other.†[39] In such a situation the rivalry of values is meaningless. In order for value-experience to be meaningful, then, there must be a God eternal enough to conserve values. God must be identified not only with the production or emergence of values, but also with the indestructibility of them.‡

---

* Cf. Calhoun, Art. (1936), 345.
† This argument can be used in favor of the doctrine of personal immortality—a doctrine which Wieman rejects. At bottom personal immortality represents the faith that good purpose never fails to all eternity. The basis of all human endeavor is in the hope that purpose can achieve values. Without personal immortality all of our efforts are worthless and the whole universe seems to be destructive of supreme value.
‡ CF. Hartshorne and Reese, PSG, 404–405.

---

37. Calhoun, "God as More than Mind," p. 345: "But in avoiding one sort of abstraction, namely, one which leaves out 'becoming,' they fall into another, and leave out *that* which 'becomes.'"

38. Hartshorne and Reese, *Philosophers Speak of God*, pp. 404–405: "Production of good, we are told, is also destruction of good. New goods displace old. . . . But what about the displaced goods? Are they simply nullified and as though they had never been? In that case all our specific objectives must in the long run prove vain."

39. Hartshorne and Reese, *Philosophers Speak of God*, p. 405: "Even if the earth were to be inhabitable forever—an astronomical impossibility, one gathers—or if man may hope to escape to another planet, still there just is not room, with the limitations of the human attention span, for any appreciable *proportion* of the values of past generations . . . to house themselves in the

7. The goodness of God

The question of the goodness of God is one that stands in the forefront of Wieman's thinking. Tillich, as we have seen, is more impressed with the power of God. For Tillich it is power that makes God God. But, for Wieman, it is goodness or value that makes God God. These are the important words in Wieman's discussion of God. God is the "source of human good"; He is "supreme value." Says Wieman: "I maintain . . . that the basic category for God must be goodness and value."*

Wieman contends that God is the only absolute good. As we have seen, he seeks to defend this claim by defining absolute in a fivefold sense.† First of all, absolute good refers to that which is good under all circumstances and conditions. It is good that is not relative to time or place or race or class or need or desire. It is good that remains changelessly and identically the same. A second mark of absolute good is that its demands are unlimited. God is good in this sense because he demands our wholehearted surrender. A third mark of absolute good is its infinite value. Fourth, absolute good is unqualified good. Finally, absolute good is entirely trustworthy.

God's goodness meets all these requirements. His goodness is not relative to time or place or desire or even human existence. He demands our wholehearted surrender. His worth is incommensurable with any finite quantity of created good. There is no perspective from which his goodness can be modified. God is entirely trustworthy. Wieman is certain that the outcome of the working of God will always be the best possible under the conditions, even when it may seem to be otherwise.

Wieman holds that God is supreme value because he brings lesser values into relations of maximum mutual support and mutual enhancement. This mutual support and enhancement is not only between contemporaries but also between successive generations, ages and cultures. All of this is Wieman's way of stressing the fact that God is supreme value and the only absolute Good.

Tillich, like Wieman, uses the terms goodness and value in referring to God. In one passage he says:

> The very fact that the one God is called "good" gives him a divine character superior to that of the evil god, for God as the expression of man's ultimate concern is supreme not only in power but also in value.‡

---

* Wieman, Art. (1943)³, 266.
† See Chap. IV, sec. 1.⁴⁰
‡ Tillich, ST, I, 225.

---

consciousness of any given human present. . . . It would really mean that our efforts are worthless, that no act can in the long run have better consequences than any other."

40. This paragraph, and the two following it, are condensed from passages in chapter 4; see pp. 466–468 and 477 in this volume.

In another context Tillich speaks of true being as the ultimate good.* Yet, in spite of these passages, instances in which he refers to the goodness of God are very scanty. In his whole <u>Systematic Theology</u> one can hardly find a page of references in which Tillich affirms the essential goodness of God. Even when the terms goodness and value are used, they are defined in terms of being. Herein lies a basic difference between Wieman and Tillich. Wieman is basically concerned with the goodness of God. Tillich, on the other hand, is basically concerned with the power of God. Wieman's basic emphasis is axiological while Tillich's is ontological.

Now we may give some critical comments on the questions of God's power and goodness as treated by Wieman and Tillich. In the judgement of the present writer, both Wieman and Tillich are partially correct in what they affirm and partially wrong in what they deny. Wieman is right in emphasizing the goodness of God, but wrong in minimizing his power. Likewise Tillich is right in emphasizing the power of God, but wrong in minimizing his goodness. Both Tillich and Wieman overstress one aspect of the divine nature to the neglect of another basic aspect. God is not <u>either</u> powerful <u>or</u> good; he is <u>both</u> powerful <u>and</u> good. Matthew Arnold's simple, almost trite, phrase contains the gist of the matter: God is a power, not ourselves, making for righteousness. Not power alone, nor righteousness alone, but a combination of the two constitutes the meaning of God. Value by itself is impotent; being by itself is morally indifferent. On the one hand, there is the view of Wieman which erects the idea of value as the sole utlimate principle. On the other hand, there is the view of Tillich which erects power or being-itself as the sole ultimate principle. Neither viewpoint adequately formulates the Christian doctrine of God.[41]

Wieman talks continually about the goodness of God. But one is forced to wonder whether Wieman's God is capable of bringing this goodness into being. As we stated above, value in itself is impotent. Hence a God devoid of power is ultimately inacapable of actualizing the good. But if God is truly God and warrants man's ultimate devotion, he must have not only an infinite concern for the good but an infinite power to actualize the good. This is the truth expressed in the somewhat misleading doctrine of the divine omnipotence. It does not mean that God can do the nondoable; neither does it mean that God has the power to act contrary to his own nature. It means, rather, that God

---

* Tillich, TPE, 27.

---

41. Demos, Review of *Systematic Theology*, p. 706: "Matthew Arnold's simple, almost platitudinous, phrase contains the gist of the matter: God is a power, not ourselves, making for righteousness. Not power alone, nor righteousness alone, but the blend of the two constitutes the meaning of God. Value by itself is impotent; being by itself is morally indifferent. On the one side, there is Platonism which erects the Idea of the Good (Value) as the sole ultimate principle. On the other side, there is the view of this book which erects beingness as the sole ultimate principle. Neither viewpoint adequately formulates Christian theology."

has the power to actualize the good and realize his purpose. Moral perfection would be an empty possession apart from a corresponding and sustaining power. It is power that gives reality to the divine being. Wieman's failure to see this causes us to doubt the adequacy of his conception of God as a meaningful theistic position.

One may well question the adequacy and significance of Tillich's statement that God is being-itself. Everybody knows that there are existing things, and if one wants to become more philosophical, one can go on and say that there is an existing ground of the existence of everything. But this is saying little more than the tautology that the universe exists. Every intelligent person admits that the universe is immense, infinite and awesome; but this does not make him a believer. What one wants to know is whether the universe is good, bad, or indifferent. It is the failure to grapple sufficiently with this question that seriously weakens Tillich's God-concept. It is true that Tillich uses the terms goodness and value, but he defines these in terms of being. To be good means to be. It will be recalled that Spinoza speaks of the perfection of the universe, but defines perfection in terms of substance. So, too, Tillich speaks of value, but defines it in terms of being. (We have noticed already that divine love is declared to be a wholly ontological concept.)[42]

Tillich's tendency to relegate value to an almost insignificant rank is clearly manifested in his analysis of value-categories in relation to being-itself. Structure, according to Tillich, is derived from being-itself; in turn, value is derived from structure. So to this point value is at a second remove from reality. But this is not all; value-concepts presuppose the contrast between ideal and actualities, and hence a split between essence and existence.* In other words, value is now a <u>third</u> remove from reality. Value-categories are relegated to the realm of finite being.†[43]

---

* See Tillich, ST, I, 202–204.
† Cf. Demos, Rev. (1952), 707.

---

42. Demos, Review of *Systematic Theology*, pp. 706–707: "One may well question what of genuine significance there is in the author's statement that God is being-itself. Everybody knows that there are existing things, and if one wants to speak causally, one can go on and say that there is an existing ground of the existence of everything. But this essentially amounts to no more than the tautology that the universe exists. . . . All sensible people grant that the universe is grand, infinite, immense, awesome; but this does not make them believers. What one wants to know is whether the universe is good or bad or worse (i.e., morally indifferent). . . . It will be recalled that Spinoza speaks of the perfection of the universe, but defines perfection in terms of substance. So, too, our author uses the terms goodness and value (incidentally, how scanty are such references in this book!) but then defines these in terms of being. (To be good means to be; we have noticed already that divine love is declared to be a wholly ontological concept.)"

43. Demos, Review of *Systematic Theology*, p. 707: "Structure (meaning) according to the author is derived from being-itself; in turn, value is derived from structure. Thus value is at a second remove from reality. This is not all, however; value-concepts presuppose the contrast between

Tillich speaks continually of the holiness of God, but even here he is not endowing being-itself with moral perfection. The holy means the sacred, and not the righteous or the morally good.*[44]

So in almost all of Tillich's references to God it is power that stands in the forefront. In a real sense, this emphasis is dangerous, because it leads toward a worship of power for its own sake. Divine power, like any other power, can become despotic power if it is not controlled by divine goodness. In short, neither Tillich's notion of being-itself, nor any other purely ontological notion is adequate for the Christian idea of God. The latter is a synthesis of the two independent concepts of value and being.[45]

We have quoted above two passages in which Tillich referred to the goodness of God. These passages reveal that he is at least aware of the significance of the category of value for an adequate God-concept. But his definition of God as being-itself prevents him from affirming it. He realizes that if he refers to God as good, he thereby conditions the unconditioned, and drags God into a subject-object relationship making him a being beside others. So in order to be consistent with his ontological analysis, Tillich talks of God as being good in the sense that he is the ground of goodness. This, however, gives rise to the same criticism that was raised concerning the personal status of God. If God is good only in the sense that he is the ground of goodness, it follows that he is evil since he is the ground of evil. If the attribute of goodness means anything it must have content and it must be a quality of some rational substance. To state that God is the ground of goodness is merely an abstraction. One wishes to get behind this abstraction to an ontological substance in which the attribute of goodness inheres. So here again we see the inadequacy of Tillich's being-itself for the Christian idea of God.

To sum up, neither Tillich nor Wieman gives and adequate conception of God's nature. The former places an undue emphasis on being to the neglect of value; the latter places an undue emphasis on value to the neglect of being.

---

* See Tillich, ST, I, 216–217.

---

ideals and actualities, and hence a split between essence and existence; they apply in the creaturely and finite world (pp. 202–204). In other words, value is at a *third* remove from reality. Value-categories are relegated to the realm of finite being."

44. Demos, Review of *Systematic Theology*, p. 707: "Professor Tillich speaks of God as holy. . . . God is not just pure being; he is a being endowed with moral perfection. But wait: the holy means the sacred essentially; it stands in *contrast* with the 'righteous' or the 'morally good,' or with 'moral perfection' (pp. 216–217)."

45. Demos, Review of *Systematic Theology*, p. 707: "All this seems to me dangerously romantic—dangerous because it easily slips into a worship of power for its own sake. If we are to save divine power from becoming despotic power we must cling to the notion of the goodness of God as an irreducible element in his essence. To sum up, neither the Thomistic notion of complete actuality, nor the author's notion of being-itself, nor any other purely ontological notion is adequate for the Christian idea of God. The latter is a synthesis of the two independent concepts of value and being."

A more adequate view is to maintain that <u>both</u> value <u>and</u> being are basic in the meaning of God, each blending with the other but neither being reduced to the other.[46]

8. God's creative activity

In traditional theology creation referred to the act whereby the underived self-existent God brought into being what had no form of independent existence hitherto. So strong was the Christian, theistic belief in an absolute, transcendent God who worked under no external limitation, that creation was said to be <u>ex nihilo</u>, i.e. generation out of nothing. With this traditional concept both Wieman and Tillich are in radical disagreement. Wieman contends that the doctrine of creation <u>ex nihilo</u> is self-contradictory; moreover, it would be impossible for Wieman on the basis of his method to get any knowledge of such an initial generation, supposing it ever occurred. Tillich disagrees with this traditional theory because it looks upon creation as an act or an event which took place "once upon a time." Creation, for Tillich, does not refer to an event, it rather indicates a condition, a relationship between God and the world.[47]

So, for Tillich, as for Wieman, there is no supernatural being before and above all beings as their creator. Instead of being a supernatural creator, Tillich's God is "the ground of Being."* Tillich's desire to place all theological matter under the scrutiny of strict ontological analysis causes him to go beyond Wieman in interpreting the meaning of the traditional doctrine. Thus he is able to find some meaning in the traditional doctrine of creation <u>ex nihilo</u>. The phrase is taken to mean that God creates the world out of not-being; hence human nature (and all nature) is constituted by not-being; natu-

---

* Ground, according to Tillich, is neither cause nor substance, taken literally, but something "underlying" all things in a manner which we can only symbolize through causation or substantiality. Literal causes always are also effects, something conditioned (whereas God is unconditioned), while "substance" and "accidents" lack the freedom with respect to each other which Christianity affirms both of God and of creatures.[48]

---

46. Demos, Review of *Systematic Theology*, p. 706: "It will be noticed that, for Plato, the Idea of the Good is a source of being; and as we will see, our author regards being as a source of value. I would maintain that the notions of value and being are *coördinate* in the meaning of God; each blending with the other but neither being reduced to the other."

47. The first four sentences of this paragraph appear in chapter 4 and the last two are in chapter 3; see pp. 481 and 425 in this volume.

48. Hartshorne, "Tillich's Doctrine of God," p. 165: "'Ground' is neither cause nor substance, taken literally, but something 'underlying' all things in a manner which we can only *symbolize* through causation or substantiality. Literal causes always are also effects, something conditioned (whereas God is unconditioned), while 'substance' and 'accidents' lack the freedom with respect to each other which Christianity affirms both of God and of creatures."

ral existence is a limitation of being; and man, just because of his heritage of not-being, is afflicted with anxiety, striving, and imperfection. We have already seen how Tillich uses all three modes of time to symbolize God's creative activity. All of this gives evidence of the fact that creation, for Tillich, does not refer to an event; it is rather the word given to the process which actualizes man in existence.

In spite of his rejection of the doctrine of creation <u>ex nihilo</u>, there is a sense in which Wieman speaks of God as creator. God is the creator of all created values. God is the sum-total of all the natural conditions of value-achievement.

Many problems arise from these analyses of God's creative activity. The basic problem in Wieman is whether or not he has raised more problems in his denial of creation than he has solved. The basic problem in Tillich is whether the man who is actualized in existence is properly "man" or "God"; whether the view of Tillich is an ultimate monism or pluralism. These problems will be discussed in the next two sections. Suffice it to say at this point that neither Wieman nor Tillich has taken seriously the scriptural witness to God's creation of man, God's imparting to man a center of consciousness with freedom and responsibility, a will with co-creative powers.*

9. God and evil

Wieman looks upon the "problem of evil" as a false problem; it arises only when one departs from the empirical evidence for God as "the good," or the chief factor for good in nature, and begins to speculate about God as also something the creator of all existence. When the idea of God as creator is relinquished, the problem disappears. The more empirical problem is to define the actual nature and scope of evil, and not to indulge in unempirical speculation as to its origin. We have already seen above how Wieman takes pains to describe the nature and scope of evil.†

This view of God is avowedly finitistic. God is only the source of good. He is therefore limited by evil forces external to his nature. He is not the ultimate ground of all existence because of the very existence of these evil forces. Wieman asks:

> Why is God not the ultimate ground of all existence? Because he is not the ultimate ground of murder, lust, treachery and all the horrors of existence. To try to revere such a reality as God, is to try to initiate a religion that is worse than voodooism.‡

---

* Gen. 1:27–31; 2:7–8;   † See Chap. IV, sec. 3.[49]
Psalms 8; Mark 12:30; Mt.   ‡ Wieman, Art. (1932)[2],
23:37.   111.

---

49. See p. 483 in this volume.

Thus Wieman avoids the problem of evil by positing a finite God who is in no way the creator of all existence.

Tillich cannot dismiss the problem of evil as easily as Wieman, because of his contention that God is the ultimate ground of all reality. As we have seen, Tillich divides evil into three classes.* (a) Physical evil, pain, and death), according to him, offer no real problem because they are natural implications of creaturely finitude. (b) Then there is moral evil which is the tragic implication of creaturely freedom. (c) Finally, there is the apparent fact of meaninglessness and futility— and this, according to Tillich, is the only sort of evil which offers genuine difficulty for theological belief. Tillich's solution to the problem of evil of this third sort is very difficult to understand, partly because of its excessive conciseness. Such evil is described as "the negativities of creaturely existence."[50]

Tillich hints at another solution to the problem of evil. This solution is found in his positing a nonrational aspect in God's nature. This is set forth in the concept of God as "abyss." As we have seen, the abysmal nature of God is a nonrational, unformed dimension of incalculable power.† There are two aspects to God's nature, viz., the logos and the abyss. The former is the rational aspect and the latter is the nonrational. It is this nonrational aspect that accounts for much of the evil in the world. So Tillich attempts to solve the problem of evil by finding a nonrational aspect in God's nature. Like Wieman, he ends up with a finitistic view of God. His language and method seem extremely absolutistic, but his stress on the abysmal aspect of God's nature is definitely finitistic. Tillich's finitism is to be distinguished from Wieman's in one significant respect: in Wieman's conception the limitation of God's power is external to his nature, while in Tillich's thought the limitation is an aspect within God's nature.

How adequate are these views? Wieman seeks to avoid the problem of evil by a complete denial of creation. He holds to the finiteness of God, yet without being subject to the criticism which may be directed against belief in a Creator-God. But the denial of a Creator-God raises more problems than it solves. Such a denial gives no explanation of the source of consciousness and value. Moreover, it fails to explain the unity of nature. This easy solution of the problem of evil fails to grapple thoroughly with the problem of good. Its impersonalism is philosophically inadequate.

Some questions may be raised concerning Tillich's solution to the problem of evil. At one point he says that physical evil offers no real problem because it is a natural implication of creaturely finitude. But this is no solution to the problem. Physical evils are surely evil, and the fact that they are implicated in

---

* See Chap. III, sec. 5.
† See Chap. III, sec. 4.[51]

---

50. This paragraph is similar to a paragraph in chapter 3; see p. 431 in this volume.
51. See p. 418 in this volume.

the finitude of all creaturely being does not help at all. For if creation is finite, and finitude be evil, then God is the creator of evil.[52]

By attributing evils in the world to some nonrational aspect in God's nature, Tillich introduces a dualism into the divine nature that can hardly be regarded as satisfactory either religiously or intellectually. This conception suffers from all of the inadequacies of any ultimate metaphysical dualism. Tillich leaves such a tremendous gap between God as <u>abyss</u> and God as <u>logos</u> that there hardly appears to be a point of contact between the two. Nowhere does Tillich adequately explain the relationship of these two aspects of God's nature. So great is the mystery between the <u>abyss</u> and the <u>logos</u> that one is compelled to wonder why the two should be called God.*[53]

10. The question of monism versus pluralism

As we have seen above, Wieman seeks to maintain an ultimate pluralism in which God is in no way responsible for evil. Wieman is emphatic in the assertion that God is not the ultimate ground of all existence. He is probably one of several ultimate realities.†[54] With this ultimate pluralism Tillich would not concur. For Tillich God is the one ultimate reality, the ultimate ground of all existence. Tillich, then, is monistic in his emphasis, while Wieman is pluralistic. As we attempted to show above, Tillich's monism is not only qualitative, but also quantitative.‡ Tillich holds to an ultimate ontological monism, both qualitative and quantitative. God is ultimately the only metaphysical reality. The life of man is a phase of the actualization of God and not a separate metaphysical reality.

If there is any one point at which Wieman and Tillich are in basic disagreement, it is here. Wieman holds to an ultimate pluralism, both quantitative and qualitative. Tillich, on the other hand, holds to an ultimate monism, both qualitative and quantitative.

Here again we find Wieman and Tillich each overstressing one phase of

---

* Cf. DeWolf, TLC, 134.

† Wieman, Art. (1932)[2]

‡ See Chap. III, sec. 11.[55]

---

52. This paragraph is similar to a paragraph in chapter 3; see p. 431 in this volume.

53. L. Harold DeWolf, *A Theology of the Living Church* (New York: Harper, 1953), p. 134: "In Tillich's view the relation between God as *abyss* and God as *logos* is left so completely in mystery that it is unclear why the two should both be called God."

54. Wieman, "Theocentric Religion," p. 111: "The only point we want to make is that God is not *the one* ultimate reality. He may be one of several ultimate realities."

55. See p. 477 in this volume. The following three sentences are also from section 11 in chapter 3.

reality while minimizing another. Wieman is so impressed with manyness that he overlooks oneness. Tillich, on the other hand, is so impressed with oneness that he overlooks manyness.

Neither of these views is basically sound. Wieman's ultimate pluralism fails to satisfy the rational demand for unity. Sense-experience is manifold and pluralistic; but reason is unitary and systematic. Monism, as Kant recognized, is the deepest demand of reason. A unitary world-ground is implied in the principle of causality. Moreover, there is system in this universe; cognition would be impossible without it. Further, no ultimate system can be made up of independent units. If the system be real, the units must be subordinated to the system.*[56]

Certainly this quest for ultimate unity haunts the religious man. One of the main things that the religious worshiper is seeking is a Being who is able to reduce all multiplicity to unity. Wieman's failure to discover this unity leaves him with a conception of God that is both religiously and intellectually inadequate.

As Wieman's ultimate pluralism is unsatisfactory, so is Tillich's ultimate monism. There is much in Tillich that is reminiscent of Spinoza and Hegel. In each of these systems finite individuality is swallowed up in the unity of being. Individual persons become merely transitory modes of the one substance, having no substantial character of their own.

One of the greatest dangers of Tillich's system is that it tends toward pantheism. This type of thinking makes God impersonal and breaks down the separateness and independence of finite personality. In this sense it brings havoc to true religion. True religion is not concerned about metaphysical union of the human with the divine, but with a relation of mutual understanding between them, a relation that expresses itself in worship and love. Such a relationship is possible only between persons who maintain their distinct individuality. To make human personality a mere phase or mode of the absolute is to render real religious experience impossible. Pantheism is both practically and theorectically disastrous.

Tillich talks a great deal about the freedom of man. The most pervasive idea in all of Tillich's utterances about man is that man is free. In numerous instances man's nature is spoken of as "finite freedom." He says: "Man is man because he has freedom."† Again he says: "Freedom makes man man."‡[57]

---

* Cf. Knudson, POP, 202.
† Tillich, ST, I, 182.

‡ Tillich, Art. (1940)³, 123.

---

56. Albert C. Knudson, *The Philosophy of Personalism* (New York: Abingdon Press, 1927), p. 202: "But there is at least system; cognition would be impossible without it. And no ultimate system can be made up of independent units. If the system be real, the units must be subordinated to the system."

57. Boozer, "Place of Reason," p. 10: "In numerous instances man's nature is spoken of as 'finite freedom.' . . . Tillich writes again: 'Man is man because he has freedom.' . . . 'Freedom makes man man.'"

Man has in a sense left the divine ground to "stand upon" his own feet. He is to some extent "outside" the divine life. "To be outside the divine life means to stand in actualized freedom, in an existence which is no longer united with essence."*[58] But the question that inevitably arises at this point is, how can Tillich have both his monism and human freedom? We have seen how he tries to maintain both, and thereby presents a contradiction which he never completely resolves. The fact is that freedom is nonexistent in a monistic system. Freedom requires metaphysical otherness. But in a monistic system there is no otherness on the part of finite persons. Finite beings are parts of the Infinite or absolute and issue forth from its being by a kind of logical necessity.

In order for freedom to exist there must be distinct individuality and independence on the part of the finite soul. This the individual is deprived of in a thoroughgoing monism. Such monism breaks down the exclusiveness of personality, and erases the boundary lines between personal beings, making the finite person simply a part of the absolute. All of this reveals the futility of Tillich's attempt to stress the freedom of man in his monistic system. When taken in all of its logical implications, Tillich's system provides no place for finite freedom.

A final weakness of Tillich's system, as with all monistic systems, is its failure to grapple with the problem of error. It makes error as necessary as truth, and thus leaves us with no standard that would enable us to distinguish between them and no means of using the standard if we had it.

To sum up, both Wieman's pluralism and Tillich's monism are inadequate as philosophical and religious world-views. Each overemphasizes one phase of reality while totally neglecting another important phase. Here again, the solution is not <u>either</u> monism <u>or</u> pluralism; it is <u>both</u> monism <u>and</u> pluralism. Tillich and Wieman fail to see that both positions can be meaningfully maintained. It is possible to hold a quantitative pluralism while holding a qualitative monism. In this way both oneness and manyness are preserved. Neither swallows the other. Such a view defends, on the one hand, individuality against the impersonalism and all-engulfing universalism of any type of ultimate monism. On the other hand, it vindicates the idea of a basal monism against the attacks of any ultimate pluralism.

---

* Tillich, ST, I, 255.

---

58. Boozer, "Place of Reason," pp. 62–63: "Man has in a sense left the divine ground to 'stand upon' his own feet. He is to some extent 'outside' the divine life. 'To be outside the divine life means to stand in actualized freedom, in an existence which is no longer united with essence.'"

Chapter VI

CONCLUSIONS

The following theses may be stated as conclusions drawn from this investigation of the conceptions of God in the thinking of Tillich and Wieman.

1. Tillich's basic and most persistent definition of God is "being-itself," <u>esse ipsum</u>. In affirming that God is being-itself, Tillich is denying that God is a being beside other beings. In this conception he intends to convey the idea of the power of being. God is the power of being in everything and above everything.

2. Wieman's basic definition of God is the "creative event." This definition is an amplification of what Wieman means when he speaks of God as growth. He further defines God as "supreme value" and as "the unlimited connective growth of value-connections." But these definitions seem to have three different meanings. When Wieman characterizes God as "supreme value" he seems to mean the ideal of perfection or of the achievement of maximum value. When he speaks of God as "the unlimited corrective growth of value-connections" he seems to mean the human and social processes which aim at the achievement of value. When he describes God as the creative event he seems to mean the natural forces underlying the achievement of value. These three meanings cannot be viewed as constituting a unity except in a highly figurative sense, and positively not for a religious philosophy which would be consistently empirical. At this point Wieman has failed to be consistently empirical.

3. Both Tillich and Wieman agree that God is an undeniable reality. They are so convinced of the reality of God that they would dismiss all arguments for his existence as futile and invalid. They further agree in seeking to assure the reality of God through the definition of God. But in attempting to formulate the idea of God so as to make the question of his existence a dead issue, Tillich and Wieman have given up much that is most essential from the religious point of view in the idea of God. Both sacrifice too much for the sake of getting rid of a troublesome question.

4. Both Tillich and Wieman deny the category of personality to God. They think that to refer to God as a person is to limit him. This denial of personality to God does not mean, they insist, that God is impersonal. Instead of being impersonal or sub-personal, God is supra-personal. Despite their warnings that God is not less than personal, however, we have seen traits throughout their thinking that point to a God that is less than personal. Wieman's God is an interaction, that is, a behavior-process. He is not a concrete object or a continuing entity. In short, he is an unconscious process devoid of any true purpose. Tillich's "being-itself" is little more than a sub-personal reservoir of power. In this respect Tillich's thought is somewhat akin to the impersonalism of Oriental Vedantism. "Being-itself" is a pure absolute devoid of consciousness and life.

5. Wieman's naturalistic position causes him to place great emphasis on the immanence of God. Like everything else that exists God is found within the natural order. Whatever transcendence God has is seen to arise out of his very

534

immanence in the world of events. There is much in Tillich's view that comes close to the naturalistic position. He revolts against the view that there is a world behind the world. The Divine does not inhabit a transcendent world above nature; it is found in the "ecstatic" character of this world as its transcendent depth and ground.

6. Tillich's desire to protect the majesty of God and his complex ontological analysis cause him to stress the transcendence of God as much as his immanence. He finds a basis for God's transcendence in the conception of God as abyss. There is a basic inconsistency in Tillich's thought at this point. On the one hand he speaks as a religious naturalist making God wholly immanent in nature. On the other hand he speaks as an extreme supernaturalist making God almost comparable to the Barthian "wholly other."

7. Tillich and Wieman have at the forefront of their thinking a deep theocentric concern. Both are convinced that God is the most significant Fact in the universe. This theocentric concern leads Tillich and Wieman to the further assertion that God is not man. They see a qualitative difference between God and man.

8. Tillich and Wieman are at one in rejecting the traditional formulations of the attributes of God. Tillich goes beyond Wieman, however, by seeking to set forth the qualitative and symbolic meaning of the attributes.

9. Tillich includes within the divine life both temporality and eternality. Wieman's stress is on the the temporality of God. His failure to emphasize the factor of permanence in the idea of God weakens Wieman's doctrine of God at many points. It leaves a God who is the increaser of value without being the conserver of value. In such a situation, value-experience becomes meaningless.

10. The most important words in Tillich's conception of God are "power" and "being". The most important words in Wieman's conception of God are "goodness" and "value." Wieman's basic emphasis is axiological while Tillich's is ontological. Now both Wieman and Tillich are partially correct in what they affirm, but partially wrong in what they deny. Both overstress one aspect of the divine nature to the neglect of another basic aspect. Tillich places an undue emphasis on being to the neglect of value; Wieman places an undue emphasis on value to the neglect of being. A more adequate view is to maintain that both value and being are basic in the meaning of God; each blending with the other but neither being reduced to the other.

11. Both Tillich and Wieman reject the traditional doctrine of creation. For neither of them is there a supernatural being before and above all beings as their creator.

12. Tillich and Wieman are theistic finitists. However, they differ in one significant respect: in Wieman's conception the limitation to God's power is external to his nature, while in Tillich's thought the limitation is an aspect within God's nature.

13. Wieman holds to an ultimate pluralism, both quantitative and qualitative. Tillich, on the other hand, holds to an ultimate monism, both qualitative and quantitative. Both of these views have been found to be inadequate. Wieman's ultimate pluralism fails to satisfy the rational demand for unity. Tillich's ultimate monism swallows up finite individuality in the unity of being. A more

adequate view is to hold a quantitative pluralism and a qualitative monism. In this way both oneness and manyness are preserved.

BIBLIOGRAPHY

Adams, James Luther—Art. (1948)
  "Tillich's Concept of the Protestant Era."
  Tillich, PE, 273–316.
Aubrey, Edwin.—Rev. (1952)
  Rev. of Tillich, Systematic Theology, I (1951).
  Jour. of Bib. and Rel., 20 (1952), 31–32.
Baillie, D. M.—Rev. (1950)
  Rev. of Tillich The Protestant Era, (1948).
  Theology Today, 6 (1950), 551–552.
Baillie, John.—Rev. (1952)
  Rev. of Tillich, Systematic Theology, I (1951).
  Theology Today, 8 (1952), 566–568.
Bernhardt, William H.—Art. (1943)[1]
  "The Cognitive Quest for God."
  Jour. of Rel., 23 (1943), 91–102.
——— Art. (1943)[2]
  "God as Dynamic Determinant."
  Jour. of Rel., 23 (1943), 276–285.
Boozer, Jack.—PRTCG
  The Place of Reason in Paul Tillich's Conception of God.
  An unpublished dissertation in Boston University, 1952.
Bowne, Borden P.—PER
  Personalism.
  Boston: Houghton Mifflin Company, 1908.
Brightman, Edgar S.—ITP, Rev. ed.
  An Introduction to Philosophy
  New York: Henry Holt and Company, (1925) 1951.
——— POR
  Philosophy of Religion.
  New York: Prentice Hall, Inc., 1940.
Buckham, John Wright.—Art. (1935)
  "Religious Experience and Personality: A Reply to Professor Wieman."
  Jour. of Rel., 15 (1935), 309–315.
Calhoun, Robert L.—Art. (1936)[1]
  "God as More than Mind."
  Christendom, 1 (1936), 333–349.
——— Art. (1936)[2]
  "How Shall We Think of God?"
  Christendom, 1 (1936), 593–611.
——— Art. (1937)[1]
  "The Power of God and the Wisdom of God."
  Christendom, 2 (1937), 36–49.

——— Art. (1937)[2]
"A Final Statement."
Christendom, 2 (1937), 215–218.
——— Rev. (1939)
Rev. of Wieman and Horton, The Growth of Religion.
The Christian Century, 56 (1939), 152–154.
Demos, Raphael.—Rev. (1952)
Rev. of Tillich, Systematic Theology I, (1951).
Journal of Philosophy, 49 (1952), 692–708.
Dessoir, Max (ed.).—LDP
Lehrbuch der Philosophie.
Berlin: Verlag Ullstein, 1925.
Dewey, John.—EN
Experience and Nature.
Chicago: Open Court Publishing Co., 1925.
——— Rev. (1933)
Rev. of Morrison, Is There a God, (1932).
Christian Century, 40 (1933), 193–196.
——— CF
A Common Faith.
New Haven: Yale University Press, 1934.
DeWolf, L. Harold.—RRR
The Religious Revolt Against Reason.
New York: Harper and Brothers, 1949.
——— TLC
A Theology of the Living Church.
New York: Harper and Brothers, 1953.
Dubbs, H. H.—Art. (1931)
"The Problem of Evil—A Modern Solution."
Jour. of Rel., 11 (1931), 554–562.
——— Art. (1942)
"God in Modern Philosophies of Religion."
Religion in the Making, 3 (1942), 18–24.
——— Art. (1943)
"Religious Naturalism—An Evaluation."
Jour. of Rel., 23 (1943), 258–265.
Eckardt, A. R.—Rev. (1950)
Rev. of Tillich, The Protestant Era, (1948).
Jour. of Bib. and Rel., 18 (1950), 261–262.
Ferm, Vergilius (ed.).—CAT
Contemporary American Theology, I.
New York: Round Table Press, 1932.
——— (ed.).—EOR
An Encyclopedia of Religion.
New York: The Philosophical Library, 1945.
Harkness, Georgia.—Art. (1938)
"The Abyss and the Given."
Christendom, 3 (1938), 508–520.

15 Apr   Hartshorne, Charles, and William L. Reese.—PSG
1955   Philosophers Speak of God.
             Chicago: The University of Chicago Press, 1953.
          Hegel, Georg W. F.—POM
             The Phenomenology of Mind (tr. John B. Baillie) (Rev. ed.).
             New York: The Macmillan Company, (1910) 1931.
          Heinecken, R.—Rev. (1949)
             Rev. of Tillich, The Protestant Era, (1948).
             Lutheran Quarterly, 1 (1949), 471–472.
          Horton, Walter M.—Art. (1952)
             "Tillich's Role in Contemporary Theology."
             Kegley and Bretall (ed.), TPT, 26–47.
          Hough, L. H.—Rev. (1947)
             Rev. of Wieman, Source of Human Good, (1946).
             Christendom, 12 (1947), 105–106.
          Kantonen, R.—Rev. (1951)
             Rev. of Tillich, Systematic Theology, I (1951).
             Lutheran Quarterly, 3 (1951), 419–420.
          Kegley, Charles W., and Robert W. Bretall (ed.).—TPT
             The Theology of Paul Tillich.
             New York: The Macmillan Company, 1952.
          Kepler, Thomas S. (ed.).—CTAJ
             Contemporary Thinking About Jesus.
             New York: Abingdom-Cokesbury Press, 1944.
          Knudson, Albert C.—POP
             The Philosophy of Personalism.
             New York: The Abingdon Press, 1927.
          ——— DOG
             The Doctrine of God.
             New York: The Abingdon-Cokesbury Press, 1930.
          ——— Rev. (1951)
             Rev. of Tillich, Systematic Theology, I (1951).
             The Pastor, 14 (1951), 29.
          Loomer, Bernard M.—Art. (1948)
             "Neo-Naturalism and Neo-Orthodoxy."
             Jour. of Rel., 28 (1948), 79–91.
          Lotze, Herman.—MET
             Metaphysics (tr. E. Bosaquet), 2 vols.
             Oxford: The Clarendon Press, 1887.
          Macintosh, D. C. (ed.).—RR
             Religious Realism.
             New York: The Macmillan Company, 1931.
          ——— Art. (1932)
             "Is There a God?"
             Morrison (ed.). ITG, 21–29.
          Morrison, C. C. (ed.).—ITG
             Is There a God?
538   Chicago: Willett, Clark, and Co., 1932.

———— Rev. (1946)
　　Rev. of Wieman, <u>The Source of Human Good</u>, (1946).
　　<u>Christian Century</u>, 62 (1946), 1374–1376.
Outler, A. C.—Rev. (1951)
　　Rev. of Tillich, <u>Systematic Theology</u>, I (1951).
　　<u>Interpretation</u>, 5 (1951), 476–480.
Randall, John Herman.—Art. (1952)
　　"The Ontology of Paul Tillich."
　　Kegley and Bretall (ed.), TPT, 132–164.
Stanley, C. L.—Rev. (1951)
　　Rev. of Tillich, <u>Systematic Theology</u>, I (1951).
　　<u>Anglican Theological Review</u>, 33 (1951), 247–250.
Thomas, George F.—Art. (1952)
　　"The Method and Structure of Tillich's Theology."
　　Kegley and Bretall (ed.), TPT, 86–106.
Tillich, Paul.—Art. (1922)[1]
　　"Anthroposophie und Theologie."
　　<u>Theologische Blatter</u>, 1 (1922).
———— Art. (1922)[2]
　　"Kairos."
　　<u>Die Tat</u>, 14 (1922), 3303–350.
———— SGV
　　<u>Sammlung Gemeinverstandlicher Vortrage</u>.
　　Tubingen: Verlag S. C. B. Mohr, 1924.
———— Art. (1925)
　　"Religionsphilosophie."
　　Dessoir (ed.), LDP, 765–835.
———— Art. (1926)
　　"Der Begriff des Dämonsichen und seine Bedeutung für die Systematic
　　　　Theologie."
　　<u>Theologische Blätter</u>, 5 (1926).
———— Art. (1927)
　　"Eschatologie und Geschichte."
　　<u>Christliche Welt</u>, 22 (1927), 1034–1042.
———— RS
　　<u>The Religious Situation</u> (tr. H. R. Niebuhr).
　　New York: Henry Holt and Co., 1932.
———— Art. (1935)[1]
　　"What is Wrong with Dialectical Theology."
　　<u>Jour. on Rel.</u>, 15 (1935), 127–145.
———— Art. (1935)[2]
　　"Natural and Revealed Religion."
　　<u>Christendom</u>, 1 (1935), 158–170.
———— IOH
　　<u>The Interpretation of History</u> (tr. N. A. Rosetzki and Elsa L. Talmey).
　　New York: Charles Scribner's Sons, 1936.
———— Art. (1939)
　　"The Conception of Man in Existential Philosophy."
　　<u>Jour. of Rel.</u>, 19 (1939), 201–215.

15 Apr ——— Art. (1940)[1]
1955 "The Religious Symbol."
Journal of Liberal Rel., 2 (1940), 13–33.
——— Art.(1940)[2]
"The Idea of a Personal God."
Union Review, 2 (1940), 8–10.
——— Rev. (1940)
Rev. of Wieman and Horton, The Growth of Religion, 1938.
Jour. of Rel., 20 (1940), 69–72.
——— Art. (1941)[1]
"Philosophy and Theology."
Religion in Life 10 (1941), 21–30.
——— Art. (1941)[2]
"Existential Thinking in American Theology."
Rel. in Life, 10 (1941), 452–455.
——— Art. (1943)
"Flight to Atheism."
The Protestant, 4 (1943), 43–48.
——— Art. (1944)[1]
"The God as History."
Christianity and Crisis, 6 (1944), 5–6.
——— Art. (1944)[2]
"What is Divine Revelation?"
The Witness, 26 (1943), 8–9.
——— Art. (1944)[3]
"Christ as the Center of History."
Kepler (ed.), CTAJ, 217–222.
——— Art. (1944)[4]
"Depth."
Christendom, 9 (1944), 317–325.
——— Art. (1945)
"The Redemption of Nature."
Christendom, 10 (1945), 299–306.
——— Art. (1946)[1]
"The Nature of Man."
Jour. of Philosophy 43 (1946), 675–677.
——— Art. (1946)[2]
"The Two Types of Philosophies of Religion."
Union Seminary Quarterly Rev., 1 (May, 1946), 3–13.
——— Art. (1947)
"The Problem of the Theological Method."
Jour. of Rel., 27 (1947), 16–26.
——— SOF
The Shaking of the Foundations.
New York: Charles Scribner's Sons, 1948.
——— PE
The Protestant Era (tr. J. L. Adams).
Chicago: University of Chicago Press, 1948.

————— Art. (1949)[1]
"Beyond Religious Socialism."
Christian Century, 55 (1949), 732–733.

————— Art. (1949)[2]
"Fragment of an Ontology of Love."
Mimeographed copy.

————— Art. (1949)[3]
"A Misinterpretation of the Doctrine of Incarnation."
Church Quarterly Review, 147 (1949), 113–148.

————— Art. (1950)
"The New Being."
Rel. in Life, 19 (1950), 511–517.

————— ST
Systematic Theology I.
Chicago: The University of Chicago Press, 1951.

————— STP
Systematic Theology Propositions.
Mimeographed draft for class use. No date.

————— CTB
The Courage to Be.
New Haven: Yale University Press, 1952.

————— LPJ
Love Power, and Justice.
New York and London: Oxford University Press, 1954.

Urban, Wilbur M.—LR
Language and Reality.
London: George Allen and Unwin, Ltd., 1939.

————— Art. (1940)
"A Critique of Professor Tillich's Theory of the Religious Symbol."
Jour. of Liberal Rel., 2 (1940), 34–36.

Van Dusen, Henry P.—Art. (1931)
"How do we Know?"
Christian Century, 48 (1931), 711.

Weigle, Luther A.—Rev. (1936)
Rev. of Wieman and Wieman, Normative Psychology of Religion.
Jour. of Rel., 16 (1936), 227–229.

Whitehead, Alfred N.—AOI
Adventures of Ideas.
New York: The Macmillan Company, 1933.

Wieman, Henry Nelson.—Art. (1924)
"Experience, Mind and the Concept."
Jour. of Philosophy, 21 (1924), 561–567.

————— Art. (1925)[1]
"Religion in Dewey's Experience and Nature."
Jour. of Rel., 5 (1925), 519–544.

————— Art. (1925)[2]
"How do we Know God?"
Jour. of Rel., 5 (1925), 113–127.

15 Apr   ——— Art. (1926)
1955   "Values and the Individual."
     Jour. of Philosophy, 25 (1928), 233–239.
  ——— Rev (1927)
     Rev. of Whitehead, Religion in the Making.
     Jour. of Rel., 7 (1927), 487–490.
  ——— RESM
     Religious Experience and Scientific Method.
     New York: The Macmillan Co., 1927.
  ——— WRT
     The Wrestle of Religion with Truth.
     New York: The Macmillan Co., 1927.
  ——— Rev. (1928)
     Rev. of Knudson, The Philosophy of Personalism, (1927).
     Jour. of Rel., 8 (1928), 291–296.
  ——— MPRL
     Methods of Private Religious Living.
     New York: The Macmillan Co., 1929.
  ——— IOF
     The Issues of Life.
     New York: The Abingdon Press, 1930.
  ——— Rev. (1930)
     Rev. of Whitehead, Process and Reality.
     Jour. of Rel., 10 (1930), 137–139.
  ——— Art. (1930)
     "Right Ways to Justify Religion."
     The Christian Century, 47 (1939), 139–142.
  ——— Art. (1931)[1]
     "How Do We Know."
     The Christian Century, 48 (1931), 711–715.
  ——— Art. (1931)[2]
     "God, the Inescapable."
     The Christian Century, 48 (1931), 1170–1172, 1209–1221.
  ——— Art. (1931)[3]
     "God and Value."
     Macintosh (ed.), RR, 155–179.
  ——— Art. (1932)[1]
     "Theocentric Religion."
     Ferm (ed.), CAT, 339–351.
  ——— Art. (1932)[2]
     "Theocentric Religion."
     Religion in Life, 1 (1932), 102–114.
  ——— Art. (1932)[3]
     "Is There a God?"
     Morrison (ed.), ITG, 11–19; 43–53; 81–90; 117–128; 155–166; 195–207; 235–245; 275–286; 317–328.
  ——— and Regina Westcott-Wieman.—NPR
542   Normative Psychology of Religion.
     New York: Thomas Y. Crowell Company, 1935.

—— , and Bernard Eugene Meland.—APR
American Philosophies of Religion.
Chicago: Willett, Clark and Co., 1936.
—— Art. (1936)[1]
"Authority and the Normative Approach."
Jour. of Rel., 16 (1936), 175–202.
—— Art. (1936)[2]
"God is More Than We Can Think."
Christendom, 1 (1936), 428–442.
—— Art. (1936)[3]
"Faith and Knowledge."
Christendom, 1 (1936), 762–778.
—— Art. (1936)[4]
"Values: Primary Data for Religious Inquiry."
Jour. of Rel., 16 (1936), 379–405.
—— Art. (1937)
"The Absolute Commitment of Faith."
Christendom, 2 (1937), 202–214.
—— , and Walter Marshall Horton,—GOR
The Growth of Religion.
Chicago: Willett, Clark and Co., 1938.
—— Art. (1938)
"The New Supernaturalism."
Christendom, 3 (1938), 68–81.
—— Art. (1939)
"Some Blind Spots Removed."
The Christian Century, 56 (1939), 115–119.
—— Art. (1940)[1]
"On Using Christian Words."
Jour. of Rel., 20 (1940), 257–269.
—— Art. (1940)[2]
"What is Most Important in Christianity."
Religion In the Making, 1 (1940), 149–166.
—— Rev. (1941)
Rev. of Brightman, A Philosophy of Religion.
Jour. of Rel., 21 (1941), 197–200.
—— Art. (1941)
"Theology and the Philosophy of Religion."
Jour. of Liberal Rel., 2 (1941), 163–175.
—— Art. (1943)[1]
"Can God be Perceived."
Jour. of Rel., 23 (1943), 23–32
—— Art. (1943)[2]
"Perception and Cognition."
Jour. of Philosophy, 40 (1943), 73–77.
—— Art. (1943)[3]
"The Power and Goodness of God."
Jour. of Rel., 23 (1943), 266–276.

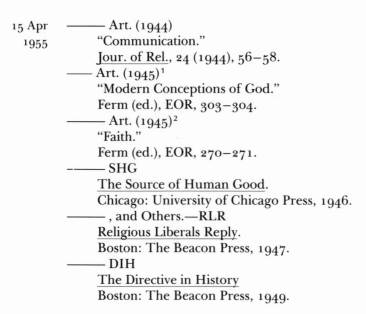

15 Apr
1955

——— Art. (1944)
"Communication."
Jour. of Rel., 24 (1944), 56–58.
—— Art. (1945)[1]
"Modern Conceptions of God."
Ferm (ed.), EOR, 303–304.
——— Art. (1945)[2]
"Faith."
Ferm (ed.), EOR, 270–271.
-——— SHG
The Source of Human Good.
Chicago: University of Chicago Press, 1946.
——— , and Others.—RLR
Religious Liberals Reply.
Boston: The Beacon Press, 1947.
——— DIH
The Directive in History
Boston: The Beacon Press, 1949.

TD. MLKP-MBU: Box 116.

A COMPARISON OF THE CONCEPTIONS OF GOD IN THE THINKING OF PAUL TILLICH AND HENRY NELSON WIEMAN

Abstract of a Dissertation

Submitted in partial fulfillment of the requirements
for the degree of Doctor of Philosophy

BOSTON UNIVERSITY GRADUATE SCHOOL

By

MARTIN LUTHER KING, Jr.

A.B., Morehouse College, 1948
B.D., Crozer Theological Seminary, 1951

Department: Systematic Theology
Major Instructor: Professor L. Harold DeWolf

1 9 5 5

Abstract of "A Comparison of the Conceptions of God in the Thinking of Paul Tillich and Henry Nelson Wieman"

[*15 April 1955*]
[*Boston, Mass.*]

A. Statement of Problem

The problem of this dissertation was to compare and evaluate the conceptions of God in the thinking of Paul Tillich and Henry Nelson Wieman.

The concept of God was chosen because of the central place which it occupies in any religion; and because of the ever-present need to interpret and clarify the God-concept. Tillich and Wieman were chosen because they represent different types of theology; and because each of them, in the last few years, has had an increasing influence upon theological and philosophical thought.

B. The Methods of Procedure

Several methods of procedure were employed in the investigation of the problem stated for this dissertation. First, the expository method was used. In this method the investigator sought to give a comprehensive and sympathetic exposition of the conceptions of God held by Wieman and Tillich. Second, the comparative method was employed. Here the thought of Wieman and Tillich was brought together with a view to determining their convergent and divergent points. Third, the critical method was employed. The investigator sought to give a critical evaluation of the conceptions of God held by Wieman and Tillich. In seeking to give this critical appraisal, two norms were employed: (i) adequacy in expressing the religious values of historic Christianity; and (ii) adequacy in meeting the requirements of consistency and coherence.

It was necessary to begin the study with a discussion of the methodologies of Tillich and Wieman, since the question of method is of such vital importance in theological and philosophical construction.

Throughout his theology Tillich undertakes the difficult task of setting forth a systematic theology which is at the same time an apologetic. The method used to effect this apologetic task is the "method of correlation." This method shows the interdependence between the ultimate questions to which philosophy is driven and the answers given in the Christian message. In this method question and answer determine each other. Philosophy and theology are not separated, and they are not identical, but they are correlated.

The method which Wieman employs is the "scientific method." He contends that this is the only method by which truth can be obtained, whether in the field of common sense, science, philosophy, or religion. The scientific method is defined as the method in which sensory observation, experimental behavior, and rational inference are working together. The methodologies of

545

Tillich and Wieman are quite antithetical at many points. Wieman's scientific method is basically naturalistic. Tillich's method of correlation seeks to overcome the conflict between the naturalistic and supernaturalistic methods.

It was necessary to begin the exposition of Tillich's conception of God with a discussion of his ontology as a whole, since it is his ultimate conviction that God is "being-itself." It was also necessary to include a section on Wieman's theory of value in the exposition of his conception of God, since he holds that God is supreme value and supreme source of value.

C. Conclusions

The following theses may be stated as conclusions drawn from this investigation of the conceptions of God in the thinking of Tillich and Wieman.

1. Tillich's basic and most persistent definition of God is "being-itself," esse ipsum. In affirming that God is being-itself, Tillich is denying that God is a being beside other beings. In this conception he intends to convey the idea of power of being. God is the power of being in everything and above everything.

2. Wieman's basic definition of God is the "creative event." This definition is an amplification of what Wieman means when he speaks of God as growth. He further defines God as "supreme value" and as "the unlimited connective growth of value-connections." But these definitions seem to have three different meanings. When Wieman characterizes God as "supreme value" he seems to mean the ideal of perfection or of the achievement of maximum value. When he speaks of God as "the unlimited connective growth of value-connections" he seems to mean the human and social processes which aim at the achievement of value. When he describes God as the creative event he seems to mean the natural forces underlying the achievement of value. These three meanings cannot be viewed as constituting a unity except in a highly figurative sense, and positively not for a consistently empirical religious philosophy. At this point Wieman has failed to be consistently empirical.

3. Both Tillich and Wieman agree that God is an undeniable reality. They are so convinced of the reality of God that they would dismiss all arguments for his existence as futile and invalid. They further agree in seeking to assure the reality of God through the definition of God. But in attempting to formulate the idea of God so as to make the question of his existence a dead issue, Tillich and Wieman have given up much that is most essential from the religious point of view in the idea of God. Both sacrifice too much for the sake of getting rid of a troublesome question.

4. Both Tillich and Wieman deny the category of personality to God. They think that to refer to God as a person is to limit him. This denial of personality to God does not mean, they insist, that God is impersonal. Instead of being impersonal or sub-personal, God is supra-personal. Despite their warnings that God is not less than personal, however, we have seen traits throughout their thinking that point to a God that is less than personal. Wieman's God is an interaction, that is, a behavior-process. He is not a concrete object or a continuing entity. In short, he is an unconscious process devoid of any true purpose. Tillich's "being-itself" is little more than a sub-personal reservoir of

power. In this respect Tillich's thought is somewhat akin to the impersonalism of Oriental Vedantism. "Being-itself" is a pure absolute, devoid of consciousness and life.

5. Wieman's naturalistic position causes him to place great emphasis on the immanence of God. Like everything else that exists, God is found within the natural order. Whatever transcendence God has is seen to arise out of his very immanence in the world of events. There is much in Tillich's view that comes close to the naturalistic position. He revolts against the view that there is a world behind the world. The Divine does not inhabit a transcendent world above nature; it is found in the "ecstatic" character of this world as its transcendent depth and ground.

6. Tillich's desire to protect the majesty of God and his complex ontological analysis cause him to stress the transcendence of God as much as his immanence. He finds a basis for God's transcendence in the conception of God as abyss. There is a basic inconsistency in Tillich's thought at this point. On the one hand he speaks as a religious naturalist making God wholly immanent in nature. On the other hand he speaks as an extreme supernaturalist making God almost comparable to the Barthian "wholly other."

7. Tillich and Wieman have at the forefront of their thinking a deep theocentric concern. Both are convinced that God is the most significant Fact in the universe. This theocentric concern leads Tillich and Wieman to the further assertion that God is not man. They see a qualitative difference between God and man.

8. Tillich and Wieman are at one in rejecting the traditional formulations of the attributes of God. Tillich goes beyond Wieman, however, by seeking to set forth the qualitative and symbolic meaning of the attributes.

9. Tillich includes within the divine life both temporality and eternality. Wieman's stress is on the temporality of God. His failure to emphasize the factor of permanence in the idea of God weakens Wieman's doctrine of God at many points. It leaves a God who is the increaser of value without being the conserver of value. In such a situation, value-experience becomes meaningless.

10. The most important words in Tillich's conception of God are "power" and "being." The most important words in Wieman's conception of God are "goodness" and "value." Wieman's basic emphasis is axiological while Tillich's is ontological. Both Wieman and Tillich are partially correct in what they affirm, but partially wrong in what they deny. Both overstress one aspect of the divine nature to the neglect of another basic aspect. Tillich places an undue emphasis on being to the neglect of value; Wieman places an undue emphasis on value to the neglect of being. A more adequate view is to maintain that both value and being are basic in the meaning of God; each blending with the other neither being reduced to the other.

11. Both Tillich and Wieman reject the traditional doctrine of creation. For neither of them is there a super-natural being before and above all beings as their creator.

12. Tillich and Wieman are finitistic theists. However, they differ in one significant respect: in Wieman's conception the limitation to God's power is external to his nature, while in Tillich's thought the limitation is an aspect within God's nature.

13. Wieman holds to an ultimate pluralism, both quantitative and qualita-

tive. Tillich, on the other hand, holds to an ultimate monism, both qualitative and quantitative. Both of these views have been found to be inadequate. Wieman's ultimate pluralism fails to satisfy the rational demand for unity. Tillich's ultimate monism swallows up finite individuality in the unity of being. A more adequate view is to hold a quantitative pluralism and a qualitative monism. In this way both oneness and manyness are preserved.

PD. MLKP-MBU: Box 2.

From Samuel D. Proctor

18 April 1955
Richmond, Va.

Proctor confirms his plan to preach at Dexter's Spring Lecture Series.

Rev. M. L. King, Jr.
309 South Jackson Street
Montgomery, Alabama

Dear Rev. King:

I am expecting to be with you on the 27th, 28th, and 29th of April. I will be coming to Montgomery from Baton Rouge, Louisiana and it is impossible now to give the exact travel plans. There is a direct airline connection which makes it simple, but I have not bothered to get reservations from this far away.

Best wishes on your final examinations for your degree. As we say in Virginia, I am "tickled to death" over this.

Best regards,
[*signed*] Samuel D. Proctor/mem
Samuel D. Proctor, Dean
School of Religion

SDP: mem

TLSr. MLKP-MBU: Box 117.

From H. Edward Whitaker

19 April 1955
Niagara Falls, N.Y.

Whitaker notes that his church program has "involved people of all the races and nationalites and faiths" and invites King to visit. He also mentions his discussion of King's "Recommendations" for Dexter's governance with Sandy Ray, a friend of King, Sr.

Dear Mike,

For quite a long while I have been trying to get around to replying to your letter which you were so kind to respond to immediately upon my previous writing. We are getting along somehow and our work here is progressing nicely in so far as it pertains to our building program, but the situation is still ver precarious. I really don't know what to expect in the next six months, but I am sure that at least I have this year to continue my ministry here. It may well be that after that time things will straighten themselves out fairly well. I would like to have things to end here very satisfactory.

In the meantime I am counting on you keeping your eyes open in those parts for anything that you think I might be able to fit in, and of course I shall be glad to do everything I can to hold up the standards.

One of the chief difficulties involved in many of the churches in this part of the country is that as it relates to the newness of the community. During the war, many persons migrated from other sections of the country with varied background, and here we find them involved in the program of the same church, promoting the ideas from their various areas from which they have come. They have certain loyalties, and they find themselves seeking to work only with certain groups, especially those persons who have come from their particular locale. This brings about a great deal of confusion sometimes. Rather than to seek to cooperate on the basis of something being right or wrong, good or bad, many support issues or reject them merely because we did not do this at home.

But aside from the many problems, something has been accomplished here for which of course I cannot begin to take credit for, although it did not happen until I came. I am confident that it has been the hand of God, and I am grateful that I have had some small part to play in it. Our program here has involved people of all the races and nationalities and faiths. It is a community wide effort and yet this is a Baptist church in the truest sense. I certainly would like to have you come up and see the development. So I am going to renew the the ~~invivt~~ invitation to have you come in the first week in November to give a series of sermons in connection with our mass evangelistic program. With our mortgage ~~olbi~~ obligations we will be in a position to do only part of what we would like to do, but if you could afford to come and give us a hand, I am sure we can make it worth your while. Of course we would be very happy to have you to bring the Madam since we have not met ~~here~~ her.

I do hope that your work is going well there and that everything is turning out the way you planned it. I was talking the other day with Dr. Sandy Ray and he mentioned you. We were discussing your program which you submitted to the church last year, and agreed that you were really going out after it. We are pulling for you and hope that everything will work out satisfactory. I am sure that what many of the churches need in the south is a program that will in effect be a shot in the arm. Dr. Ray is the President of our State Convention and was in our area speaking in connection with that work.

We have one or two fellows coming in our area now who will be quite an asset to the religious life of Western New York.

Well take it easy Mike and let me hear from you sometime when you are not too busy. Hope to see you before long. Kind regards and best wishes, I remain

Sincerely,
[*signed*] Whit
H. Edw. Whitaker

TLS. MLKP-MBU: Box 117.

From H. Councill Trenholm

2 May 1955
Montgomery, Ala.

Trenholm, president of Alabama State College and a deacon at Dexter, invites King to give the baccalaureate sermon at Alabama State's commencement.[1] King accepted the invitation.[2]

Dr. M. L. King, Jr.
303 S. Jackson Street
Montgomery, Alabama

IN RE: Sunday Afternoon, May 15

Dear Dr. King:

I herewith extend to you the invitation to serve as the baccalaureate minister for our 1955 May commencement on Sunday afternoon, May 15, at 3:30 at the College Gymnasium.

At that time we will have approximately 300 candidates for the baccalaureate degree and possibly 8 candidates for the master of education degree. The nineteen candidates for the senior high school diploma also share that baccalaureate service although their graduation is not until May 27.

From the enclosed copy of the program of last year, you will note the organization of the program. We have just the brief "atmosphere program" preceding your message. We also "introduce you" through the statement on the program for which we will ask Mr. Brooks to obtain the necessary information. It is our pleasure to have our baccalaureate minister to share the recep-

---

1. Harper Councill Trenholm (1900–1963) received his A.B. from Morehouse in 1920 and his baccalaureate in philosophy from the University of Chicago in 1921. He was president of Alabama State College from 1925 to 1960.

2. Trenholm to King, Jr., 15 May 1955, MLKP-MBU: Box 117, confirms participation.

tion to the graduates and we shall be hopeful that it will be convenient for you and Mrs. King to share that occasion.

We should like also to extend to you and Mrs. King the invitation to be our house guests for the dinner courtesy preceding the exercises and at such hour as may be most acceptable in relation to your obligations for that day.

I also take this occasion to extend congratulations upon your having completed the work for your doctor's degree.

Pleased to look forward to your reply in confirmation of the preliminary indication which you made in my requested exploratory conversation through Mr. Brooks, I am

Yours very truly,
[*signed*]
H. Councill Trenholm

HCT:A

cc: Mr. J. T. Brooks

TLS. MLKP-MBU: Box 117.

From Walter R. McCall

6 May 1955
Fort Valley, Ga.

McCall describes his plan to build a soda shop at Fort Valley State College and says that he may ask King for a loan. King's response is not documented.

Dear Mike,

At last, I have an opportunity to sit down and write a letter! Boy! I have been a busy fellow: Work! Work! everywhere I turn, but things have slowed down a bit now. In spite of things being in a whirl, I have no reason to complain, I guess.

Hope things are going your way. I wanted to drop in on you on last Sunday past, but I discovered that I was too far off the Montgomery route from Talladega, therefore I had to take the shortest route back. Had an exceedingly good time there, as ever. By the way, I recommended you to Dr. J. R. Pross, Dean of Philosophy and Psychology and Head of Chaplaincy at Talladega. You may hear from him relative to speaking there. He is a very fine fellow. He and his wife holds the Ph.D. degree in philosophy from the University of Chicago. I hope that you both get to know each other.

By the way, I have gone a long way on the plans for constructing the College Soda Shop here: Have bought six thousand dollars ($6,000.00) worth of equipment, and will pick it up on Saturday. It is bought on a good bargain.

Fellow is going out of business in downtown Atlanta, and has a whole completely furnished-elaborately furnished drug stroe, and he is giving me everything we need to equip our place. So, I have already bought a 50 gal tank, soda fountain 12 ft. long, bar bar, mirror; steamer with 8 holes; meat ei slicer (electric), cash register (electric), coke dispenser, 12 lights (neon), 150 pots, pans, knives, forks, plates, etc., 3 show cases, a whole side of enclosed shelves—a whlae of a lot of stuff—much more than I can name off hand. At any rate, I have bought every piece of equipment and fixture the business needs from him. He is the brother of a local druggist of this city, with whom I am very familar. Every iota is completed for building, so as soon as we go to Atlanta and pick the stuff up and get the measurements on the drain pipes on the fountain and steamer etc. the building will be underway. Hope to complete it by the last of July, but if at all possible by the last of June. It will be a dream, though a somewhat small place—only 35' × 50'. All plans are completed to stock it up as soon as it is completed. I will be a happy fellow when this is completed, as I am putting a lot of blood, sweat, tears, and dollars in it. Though we are getting out very cheaply.

Look out, I may call upon you for a small loan of two or three hundred bucks in June until Christmas of this year—really. Of course, I will pay you interest on it. Mike there is a dire need for this kind of business here, and I am absolutely sure that it will go in a big way here as we have the clientele and have the best possible location in town—just behind the Academic buld bildi building with only a street dividing it from the college campus! I am trying like Hell to build as I am young so by the time I am a bit older these investments will pay off. I plan to go back to school next year, or the year after. I hope to study for two or three straight years before stopping. Let me mention another factor or so about this business as I think it's important: three of us are in it: a Maddox who was in Morehouse along with us for a while, but left to study photography in Connecticut, and has a studio here; he owns the land and is giving us a 15 yrs. lease on it free from rent for the first five years. Good! I have bought more than an acre of land which is being used now as a basis of foodstuff for the business free from rent for the first five yrs. As Maddox is giving us an option on the renewal of the lease after 15 yrs., I also am giving the owners an option on the land I own after the first 5 yrs. for renewal of release. The other fellow is a young buck in our age category (27 yrs.), as Maddox and I are the same age. This fellow's wife holds the Ph.D. degree and works on here at the college, as professor of sec. education! Each has a good reputation in the town, and is sober in all conduct and thinking. We have the business so organized that no one can infringe upon the rights of the other. It is legally constructed. We all will be a batch of proud JACK ASSES when this thing is finished.

By the way, Norma is in school down here, and is in my class! Why don't you and Coretta spend a week or so here with me in the Summer? Will look for you.

Remember, Doctor, I may wish to borrow that sum from you in June. I am struggling! Don't worry, I will be able to loan you a few thousand in a few years! Watch me.

Best wishes, OLE TIMER, and a bigh hello to Coretta, and my good ac- quaintances there.

A Pal,
[*signed*]
Mac.

TLS. MLKP-MBU: Box 117.

From Melvin H. Watson

6 May 1955
Atlanta, Ga.

Reverend M. L. King, Jr., Pastor
Dexter Avenue Baptist Church
Dexter Avenue at Decatur Street
Montgomery, Alabama

Dear Doctor (elect):

Things happen in peculiar ways sometime. I had already composed a letter to you when yours arrived this morning. It was just a word to express Agnes' and my deep satisfaction in the knowledge that you have now jumped over the last hurdle necessary to the achievement of the doctoral goal. We are both very happy that this milestone in your career has been reached at what is indeed a young age. That you and Coretta need to rest is easy to understand.

Against my better judgment the check which you were kind enough to en- close in your letter has been given to my wife. Experience has taught me that when I spend her money, it is generally more <u>wisely</u> spent. She will probably send you a note on her own later.

I wrote Dean Frank T. Wilson of the School of Religion, Howard University, and requested that your name be included on the Institute mailing list and he returned a favorable reply.

With every good wish to you and Miss Coretta, I am

Sincerely yours,
[*signed*]
Melvin Watson

TLS. MLKP-MBU: Box 117.

From William A. Bell

11 May 1955
Sheppard AFB, Tex.

*Bell, a member of Ebenezer Baptist Church, graduated from Morehouse College in
1950. In this letter from Sheppard Air Force Base he discusses his plan to return
to Atlanta.*

Hello M. L. :

Hope this letter finds you and your wife well and in the best of health.
Virginia and I are doing fine at the present time, but still anxiously counting
the days until my separation from the Service, so that again we can be on our
way back to Atlanta! Do you know that we have not been there since March
of 1953? Boy, that is certainly a long time. I can hardly imagine what the place
must look like at this time. All I know is that we will be greatly overjoyed to
go back there.

We received your letter a couple of days ago, and were more than pleased
to learn that you are doing so well. But, it is no more than was expected by
us. We are still undecided as to what route we will be taking going back to
Atlanta, as I am still awaiting a letter from Atlanta U. as to when I will have
to report for my Field Work assignment. If it should happen to be the first of
September, as I am afraid it will be, then we will probably have to forego any
stops we might have been anticipating. If I shouldn't have to report until a
later date than anticipated, then we will be going by way of San Antonio, and
possibly a trip through Montgomery. We sure hope that this is possible, as we
do so want to meet your wife, and see your Church, as we have heard so much
about it and the fine work you are doing through the family.

We took a brief trip this past weekend to San Antonio to visit Charles Price
and his wife Gwendolyn—perhaps you remember some of the Prices that
were at the 'House—who last week had another addition to their family. They
had a boy, which is their third child. Virginia wanted to go down there, as she
and "Gwen" are quite friendly, so I had to drive her down. As it turned out,
we had quite a nice time. But I suppose after living in this place for awhile,
any town would be quite a pleasant change. This town is about the closest
thing to nothing that I have ever seen! If you could visit here you would see
what I mean. And the people here don't seem to be progressive at all! I sure
hope they will change, or they will be in pretty sad shape before long.

I guess this is about all for now, as I must get back to work before I get
"fired" (smile). If the opportunity should avail itself drop us a line. We will be
looking to hear from you, and as soon as I hear from A.U. I will let you know
if we will be able to come by there.

[*signed*]
WILLIAM A BELL

TLS. MLKP-MBU: Box 117.

J. Raymond Henderson
to Martin Luther King, Sr.

12 May 1955
Los Angeles, Calif.

Henderson became friends with King, Sr., while serving as pastor of Wheat Street Baptist Church in Atlanta during the 1930s.[1] Henderson later moved to Los Angeles to become pastor of Second Baptist Church. Henderson encloses a letter to King, Jr.

Rev. M. L. King, Sr.
169 Boulevard, N.E.
Atlanta, Ga.

Dear Brother King:

They told me you have a son that can preach rings around you any day you ascend the pulpit. How about that? If it is so, it is a compliment to you. I hope you are well and that your work moves on nicely. The Lord has been good to the work here. I am deeply grateful. I hope to see you in Atlantic City at the Congress.[2]

Please address enclosure and mail to M. L., Jr. at Montgomery. Best wishes to your dear wife.

Fraternally,
[*signed*]
J. Raymond Henderson

encl.

TLS. MLKP-MBU: Box 117.

---

1. J. Raymond Henderson (1898–1985) graduated from Virginia Union University, Oberlin College, and Andover-Newton Theological Seminary. After serving churches in New York, Pennsylvania, and West Virginia he was called to Atlanta's Wheat Street Baptist Church, where he remained from 1931 to 1937. In 1937, he became pastor of Bethesda Baptist Church in New Rochelle, New York, but soon moved to Second Baptist Church in Los Angeles, California, the largest Baptist congregation in the city. By 1953 its social ministry had built the Henderson Community Center, which housed a day nursery, a home for the aged, two dormitories for working women, and a recreation building. Several years after King led a week-long revival at Second Baptist, Henderson chose King as his first choice to succeed him as pastor. King declined the call. See Velva Henderson to King Papers Project, 3 July 1990.

2. King attended the National Baptist Sunday School and Baptist Training Union Congress that met in Atlantic City, New Jersey, in June.

From J. Raymond Henderson

12 May 1955
Los Angeles, Calif.

Rev. M. L. King, Jr.

Dear Young Brother:

Do you plan to attend the Congress in Atlantic City? If so, let me know at once and I'll try to arrange a preaching engagement for you. I have had you much in my thoughts and prayers from time to time. You have a great heritage in your grandfather and father. I understand you are developing into a good preacher in your own right.

Remain careful of your conduct. Steer away from "trashy" preachers. Be worthy of the best. It may come to you some day. Write to me, and send me one of your bulletins. Best wishes.

Yours fraternally,
[*signed*]
J. Raymond Henderson

TLS. MLKP-MBU: Box 117.

Martin Luther King, Sr., to J. Raymond Henderson

16 May 1955

Dr. J. Raymond Henderson
Second Baptist Church
Griffith Ave at 24th Street
Los Angles 11, California

My dear Brother Henderson:

You have every right to believe me to be an ingrate. I received your church calendar back in January which I thought was very uniquely planned. It was my fullest intention to write you at that particular time, but somehow I mislaid the letter, thus the delay.

I am now in receipt of your letter, both to M. L. Jr and me. Thanks so much for your fine encouraging words concerning my son. He is very fond of you and speaks often of you and your work. He has completed all requirement for his Ph.D which is to be conferred the First Sunday June 5th. The information you received is correct, he can preach rings around me any day. But being a father yourself you know how ~~happ;~~ happy this makes me feel. Frankly Joe, he <u>is somebodys preacher</u>, and yet hs is but a lad. He delivered the Baccalaurate yesterday at Alabama State. They tell me he swept. He is already in great demand. Continue to pray for us for there is always a need. As you know the devil can clip one so easily. I am forwarding the letter on to M. L. that you sent. I am sure you will hear from him in a few days.

I keep hearing that oldest son of yours is a genius in music. Certainly that makes parents proud when their children do well. Many congratulations and good luck.

When ever you are coming this way drop me a line, we shall be happy to have you preach at Ebenezer. Glad to know that the work is moving on in a fine way at Second Baptist. We are just about to get underway with the erection of our Christian Education Bldg. It is a job I dread for I had hope to have gotten through with this ten years ago. As you know we were held up because of land. We were finally able to purchase the Big Bethel AM.E. Church parsonage, immediately next door to our church building.

It is always good to hear from you and to know your whereabouts My entire family joins me in sending warmest regards to you, Mrs. Henderson and the children.

With every great wish,

Most cordially yours,
M. L. King Sr.

TLc. EBCR.

From L. Harold DeWolf

28 May 1955
Boston, Mass.

Dear Martin:

This is terribly late to be writing this letter, but perhaps you will forgive me in view of the fact that my daughter is to be married on June 23rd, we leave the next day for fourteen months abroad and we have been passing through an unusually crowded finishing of the University year.

Madeleine and I hope that we are not too late to find you able to accept an invitation for supper with us on the evening of Commencement Day, June 5th. We mean, of course, to invite both you and your wife. I hope she can be with you for the big day.

I have just recommended you for a college teaching position in a western school. You may not feel free to leave your church so soon, you might not want the place if offered and different officials of the college already have other candidates in mind. However, it would be a good place to break into the college field if it should open and you were free to take it.

Most cordially yours,
[*signed*] Harold.

TLS. MLKP-MBU: Box 117.

From Duncan E. MacDonald

31 May 1955
Boston, Mass.

Mr. Martin L. King, Jr.
309 South Jackson St.,
Montgomery, Alabama

Dear Mr. King,

I am glad to be able to report that the Faculty of the Graduate School, at their meeting held today, voted to recommend you to the Trustees for the degree of Doctor of Philosophy, which will be conferred at Commencement.

Please accept my personal congratulations.

Sincerely yours,
[*signed*]
Duncan E. MacDonald
Dean

TLS. MLKP-MBU: Box 117.

From Major J. Jones

[*May 1955*]
Boston, Mass.

Having just taken his qualifying examinations at Boston University, Jones asks whether King would attend the graduation ceremony. King remained in Montgomery.

Dear Dr. King, Ph.D.

This is just a note to say that I will be there for the week end of the 12th of June. If that is not a good Sunday for you I will have to come on another occasion of a visit to the fair city of Atlanta.

Things are going well with me here and I am not so sure how long they will be so. They examined me on May the 9th and I have you to know they did just that too. Don't you tell me anything about B. U. any more. I don't know what the man was thinking about when he made that exam. I have never taken anything like that before in all my life. I have not had the word as yet as to what I did, but I do hope I made it. I don't want to go through that again.

Other than that I am going on with the other work. I don't have any axams so I can get to work on my dissertation as soon as I get the word. I hope to get a lot of the word done by the end of the Summer so that I might be able to get it over with this next year.

Well, think of it Dr. and let me hear from you. Are you going to come up for the graduation? I know you said you did not know as you would when you were here last. I suppose when you do get the thing out of the way you don't care for anything but that you have done all of this work. But those 35 books really did me in, but I got them read some kind of way. I don't know yet how.

Tell you more about it when I see you. Tell all Hi!

Very truly yours,
[*signed*]
Major

TLS. MLKP-MBU: Box 117.

From Major J. Jones

[*June 1955*]

Jones reports that he delivered photographs of King to the Graduate School for placement in King's dissertation.

Hello Martin,

This is just a note to say that I went over and got the photos in the dissertation. The lady in the office of the Graduate School helped me to get them in, and after I did so she checked them and said they were Ok!

When I sent you my last letter I had not heard from my comprehensives, I have now come to the the last two things, My dissertation and the exam. on that. I was sure glad to get that exam. out of the way.

I will see you on the second Sunday. As I can see it now, I will be coming down that Sat. Mor. I will let you know more of my plans later. But just now these are how they stand now.

Give my love to all.

Major

TL. MLKP-MBU: Box 117.

From L. Harold DeWolf

4 June 1955
Boston, Mass.

Dr. Martin Luther King
309 South Jackson Street
Montgomery, Alabama

Dear Martin,

Although you are not Dr. King as I write you will be long before this letter arrives, so I address you according to the degree you have earned and which will be conferred tomorrow.

I greatly regret, as does my wife also, that you will be unable to be here. We especially regret that this means also that we shall not have the opportunity to meet your wife just now. I understand the reasons very well and hope that before many years some opportunity may offer itself to bring the four of us together in Boston or elsewhere.

Thank you for the generous comment about my teaching and our personal relationships. I shall be deeply interested in following both your professional and your personal career and the fortunes of your new family.

I should be very happy to hear from you in Africa. My address there will be: Old Umtali, P. O. Box 24, Umtali, Southern Rhodesia.

I expect splendid achievements from you and shall always regard you with high appreciation and pride.

Fraternally yours,
[*signed*] Harold DeWolf.

TLS. MLKP-MBU: Box 117.

From Archibald James Carey, Jr.

7 June 1955
Chicago, Ill.

Carey, pastor of Chicago's Quinn Chapel AME Church and a prominent Republican politician, thanks King for the hospitality extended him during Carey's visit to Montgomery.[1] Carey spoke at a 1 June citizenship rally sponsored by the local chapter of the Alpha Phi Alpha fraternity. King gave the benediction at the rally.

---

1. Archibald James Carey, Jr. (1908–1981), received his B.A. from Lewis Institute in Chicago in 1929 and his B.D. from Northwestern University's Garrett Biblical Institute in 1932. In 1935 he received his law degree from Chicago-Kent College of Law, and he was admitted to the Illinois

Reverend M. L. King   7 June
309 Jackson   1955
Montgomery, Alabama

Dear M. L.:

I can't tell you how very much I enjoyed the afternoon and night that I spent with you and your charming wife, Coretta and the distinguished Dr. M. L., Sr., when I came to speak at Alabama State College. I had no idea, when I approached the campus, that I was going to be in a good, old fashioned "preachers' meeting", in addition. But it was most enjoyable to reminisce and reflect and prognosticate (how'm I doing?) with you and your dad.

When you write him, please give him my kind regards and please tell your wife how much I appreciate every courtesy that both of you showed me so graciously. Remember, you have a pulpit in Chicago whenever you are coming this way and, meanwhile, I hope to see you again (either two or three of you—and I don't mean your dad) before too long.[2]

Very sincerely,
[*signed*] Arch.

AJC:gt

TLS. MLKP-MBU: Box 117.

From Daniel W. Wynn

7 June 1955
Tuskegee, Ala.

Wynn, a fellow graduate of Boston University and chaplain of Tuskegee Institute, asks King to preach there on 31 July 1955.[1] King's sermon topic was "The Three Dimensions of a Complete Life."

---

bar the next year. From 1930 to 1949 he served as pastor of Woodlawn AME Church in Chicago. In 1949 he became pastor of Chicago's Quinn Chapel AME Church, where he served until 1967. He was elected alderman of Chicago's Third Ward in 1947 and 1951, and was the Republican nominee for the First Congressional District in 1950. In January 1955 President Dwight David Eisenhower appointed Carey vice-chair of the President's Committee on Government Employment Policy. In 1966, after changing his party affiliation to the Democratic party, he was elected a circuit court judge in Cook County, Illinois.

2. Coretta Scott King was four months pregnant at the time.

1. Daniel Webster Wynn (1919–) graduated from Langston University in Oklahoma in 1941 and received the B.D. and M.A. from Howard University in 1944 and 1945, respectively. He   561

28 June
1955
Dr. W. L. King, Pastor
Dexter Avenue Baptist Church
Montgomery, Alabama

Dear Dr. King,

   Kindly advise if you can deliver the sermon in the Tuskegee Institute Chapel on Sunday morning, July 31, 1955 at eleven o'clock. The service lasts one hour. About twenty-five minutes are alloted to the speaker.

   Our summer chapel attendance consists primarily of in-service teachers as well as our regular students, staff members, and friends.

   We can offer you an honorarium of $35.00 for this service.

Sincerely yours,
[*signed*]
Daniel W. Wynn
Chaplain

DWW:mb

TLS. MLKP-MBU: Box 48.

To Benjamin Elijah Mays

28 June 1955
Montgomery, Ala.

Dr. B. E. Mays, President
Morehouse College
Atlanta, Georgia

Dear Dr. Mays:

   This is just a note to let you know we are looking forward with great anticipation to your coming to us as Men's Day Speaker at the 11:00 o'clock service on the second Sunday in July. Please let me know how you will be traveling and what time you will arrive.

---

received the Ph.D. from Boston University in 1954, a year before King. He was dean of religion at Bishop College in Marshall, Texas, from 1947 until 1953, when he became acting chaplain of Tuskegee Institute for a year. He was then dean of students at Langston University for a year before returning to Tuskegee as chaplain in 1955. After ten years of service at Tuskegee he became associate director, division of higher education, for the Board of Higher Education and Ministry of the United Methodist Church, where he remained until 1976. His publications include *The NAACP Versus Negro Revolutionary Protest: A Comparative Study of the Effectiveness of Each Movement*, based on his doctoral dissertation (1955); *Moral Behavior and the Christian Ideal* (1961); *Timeless Issues* (1967); and *The Black Protest Movement* (1974).

I am off now to the National Baptist Congress. I will be returning to Montgomery by Tuesday or Wednesday of next week. With every good wish, I am

Sincerely yours,
[*signed*]
M. L. King, Jr.

MLK:cpc

TLS. BEMP-DHU: Box 16.

From Major J. Jones

[*June 1955*]
Boston, Mass.

Jones stayed with the King family in Montgomery during the second week of June and returned to Boston to write his dissertation. Jones mentions other members of the black graduate student community in Boston, including Wayman "Mac" McLaughlin and Philip Lenud, King's former roommate.

Dear Friends:

May I take this time to say how nice it was to have had a week end in your home and church. It was sure nice to be there with you people for a few days, and more than that to see that you are doing so very well there at Dexter. It was a real inspiration to me to see your great success. I also think that you have a great opportunity there and that you are making a great contribution to Alabama.

I checked with the man about the dissertation, he said that he had sent it to you. But if you have not recieved it I will go back by there and see what has come of it. But he would not have me say that he had not sent it. I did not press the issue because I thought that you may have recieved it by now. Please let me know if you have not.

Well, at the time I was there I had to not say what my plans were about marriage this summer. But now that I am sure you people are on my list of letter writing. Mattie and I are to be married some time the last of the summer. We will let you know more of our plans later. I was not so sure when I was there. But since I am back here and things went well with me in other respects we have made plans.

The work here is going on, I hope, to be completed with this reading and the like and have that copy fairly put together by the last of August. Other than that I do not know what I will be doing this fall as I have not had any word for sure about a job.

Mac was by today and he said that he got by his exams ok and has nothing to do now but his writing. He is happy about that thing too. He really would have liked to had his degree with you. It rather hurt him that he did not get it with you. But things look bright for him now. We are trying to make it next June.

I suppose you will see Phil there in A.C. and he will bring you up on much of the news. He was by today and told me he was to be there this or next week.

Take care of things now and I will see you before the summer is over. I hope that things will go well with you and that all will be good for the little one to come.

Very truly yours,
[*signed*]
Major

TLS. MLKP-MBU: Box 117.

From J. Pius Barbour

21 July 1955
Chester, Pa.

King had invited Barbour to participate in Dexter's Spring Lecture Series on 27–29 April 1956. Barbour accepts the invitation for a different Sunday, 15 April; he gave a sermon and three lectures on 15–17 April 1956. Barbour reports on the progress of his building campaign at Calvary Baptist Church in Chester, Pennsylvania.

Dear Mike:

April 29th is my Women's Day and I am in the midst of a building programme and I have to stick around on these financial days. I can come of the Third Sunday In April if you can arrange it. Then too I wonder if I am your man. I am distinctly a "preacher's preacher" and a college lecture man. I can preach "Mob-sermons" but I cant lecture to mobs. I am filled up with three lectures:

(1) Should we open the Canon? . this deals with adding to the Bible and Revelation.
(2) Has Marx outmoded the Christian Ethic? . this deals with the historical process.
(3) Is the Baptist Church Doomed? . this deals with the New concept of the Church.

Now I cant make any more preparation as I am filled with the above and I have always stuck to one rule: Fill yourself up with some deep stuff and stick to it until it is out of your system. I heard Proctor on "success". Trite! Trite!

Trite! for a "TH.D."[1] (See my article on the New England Convention in the "Voice" I am sending you.) Now think on these things and write me your conclusions.

My annex is finished . . . the hottest thing on the Eastern seaboard. Paid sixty-two thousand <u>CASH</u>, have'nt borrowed one penny. Now I will turn the Church into a Catholic Sanctuary. This will cost fortyfive {thosa} thousand and the furnishings twenty five thousand. I will sweat the Spooks and then BORROW to finish. I have it all planned and it is working as a clock.

I put a colonial front on and The white folks are eating me {up} as you know the Church is on the high way and they see it. The Banks are calling me to LEND me money! How is that? I raised $,4,024.00 Sunday July 17th, the hottest day of the year and the "Spooks" were standing around the wall. Besides I have taken in 114 members since December and raised $16,000. {EXTRA} in special efforts in FIVE MONTHS. PREACHED IT UP!

Yet all of this leaves me cold as I am no Caiaphas. I am a Paul. Buildings dont impress me. I went to sleep in the Cathedral of Notre Dame in Paris. Not impressed. Harkness is right.[2] Emphasis on buildings and ritual is a sign of religious and spiritual decadence. Nobody said much when I baptized NINETY TWO at one time EASTER, but every body is talking about the building. SAD! SAD! SAD! Although I am the deepest theologian in the Baptist Church nobody paid me any attention. Even you had it in the back of your head that I was a loafer. Now that I have turned "My Father's House into a den of thieves" even you say: "Doc I did not know it was in you." SAD! SAD! SAD!

Littlejohn is Pastor of the Bethesda Baptist Church Minneapolis, Minn.[3] I just got a letter from him and he wants to leave because the "Niggers" have up hell about the Choir and Gospel chorus singing. Poor boy . . he does not know that Hell is the natural habitat of the average Baptist member.

Copy this article and send me your cut AIR MAIL SPECIAL and I will put you in the Convention issue of the VOICE. I warn you. Dont get stuck there. Move on to a big metropolitan center in THE NORTH, or some town as ATLANTA. You will dry rot there. I feel sorry for you with all that learning. I wrote a two hundred page thesis on RELIGION AND PHYSIOLOGICAL PSYCHOLOGY and with the exception of lectures to colleges have been unable to use ONE SINGLE IDEA in the Baptist Church. The coutry Negroes have swept into town and REDUCED the intellectual level of RELIGION. This is the day of Mass preachers except in certain spots. Hurry and get one. Curry is trying to put the heat on me to come to Bishop but I am satisfied where I am.[4] I have my house air-conditioned and I have not been out of this "hole" up on the second floor in a month. I just read and sleep and look out

---

1. Samuel D. Proctor received his Th.D. from Boston University in 1950.

2. Barbour may be referring to R. E. E. Harkness, who was a professor at Crozer Theological Seminary.

3. Worth Littlejohn Barbour was Barbour's son.

4. Barbour refers to M. K. Curry, Jr., president of Bishop College in Marshall, Texas.

the window at the men working on my Church! "All this and Heaven too"! Hurry up and reply. You ~~are~~ {and} Coretta are going to rue the day you have children. The Catholics are right. Preachers should be celibates.

Your Old Friend
[*signed*] JPB

P.S. Be sure and show Coretta the article in the Voice. I like her and this is a compliment as I do not like preachers wives . . most of them are empty headed and butt in their husbands business too much.

Tillich is all wet. There is no "being-itself. "Das Ding im Sich" is Non-Being! Kant proved that. Being-Itself is a meaningless abstraction. As Marx said. Read Tillich "The Courage To Be."[5] He has a good section "Existentialism"— The Latest Philosophical "Fad". Can man <u>hurry</u> up the historical process? This occupies my mind at present.

I am killing the church on "Job." Eliphaz made 3 indictments against Job.

(1). You have no right to complain
(2). You have a secret sin
(3). You question the justice of God

Job <u>answers</u>

July 10 (1) "Freedom Implies Freedom to Question God"—Subject: "<u>Boundless Freedom</u>" Results: "Hari-Kari"
July 17 (2) "<u>Worried Minds</u>"—Text—"The Almighty Troubles Me—Job 23:16
Thesis: Unexplained Suffering Worries Us—Attack on Norman Vincent Peale
I have no sin, said Job—Your doctrine is outmoded
(2). Can Christianity Handle Worried Minds?—(Double "Hari-Kari" The old approach has failed! So what?
July 24 (3) "<u>The Justice of God</u>"—Working on this now.

All of these
Deep! Deep! Deep!

TALI. MLKP-MBU: Box 121.

---

5. Barbour refers to Paul Tillich, *The Courage to Be* (New Haven: Yale University Press, 1952).

The National Baptist Voice

OFFICIAL ORGAN OF

NATIONAL BAPTIST CONVENTION, INC., U. S. A.

27,000 Churches   25,000 Ministers   4,000,000 Members

J. PIUS BARBOUR, A. B., B. D., TH. M., Editor

1614 West Second Street

CHESTER, PA.

July 21st 1955

Dear Mike:

April 29th is my Women's Day and I am in the midst of a building programme and I have to stick around on these financial days. I can come of the Third Sunday In April if you can arrange it. Then too I wonder if I am your man. I am distinctly a "preacher's preacher" and a college lecture man. I can preach "Mob-sermons" but I cant lecture to mobs. I am filled up with three lectures:

    (1) Should we open the Canon?..this deals with adding to the Bible and Revelation.

    (2) Has Marx outmoded The Christian Ethic?..this deals with the historical process.

    (3) Is the Baptist Church Doomed?..this deals with the New concept of the Church.

Now I cant make any more preparation as I am filled with the above and I have always stuck to one rule: Fill yourself up with some deep stuff and stick to it until it is out of your system. I heard Proctor on " success ". Trite. Trite. Trite for a TH. D. (See my article on the New England Convention in the "Voice" I am sending you.) Now think on these things and write me your conclusions.

My annex is finished...the hottest thing on the Eastern seaboard. Paid sixty-two thousand CASH, have'nt borrowed one penny. Now I will turn the Church into a Catholic Sanctuary. This will cost forty five thousand and the furnishings twenty five thousand. I will sweat the Spooks and then BORROW to finish. I have it all planed and it is working as a clock.

The National Baptist Voice

OFFICIAL ORGAN OF

NATIONAL BAPTIST CONVENTION, INC., U. S. A.

27,000 Churches   25,000 Ministers   4,000,000 Members

J. PIUS BARBOUR, A. B., B. D., TH. M., Editor

1614 West Second Street

CHESTER, PA.

I put a colonial front on and The white folks are eating me, as you
know the Church is on the high way and they see it. The Banks are calling
me to LEND me money. How is that ? I raised $,4,024.00 Sunday July
17th, the hottest day of the year and the "Spooks" were standing around
the wall. Besides I have taken in 114 members since December and raised
$16,000. in special efforts in FIVE MONTHS. PREACHED IT UP.

Yet all of this leaves me cold as I am no Caiaphas. I am a
Paul. Buildings dont impress me. I went to sleep in the Cathedral of
Notre Dame in Paris. Not impressed. Darkness is right. Emphasis on buildings and ritual is a sign of religious and spiritual decadence. Nobody
said much when I baptized NINETY TWO at one time EASTER, but every body
is talking about the building. BAD. SAD. SAD. Although I am the deepest
theologian in the Baptist Church nobody paid me any attention. Even you
had it in the back of your head that I was a loafer. Now that I have
turned " My Fathers House into a den of thieves " even you say: Doc
I didnot know it was in you. SAD. SAD. SAD.

Littlejohn is Pastor of the Bethesda Baptist Church Minneapolis,
Minn. I just got a letter from him and he wants to leave because the
"Niggers" have up hell about the Choir and Gospel chorus singing. Poor boy
..he does not know that Hell is the natural habitat of the average
Baptist member.

Copy this article and send me your cut AIR MAIL SPECIAL and I
will put you in the Convention issue of the VOICE. I warn you.
Dont get stuck there. Move on to a big metropolitan center in THE
NORTH, or some town as ATLANTA. You will dry rot there. I feel sorry for

The National Baptist Voice

OFFICIAL ORGAN OF

NATIONAL BAPTIST CONVENTION, INC., U. S. A.

27,000 Churches · · · · · · 25,000 Ministers · · · · · · 4,000,000 Members

J. PIUS BARBOUR, A. B., B. D., TH. M., Editor

1614 West Second Street

CHESTER, PA.

②

you with all that learning. I wrote a two hundred page thesis on
RELIGION AND PHYSIOLOGICAL PSYCHOLOGY and with the exception of
lectures to colleges have been unable to use ONE SINGLE IDEA in the
Baptist Church. The coutry Negroes have swept into town and REDUCED the
intellectual level of RELIGION. This is the day of Mass preachers
except in certain spots. Hurry and get one. Curry is trying to put the
heat on me to come to Bishop but I am satisfied where I am. I have my
house air-conditioned and I have not been out of this "hole" up on the
second floor in a month. I just read and sleep and look out the window
at the men working on my Church. "All this and Heaven too." Hurry up and
reply. You and Coretta are going to rue the day you have children.
The Catholics are right. Preachers should be celibates.

                              Your Old Friend

                              JPB

P. S. Be sure and show Coretta the article in the Voice. I like her
and this is a compliment as I do not like preachers wives..most of them
are empty headed and butt in their husbands business too much.

Tillich is all wet. There is no "Being-itself"
"Das Ding im Sich" is Non-Being. KANT proved that. Being-itself
is a MEANINGLESS ABSTRACTION. As MARX SAID " the
Read Tillich. "THE has
courage to Be". He "EXISTENTIALISM"
a new school PHILOSOPHICALLY
the latest philosophers HURRY OLD MAN
"GOD." The HISTORICAL PROCESS
this is occupied by time
at present. (OVER)

I AM KILLING THE CHURCH ON
"JOB." ELIPHAZ MADE 3 INDICTMENTS
AGAINST JOB.
① YOU HAVE NO RIGHT TO COMPLAIN
② YOU HAVE A SECRET SIN
③ YOU QUESTION THE JUSTICE OF GOD

JOB. ANSWERS

July 10 ① "FREEDOM IMPLIES FREEDOM TO QUESTION
GOD" - SUBJECT: "BOUNDLESS FREEDOM"
RESULTS: "HARI-HARI"

"17 ② "WORRIED MINDS" - TEXT - THE ALMIGHTY
TROUBLES ME - JOB 23:16
- THESIS: UNEXPLAINED SUFFERING WORRIES US -
ATTACK ON NORMAN VINCENT PEALE
- I HAVE NO SIN, SAID JOB - YOUR DOCTRINE
IS OUTMODED
② CAN CHRISTIANITY HANDLE WORRIED MINDS?
- (DOUBLE "HARI-KARI")

July 24 (3) "THE JUSTICE OF GOD"
- WORKING ON THIS NOW.

ALL OF THESE
DEEP! DEEP! DEEP!

THE OLD APPROACH
HAS FAILED! SO
WHAT?

25 July 1955
New Orleans, La.

*King had flown to New Orleans for a meeting with Dent, the president of Dillard
University.[1] They discussed King's leaving Dexter Avenue Baptist Church and
becoming dean of Dillard's new chapel. King stayed at Dexter.*

Dr. M. L. King
309 South Jackson Street
Montgomery, Alabama

Dear Doctor King:

There is enclosed a University check to reimburse your plane fare for the
visit to New Orleans to talk with me last Friday. As I proceed with planning
our program for the new chapel, I will bear in mind our telephone conversation of this morning.

With best wishes, I am

Sincerely yours,
[*signed*]
A. W. Dent
President

AWD:db

TLS. MLKP-MBU: Box 117.

---

1. Albert Walter Dent (1904–1984) received his B.A. from Morehouse in 1926. He was Morehouse alumni secretary for several years before becoming superintendent of Dillard's Flint-
Goodridge Hospital in 1932. He also served as Dillard's business manager from 1935 until 1941,
when he became president of the university. He retired as president in 1969. He chaired the
National Health Council in 1953–1955 and the United Negro College Fund in 1965–1970.

From Major J. Jones

[*August 1955*]
Boston, Mass.

Jones describes fellow Boston University graduate Thomas J. Pugh's guest sermon at Twelfth Baptist Church in Roxbury. A member of the Dialectical Society and a Baptist minister, Pugh had received his Ph.D. in systematic theology in 1955.[1]

Dear Martin, The Wife and the One to be:

I hope by now you have gotten your mastercopy and that you have reread it after having been out of school and on the world a little while—Smile. Seriously, I do hope it got there ok. Let me know because I put a $100.00 on it just in case. Forget the $ it took to send it, I will see you some time.

Boy the "cloud" sure got here this summer. There are more of us here this year than before, and the looks are not as good. It seems as if all the looks got off in New York or some place other than this place. It is sure not here. I do not have any worry working this summer, there is nothing here to take my mind off of study.

I went to hear Dr. Pugh and it seems as if he has not become a bit better since he got his Ph.D. I was more confused about what took place between Christ and Nicodemus than ever after his sermon. Rev. Hester had him and the people were just as mad as I was confused—Smile.

The Wedding is the 28th of August in Oxford, N.C. at the Methodist Church there at 5:31. I hope that you might find the time to come, I would hope that Mrs. King could also, but the little one might be so near until I will understand if that is impossible.

Take Care, and yours,
[*signed*]
Major

TLS. MLKP-MBU: Box 117.

---

1. Thomas Jefferson Pugh (1917–) received an A.B. from Clark College in 1940, a B.D. from Gammon Theological Seminary in 1942, and an M.A. from Atlanta University in 1947. Pugh was a public school principal and Baptist pastor in southern Georgia before joining the faculty of Atlanta's Bryant Theological Seminary in 1944 and serving as chaplain at Albany State College from 1948 to 1958. In 1958 he joined the faculty of Atlanta's Interdenominational Theological Center, where he taught for the rest of his career.

From Sankey L. Blanton

1 August 1955
Chester, Pa.

Blanton congratulates King on his doctorate and inquires about an applicant for admission to Crozer.

Dr. M. L. King, Jr.
309 South Jackson Street
Montgomery, Alabama

Dear Dr. King:

Thank you for your letter and the enclosed abstract of your dissertation leading to the doctorate. I congratulate you now that the Ph.D. is in hand, and I assure you of my continued interest in your career. I have abounding confidence in your ability and integrity, and would like to see more of you.

When I am through Alabama again in the Fall, I will try to give you prior notice of my arrival in Montgomery.

Incidentally, we had some correspondence with the young man who works with you. At the time I left the office, he had not completed his application papers with us. We would certainly be glad to have him in our student body next year, and if he has not completed said papers, I would appreciate your giving him a gentle shove in the right direction.[1] Please remember me kindly to Mrs. King.

Yours sincerely,
[*signed*] Sankey L. Blanton/hd
Sankey L. Blanton

SLB/hd

Dict. Wilmington, N.C.
7/28/55

TLSr. MLKP-MBU: Box 117.

---

1. Blanton refers to John Thomas Porter (1931–), a student applicant. Crozer's acting registrar, Lucile B. Knapp, also wrote King about Porter's plans; see Knapp to King, 29 June 1955, MLKP-MBU: Box 117. In the fall of 1955 Porter enrolled in Morehouse's School of Religion rather than at Crozer. He received his B.S. from Alabama State College in 1955 and his B.D. from Morehouse in 1958. After serving as an assistant to King at Dexter during the 1954–1955 academic year, Porter interned with King, Sr., at Ebenezer while at Morehouse. He became pastor of Detroit's First Baptist Institutional Church in 1958 before being called to Birmingham's Sixth Avenue Baptist Church in 1962. King spoke at Porter's installation service in Birmingham on 9 December 1962. Porter was active in the Birmingham movement with King and Fred Shuttlesworth during the 1960s. He still serves at Sixth Avenue. See John Thomas Porter to King Papers Project, 10 August 1990.

From Kelly Miller Smith

8 August 1955
Nashville, Tenn.

*Smith, pastor of First Baptist Church in Nashville, accepts King's invitation to
preach at Dexter in March 1956.[1] He mentions that he will see King at the
National Baptist Convention's annual meeting in Memphis in September.*

Dr. M. L. King, Jr.
Dexter Avenue Baptist Church
454 Dexter Avenue
Montgomery, Alabama

Dear Mike,

I shall be honored, indeed to share with you the 11 o'clock services on the
second Sunday in March. You see, I have no alternative, for I have not
thought that far ahead in the matter of scheduling. I think you are taking
advantage of the fact that the average cleric of this denominational and ethnic
identification does no advance planning. You are showing us old veterans up.
I am getting busy on my 1956 program tomorrow.

Seriously, though I shall be pleased to be with you and I am placing that
date on my calendar. I don't know how wise that is, however, as the following
Sunday will be my fifth anniversary occasion (but without fanfare).

I am just back from a very revealing and educational trip to Europe and
the Middle East,—thus the delay in answering.

I know you are still doing a monumental job there at Dexter and you have
my sincerest prayers and best wishes.

See you in Memphis.

Yours sincerely,
[*signed*] Kelly
Kelly Miller Smith

KMS:prp

TLS. MLKP-MBU: Box 121.

---

1. Kelly Miller Smith (1920–1984) received his B.A. from Morehouse in 1942 and his B.D.
from Howard University's School of Religion in 1945. He was pastor of Mount Heroden Baptist
Church in Vicksburg, Mississippi, from 1946 until 1951, when he became pastor of First Baptist
Church in Nashville; he served that congregation until his death. He was also assistant dean of
Vanderbilt University Divinity School from 1968 until 1984, a member of Morehouse School of
Religion's board of directors from 1975 until his death, and president of the National Conference
of Black Christians from 1979 to 1982. He was a founding member and chaplain of the Southern
Christian Leadership Conference and the Nashville Christian Leadership Council, an affiliate of
SCLC. His publications include *Social Crisis Preaching* (1984).

From Sylvester Jones

20 August 1955
Colfax, La.

*Jones, president of Raven Camp School in Colfax, asks for a copy of King's sermon
"The Three Dimensions of a Complete Life," delivered at Tuskegee Institute's
chapel on 31 July.*

Dr. M. L. King Jr.
309 South Jackson St.
Montgomery, Alabama

Dear Dr. King:

After listening to your wonderful sermon in Tuskegee's Chapel a few sundays
ago entitled, "The Three Dimensions of Life" I became rather inspired, so
inspired, that I would appreciate having a copy of that particular sermon. Whatever method is used for securing a copy of such sermon, I am willing to apply.

Very truly yours,
[*signed*]
Sylvester Jones

TLS. MLKP-MBU: Box 117.

To Sylvester Jones

26 August 1955
[*Montgomery, Ala.*]

Mr. Sylvester Jones, Principal
Raven Camp School
Colfax, Louisiana

Dear Mr. Jones:

Thanks very much for your very complimentary letter concerning my sermon in the Tuskegee Chapel a few Sundays ago. Unfortunately, the sermon
that I preached at Tuskegee is one of the sermons that I do not have written
in manuscript form. However, since you have expressed an interest in its content, I will attempt at some future date to take some time out to write it. When
this is done, I will be sure to mail you a copy.

With every good wish, I am

Sincerely yours,
Martin L. King, Jr.

MLK/csk

TLc. MLKP-MBU: Box 116.

From Rosa Parks

26 August 1955
Montgomery, Ala.

*After King addressed the Montgomery branch of the NAACP on 14 August, the
branch president, Robert L. Matthews, requested that King join the executive
committee. Parks, secretary of the local branch, informs King of his selection to
serve on the committee.[1]*

Rev. M. L. King
309 S. Jackson Street
Montgomery 5, Alabama

Dear Rev. King:

This is to inform you, as requested by Montgomery Branch NAACP president, Mr. R. L. Matthews, that you are a member of the executive committee of the branch. You are most cordially welcomed to be a part of the official staff. Your outstanding contribution merits this action.

There will be a meeting of the executive committee and branch members at the Pilgrim Health and Life Insurance Company office, 131 Monroe Street Monday August 29 at 7:30 P.M. Please be present for very important business.

Respectfully yours,
[*signed*]
Rosa L. Parks, Secretary
Montgomery Branch NAACP

P. S. There will not be a meeting Sunday August 28.

RLP

TLS. MLKP-MBU: Box 117.

---

1. Rosa Louise McCauley Parks was born in Tuskegee, Alabama, in 1913. She attended the laboratory school of Alabama State College in Montgomery but had to leave before graduating to begin working as a seamstress at age sixteen. After her marriage to Raymond A. Parks in December 1932 she returned to school, receiving her high school diploma in 1933. In 1943 she was elected secretary of the Montgomery branch of the NAACP. After several attempts, Parks became registered to vote in 1945. On 1 December 1955, after a dozen years of civil rights activism, Parks refused to move from her seat when a bus driver attempted to enforce Montgomery's segregation ordinance. Her arrest sparked the Montgomery bus boycott. As a result of their involvement in the movement, Parks and her husband lost their jobs, and after several months of continued intimidation they moved to Detroit, where she still lives. In 1965 Parks began working for Congressman John Conyers in Detroit, retiring from her position in 1988. In 1987 Parks founded the Rosa and Raymond Parks Institute for Self-Development. See her autobiography, with Jim Haskins, *Rosa Parks: My Story* (New York: Dial Books, 1992).

From J. H. Jackson

28 September 1955
Chicago, Ill.

*Jackson, president of the National Baptist Convention, declines King's invitation
to preach at Dexter in July 1956.*[1]

Dr. M. L. King, Jr.
309 South Jackson Street
Montgomery, Alabama

Dear Dr. King:

Thanks for your kind letter of September 26th.

I would be delight to serve you and your congregation the second Sunday
in July, 1956, but a previous engagement will hinder my fellowship with you.

I am delighted to know of the great work that you are doing at Dexter. I
know we can count on you and your congregation to help us build the kind
of National Baptist Convention that will reflect credit on our founding fathers, and will be an inspiration both to the present and future generation.

Yours truly,
[*signed*]
J. H. Jackson

JHJ:nb

TLS. MLKP-MBU: Box 117.

---

1. Joseph Harrison Jackson (1900–1990) received his B.A. from Jackson College (later Jackson State University) in 1926 and his B.D. from Colgate Rochester Divinity School in 1932. He
later received an M.A. from Creighton University in Omaha, Nebraska. After serving churches
in Nebraska, Pennsylvania, and his home state of Mississippi, he became pastor of Chicago's
Olivet Baptist Church in 1941. Jackson succeeded the late president of the National Baptist Convention, L. K. Williams, as pastor of Olivet, which was one of the largest churches in the United
States. After serving as secretary of the foreign mission board and vice-president of the National
Baptist Convention, Jackson was elected president of the organization in 1953. Jackson presided
during a time of deep disagreement among the group's members over the role the church should
play in the civil rights movement, a conflict that eventually led to the 1961 formation of an opposition group committed to church involvement, the Progressive National Baptist Convention.
He resigned as president of the National Baptist Convention in 1982. Jackson's publications include *Unholy Shadows and Freedom's Holy Light* (1967) and *A Story of Christian Activism: The History
of the National Baptist Convention, U.S.A., Inc.* (1980).

From Walter R. McCall

29 September 1955
Fort Valley, Ga.

*In a letter of 19 August McCall had invited King to participate in the Fort Valley
State College's Religious Emphasis Week that October. King accepted the
invitation, whereupon McCall sent this letter outlining his friend's responsibilities
for the week. King's sermons at the event included "The Dimensions of a Complete
Life" and "Going Forward by Turning Back," another title for "Rediscovering
Lost Values."[1]*

Dr. M. L. King, Jr., Minister
The Dexter Avenue Baptist Church
Montgomery, Alabama

Dear Mike,

   This letter is a bit late due to our failure to get the necessary meetings
underway pertaining thereto. Below is information relative to your expected
responsibilities in regard to our Religious Emphasis Week:

1. You will be expected to preach on M., W., and Friday during our regular
    Chapel period. We have about thirty (30) minutes. May be 15 to 20 min-
    utes of that time can be used by the speaker.
2. Your preaching activities will reach their climax during our Vesper
    Hour—4:30 p.m. on that following Sunday. About 25 to 35 minutes are
    given to the Messenger (Preacher).
3. Be prepared to lead a discussion on the topics appearing on the pro-
    gram. Note: The topic "E" refers to "lands, property, lawn, etc". In other
    words, what has Christianity has to say to us about keeping, or creating
    a wholesome physical environment?
4. You will be expected to be available for consultation with students.
5. Drop me a line suggesting any thing you would have me do that will aid
    you in our success during the Week.
6. When possible, forward the topics of your sermons.
7. Note in "D" the term 'business' refers to manufacturing enterprises, hir-
    ing etc.
8. If you say, I will have Charles W. Ward to schedule you to speak to his
    congregation on Sunday October 23, 1955 at 11:00 o'clock.[2]

---

1. For a complete list of King's sermons and speeches at Fort Valley, see the Chronology,
17–23 October 1955, at the beginning of this volume.

2. Charles W. Ward (1915–) was executive secretary of Georgia's Missionary and Educational
Convention. A fellow Baptist preacher, Ward graduated from Morehouse in 1942, six years before King and McCall.

All things are going relatively well for us. As you can imagine, we are kept quite busy as Norma is in school. With best wishes and many regards to all, I am

Sincerely yours,
[*signed*] (Walter) <u>Mac</u>
Walter R. McCall

TLS. MLKP-MBU: Box 117.

From Walter R. McCall

22 October 1955
Fort Valley, Ga.

The Reverend Dr. M. L. King, Jr.
Fort Valley State College Campus

Dear Brother King:

Please find enclosed an honorarium of one hundred sixty eight dollars ($168.00) for the exceptionally able service which you have rendered during our Religious Emphasis Week Observance.

We are sure that this small honorarium is {not} given with the idea of paying you for your fine fellowship and most relevant and dynamic services, but we give it as a token of our appreciation for what you have done.

It was indeed a pleasure to have had you with us, and we pray for your continued success as a good man and a Gospel Carrier for Christ.

I am,

Sincerely Yours,
[*signed*]
Walter R. McCall

TALS. MLKP-MBU: Box 117.

From Nathaniel Garth

27 October 1955
Chattanooga, Tenn.

Garth, pastor of Westside Baptist Church in Chattanooga, describes King's role in the National Sunday School and Baptist Training Union's fall institute.

Dear Rev. King,

This comes as a method of informing you of the outlay of our Fall Institute. As you already know our fall institute will begin November 7, 1955 at 7:00 p.m. The first class period will run from 7:00–7:40; from 7:40–7 45 will be a short recess. The second class period will begin at 7:45 and end at 8:25. At this point there will be a very short devotion and you will be introduced to give your message. Then we will have our announcements and benediction after you have spoken. You will have from 25 to 30 minutes, more or less.

We are not using a theme this time only a Motto: "Teach—Reach—Win." So you are at liberty to use your own discretion to your theme or topic. However you may point out to us the need of prepared leaders in the Christian Church. Then too, you may touch upon some or any of these courses we are teaching.

You will not worry about teaching any course. However you may find something to add to them in your message. They are as follow:

A Survey of the Old Testament
    Rev. H. H. Battle, Morehouse man
Christian Doctrines, Rev. W. J. Thomas
    another Morehouse graduate
Administering the Sunday School
    Rev. W. A. Dennis, a product of Drew
Stewardship—Rev. C. L. Robinson
Church Leaders and Their Responsibilities
    Rev. E. L. Hicks
Preparation for Marriage
    Mrs. J. C. Bonner
Church Music, Mrs. C. L. Robinson
Ushers and First Aid
    Mrs. B. Johnson
Administering the Baptist Training Union—T. D. Lewis

All of the above ministers are local pastors.

I had hoped to contact you Thurs night but there was a misunderstanding on the part of the operator. I wanted to see if you had any question that you would would like for us to answer for you.

You will have the opportunity of meeting many people from Alabama and

Georgia. We are praying for you, and we hope that your week in Chattanooga will be a blessing.

The school will close on Friday evening.

Yours truly,
[*signed*] Rev. N. Garth, Jr.

ALS. MLKP-MBU: Box 117.

To Dexter Avenue Baptist Church Members

27 October 1955
Montgomery, Ala.

King distributed this letter and the annual report to the members of Dexter at the end of his first year as pastor. In his annual message King summarizes the accomplishments of the church, including the liquidation of its substantial debt and the "superb" work of the Social and Political Action Committee. "Through the work of this committee many persons have become registered voters and Dexter has led all other church[es] of Montgomery in contributions to the NAACP." King presents recommendations for the next year and asks the congregation to increase their financial contributions to the church.

Dear Member:

As we come to the end of another church year and stand on the threshold of a new church year, we have much to be proud of. The horizons in the life of Dexter were greatly extended in 1954–55. The church year 1954–55 is about to become history now, but for Dexter it is blessed history.

Words can never adequately express appreciation. Real appreciation must flow from the deep seas of the heart. But with my stumbling words, I want to express my deepest appreciation to you for your cooperation with the church program, and for the financial contributions you have made.

Now we prepare for the new church year. Our new church year begins Sunday November 5, and goes thru the last Sunday in October, 1956. We solicit your cooperation and prayers that our work for Kingdom building will reach new heights in the 1955–56 church year. As you can see from the enclosed budget, our financial responsibilities are even greater than last year. This is naturally the case, since we are determined to move forward every year, rather than remain stagnant. Since our budget is higher this year, we are expecting every loyal member to make a pledge to the Unified Budget of the church, and we are requesting every member to increase his pledge over last year. We need the help of every member. We need your help. As you prayerfully consider your part, would you kindly sign and return the enclosed Commitment Card, stating how much you will pledge. At the bottom of the budget you will notice a list of possible commitments. Please seek to make your pledge within one of these categories. Seek to fit into the highest category possible. We need a minimum of $20,000.00 in pledges.

It would be a fine idea for you to consider tithing this year. This is a debt that we all owe to God. If your income is $300.00 per month, 10 percent is $30.00. This should be the minimum that you consider giving. Most of us, "out of speechless gratitude for the redemption of Jesus Christ," know that we should give more.

May I close by asking you to consider this question: Where else in all the world can a dollar buy so much?

May God bless you abundantly.

Yours in His service,
M. L. King, Jr., Pastor

MLK/ehr

P.S. Be sure to fill out the Information Card in detail, and return it to the church office with the Commitment Card. This information is of vital importance for our church records.

PD. Zelia S. Evans and J. T. Alexander, eds., *Dexter Avenue Baptist Church, 1877–1977* (Montgomery, Ala.: Dexter Avenue Baptist Church, 1978), pp. 79–80.

Annual Report,
Dexter Avenue Baptist Church

1 October 1954–31 October 1955
Montgomery, Ala.

INTRODUCTORY EXPRESSIONS

As we come to the end of another church year and stand on the threshold of a new church year, we have much to be proud of. The horizons in the life of Dexter were greatly extended in 1954–55. The church year 1954–55 is history now, but for Dexter it is blessed history.

About thirty new members have joined the fellowship of Dexter this year. This group includes children, young people and adults. A great majority of these new members are now active participants in the life of the church. They have joined with other members in inspiring worship services each Lord's Day, and in other activities which make up the total work of the church.

Financially, we have done extraordinarily well. Receipts from all sources have exceeded twenty-two thousand dollars ($22,000.00). Of this amount we have given generously for benevolent purposes, missions, and education. Over one thousand dollars

($1,000.00) has been paid into the building fund, and our debt of forty-five hundred dollars ($4,500.00) has been totally liquidated. These figures represent more than cold statistics; rather they express the soul of a church.

Several improvements have been made in the physical structure of the church. These include: carpeting the main auditorium; a public address system; a communion table;* and painting the basement. Under the leadership of a fine group of ladies from the church, a Sunday nursery has been established in the basement of the church.

Many other wonderful things happened in our church-life this year. Mention will be made here of only a few. For the first time in its history, the church employed a full-time secretary. The benefits from this undertaking have been so tremendous that every member has come to see the indispensability of this office for the general welfare of the church. Twelve month clubs, representing the twelve months of the year, were organized. These clubs have been a great blessing to the church both financially and spiritually. Under the direction of the Scholarship Fund Committee, a scholarship of one hundred dollars ($100.00) was awarded to one of the fine young members of our church who is now a freshman in college. The Cultural Committee brought to Dexter and the Montgomery Community the celebrated choir of the Ebenezer Baptist Church, Atlanta, Georgia. This event was both culturally uplifting and spiritually stimulating. For the first time in several years, the church, under the dynamic leadership of the Board of Religious Education, undertook a Daily Vacation Bible School. This undertaking was a great success. A Social and Political Action Committee was organized at the beginning of the church year to keep the membership informed concerning social, political, and economic issues. The work of this committee has been superb, and every member of Dexter has felt its influence. Through the work of this committee many persons have become registered voters and Dexter has led all other church of Montgomery in contributions to the NAACP. The "special days" through the church year have been tremendously successful. Through these occasions we have been able to bring to Dexter some of the great minds and pulpiteers of our nation. The various auxiliaries of the church are alive and growing stronger; each of them stands ready to lend its cooperation to the overall work of the church. All of

* This lovely communion table was a gift to the church from Mr. William J. Cole of Chicago in memory of his mother.

these events speak loudly of the extended horizons of Dexter. We will always remember 1954–55 as the church year in which we reached great heights in fellowship and working together.

Words can never adequately express appreciation. Real appreciation must flow from the deep seas of the heart. But in my little way and with my stumbling words, I would like to express my deepest appreciation to each of you. The wonders that have come about at Dexter this year were not due so much to my leadership, but to the greatness of your followship. The Official Board has worked as a unit and has distinguished itself for peace and harmony and a higher spiritual life. The heads of the various organizations of the church deserve the highest praise. Most of them have worked indefatiguably and assiduously for the success of the overall program of the church.

Now, although these achievements are marvelous, and deserve our highest praise, we must not become so involved in passively idolizing them that we forget the tremendous responsibilities which lie ahead. Institutions, like men, can so easily fall into moribund conditions when they project their visions merely to past achievements rather than future challenges. There is nothing more tragic than to see a church drowning in the deep waters of spiritual stagnancy, and at the last moment reaching out for some thin straw of past achievement in an attempt to survive. We must take these noble achievements of the last church year as challenges to even greater achievements for the new church year. Those great yesterdays must inspire us to work courageously for more noble tomorrows. As we have worked so nobly in the past for this great church which is so near and dear to our hearts, and whose efforts God has so richly crowned with success, so let us work in the future; let each of us go out at this moment with grim and bold determination to extend the horizons of Dexter to new boundaries, and lift the spire of her influence to new heights, so that we will be able to inject new spiritual blood into the veins of this community, transforming its jangling discords into meaningful symphonies of spiritual harmony.

M. L. K., Jr. [. . .][1]

---

1. A page listing "Outstanding Events" is omitted here; the information can be found in the Chronology at the beginning of this volume.

Sermons preached at Dexter   46
Sermons preached at other churches   7
Sermons and lectures at Colleges   13
Community and Civic Meetings attended   36
Pastoral visits   87
Sick visits   49
Baptized   12
Marriages performed   5
Funerals preached   5
Children dedicated   2
Personal Interviews and Conferences   22
Books read   26
Periodicals read   102
Represented the Church in District, State & National Conventions   10
Doctoral Dissertation completed
  Title: <u>A Comparison of the Conceptions of God in the thinking of Paul Tillich and Henry Nelson Wieman</u>   343 pages. [. . .][2]

Recommendations

The following are recommendations submitted by the pastor for the 1955–56 church year:

1. In order to increase the membership of the church as well as extend the spiritual influence of the church throughout the community, a serious evangelistic campaign shall be undertaken, extending throughout the church year. This campaign shall be carried out by twenty-five evangelistic teams, each consisting of a captain and at least three other members. Each team shall be urged to bring in at least five new members within the church year. The team that brings in the highest number of members shall be duly recognized at the end of the church year. Each captain shall call his team together at least once a month to discuss findings and possibilities. The pastor shall serve as general chairman of this campaign. The initial meeting of the

2. Two sections, "Special Sermons and Lectures Away from Home" and "Members Added to the Church," are omitted; the sermons and lectures are listed in the Chronology.

campaign shall be held at the church on October 31, at which time the pastor will set forth the general outlay of the campaign to all team captains as well as all members of teams. The teams are as follows: [. . .][3]

2. In order to further strengthen the spiritual life of the church, the regular mid-week prayer services shall be rejuvenated. Each week some organization from the church shall be called on to lead the prayer service. At a very early date the paster shall post a list of these organizations for the entire church year. The prayer service shall begin each Wednesday at 7:45 going thru 8:30.

3. The Men's Brotherhood shall be reorganized with Mr. J. H. Gilchrist serving as chairman. This organization will include every man in the church. It is hoped that this will be one of the most dynamic organizations in the church.

4. The Youth Council, as set up last year, shall be dissolved. All youth work shall now grow out of the missionary society. The youth work shall be divided into four groups: Sunshine Band Circle (boys and girls, ages 5–9); Red Circle (ages 14–18); Crusaders (ages 9–14); Young Matron's League (19 to 35). Each of these groups shall have a counselor from the missionary society. The counselors shall be as follows: Sunshine Band, Miss Cherrye Ballard; Red Circle, Mrs. Coretta King; Crusaders, Miss Verdie Davie; Young Matron's League, Mrs. E. M. Arrington.

5. That persons who join the church on Sundays shall no longer be voted in the church from the floor. As soon as a person joins the church, the chairman of the Deacon Board and the clerk of the church shall take him to the pastor's study in the first unit of the church and interview him concerning how he wishes to join and other important details. The person or persons joining shall wait in the study to be interviewed by the New Member Committee. The duties of this committee shall be the same as listed in the last year's recommendations. (See 1954–55 recommendations, p. 2). The following persons shall comprise the New Member Committee: Mrs. B. P. Brewer, Chairman; Mr. Julius Alexander,

3. The names have been omitted.

Vice-Chairman; Mrs. R. E. Harris, Secretary; 31 Oct
Mrs. Mary Morgan; Mrs. E. M. Arrington; Mrs. 1955
Mary Louise Williams; Mr. Jerome Morris. The
names of the person or persons joining shall be
listed in the Church Bulletin on the Sunday after they join, and they will be officially welcomed
into the church on the First Sunday night with
the right hand of fellowship. [. . .][4]

TD. MLKP-MBU: Box 77.

---

4. A listing of the church members and officers is omitted, as is the detailed financial report.

To Howard Thurman

31 October 1955
Montgomery, Ala.

*King invites Thurman, dean of Boston University's Marsh Chapel, to speak for
Men's Day.*[1]

Dr. Howard Thurman
Boston University School of Theology
745 Commonwealth Avenue
Boston, Mass.

Dear Dr. Thurman:

I am in the process of setting up my program for the coming church year.
The second Sunday in July is the date set aside for our annual Men's Day. I

---

1. Howard Thurman (1899–1981) received his B.A. from Morehouse College in 1923 and his
M.Div. from Rochester Theological Seminary in 1926. After serving as pastor of Mount Zion
Baptist Church in Oberlin, Ohio, Thurman returned to Morehouse as professor of religion in
1929. He joined Howard University's faculty in 1932 and three years later became dean of the
university's chapel. Just prior to his appointment as dean, Thurman and his wife, Sue Bailey
Thurman, traveled to India on a "Pilgrimage of Friendship" and met Mohandas K. Gandhi. Thur-
man resigned from Howard in 1943 to help establish San Francisco's Church for the Fellowship
of All Peoples, one of the first churches composed of African-Americans, Asian-Americans, and
Euro-Americans. In 1953 he became dean of Boston University's Marsh Chapel, where he served
until 1965. His many publications include an autobiography, *With Head and Heart* (1979); *Deep
River: Reflections on the Religious Insight of Certain of the Negro Spirituals* (1946, rev. ed. 1955); *The
Negro Speaks of Life and Death* (1947); *Jesus and the Disinherited* (1949); *Deep Is the Hunger* (1951);
Meditations of the Heart (1953); *The Creative Encounter* (1954); *Footprints of a Dream* (1959); *The
Inward Journey* (1961); *The Luminous Darkness* (1965); and *The Centering Moment* (1969).

583

am seeking each year to bring some of the great preachers of our nation to Dexter Avenue Baptist Church for this occasion. Our last Men's Day speaker was Dr. Benjamin E. Mays of Morehouse College. I would like to extend to you an invitation to preach the Men's Day sermon the second Sunday in July, 1956.

This is one of the outstanding events of our church year. I sincerely hope that you can accept the invitation. Your presence as well as your message would mean so much to our church and to our community.

The Dexter Avenue Baptist Church has a rich history. Probably you are already familiar with the church. Many outstanding ministers have served here. My immediate predecessor was your friend, Dr. Vernon Johns.[2] You will probably remember me from my recent studies at Boston University. I received my Ph.D. degree from the University in June of this year.

I will look forward to hearing from you at your earliest convenience concerning this matter so that I may proceed in setting up my church calendar for the year. Please give my best regards to Mrs. Thurman.[3] With every good wish, I am

Sincerely yours,
M. L. King, Jr.

MLK:lmt

TL. HTC-MBU: Box 43.

To W. T. Handy, Jr.

2 November 1955
[*Montgomery, Ala.*]

Both King and Handy preached at Southern University in Baton Rouge in October.

---

2. Vernon Johns (1892–1965) was pastor of Dexter from 1947 until 1952. Johns received his A.B. from Virginia Theological Seminary and College in 1915 and his B.D. from Oberlin College in 1918. After pastoring churches in Virginia, West Virginia, and Pennsylvania, Johns was called to Dexter in 1947. Johns preached economic self-sufficiency and civil rights militancy, arousing the ire of local authorities. See Charles Emerson Boddie, "Vernon Johns," in *God's Bad Boys* (Valley Forge, Pa.: Judson Press), pp. 61–75.

3. Sue Bailey Thurman (1903–) was a contemporary of Alberta Williams King at Spelman and graduated from Oberlin in 1926. She became traveling secretary of the national YWCA in 1928, remaining in that position until her marriage to Howard Thurman in 1932. In 1940 she helped found and edit the official organ of the National Council of Negro Women, the *Aframerican Women's Journal*. Her publications include *Pioneers of Negro Origin in California* (1952) and *The Historical Cookbook of the American Negro* (1958).

Rev. W. T. Handy, Jr.
1616—8th. Street
Alexanderia, La.

2 Nov
1955

Dear W. T. :

Thanks for your very kind letter. I am sorry you beat me to the point of writing, for I have been planning to write you for several weeks to congratulate you for building a church. I saw a picture of the edifice in the Courier, and it appears to be quite elaborate. You are to be commended for building at such an early age. The Methodist Church will be deeply indebted to you for many years to come. Although I have never built a church, I do know something of the strain that a minister goes through in such an undertaking.

I know you did a most acceptable job at Southern. I wish I could have been there to hear you. It is quite coincidental that we came so close together.

Please make it your business to stop in Montgomery on your way to Gammon next March. It would be a wonderful experience to have you and Ruth visit us for a few days. Be sure to put this on your agender.

Corretta and I are doing very well. We are expecting a baby within a matter of days now, and we are going through the normal excitement of such anticipation. Give my best regards to Ruth. Continue in making the excellent contribution that you have already made to the christian ministry.

Sincerely yours,
M. L. King, Jr.

MLK:lmt

TLc. DABCC.

To Vernon O. Rogers

2 November 1955
[Montgomery, Ala.]

Rogers preached at Dexter during King's week-long visit to Fort Valley State College in October.

Chaplin Vernon O. Rogers
4071 Gaston Avenue
Montgomery, Alabama

Dear Chaplin Rogers:

All week long members have been telling me of the effectiveness of your message to our congregation on Sunday before last. I am indeed grateful to you for the excellent contributions that you have made to our congregation on both occasions of my absence. You can be assured that you have a standing invitation to come to Dexter.

I hope in the very near future it will be possible for me to meet you. With every good wish, I am

Sincerely Yours,
M. L. King, Jr.

MLK:lmt

TLc. DABCC.

To Roosevelt Smitherman

2 November 1955
[*Montgomery, Ala.*]

King welcomes a new member to Dexter.

Mr. Roosevelt Smitherman
D. R.
Route 3 Box 115
Montgomery, Alabama

Dear Mr. Smitherman:

I have been intending to write to you ever since I met you, but absence from the city for several days has delayed my doing so. I presented your name to the church on the following Sunday, and they readily voted you in as a candidate for baptism. The baptism was to take place on last Sunday afternoon, but after talking with Chaplin Pearson I discovered that the baptismal pool had not been repaired. So we will have to wait a week or so now. In any event I will have Chaplin Pearson let you know exactly when the baptism will be. We plan to bring several members of the church out on the Sunday of the baptism to witness the ceremony.

You are constantly in my prayers. I hope you will keep the faith and keep looking up. In thses moments you need God, and He will be with you if you will properly commit yourself to Him. Feel free to write me at any time, and remember that the members of the Dexter Avenue Baptist Church are continually thinking about you.

Sincerely Yours,
M. L. King, Jr.

P. S. Enclosed you will find one or two of our church bulletins.

MLK:lmt

TLc. DABCC.

From John Thomas Porter

3 November 1955
Atlanta, Ga.

Porter, who had assisted King at Dexter, inquires about future preaching opportunities.

Dear Rev. King:

I trust this letter will find you and Mrs. King in the best of health and enjoying life. At the present time I am doing fine and studying hard.

I had wanted to come to Montgomery the first of this month but due to a rapidly disappearing treasure I thought I better wait until Thanksgiving. I will be in Montgomery on the Thanksgiving weekend without fail.

Rev. King, as you know, there comes a time in every man's life when he must take on the responsibilities of manhood. When I came to Atlanta I was in hope of getting an assistantship with a small income. I am a little doubtful now about the possibilities of such a thing becoming a reality. Dr. Watson is trying to work out some appointments. Your Father is one of the few Ministers who is quite liberal in matters of this sort. But due to the building program that he is in the midst off, I can see where it will be hard for him to take on extra responsibility. Therefore I will have to locate engagements in order to have a little something coming in. I would be more than appreciative if you would let me preach for you on Sundays when you are away. I can pay my own train fare and still have 5 or 6 dollars left. You will never know how much just a few dollars will mean to me. On second thought, I know you are aware of how much a few dollar can mean. If you have somebody working with you already I will understand. I can never repay you already for your kindness. If you care to discuss the matter further I will look forward to doing so on the 4th sunday.

You asked me about my love life when you were passing through. Well, sometime I think I'll just be a bachelor. I'll tell you more about it when I see you. (smile)

Please give my regards to Mrs. King and the rest of the church. I will write again very soon.

Yours in Christ,
[*signed*]
John T. Porter

TLS. MLKP-MBU: Box 117.

From Howard Thurman

14 November 1955

Rev. Martin L. King, Jr.
Dexter Avenue Baptist Church
Dexter Avenue at Decatur Street
Montgomery, Alabama

Dear Rev. King:

I am delighted to get your letter and to know that you are deeply involved in your work as the minister of the historic Dexter Avenue Baptist Church.

I am sorry that I cannot accept your invitation for July, 1956 because, according to my present schedule, I will be in California.

Mrs. Thurman asked me to send you her special greetings and to say that her hopes are very high for the kind of future which your ability and equipment will indicate.

Please know how sorry I am that I cannot be with you.

Sincerely yours,
Howard Thurman
Dean

TLc. HTC-MBU: Box 43.

To Ralph W. Riley

15 November 1955
[*Montgomery, Ala.*]

King confirms Riley's preaching engagement on 11 December.

Dr. R. W. Riley, President
American Baptist Theological Seminary
Nashville, Tenn.

Dear Dr. Riley:

This is just a note to say that we are still expecting you to give the Anniversary sermon at 11:00 o'clock service on the second Sunday in December. As you know this is the Seventy-eighth Anniversary of this church. Please send me within the next ten days one of your cuts and an "immodest" biographical statement for publicity purposes.

At your earliest convenience let me know when you will arrive and how you will be traveling. We hope it will be possible for Mrs. Riley to come.

With every good wish, I am

Sincerely yours,
M. L. King, Jr.,

MLK:lmt

TLc. DABCC.

To Rev. and Mrs. J. C. Bonner

16 November 1955
[*Montgomery, Ala.*]

*King stayed with the Bonners during a week-long Baptist Training Union institute
in Chattanooga.*

Rev. and Mrs. J. C. Bonner
1400 Kirkland Avenue
Chattanooga, Tennessee

Dear Rev. and Mrs. Bonner:

There is a word in Catholic theology called "supererogation." This word means in substance, "more than justice requires." I assure you that the kindness that you showed toward me was a work of supererogation. I will long remember the hospitality and the fellowship.

Please extend my gratitude to the very fine members of your church, and give my best regards to the children. I will be looking forward to this rich fellowship again next year.

With every good wish, I am

Sincerely yours,
M. L. King, Jr.,

MLK:lmt

P.S. The baby has not arrived yet. We are still waiting and hoping. Maybe after that I will be able to come back down to earth.

TLc. DABCC.

To John Thomas Porter

18 November 1955
[*Montgomery, Ala.*]

King confirms Porter's preaching engagement at Dexter on 27 November. King also reports the birth of Yolanda Denise King, who was born on 17 November, the night before King wrote this letter.

Rev. John Porter
Morehouse College
Atlanta, Georgia

Dear Porter:

This is just a note to say that I received your letter, and I will be looking forward to your preaching for me on the fourth Sunday morning. I will discuss with you the other matters that you raised when you come down.

Just last evening Coretta brought into the world a "big" little girl. She weighs nine pounds and eleven ounces. You will get a chance to see the new arrival when you come down on the week-end.

Sincerely yours,
M. L. King, Jr.

MLK:lmt

TLc. DABCC.

To Samuel D. Proctor

18 November 1955
[*Montgomery, Ala.*]

King invites Proctor to deliver the Men's Day sermon at Dexter. Proctor had been recently appointed president of Virginia Union University. He accepted the invitation.

Dr. Samuel D. Proctor, President
Virginia Union University
Richmond, Virginia

Dear Proctor:

You will probably remember that I spoke to you in Memphis concerning our annual Men's Day observance. I am seeking to bring each year some of

THE MORNING WORSHIP
Eleven O'clock

Organ Prelude: "Prelude in B Major" — Bach
*Processional Hymn: #7
Call to Worship

Invocation

The Responsive Reading: No. 537

*Gloria Patri — Scott

Anthem: "Come Ye Blessed"

The Morning Lesson: Luke 10:25-37

Prayer

Choral Response

Announcements

The Worship of God in Offering

*Offertory: All Things come of Thee, O Lord; and of Thine own have we given Thee. Amen

The Meditation Hymn: #479 (Stanzas 1 & 3)

Sermon: "The One-sided Approach of the Good Samaritan" — The Pastor

*Hymn of Invitation: #390

*Recessional Hymn: #38

The Benediction (Congregation seated)
The Choral Amen
Postlude: Fugue in B Major — Bach

CHURCH NOTES

We are happy to welcome into our fellowship Miss Eleanor Hatcher. Miss Hatcher joined the church last Sunday through Watch Care. She is a student of Alabama State College, and comes from John the Baptist Church, Abbeville, Ala. Mrs. Pressie B. Maxwell is responsible for Miss Hatcher joining this church.

****

This evening at 6:30 the rite of Baptism will be administered. At 7:00 o'clock, immediately following Baptism, there will be a service for the installation of all officers for the 1955-55 church year. Officers of all organizations of the church are urged to be present. Both of these services are open to the entire membership.

****

The November Club has been meeting weekly at the home of Mrs. Pressie B. Maxwell. In an effort to carry out the Thanksgiving theme and spirit this club will sell a 15 lb. turkey at the home of Mrs. Pressie B. Maxwell, 912 Hutchinson St., Monday evening at 7 p.m. All members and friends are invited to share. This turkey was donated to the club by the Alabama Appliance Co.

****

The June Club will meet at the residence of Dr. E. L. Smiley, 2402 W. Edgemont, Tuesday evening at 7:00 o'clock, November 22.

****

1. Visitor
2. New baby
3. Installation Program
4. Baptism
5. Philip Cade
6. Anniversary
7. Mobile Cross
8. See is present at the office
J.
Yolanda

King notes the birth of his daughter Yolanda on this church program of 20 November 1954.

the great preachers of our nation to Dexter Avenue Baptist Church for this occasion. I would like to extend to you an invitation to preach the Men's Day sermon on the second Sunday in July 1956.

I sincerely hope that you can accept the invitation. Your presence as well as your message would mean so much to our church and community. The members of Dexter and the whole Montgomery community have talked so much of the effectiveness of your preaching and of their desire to hear you again, that your presence would inevitably make this an epic making occasion.

I will look forward to hearing from you at your earliest convenience concerning this matter so that I may proceed in setting up my church calendar for the year. I have been reading of your inauguration. Again let me commend you for the great strides you have made, and you have my prayers and best wishes for a great future at Virginia Union.

Just last evening Coretta brought into the world a "big" little girl. She weighs nine pounds and eleven ounces. So you must see the new addition soon.

Sincerely yours,
M. L. King, Jr.,

MLK:lmt

TLc. DABCC.

From C. R. Williams

25 November 1955
Montgomery, Ala.

Williams, the president of Pilgrim Health and Life Insurance Company, asks King to speak at a program in Montgomery on 1 January 1956 commemorating the Emancipation Proclamation.

Dr. M. L. King, Jr.,
309 So. Jackson St.,
Montgomery, Alabama.

Dear Dr. King:

The Emancipation Proclamation Committee of Montgomery is considering a speaker for program to be had January 1, 1956 at Alabama State College. Your name is prominently suggested; hence, we would like to know if you are available for that date.

Since you have participated freely in committee activities, and are well aware of the character of programs previously presented, we will not go into further details. However, we would consider it a favor if we could have your immediate response as to availability and any other particulars.

Very truly yours,
Emancipation Proclamation Committee,
[*signed*]
C.R. Williams, President.

CRW:JEO

TLS. MLKP-MBU: Box 117.

To C. R. Williams

29 November 1955
[*Montgomery, Ala.*]

Mr. C. R. Williams
Pilgrim Health & Life Insurance Co.
131 Monroe Street
Montgomery, Alabama

Dear Mr. Williams:

Thanks for your very kind letter of November 25.

After checking my schedule, I find that I will be available to serve as guest speaker for the Emancipation Proclamation Program, Sunday, January 1. Please feel free to contact me concerning further developments.

With every good wish, I am

Sincerely yours,
M. L. King, Jr.

MLK:lmt

TLc. DABCC.

To H. Edward Whitaker

30 November 1955
[*Montgomery, Ala.*]

After several years of construction, Whitaker's New Hope Baptist Church was finished. Although King had declined an invitation to preach, he would eventually speak there in 1956.

Rev. H. Edward Whitaker
1122 Buffalo Avenue
Niagara Falls, New York

Dear Whit:

I have been intending to write you for several weeks now, but an extremely busy schedule has prevented it. I was very happy to get the picture of your church. It is simply beautiful, and you and your members are to be commended for such good taste. I can assure you that your one hundred-thousand dollars were well spent.

I am very sorry that I was unable to be with you on the dates we had previously discussed. I am sure that the fellowship would have been very rich indeed. However, I hope that it will be possible to come up for the special services during Holy Week. If such can be worked out I am sure that I can fit it into my schedule.

I am now the proud father of a little daughter. Her name is Yolonda Denise. She is now about thirteen days old, and she is keeping her father quite busy walking the floor. I hope every thing goes well with you and your family. Give all my best regards. Let me hear from you at your earliest convenience.

Sincerely yours,
M. L. King, Jr.

MLK:lmt

P.S. I am mailing the photograph of your church under separate cover.

TLc. DABCC.

Each volume of *The Papers of Martin Luther King, Jr.* includes a "Calendar of Documents" that provides an extensive list of significant King-related material for the period. In addition to specifying those documents selected for publication, the calendar includes other research material relevant to the study of King's life and work. It is generated from an online database maintained at the King Project's Stanford University office.

Space limitations prevent the publication of all documents from the online database, but researchers can utilize the information in the calendar to identify documents of interest among the many available in archives. This inventory includes not only all significant documents in the King collection at Boston University, but also documents obtained from King's relatives and acquaintances as well as material in archives such as the Moorland-Spingarn Research Center at Howard University. The calendar lists, for example, citations to all extant King-authored material, correspondence sent to King, and programs of events in which King participated.

School essays and notes constitute the bulk of the documentary material. Such items include class syllabi, lecture notes, papers written by his classmates, and other materials relating to King's intellectual development and his interaction with academic mentors. Although many papers lack identifying information, we determined their provenance by examining class notes and syllabi, course catalogues, and other documentary material. In this way, many documents from King's schooling could be assigned to a time span corresponding to one of the courses King completed during his nine years of postsecondary education. Documents that could not be identified with a specific course were assigned generally to the years King spent at Morehouse College, Crozer Theological Seminary, or Boston University. The calendar does not include published material about King unless the document appeared in a relatively obscure publication such as the *Morehouse College Bulletin*.

Each calendar entry provides essential information about the document. Italics and brackets indicate information assigned by the editors based on evidence contained in the document; in addition to brackets, question marks are used when the evidence is not conclusive. The entry adheres to the following format:

Date   Author (Affiliation). "Document Title." Date. Place of origin. (Physical description codes) Number of pages. (Notes.) Archival location. King Papers Project identification number.

5/9/52   King, Martin Luther, Jr. (Boston University). "Reinhold Niebuhr's Ethical Dualism, paper for Seminar in Systematic Theology." [5/9/52]. [*Boston, Mass.*] (THD) 14 pp. (Marginal comments by L. Harold DeWolf.) MLKP-MBU: Box 113. 520509–000.

Date. In those cases where the original document bears no date, the editors have assigned a date and enclosed it in brackets. Range dates that correspond to the dates of a school term are given to some undated papers such as school essays. Those documents bearing range dates are arranged after precisely dated documents, unless logic dictates another order. The date of photographs is presented without brackets if the donor provided a date. The date of published or printed papers is the date of publication or public release rather than the date of composition. The date in the left margin is intended to aid the reader in looking up specific documents. Complete date information is provided in the entry.

Author. A standardized form of an individual's name (based on *Anglo-American Cataloging Rules*, Second Edition) is provided in both the author and title fields. Forms of address are omitted unless necessary for identification, as in the case of a woman who used her husband's name. The calendar provides only one author for documents with multiple authors. For photographs, the photographer is considered the author. Since King's script is distinctive, his unsigned handwritten documents are identified as of certain authorship. Institutional authorship is provided when appropriate.

Affiliation. Affiliation information is provided if the author wrote in his or her capacity as an official of an organization. No brackets or italics have been used in the affiliation field. King's affiliation as a student at Morehouse, Crozer, or Boston is indicated in entries for documents produced during his formal education.

Title. In general, the title as it appears on the document is used, with minor emendations of punctuation, capitalization, and spelling for clarity. Phrases such as "Letter to," "Photo of," "Examination answers" are used to create titles for otherwise untitled documents; in such titles, words are generally in lower-case letters and names are standardized. For academic essays, the name of the course is provided in the title.

Place of Origin. This field identifies where the document was completed or, in the case of a published document, the place of publication. If the document does not contain the place of origin and the information can be obtained, it is provided in brackets; such information is offered only for documents written by King or his secretary.

Physical Description. This field describes the format of presentation, type of document, version of document, and character of the signature (see "List of Abbreviations"). Documents that consist of several formats are listed with the predominant one first.

Notes. In this optional field, miscellaneous information pertaining to the document is provided. This information includes enclosures to a letter, routing information ("copy to King"), and remarks concerning the legibility of the document or the authorship of marginalia. For tapes, information about the media used is also indicated in this field.

Archival Location. The location of the original document is identified using standard abbreviations based on the Library of Congress's *Symbols of American Libraries* (see "List of Abbreviations"). When available, box numbers are provided.

Identification Number. The nine-digit identification number is based on the date and uniquely identifies the document.

Documents that are published in the volume are set in boldface type.
Published documents contain bibliographic citations that adhere to the *Chicago Manual of Style*: name of journal, volume number (date of issue): page number.

7/26/48   **Mosley, John W. "Photo of Coretta Scott." 7/25–7/26/48. Philadelphia, Pa. (Ph) 1 p. CLBAA-PPT. 480726-000.**

9/16/51   Concord Baptist Church. "Program, Sunday services." 9/16/51. Brooklyn, N.Y. (TD) 4 pp. MLKP-MBU: Box 113. 510916-000.

9/27/51   [*Brightman, Edgar S.*] (Boston University). "Home Quiz I, Philosophy of Religion." 9/27/51. (THD) 1 p. (Marginal comments by King.) MLKP-MBU: Box 114. 510927-000.

10/3/51   Blanton, Sankey L. (Crozer Theological Seminary). "Letter to Martin Luther King, Jr." 10/3/51. Chester, Pa. (TLS) 1 p. CSKC. 511003-000.

10/3/51   "*Universal Jewish Encyclopedia*, paper for Seminar in Systematic Theology." [*10/3/51*]. (TD) 1 p. MLKP-MBU: Box 114. 511003-001.

10/10/51   "*Encyclopedia of Religion and Ethics*, paper for Seminar in Systematic Theology." [*10/10/51*]. (THD) 1 p. (Marginal comments by King.) MLKP-MBU: Box 114. 511010-000.

10/15/51   **[*King, Martin Luther, Jr.*] "Letter to Sankey L. Blanton." 10/15/51. Boston, Mass. (TLc) 1 p. MLKP-MBU: Box 116. 511015-000.**

10/16/51   King, Martin Luther, Jr. (Boston University). "Examination answers, Personalism." 10/16/51. [*Boston, Mass.*] (AHDS) 10 pp. (Marginal comments by L. Harold DeWolf.) MLKP-MBU: Box 115. 511016-000.

10/17/51   "*Religion in Life*, paper for Seminar in Systematic Theology." [*10/17/51*]. (TD) 1 p. MLKP-MBU: Box 114. 511017-000.

10/18/51   [*Brightman, Edgar S.*] (Boston University). "Home Quiz II, Philosophy of Religion." 10/18/51. (TD) 1 p. MLKP-MBU: Box 114. 511018-000.

10/24/51   Mills, E. (Boston University). "*Ecumenical Review*, paper for Seminar in Systematic Theology." [*10/24/51*]. (TD) 1 p. MLKP-MBU: Box 114. 511024-000.

10/25/51   King, Martin Luther, Jr. (Boston University). "A Comparison and Evaluation of the Views Set Forth in J. M. E. McTaggart's *Some Dogmas of Religion* with Those Set Forth by Edgar S. Brightman in His Course on 'Philosophy of Religion.'" [*10/25/51*]. [*Boston, Mass.*] (THDS) 12 pp. (Marginal comments by Edgar S. Brightman.) MLKP-MBU: Box 112. 511025-000.

10/26/51   **Enslin, Morton Scott (*Crozer Quarterly*). "Letter to Martin Luther King, Jr." 10/26/51. Chester, Pa. (ALS) 2 pp. MLKP-MBU: Box 117. 511026-000.**

10/31/51   "*Interpretation: A Journal of Bible and Theology*, paper for Seminar in Systematic Theology." [*10/31/51*]. (TD) 1 p. MLKP-MBU: Box 114. 511031-000.

10/31/51   "*Journal of Religious Thought*, paper for Seminar in Systematic Theology." [*10/31/51*]. (TD) 1 p. MLKP-MBU: Box 114. 511031-001.

11/13/51   [*Brightman, Edgar S.*] (Boston University). "Home Quiz III, Philosophy of Religion." 11/13/51. (TD) 1 p. MLKP-MBU: Box 114. 511113-000.

11/14/51   "*Theology Today*, paper for Seminar in Systematic Theology." [*11/14/51*]. (TD) 1 p. MLKP-MBU: Box 114. 511114-000.

11/16/51   King, Martin Luther, Jr. (Boston University). "Examination answers, Personalism." 11/16/51. [*Boston, Mass.*] (AHDS) 9 pp. (Marginal comments by L. Harold DeWolf.) MLKP-MBU: Box 115. 511116-000.

11/19/51   [*Scarrow, David S.*] (Boston University). "Examination questions, Formal Logic." [*11/19/51*]. (THD) 1 p. (Marginal comments by King.) MLKP-MBU: Box 113. 511119-000.

11/19/51   King, Martin Luther, Jr. (Boston University). "Examination answers, Formal Logic." [*11/19/51*]. [*Boston, Mass.*] (AHDS) 7 pp. (Marginal comments by David S. Scarrow.) MLKP-MBU: Box 113. 511119-001.

11/22/51   King, Martin Luther, Sr. "Invitation to 25th Wedding Anniversary Celebration of Martin Luther King, Sr. and Alberta Williams King." 11/22/51. Atlanta, Ga. (PD) 1 p. CKFC. 511122-000.

11/22/51   **"Photo of Christine King, Martin Luther King, Jr., Alberta Williams King, Naomi King, Alveda King, Alfred Daniel King, and Martin Luther King, Sr., 25th Wedding Anniversary Celebration." 11/22/51. Atlanta, Ga. (Ph) 1 p. CKFC. 511122-001.**

11/22/51   **"Photo of Martin Luther King, Sr. and Alberta Williams King, 25th Wedding Anniversary Celebration." 11/22/51. Atlanta, Ga. (Ph) 1 p. CKFC. 511122-002.**

11/22/51   "Photo of Martin Luther King, Jr., Christine King, Martin Luther King, Sr., Alberta Williams King, Alfred Daniel King, Naomi King, Jerome Brown, and Woodie Clara King Brown, 25th Wedding Anniversary Celebration." 11/22/51. Atlanta, Ga. (Ph) 1 p. CKFC. 511122-003.

597

11/22/51   "Photo of Martin Luther King, Sr. and Alberta Williams King, 25th Wedding Anniversary Celebration." 11/22/51. Atlanta, Ga. (Ph) 1 p. CKFC. 511122–004.

11/28/51   "*Journal of Bible and Religion*, paper for Seminar in Systematic Theology." [*11/28/51*]. (THD) 1 p. (Marginal comments by King.) MLKP-MBU: Box 114. 511128–000.

11/51   **"Photo, Some Morehouse Men of Philadelphia." 11/51. Atlanta, Ga. From: *Morehouse College Bulletin* 19 (November 1951): 6. (PPh) 1 p. TAP. 511100–004.**

12/4/51   **King, Martin Luther, Jr. (Boston University). "The Personalism of J. M. E. McTaggart Under Criticism, paper for Personalism." 12/4/51. [*Boston, Mass.*] (THDS) 17 pp. (Marginal comments by L. Harold DeWolf.) MLKP-MBU: Box 112. 511204–000.**

12/5/51   "*Personalist*, paper for Seminar in Systematic Theology." [*12/5/51*]. (TD) 1 p. MLKP-MBU: Box 114. 511205–000.

12/6/51   **King, Martin Luther, Jr. (Boston University). "Letter to Edgar S. Brightman." [*12/6/51*]. [*Boston, Mass.*] (AHLS) 2 pp. (Marginal comments by Edgar S. Brightman.) MLKP-MBU: Box 114. 511206–001.**

12/6/51   **King, Martin Luther, Jr. (Boston University). "A Comparison and Evaluation of the Philosophical Views Set Forth in J. M. E. McTaggart's *Some Dogmas of Religion*, and William E. Hocking's *The Meaning of God in Human Experience* with Those Set Forth in Edgar S. Brightman's Course on 'Philosophy of Religion.'" [*12/6/51*]. [*Boston, Mass.*] (THDS) 19 pp. (Marginal comments by Edgar S. Brightman.) MLKP-MBU: Box 112. 511206–000.**

12/12/51   King, Martin Luther, Jr. (Boston University). "Draft, *Crozer Quarterly*, paper for Seminar in Systematic Theology." [*12/12/51*]. [*Boston, Mass.*] (ADd) 8 pp. MLKP-MBU: Box 114. 511212–000.

12/12/51   **King, Martin Luther, Jr. (Boston University). "*Crozer Quarterly*, paper for Seminar in Systematic Theology." [*12/12/51*]. [*Boston, Mass.*] (TD) 1 p. MLKP-MBU: Box 114. 511212–001.**

1951   Reid, Ira (Baptist Inter-Convention Committee). "Negro Baptist Ministry: An Analysis of its Profession, Preparation, and Practices." 1951. (PDf) 18 pp. BEMP-DHU: Box 77. 510000–013.

1951   **"Photo of Coretta Scott." [*1951*]. (Ph) 1 p. BNC-OYesA. 510000–017.**

1/2/52   **King, Martin Luther, Jr. (Boston University). "Karl Barth's Conception of God, paper for Directed Study in Systematic Theology." 1/2/52. [*Boston, Mass.*] (THDS) 15 pp. (Marginal comments by L. Harold DeWolf.) MLKP-MBU: Box 113. 520102–000.**

1/9/52   [*Brightman, Edgar S.*] (Boston University). "Final examination questions, Philosophy of Religion." 1/9/52. (TD) 1 p. MLKP-MBU: Box 114. 520109–000.

1/9/52   **King, Martin Luther, Jr. (Boston University). "Final examination answers, Philosophy of Religion." [*1/9/52*]. [*Boston, Mass.*] (AHDS) 17 pp. (Marginal comments by Edgar S. Brightman.) MLKP-MBU: Box 115. 520109–002.**

1/11/52   [*Scarrow, David S.*] (Boston University). "Final examination questions, Formal Logic." 1/11/52. (THD) 2 pp. (Marginal comments by King.) MLKP-MBU: Box 115. 520111–000.

1/52   **King, Martin Luther, Jr. (Boston University). "Final examination answers, Personalism." 1/52. [*Boston, Mass.*] (AHDS) 16 pp. (Marginal comments by L. Harold DeWolf.) MLKP-MBU: Box 113. 520100–000.**

1/15/52   [*Brightman, Edgar S.*] (Boston University). "Syllabus, Philosophy of Religion." 9/13/51–1/15/52. (THD) 13 pp. (Marginal comments by King.) MLKP-MBU: Box 114. 520115–010.

1/15/52   [*Brightman, Edgar S.*] (Boston University). "Principles for All Four Home Quizzes, Philosophy of Religion." 9/13/51–1/15/52. (TD) 1 p. MLKP-MBU: Box 114. 520115–013.

1/15/52   King, Martin Luther, Jr. (Boston University). "Class notes, Philosophy of Religion." [*9/18/51–1/15/52*]. [*Boston, Mass.*] (AD) 15 pp. MLKP-MBU: Box 114. 520115–033.

1/15/52   King, Martin Luther, Jr. (Boston University). "Notes on evil, Philosophy of Religion." [*9/13/51–1/15/52*]. [*Boston, Mass.*] (AD) 2 pp. MLKP-MBU: Box 114. 520115–034.

1/15/52	King, Martin Luther, Jr. (Boston University?). "Notes on Luccock, chapters 12 and 13." [9/13/51–1/15/52?]. [Boston, Mass.?] (ADf) 1 p. MLKP-MBU: Box 113. 520115–035.
1/15/52	[Brightman, Edgar S.] (Boston University). "Card file for Martin Luther King, Jr." [1/15/52]. (TD) 1 p. ESBC-MBU. 520115–040.
1/15/52	DeWolf, L. Harold (Boston University). "Syllabus, Seminar in Systematic Theology." 9/13/51–1/15/52. (THD) 2 pp. (Marginal comments by King.) MLKP-MBU: Box 114. 520115–014.
1/15/52	King, Martin Luther, Jr. (Boston University). "Class notes, Seminar in Systematic Theology." [9/13/51–1/15/52]. [Boston, Mass.] (AD) 19 pp. MLKP-MBU: Box 114. 520115–023.
1/15/52	"Scottish Journal of Theology, paper for Seminar in Systematic Theology." [9/13/51–1/15/52]. (TD) 1 p. MLKP-MBU: Box 114. 520115–017.
1/15/52	"List of the Most Important Theological Journals in German Language, paper for Seminar in Systematic Theology." [9/13/51–1/15/52]. (THD) 2 pp. (Marginal comments by King.) MLKP-MBU: Box 114. 520115–019.
1/15/52	"Theology—A Monthly Journal of Historic Christianity, paper for Seminar in Systematic Theology." [9/13/51–1/15/52]. (TD) 1 p. MLKP-MBU: Box 114. 520115–022.
1/15/52	"Philosophy, paper for Seminar in Systematic Theology." [9/13/51–1/15/52]. (TD) 1 p. MLKP-MBU: Box 114. 520115–030.
1/15/52	"Hibbert Journal, paper for Seminar in Systematic Theology." [9/13/51–1/15/52]. (THD) 1 p. (Marginal comments by King.) MLKP-MBU: Box 114. 520115–031.
1/15/52	"Philosophical Review, paper for Seminar in Systematic Theology." [9/13/51–1/15/52]. (TAD) 1 p. MLKP-MBU: Box 114. 520115–032.
1/15/52	**King, Martin Luther, Jr. (Boston University?). "Contemporary Continental Theology, paper for Seminar in Systematic Theology." [9/13/51–1/15/52?]. [Boston, Mass.?] (THDS) 25 pp. (Marginal comments by L. Harold DeWolf.) MLKP-MBU: Box 112. 520115–039.**
1/15/52	[DeWolf, L. Harold] (Boston University). "Syllabus, Personalism." 9/13/51–1/15/52. (THD) 12 pp. (Marginal comments by King.) MLKP-MBU: Box 113. 520115–003.
1/15/52	King, Martin Luther, Jr. (Boston University). "Class notes, Personalism." [9/13/51–1/15/52]. [Boston, Mass.] (AD) 81 pp. MLKP-MBU: Box 113. 520115–008.
1/15/52	[Scarrow, David S.] (Boston University). "Examination questions, Formal Logic." [9/13/51–1/15/52]. [Boston, Mass.] (THD) 1 p. (Marginal comments by King.) MLKP-MBU: Box 113. 520115–005.
1/15/52	King, Martin Luther, Jr. (Boston University). "Examination answers, Formal Logic." [9/13/51–1/15/52]. [Boston, Mass.] (AHDS) 5 pp. (Marginal comments by David S. Scarrow.) MLKP-MBU: Box 113. 520115–037.
1/15/52	King, Martin Luther, Jr. (Boston University). "Class notes, Formal Logic." [9/13/51–1/15/52]. [Boston, Mass.] (AD) 34 pp. MLKP-MBU: Box 113. 520115–007.
1/15/52	King, Martin Luther, Jr. (Boston University). "Exercises, Formal Logic." [9/13/51–1/15/52]. [Boston, Mass.] (AD) 2 pp. MLKP-MBU: Box 113. 520115–004.
1/15/52	King, Martin Luther, Jr. (Boston University). "Exercises, Formal Logic." [9/13/51–1/15/52]. [Boston, Mass.] (AD) 32 pp. MLKP-MBU: Box 113. 520115–006.
1/15/52	King, Martin Luther, Jr. (Boston University). "Exercises, Formal Logic." [9/13/51–1/15/52]. [Boston, Mass.] (ADS) 2 pp. MLKP-MBU: Box 113. 520115–036.
1/15/52	King, Martin Luther, Jr. (Boston University). "Philosophy, exercise for Formal Logic." [9/13/51–1/15/52]. [Boston, Mass.] (ADS) 3 pp. MLKP-MBU: Box 113. 520115–038.
1/23/52	[Keller, Ed] (Boston University). "Walter Marshall Horton, paper for Seminar in Systematic Theology." [1/23/52]. (TAD) 1 p. MLKP-MBU: Box 114. 520123–000.
1/52	King, Martin Luther, Jr. (Boston University). "List of classes to be taken at Boston University." [1/52]. [Boston, Mass.] (AD) 2 pp. MLKP-MBU: Box 113. 520100–001.
2/6/52	[Baker, Luther G.] (Boston University). "Edwin Lewis, paper for Seminar in

Systematic Theology." [*2/6/52*]. (TD) 1 p. MLKP-MBU: Box 114. 520206–000.

2/20/52 "William Norman Pittenger, paper for Seminar in Systematic Theology." [*2/20/52*]. (THD) 1 p. (Marginal comments by King.) MLKP-MBU: Box 114. 520220–000.

2/27/52 Metallides (Boston University). "Nels F. S. Ferré, paper for Seminar in Systematic Theology." [*2/27/52*]. (THD) 1 p. (Marginal comments by King.) MLKP-MBU: Box 114. 520227–000.

2/27/52 Kirche, Roland (Boston University). "Nels Ferré, paper for Seminar in Systematic Theology." [*2/27/52*]. (THD) 1 p. (Marginal comments by King.) MLKP-MBU: Box 114. 520227–001.

2/52 [*DeWolf, L. Harold*] (Boston University). "Examination questions, Systematic Theology." 2/52. (TD) 1 p. MLKP-MBU: Box 113. 520200–000.

3/5/52 McLaughlin, Wayman (Boston University). "Robert Lowry Calhoun, paper for Seminar in Systematic Theology." [*3/5/52*]. (THD) 1 p. (Marginal comments by King.) MLKP-MBU: Box 114. 520305–000.

3/21/52 [*Demos, Raphael*] (Harvard University). "Examination questions, History of Modern Philosophy." [*3/21/52*]. (TD) 1 p. MLKP-MBU: Box 115. 520321–000.

3/21/52 King, Martin Luther, Jr. (Harvard University). "Examination answers, History of Modern Philosophy." [*3/21/52*]. [Cambridge, Mass.] (AHD) 9 pp. (Marginal comments by Raphael Demos.) MLKP-MBU: Box 115. 520321–002.

3/26/52 Fehlman, Robert B. (Boston University). "John Coleman Bennett, paper for Seminar in Systematic Theology." 3/26/52. (TDS) 1 p. MLKP-MBU: Box 114. 520326–000.

4/2/52 Kopelke, William F. (Boston University). "Ethics of Reinhold Niebuhr, paper for Seminar in Systematic Theology." 4/2/52. (TD) 1 p. MLKP-MBU: Box 115. 520402–000.

4/2/52 King, Martin Luther, Jr. (Boston University). "Draft, Reinhold Niebuhr, paper for Seminar in Systematic Theology." [*4/2/52*]. [*Boston, Mass.*] (ADdS) 6 pp. MLKP-MBU: Box 115. 520402–001.

4/2/52 **King, Martin Luther, Jr. (Boston University). "Reinhold Niebuhr, paper for Seminar in Systematic Theology." [*4/2/52*]. [*Boston, Mass.*] (THDS) 1 p. MRP-GAMK. 520402–002.**

4/4/52 King, Martin Luther, Jr. (Boston University). "Examination answers, Religious Teaching of the New Testament." [*4/4/52*]. [*Boston, Mass.*] (AHDS) 10 pp. (Marginal comments by L. Harold DeWolf.) MLKP-MBU: Box 113. 520404–000.

4/9/52 Mauck, Donald M. (Boston University). "Shirley Jackson Case, paper for Seminar in Systematic Theology." 4/9/52. (TDS) 1 p. MLKP-MBU: Box 114. 520409–000.

4/9/52 Bullard, Jack L. (Boston University). "Reinhold Niebuhr, paper for Seminar in Systematic Theology." [*4/9/52*]. (THDS) 2 pp. (Marginal comments by King.) MLKP-MBU: Box 115. 520409–001.

4/16/52 Rouch, Mark (Boston University). "Henry Nelson Wieman: The Content of His Theology, paper for Seminar in Systematic Theology." 4/16/52. (THDS) 1 p. (Marginal comments by King.) MLKP-MBU: Box 114. 520416–000.

4/16/52 "Henry Nelson Wieman, paper for Seminar in Systematic Theology." [*4/16/52*]. (TD) 1 p. MLKP-MBU: Box 114. 520416–001.

4/23/52 Erb, John D. (Boston University). "Georgia Harkness, paper for Seminar in Systematic Theology." 4/23/52. (THDS) 1 p. (Marginal comments by King.) MLKP-MBU: Box 114. 520423–000.

4/23/52 Mitchell, Kenneth (Boston University). "H. Richard Niebuhr, paper for Seminar in Systematic Theology." [*4/23/52*]. (TADS) 1 p. MLKP-MBU: Box 114. 520423–001.

5/7/52 Booth, Newoel S. (Boston University). "Paul Sevier Minear, paper for Seminar in Systematic Theology." 5/7/52. (TADS) 1 p. MLKP-MBU: Box 114. 520507–000.

5/7/52 Larsen, William (Boston University). "Walter Lowrie, paper for Seminar in Systematic Theology." [*5/7/52*]. (THDS) 1 p. (Marginal comments by King.) MLKP-MBU: Box 114. 520507–001.

5/9/52 **King, Martin Luther, Jr. (Boston University). "Reinhold Niebuhr's Ethical Dualism, paper for Seminar in Systematic Theology." 5/9/52. [*Boston,***

Mass.] (THD) 16 pp. (Marginal comments by L. Harold DeWolf.) MLKP-MBU: Box 113. 520509–000.

5/9/52   King, Martin Luther, Jr. (Boston University). "A Comparison of Friedrich Schleiermacher's Christology with that of Albrecht Ritschl, paper for Directed Study in Systematic Theology." 5/9/52. [*Boston, Mass.*] (THDS) 29 pp. (Marginal comments by L. Harold DeWolf.) MLKP-MBU: Box 112. 520509–001.

5/16/52   [*DeWolf, L. Harold*] (Boston University). "Course outline, Seminar in Systematic Theology." 1/23–5/16/52. (THD) 4 pp. (Marginal comments by King.) MLKP-MBU: Box 114. 520516–008.

5/16/52   King, Martin Luther, Jr. (Boston University). "Class notes, Seminar in Systematic Theology." [*1/23–5/16/52*]. [*Boston, Mass.*] (AHD) 6 pp. MLKP-MBU: Box 113. 520516–009.

5/16/52   "Vergilius Ture Anselm Ferm, paper for Seminar in Systematic Theology." [*1/23–5/16/52*]. (TAD) 1 p. MLKP-MBU: Box 114. 520516–013.

5/16/52   "Sören Kierkegaard, paper for Seminar in Systematic Theology." [*1/23–5/16/52*]. (THD) 3 pp. (Marginal comments by King.) MLKP-MBU: Box 114. 520516–020.

5/16/52   King, Martin Luther, Jr. (Boston University). "Notes on Niebuhr's theory of history and the Kingdom of God." [*1/23–5/16/52*]. [*Boston, Mass.*] (AD) 2 pp. MLKP-MBU: Box 115. 520516–022.

5/16/52   King, Martin Luther, Jr. (Boston University). "Class notes, Religious Teachings of the New Testament." [*1/23–5/16/52*]. [*Boston, Mass.*] (AD) 41 pp. MLKP-MBU: Box 114. 520516–007.

5/16/52   King, Martin Luther, Jr. (Boston University). "Examination answers, Religious Teachings of the New Testament." [*1/23–5/16/52*]. [*Boston, Mass.*] (AHDS) 7 pp. (Marginal comments by L. Harold DeWolf.) MLKP-MBU: Box 115. 520516–001.

5/16/52   King, Martin Luther, Jr. (Boston University). "Final examination answers, Religious Teachings of the New Testament." [*1/23–5/16/52*]. [*Boston, Mass.*] (AHDS) 18 pp. (Marginal comments by L. Harold DeWolf.) MLKP-MBU: Box 115. 520516–000.

5/16/52   King, Martin Luther, Jr. (Boston University). "Notes on *The Kingdom and the Power* by Paul Sevier Minear." [*1/23–5/16/52*]. [*Boston, Mass.*] (AD) 8 pp. MLKP-MBU: Box 113. 520516–003.

5/16/52   King, Martin Luther, Jr. (Boston University). "Notes on *Biblical Theology* by Millar Burrows." [*1/23–5/16/52*]. [*Boston, Mass.*] (AD) 3 pp. MLKP-MBU: Box 113. 520516–004.

5/16/52   King, Martin Luther, Jr. (Boston University). "Notes on *New Testament Theology* by Henry Clay Sheldon." [*1/23–5/16/52*]. [*Boston, Mass.*] (AD) 13 pp. MLKP-MBU: Box 113. 520516–005.

5/16/52   King, Martin Luther, Jr. (Boston University). "Notes on *Present Theological Tendencies*, by Edwin Ewart Aubrey; *The Divine Imperative*, by Emil Brunner; and *Principles of Christian Ethics*, by Albert Cornelius Knudson." [*1/23–5/16/52*]. [*Boston, Mass.*] (AD) 3 pp. MLKP-MBU: Box 113. 520516–006.

6/10/52   [*Demos, Raphael*] (Harvard University). "Reading list, History of Modern Philosophy." [*2/4–6/10/52*]. (TD) 1 p. MLKP-MBU: Box 115. 520610–000.

6/10/52   King, Martin Luther, Jr. (Harvard University). "Class notes, History of Modern Philosophy." [*2/4–6/10/52*]. [*Cambridge, Mass.*] (AD) 80 pp. MLKP-MBU: Box 114. 520610–001.

6/10/52   King, Martin Luther, Jr. (Harvard University). "Notes, History of Modern Philosophy." [*2/4–6/10/52*]. [*Cambridge, Mass.*] (AD) 3 pp. MLKP-MBU: Box 115. 520610–003.

6/10/52   King, Martin Luther, Jr. (Harvard University). "Descartes, paper for History of Modern Philosophy." [*2/4–6/10/52*]. [*Cambridge, Mass.*] (AHDS) 1 p. (Marginal comments by Raphael Demos.) MLKP-MBU: Box 115. 520610–002.

6/22/52   **Alpha Phi Alpha Fraternity. "Membership Certificate for Martin Luther King, Jr." [*6/22/52*]. Boston, Mass. (TFmS) 1 p. MLKP-MBU: Box 113. 520622–000.**

6/52   [*Demos, Raphael*] (Harvard University). "Final examination questions, History of Modern Philosophy." 6/52. (THD) 2 pp. (Marginal comments by King.) MLKP-MBU: Box 115. 520600–001.

7/5/52   King, Martin Luther, Jr. (Boston University). "Class notes, History of Recent Philosophy." [5/26–7/5/52]. [Boston, Mass.] (AD) 82 pp. MLKP-MBU: Box 114. 520705–000.

7/5/52   King, Martin Luther, Jr. (Boston University). "The Influence of Darwinian Biology on Pragmatism with Special Emphasis on William James and John Dewey, paper for History of Recent Philosophy." [5/26–7/5/52]. [Boston, Mass.] (THDS) 26 pp. (Marginal comments by Richard M. Millard.) MLKP-MBU: Box 115. 520705–004.

7/5/52   King, Martin Luther, Jr. (Boston University). "Examination answers, History of Recent Philosophy." [5/26–7/5/52]. [Boston, Mass.] (AHDS) 12 pp. (Marginal comments by Richard M. Millard.) MLKP-MBU: Box 115. 520705–001.

7/5/52   King, Martin Luther, Jr. (Boston University?). "Notes on alcohol, William James, and mysticism." [5/26–7/5/52?]. [Boston, Mass.?] (AD) 3 pp. MLKP-MBU: Box 106. 520705–006.

7/5/52   King, Martin Luther, Jr. (Boston University). "Class notes, Seminar in Historical Theology." [5/26–7/5/52]. [Boston, Mass.] (AD) 60 pp. MLKP-MBU: Box 114. 520705–002.

7/5/52   King, Martin Luther, Jr. (Boston University). "Comparison of the Theology of Luther with That of Calvin, paper for Seminar in Historical Theology." [5/26–7/5/52]. [Boston, Mass.] (THDS) 21 pp. (Marginal comments by Edward Booth.) MLKP-MBU: Box 113. 520705–005.

7/29/52   King, Martin Luther, Jr. "Letter to Charles E. Batten." 7/29/52. Atlanta, Ga. (THLS) 1 p. CRO-NRCR. 520729–000.

7/31/52   Batten, Charles E. (Crozer Theological Seminary). "Letter to Martin Luther King, Jr." 7/31/52. (TLc) 1 p. CRO-NRCR. 520731–000.

8/14/52   Watson, Melvin H. (Morehouse College). "Letter to Martin Luther King, Jr." 8/14/52. Atlanta, Ga. (ALS) 3 pp. MLKP-MBU: Box 117. 520814–000.

9/5/52   Phelps, Reginald H. (Harvard University). "Letter to Martin Luther King, Jr." 9/5/52. Cambridge, Mass. (TLS) 1 p. MLKP-MBU: Box 117. 520905–001.

9/18/52   King, Martin Luther, Jr. (Boston University). "Petition to Boston University Faculty." 9/18/52. [Boston, Mass.] (ATFmS) 2 pp. (Includes approval by Chester M. Alter.) MLKP-MBU: Box 117. 520918–000.

9/24/52   King, Martin Luther, Jr. (Boston University). "Exploratory quiz, Seminar in Hegel." [9/24/52]. [Boston, Mass.] (AHDS) 3 pp. (Marginal comments by Edgar S. Brightman.) MLKP-MBU: Box 113. 520924–007.

9/24/52   [Godwin, R. C.] (Boston University). "Seminar in Hegel, session no. 1." 9/24/52. (THD) 1 p. (Marginal comments by King.) MLKP-MBU: Box 115. 520924–000.

10/1/52   [Godwin, R. C.] (Boston University). "Seminar in Hegel, session no. 2: Life, Writings, Influence of Hegel." 10/1/52. (TD) 1 p. MLKP-MBU: Box 115. 521001–000.

10/1/52   King, Martin Luther, Jr. (Boston University). "The Development of Hegel's Thought as Revealed in his Early Theological Writings, paper for Seminar in Hegel." [10/1/52]. [Boston, Mass.] (THDS) 3 pp. (Marginal comments by Edgar S. Brightman.) MLKP-MBU: Box 115. 521001–001.

10/3/52   King, Martin Luther, Jr. (Boston University). "Examination answers, Religious Teachings of the Old Testament." 10/3/52. [Boston, Mass.] (AHDS) 9 pp. (Marginal comments by L. Harold DeWolf.) MLKP-MBU: Box 115. 521003–000.

10/8/52   [Godwin, R. C.] (Boston University). "Seminar in Hegel, session no. 3: Dialectic." 10/8/52. (TD) 1 p. MLKP-MBU: Box 115. 521008–000.

10/15/52   [Godwin, R. C.] (Boston University). "Seminar in Hegel, session no. 4: PHÄN as a Whole." 10/15/52. (THD) 1 p. (Marginal comments by King.) MLKP-MBU: Box 115. 521015–000.

10/15/52   King, Martin Luther, Jr. (Boston University). "The Transition from Sense-Certainty to Sense-Perception in Hegel's Analysis of Consciousness, paper for Seminar in Hegel." [10/15/52]. [Boston, Mass.] (THDS) 3 pp. (Marginal comments by Peter A. Bertocci.) MLKP-MBU: Box 115. 521015–001.

10/22/52   [Godwin, R. C.] (Boston University). "Seminar in Hegel, session no. 5: Bewusstsein." 10/22/52. (TD) 1 p. MLKP-MBU: Box 115. 521022–000.

10/23/52   Demos, Raphael (Harvard University). "Book review of *Systematic Theology* by

Paul Tillich." 10/23/52. New York, N.Y. From: *Journal of Philosophy* 49 (23 October 1952): 692–708. (PHDS) 17 pp. (Marginal comments by King.) MLKP-MBU: Box 107. 521023–000.

10/28/52 King, Martin Luther, Jr. (Boston University). "Examination answers, History of Christian Doctrine." [*10/28/52*]. [*Boston, Mass.*] (AHDS) 10 pp. (Marginal comments by L. Harold DeWolf.) MLKP-MBU: Box 115. 521028–000.

10/29/52 [*Godwin, R. C.*] (Boston University). "Seminar in Hegel, session no. 6: Selbstbewusstsein." 10/29/52. (TAD) 1 p. MLKP-MBU: Box 115. 521029–000.

10/29/52 King, Martin Luther, Jr. (Boston University). "The Transition from Sense-Perception to Understanding, paper for Seminar in Hegel." [*10/29/52*]. [*Boston, Mass.*] (THDS) 6 pp. (Marginal comments by Peter A. Bertocci.) MLKP-MBU: Box 115. 521029–001.

10/31/52 **Whitaker, H. Edward. "Letter to Martin Luther King, Jr." 10/31/52. Niagara Falls, N.Y. (ALS) 2 pp. MLKP-MBU: Box 117. 521031–000.**

11/6/52 **Strassner, William R. (Shaw University). "Letter to Martin Luther King, Jr." 11/6/52. Raleigh, N.C. (TLS) 1 p. (Contains enclosure 521106–001.) MLKP-MBU: Box 117. 521106–000.**

11/6/52 Shaw University. "Faculty Application." [*11/6/52*]. Raleigh, N.C. (Fm) 4 pp. (Enclosure in 521106–000.) CSKC. 521106–001.

11/12/52 [*Godwin, R. C.*] (Boston University). "Seminar in Hegel, session no. 7." 11/12/52. (THD) 1 p. (Marginal comments by King.) MLKP-MBU: Box 115. 521112–000.

11/13/52 King, Martin Luther, Jr. (Boston University). "Examination answers, Seminar in History of Philosophy." [*11/13/52*]. [*Boston, Mass.*] (AHDS) 14 pp. (Marginal comments by Peter A. Bertocci.) MLKP-MBU: Box 113. 521113–000.

11/13/52 [*Demos, Raphael*] (Harvard University). "Examination questions, Philosophy of Plato." 11/13/52. (TD) 1 p. MLKP-MBU: Box 113. 521113–003.

11/13/52 King, Martin Luther, Jr. (Harvard University). "Examination answers, Philosophy of Plato." [*11/13/52*]. [*Cambridge, Mass.*] (AHDS) 9 pp. (Marginal comments by Raphael Demos.) MLKP-MBU: Box 113. 521113–001.

11/18/52 **Handy, W. T., Jr. (Newman Methodist Church). "Letter to Martin Luther King, Jr." 11/18/52. Alexandria, La. (TALS) 2 pp. MLKP-MBU: Box 117. 521118–001.**

11/19/52 [*Godwin, R. C.*] (Boston University). "Seminar in Hegel, session no. 8." 11/19/52. (THD) 1 p. (Marginal comments by King.) MLKP-MBU: Box 115. 521119–000.

12/3/52 **Blanton, Sankey L. (Crozer Theological Seminary). "Letter to William R. Strassner." 12/3/52. (TLc) 1 p. (Copy sent to King.) MLKP-MBU: Box 117. 521203–000.**

12/3/52 [*Godwin, R. C.*] (Boston University). "Seminar in Hegel, session no. 10." 12/3/52. (TD) 1 p. MLKP-MBU: Box 115. 521203–001.

12/3/52 [*Bertocci, Peter A.*] (Boston University). "Phenomenology of Mind, Seminar in Hegel." [*12/3/52*]. (THD) 10 pp. (Marginal comments by King.) MLKP-MBU: Box 115. 521203–002.

12/17/52 [*Godwin, R. C.*] (Boston University). "Seminar in Hegel, session no. 12." 12/17/52. (THD) 1 p. (Marginal comments by King.) MLKP-MBU: Box 115. 521217–000.

1952 "Photo of William H. (William Herbert) Gray, Jr., Christine King, Martin Luther King, Jr., Alberta Williams King, Martin Luther King, Sr., at Bright Hope Baptist Church." 1952. Philadelphia, Pa. From: *Dedicatory Program of the Bright Hope Baptist Church* (Philadelphia: Bright Hope Baptist Church, 1965):28. 1 p. (PPh) MLKJrP-GAMK. 520000–026.

1/2/53 Strassner, William R. (Shaw University). "Letter to Martin Luther King, Jr." 1/2/53. Raleigh, N.C. (TLS) 1 p. MLKP-MBU: Box 117. 530102–000.

1/8/53 Phelps, Reginald H. (Harvard University). "Letter to Martin Luther King, Jr." 1/8/53. Cambridge, Mass. (TLS) 1 p. MLKP-MBU: Box 117. 530108–000.

1/9/53 King, Martin Luther, Jr. (Boston University). "A Critical Evaluation of Augustine's Conception of Evil, paper for History of Christian Doctrine." 1/9/53. [*Boston, Mass.*] (THDS) 24 pp. (Marginal comments by L. Harold DeWolf.) MLKP-MBU: Box 115. 530109–000.

1/20/53 DeWolf, L. Harold (Boston University). "Final examination questions, History of Christian Doctrine." 1/20/53. (THD) 1 p. (Marginal comments by King.) MLKP-MBU: Box 114. 530120–000.

1/20/53   King, Martin Luther, Jr. (Boston University). "Final examination answers, History of Christian Doctrine." [*1/20/53*]. [*Boston, Mass.*] (AHDS) 21 pp. (Marginal comments by L. Harold DeWolf.) MLKP-MBU: Box 113. 530120–001.

1/26/53   [*Demos, Raphael*] (Harvard University). "Syllabus, Philosophy of Plato." [*9/22/52–1/26/53*]. (THD) 1 p. (Marginal comments by King.) MLKP-MBU: Box 114. 530126–000.

1/26/53   King, Martin Luther, Jr. (Harvard University). "Class notes, Philosophy of Plato." [*9/22/52–1/26/53*]. [*Cambridge, Mass.*] (AD) 48 pp. MLKP-MBU: Box 114. 530126–003.

1/26/53   King, Martin Luther, Jr. (Harvard University?). "Notes on Plato." [*9/22/52–1/26/53?*]. [*Cambridge, Mass.?*] (AD) 1 p. MLKP-MBU: Box 114. 530126–002.

1/26/53   [*King, Martin Luther, Jr.?*] (Harvard University?). "Plato's ideas about God and gods, paper for Philosophy of Plato." [*9/22/52–1/26/53?*]. [*Cambridge, Mass.?*]. (TD) 17 pp. MLKP-MBU: Box 112. 530126–001.

1/53   [*Demos, Raphael*] (Harvard University). "Final examination questions, Philosophy of Plato." 1/53. (TD) 2 pp. MLKP-MBU: Box 114. 530100–001.

1/28/53   **King, Martin Luther, Jr. (Boston University). "Notecards on books of the Old Testament." [*9/22/52–1/28/53*]. [*Boston, Mass.*] (AD) 834 pp. CSKC. 530128–014 through 530128–048.**

1/28/53   King, Martin Luther, Jr. (Boston University). "Notecards on Old Testament Biblical references and comments." [*9/22/52–1/28/53*]. [*Boston, Mass.*] (AD) 19 pp. CSKC. 530128–049.

1/28/53   King, Martin Luther, Jr. (Boston University). "Examination answers, Religious Teachings of the Old Testament." [*9/22/52–1/28/53*]. [*Boston, Mass.*] (AHDS) 11 pp. (Marginal comments by L. Harold DeWolf.) MLKP-MBU: Box 115. 530128–000.

1/28/53   **King, Martin Luther, Jr. (Boston University). "Final examination answers, Religious Teachings of the Old Testament." [*9/22/52–1/28/53*]. [*Boston, Mass.*] (AHDS) 16 pp. (Marginal comments by L. Harold DeWolf.) MLKP-MBU: Box 112. 530128–013.**

1/28/53   DeWolf, L. Harold (Boston University). "Syllabus, History of Christian Doctrine." 9/22/52–1/28/53. (TD) 1 p. MLKP-MBU: Box 114. 530128–002.

1/28/53   King, Martin Luther, Jr. (Boston University). "Class notes, History of Christian Doctrine." [*9/22/52–1/28/53*]. [*Boston, Mass.*] (AD) 57 pp. MLKP-MBU: Box 114. 530128–003.

1/28/53   King, Martin Luther, Jr. (Boston University). "Outlines of Ancient, Medieval, and Modern Philosophy." [*9/22/52–1/28/53?*]. [*Boston, Mass.*] (AHD) 62 pp. MLKP-MBU: Box 112. 530128–004.

1/28/53   Brightman, Edgar S. (Boston University). "Outline of History of Philosophy." [*9/22/52–1/28/53?*]. (TD) 7 pp. MLKP-MBU: Box 115. 530128–005.

1/28/53   King, Martin Luther, Jr. (Boston University). "Class notes, Seminar in History of Philosophy." [*9/22/52–1/28/53*]. [*Boston, Mass.*] (AD) 20 pp. MLKP-MBU: Box 114. 530128–001.

1/28/53   King, Martin Luther, Jr. (Boston University). "Notes, History of Philosophy." [*9/22/52–1/28/53?*]. [*Boston, Mass.*] (AD) 4 pp. CSKC. 530128–007.

1/28/53   King, Martin Luther, Jr. (Boston University). "Notes, Seminar in History of Philosophy." [*9/22/52–1/28/53*]. [*Boston, Mass.*] (AD) 17 pp. MLKP-MBU: Box 114. 530128–011.

1/28/53   King, Martin Luther, Jr. (Boston University?). "Notes on *The Instructor*, Book I, by Clement of Alexandria." [*9/22/52–1/28/53?*]. [*Boston, Mass.?*] (AD) 2 pp. MLKP-MBU: Box 113. 530128–012.

2/4/53   **King, Martin Luther, Jr. (Boston University). "Petition to the Boston University Faculty." 2/4/53. [*Boston, Mass.*] (ATFmS) 2 pp. (Includes approval by Chester M. Alter.) MLKP-MBU: Box 117. 530204–000.**

2/17/53   **King, D. E. (Zion Baptist Church). "Letter to Martin Luther King, Jr." 2/17/53. Louisville, Ky. (TLS) 1 p. MLKP-MBU: Box 117. 530217–000.**

2/18/53   Loverude, Otto R. (First United Baptist Church). "Letter to Martin Luther King, Jr." 2/18/53. Lowell, Mass. (TLS) 1 p. MLKP-MBU: Box 117. 530218–000.

2/18/53   "Final examination questions, German." [*9/13/51–2/18/53?*]. (THD) 1 p. (Marginal comments by King.) CSKC. 530218–001.

2/18/53 King, Martin Luther, Jr. (Boston University). "German vocabulary." [9/13/51– 2/18/53]. [Boston, Mass.] (AD) 36 pp. CSKC. 530218–002.

2/18/53 King, Martin Luther, Jr. (Boston University). "German vocabulary." [9/13/51– 2/18/53]. [Boston, Mass.] (AD) 5 pp. MLKP-MBU: Box 115. 530218–003.

2/24/53 Beshai, Jimmy. "Letter to Martin Luther King, Jr." 2/24/53. Cairo, Egypt. (TLS) 1 p. MLKP-MBU: Box 117. 530224–000.

2/53 **"Photo of Martin Luther King, Jr., and friends." 2/53. Boston, Mass. (Ph) 1 p. JMBC. 530200–005.**

2/53 **"Photo of Martin Luther King, Jr., Reuben Dawkins, and Sybil Haydel Morial." 2/53. Boston, Mass. (Ph) 1 p. JMBC. 530200–004.**

2/53 [*King, Martin Luther, Jr.*] "Letter to Mrs. Ford." [2/53]. [Boston, Mass.] (HLd) 1 p. MLKP-MBU: Box 116. 530200–002.

2/53 [*King, Martin Luther, Jr.*] "Letter to Henry Kelley." [2/53]. [Boston, Mass.] (HLd) 3 pp. MLKP-MBU: Box 116. 530200–003.

3/16/53 King, Martin Luther, Jr. (Harvard University). "Examination answers, Philosophy of Whitehead." [3/16/53]. [Cambridge, Mass.] (AHDS) 12 pp. (Marginal comments by Nathaniel M. Lawrence.) MLKP-MBU: Box 115. 530316–000.

3/24/53 King, Martin Luther, Jr. (Boston University). "Examination answers, History of Christian Doctrine." [3/24/53]. [Boston, Mass.] (AHDS) 12 pp. (Marginal comments by L. Harold DeWolf.) MLKP-MBU: Box 115. 530324–000.

3/53 **King, Martin Luther, Jr. "Letter to Otto R. Loverude." [3/53]. [Boston, Mass.] (ALdS) 1 p. MLKP-MBU: Box 116. 530300–000.**

3/53 **[King, Martin Luther, Jr.] "Letter to D. E. King." [3/53]. [Boston, Mass.] (AHLd) 1 p. MLKP-MBU: Box 116. 530300–001.**

4/12/53 First United Baptist Church. "United Baptist Church Messenger." 4/12/53. Lowell, Mass. (PD) 2 pp. FUBCR. 530412–000.

4/53 Boston University. "Regulations on the Preparation of the Dissertation for the Degree of Doctor of Philosophy." 4/53. Boston, Mass. (PD) 5 pp. (Enclosure in 531009–000.) CSKC. 530400–000.

5/15/53 **King, Martin Luther, Jr. (Boston University). "A Comparison and Evaluation of the Theology of Luther with That of Calvin, paper for History of Christian Doctrine." 5/15/53. [Boston, Mass.] (THDS) 26 pp. (Marginal comments by L. Harold DeWolf.) MLKP-MBU: Box 112. 530515–000.**

5/19/53 [*DeWolf, L. Harold*] (Boston University). "Final examination questions, History of Christian Doctrine." 5/19/53. (TD) 1 p. MLKP-MBU: Box 114. 530519–001.

5/19/53 **King, Martin Luther, Jr. (Boston University). "Final examination answers, History of Christian Doctrine." 5/19/53. [Boston, Mass.] (AHDS) 19 pp. (Marginal comments by L. Harold DeWolf.) MLKP-MBU: Box 115. 530519–003.**

5/22/53 DeWolf, L. Harold (Boston University). "Syllabus, History of Christian Doctrine." 2/4–5/22/53. (THD) 3 pp. (Marginal comments by King.) MLKP-MBU: Box 113. 530522–028.

5/22/53 King, Martin Luther, Jr. (Boston University). "Notes on *History of Christian Doctrine* by George Park Fisher." [9/22/52–5/22/53]. [Boston, Mass.] (AD) 66 pp. MLKP-MBU: Box 114. 530522–006.

5/22/53 King, Martin Luther, Jr. (Boston University?). "Notes on Plato, Hegel, Kant, and Aristotle." [9/22/52–5/22/53?]. [Boston, Mass.?] (AD) 11 pp. CSKC. 530522–007.

5/22/53 King, Martin Luther, Jr. (Boston University?). "Notecards on Thomas Aquinas and Augustine." [9/22/52–5/22/53?]. [Boston, Mass.?] (AD) 58 pp. CSKC. 530522–008.

5/22/53 King, Martin Luther, Jr. (Boston University?). "Notes on *A Compend of the Institutes of the Christian Religion* by John Calvin, edited by Hugh Thomson Kerr." [2/4–5/22/53?]. [Boston, Mass.?] (AD) 36 pp. MLKP-MBU: Box 114. 530522–011.

5/22/53 King, Martin Luther, Jr. (Boston University?). "Notes on *Luther's Primary Works*, edited by Henry Wace." [2/4–5/22/53?]. [Boston, Mass.?] (AD) 23 pp. MLKP-MBU: Box 114. 530522–021.

5/22/53 King, Martin Luther, Jr. (Boston University?). "Notes on the free-will controversy and other topics." [2/4–5/22/53?]. [Boston, Mass.?] (AD) 4 pp. MLKP-MBU: Box 114. 530522–023.

5/22/53 King, Martin Luther, Jr. (Boston University?). "Notes on suffering, sin, the person of Christ, the Christian life, and the Christian church, chapters 4–9 of a book by Albert Cornelius Knudson." [2/4–5/22/53?]. [*Boston, Mass.?*] (AD) 8 pp. MLKP-MBU: Box 114. 530522–024.

5/22/53   King, Martin Luther, Jr. (Boston University). "Objective Spirit, paper for Seminar in Hegel." [2/4–5/22/53]. [*Boston, Mass.*] (THDS) 8 pp. (Marginal comments by Peter A. Bertocci.) MLKP-MBU: Box 115. 530522–009.

5/22/53   **King, Martin Luther, Jr. (Boston University). "An Exposition of the First Triad of Categories of the Hegelian Logic—Being, Non-Being, Becoming, paper for Seminar in Hegel." [2/4–5/22/53]. [*Boston, Mass.*] (THDS) 5 pp. (Marginal comments by Peter A. Bertocci.) MLKP-MBU: Box 115. 530522–010.**

5/22/53   [*Newhall, Jannette E.*] (Boston University). "Syllabus, Thesis and Dissertation Writing." 2/4–5/22/53. (TD) 2 pp. MLKP-MBU: Box 115. 530522–013.

5/22/53   King, Martin Luther, Jr. (Boston University). "Notes on 'A Comparison of the Conceptions of God in the Thinking of Paul Tillich and Henry Nelson Wieman.'" [2/4–5/22/53]. [*Boston, Mass.*] (AD) 4 pp. MLKP-MBU: Box 107. 530522–019.

5/22/53   King, Martin Luther, Jr. (Boston University). "Draft of table of contents, 'A Comparison of the Conceptions of God in the Thinking of Paul Tillich and Henry Nelson Wieman.'" [2/4–5/22/53]. [*Boston, Mass.*] (ADd) 1 p. MLKP-MBU: Box 107. 530522–014.

5/22/53   King, Martin Luther, Jr. (Boston University). "Draft of table of contents, 'A Comparison of the Conceptions of God in the Thinking of Paul Tillich and Henry Nelson Wieman.'" [2/4–5/22/53]. [*Boston, Mass.*] (THDd) 4 pp. (Marginal comments by Jannette E. Newhall.) MLKP-MBU: Box 107. 530522–015.

5/22/53   King, Martin Luther, Jr. (Boston University). "Draft of table of contents, 'A Comparison of the Conceptions of God in the Thinking of Paul Tillich and Henry Nelson Wieman.'" [2/4–5/22/53]. [*Boston, Mass.*] (TADf) 2 pp. MLKP-MBU: Box 107. 530522–016.

5/22/53   King, Martin Luther, Jr. (Boston University). "Draft of table of contents, 'A Comparison of the Conceptions of God in the Thinking of Paul Tillich and Henry Nelson Wieman.'" [2/4–5/22/53]. [*Boston, Mass.*] (ADf) 1 p. MLKP-MBU: Box 107. 530522–017.

5/22/53   King, Martin Luther, Jr. (Boston University). "Draft of table of contents, 'A Comparison of the Conceptions of God in the Thinking of Paul Tillich and Henry Nelson Wieman.'" [2/4–5/22/53]. [*Boston, Mass.*] (ADf) 1 p. MLKP-MBU: Box 107. 530522–018.

5/22/53   King, Martin Luther, Jr. (Boston University). "Draft of table of contents, 'A Comparison of the Conceptions of God in the Thinking of Paul Tillich and Henry Nelson Wieman.'" [2/4–5/22/53]. [*Boston, Mass.*] (TADd) 3 pp. MLKP-MBU: Box 96. 530522–025.

5/22/53   King, Martin Luther, Jr. (Boston University). "Draft of table of contents, 'A Comparison of the Conceptions of God in the Thinking of Paul Tillich and Henry Nelson Wieman.'" [2/4–5/22/53]. [*Boston, Mass.*] (ADf) 2 pp. MLKP-MBU: Box 107. 530522–026.

5/22/53   King, Martin Luther, Jr. (Boston University). "Draft of table of contents, 'A Comparison of the Conceptions of God in the Thinking of Paul Tillich and Henry Nelson Wieman.'" [2/4–5/22/53]. [*Boston, Mass.*] (ADf) 3 pp. MLKP-MBU: Box 114. 530522–029.

5/22/53   King, Martin Luther, Jr. (Boston University). "Draft of chapter 1, 'A Comparison of the Conceptions of God in the the Thinking of Paul Tillich and Henry Nelson Wieman.'" [2/4–5/22/53]. [*Boston, Mass.*] (THDd) 3 pp. (Marginal comments by Jannette E. Newhall.) MLKP-MBU: Box 107. 530522–020.

5/22/53   King, Martin Luther, Jr. (Boston University). "Draft of chapter 1, Statement of Problem, 'A Comparison of the Conceptions of God in the Thinking of Paul Tillich and Henry Nelson Wieman.'" [2/4–5/22/53]. [*Boston, Mass.*] (ADd) 3 pp. MLKP-MBU: Box 107. 530522–027.

5/23/53   Hartsfield, William B. "Letter to Martin Luther King, Sr." 5/23/53. (TLc) 1 p. WHP-GEU: Box 12. 530523–000.

5/53   King, Martin Luther, Jr. (Boston University?). "Notes on *Man, Nature and Revelation*, by W. R. Taylor with notes on Reinhold Niebuhr." [9/51–5/53?]. [*Boston, Mass.?*] (AD) 11 pp. MLKP-MBU: Box 115. 530500–002.

5/53	"Bibliography, Christian Theology." [*9/51–5/53?*]. (TD) 24 pp. MLKP-MBU: Box 113. 530500–003.
5/53	King, Martin Luther, Jr. (Boston University?). "Notes on Part I, Introduction: The Province of Theology." [*9/51–5/53?*]. [*Boston, Mass.?*] (AD) 4 pp. MLKP-MBU: Box 106. 530500–004.
5/53	King, Martin Luther, Jr. (Boston University?). "Notes on Theology and the Crisis of Culture, Modernism, and the Dialectical Theology, Chapters I–III." [*9/51–5/53?*]. [*Boston, Mass.?*] (AD) 5 pp. MLKP-MBU: Box 106. 530500–005.
5/53	King, Martin Luther, Jr. (Boston University). "Notes on *The World as Will and Idea* by Arthur Schopenhauer." [*9/51–5/53*]. [*Boston, Mass.*] (AD) 1 p. MLKP-MBU: Box 107. 530500–008.
5/53	[*Lawrence, Nathaniel M.*] (Harvard University). "Final examination questions, Philosophy of Whitehead." 5/53. (TD) 2 pp. MLKP-MBU: Box 113. 530500–000.
6/2/53	King, Martin Luther, Jr. (Harvard University). "Class notes, Philosophy of Whitehead." [*1/26–6/2/53*]. [*Cambridge, Mass.*] (AD) 46 pp. MLKP-MBU: Box 114. 530602–002.
6/2/53	King, Martin Luther, Jr. (Harvard University). "Whitehead and the Problem of the One and Many, paper for Philosophy of Whitehead." [*1/26–6/2/53*]. [*Cambridge, Mass.*] (THDS) 17 pp. (Marginal comments by Nathaniel M. Lawrence.) MLKP-MBU: Box 112. 530602–001.
6/2/53	**Murphy, Rosemary (Lahey Clinic). "Letter to Martin Luther King, Jr." 6/2/53. Boston, Mass. (TLS) 3 pp. (Includes medical report.) MLKP-MBU: Box 117. 530602–000.**
6/18/53	**Scott, Obadiah. "Marriage announcement for Coretta Scott and Martin Luther King, Jr." 6/18/53. (PHD) 1 p. CRO-NRCR. 530618–002.**
6/18/53	**"Photo of Wedding Party of Martin Luther King, Jr., and Coretta Scott King." 6/18/53. Heiberger, Ala. (Ph) 1 p. CKFC. 530618–000.**
6/18/53	"Photo of Martin Luther King, Jr., and Coretta Scott King on their wedding day." 6/18/53. Heiberger, Ala. (Ph) 1 p. CKFC. 530618–001.
6/23/53	**Batten, Charles E. (Crozer Theological Seminary). "Letter to Martin Luther King, Jr." 6/23/53. (TLc) 1 p. CRO-NRCR. 530623–000.**
6/53	**"Photo of Martin Luther King, Jr., and Coretta Scott King, in wedding attire." 6/53. Atlanta, Ga. (Ph) 1 p. CKFC. 530600–004.**
7/18/53	Jemison, D. V. (National Baptist Convention of the United States of America). "Letter to Benjamin Elijah Mays." 7/18/53. Selma, Ala. (TLS) 1 p. BEMP-DHU: Box 12. 530718–000.
7/25/53	Mays, Benjamin Elijah (Morehouse College). "Letter to D. V. Jemison." 7/25/53. (TLc) 2 pp. BEMP-DHU: Box 12. 530725–000.
7/27/53	Mays, Benjamin Elijah (Morehouse College). "Letter to D. V. Jemison." 7/27/53. (TLc) 1 p. BEMP, DHU: Box 12. 530727–000.
8/4/53	Jemison, D. V. (National Baptist Convention of the United States of America). "Letter to Benjamin Elijah Mays." 8/4/53. Selma, Ala. (TLS) 1 p. BEMP-DHU: Box 12. 530804–000.
8/13/53	Ryan, Lois (Harvard University). "Letter to Martin Luther King, Jr." 8/13/53. Cambridge, Mass. (TLS) 1 p. (Contains enclosure 530813–001.) CSKC. 530813–000.
8/13/53	Harvard University. "Transcript for Martin Luther King, Jr." 8/13/53. (TFmS) 1 p. (Enclosure in 530813–000.) CSKC. 530813–001.
8/14/53	**Wieman, Henry Nelson (Washington University). "Letter to Martin Luther King, Jr." 8/14/53. St. Louis, Mo. (TALS) 1 p. CSKC. (Contains enclosure 530814–001.) 530814–000.**
8/14/53	Wieman, Henry Nelson. "Moral and Spiritual Values in Education, Sections I and II: 'Spiritual Values Interpreted for Education' and 'The Problem of Religion in Education.'" [*8/14/53*]. (TDS) 43 pp. (Enclosure in 530814–000.) CSKC. 530814–001.
9/16/53	Jackson, J. H. (Joseph Harrison) (Olivet Baptist Church). "Letter to Benjamin Elijah Mays." 9/16/53. Chicago, Ill. (THLS) 1 p. (Marginal comments by Benjamin Elijah Mays.) BEMP, DHU: Box 12. 530916–000.
9/19/53	Mays, Benjamin Elijah (Morehouse College). "Letter to J. H. Jackson." 9/19/53. (TLc) 2 pp. BEMP-DHU: Box 10. 530919–000.
9/22/53	**Tillich, Paul. "Letter to Martin Luther King, Jr." 9/22/53. Ascona, Switzerland. (TLS) 1 p. MLKP-MBU: Box 117. 530922–000.**

9/25/53   Mays, Benjamin Elijah (Morehouse College). "Letter to Robert S. Bilheimer." 9/25/53. (TLc) 2 pp. BEMP-DHU: Box 13. 530925–000.

9/53   Mays, Benjamin Elijah (Morehouse College). "List of suggested delegates to World Council of Churches." [9/53]. (TAD) 2 pp. BEMP-DHU: Box 12. 530900–001.

9/53   **"Photo of Martin Luther King, Jr., and Morehouse College alumni at the National Baptist Convention, U.S.A., Inc." 9/53. Miami, Fla. (Ph) 1 p. LECC. 530900–002.**

10/9/53   Ring, Bessie A. (Boston University). "Letter to Graduate School Faculty and Candidates for the Ph.D. Degree." 10/9/53. Boston, Mass. (TL) 1 p. (Contains enclosure 530400–000.) CSKC. 531009–000.

10/27/53   [*Boston University.*] "Qualifying examination questions, Theology of the Bible." 10/27/53. (THD) 1 p. (Marginal comments by King.) CSKC. 531027–000.

11/2/53   **King, Martin Luther, Jr. (Boston University). "Qualifying examination answers, Theology of the Bible." [*11/2/53*]. [*Boston, Mass.*] (AHDS) 28 pp. (Marginal comments by L. Harold DeWolf.) MLKP-MBU: Box 115. 531102–000.**

11/3/53   **Boddie, J. Timothy (New Shiloh Baptist Church). "Letter to Martin Luther King, Sr." 11/3/53. Baltimore, Md. (TLS) 1 p. MLKP-MBU: Box 117. 531103–000.**

11/16/53   **Brooks, J. T. (Alabama State College for Negroes). "Letter to Martin Luther King, Sr., and Alberta Williams King." 11/16/53. Montgomery, Ala. (TLS) 1 p. CSKC. 531116–000.**

11/19/53   **Watson, Melvin H. (Morehouse College). "Letter to Martin Luther King, Jr." 11/19/53. Atlanta, Ga. (TLS) 1 p. MLKP-MBU: Box 117. 531119–000.**

11/20/53   [*Boston University.*] "Qualifying examination questions, History of Doctrine." 11/20/53. (THD) 1 p. (Marginal comments by King.) MLKP-MBU: Box 115. 531120–000.

11/20/53   **King, Martin Luther, Jr. (Boston University). "Qualifying examination answers, History of Doctrine." [*11/20/53*]. [*Boston, Mass.*] (AHDS) 33 pp. (Marginal comments by L. Harold DeWolf.) MLKP-MBU: Box 115. 531120–001.**

11/24/53   **King, Martin Luther, Jr. "Letter to Melvin H. Watson." 11/24/53. Boston, Mass. (TLc) 1 p. MLKP-MBU: Box 117. 531124–000.**

11/24/53   **King, Martin Luther, Jr. "Letter to J. Timothy Boddie." 11/24/53. Boston, Mass. (TLc) 1 p. MLKP-MBU: Box 116. 531124–001.**

11/24/53   **King, Martin Luther, Jr. "Letter to J. L. Henry." 11/24/53. Boston, Mass. (TLc) 1 p. MLKP-MBU: Box 116. 531124–002.**

11/24/53   **King, Martin Luther, Jr. "Letter to J. T. Brooks." 11/24/53. Boston, Mass. (TLc) 1 p. MLKP-MBU: Box 116. 531124–003.**

11/53   [*Boston University.*] "Special Regulations for the Ph.D. in Theological Studies with Concentration in Systematic Theology." [*9/51–11/53*]. Boston, Mass. (THD) 4 pp. (Marginal comments by King.) CSKC. 531100–002.

12/1/53   **King, Martin Luther, Jr. (Boston University). "Letter to Werner Rode." 12/1/53. Boston, Mass. (TLc) 1 p. MLKP-MBU: Box 117. 531201–000.**

12/1/53   **King, Martin Luther, Jr. (Boston University). "Letter to Reinhold Niebuhr." 12/1/53. Boston, Mass. (TLc) 1 p. MLKP-MBU: Box 116. 531201–001.**

12/1/53   King, Martin Luther, Jr. (Boston University). "Letter to Bernard M. Loomer." 12/1/53. Boston, Mass. (TLc) 1 p. MLKP-MBU: Box 116. 531201–002.

12/1/53   King, Martin Luther, Jr. (Boston University). "Letter to John Dillenberger." 12/1/53. Boston, Mass. (TLc) 1 p. MLKP-MBU: Box 116. 531201–003.

12/1/53   King, Martin Luther, Jr. (Boston University). "Letter to Edward H. Roberts." 12/1/53. Boston, Mass. (TLc) 1 p. MLKP-MBU: Box 116. 531201–004.

12/1/53   **King, Martin Luther, Jr. (Boston University). "Letter to George W. Davis." 12/1/53. Boston, Mass. (TALS) 2 pp. IGZ. 531201–005.**

12/2/53   Meade, Nola E. (Union Theological Seminary). "Letter to Martin Luther King, Jr." 12/2/53. New York, N.Y. (TLS) 1 p. MLKP-MBU: Box 117. 531202–000.

12/3/53   **King, Joel Lawrence. "Letter to Martin Luther King, Jr., and Coretta Scott King." 12/3/53. Lansing, Mich. (ALS) 2 pp. MLKP-MBU: Box 117. 531203–000.**

    12/3/53   Bilheimer, Robert S. (World Council of Churches). "Letter to Benjamin Elijah Mays." 12/3/53. New York, N.Y. (TLS) 2 pp. (Includes enclosure.) BEMP-DHU: Box 13. 531203–001.

12/7/53   **Davis, George W. (Crozer Theological Seminary). "Letter to Martin Luther King, Jr." 12/7/53. Chester, Pa. (TLS) 1 p. MLKP-MBU: Box 117. 531207–000.**

12/8/53   **Loomer, Bernard M. (University of Chicago Divinity School). "Letter to Martin Luther King, Jr." 12/8/53. Chicago, Ill. (TLS) 1 p. MLKP-MBU: Box 117. 531208–000.**

12/8/53   King, Martin Luther, Jr. "Letter to James H. Ward." 12/8/53. Boston, Mass. (TLc) 1 p. MLKP-MBU: Box 116. 531208–001.

12/9/53   **King, Martin Luther, Jr. "Letter to Joel Lawrence King." 12/9/53. Boston, Mass. (TLc) 1 p. MLKP-MBU: Box 116. 531209–000.**

12/11/53   Dillenberger, John (Columbia University). "Letter to Martin Luther King, Jr." 12/11/53. New York, N.Y. (TLS) 1 p. MLKP-MBU: Box 117. 531211–000.

12/11/53   Roberts, Edward H. (Princeton Theological Seminary). "Letter to Martin Luther King, Jr." 12/11/53. Princeton, N.J. (TLS) 1 p. MLKP-MBU: Box 117. 531211–001.

12/11/53   Mays, Benjamin Elijah (Morehouse College). "Letter to Robert S. Bilheimer." 12/11/53. (TLc) 1 p. BEMP-DHU: Box 13. 531211–002.

12/17/53   **King, Martin Luther, Jr. (Boston University). "Qualifying examination answers, Systematic Theology." [*12/17/53?*]. [*Boston, Mass.*] (AHDS) 30 pp. (Marginal comments by L. Harold DeWolf.) MLKP-MBU: Box 115. 531217–000.**

12/30/53   **DeWolf, L. Harold. "Letter to Martin Luther King, Jr." 12/30/53. (ALS) 1 p. MLKP-MBU: Box 115. 531230–000.**

1953   "Photo of Martin Luther King, Jr." [*1952–1953*]. (Ph) 1 p. RKC-WHi. 530000–009.

1953   "Photo of Alfred Daniel King and Martin Luther King, Jr." [*1952–1953*]. (Ph) 1 p. CSKC. 530000–014.

1953   **"Photo of Coretta Scott and Martin Luther King, Jr., at Boston University." 1952–1953. Boston, Mass. (Ph) 1 p. CSKC. 530000–017.**

1953   **"Photo of Coretta Scott and Martin Luther King, Jr., at Boston University." 1952–1953. Boston, Mass. (Ph) 1 p. CSKC. 530000–018.**

1953   **"Photo of Coretta Scott and Martin Luther King, Jr., at Boston University." 1952–1953. Boston, Mass. (Ph) 1 p. CSKC. 530000–019.**

1953   "Photo of Coretta Scott and Martin Luther King, Jr., at Boston University." [*1952–1953*]. Boston, Mass. (Ph) 1 p. RKC-WHi. 530000–020.

1953   "Photo of Coretta Scott and Martin Luther King, Jr." 1952–1953. (Ph) 1 p. CSKC. 530000–021.

1/12/54   **Key, G. A. (First Baptist Church). "Letter to Martin Luther King, Jr." 1/12/54. Chattanooga, Tenn. (TLS) 1 p. MLKP-MBU: Box 117. 540112–000.**

1/16/54   **Brooks, J. T. (Alabama State College for Negroes). "Letter to Martin Luther King, Jr." 1/16/54. Montgomery, Ala. (TLI) 1 p. MLKP-MBU: Box 117. 540116–000.**

1/17/54   **McCall, Walter R. (Fort Valley State College). "Letter to Martin Luther King, Jr." 1/17/54. Fort Valley, Ga. (TL) 1 p. MLKP-MBU: Box 117. 540117–000.**

1/25/54   **Banks, A. A., Jr. (Second Baptist Church). "Letter to Martin Luther King, Sr." 1/25/54. Detroit, Mich. (TLS) 1 p. MLKP-MBU: Box 117. 540125–000.**

1/25/54   **King, Alberta Williams. "Letter to Martin Luther King, Jr." [*1/25/54*]. (ALS) 1 p. (On verso of 540125–000.) MLKP-MBU: Box 117. 540125–001.**

2/4/54   **King, Joel Lawrence. "Letter to Martin Luther King, Jr." 2/4/54. Lansing, Mich. (TALS) 1 p. MLKP-MBU: Box 117. 540204–000.**

2/8/54   **King, Joel Lawrence. "Letter to Martin Luther King, Jr." 2/8/54. Lansing, Mich. (TLS) 1 p. MLKP-MBU: Box 117. 540208–001.**

2/8/54   **Crockett, R. D. (Alabama State College for Negroes). "Letter to Martin Luther King, Jr." 2/8/54. Montgomery, Ala. (TLS) 1 p. MLKP-MBU: Box 117. 540208–000.**

2/13/54   **Lee, J. McKinley, Sr. (NAACP). "Letter to Martin Luther King, Jr." 2/13/54. Lansing, Mich. (TLS) 1 p. MLKP-MBU: Box 117. 540213–000.**

2/19/54   **Banks, A. A., Jr. (Second Baptist Church). "Letter to Martin Luther King, Jr." 2/19/54. Detroit, Mich. (TLS) 1 p. MLKP-MBU: Box 117. 540219–000.**

2/24/54   [*Boston University.*] "Qualifying examination questions, History of Philosophy." 2/24/54. (TD) 1 p. MLKP-MBU: Box 115. 540224–000.

2/24/54   **King, Martin Luther, Jr. (Boston University). "Qualifying examination answers, History of Philosophy." 2/24/54. [*Boston, Mass.*] (AHDS) 30 pp. (Marginal comments by L. Harold DeWolf.) MLKP-MBU: Box 115. 540224–001.**

2/28/54   **King, Martin Luther, Jr. "Rediscovering Lost Values, sermon at Second Baptist Church." 2/28/54. Detroit, Mich. (At) 32 min. (1 sound cassette: analog.) SdBCC. 540228–001.**

2/28/54   **Townsend, Julian (Second Baptist Church). "Photo of Martin Luther King, Jr." 2/28/54. Detroit, Mich. (Ph) 1 p. SdBCC. 540228–002.**

2/28/54   **Leach, Nathaniel. "Photo of Martin Luther King, Jr., Justina Leach, and Charles Nicks, Jr." 2/28/54. Detroit, Mich. From: Nathaniel Leach, *Reaching Out to Freedom: The Second Baptist Connection* (Detroit, Mich.: Second Baptist Church, 1988): 85. (PPh) 1 p. SdBCC. 540228–003.**

3/7/54   **Nesbitt, R. D. (Dexter Avenue Baptist Church). "Telegram to Martin Luther King, Jr." 3/7/54. Montgomery, Ala. (PWSr) 2 pp. MLKP-MBU: Box 117. 540307–000.**

3/10/54   **Parker, Joseph C., Sr. "Letter to Martin Luther King, Jr." 3/10/54. Montgomery, Ala. (ALS) 4 pp. MLKP-MBU: Box 117. 540310–000.**

3/10/54   **King, Martin Luther, Jr. "Letter to Pulpit Committee, Dexter Avenue Baptist Church." 3/10/54. Boston, Mass. (TLc) 1 p. MLKP-MBU: Box 116. 540310–001.**

3/15/54   **Nesbitt, R. D. (Dexter Avenue Baptist Church). "Letter to Martin Luther King, Jr." 3/15/54. Montgomery, Ala. (TLS) 1 p. MLKP-MBU: Box 117. 540315–000.**

4/14/54   **King, Martin Luther, Jr. "Letter to Dexter Avenue Baptist Church." 4/14/54. Boston, Mass. (TLc) 1 p. MLKP-MBU: Box 116. 540414–000.**

4/15/54   **Brooks, J. T. (Alabama State College for Negroes). "Letter to Martin Luther King, Jr." 4/15/54. Montgomery, Ala. (TLS) 1 p. MLKP-MBU: Box 117. 540415–000.**

4/16/54   **Carr, Leonard G. (Vine Memorial Baptist Church). "Letter to Martin Luther King, Jr." 4/16/54. Philadelphia, Pa. (TLS) 1 p. MLKP-MBU: Box 117. 540416–000.**

4/19/54   **Nesbitt, R. D. (Dexter Avenue Baptist Church). "Letter to Martin Luther King, Jr." 4/19/54. Montgomery, Ala. (TLS) 1 p. MLKP-MBU: Box 117. 540419–000.**

4/27/54   Watson, Melvin H. (Morehouse College). "Letter to Martin Luther King, Jr." 4/27/54. Atlanta, Ga. (TALS) 1 p. MLKP-MBU: Box 117. 540427–000.

5/8/54   **Whitaker, H. Edward (New Hope Baptist Church). "Letter to Martin Luther King, Jr." 5/8/54. Niagara Falls, N.Y. (TLS) 2 pp. MLKP-MBU: Box 117. 540508–000.**

5/9/54   Dexter Avenue Baptist Church. "Program, Organ Dedication and Recital." 5/9/54. Montgomery, Ala. (PD) 4 pp. CSKC. 540509–000.

5/10/54   [*Carter, Percy A., Jr.*] "Notes, meeting of the Dialectical Society." 5/10/54. (AD) 4 pp. PACC. 540510–000.

5/10/54   King, Martin Luther, Jr. "Notes, meeting of the Dialectical Society." [5/10/54]. [*Boston, Mass.*] (AD) 1 p. CSKC. 540510–001.

5/13/54   **Nesbitt, R. D. "Letter to Martin Luther King, Jr." 5/13/54. Montgomery, Ala. (ALS) 2 pp. MLKP-MBU: Box 117. 540513–000.**

5/15/54   **King, Martin Luther, Jr. "Letter to L. Harold DeWolf." 5/15/54. Boston, Mass. (TLc) 1 p. MLKP-MBU: Box 116. 540515–000.**

5/15/54   **King, Martin Luther, Jr. "Letter to Joseph C. Parker, Sr." 5/15/54. Boston, Mass. (TLc) 1 p. MLKP-MBU: Box 116. 540515–001.**

5/15/54   **King, Martin Luther, Jr. "Letter to Leonard G. Carr." 5/15/54. Boston, Mass. (TLc) 1 p. MLKP-MBU: Box 116. 540515–002.**

5/16/54   Pullman Porters' Benefit Association of America. "Program, Thirty-third Annual Memorial Service." 5/16/54. Cambridge, Mass. (PD) 4 pp. MLKP-MBU: Box 80. 540516–000.

5/22/54   **King, Martin Luther, Jr. (Dexter Avenue Baptist Church). "Form letter to Montgomery pastors." 5/22/54. Boston, Mass. (TLSr) 1 p. MLKP-MBU: Box 116. 540522–000.**

6/7/54   King, Martin Luther, Jr. "Expenditures Notebook." 10/28/53–6/7/54. [*Boston, Mass.*] (AD) 38 pp. MLKP, MBU: Box 114. 540607–000.

6/15/54	New England Conservatory of Music. "Program, Eighty-Fourth Commencement Concert and Exercises." 6/15/54. Boston, Mass. (PD) 6 pp. CKFC. 540615–000.
6/20/54	Union Baptist Church. "*Christian Sentinel*, Men's Day Program." 6/20/54. Cambridge, Mass. (PD) 4 pp. MLKP-MBU: Box 80. 540620–000.
6/24/54	**Kilgore, Thomas, Jr. (Friendship Baptist Church). "Letter to Martin Luther King, Jr." 6/24/54. New York, N.Y. (TLS) 1 p. MLKP-MBU: Box 117. 540624–000.**
6/24/54	**King, Martin Luther, Jr. "Letter to Thomas Kilgore, Jr." 6/24/54. Boston, Mass. (TLc) 1 p. MLKP-MBU: Box 116. 540624–001.**
6/54	Bivens, Isaac H. "Conclusions from the discussion of the paper on Walter Rauschenbusch, paper for the Dialectical Society." [4/53–6/54]. (TADS) 1 p. PACC. 540600–000.
6/54	Jones, Major J. "A Compend of Edwin Lewis's Theology, paper for the Dialectical Society." [4/53–6/54]. (TDS) 1 p. PACC. 540600–001.
6/54	Pugh, Thomas J. "Suffering: A Psychological Interpretation, paper for the Dialectical Society." [4/53–6/54]. (THDS) 14 pp. (Marginal comments by King.) PACC. 540600–002.
6/54	King, Martin Luther, Jr. "Draft, The Theology of Reinhold Niebuhr, paper for the Dialectical Society." [4/53–6/54]. [*Boston, Mass.*] (AHDd) 18 pp. (Marginal comments by L. Harold DeWolf.) MLKP-MBU: Box 113. 540600–007.
6/54	**King, Martin Luther, Jr. "The Theology of Reinhold Niebuhr, paper for the Dialectical Society." [4/53–6/54]. [*Boston, Mass.*] (TADS) 12 pp. PACC. 540600–004.**
6/54	**"Photo of Zenobia McLaughlin and Wayman McLaughlin, Ella Clark and Jack Clark, Coretta Scott King, and Martin Luther King, Jr., at home of Percy A. Carter, Jr." [4/53–6/54]. Woburn, Mass. (Ph) 1 p. PACC. 540600–003.**
6/54	King, Martin Luther, Jr. (Boston University). "Notes on Aristotle's *Metaphysics* and Plato's theory of ideas." [4/53–6/54]. [*Boston, Mass.*] (AD) 4 pp. MLKP-MBU: Box 115. 540600–006.
7/26/54	**King, Martin Luther, Jr. "Letter to Francis E. Stewart." 7/26/54. Roxbury, Mass. (ALS) 4 pp. (Water damaged.) FESP. 540726–000.**
7/29/54	**Stewart, Francis E. (Monticello Baptist Church). "Letter to Martin Luther King, Jr." 7/29/54. Monticello, Ga. (TLS) 1 p. MLKP-MBU: Box 117. 540729–000.**
8/3/54	**Burroughs, Nannie H. (National Baptist Convention of the United States of America, Woman's Auxiliary). "Letter to Martin Luther King, Jr." 8/3/54. (TLc) 1 p. NHBP-DLC. 540803–000.**
8/5/54	**McCall, Walter R. (Fort Valley State College). "Letter to Martin Luther King, Jr." 8/5/54. Fort Valley, Ga. (TALS) 2 pp. MLKP-MBU: Box 117. 540805–000.**
8/24/54	Spencer, M. H. (Calvary Baptist Church). "Letter to Martin Luther King, Jr." 8/24/54. Chester, Pa. (TLS) 1 p. MLKP-MBU: Box 117. 540824–000.
9/5/54	**King, Martin Luther, Jr. (Dexter Avenue Baptist Church). "Recommendations to the Dexter Avenue Baptist Church for the Fiscal Year 1954–1955." [9/5/54]. [*Montgomery, Ala.*] (TD) 7 pp. MLKP-MBU: Box 117. 540905–000.**
9/5/54	King, Martin Luther, Jr. (Dexter Avenue Baptist Church). "List of Proposed Parsonage Repairs." [9/5/54]. [*Montgomery, Ala.*] (TAD) 3 pp. CSKC. 540905–002.
1954	**National Baptist Convention of the United States of America, Woman's Auxiliary. "Notes, speech by Martin Luther King, Jr., at Woman's Auxiliary Convention on 9/9/54." 1954. From: *Record of the 74th Annual National Baptist Convention*, 1954. (PD) 1 p. SBHL-TNSB. 540000–021.**
9/15/54	**Whitaker, H. Edward (New Hope Baptist Church). "Letter to Martin Luther King, Jr." 9/15/54. Niagara Falls, N.Y. (ALS) 3 pp. MLKP-MBU: Box 117. 540915–000.**
9/16/54	Dudley, George W. (Liberty Baptist Church). "Letter to Martin Luther King, Jr." 9/16/54. Atlanta, Ga. (ALS) 1 p. MLKP-MBU: Box 117. 540916–000.
9/21/54	**Burroughs, Nannie H. (National Baptist Convention of the United States of America, Woman's Auxiliary). "Letter to Martin Luther King, Jr."**

9/23/54

9/21/54. **Washington, D.C. (TLS) 1 p. MLKP-MBU: Box 117. 540921–000.**

Bowden, Henry J. C. (Veterans Administration Hospital). "Letter to Martin Luther King, Jr." 9/23/54. Tuskegee, Ala. (TLS) 1 p. MLKP-MBU: Box 117. 540923–000.

9/24/54

Jackson, Estelle. "Letter to Martin Luther King, Jr." 9/24/54. Roxbury, Mass. (ALS) 2 pp. MLKP-MBU: Box 117. 540924–000.

9/29/54

Riley, Ralph W. (American Baptist Theological Seminary). "Letter to Martin Luther King, Jr." 9/29/54. Nashville, Tenn. (TLS) 1 p. MLKP-MBU: Box 117. 540929–000.

10/54

King, Martin Luther, Jr. (Dexter Avenue Baptist Church). "Letter to Samuel D. Proctor." [10/54]. [Montgomery, Ala.] (TLc) 2 pp. MLKP-MBU: Box 117. 541000–000.

10/4/54

Pinkston, Harold Edward. (Virginia Union University). "Letter to Martin Luther King, Jr." 10/4/54. Richmond, Va. (TALS) 1 p. MLKP-MBU: Box 117. 541004–000.

10/4/54

King, Martin Luther, Jr. "Letter to Henry J. C. Bowden." 10/4/54. Montgomery, Ala. (TLc) 1 p. MLKP-MBU: Box 116. 541004–001.

10/9/54

Reynolds, Clyde L. (Dexter Avenue Baptist Church). "Letter to Martin Luther King, Jr." 10/9/54. (ALS) 1 p. MLKP-MBU: Box 117. 541009–000.

10/15/54

Mitchell, Florence (Boston University). "Letter to Martin Luther King, Jr." 10/15/54. Boston, Mass. (TLS) 1 p. MLKP-MBU: Box 117. 541015–000.

10/17/54

King, Coretta Scott. "Answers, Voter Registration Questionnaire of the Dexter Avenue Baptist Church Social and Political Action Committee." 10/17/54. Montgomery, Ala. (AFmS) 1 p. MLKP-MBU: Box 77. 541017–000.

10/19/54

King, Martin Luther, Jr. "Letter to Paul Tillich." 10/19/54. Montgomery, Ala. (TLc) 1 p. MLKP-MBU: Box 116. 541019–000.

10/19/54

King, Martin Luther, Jr. "Letter to Ralph W. Riley." 10/19/54. Montgomery, Ala. (TLc) 1 p. MLKP-MBU: Box 116. 541019–001.

10/19/54

King, Martin Luther, Jr. "Letter to E. A. Jones." 10/19/54. Montgomery, Ala. (TLc) 1 p. MLKP-MBU: Box 116. 541019–002.

10/19/54

King, Martin Luther, Jr. "Letter to Walter R. McCall." 10/19/54. Montgomery, Ala. (TLc) 1 p. MLKP-MBU: Box 116. 541019–003.

10/20/54

Watson, Melvin H. (Morehouse College). "Letter to Martin Luther King, Jr." 10/20/54. Atlanta, Ga. (TLS) 1 p. MLKP-MBU: Box 117. 541020–000.

10/20/54

Nesbitt, James E. "Telegram to Martin Luther King, Jr." 10/20/54. Los Angeles, Calif. (PWSr) 1 p. MLKP-MBU: Box 117. 541020–001.

10/21/54

McCall, Walter R. (Fort Valley State College). "Letter to Martin Luther King, Jr." 10/21/54. Fort Valley, Ga. (TALS) 1 p. MLKP-MBU: Box 117. 541021–000.

10/25/54

Riley, Ralph W. (American Baptist Theological Seminary). "Letter to Martin Luther King, Jr." 10/25/54. Nashville, Tenn. (TLS) 1 p. MLKP-MBU: Box 117. 541025–000.

10/26/54

King, Martin Luther, Jr. "Letter to William H. Hester." 10/26/54. [Montgomery, Ala.] (TLc) 1 p. MLKP-MBU: Box 116. 541026–000.

10/26/54

King, Martin Luther, Jr. "Letter to Sankey L. Blanton." 10/26/54. [Montgomery, Ala.] (TLc) 1 p. MLKP-MBU: Box 116. 541026–001.

10/26/54

King, Martin Luther, Jr. "Letter to Manager, Boston Young Men's Christian Association (YMCA)." 10/26/54. [Montgomery, Ala.] (TLc) 1 p. MLKP-MBU: Box 116. 541026–002.

10/26/54

King, Martin Luther, Jr. "Letter to Manager, Statler Hotel." 10/26/54. [Montgomery, Ala.] (TLc) 1 p. MLKP-MBU: Box 116. 541026–003.

10/28/54

Proctor, Samuel D. (Virginia Union University). "Letter to Martin Luther King, Jr." 10/28/54. Richmond, Va. (TLSr) 1 p. MLKP-MBU: Box 117. 541028–000.

10/29/54

King, Martin Luther, Jr. "Letter to Florence Mitchell." 10/29/54. Montgomery, Ala. (TLc) 1 p. MLKP-MBU: Box 116. 541029–000.

10/30/54

Whitehead, Elizabeth P. "Telegram to Martin Luther King, Jr." 10/30/54. Atlanta, Ga. (PWSr) 1 p. MLKP-MBU: Box 117. 541030–000.

10/30/54

Gideons, Charlie. "Telegram to Martin Luther King, Jr." 10/30/54. Atlanta, Ga. (PWSr) 1 p. MLKP-MBU: Box 117. 541030–001.

10/31/54

Dexter Avenue Baptist Church. "Program, Installation of the Rev. Martin Luther King, Jr., as Pastor." 10/31/54. Montgomery, Ala. (PHD) 11 pp. CKFC. 541031–000.

10/31/54   Burks, Mary Fair (Dexter Avenue Baptist Church). "Social and Political Action Committee, Report 3." 10/31/54. Montgomery, Ala. (TD) 1 p. MLKP-MBU: Box 77. 541031–001.

10/54   **King, Martin Luther, Jr. (Dexter Avenue Baptist Church). "Letter to Benjamin Elijah Mays."** [*10/54*]. [*Montgomery, Ala.*] (TLc) 1 p. MLKP-MBU: Box 116. 541000–004.

11/54   **Jones, Major J. "Letter to Martin Luther King, Jr."** [*11/54*.] Boston, Mass. (TALS) 1 p. MLKP-MBU: Box 117. 541100–000.

11/1/54   **Blanton, Sankey L. (Crozer Theological Seminary). "Letter to Martin Luther King, Jr."** 11/1/54. Chester, Pa. (TLS) 1 p. MLKP-MBU: Box 117. 541101–000.

11/2/54   Bourgeois, Ernest (YMCA). "Letter to Martin Luther King, Jr." 11/2/54. Boston, Mass. (TLS) 1 p. MLKP-MBU: Box 117. 541102–000.

11/2/54   **Hester, William H. (Twelfth Baptist Church). "Letter to Martin Luther King, Jr."** 11/2/54. Roxbury, Mass. (TLS) 1 p. MLKP-MBU: Box 117. 541102–001.

11/2/54   King, Martin Luther, Jr. "Letter to Samuel D. Proctor." 11/2/54. [*Montgomery, Ala.*] (TLc) 1 p. MLKP-MBU: Box 116. 541102–002.

11/2/54   **King, Martin Luther, Jr. "Letter to Melvin H. Watson."** 11/2/54. [*Montgomery, Ala.*] (TLc) 1 p. MLKP-MBU: Box 116. 541102–003.

11/3/54   **Tillich, Paul. "Letter to Martin Luther King, Jr."** 11/3/54. Aberdeen, Scotland. (TLS) 1 p. MLKP-MBU: Box 117. 541103–000.

11/4/54   **Mays, Benjamin Elijah (Morehouse College). "Letter to Martin Luther King, Jr."** 11/4/54. Atlanta, Ga. (TLS) 1 p. MLKP-MBU: Box 117. 541104–000.

11/4/54   Mays, Benjamin Elijah (Morehouse College). "Letter to Martin Luther King, Jr." 11/4/54. Atlanta, Ga. (TLS) 1 p. MLKP-MBU: Box 117. 541104–001.

11/4/54   **King, Martin Luther, Jr. "Montgomery-Antioch Ass'n. Endorses Wilson and Washington."** 11/4/54. From: *Baptist Leader*, 4 November 1954, p. 3. (PD) 1 p. A-Ar. 541104–002.

11/6/54   **King, Martin Luther, Jr. "Letter to Ebenezer Baptist Church members."** 11/6/54. [*Montgomery, Ala.*] (TLc) 1 p. MLKP-MBU: Box 116. 541106–000.

11/12/54   Watson, Melvin H. (Morehouse College). "Letter to Martin Luther King, Jr." 11/12/54. Atlanta, Ga. (TLS) 1 p. MLKP-MBU: Box 117. 541112–000.

11/18/54   **Williams, Samuel W. (Friendship Baptist Church). "Letter to Martin Luther King, Jr."** 11/18/54. Atlanta, Ga. (TLSr) 1 p. MLKP-MBU: Box 117. 541118–000.

11/22/54   King, Martin Luther, Jr. "Letter to Samuel W. Williams." 11/22/54. [*Montgomery, Ala.*] (TLc) 1 p. MLKP-MBU: Box 116. 541122–000.

11/24/54   **King, Martin Luther, Jr. "Letter to Ralph Abernathy."** 11/24/54. [*Montgomery, Ala.*] (TLc) 1 p. MLKP-MBU: Box 116. 541124–000.

11/24/54   King, Martin Luther, Jr. "Letter to T. M. Alexander." 11/24/54. [*Montgomery, Ala.*] (TLc) 1 p. MLKP-MBU: Box 116. 541124–001.

11/24/54   King, Martin Luther, Jr. "Letter to Melvin H. Watson." 11/24/54. [*Montgomery, Ala.*] (TLc) 1 p. MLKP-MBU: Box 116. 541124–002.

11/24/54   King, Martin Luther, Jr. "Letter to M. C. Cleveland." 11/24/54. [*Montgomery, Ala.*] (TLc) 1 p. MLKP-MBU: Box 116. 541124–003.

11/24/54   King, Martin Luther, Jr. "Letter to H. H. Johnson." 11/24/54. [*Montgomery, Ala.*] (TLc) 1 p. MLKP-MBU: Box 116. 541124–004.

11/24/54   King, Martin Luther, Jr. "Letter to B. D. Lambert." 11/24/54. [*Montgomery, Ala.*] (TLc) 1 p. MLKP-MBU: Box 116. 541124–005.

11/24/54   King, Martin Luther, Jr. "Letter to Joseph C. Parker, Sr." 11/24/54. [*Montgomery, Ala.*] (TLc) 1 p. MLKP-MBU: Box 116. 541124–006.

11/24/54   **King, Martin Luther, Jr. "Letter to William H. Hester."** 11/24/54. [*Montgomery, Ala.*] (TLc) 1 p. MLKP-MBU: Box 116. 541124–007.

11/24/54   **King, Martin Luther, Jr. "Letter to Benjamin Elijah Mays."** 11/24/54. [*Montgomery, Ala.*] (TLc) 1 p. MLKP-MBU: Box 116. 541124–008.

11/24/54   King, Martin Luther, Jr. "Letter to W. J. Powell." 11/24/54. [*Montgomery, Ala.*] (TLc) 1 p. MLKP-MBU: Box 116. 541124–009.

11/24/54   King, Martin Luther, Jr. "Letter to Melvin H. Watson." 11/24/54. [*Montgomery, Ala.*] (TLc) 1 p. MLKP-MBU: Box 116. 541124–010.

11/24/54   King, Martin Luther, Jr. (Dexter Avenue Baptist Church). "Letter to G. Franklin Lewis." 11/24/54. [*Montgomery, Ala.*] (TLc) 1 p. MLKP-MBU: Box 116. 541124–011.

11/29/54   **Watson, Melvin H. (Morehouse College). "Letter to Martin Luther King, Jr."** 11/29/54. Atlanta, Ga. (TLS) 2 pp. (Includes enclosure.) MLKP-MBU: Box 117. 541129–000.

11/30/54   **Mays, Benjamin Elijah (Morehouse College). "Letter to Martin Luther King, Jr."** 11/30/54. Atlanta, Ga. (TLS) 1 p. MLKP-MBU: Box 117. 541130–000.

11/54   "Biographical entry on Martin Luther King, Jr." 11/54. Atlanta, Ga. From: *Morehouse College Bulletin* 22 (November 1954): 6–7. (PD) 2 pp. MLKP-MBU: Box 117. 541100–001.

12/2/54   **King, Martin Luther, Sr. (Ebenezer Baptist Church). "Letter to Martin Luther King, Jr."** 12/2/54. Atlanta, Ga. (TLS) 1 p. MLKP-MBU: Box 117. 541202–000.

12/2/54   Burroughs, Nannie H. (National Baptist Convention of the United States of America, Woman's Auxiliary). "Letter to Martin Luther King, Sr." 12/2/54. (TLc) 1 p. NHBP-DLC: Box 39. 541202–001.

12/10/54   **Smith, Roland (National Baptist Training Union Board). "Letter to Martin Luther King, Jr."** 12/10/54. Nashville, Tenn. (TLS) 1 p. MLKP-MBU: Box 117. 541210–000.

12/10/54   Watson, Melvin H. (Morehouse College). "Letter to Martin Luther King, Jr." 12/10/54. Atlanta, Ga. (TLS) 1 p. MLKP-MBU: Box 117. 541210–001.

12/15/54   **Watson, Melvin H. (Morehouse College). "Letter to Martin Luther King, Jr."** 12/15/54. Atlanta, Ga. (TLS) 1 p. MLKP-MBU: Box 117. 541215–000.

12/16/54   Harris, R. E. (Dexter Avenue Baptist Church). "Letter to Martin Luther King, Jr." 12/16/54. Montgomery, Ala. (ALS) 1 p. MLKP-MBU: Box 117. 541216–000.

12/21/54   **Barbour, J. Pius (*National Baptist Voice*). "Letter to Martin Luther King, Jr."** 12/21/54. Chester, Pa. (TALS) 4 pp. MLKP-MBU: Box 63. 541221–000.

12/23/54   Jordan, G. K. (Advertiser Company, Inc.). "Letter to Martin Luther King, Jr., Ralph Abernathy, P. M. Blair, and Thomas Lowery." 12/23/54. Montgomery, Ala. (TLS) 1 p. MLKP-MBU: Box 117. 541223–000.

1954   King, Martin Luther, Jr. "Excerpt from a Marriage Ceremony." [*1954?*]. [*Montgomery, Ala.?*] (TAD) 2 pp. CSKC. 540000–017.

1954   King, Martin Luther, Jr. "Notes, Program for Morning Worship." [*1954?*]. [*Montgomery, Ala.?*] (AD) 1 p. CSKC. 540000–018.

1955   **"Photo of Dexter Avenue Baptist Church."** [*1952–1955*]. Montgomery, Ala. (Ph) 1 p. RKC-WHI. 550000–125.

1955   **Carter, Percy A., Jr. (Second Baptist Church). "Letter to Martin Luther King, Jr."** [*1955?*]. Dixon, Ill. (TLS) 1 p. MLKP-MBU: Box 117. 550000–002.

1955   King, Martin Luther, Jr. "Notecards on topics arranged alphabetically." [*1948–1955*]. (AD) 822 pp. CSKC. 550000–064 through 550000–086.

1955   King, Martin Luther, Jr. "Miscellaneous notecards." [*1948–1955*]. (ATD) 9 pp. CSKC. 550000–087.

1955   King, Martin Luther, Jr. "Notecards and heading cards." [*1948–1955*]. (AD) 34 pp. CSKC. 550000–088.

1955   **King, Martin Luther, Jr. (Boston University?). "Notecards on the Challenge of the Book of Jonah."** [*1951–1955?*]. [*Boston, Mass.?*] (AD) 5 pp. CSKC. 550000–018.

1955   **King, Martin Luther, Jr. (Boston University?) "Notecards on the Bigness of God."** [*1951–1955?*]. [*Boston, Mass.?*] (AD) 4 pp. MLKP, MBU: Box 118. 550000–121.

1955   **King, Martin Luther, Jr. (Boston University?). "Notecards on God's Love."** [*1951–1955?*]. [*Boston, Mass.?*] (AD) 3 pp. CSKC. 550000–016.

1955   King, Martin Luther, Jr. (Boston University). "Author index file notecards." [*1951–1955*]. [*Boston, Mass.*] (AD) 4 pp. CSKC. 550000–020.

1955   King, Martin Luther, Jr. (Boston University). "Notecards on Barth, Batten, Brunner, Bultman, and Burton." [*1951–1955*]. [*Boston, Mass.*] (AD) 8 pp. CSKC. 550000–023.

1955   King, Martin Luther, Jr. (Boston University). "Notecards on Case, Chesterton, Colwell, Cope, and Copleston." [*1951–1955*]. [*Boston, Mass.*] (AD) 5 pp. CSKC. 550000–024.

1955   King, Martin Luther, Jr. (Boston University). "Notecards on L. Harold DeWolf." [*1951–1955*]. [*Boston, Mass.*] (AD) 2 pp. CSKC. 550000–025.

1955   King, Martin Luther, Jr. (Boston University). "Notecards on Ferm and Ferré." [*1951–1955*]. [*Boston, Mass.*] (AD) 4 pp. CSKC. 550000–026.

1955   King, Martin Luther, Jr. (Boston University). "Notecards on Harkness, Har-

ris, Hegel, Kant, Hibben, and Hughes." [*1951–1955*]. [*Boston, Mass.*] (AD)
11 pp. CSKC. 550000–027.

1955   King, Martin Luther, Jr. (Boston University). "Notecard on article on Edgar S. Brightman by Paul Johnson." [*1951–1955*]. [*Boston, Mass.*] (AD) 1 p. CSKC. 550000–028.

1955   King, Martin Luther, Jr. (Boston University). "Notecards on Kepler and Knudson." [*1951–1955*]. [*Boston, Mass.*] (ATD) 8 pp. CSKC. 550000–029.

1955   King, Martin Luther, Jr. (Boston University). "Notecard on Philip Leon." [*1951–1955*]. [*Boston, Mass.*] (AD) 1 p. CSKC. 550000–030.

1955   King, Martin Luther, Jr. (Boston University). "Notecards on McEachran, McTaggart, Mackay, Macintosh, Minear, Muelder, and Muirhead." [*1951–1955*]. [*Boston, Mass.*] (AD) 10 pp. CSKC. 550000–031.

1955   King, Martin Luther, Jr. (Boston University). "Notecards on Reinhold Niebuhr." [*1951–1955*]. [*Boston, Mass.*] (AD) 5 pp. CSKC. 550000–032.

1955   King, Martin Luther, Jr. (Boston University). "Notecard on James Orr." [*1951–1955*]. [*Boston, Mass.*] (AD) 1 p. CSKC. 550000–033.

1955   King, Martin Luther, Jr. (Boston University). "Notecards on Puitt and Przywara." [*1951–1955*]. [*Boston, Mass.*] (AD) 2 pp. CSKC. 550000–034.

1955   King, Martin Luther, Jr. (Boston University). "Notecard on H. Wheeler Robinson." [*1951–1955*]. [*Boston, Mass.*] (AD) 1 p. CSKC. 550000–035.

1955   King, Martin Luther, Jr. (Boston University). "Notecards on Schleiermacher, Shrag, Scott, Sheen, and Spurrier." [*1951–1955*]. [*Boston, Mass.*] (AD) 9 pp. CSKC. 550000–036.

1955   King, Martin Luther, Jr. (Boston University). "Notecard on Cornelius Van Til." [*1951–1955*]. [*Boston, Mass.*] (AD) 1 p. CSKC. 550000–038.

1955   King, Martin Luther, Jr. (Boston University). "Notecards on Fannie and Roland Haynes and Julian Huxley." [*1951–1955*]. [*Boston, Mass.*] (AD) 3 pp. CSKC. 550000–039.

1955   King, Martin Luther, Jr. (Boston University). "Notecards on Aristotle, U.S. policy on Asia, Atheism, and Augustine." [*1951–1955*]. [*Boston, Mass.*] (AD) 8 pp. CSKC. 550000–040.

1955   King, Martin Luther, Jr. (Boston University). "Notecards on Karl Barth, Bergson, the Bible, Biblical authority, and Edgar S. Brightman." [*1951–1955*]. [*Boston, Mass.*] (AD) 22 pp. CSKC. 550000–041.

1955   King, Martin Luther, Jr. (Boston University). "Notecards on Capitalism, Christianity, Church unity, Civil rights, Colleges (private and Negro), Conversion, and Counseling procedures." [*1951–1955*]. [*Boston, Mass.*] (AD) 9 pp. CSKC. 550000–042.

1955   King, Martin Luther, Jr. (Boston University). "Notecards on Charles Drew, Death, Réné Descartes, and Dialectical theology." [*1951–1955*]. [*Boston, Mass.*] (ATD) 6 pp. CSKC. 550000–043.

1955   King, Martin Luther, Jr. (Boston University). "Notecards on Religious education, Eisenhower, Ethics, Evil, and Existentialism." [*1951–1955*]. [*Boston, Mass.*] (AD) 18 pp. CSKC. 550000–044.

1955   King, Martin Luther, Jr. (Boston University). "Notecards on Faith, Reason, and Freedom." [*1951–1955*]. [*Boston, Mass.*] (AD) 6 pp. CSKC. 550000–045.

1955   King, Martin Luther, Jr. (Boston University). "Notecards on God." [*1951–1955*]. [*Boston, Mass.*] (AD) 3 pp. CSKC. 550000–046.

1955   King, Martin Luther, Jr. (Boston University). "Notecards on George Hourison, Hegel, Holy Spirit, and Julian Huxley." [*1951–1955*]. [*Boston, Mass.*] (AD) 11 pp. CSKC. 550000–047.

1955   King, Martin Luther, Jr. (Boston University). "Notecards on Kant, Theodicy, and the Kingdom." [*1951–1955*]. [*Boston, Mass.*] (AD) 4 pp. CSKC. 550000–048.

1955   King, Martin Luther, Jr. (Boston University). "Notecards on Labor and Religion, Leibniz, Life, and Love." [*1951–1955*]. [*Boston, Mass.*] (AD) 4 pp. CSKC. 550000–049.

1955   King, Martin Luther, Jr. (Boston University). "Notecards on Magic, Mythology, Man, Marriage, Mind, Miracles, Money, Music, Monism, Mystical religion, and Mysticism." [*1951–1955*]. [*Boston, Mass.*] (AD) 16 pp. CSKC. 550000–050.

1955   King, Martin Luther, Jr. (Boston University). "Notecards on Nature and grace, the Negro, Negro education, Neo-Thomism, and Reinhold Niebuhr." [*1951–1955*]. [*Boston, Mass.*] (AD) 43 pp. CSKC. 550000–051.

1955 King, Martin Luther, Jr. (Boston University). "Notecards on Personalism, Pragmatism, Prayer, Theology and psychology of prophecy, and Protestantism." [*1951–1955*]. [*Boston, Mass.*] (AD) 10 pp. CSKC. 550000–052.

1955 King, Martin Luther, Jr. (Boston University). "Notecards on Walter Rauschenbusch, Religion, Resurrection, Revelation and human discovery, Friedrich Schleiermacher, and Albrecht Ritschl." [*1951–1955*]. [*Boston, Mass.*] (AD) 35 pp. CSKC. 550000–053.

1955 King, Martin Luther, Jr. (Boston University). "Notecards on Schleiermacher, Segregation and the Brown decision, Self, Sin, and Suffering." [*1951–1955*]. [*Boston, Mass.*] (AD) 62 pp. CSKC. 550000–054.

1955 King, Martin Luther, Jr. (Boston University). "Notecard on Unemployment." [*1951–1955*]. [*Boston, Mass.*] (AD) 1 p. CSKC. 550000–055.

1955 King, Martin Luther, Jr. (Boston University). "Notecard on Wealth." [*1951–1955*]. [*Boston, Mass.*] (AD) 1 p. CSKC. 550000–056.

1955 King, Martin Luther, Jr. (Boston University). "Notes from the Bible on Reason, Knowledge, Revelation, Biblical authority, Man, Jesus, the Holy Spirit and the Trinity, Judgment, Salvation, the Kingdom, Church, Sacraments, and Prayer." [*1951–1955*]. [*Boston, Mass.*] (AD) 64 pp. CSKC. 550000–058.

1955 King, Martin Luther, Jr. (Boston University). "Notecards on Wace, Buchheim, Walker, Weatherhead, Weigle, White, Whitehead, and Wieman." [*1951–1955*]. [*Boston, Mass.*] (AD) 176 pp. CSKC. 550000–060.

1955 King, Martin Luther, Jr. (Boston University). "Notecards on Theological seminary and its function, Theology, Traditionalism, Trinity, and Truth." [*1951–1955*]. [*Boston, Mass.*] (AD) 17 pp. CSKC. 550000–061.

1955 King, Martin Luther, Jr. (Boston University). "Notecards on Anselm and Grotius." [*1951–1955*]. [*Boston, Mass.*] (AD) 2 pp. CSKC. 550000–111.

1955 King, Martin Luther, Jr. (Boston University). "Notecard on philosophers." [*1951–1955*]. [*Boston, Mass.*] (AD) 1 p. CSKC. 550000–112.

1955 King, Martin Luther, Jr. (Boston University). "Notecard on Jesus." [*1951–1955*]. [*Boston, Mass.*] (AD) 1 p. CSKC. 550000–113.

1955 King, Martin Luther, Jr. (Boston University). "Dissertation notecards on Paul Tillich." [*1953–1955*]. [*Boston, Mass.?*] (AD) 9 pp. MLKP-MBU: Box 107. 550000–014.

1955 King, Martin Luther, Jr. (Boston University). "Dissertation notecards on Paul Tillich." [*1953–1955*]. [*Boston, Mass.?*] (AD) 43 pp. CSKC. 550000–019.

1955 King, Martin Luther, Jr. (Boston University). "Dissertation notecards on Henry Nelson Wieman." [*1953–1955*]. [*Boston, Mass.?*] (AD) 53 pp. CSKC. 550000–022.

1955 King, Martin Luther, Jr. (Boston University). "Dissertation notecards." [*1953–1955*]. [*Boston, Mass.?*] (ATD) 122 pp. MLKP-MBU: Box 118. 550000–004.

1955 King, Martin Luther, Jr. (Boston University). "Dissertation notecards on *Systematic Theology* by Paul Tillich." [*1953–1955*]. [*Boston, Mass.?*] (AD) 89 pp. CSKC. 550000–037.

1955 King, Martin Luther, Jr. (Boston University). "Dissertation notes on Henry Nelson Wieman." [*1953–1955*]. [*Boston, Mass.?*] (AD) 12 pp. MLKP-MBU: Box 107. 550000–089.

1955 King, Martin Luther, Jr. (Boston University). "Dissertation notes on articles by Henry Nelson Wieman." [*1953–1955*]. [*Boston, Mass.?*] (AD) 4 pp. MLKP-MBU: Box 107. 550000–090.

1955 King, Martin Luther, Jr. (Boston University). "Dissertation notes on a book by Henry Nelson Wieman." [*1953–1955*]. [*Boston, Mass.?*] (AD) 11 pp. MLKP-MBU: Box 107. 550000–091.

1955 King, Martin Luther, Jr. (Boston University). "Dissertation notes on C. C. Morrison's review of *The Source of Human Good* by Henry Nelson Wieman." [*1953–1955*]. [*Boston, Mass.?*] (AD) 2 pp. MLKP-MBU: Box 107. 550000–092.

1955 King, Martin Luther, Jr. (Boston University). "Draft of title page, table of contents and bibliography, 'A Comparison of the Conceptions of God in the Thinking of Paul Tillich and Henry Nelson Wieman.'" [*1954–1955*]. (TDd) 14 pp. MLKP, MBU: Box 116. 550000–119.

1955 **King, Martin Luther, Jr. (Boston University). "Draft of chapters 1–3, 'A Comparison of the Conceptions of God in the Thinking of Paul Tillich**

and Henry Nelson Wieman.'" [*1954–1955*]. (ATDd) 181 pp. **MLKP-MBU: Box 97. 550000–106.**

1955   King, Martin Luther, Jr. (Boston University). "Draft of chapter 2, 'A Comparison of the Conceptions of God in the Thinking of Paul Tillich and Henry Nelson Wieman.'" [*1954–1955*]. (THDd) 41 pp. MLKP-MBU: Box 96. 550000–107.

1955   King, Martin Luther, Jr. (Boston University). "Draft of chapter 2, 'A Comparison of the Conceptions of God in the Thinking of Paul Tillich and Henry Nelson Wieman.'" [*1954–1955*]. (THDd) 41 pp. (Marginal comments by S. Paul Schilling.) MLKP-MBU: Box 96. 550000–093.

1955   King, Martin Luther, Jr. (Boston University). "Draft of chapter 2, 'A Comparison of the Conceptions of God in the Thinking of Paul Tillich and Henry Nelson Wieman.'" [*1954–1955*]. (TDd) 45 pp. MLKP-MBU: Box 97A. 550000–094.

1955   King, Martin Luther, Jr. (Boston University). "Draft of chapter 3, 'A Comparison of the Conceptions of God in the Thinking of Paul Tillich and Henry Nelson Wieman.'" [*1954–1955*]. (ADd) 29 pp. MLKP-MBU: Box 107. 550000–011.

1955   King, Martin Luther, Jr. (Boston University). "Draft of chapter 3, 'A Comparison of the Conceptions of God in the Thinking of Paul Tillich and Henry Nelson Wieman.'" [*1954–1955*]. (TADd) 24 pp. MLKP-MBU: Box 96A. 550000–095.

1955   King, Martin Luther, Jr. (Boston University). "Draft of chapter 3, 'A Comparison of the Conceptions of God in the Thinking of Paul Tillich and Henry Nelson Wieman.'" [*1954–1955*]." (THDd) 74 pp. (Marginal comments by S. Paul Schilling.) MLKP-MBU: Box 96A. 550000–096.

1955   King, Martin Luther, Jr. (Boston University). "Draft of chapter 3, 'A Comparison of the Conceptions of God in the Thinking of Paul Tillich and Henry Nelson Wieman.'" [*1954–1955*]. (TADd) 74 pp. (Marginal comments by L. Harold DeWolf.) MLKP-MBU: Box 96. 550000–097.

1955   King, Martin Luther, Jr. (Boston University). "Draft of chapter 3, 'A Comparison of the Conceptions of God in the Thinking of Paul Tillich and Henry Nelson Wieman.'" [*1954–1955*]. (TDd) 87 pp. MLKP-MBU: Box 97. 550000–098.

1955   King, Martin Luther, Jr. (Boston University). "Draft of chapter 4, 'A Comparison of the Conceptions of God in the Thinking of Paul Tillich and Henry Nelson Wieman.'" [*1954–1955*]. (ADd) 111 pp. MLKP-MBU: Box 97. 550000–099.

1955   King, Martin Luther, Jr. (Boston University). "Draft of chapter 4, 'A Comparison of the Conceptions of God in the Thinking of Paul Tillich and Henry Nelson Wieman.'" [*1954–1955*]. (THDd) 60 pp. (Marginal comments by S. Paul Schilling.) MLKP-MBU: Box 97. 550000–100.

1955   King, Martin Luther, Jr. (Boston University). "Draft of chapter 4, 'A Comparison of the Conceptions of God in the Thinking of Paul Tillich and Henry Nelson Wieman.'" [*1954–1955*]. (TADd) 60 pp. (Marginal comments by L. Harold DeWolf.) MLKP-MBU: Box 97. 550000–102.

1955   **King, Martin Luther, Jr. (Boston University). "Draft of chapter 5, 'A Comparison of the Conceptions of God in the Thinking of Paul Tillich and Henry Nelson Wieman.'" [*1954–1955*]. (ADd) 84 pp. MLKP-MBU: Box 97. 550000–103.**

1955   King, Martin Luther, Jr. (Boston University). "Draft of chapter 5, 'A Comparison of the Conceptions of God in the Thinking of Paul Tillich and Henry Nelson Wieman.'" [*1954–1955*]. (TADd) 57 pp. MLKP-MBU: Box 96A. 550000–104.

1955   King, Martin Luther, Jr. (Boston University). "Draft of chapter 5 and bibliography, 'A Comparison of the Conceptions of God in the Thinking of Paul Tillich and Henry Nelson Wieman.'" [*1954–1955*]. (THDd) 63 pp. MLKP-MBU: Box 96. 550000–105.

1955   King, Martin Luther, Jr. (Boston University). "Draft of chapter 6, 'A Comparison of the Conceptions of God in the Thinking of Paul Tillich and Henry Nelson Wieman.'" [*1954–1955*]. (ADd) 8 pp. MLKP-MBU: Box 97. 550000–125.

1955   "Biographical sketch of Martin Luther King, Jr." [*1955?*]. (TD) 1 p. MLKP-MBU: Box 117. 550000–003.

1955   "Biographical sketch of Martin Luther King, Jr." [*1955?*]. (TD) 1 p. CSKC. 550000–110.

1/9/55   Parks, Rosa (NAACP). "Minutes, Montgomery branch meeting." 1/9/55. Montgomery, Ala. (AD) 3 pp. MNAACP-NN-Sc. 550109–000.

1/12/55   **Jackson, Emory O. (*Birmingham World*). "Letter to Martin Luther King, Jr." 1/12/55. Birmingham, Ala. (TLSr) 1 p. MLKP-MBU: Box 117. 550112–000.**

1/14/55   Reynolds, Clyde L. "Letter to Martin Luther King, Jr." 1/14/55. (ALS) 1 p. MLKP-MBU: Box 117. 550114–000.

1/14/55   **Law, W. W. "Letter to Martin Luther King, Jr." 1/14/55. Savannah, Ga. (TLS) 1 p. MLKP-MBU: Box 117. 550114–001.**

1/25/55   **"Apathy Among Church Leaders Hit in Talk By Rev. M. L. King." 1/25/55. Birmingham, Ala. From: *Birmingham World*, 25 January 1955. (PD) 2 pp. 550125–000.**

1/55   Dexter Avenue Baptist Church. "Social and Political Action Committee Digest, Number 2." 1/55. Montgomery, Ala. (TD) 2 pp. MLKP-MBU: Box 77. 550100–002.

2/5/55   **Cole, William J. "Letter to Martin Luther King, Jr." 2/5/55. Chicago, Ill. (ALS) 2 pp. MLKP-MBU: Box 117. 550205–000.**

2/7/55   McCall, Walter R. (Fort Valley State College). "Letter to Martin Luther King, Jr." 2/7/55. Fort Valley, Ga. (TLS) 1 p. MLKP-MBU: Box 117. 550207–000.

2/10/55   Thomas, D. E. (J. P. Rendington & Company, Inc.) "Letter to Martin Luther King, Jr." 2/10/55. Scranton, Pa. (TLS) 1 p. MLKP, MBU: Box 117. 550210–000.

2/24/55   **Smith, Roland (National Baptist Training Union Board). "Letter to Martin Luther King, Jr." 2/24/55. Nashville, Tenn. (TLS) 1 p. MLKP-MBU: Box 117. 550224–000.**

2/26/55   **DeWolf, L. Harold (Boston University). "First Reader's Report on Dissertation by Martin Luther King, Jr." 2/26/55. Boston, Mass. (TFmS) 2 pp. SPS. 550226–000.**

2/26/55   **Schilling, S. Paul (Boston University). "Second Reader's Report on Dissertation by Martin Luther King, Jr." 2/26/55. Boston, Mass. (TFmS) 1 p. SPS. 550226–001.**

3/2/55   **King, Martin Luther, Jr. (Dexter Avenue Baptist Church). "Letter to Julian O. Grayson." 3/2/55. Montgomery, Ala. (TLS) 1 p. JOG. 550302–000.**

3/3/55   **McCall, Walter R. (Fort Valley State College). "Letter to Martin Luther King, Jr." 3/3/55. Fort Valley, Ga. (TLS) 1 p. MLKP-MBU: Box 117. 550303–000.**

3/3/55   Franklin, L. L. (Talladega County Training School). "Letter to Martin Luther King, Jr." 3/3/55. Renfroe, Ala. (TLS) 1 p. MLKP-MBU: Box 117. 550303–001.

3/3/55   Ring, Bessie A. (Boston University). "Letter to Martin Luther King, Jr." 3/3/55. Boston, Mass. (TLS) 1 p. MLKP-MBU: Box 96A. 550303–002.

3/4/55   Carpenter, Alfreda Gibbs (Stillman College). "Letter to Martin Luther King, Jr." 3/4/55. Tuscaloosa, Ala. (TLS) 1 p. MLKP-MBU: Box 117. 550304–000.

3/13/55   Dexter Avenue Baptist Church. "Program, Symposium on 'The Meaning of Integration for American Society.'" 3/13/55. Montgomery, Ala. (TD) 1 p. MLKP-MBU: Box 117. 550313–000.

3/14/55   **James, Julius (Shiloh Baptist Church). "Letter to Martin Luther King, Jr." 3/14/55. Brunswick, Ga. (TLS) 1 p. MLKP-MBU: Box 117. 550314–000.**

3/21/55   Nesbitt, James E. "Letter to Martin Luther King, Jr." 3/21/55. Los Angeles, Calif. (TLS) 1 p. MLKP-MBU: Box 117. 550321–000.

3/28/55   Bennett, Ambroe (National Baptist Missionary Training School). "Letter to Martin Luther King, Jr." 3/28/55. Nashville, Tenn. (TLS) 1 p. MLKP-MBU: Box 117. 550328–000.

4/5/55   McCall, Walter R. (Fort Valley State College). "Letter to Martin Luther King, Jr." 4/5/55. Fort Valley, Ga. (TLS) 1 p. MLKP-MBU: Box 117. 550405–000.

4/14/55   Macdonald, Duncan E. (Boston University). "Announcement of the Final Oral Examination of Martin Luther King, Jr., for the Degree of Doctor of Philosophy." 4/14/55. Boston, Mass. (TD) 2 pp. WMP-MBU. 550414–000.

  4/15/55   **King, Martin Luther, Jr. (Boston University). "A Comparison of the Conceptions of God in the Thinking of Paul Tillich and Henry Nelson Wie-**

man." [*4/15/55*]. [*Boston, Mass.*] (TD) 343 pp. MLKP-MBU: Box 116.
550415–000.

4/15/55   King, Martin Luther, Jr. (Boston University). "Abstract of 'A Comparison of the Conceptions of God in the Thinking of Paul Tillich and Henry Nelson Wieman.'" [*4/15/55*]. [*Boston, Mass.*] (PD) 4 pp. MLKP-MBU: Box 2. 550415–002.

4/15/55   "Photo of Martin Luther King, Jr." [*4/15/55*]. [*Boston, Mass.*] 1 p. (Ph) MLKP-MBU. 550415–003.

4/18/55   Proctor, Samuel D. (Virginia Union University). "Letter to Martin Luther King, Jr." 4/18/55. Richmond, Va. (TLSr) 1 p. MLKP-MBU: Box 117. 550418–000.

4/19/55   Whitaker, H. Edward. "Letter to Martin Luther King, Jr." 4/19/55. Niagara Falls, N.Y. (TLS) 2 pp. MLKP-MBU: Box 117. 550419–000.

4/25/55   Reed, Dunbar (YMCA). "Letter to Martin Luther King, Jr." 4/25/55. Atlanta, Ga. (TLSr) 1 p. CSKC. 550425–000.

5/2/55   Trenholm, H. Councill (Alabama State College). "Letter to Martin Luther King, Jr." 5/2/55. Montgomery, Ala. (TLS) 1 p. MLKP-MBU: Box 117. 550502–000.

5/6/55   McCall, Walter R. (Fort Valley State College). "Letter to Martin Luther King, Jr." 5/6/55. Fort Valley, Ga. (TLS) 2 pp. MLKP-MBU: Box 117. 550506–000.

5/6/55   Watson, Melvin H. (Morehouse College). "Letter to Martin Luther King, Jr." 5/6/55. Atlanta, Ga. (TLS) 1 p. MLKP-MBU: Box 117. 550506–001.

5/11/55   Bell, William A. "Letter to Martin Luther King, Jr." 5/11/55. Sheppard Air Force Base, Tex. (TLS) 2 pp. MLKP-MBU: Box 117. 550511–000.

5/12/55   Henderson, J. Raymond (Second Baptist Church). "Letter to Martin Luther King, Sr." 5/12/55. Los Angeles, Calif. (TLS) 1 p. (Contains enclosure 550512–000.) MLKP-MBU: Box 117. 550512–001.

5/12/55   Henderson, J. Raymond (Second Baptist Church). "Letter to Martin Luther King, Jr." 5/12/55. Los Angeles, Calif. (TLS) 1 p. (Enclosure in 550512–001.) MLKP-MBU: Box 117. 550512–000.

5/15/55   Trenholm, H. Councill (Alabama State College). "Letter to Martin Luther King, Jr." 5/15/55. Montgomery, Ala. (TLS) 1 p. MLKP-MBU: Box 117. 550515–000.

5/16/55   Alabama State College. "Program, Baccalaureate Service of the 1955 Spring Commencement." 5/16/55. Montgomery, Ala. (PD) 4 pp. CKFC. 550516–000.

5/16/55   Franklin, L. L. (Talladega County Training School). "Letter to Martin Luther King, Jr." 5/16/55. Renfroe, Ala. (TLS) 1 p. MLKP-MBU: Box 117. 550516–001.

5/16/55   Finkelstein, Mrs. J. C. (Congregation Agudat Israel). "Letter to Martin Luther King, Jr." 5/16/55. Montgomery, Ala. (TLS) 1 p. MLKP-MBU: Box 117. 550516–002.

5/16/55   King, Martin Luther, Sr. "Letter to J. Raymond Henderson." 5/16/55. (TLc) 1 p. EBCR. 550516–003.

5/16/55   "Photo of Martin Luther King, Jr., and John Thomas Porter, Alabama State Commencement." 5/16/55. Montgomery, Ala. (Ph) 1 p. JTPP. 550516–004.

5/24/55   Nickerson, Oscar M. (Nazarene Baptist Church). "Letter to Martin Luther King, Jr." 5/24/55. Philadelphia, Pa. (ALS) 1 p. MLKP-MBU: Box 117. 550524–000.

5/28/55   DeWolf, L. Harold (Boston University). "Letter to Martin Luther King, Jr." 5/28/55. Boston, Mass. (TLS) 1 p. MLKP-MBU: Box 117. 550528–000.

5/31/55   MacDonald, Duncan E. (Boston University). "Letter to Martin Luther King, Jr." 5/31/55. Boston, Mass. (TLS) 1 p. MLKP-MBU: Box 117. 550531–000.

5/31/55   Cole, William J. "Letter to Martin Luther King, Jr." 5/31/55. Chicago, Ill. (ALS) 1 p. MLKP-MBU: Box 117. 550531–001.

5/55   Jones, Major J. "Letter to Martin Luther King, Jr." [*5/55*]. Boston, Mass. (TLS) 1 p. MLKP-MBU: Box 117. 550500–002.

6/55   Jones, Major J. "Letter to Martin Luther King, Jr." [*6/55*]. (TL) 1 p. MLKP-MBU: Box 117. 550600–003.

6/1/55   Nickerson, Oscar M. (Nazarene Baptist Church). "Letter to Martin Luther King, Jr." 6/1/55. Philadelphia, Pa. (ALS) 1 p. MLKP-MBU: Box 117. 550601–000.

6/1/55   Alpha Phi Alpha Fraternity. "Program, Citizenship Rally: Operation 5000."

[*6/1/55*]. Montgomery, Ala. (TD) 8 pp. AJC-ICHi: Box 24. 550601–002.

6/3/55   Brooks, J. T. (Alabama State College). "Letter to Martin Luther King, Jr." 6/3/55. Montgomery, Ala. (TLS) 1 p. MLKP-MBU: Box 117. 550603–000.

6/3/55   Proctor, Samuel D. (Virginia Union University). "Letter to Martin Luther King, Jr." 6/3/55. Richmond, Va. (TLSr) 1 p. MLKP-MBU: Box 117. 550603–001.

6/4/55   **DeWolf, L. Harold (Boston University). "Letter to Martin Luther King, Jr." 6/4/55. Boston, Mass. (TLS) 1 p. MLKP-MBU: Box 117. 550604–000.**

6/5/55   Boston University. "Transcript of Record for the Degree of Doctor of Philosophy for Martin Luther King, Jr." 6/5/55. Boston, Mass. (THFm) 2 pp. BUR-MBU. 550605–000.

6/7/55   **Carey, Archibald J. "Letter to Martin Luther King, Jr." 6/7/55. Chicago, Ill. (TLS) 1 p. MLKP-MBU: Box 117. 550607–000.**

6/7/55   **Wynn, Daniel W. (Tuskegee Institute). "Letter to Martin Luther King, Jr." 6/7/55. Tuskegee, Ala. (TLS) 1 p. MLKP-MBU: Box 48. 550607–001.**

6/9/55   Nickerson, Oscar M. (Nazarene Baptist Church). "Letter to Martin Luther King, Jr." 6/9/55. Philadelphia, Pa. (ALS) 1 p. MLKP-MBU: Box 117. 550609–000.

6/16/55   Coston, W. H. (Alpha Phi Alpha Fraternity). "Letter to Martin Luther King, Jr." 6/16/55. Montgomery, Ala. (TLS) 1 p. MLKP-MBU: Box 117. 550616–000.

6/19/55   Dexter Avenue Baptist Church. "Program, Sunday services." 6/19/55. Montgomery, Ala. (TD) 4 pp. MLKP-MBU: Box 76. 550619–000.

6/19/55   Parks, Rosa (NAACP). "Minutes, Mass meeting." 6/19/55. Montgomery, Ala. (ADf). 2 pp. MNAACP-NN-Sc. 550619–001.

6/22/55   King, Martin Luther, Jr. (Dexter Avenue Baptist Church). "Form letter to church members." 6/22/55. Montgomery, Ala. (THLd) 1 p. DABCC. 550622–000.

6/26/55   Dexter Avenue Baptist Church. "Program, Sunday services." 6/26/55. Montgomery, Ala. (THD) 4 pp. MLKP-MBU: Box 76. 550626–000.

6/28/55   **King, Martin Luther, Jr. (Dexter Avenue Baptist Church). "Letter to Benjamin Elijah Mays." 6/28/55. Montgomery, Ala. (TLS) 1 p. BEMP-DHU: Box 16. 550628–000.**

6/29/55   Knapp, Lucile B. (Crozer Theological Seminary). "Letter to Martin Luther King, Jr." 6/29/55. Chester, Pa. (TLS) 1 p. MLKP-MBU: Box 117. 550629–000.

6/55   Dexter Avenue Baptist Church. "Social and Political Action Committee Digest." 6/55. Montgomery, Ala. (TD) 3 pp. MLKP-MBU: Box 77. 550600–000.

6/55   **Jones, Major J. "Letter to Martin Luther King, Jr." [*6/55*]. Boston, Mass. (TLS) 1 p. MLKP-MBU: Box 117. 550600–002.**

7/1/55   Mays, Benjamin Elijah (Morehouse College). "Letter to Martin Luther King, Jr." 7/1/55. Atlanta, Ga. (TLS) 1 p. MLKP-MBU: Box 117. 550701–000.

7/10/55   Nickerson, Oscar M. (Nazarene Baptist Church). "Letter to Martin Luther King, Jr." 7/10/55. Philadelphia, Pa. (ALS) 1 p. MLKP-MBU: Box 117. 550710–000.

7/18/55   Dumire, Helen E. (Crozer Theological Seminary). "Letter to Martin Luther King, Jr." 7/18/55. Chester, Pa. (TLS) 1 p. MLKP-MBU: Box 117. 550718–000.

7/21/55   **Barbour, J. Pius (*National Baptist Voice*). "Letter to Martin Luther King, Jr." 7/21/55. Chester, Pa. (TALI) 4 pp. MLKP-MBU: Box 121. 550721–000.**

7/22/55   Robinson, Avis P. (Howard University). "Letter to Martin Luther King, Jr." 7/22/55. Washington, D.C. (TLS) 1 p. MLKP-MBU: Box 117. 550722–000.

7/24/55   Dexter Avenue Baptist Church. "Program, Sunday services." 7/24/55. Montgomery, Ala. (TD) 4 pp. MLKP-MBU: Box 76. 550724–000.

7/25/55   **Dent, Albert W. (Dillard University). "Letter to Martin Luther King, Jr." 7/25/55. New Orleans, La. (TLS) 1 p. MLKP-MBU: Box 117. 550725–000.**

8/55   **Jones, Major J. "Letter to Martin Luther King, Jr., and Coretta Scott King." [*8/55*]. Boston, Mass. (TLS) 1 p. MLKP-MBU: Box 117. 550800–000.**

8/1/55   **Blanton, Sankey L. (Crozer Theological Seminary). "Letter to Martin Luther King, Jr." 8/1/55. Chester, Pa. (TLSr) 1 p. MLKP-MBU: Box 117. 550801–000.**

  8/4/55   Sparling, Judd (Southland Broadcasting Co.). "Letter to Martin Luther

King, Jr." 8/4/55. Montgomery, Ala. (TLS) 1 p. MLKP-MBU: Box 117. 550804–000.

8/5/55   King, Martin Luther, Sr. (Ebenezer Baptist Church). "Letter to Melvin H. Watson." 8/5/55. Atlanta, Ga. (TLc) 1 p. EBCR. 550805–000.

8/8/55   **Smith, Kelly Miller (First Baptist Church). "Letter to Martin Luther King, Jr." 8/8/55. Nashville, Tenn. (TLS) 1 p. MLKP-MBU: Box 121. 550808–000.**

8/12/55   Riley, Ralph W. (American Baptist Theological Seminary). "Letter to Martin Luther King, Jr." 8/12/55. Nashville, Tenn. (TLS) 1 p. MLKP-MBU: Box 117. 550812–000.

8/14/55   Parks, Rosa (NAACP). "Minutes, Montgomery branch executive committee meeting." 8/14/55. Montgomery, Ala. (AD) 1 p. MNAACP-NN-Sc. 550814–000.

8/19/55   Hughes, Robert E. (Alabama Council on Human Relations). "Letter to R. E. Whatley." 8/19/55. Montgomery, Ala. (TLc) 1 p. (Copy to King.) MLKP-MBU: Box 117. 550819–000.

8/19/55   McCall, Walter R. (Fort Valley State College). "Letter to Martin Luther King, Jr." 8/19/55. Fort Valley, Ga. (THLS) 1 p. MLKP-MBU: Box 117. 550819–001.

8/20/55   **Jones, Sylvester (Raven Camp School). "Letter to Martin Luther King, Jr." 8/20/55. Colfax, La. (TLS) 1 p. MLKP-MBU: Box 117. 550820–000.**

8/23/55   Forte, Maggie Y. (Montgomery Public Schools). "Letter to Martin Luther King, Jr." 8/23/55. Montgomery, Ala. (TLS) 1 p. MLKP-MBU: Box 117. 550823–000.

8/26/55   **King, Martin Luther, Jr. "Letter to Sylvester Jones." 8/26/55. [*Montgomery, Ala.*] (TLc) 1 p. MLKP-MBU: Box 116. 550826–001.**

8/26/55   **Parks, Rosa (NAACP). "Letter to Martin Luther King, Jr." 8/26/55. Montgomery, Ala. (TLS) 1 p. MLKP-MBU: Box 117. 550826–000.**

8/26/55   King, Martin Luther, Jr. "Letter to Maggie Y. Forte." 8/26/55. [*Montgomery, Ala.*] (TLc) 1 p. MLKP-MBU: Box 116. 550826–002.

8/27/55   Neill, John H. (American Red Cross). "Telegram to Martin Luther King, Jr." 8/27/55. Montgomery, Ala. (PWSr) 1 p. MLKP-MBU: Box 121. 550827–000.

9/3/55   Hayes, Robert (Friendship Baptist Church). "Letter to Martin Luther King, Jr." 9/3/55. Anniston, Ala. (TLS) 1 p. MLKP-MBU: Box 117. 550903–000.

9/13/55   King, Martin Luther, Jr. "Letter to Robert Hayes." 9/13/55. [*Montgomery, Ala.*] (TLc) 1 p. MLKP-MBU: Box 116. 550913–000.

9/13/55   King, Martin Luther, Jr. "Letter to Daniel W. Wynn." 9/13/55. [*Montgomery, Ala.*] (TLc) 1 p. MLKP-MBU: Box 116. 550913–001.

9/28/55   **Jackson, J. H. (Joseph Harrison) (National Baptist Convention of the United States of America). "Letter to Martin Luther King, Jr." 9/28/55. Chicago, Ill. (TLS) 1 p. MLKP-MBU: Box 117. 550928–000.**

9/29/55   **McCall, Walter R. (Fort Valley State College). "Letter to Martin Luther King, Jr." 9/29/55. Fort Valley, Ga. (TLS) 1 p. MLKP-MBU: Box 117. 550929–000.**

10/7/55   Thomas, E. S. "Letter to Martin Luther King, Jr." 10/7/55. Oakland, Calif. (ALS) 2 pp. MLKP-MBU: Box 117. 551007–000.

10/15/55   Bickers, Lynette. "Letter to Martin Luther King, Jr." 10/15/55. Atlanta, Ga. (ALS) 1 p. MLKP-MBU: Box 117. 551015–000.

10/16/55   Southern University. "Program, Sunday Vespers." 10/16/55. (PD) 5 pp. MLKP-MBU: Box 80. 551016–000.

10/18/55   Harvey, Martin L. (Southern University). "Letter to Martin Luther King, Jr." 10/18/55. Baton Rouge, La. (TLS) 1 p. MLKP-MBU: Box 117. 551018–000.

10/22/55   **McCall, Walter R. (Fort Valley State College). "Letter to Martin Luther King, Jr." 10/22/55. Fort Valley, Ga. (TALS) 1 p. MLKP-MBU: Box 117. 551022–000.**

10/23/55   Fort Valley State College. "Program, Vespers." 10/23/55. Fort Valley, Ga. (TD) 4 pp. CSKC. 551023–000.

10/27/55   **Garth, Nathaniel (National Baptist Training Union Board). "Letter to Martin Luther King, Jr." 10/27/55. Chattanooga, Tenn. (ALS) 3 pp. MLKP-MBU: Box 117. 551027–000.**

10/27/55   **King, Martin Luther, Jr. (Dexter Avenue Baptist Church). "Letter to church**

members." 10/27/55. Montgomery, Ala. From: Zelia S. Evans and J. T. Alexander, eds. *Dexter Avenue Baptist Church: 1877–1977* (Montgomery, Ala.: Dexter Avenue Baptist Church, 1978), pp. 79–80. (PD) 2 pp. 551027–001.

10/29/55 Spears, Henry A. (YMCA). "Letter to Martin Luther King, Jr." 10/29/55. Montgomery, Ala. (TLS) 1 p. MLKP-MBU: Box 117. 551029–000.

10/30/55 Dexter Avenue Baptist Church. "Program, Sunday services." 10/30/55. Montgomery, Ala. (TD) 4 pp. MLKP-MBU: Box 76. 551030–000.

10/31/55 **King, Martin Luther, Jr. (Dexter Avenue Baptist Church). "Annual Report, Dexter Avenue Baptist Church." 10/1/54–10/31/55. Montgomery, Ala. (TD) 36 pp. MLKP-MBU: Box 77. 551031–000.**

10/31/55 **King, Martin Luther, Jr. (Dexter Avenue Baptist Church). "Letter to Howard Thurman." 10/31/55. Montgomery, Ala. (TL) 1 p. HTC-MBU: Box 43. 551031–001.**

11/2/55 King, Martin Luther, Jr. "Letter to Nathaniel Garth." 11/2/55. [*Montgomery, Ala.*] (TLc) 1 p. DABCC. 551102–000.

11/2/55 **King, Martin Luther, Jr. "Letter to W. T. Handy, Jr." 11/2/55. [*Montgomery, Ala.*] (TLc) 1 p. DABCC. 551102–001.**

11/2/55 **King, Martin Luther, Jr. "Letter to Vernon O. Rogers." 11/2/55. [*Montgomery, Ala.*] (TLc) 1 p. DABCC. 551102–002.**

11/2/55 **King, Martin Luther, Jr. (Dexter Avenue Baptist Church). "Letter to Roosevelt Smitherman." 11/2/55. [*Montgomery, Ala.*] (TLc) 1 p. DABCC. 551102–003.**

11/3/55 **Porter, John Thomas (Morehouse College). "Letter to Martin Luther King, Jr." 11/3/55. Atlanta, Ga. (TLS) 1 p. MLKP-MBU: Box 117. 551103–000.**

11/5/55 Thomas, E. S. "Letter to Martin Luther King, Jr." 11/5/55. Oakland, Calif. (ALS) 1 p. MLKP-MBU: Box 117. 551105–000.

11/8/55 Creecy, Howard W. (Mount Pilgrim Baptist Church). "Letter to Martin Luther King, Jr." 11/8/55. Morgan City, La. (TLS) 1 p. MLKP-MBU: Box 117. 551108–000.

11/14/55 **Thurman, Howard (Boston University). "Letter to Martin Luther King, Jr." 11/14/55. (TLc) 1 p. HTC-MBU: Box 43. 551114–000.**

11/15/55 **King, Martin Luther, Jr. (Dexter Avenue Baptist Church). "Letter to Ralph W. Riley." 11/15/55. [*Montgomery, Ala.*] (TLc) 1 p. DABCC. 551115–000.**

11/16/55 **King, Martin Luther, Jr. "Letter to Rev. and Mrs. J. C. Bonner." 11/16/55. [*Montgomery, Ala.*] (TLc) 1 p. DABCC. 551116–000.**

11/18/55 Riley, Ralph W. (American Baptist Theological Seminary). "Letter to Martin Luther King, Jr." 11/18/55. Nashville, Tenn. (TLS) 1 p. MLKP-MBU: Box 117. 551118–000.

11/18/55 King, Martin Luther, Jr. "Letter to A. B. O'Reilly." 11/18/55. [*Montgomery, Ala.*] (TLc) 1 p. DABCC. 551118–001.

11/18/55 **King, Martin Luther, Jr. "Letter to John Thomas Porter." 11/18/55. [*Montgomery, Ala.*] (TLc) 1 p. DABCC. 551118–002.**

11/18/55 **King, Martin Luther, Jr. "Letter to Samuel D. Proctor." 11/18/55. [*Montgomery, Ala.*] (TLc) 1 p. DABCC. 551118–003.**

11/20/55 **Dexter Avenue Baptist Church. "Program, Sunday services and Installation Services." 11/20/55. Montgomery, Ala. (THD) 4 pp. (Marginal comments by King.) MLKP-MBU: Box 76. 551120–000.**

11/25/55 **Williams, C. R. (Emancipation Proclamation Committee of Montgomery). "Letter to Martin Luther King, Jr." 11/25/55. Montgomery, Ala. (TLS) 1 p. MLKP-MBU: Box 117. 551125–000.**

11/29/55 **King, Martin Luther, Jr. "Letter to C. R. Williams." 11/29/55. [*Montgomery, Ala.*] (TLc) 1 p. DABCC. 551129–000.**

11/30/55 King, Martin Luther, Jr. (Dexter Avenue Baptist Church). "Letter to Mr. Krechel." 11/30/55. [*Montgomery, Ala.*] (TLc) 1 p. DABCC. 551130–000.

11/30/55 King, Martin Luther, Jr. "Letter to Samuel D. Proctor." 11/30/55. [*Montgomery, Ala.*] (TLc) 1 p. DABCC. 551130–001.

11/30/55 **King, Martin Luther, Jr. "Letter to H. Edward Whitaker." 11/30/55. [*Montgomery, Ala.*] (TLc) 1 p. DABCC. 551130–002.**

INDEX

Boldfaced page numbers in entries indicate that the material can be found in documents authored by Martin Luther King, Jr.

Italicized page numbers in entries are used to indicate the location of the main biographical entry for an individual.

Compositor: G&S Typesetters, Inc.
Text: 10/12 Baskerville
Display: Baskerville
Printer: Edwards Brothers, Inc.
Binder: Edwards Brothers, Inc.